Security and Loss Prevention

Security and Loss Prevention:
An Introduction

5th Edition

Philip P. Purpura

AMSTERDAM • BOSTON • HEIDELBERG • LONDON
NEW YORK • OXFORD • PARIS • SAN DIEGO
SAN FRANCISCO • SINGAPORE • SYDNEY • TOKYO

Butterworth-Heinemann is an imprint of Elsevier

ELSEVIER

Publisher:	Amy Pedersen
Acquisitions Editor:	Pam Chester
Project Manager:	Jay Donahue
Marketing Manager:	Marissa Hederson
Designer:	Elsevier Design Group

Elsevier Butterworth-Heinemann
30 Corporate Drive, Suite 400, Burlington, MA 01803, USA
525 B Street, Suite 1900, San Diego, California 92101-4495, USA
84 Theobald's Road, London WC1X 8RR, UK

This book is printed on acid-free paper. ∞

Library of Congress Cataloging-in-Publication Data
Application Submitted

British Library Cataloguing in Publication Data
A catalogue record for this book is available from the British Library

ISBN 978-0-12-372525-7

For all information on all Butterworth-Heinemann publications visit our Web site at www.books.elsevier.com/security

Printed in The United States of America
09 10 9 8 7 6 5 4 3

Dedication

To my family.
To the millions of military, public safety, security and loss prevention, and other professionals who seek global security and safety.

Table of Contents

About the Author

Philip P. Purpura, Certified Protection Professional, is a college educator, consultant, expert witness, and writer. He is Director of the Security Training Institute and Resource Center and Coordinator of the Security for Houses of Worship Project in South Carolina. Purpura began his security career in New York City and held management and proprietary and contract investigative positions. He also worked with a public police agency. Purpura is the author of six other books: *Terrorism and Homeland Security: An Introduction with Applications* (Burlington, MA: Elsevier Butterworth-Heinemann, 2007); *Security Handbook, 2nd ed.* (Boston, MA: Butterworth-Heinemann, 2003; Albany, NY: Delmar, 1991); *Police & Community: Concepts & Cases* (Needham, MA: Allyn & Bacon, 2001); *Criminal Justice: An Introduction* (Boston, MA: Butterworth-Heinemann, 1997); *Retail Security & Shrinkage Protection* (Boston, MA: Butterworth-Heinemann, 1993); and *Modern Security & Loss Prevention Management* (Boston, MA: Butterworth, 1989). Purpura was contributing editor to three security periodicals; wrote numerous articles published in journals, magazines, and newsletters; and has been involved in a variety of editorial projects for publishers. He holds an associate's degree in police science from the State University of New York at Farmingdale, and bachelor's and master's degrees in criminal justice from the University of Dayton and Eastern Kentucky University, respectively. He also studied in several foreign countries. He serves on the ASIS International Council on Academic Programs.

Preface

The fifth edition of *Security and Loss Prevention: An Introduction* continues to draw on many disciplines for answers to protection challenges facing practitioners while helping the reader to understand the security and loss prevention profession. A major focus is placed on loss problems and countermeasures.

Terminology, concepts, and theories, at the foundation of this profession, are emphasized. The book has been updated with newer laws, statistics, research, strategies of protection, technology, events, and issues. At the same time, the contents retain basic information on the body of knowledge of security and loss prevention.

The many disciplines within this book include law, criminal justice, business, accounting, risk management, emergency management, fire protection, safety, sociology, and psychology. The publications supporting this book include articles from journals and a variety of other periodicals, books, research reports from numerous organizations, codes, and guidelines. The book has been updated and aligned with ASIS International research on security tasks, knowledge, and skills of practitioners.

A major change is the inclusion of Chapters 12, 13, 15, and 16. These chapters explain the threats of terrorism, natural disasters, and accidents, while including an "all hazards" preparation and protection approach. Public and private sector strategies and issues are explained. The book shows an awareness that, beyond the attention terrorism has received since the 9/11 attacks, security and loss prevention practitioners continue to face the same basic challenges they faced prior to the attacks, such as violence in the workplace, theft, and cybercrime.

Several new topics are included in the fifth edition. Examples are internal and external metrics, competitive bidding, contract life management, digital evidence, globalization, homeland security, pandemics, quarantine enforcement, and the cascade effect.

Because we are in the "information age" and the protection of both information technology (IT) and information are so important today, a major theme of this book is to connect the traditional security manager and physical security specialist to IT security. This is not a claim to make the reader an IT security expert. Rather, the reader will learn about similarities and differences of physical and IT security; internal and external IT risks and countermeasures; and the mindset of the IT security specialist. The convergence of physical security and IT security, as covered in the contents, makes an understanding of IT especially important to the security and loss prevention practitioner. Our "information age" has brought with it an explosion of data, information, and "hype" that challenge us to probe and shape knowledge for our personal and professional life. To assist the reader, critical thinking skills are presented as a tool to go beyond collecting "facts" as we seek to understand causes, motives, and change. In addition, because all security strategies either protect people and assets, accomplish nothing, or help offenders (see Chapter 3), practitioners will benefit by thinking critically as they plan, select vendors, and implement and manage security strategies that will make or break their careers.

The fifth edition includes learning objectives and key terms at the beginning of each chapter, key terms in bold within each chapter, definitions, examples, illustrations, photos, boxed scenarios, boxed international topics for global perspectives, and career boxes that explain various specializations in security.

The student or practitioner will find this book to be user-friendly and interactive, as in previous editions. Several features will assist the reader in understanding not only the basics but also the "reality" of the field. The reader is placed in the role of the practitioner through various exercises. Within each chapter, the loss problems are described and are followed by a discussion of the nuts-and-bolts countermeasures. Sidebars in each chapter emphasize significant points and facilitate critical thinking about security issues. Cases titled "You Be the Judge" appear in the text. These fictional accounts of actual cases deal with security-related legal problems. The reader is asked for a verdict based on the material at hand and then is directed to the end of the chapter for the court's ruling. Additional boxed cases appear in chapters and offer bits of interesting information or analyze a loss problem relevant to the subject matter of the chapter. The case problems at the ends of chapters bridge theory to practice and ask the reader to apply the general concepts of the chapter to real-world situations. These exercises enable the student to improve analytical and decision-making skills, consider alternative strategies, stimulate controversy in group discussions, make mistakes and receive feedback, and understand corporate culture and ethical guidelines.

This new edition also serves as a helpful directory; professional organizations and sources of information that enhance protection programs are included with web addresses at the ends of chapters.

This book also helps applicants prepare for the Certified Protection Professional examination, which is sponsored by ASIS International. Numerous topics included in the examination are covered in this book.

The first few chapters provide an introduction and foundation for protection programs and strategies. Chapter 1 defines security and loss prevention and presents a critical perspective of the history of security and loss prevention. The second chapter concentrates on the growth of the security industry and profession and related challenges. The next three chapters provide a foundation from which protection programs can become more efficient and effective. Chapter 3 focuses on security as a profession, risk analysis, planning, evaluation, research, and security standards and regulations. Chapter 4 provides an overview of civil and criminal law and includes discussions of premise protection, negligence, and arrest law. Chapter 5 explains the why and how of recruiting people and organizations to assist with loss prevention efforts. Chapters 6, 7, and 8 emphasize strategies for curbing internal and external crime threats. These include job applicant screening, policies, procedures, and physical security. Chapter 9, on purchasing security services and systems, is vital because not all security specialists are wise consumers, and the best plans are useless when followed by poor purchasing decisions. Chapter 10 provides practical information on investigations. The strategies of accountability, accounting, and auditing are described in Chapter 11, with an explanation as to why these tools are essential for survival. Chapter 12 focuses on risk management, business continuity, and emergency management as a foundation for Chapter 13 on life safety, fire protection, emergencies, and disasters. Chapter 14 emphasizes workplace safety and OSHA. The topics of terrorism and homeland security are discussed in Chapter 15. Chapter 16 emphasizes protecting critical infrastructures, key assets, and borders. Chapter 17 explains security and loss prevention at retail, financial, educational, and healthcare organizations. The topics of workplace violence, personnel protection, substance abuse, and information security are in Chapter 18. The final chapter focuses on trends, education, research, training, and employment.

The traditional focus of security—security officers, fences, and alarms—is too narrow to deal with an increasingly complex world. Practitioners are being asked to do more with fewer resources and prove that the money spent on protection has a return on investment. In a world of rapid change, senior management expects security and loss prevention practitioners to produce answers quickly. The true professional maintains a positive attitude and sees problems as challenges that have solutions.

The tremendous growth of the security and loss prevention profession provides fertile ground to advance in a rewarding career. In such a competitive world, the survival and protection of businesses and institutions, technological innovations, and the national interest depend greatly on security and loss prevention programs. This book should inspire and motivate students and practitioners to fulfill these vital protection needs.

Acknowledgments

I would like to thank the many people who contributed to this fifth edition. Gratitude goes to my family for their support and patience. I am thankful to security practitioners, educators, librarians, and others who helped to provide a wealth of information to support the contents of this book. The hardworking Security team at Elsevier, including Amy Pedersen, Pam Chester, Marissa Hederson, Greg deZarn-O'Hare, Jay Donahue, and Alisa Andreola, are to be recognized for their talents and skills in publishing this book. I am grateful for the team effort, among so many people, for without it this book could not be published.

Introduction to Security and Loss Prevention

1

The History of Security and Loss Prevention: A Critical Perspective

Objectives

After studying this chapter, the reader will be able to:

1. Explain the purpose of critical thinking and how to think critically.
2. Define security and loss prevention.
3. List the benefits of studying the history of security and loss prevention.
4. Trace the early development of security and policing.
5. Describe the growth of security companies in the United States.
6. Explain the convergence of IT and physical security and the convergence of enterprise security.
7. Describe 21st century/post-9/11 security challenges.

KEY TERMS
• critical thinking	• watch and ward
• security	• Henry Fielding
• loss prevention	• Bow Street Runners
• Chief Security Officer (CSO)	• Sir Robert Peel
• Great Wall of China	• Metropolitan Police Act
• Hammurabi, King of Babylon	• Allan Pinkerton
• polis	• Henry Wells
• Praetorian Guard	• William Fargo
• vigiles	• William Burns
• feudalism	• Washington Perry Brink
• comitatus	• Edwin Holmes
• posse comitatus	• George Wackenhut
• Posse Comitatus Act	• first wave societies
• frankpledge system	• second wave societies
• tithing	• third wave societies
• Magna Carta	• convergence of IT and physical security
• Statute of Westminster	• convergence of enterprise security

Why Critical Thinking?

September 11, 2001, marked a turning point in the history of security. In a devastating terrorist onslaught, knife-wielding hijackers crashed two airliners into the World Trade Center in New York City, creating an inferno that caused the 110-story twin skyscrapers to collapse. About 3,000 people were killed, including responding firefighters and police. During the same morning, another hijacked airliner crashed into the Pentagon, causing additional deaths and destruction. A fourth hijacked airliner failed to reach its target and crashed when heroic passengers learned of the other attacks and struggled with hijackers to control the airliner. The attacks were immensely successful and cost-effective for the terrorists. With a loss of 19 terrorists and expenses between $400,000 and $500,000, the attackers were able to kill thousands, cause hundreds of billions of dollars in economic damage and spending on counterterrorism, and significantly affect global history. With such a huge kill ratio and investment payoff for the terrorists, governments and the private sector must succeed in controlling terrorism.

Because of these devastating attacks, not only have homeland defenses, military strategies, public safety, and private sector security changed, but also our way of thinking has changed. We cannot afford to have failures in our planning and imagination of what criminals can do. To improve security, we must seek new tools to assist us in our thinking processes.

Here we begin with critical thinking skills to counter "business as usual." **Critical thinking** helps us to become active learners: to not only absorb information, but to probe and shape knowledge. The critical thinker cuts through "hype" and emotion and goes beyond collecting "facts" and memorizing information in an effort to understand causes, motives, and changes. Critical thinking skills provide a foundation for creative planning while helping us to anticipate future events.

The critical thinker asks many questions, and the questions are often easier to formulate than the answers. Critical thinking requires us to "jump out of our own skin" to see the world from the perspective of others. Although this is not an easy process, we are much better informed before we make our conclusions and decisions.

Critical thinking is not to be used as a tool to open up the floodgates of criticism in the workplace. It is to be applied discreetly to understand the world and to meet challenges.

A professional's success depends on his or her thinking process applied to everyday duties and long-range planning. Critical thinking adds an extra edge to the repertoire of tools available to security and loss prevention practitioners.

Safi and Burrell (2007: 54) write:

Theorists have hypothesized that critical thinking is correlated with internal motivation to think. Cognitive skills of analysis, interpretation, explanation, evaluation and correcting one's own reasoning are at the heart of critical thinking.

Critical thinking can be learned with practice and guidance by changing the actions involved in making decisions so that they become part of permanent behavior in homeland security intelligence analysis, threat protection and security planning.

Security challenges have become increasingly complex because as we plan for protection and face a multitude of threats in a rapidly changing environment, we must expect the unexpected, while staying within our budgets. The security practitioner should be creative, have an excellent imagination, apply critical thinking skills, and carefully prioritize security strategies to produce the best possible security program.

Although critical thinking skills are applied to a critical perspective of history in this chapter, students and practitioners are urged to continue this thinking process throughout this book. It is hoped that your conclusions and decisions will be enhanced to improve security and loss prevention.

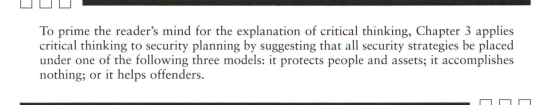

To prime the reader's mind for the explanation of critical thinking, Chapter 3 applies critical thinking to security planning by suggesting that all security strategies be placed under one of the following three models: it protects people and assets; it accomplishes nothing; or it helps offenders.

How Can We Think Critically?

Our world is filled with many efforts to influence our thinking. Examples are the media, advertisers, politicians, educators, and writers. This author is biased just like other writers, and within these pages is a North American interpretation of security. Although an effort has been made to write an objective book here, it is impossible for any writer, and biases surface. Objectivity is fostered in this book through an introduction to critical thinking skills, a multidisciplinary approach, international perspectives, boxed topics and questions, a variety of references, Web exercises, and case problems at the end of chapters that bridge theory to practice and ask the reader to make decisions as a practitioner.

With so much competition seeking to influence us, choices become difficult and confusing. And, as we think through complex challenges, we need a method of sorting conflicting claims, differentiating between fact and opinion, weighing "evidence" or "proof," being perceptive to our biases and those of others, and drawing logical conclusions. Ellis (1991: 184–185) suggests a four-step strategy for critical thinking:

Step 1: Understand the point of view.
- Listen/read without early judgment.
- Seek to understand the source's background (e.g., culture, education, experience, and values).
- Try to "live in their shoes."
- Summarize their viewpoint.

Step 2: Seek other views.
- Seek viewpoints, questions, answers, ideas, and solutions from others.

Step 3: Evaluate the various viewpoints.
- Look for assumptions (i.e., an opinion that something is true, without evidence), exceptions, gaps in logic, oversimplification, selective perception, either/or thinking, and personal attacks.

Step 4: Construct a reasonable view.
- Study multiple viewpoints, combine perspectives, and produce an original viewpoint that is a creative act and the essence of critical thinking.

Why Think Critically about the History of Security and Loss Prevention?

The intent here is to stimulate the reader to go beyond memorizing historical events, names, and dates. If you have read several books in this field, the history chapters sound very similar. Did the writers, including this one, become complacent and repeat what has been written repeatedly about the history of this field? How do you know that the history of security and loss prevention as presented in this book and in others is objective?

Recorded history is filled with bias. Historians and scholars decide what subjects, events, innovations, countries, ethnic groups, religions, men, and women should be included or excluded from recorded history. In reference to the history of security and loss prevention, what have we missed? What subjects have been overemphasized? (A case problem at the end of this chapter asks the reader to critically think about the history of security and loss prevention.) In the policing field, for example, Weisheit, Baker, and Falcone (1995: 1) note that history and research reflect a bias toward urban police, at the expense of rural police. Do security researchers and writers overemphasize large proprietary security programs and large security service firms? What about the thousands of proprietary security programs at small companies and the thousands of small security service firms? Another question is what role did women and minorities play in the history of this field?

What country do you think has had the most impact on police and security in the United States? Our language, government, public and private protection, law, and many other aspects of our lives have deep roots in England. However, what about the role of other countries in the development of police and private security methods? Stead (1983: 14–15) writes of the French as innovators in crime prevention as early as the 1600s under King Louis XIV. During that time, crime prevention was emphasized through preventive patrol and street lighting. Germann, Day, and Gallati (1974: 45–46) write of early Asian investigative methods that used psychology to elicit confessions.

A critical thinking approach "opens our eyes" to a more objective perspective of historical events. The author is not seeking to rewrite history, or to change the basic strategies of security and loss prevention. Rather, the aim is to expand the reader's perception and knowledge as a foundation for smarter protection in a complex world.

Security and Loss Prevention Defined

Within our organized society, security is provided primarily by our armed forces, law enforcement agencies, and private security. The 9/11 attacks resulted in several changes in the way in which we organize public and private security. Post-9/11 security changes are covered in subsequent chapters.

During the last decades of the 20th century, the methods of private security became more specialized and diverse. Methods not previously associated with security emerged as important components of the total security effort. Security officers, fences, and alarms have been the hallmark of traditional security functions. Today, with society becoming increasingly complex, additional specialization—auditing, safety, fire protection, information technology (IT) security, crisis management, executive protection, terrorism countermeasures, to name a few—continuously are being added to the security function. Because of the increase in diverse specializations within the security function, many practitioners favor a broader term for all of these functions, known as *loss prevention*.

Another reason for the growing shift in terminology from security to loss prevention involves the negative connotations of security. Saul Astor (1978: 27) points out:

> *In the minds of many, the very word "security" is its own impediment.*
> *... Security carries a stigma; the very word suggests police, badges, alarms, thieves, burglars, and some generally negative and even repellent mental images....*
> *Simply using the term "loss prevention" instead of the word "security" can be a giant step toward improving the security image, broadening the scope of the security function, and attracting able people.*

Because of additional specialization included in the security function and the frequently negative connotations associated with the term *security*, the all-encompassing term for describing the contents of this book is *loss prevention*. The security function and other specialized fields (auditing, safety, fire protection, etc.) are subsumed in loss prevention.

Security is narrowly defined as traditional methods (security officers, fences, and alarms) used to increase the likelihood of a crime-controlled, tranquil, and uninterrupted environment for an individual or organization in pursuit of objectives.

Loss prevention is broadly defined as almost any method (e.g., security officers, safety, auditing) used by an individual or organization to increase the likelihood of preventing and controlling loss (e.g., people, money, productivity, materials) resulting from a host of adverse occurrences (e.g., crime, fire, accident, natural disaster, error, poor supervision or management, bad investment). This broad definition provides a foundation for the loss prevention practitioner whose innovations are limited only by his or her imagination. It is hoped that these concepts not only will guide the reader through this book but also reinforce a trend in the use of these definitions.

Various employment titles are applied to individuals who perform security and loss prevention duties within organizations. The titles include Vice President, Director, or Manager of Security, Corporate Security, Loss Prevention, or Assets Protection.

Another title receiving attention is the **Chief Security Officer (CSO)**. The *Chief Security Officer Guideline* (ASIS International, 2004) is designed "… as a model for organizations to utilize in the development of a leadership function to provide a comprehensive, integrated security risk strategy to contribute to the viability and success of the organization." This guideline is a response to an increasingly serious threat environment, and it recommends that the CSO report to the most senior level executive of the organization. The guideline lists specific risks, job duties and services, and skills required. The CSO designation and the guideline supporting it provide an excellent reference from which the security profession and senior management can draw on to improve the protection of people and assets and help organizations survive in a world filled with risks.

CSO (2004) defines the CSO position as follows:

> *The title Chief Security Officer (CSO) was first used principally inside the information technology function to designate the person responsible for IT security. At many companies, the term CSO is still used in this way. CISO, for Chief Information Security Officer, is an equivalent term, and today the CISO title is becoming more prevalent for leaders with an exclusive infosecurity focus.*
>
> *The CSO title is also used at some companies to describe the leader of the "corporate security" function, which includes the physical security and safety of employees, facilities and assets. More commonly, this person holds a title such as Vice President or Director of Corporate Security. This function has historically been distinct from information security.*
>
> *Increasingly, Chief Security Officer means what it sounds like: The CSO is the executive responsible for the organization's entire security posture, both physical and digital.*

Research conducted by Booz Allen Hamilton (2005) for ASIS International, the Information Systems Security Association, and the Information Systems Audit and Control Association, found that placing all security functions under one individual ("the strongest or most powerful of the various security elements") may not be beneficial ("an obvious and flawed option") for all organizations because it can reduce the influence of important managers in enterprisewide security. The study recommended a "business-focused council of leaders" consisting of representatives from various specializations—such as risk management, law, safety, and business continuity—who "come together using the corporate strategy as a common element on which to focus."

□ □ □ ▬▬▬▬▬▬▬▬▬▬▬▬▬▬▬▬▬▬▬▬▬▬▬▬▬▬

Security is narrowly defined; *loss prevention* is broadly defined.

▬▬▬▬▬▬▬▬▬▬▬▬▬▬▬▬▬▬▬▬▬▬▬▬▬▬ □ □ □

History

Why Study the History of Security and Loss Prevention?

We should study the history of security and loss prevention because

- We learn of the origins of the profession and how it developed.
- We can see how voids in security and safety within society were filled by the private sector.

- We can learn of noted practitioners and theorists and their challenges, failures, and successes.
- We can compare security in the past to security in the present to note areas of improvement and areas requiring improvement.
- We can learn how security services and systems have been controlled and regulated.
- We can learn of the interaction of private security and public police over time.
- History repeats itself. We should strive to avoid the mistakes of the past and continue with successes.
- We can learn how social, economic, political, and technological forces have affected security over time.
- The past assists us in understanding the present, and it offers us a foundation to anticipate future events.

Early Civilizations

Prehistoric human beings depended on nature for protection because they had not learned how to build strong houses and fortifications. In cold climates, caves provided protection and shelter, whereas in the tropics, trees and thickets were used. Caves were particularly secure because rocky walls guarded tribes on all sides except at the cave mouth. To protect the entrance, redundant (i.e., duplicating to prevent failure) security was employed: large rocks acted as barriers when they were rolled in front of entrances; dogs, with their keen sense of smell, served to alarm and attack; and fires added additional defense. By living on the side of a mountain with access via a narrow, rocky ledge, cave dwellers were relatively safe from enemies and beasts. Early Pueblo Indians, living in what is now New Mexico and Arizona, ensured greater protection for themselves in their dwellings by constructing ladders that could be pulled in, and this defense proved useful until enemies attacked with their own ladders. *In fact, in early civilizations, as today, security measures have never been foolproof, and adversaries typically strive to circumvent (i.e., to go around) defenses.*

□ □ □ ▬▬▬▬▬▬▬▬▬▬▬▬▬▬▬▬▬▬▬▬▬▬▬▬▬▬▬▬▬▬▬▬

Throughout history, redundant security has been used to block adversaries attempting to circumvent defenses.

▬▬▬▬▬▬▬▬▬▬▬▬▬▬▬▬▬▬▬▬▬▬▬▬▬▬▬▬▬▬▬▬ □ □ □

The **Great Wall of China** is the longest structure ever built. It was constructed over hundreds of years beginning in the 400s BC. Hundreds of thousands of workers lived their lives near the wall and participated in this huge project that stretched 4,000 miles and reached heights of 25 feet. Unfortunately, the wall provided protection only from minor attacks; when a major invasion force struck, the defense could not withstand the onslaught. The army of Mongol leader Genghis Khan swept across the wall during the AD 1200s and conquered much of China. Since 1949, the Chinese government has restored some sections of the mostly collapsed wall, which is a major tourist attraction (Feuerwerker, 1989: 373–374).

It is interesting to note the changing character of security through history. In earlier years, huge fortifications could be built with cheap labor, and a king could secure a perimeter with many inexpensive guards. Today, physical barriers such as fences and walls are expensive, as is the posting of security forces at physical barriers. One 24-hour post can cost over $100,000 annually for security personnel and physical security systems.

As societies became more complex, the concepts of leadership, authority, and organization began to evolve. Mutual association created social and economic advantages but also inequities, so people and assets required increased protection. Intergroup and intragroup conflicts created problems whose "solutions" often took the form of gruesome punishments, including stoning, flaying, burning, and crucifying. A person's criminal record was carried right on his or her body, through branding and mutilation. By 1750 BC the laws of **Hammurabi, King of Babylon,** not only codified the responsibilities of the individual to the group and the rules for private dealings between individuals, but also discussed retributive penalties (Germann, Day, and Gallati, 1974: 43).

Ancient Greece

Between the ninth and third centuries BC, ancient Greece blossomed as an advanced commercial and culturally rich civilization. The Greeks protected their advancing civilization with the **polis,** or city-state, which consisted of a city and the surrounding land protected by a centrally built fortress overlooking the countryside. A stratified society brought the ruling classes constant fear of revolution from below. Spartans, for example, kept their secret agents planted among the lower classes and subversives. *During the time of the Greek city-states, the first police force evolved to protect local communities, although citizens were responsible for this function.* The Greek rulers did not view local policing as a state responsibility, and when internal conflicts arose, they used the army. During this era, the Greek philosopher Plato introduced an advanced concept of justice, in which an offender not only would be forced to pay a sort of retribution, but also would be forced into a method of reform or rehabilitation.

☐ ☐ ☐

Ancient Egyptians sealed the master locksmith in the tomb to prevent security leaks.

☐ ☐ ☐

Ancient Rome

The civilization of ancient Rome also developed both commercially and culturally before the birth of Christ. Rome was located only 15 miles from the sea and could easily share in the trade of the Mediterranean. This city sat on seven hills overlooking the Tiber River, which permitted ease in fortification and defense. A primitive but effective alarm system was used by placing geese at strategic locations so their very sensitive hearing would trigger squawking at the sound of an approaching army.

The Roman regime was well designed to carry on the chief business of the Roman state, which was war. A phalanx of 8,000 foot-soldiers became the basic unit of a Roman army equipped with helmets, shields, lances, and swords. Later, a more maneuverable legion of 3,600 men armed in addition with iron-tipped javelins was used. These legions also were employed to maintain law and order. The first emperor of Rome, Augustus (63 BC–AD 14), created the **Praetorian Guard** to provide security for his life and property. These urban cohorts of 500 to 600 men were deployed to keep the peace in the city. Some believe that after about AD 6 this was the most effective police force until recent developments in law enforcement. Modern-day coordinated patrolling and preventive security began with the subsequent nonmilitary **vigiles,** night watchmen who were active in both policing and firefighting (Post and Kingsbury, 1977; Ursic and Pagano, 1974).

The Romans have an interesting history in fire protection. During the 300s BC, slaves were assigned firefighting duties. Later, improved organization established divisions encompassing hundreds of people, who carried water in jars to fires or brought large pillows so victims trapped in taller structures could jump with improved chances for survival. The completion of the aqueducts to Rome aided firefighting by making water easier to obtain. Hand pumps and leather hoses were other innovations.

The Middle Ages in Europe

During the Dark Ages, the period in history after the destruction of the ancient Greek and Roman empires, **feudalism** gradually developed in Europe. Overlords supplied food and security to those who farmed and provided protection around castles fortified by walls, towers, and a drawbridge that could be raised from its position across a moat. Even then, security required registration, licensing, and a fee—Henry II of England (reigned AD 1154–1189) destroyed more than 1,100 unlicensed castles that had been constructed during a civil war (Brinton, et al., 1973: 167).

Another mutual arrangement was the war band of the early Germans, the **comitatus**, by which a leader commanded the loyalty of followers, who banded together to fight and win booty. To defend against these bands of German barbarians, many landowners throughout Europe built their own private armies. (The term **posse comitatus** denotes a body of citizens that authority can call on for assistance against offenders. The **Posse Comitatus Act** is a Civil War–era act that generally prohibits the military from engaging in civilian law enforcement. This law has been labeled as archaic because it limits the military from responding to disasters.)

Much of the United States' customs, language, laws, and police and security methods can be traced to its English heritage. For this reason, England's history of protection is examined here.

Between the 7th and 10th centuries, the frankpledge system and the concept of tithing fostered increased protection. The **frankpledge system**, which originated in France and spread to England, emphasized communal responsibility for justice and protection. The **tithing**, or group of 10 families, shared the duties of maintaining the peace and protecting the community.

In 1066, William, Duke of Normandy (in present-day France), crossed the English Channel and defeated the Anglo-Saxons at Hastings. A highly repressive police system developed under martial law as the state appropriated responsibility for peace and protection. Community authority and the tithing system were weakened. William divided England into 55 districts, or *shires*. A *reeve*, drawn from the military, was assigned to each district. (Today, we use the word *sheriff*, derived from *shire-reeve*.) William is credited with changing the law to make a crime an offense against the state rather than against the individual and was instrumental in separating police from judicial functions. A traveling judge tried the cases of those arrested by the shire-reeves.

In 1215 King John signed the **Magna Carta**, which guaranteed civil and political liberties. Local government power increased at the expense of the national government, and community protection increased at the local level.

Another security milestone was the **Statute of Westminster** (1285), issued by King Edward I to organize a police and justice system. A **watch and ward** was established to keep the peace. Every town was required to deploy men all night, to close the gates of walled towns at night, and to enforce a curfew.

□ □ □ ▬▬▬▬▬▬▬▬▬▬▬▬▬▬▬▬▬▬▬▬▬▬▬▬▬▬▬▬▬▬▬▬▬▬▬

What similarities can you draw between security strategies of earlier civilizations and those of today?

▬▬▬▬▬▬▬▬▬▬▬▬▬▬▬▬▬▬▬▬▬▬▬▬▬▬▬▬▬▬▬▬▬▬▬ □ □ □

More Contemporary Times

England

For the next 500 years, repeated attempts were made to improve protection and justice in England. Each king was confronted with increasingly serious crime problems and cries from the citizenry for solutions. As England colonized many parts of the world and as trade and commercial pursuits brought many people into the cities, urban problems and high crime rates persisted. Merchants, dissatisfied with the protection afforded by the government, hired private security forces to protect their businesses.

By the 18th century, the Industrial Revolution compounded urban problems. Many citizens were forced to carry arms for their own protection, because a strong government policing system was absent. Various police and private security organizations did strive to reduce crime; **Henry Fielding**, in 1748, was appointed magistrate, and he devised the strategy of preventing crime through police action by helping to form the famous **Bow Street Runners**, the first detective unit. The merchant police were formed to protect businesses, and the Thames River police provided protection at the docks. During this period, more than 160 crimes, including stealing food, were punishable by death. As pickpockets were being hanged, others moved among the spectators, picking pockets.

□ □ □ ▬▬▬▬▬▬▬▬▬▬▬▬▬▬▬▬▬▬▬▬▬▬

Do you think policing and justice were impotent during the early Industrial Revolution in England? Do you think we have a similar problem today in the United States?

▬▬▬▬▬▬▬▬▬▬▬▬▬▬▬▬▬▬▬▬▬▬ □ □ □

Peel's Reforms

In 1829, **Sir Robert Peel** worked to produce the **Metropolitan Police Act** that resulted in a revolution in law enforcement. Modern policing was born. Peel's innovative ideas were accepted by Parliament, and he was selected to implement the act that established a full-time, unarmed police force with the major purpose of patrolling London. Peel is credited also with reforming the criminal law by limiting its scope and abolishing the death penalty for more than 100 offenses. It was hoped that such a strategy would gain public support and respect for the police. Peel was very selective in hiring his personnel, and training was an essential part of developing a professional police force. Peel's reforms are applicable today and include crime prevention, the strategic deployment of police according to time and location, a command of temper rather than violent action, record keeping, and crime news distribution.

□ □ □ ▬▬▬▬▬▬▬▬▬▬▬▬▬▬▬▬▬▬▬▬▬▬

Although Sir Robert Peel produced a revolution in law enforcement in 1829, crime and the private security industry continued to grow.

▬▬▬▬▬▬▬▬▬▬▬▬▬▬▬▬▬▬▬▬▬▬ □ □ □

Early America

The Europeans who colonized North America had brought with them the heritage of their mother countries, including various customs of protection. The watchman system and collective responses remained popular. A central fortification in populated areas provided increased security from hostile threats. As communities expanded in size, the office of sheriff took hold in the South, whereas the functions of constable and watchman were the norm in the Northeast. The sheriff's duties involved apprehending offenders, serving subpoenas, and collecting taxes. Because a sheriff was paid a higher fee for collecting taxes, policing became a lower priority. Constables performed a variety of tasks such as keeping the peace, bringing suspects and witnesses to court, and eliminating health hazards. As in England, the watch system had its share of inefficiency, and to make matters worse, those convicted of minor crimes were sentenced to serve time on the watch.

The watch also warned citizens of fire. In colonial towns, each home had to have two fire buckets, and homeowners were subject to a fine if they did not respond to a fire, buckets in hand. A large fire in Boston in 1679 prompted the establishment of the first paid fire department in North America (Bugbee, 1978: 5).

The Growth of Policing

The period of the middle 1800s was a turning point for both law enforcement and private security in America, as it had been in England. Several major cities (e.g., New York, Philadelphia,

San Francisco) organized police forces, often modeled after the London Metropolitan Police. However, corruption was widespread. Numerous urban police agencies in the Northeast received large boosts in personnel and resources to combat the growing militancy of the labor unions in the late 1800s and early 1900s. Many of the large urban police departments originally were formed as strikebreakers (Holden, 1986: 23). Federal policing also experienced growth during this period. The U.S. Treasury had already established an investigative unit in 1864. As in England, an increase in public police did not quell the need for private security.

The History of Loss Prevention in a Nutshell

Loss prevention has its origin in the insurance industry. Before the Civil War, insurers gave minimal attention to the benefits of loss prevention. For instance, in the fire insurance business, executives generally viewed fires as good for business. Insurance rates were based on past loss experience, premiums were paid by customers, losses were paid to unfortunate customers, and a profit was expected by the insurer. When excessive fire losses resulted in spiraling premiums, the changing nature of the fire insurance business created a hardship for both the insurer and the insured. Insurance executives were forced to raise premiums to cover losses, and customers complained about high rates. The predominance of wooden construction (even wooden chimneys) in dense urban areas made fire insurance unaffordable for many. A serious fire peril persisted.

After the Civil War, loss prevention began to gain momentum as a way to reduce losses and premiums. Fire insurance companies formed the National Board of Fire Underwriters, which, through the use of engineering, investigation, research, and education, was credited with preventing losses. In 1965, the board was merged into the American Insurance Association (AIA). AIA activities have brought about the development of the National Building Code, a model code adopted by many municipalities to reduce fire losses.

Today, executives throughout the insurance industry view loss prevention as essential. Many insurers have loss prevention departments to aid themselves and customers. Furthermore, customers (i.e., the insured), to reduce premiums, have become increasingly concerned about preventing losses. Management in many businesses instituted loss prevention strategies (e.g., fire protection). The security department within businesses repeatedly handle these strategies, which results in an expanded role for security. Expansion of the security function to such fields as fire protection and safety has led to the use of the broader term *loss prevention* rather than *security*.

The Growth of Security Companies

In 1850, **Allan Pinkerton,** a cooper, opened a detective agency in the United States after becoming the Chicago Police Department's first detective. Because public police were limited by geographic jurisdiction, they were handicapped when investigating and apprehending fleeing offenders. This limitation facilitated the growth of private security. Pinkerton (see Figure 1-1) and others became famous as they pursued criminals across state boundaries throughout the country. Today, Pinkerton Service Corporation is a subsidiary of Securitas, based in Stockholm, Sweden.

During the 1800s, because public police were limited by geographic jurisdiction and restrained from chasing fleeing offenders, private security filled this need and became a growth industry.

FIGURE 1-1 Major Allan Pinkerton, President Lincoln, and General John A. McClellan, Antietam, MD, October 1862. *Courtesy:* National Archives.

To accompany Americans' expansion westward during the 19th century and to ensure the safe transportation of valuables, **Henry Wells** and **William Fargo** supplied a wide-open market by forming Wells, Fargo & Company in 1852, opening the era of bandits accosting stage-coaches and their shotgun riders. Wells Fargo was acquired by Burns International Services Corporation. The name Wells Fargo is exclusive to Wells Fargo & Company, a large financial services business.

Another security entrepreneur, **William Burns**, first was a Secret Service agent who directed the Bureau of Investigation that preceded the FBI. In 1910, this experienced investigator opened the William J. Burns Detective Agency (see Figure 1-2), which became the investigative arm of the American Bankers Association. Today, Burns International Services Corporation is a subsidiary of Securitas.

Washington Perry Brink, in 1859, also took advantage of the need for the safe transportation of valuables. From freight and package delivery to the transportation of payrolls, his service required increased protection through the years as cargo became more valuable and more vulnerable. Following the killing of two Brink's guards during a robbery, the armored truck was initiated in 1917. Today, the Brink's Company is a leading global security services company. It provides secure transportation services, and it monitors home security systems.

Edwin Holmes is another historical figure in the development of private security in the United States. He pioneered the electronic security alarm business. During 1858, Holmes had a difficult time convincing people that an alarm would sound on the second floor of a home when a door or window was opened on the first floor. His sales strategy was to carry door-to-door a small model of a home containing his electric alarm system. Soon sales soared, and

FIGURE 1-2 In 1910, William J. Burns, the foremost American investigator of his day and the first director of the government agency that became the FBI, formed the William J. Burns Detective Agency.

the first central office burglar alarm monitoring operation began. Holmes Protection Group, Inc., was acquired by ADT Security Services, Inc., at the end of the 20th century.

Since 1874, ADT Security Services, Inc., has been a leader in electronic security services. Originally known as American District Telegraph, ADT has acquired numerous security companies since its inception. Today, it is a unit of Tyco Fire and Security Services. ADT is a provider of electronic security services (i.e., intrusion, fire protection, closed-circuit television or CCTV, access control) to millions of commercial, federal, and residential customers.

The Wackenhut Corporation is another leader in the security industry. Founded in 1954 by **George Wackenhut**, a former FBI agent, the corporation extended its services to government agencies, which resulted in numerous contracts since its inception. The Wackenhut Corporation is the U.S.-based division of Group 4 Securicor, located in the United Kingdom.

Railroads and Labor Unions

The history of private security businesses in the United States must include two important events of the 19th century: the growth of railroads and labor unions.

Although railroads were valuable in providing the vital East–West link that enabled the settling of the American frontier, these powerful businesses used their domination of transportation to control several industries, such as coal and kerosene. Farmers were especially hurt in economic terms because they had no alternative but to pay high fees to transport their products via the railroads. The monopolistic practices of railroads created considerable hostility; when Jesse James and other criminals robbed trains, citizens applauded. Railroads could not rely on public police protection because of jurisdictional boundaries. Consequently, numerous states passed laws enabling railroads to organize proprietary security forces with full arrest powers and the authority to apprehend criminals transcending multiple jurisdictions. Railroad police numbered 14,000 by 1914. During World War I, they were deputized by the federal government to ensure protection of this vital transportation network.

The growth of labor unions at the end of the 19th century resulted in increased business for security firms who acted as strikebreakers for large corporations. However, this venture proved costly. A bloody confrontation between Pinkerton men and workers at the Carnegie steel plant in Homestead, Pennsylvania, resulted in eight deaths (three security men and five workers). Pinkerton's security force surrendered. The plant then was occupied by federal troops. Senate hearings followed the Homestead disaster and "anti-Pinkertonism" laws were enacted to restrict private security. However, local and state police forces began to emerge quickly to deal with strikers (Shelden, 2001: 84). Later, the Ford Motor Company and other businesses were involved in bloody confrontations. Henry Ford had a force of about 3,500 security personnel, spies, and "sluggers" (i.e., private detectives), who were augmented by various community groups such as the Knights of Dearborn and the Legionnaires. The negative image brought to the public eye by newspaper coverage tarnished many businesses and security firms. Prior to World War II, pressure from Congress, the Roosevelt Administration, labor unions, and the ACLU caused corporate management to shift its philosophy to a softer "public relations" approach (Shelden, 2001: 92).

The Great Wars

World Wars I and II brought about an increased need for protection in the United States. Sabotage and espionage were serious threats. Key industries and transportation systems required expanded and improved security. The social and political climate in the early 20th century reflected urban problems, labor unrest, and worldwide nationalism. World War I compounded these turbulent times and people's fears. Security became a primary concern. A combination of the "war to end all wars," Prohibition, intense labor unrest, and the Great Depression all overtaxed public police. Private security companies helped fill the void.

By the late 1930s, Europe was at war again, and the Japanese were expanding in the Far East. A surprise Japanese bombing of the Pacific Fleet at Pearl Harbor in 1941 jolted the United States into World War II, and security concerns appeared again. The United States went into full production, and protection of vital industries became crucial, leading the federal government to bring plant security personnel into the army as an auxiliary to military police. By the end of the war, more than 200,000 of these security workers had been sworn in.

The Third Wave

In the decades following World War II, private security expanded even more; during the 1950s, the Korean War and the unrelenting "cold war" created worldwide tension and competition between the democracies and communist regimes. The Department of Defense, in 1952, strengthened the security requirements of defense industries to protect classified information and materials. When the Soviets successfully launched the first earth satellite (Sputnik, in 1957) and first reached the moon with an unmanned rocket (1959), Americans were stunned. The technological race became more intense, and information protection became more important.

The turbulent 1960s created massive social and political upheaval in the United States, and public police forces were overwhelmed by responses to the unpopular Vietnam war; protests over the denial of civil rights to minority groups; the assassinations of President John F. Kennedy, Senator Robert Kennedy, and the Reverend Martin Luther King, Jr.; and rising crime and drug problems. Private security boomed.

Protests, crime, terrorism, and limited public police resources marked the 1970s, 1980s, and 1990s. By this time, the advanced nations of the world had developed into what Alvin Toffler's (1980) *The Third Wave* and John Naisbitt's (1982) *Megatrends* call **third wave societies**: societies based on information and technology. (**First wave societies** had agriculture as a foundation, and these dominated the world for thousands of years, deriving energy from human and animal power. Offenders stole cattle, gold, and other valuables. **Second wave societies** occurred during the Industrial Revolution when production was powered by irreplaceable energy sources such as coal and oil. Criminals focused on money and booming economic conditions.) With the depletion of world resources, the world is becoming more dependent on technology and information; and "third wave" criminals exploit technology to commit their crimes, the extent of which is limited only by technological innovation and the offenders' imaginations.

"Has Cybercrime Surpassed Physical Crime?"

Gips (2006: 24) asked the preceding question in response to an IBM survey of mostly chief information officers. Sixty percent viewed cybercrime as more costly to their business than physical crime. Gips notes that it is difficult to measure and compare cybercrime and physical crime because "studies that attempt to quantify security losses across sectors and types of crime are based on extrapolation and guesswork." He argues that the cost of physical crime in the United States easily outpaces the cost of cybercrime. Gips refers to several sources on annual costs of crime: the FBI estimates that cybercrime costs about $400 billion and counterfeit goods cost about $250 billion; the Association of Certified Fraud Examiners estimates that occupational crime (e.g., altering checks, setting up fictitious accounts) costs about $652 billion; cargo theft costs "tens of billions" of dollars according to the International Cargo Security Council; retailers lose about $40 billion from shrinkage and inventory loss; and physical crime losses often exclude indirect costs, such as defending and paying judgments on lawsuits alleging negligent security. Gips concludes his arguments by noting that "if you think you are at risk for cybercrime, that's likely where you will devote your resources. And if the risk lies elsewhere, that could mean that the company's more costly vulnerabilities will not be adequately addressed."

Convergence of IT and Physical Security

Today, the third wave is continuing with three notable occurrences affecting security. First, terminology is changing. Examples are *cybercrime* and *denial of service*. Second, two distinct security camps have emerged: information technology (IT) security specialists and physical security specialists. Generally, the former possess a background geared to protect against computer-related crime and unauthorized intrusions into IT systems, whereas the latter focus on traditional security duties (e.g., perimeter security, access controls, and contract security forces). Third, both camps often use similar terminology and perform similar duties. Terms common to both groups include *denial of access* and *intrusion detection*. Similar duties can be far reaching and include investigations, information security, loss prevention, and risk management. Jim Spencer (2000: 1-13), writing in *iSecurity*, adds that these two groups have their own suppliers, consultants, publications, associations, and trade shows.

For several years, *cross-training* has been a buzzword for various vocations, such as for investigators and auditors. History repeats itself and we have a need for cross-training for IT and physical security specialists. Each specialist can assist the other with data, technologies, access controls, biometrics, investigations, and business continuity, among other areas. Cooperative planning is essential. Suppose an employee is fired at a company. Security officers and access control systems customarily deny the former employee entrance to the company facility. However, today, protection requires broader applications because of remote access to IT systems. *An offender no longer has to physically trespass to steal and do harm to an organization.* We can only guess at the number of times the traditional security manager has done an excellent job of ensuring that security officers are patrolling, physical security is operational, and the facility is protected, except that a hacker has penetrated the corporate IT system and stolen proprietary information or caused other harm to the business. Physical security specialists and IT specialists must work together for comprehensive protection. As explained earlier, an executive with a title such as Vice President of Security, Vice President of Loss Prevention, or Chief Security Officer can manage all aspects of security (i.e., physical and digital), work to ensure organizational survival, and report to senior executives.

Convergence of IT and physical security means that both specializations and related technologies unite for common objectives. Efforts to secure access to databases, e-mail, and organizational intranets are merging with access controls, fire and burglar alarm systems, and video surveillance. Physical security is increasingly relying on IT systems and related software. Both IT systems and physical security systems have sensors that generate data that is managed. As examples, an IT system will have an antivirus program and a physical security system will have motion detectors.

Bernard (2007: 475) notes that "convergence relating to security is occurring at two levels: technology and management." At the technology level is the convergence of digital information technology with electronic security systems. At the security management level, convergence is the integration of physical security functions, IT security, and security risk management.

There are advantages from the convergence of IT and physical security. These include the opportunity for security personnel to monitor physical security remotely from almost anywhere in the world, less travel time and expenses for monitoring and investigations, and easier software upgrades. Two disadvantages are a virus may affect physical security when sharing a single server; and an organization's bandwidth may reach its limit from the requirements of video surveillance.

Gural (2005: 9) cites a report from Forrester Research that shows increases in organizational spending that brings traditional security functions—CCTV, access controls, and security officer duties—onto the same platform as such functions as IT network access management. In addition, software is increasingly being used for detection and response instead of relying on only personnel. *Security Management* (Tech Talk, 2004: 45) notes that as traditional physical security increasingly relies on IT systems, IT specialists in organizations are playing a larger role in physical security decisions. IT specialists want to ensure that physical security technology is compatible with the network and safe from virus infections and hackers. Physical security purchasing decisions in organizations often consist of a committee of personnel from security or loss prevention, IT, and operations. Generally, the IT department has a larger budget than the security department, and this may increase the clout of IT in purchasing decisions. Furthermore, if IT managers can convince senior management that cybercrime is a greater threat than physical crime, then this also will influence the direction of the security budget (Computer Business Review, 2006).

Another player in corporate management change is the facility manager. This individual, often an engineer, ensures that the company's infrastructure, which houses people and operations, functions at optimum efficiency to support business goals. The traditional security department is likely to feel a "pull" toward IT or the facility manager because its boundaries are dissolving as a result of information and communications technology. The process of management is increasingly dependent on information, who controls it, what is done with it, and its dissemination. The power of IT especially is growing (Freeman, 2000: 10).

There are those who may claim the demise of the traditional security manager, who will be replaced by the IT manager or facility manager. The argument is that if an offender enters a facility and steals a computer, this crime is minor in comparison to, say, the potential harm from a hacker accessing a company's IT system. Such reasoning misses the broad, essential functions performed by the traditional security manager and staff. Examples are preventing crimes against people, responding to crimes, rendering first aid, conducting investigations, working with public police to arrest offenders, life safety, and fire protection. At the same time, traditional security practitioners must be put on notice to become involved in lifelong learning of IT systems, which touch all aspects of their traditional duties.

Convergence of Enterprise Security

Convergence of enterprise security refers to the merging of security functions throughout the entire business enterprise (i.e., business organization). Research conducted by Booz Allen Hamilton (2005) for ASIS International, and others, showed a trend of convergence of all components of security in organizations. The research report titled *Convergence of Enterprise Security Organizations* explains convergence in broad business terminology and emphasizes an enterprisewide view of risk. "Delivering on convergence is not just about organizational integration; rather it is about integrating the security disciplines with the business' mission to deliver shareholder value." "To be effective this converged approach should reach across people, processes, and technology, and enable enterprises to prevent, detect, respond to, and recover from any type of security incident." The research report referred to an incident at the Sumitomo Mitsui Bank in London, England, to illustrate the importance of merging security functions throughout the entire business enterprise. Although the bank had strong IT security measures, hackers took advantage of a lapse in physical security by posing as janitors and installing devices on computer keyboards that permitted them to obtain valuable login information. In 2004, in only three days the MyDoom e-mail virus caused about $22.6 billion in damages as it spread to more than 200 countries. Besides the initial costs of such incidents, long-term harm can damage reputation and brand, and if the incident threatens the public good, regulators may enact stricter regulations of business practices.

Surveys and interviews from the Booz Allen Hamilton research point to several internal and external drivers that are influencing the trend in convergence. They are

- *Rapid expansion of the enterprise ecosystem.* Enterprises are becoming more complex in a global economy of external partners.
- *Value migration from the physical to information-based and intangible assets.* Value is continuing to shift from physical to information-based assets.
- *New protective technologies blurring functional boundaries.* Technology is causing an overlap between physical and IT security.
- *New compliance and regulatory regimes.* Regulations are increasing in response to new threats and business interactions.
- *Continuing pressure to reduce cost.* Enterprises are constantly striving to efficiently reduce risk.

Many companies have two security directors, one for IT and the other for physical security. Do you agree with this approach? Why or why not?

Twenty-First Century/Post-9/11 Security Challenges

The last decade of the 20th century offered warnings of what was to come in the next century. The 1990s brought the first bombing of the World Trade Center, the bombing of the Murrah Federal Building in Oklahoma City, the first war with Iraq, crimes resulting from the Internet, the increased value of proprietary information, and attention to violence in the workplace.

As we know, not long into the 21st century, on September 11, 2001, terrorists attacked the World Trade Center and the Pentagon. Following the attacks, a crisis in confidence in government occurred. Citizens asked: How could the most powerful nation on earth be subject to such a devastating attack? What went wrong? Who is to blame? In response to the crisis, President George Bush declared war on terrorism. He appointed a new Cabinet position, the Office of Homeland Defense, to coordinate counterterrorism. The attacks also led to greater police powers for search and seizure and electronic surveillance, and the age-old question of how to balance police powers and constitutional rights.

These bold, surprise attacks, subsequent bioterrorism (i.e., anthrax attacks through the U.S. Postal System), the war in Afghanistan, and the second war in Iraq show the difficult challenges facing our world in this new century. The United States and its allies are not only faced with conflict in Iraq, Afghanistan, and other regions, but also old and emerging state competitors and the proliferation of weapons of mass destruction.

The 21st century has also recorded huge natural disasters that—along with the problem of terrorism—necessitate a rethinking of emergency management and business continuity. Hurricanes Katrina and Rita, in 2005, devastated Gulf-coast states. Katrina flooded New Orleans. The December 2004 Sumatran Tsunami killed almost 300,000 people and affected 18 countries around the Indian Ocean. The human and financial strain on nations in preparing for and responding to natural and accidental threats is overwhelming. These challenges require global cooperation, a broad base of knowledge, skills from many disciplines, and continued research.

From a business perspective, security and loss prevention practitioners are faced with serious challenges and questions as they assist their employers with surviving in a constantly changing world filled with risks. How can businesses and institutions protect employees, assets, and operations from terrorism and other risks? What does the future hold? Who will pay for protection? Although this book offers some insight into these questions, the answers are still being developed.

A rethinking of strategies will meet these threats. Through improved education, training, research, professionalism, creativity, astute planning, and support from our business and government leaders, security professionals will provide a safer environment.

Search the Web

Access the Web and seek an international perspective by visiting the New Scotland Yard, which includes links to history: http://www.met.police.uk

Use your favorite search engines to check the sites of major security companies. For example: http://www.pinkertons.com/

What did you learn from these sites?

Case Problems

1A. As a security manager you are asked to speak to a local college class on the history and development of the security and loss prevention field. What five significant points in the history of this field do you emphasize?

1B. As a part-time security officer and a full-time college student, you are now working on an assignment to think critically about the history of security and loss prevention and prepare a typed report. The assignment requires you to focus on some aspect of the history of security and loss prevention that you believe is biased or inaccurate, and to explain your interpretation of historical events.

1C. As Director of Security for a corporation, you are responsible for security officer operations, investigations, and physical security. You presently report to the Senior Vice President. A pending reorganization may place you, your department, and its budget under the supervision of either the Director of IT or the Director of Facilities. You may become an Assistant Director. Time is now available for possible negotiation. Changes will be finalized in three months. Soon you will be meeting with the Senior Vice President. Are you in favor of the pending changes? What suggestions do you offer? If you would like to maintain the present position of security, what justification and value do you offer your supervisor and the corporation? What justification and value do you think your supervisor will present to you to support change?

References

ASIS International. (2004). *Chief Security Officer Guideline*. www.asisonline.org, retrieved May 1, 2006.

Astor, S. (1978). *Loss Prevention: Controls and Concepts*. Stoneham, MA: Butterworth.

Bernard, R. (2007). "Convergence of Physical Security and IT." In J. Fay (Ed.), *Encyclopedia of Security Management*, 2nd ed. Burlington, MA: Elsevier Butterworth-Heinemann Pub.

Booz Allen Hamilton. (2005). *Convergence of Enterprise Security Organizations*. (November 8). www.securitymanagement.com, retrieved January 27, 2006.

Brinton, C., et al. (1973). *Civilization in the West*. Englewood Cliffs, NJ: Prentice-Hall.

Bugbee, P. (1978). *Principles of Fire Protection*. Boston: National Fire Protection Association.

CSO. (2004). "What Is a Chief Security Officer?" *CSO* (September 13). http://www.csoon-line.com/research/leadership/cso_role.html, retrieved May 1, 2006.

Computer Business Review. (2006). "Survey Says Cyber Crime Overtakes Physical Crime." *Computer Business Review Online*. www.cbronline.com, retrieved March 24, 2006.

Ellis, D. (1991). *Becoming a Master Student*, 6th ed. Rapid City, SD: College Survival, Inc.

Feuerwerker, A. (1989). "Great Wall of China." *World Book Encyclopedia*. Chicago, IL.

Freeman, J. (2000). "Security Director as Politician." *Security Technology & Design* (August).

Germann, A., Day, F., and Gallati, R. (1974). *Introduction to Law Enforcement and Criminal Justice*. Springfield, IL: Thomas Pub.

Gips, M. (2006). "Has Cybercrime Surpassed Physical Crime?" *Security Management*, 50 (July).

Gural, A. (2005). "Convergence Proves More Than Fad." *Security Director News*, 2 (February).

Holden, R. (1986). *Modern Police Management*. Englewood Cliffs, NJ: Prentice-Hall.

Naisbitt, J. (1982). *Megatrends*. New York: Warren Books.

Post, R., and Kingsbury, A. (1977). *Security Administration: An Introduction*, 3rd ed. Springfield, IL: Charles C. Thomas.

Safi, A., and Burrell, D. (2007). "Developing Critical Thinking Leadership Skills in Homeland Security Professionals, Law Enforcement Agents and Intelligence Analysts." *Homeland Defense Journal*, 5 (June).

Shelden, R. (2001). *Controlling the Dangerous Classes*. Boston, MA: Allyn & Bacon.

Spencer, J. (2000). "Of a Single Mind." *iSecurity* (November).

Stead, P. (1983). *The Police of France*. New York: Macmillan.

Tech Talk. (2004). "IT Gains Clout in Making Security Decisions." *Security Management*, 48 (June).

Toffler, A. (1980). *The Third Wave*. New York: Morrow.

Ursic, H., and Pagano, L. (1974). *Security Management Systems*. Springfield, IL: Charles C. Thomas.

Weisheit, R., Baker, L., and Falcone, D. (1995). *Crime and Policing in Rural and Small Town America: An Overview of the Issues*. Washington, DC: National Institute of Justice.

2

The Business, Careers, and Challenges of Security and Loss Prevention

Objectives

After studying this chapter, the reader will be able to:

1. Explain the risks and losses facing our society.
2. Define and illustrate metrics and explain why it is important.
3. Describe the security industry.
4. Define and explain privatization.
5. Describe the types of employment available in the security and loss prevention vocation.
6. Explain the limitations of the criminal justice system.
7. List and discuss the challenges of the security industry.

KEY TERMS	
• private sector	• direct losses
• public sector	• indirect losses
• human resources	• external metrics
• asset	• contract security
• operations of enterprises	• proprietary security
• risk	• privatization
• threat	• mercenary
• hazard	• deterrence
• all-hazards	• reactive strategies
• all hazards preparedness concept	• proactive strategies
• metrics	• Private Security Officer Employment Authorization Act of 2004
• internal metrics	• ethics
• methodological problems	

☐ ☐ ☐

> **The millions of employees in the security and loss prevention vocation protect people, assets, and the operations of enterprises.**

☐ ☐ ☐

Introduction

Security is "big business" globally, and there are many career opportunities and challenges in this profession. Several drivers are affecting the growth of this industry:

- Crimes, fires, accidents, and natural and other disasters pose threats to the general public and the public and private sectors worldwide.
- Offenders from throughout the world are constantly seeking to exploit vulnerabilities that they can pinpoint in government, businesses, institutions, nonprofits, and individuals.
- The 9/11 attacks, other terrorist threats, and the conflicts in Iraq, Afghanistan, and other locations illustrate the need for global security and safety.
- Government laws and mandates to improve homeland security and protect critical infrastructure and key assets are placing increasing responsibilities on protection programs.
- The challenges of risk management, such as increasing insurance premiums, are forcing businesses, institutions, and organizations to enhance their security and loss prevention programs to reduce risks.
- There is increased pressure on the security and loss prevention vocation and industry to improve professionalism, performance, and value to enterprises.

This chapter begins with basic definitions as a foundation for an explanation of what this business is about and what it seeks to accomplish. Subsequent paragraphs explain the importance of metrics as a way to show the value and performance of security and loss prevention. Another important topic in this business is customer service (explained in Chapter 5). The practitioners in this vocation must be mindful of value, performance, and customer service as vital strategies to survive in this business. These strategies are important for both proprietary and contract security organizations.

Businesses, often referred to as the **private sector**, exist to generate profit. Government, often referred to as the **public sector**, serves the general public and is supported by tax dollars. Both sectors contain security and loss prevention programs to protect *people*, *assets*, and the *operations of enterprises* from a broad variety of *threats* and *hazards* that can result in harm and losses. Here we emphasize protecting people connected in some way to organizations, as opposed to protecting the general public through the efforts of our armed forces and law enforcement agencies and other first responders. The people in organizations are referred to as employees or **human resources**. They must be protected if an enterprise is to continue its operations and pursue its objectives. However, other groups of people are connected to organizations and require protection. Examples are customers, vendors, and visitors. In fact, people are not required to be on the premises to receive protection, as in the case of an organization protecting customer information as required by law. From a business perspective, an **asset** is a resource controlled by an organization that can produce economic benefit. Examples are many and include cash, stocks, inventory, property, equipment, patents, copyrights, and goodwill. The **operations of enterprises** refer to the utilization of human resources and assets to pursue organizational objectives.

☐ ☐ ☐

> **The practitioners in the security and loss prevention vocation must be mindful of value, performance, and customer service as vital strategies to survive in this business.**

☐ ☐ ☐

Quinley and Schmidt (2002: 4), from the insurance and risk management discipline, define risk as "a measure of the frequency or probability of a negative event and the severity or consequences of that negative event." Leimberg et al. (2002: 82), from the same discipline, define risk as "exposure to damages that arises from property damage or bodily injury." Haddow and Bullock (2003: 15), from the emergency management discipline, use the definition of risk from the National Governors Association: "... susceptibility to death, injury, damage, destruction, disruption, stoppage and so forth." ASIS International (2003: 5), from the security discipline, defines risk as "the possibility of loss resulting from a threat, security incident, or event." **Risk** is defined here as the measurement of the frequency, probability, and severity of losses from exposure to threats or hazards. The management and measurement of risk are important processes that are continually being developed. These topics are explained in subsequent chapters.

A **threat** is a serious, impending, or recurring event that can result in loss, and it *must be dealt with immediately*. For instance, management in a corporation is informed that an employee stated that he intends to kill other employees, or, in another corporation, an increase in workplace violence occurs. A retailer typically incurs losses from internal theft and shoplifting. The expansion of e-commerce presents retailers with additional security concerns.

The U.S. Department of Homeland Security (2004: 66) defines hazard as "something that is potentially dangerous or harmful, often the root cause of an unwanted outcome." The U.S. Department of Justice (2000: 37) defines hazard as "any circumstances, natural or manmade, that may adversely affect or attack the community's businesses or residences." **Hazard** is defined here as a source of danger that has the potential to cause unwanted outcomes such as injury, death, property damage, economic loss, and environmental damage that adversely impact our society.

Table 2-1 depicts several threats/hazards that can cause losses. The frequency and cost of each loss vary. Each type of threat/hazard has its own specialist to work toward solutions.

Table 2-1 Threats/Hazards

Criminal Acts	Natural Disasters	Miscellaneous
Arson	Earthquake	Accident
Assault	Excessive Snow/Ice	Bad Investment
Burglary	Floods/Excessive Rain	Business
Computer Crime	Hurricane	Interruption
Counterfeiting	Landslide	Equipment Failure
Embezzlement	Lightning	Error
Espionage	Pandemic	Explosion
Extortion	Pestilence	Fire
Fraud	Tidal Wave	Litigation
Identity Theft	Tornado	Mine Disaster
Kidnapping	Tsunami	Nuclear
Larceny/Theft	Volcanic Eruption	Accident
Murder		Oil Spill
Product Tampering		Pollution
Riot		Poor Safety
Robbery		Poor Supervision
Sabotage		Power Outage
Sexual Assault		Sexual Harassment
Shoplifting		Sonic Boom
Substance Abuse		Strike
Terrorism		Unethical Conduct
Vandalism		War
		Waste

For instance, a rash of robberies in a liquor store may require additional public law enforcement assistance and the installation of a more sophisticated alarm system from the private sector. Numerous injuries at a manufacturing plant may require assistance from a safety specialist. The loss prevention manager—a specialist in his or her own right or with the assistance of a specialist—must plan, implement, and monitor programs to anticipate, prevent, and reduce loss.

Another important term is **all-hazards**. It refers to multiple types of hazards, including natural disasters (e.g., hurricane) and human-made events (e.g., inadvertent accidents, such as an aircraft crash, and deliberate events, such as the terrorist bombing of an aircraft). Another type is technological events. An example is an electric service blackout resulting from a variety of possible causes. The term *all-hazards* is important because it relates to the **all-hazards preparedness concept**. This means that different hazards contain similarities, and organizations can benefit, to a certain degree, from generic approaches to emergency management and business continuity. This provides an opportunity for efficient and cost-effective planning. In other words, how you prepare for one hazard may be similar for other hazards. This topic is covered in greater depth in a later chapter.

Metrics

Since *the business* of security and loss prevention is to protect people, assets, and the operations of enterprises, it is imperative that management in this vocation develop methods to measure security and loss prevention, loss events, and the cost of losses. Senior executives are sure to ask for evidence of the program's successes, effectiveness, return on investment, and when losses do occur, the cost and why it occurred. Methods of measurement can also be used to brief senior executives, help support a budget increase and additional resources, and justify human resources (e.g., proving one's value to the organization). Senior executives are also interested in what is driving the security and loss prevention program. Is it risks, legal requirements, regulations, or other factors?

Methods of measurement are referred to as **metrics**. These measurements show the *value* and *performance* that security and loss prevention brings to the business enterprise. Metrics are a vital component of quality management and essential when communicating with senior executives. Examples of metrics related to security are numerous and depend on business objectives and need. What may be a high priority metric for one business may not be important in another business.

Modern technology provides the opportunity to remotely monitor global operations, collect data, and report. In addition, the Web provides easy access to a variety of information and data to assist metrics.

Internal Metrics

Internal metrics focus on measurements within an organization. Examples of internal metrics include the annual number of theft incidents and the monetary value of company assets recovered; the percentage of employees hired and then released each year because it was later learned that they had falsified their backgrounds; the number of malfunctions of an access control system each month; and the number of contract security officers that are replaced each year due to poor performance.

Kovacich and Halibozek (2006: xxvii) define a security metric as "the application of quantitative, statistical, and/or mathematical analyses to measuring security functional costs, benefits, successes, failures, trends and workload—in other words, tracking the status of each security function in those terms." They describe two basic methods of tracking costs and benefits. The first is through recurring costs from day-to-day operations, such as security officer duties and investigations of loss of assets. Metrics can depict trends, such as whether the cost of protection is going up or down. The second method is through formal project plans that have a set schedule of beginning and ending dates, with specific objectives and costs that serve to track (i.e., metrics) time, expenses, and accomplishments.

Wailgum (2005) writes that metrics provide the numbers and context on performance of the security function. He adds that metrics vary by security executive, organization, and industry. Wailgum offers examples of how metrics are used by various businesses. He refers to a retail chain of thousands of stores. One metric used is the number of robberies per 1,000 stores. This figure is compared to the rates of other similar retail chains. Another metric is cash loss as a percentage of sales for every retail unit. The retailer uses many other metrics.

Wailgum provides another illustration through a utility company that uses metrics to gauge its compliance with federal regulations. It compares performance on "readiness reviews" among different facilities. Readiness reviews assess whether employees understand threat plans and what to do when the threat level is raised or lowered. It also covers physical security and emergency action plans, among other areas. Another example is penetration testing to breach security. How far can someone reach without a badge? Can someone talk his or her way around delivery procedures? These evaluations can be quantified and compared over time.

Metrics are subject to **methodological problems.** This means that measurements are not perfect and subject to a host of factors that may result in inaccuracies. Factors that can distort metrics include variations and inconsistencies in the use of definitions, exclusion of indirect losses, inconsistencies in reporting, bias, miscalculations, the possibility of fraud, and difficulty when making comparisons among organizations. Furthermore, *metrics may produce more evidence about the way in which the enterprise is managed than about actual events and losses.* For instance, one company that maintains a zero tolerance for violence in the workplace shows data indicating numerous incidents of threats and violence, while another similar company, with a corporate culture that almost ignores the problem, shows few incidents.

Why Emphasize Both Direct and Indirect Losses?

The methodology of metrics should include direct and indirect losses. Businesses, institutions, and organizations can suffer extensive direct losses from threats and hazards. Additionally, indirect losses can be devastating and often surpass direct losses. **Direct losses** are immediate, obvious losses, whereas **indirect losses** are prolonged and often hidden. A burglary at a business, for example, may show the loss of, say, $1,000 from a safe. However, on close inspection of indirect losses, total losses may include the following: damage to the door or window where the break-in occurred; replacement of the destroyed safe; insurance policy deductible; increase in insurance premium; loss of sales from a delay in opening the business; customer dissatisfaction; and employee time required to speak with police, insurance representatives, and repair people. Depending on the seriousness of the loss, additional indirect losses could include adverse media attention, permanent loss of customers, employee morale problems, turnover, and negative reactions from shareholders. *Security practitioners can help justify their position and their value to the business community by demonstrating total losses resulting from each incident and all hazards.*

External Metrics

External metrics focus on society-wide measurements. Examples include the risk of crimes or natural disaster in a geographic area. External metrics help enterprises make business decisions, such as the geographic location for business investment and the types of insurance to purchase. They have many uses for security and loss prevention programs, including planning and budgeting for strategies to prevent crimes, fires, and accidents.

Several external sources measure risk, society-wide loss events, and the cost of losses. Public and private sector organizations collect data and publish reports that may or may not be available to the general public. The U.S. Department of Justice publishes crime statistics that are easily accessible on the Web. The U.S. Department of State publishes information on terrorism and safety in other countries that is also easily accessible on the Web. Risk management and insurance firms offer services for a fee that estimate risks and costs from all-hazards. A government agency may withhold data and reports due to reasons of national security, whereas a corporation may see its data and reports as proprietary information and/or subject to sale. As with internal metrics, methodological problems exist with external metrics.

Here we take a look at some public and private sector organizations that serve as a gauge of risks facing not only society, but also business enterprises, institutions, and other organizations within society. An emphasis is placed on the risk of crimes, fires, and accidents because, traditionally, security and loss prevention practitioners have expended considerable time and resources on these problems. However, as explained in this book, our world is becoming increasingly complex and practitioners are facing a broader variety of risks.

Crimes

In 1930, Congress passed the first legislation mandating the collection of crime data. The task was assigned to the Federal Bureau of Investigation (FBI), within the U.S. Department of Justice, and each year the *Uniform Crime Report* (UCR) provides data on crime trends. It helps to calculate quality of life in communities throughout the country; set government policy; plan funding; and gauge the effectiveness of anticrime strategies. The data are collected by police agencies that report it to the FBI. There are many weaknesses of the UCR, and the data have been called notoriously inaccurate. Examples of UCR problems are as follows: it represents *reported* crimes, and many crimes are not reported to police; only local and state crimes are reported, not federal crimes or crimes at institutions (e.g., jails and prisons); definitions of crimes vary among states; and the data have been subject to political manipulation. To improve the UCR, the FBI is refining a newer system—the National Incident-Based Reporting System—that collects data that are more specific. In 1972, because of the shortcomings of the UCR, the National Crime Victim Survey (NCVS) began to collect crime data from households. It was found that there was a significantly higher rate of crime than what was reported in the UCR. Forcible rape, robbery, aggravated assault, burglary, and larceny were reported by the NCVS at rates two to three times greater than rates reported in UCR data. NCVS data are gathered by the Bureau of Justice Statistics (U.S. Department of Justice) and the U.S. Census Bureau (Fagin, 2005: 34–41).

Although the methodology of collecting crime data by official sources is problematic, crime is a serious problem, and millions of crimes are committed each year in the United States. In 2004, the UCR showed 1,367,009 violent crimes and 10,328,255 property crimes. Both categories showed a decrease in crime by about 1% from the previous year (FBI, 2006). Other sources of crime data are available from individual states, educational institutions, and self-report surveys conducted by researchers who use questionnaires to gather anonymous input on crimes committed by offenders.

Barkan (2006: 75) writes that crime data gathered outside the United States is highly inconsistent. Some nations gather crime data similar to the United States, while other nations do not collect such data. Three major sources of international crime data are the International Criminal Police Organization (INTERPOL), the World Health Organization, and the United Nations. The collection of global crime data also suffers from methodological problems.

Chamard (2006: 2) notes that there are few studies on the victimization of businesses in the United States, even though crime costs the U.S. economy at least $186 billion annually and businesses suffer disproportionately from crime in comparison to households and individuals. She argues that the UCR underreports crimes against businesses. Chamard refers to a British study of small businesses that found that nearly two-thirds had suffered some form of victimization over a five-year span. She reports on cross-national surveys that suggest, "retail businesses may have an overall burglary risk that is ten times greater than the risk faced by households."

Fires

Fire represents another serious hazard facing organizations. Two major sources that measure the fire problem are the National Fire Protection Association (NFPA) and the U.S. Fire Administration (USFA). The National Fire Data Center (NFDC) of the USFA periodically publishes *Fire in the United States*, a 10-year overview of fires in the United States. It is designed to motivate corrective action, set priorities, serve as a model for state and local analysis of fire data, and serve as a baseline for evaluating programs. Because of the time it takes for states to submit data, the publication lags the date of data collection.

The U.S. Fire Administration (2005) reported that the U.S. fire problem is one of the worst in the industrial world. In 2005, the fire problem resulted in the following losses: 3,675 civilian deaths and 17,925 injuries; 115 firefighter deaths while on duty; 1.6 million fires reported and many went unreported; property loss at about $10.7 billion; and there were 31,500 intentionally set structure fires resulting in 315 civilian deaths. Furthermore, fire killed more Americans than all natural disasters combined and 83% of all civilian fire deaths occurred in residences (U.S. Fire Administration, 2006).

Accidents

Accidents pose another serious hazard facing organizations and their employees when on and off the job. The Occupational Safety & Health Administration (2006) reported 4.4 million injuries and illnesses among private sector firms in 2003, with about 32% of work-related injuries occurring in goods-producing industries and 68% in services. The same year recorded 5,559 worker deaths, including 114 additional deaths from the previous year among self-employed workers and 61 more from workplace violence.

The National Center for Injury Prevention and Control (2006) reported that society-wide there are about 160,000 deaths each year from injuries, and millions more people are injured and survive. In 2000, the 50 million injuries that required medical treatment will ultimately cost $406 billion, including $80.2 billion in medical care costs and $326 billion in productivity losses.

The Security Industry

The security industry is a multibillion-dollar business. Every decade seems to bring an increased need for security. Internal theft, computer crime, street crime, terrorism, natural disasters, and so on bring greater demands for protection. In the United States, thousands of companies provide contract security services and investigations. In addition, there are manufacturers of products and systems and thousands of alarm installation firms.

The Freedonia Group (2006), a market research firm, publishes "World Security Services." It reported the following:

- U.S. demand for private contracted security services will grow 4.3% annually through 2010. This is a $39 billion industry. Guarding and alarming monitoring will remain dominant. Other services include security consulting, systems integration, armored transport, prison management, and private investigations.
- World demand for private contracted security services will grow 7.7% annually through 2008 based on heightened fears of global terrorism and rising crime. This is a $95 billion industry. Guarding will remain dominant.
- U.S. demand for electronic security products and systems will grow 8.7% annually through 2008. This is a $10 billion industry.
- World demand for electronic security products and systems will grow at 8.4% yearly through 2008. This is a $49 billion industry.

The American Society for Industrial Security, known as ASIS International (ASIS), is a major organization of security professionals who are at the forefront of improving the security industry through education and training, certifications, research, security guidelines, and global collaborative initiatives. The ASIS Foundation funded research by Eastern Kentucky University, with support from the National Institute of Justice, to focus on three primary areas: (1) the size and economic strength of the various security sectors, including security services and providers of security technology; (2) changes in security trends pre and post 9/11; and (3) the nature of the relationship between private security and law enforcement. Preliminary findings included the following (ASIS Foundation, 2004):

- Company security budgets in the United States increased 14% from 2001 to 2002, decreased slightly in 2003, and increased 10% in 2004.

- More companies are purchasing computer/network security systems (40%), burglar alarms (26%), and closed-circuit television (CCTV; 24%) than any other types of security systems or products.
- Ninety percent of companies stated that security-related contacts with law enforcement had remained the same.

In 2005, the final report was released, and it contained results of four different nation-wide surveys: (1) all U.S. companies; (2) ASIS companies (ASIS members identified as security managers for companies); (3) ASIS security services (ASIS members identified as managers of companies that provide security services); and (4) local law enforcement agencies. A sample of the findings is listed next (Collins et al., 2005):

- In the next fiscal year, all three types of companies expected increases in security budget/revenue.
- ASIS companies were about 20% more likely than all U.S. companies to report increased investments in security as a result of the 9/11 attacks.
- Over one-half of ASIS companies indicated an increased emphasis on information security following the 9/11 attacks, compared to 31% of all U.S. companies.
- Of all U.S. companies, finance–insurance–real estate continue to be most impacted by 9/11, in comparison to transportation–communication–utilities, agriculture–mining–construction, manufacturing, and wholesale–retail.
- For all U.S. companies, the top three concerns were computer/network security, liability insurance, and employee theft. For ASIS companies, the top three were access control, property crime, and a tie between workplace violence and terrorism.
- One-half of ASIS companies reported increased contact with police agencies since 9/11, whereas only 10% of all U.S. companies reported increased contact. The researchers concluded that larger companies and those with professional security personnel have been much more likely to develop public-private partnerships than smaller companies have.
- The least common type of contact with police agencies among ASIS companies and U.S. companies was on cyber-crimes. The researchers surmise that the reason could be attributed to limited knowledge of cyber-crime by police or inadequate response.

Contract versus Proprietary Security

Contract security refers to businesses that seek a profit by offering a host of security services to businesses, institutions, and organizations. Examples of services include security officers, investigations, consulting, and monitoring alarm systems. Depending on its unique needs and weighing several factors, an entity requiring security may prefer to establish its own security, known as **proprietary** (in-house) **security**, of which there are thousands. In addition, an organization may use both contract and proprietary security (see Figure 2-1).

The *Report of the Task Force on Private Security* (U.S. Department of Justice, 1976b: 146–147 and 249–257) lists several factors to consider concerning contract versus proprietary security officers. Contract security generally is less expensive, although there are exceptions. The service company typically handles recruitment, selection, training, and supervision. Hiring unqualified security officers and rapid turnover are two primary disadvantages of con-tract services. Many contract officers are "moonlighting" and subject to fatigue. Questions concerning insurance and liability between the security company and the client may be hazy.

A major advantage of a proprietary force is that greater control is maintained over personnel, including selection, training, and supervision, and of course, such a force is more familiar with the unique needs of the company. Salaries and benefits, however, often make establishment of a proprietary force more expensive.

Research is needed to ascertain the number of security officers employed in both contract and proprietary security in the United States and the impact the 9/11 attacks has had on these numbers. Wagner (2006: 2) reports that 1.5 million are employed in

FIGURE 2-1 Businesses often employ both proprietary and contract security personnel.

the nation's security companies. The U.S. Department of Justice, Office of Community Oriented Policing Services (2004: 1–2) states that studies of the private security industry suggest there may be as many as 90,000 private security organizations employing about 2 million security officers and other practitioners in the United States. Parfomak (2004: 8–9) writes that overall employment of U.S. security officers has declined, although increases have occurred in certain infrastructure sectors. He notes that there was a sharp increase in demand for security officers following the 9/11 attacks, but it was short term. For decades, security officers have outnumbered public police in most locales.

The U.S. Department of Justice, Bureau of Justice Statistics (2006: 6) reports 1.1 million employed in police protection, in 2003, as follows: 157,000 federal, 106,000 state, and 856,000 local. According to the FBI (2006), in 2004, 14,254 state, city, university and college, metropolitan and nonmetropolitan county, and other law enforcement agencies employed 675,734 sworn officers and 294,854 civilians, who provided law enforcement services to more than 278 million people nationwide. The FBI-UCR Program defines sworn law enforcement officers as individuals who carry a firearm and a badge, have full arrest powers, and are paid from government funds. Civilians working in law enforcement agencies perform a variety of functions (e.g., dispatch, records) at a lower cost than if sworn officers performed the tasks.

□ □ □ ▬▬▬▬▬▬▬▬▬▬▬▬▬▬▬▬▬▬▬▬▬▬▬▬

Privatization

Privatization is the contracting out of government programs, either wholly or in part, to for-profit and not-for-profit organizations. There is a growing interdependence of the public and private sectors. A broad array of services is provided to government agencies by the private sector today, from consulting services to janitorial services. Both government and the private sector are operating hospitals, schools, and other institutions formerly dominated by government. For crime control efforts, we see private security patrols in residential areas, private security officers in courts, and private prisons. Business people make themselves attractive to governments when they claim that they can perform services more efficiently and at a lower cost than the public sector.

Privatization is not a new concept. In the late 1600s, much security and incarceration for early urban areas was supplied by the private sector. By the 1700s, government dominated these services. Today, privatization can be viewed as a movement to demonopolize and decentralize services dominated by government. This movement to privatize criminal justice services encourages shared responsibility for public safety (Bowman, 1992: 15–57).

Another factor fueling the privatization movement is victim and citizen dissatisfaction with the way in which government is handling crime. Increasing numbers of citizens are confronting crime through neighborhood watches, citizen patrols, crime stoppers, hiring private attorneys to assist prosecutors, and dispute resolution.

Critics of privatization argue that crime control by government is rooted in constitutional safeguards and crime control should not be contracted to the private sector. Use of force and searches by the private sector, punishment in private prisons, and liabilities of governments and contractors are examples of the thorny issues that face privatization.

Since the 9/11 attacks, and because U.S. military engagements in Afghanistan and Iraq have strained U.S. military resources, private security companies have been increasingly guarding military installations in the United States. Supporters note that these private security officers are supervised and trained by Department of Defense (DOD) specifications, and they provide an invaluable service. Critics argue that there is concern about the caliber and training of these security officers and some work for American subsidiaries of foreign-owned companies. This concern led to a U.S. Government Accountability Office (GAO) investigation that found that some contractors had hired felons and that training records had been falsified. The GAO found that the contracts cost 25% more than contracts later put out for bid. And, the Army relied on what the contractors said they were doing and provided very little monitoring. The DOD pledged to improve management and oversight of private security officers (Marks, 2006; U.S. Government Accountability Office, 2006).

Private military and private security companies (PMPSCs) are providing a wide variety of services for a profit in geographic areas facing conflict. These firms are growing rapidly worldwide. Governments, corporations, organizations, and individuals are relying on these companies for many reasons. A national government, for example, may need additional personnel because human resources and expertise are stretched to the limit and a rebel group is gaining strength. A corporation, organization (e.g., nonprofit aid group), or individual may require protection for operations in a foreign country containing an insurgency and weak police and military forces. In addition, a country may be dangerous because of a hodgepodge of self-defense forces, mercenary units, militias, and vigilante squads that maintain their own agendas. The uncontrolled proliferation of conventional arms has hastened the growth of armed groups (Purpura, 2007).

Zarate (1998) writes that the term *mercenary* is difficult to define and United Nations members disagree on its definition. He refers to a **mercenary** as "a soldier-for-hire, primarily motivated by pecuniary interests, who has no national or territorial stake in a conflict and is paid a salary above the average for others of his rank." Zarate sees the legal issues involving mercenaries as unclear, but views the legal status of companies that provide military and security services—such as training, security and other noncombat activities—as outside the mercenary concerns of the international community.

Zarate offers two concerns: (1) PMPSCs could be hired by insurgents or foreign governments to destabilize an established regime, or a government could hire a PMPSC to suppress a national liberation movement (e.g., group fighting colonialism or racism); and (2) PMPSCs that assist multinational corporations will act solely for the benefit of the corporation in foreign countries and create semi-sovereign entities supported by the government. He adds that PMPSCs are regulated in most countries. In the United States, regulations are stringent, and registration with the U.S. government is required.

In Iraq, companies helping to rebuild the country with multibillion dollar U.S. government appropriations initially relied on U.S. forces for protection. However, the growing insurgency forced U.S. forces to be redirected, and companies quickly sought assistance from PMPSCs (Flores and Earl, 2004).

The hostilities in Iraq and Afghanistan provide excellent opportunities for PMPSCs, and especially those firms with employees possessing military backgrounds that can provide support to the U.S. military and train the armies of weak countries. The U.S. Army (2006: 6–4 and 8–17) notes, "training support from contractors enables commanders to use Soldiers and Marines more efficiently." The support includes institutional training, developing security ministries and headquarters, and establishing administrative and logistic systems. In addition, theater support contractors (i.e., local vendors in hostile areas) supply a host of products and services. Examples are concrete security barriers, fencing, construction, sanitation, and trucking. As the United States pursues a global war on terrorism, with limited armed forces, private contractors are in demand.

☐ ☐ ☐ ▬▬▬▬▬▬▬▬▬▬▬▬▬▬▬▬▬▬▬▬▬▬▬▬

What are your views on privatization?

▬▬▬▬▬▬▬▬▬▬▬▬▬▬▬▬▬▬▬▬▬▬▬▬ ☐ ☐ ☐

Careers: Loss Prevention Services and Specialists

Many services and specialists from the private sector can help the practitioner develop an effective loss prevention program. These services and specialists can be proprietary or attainable through outside sources. Table 2-2 lists various facilities requiring security and loss prevention programs. Since the 9/11 attacks, many of these facilities have been referred to as "critical infrastructure." Table 2-3 lists security and loss prevention services and products from the private sector. Table 2-4 lists specialists and consultants who can aid loss prevention efforts. These tables are not conclusive because protection programs are becoming increasingly specialized and diversified. Therefore, additional specialization will evolve to aid these programs.

Most loss prevention managers are generalists, which means that they have a broad knowledge of the field plus specialized knowledge of the risks facing their employer. When feasible, these managers should develop a multidisciplinary staff to assist in protection objectives. The staff should represent various specializations as appropriate, such as security, safety, and fire protection.

☐ ☐ ☐ ▬▬▬▬▬▬▬▬▬▬▬▬▬▬▬▬▬▬▬▬▬▬▬▬

Career: Manufacturing Security

Manufacturers make products, which, in turn, are sold, either to wholesalers, distributors, or directly to consumers. Professionals within the manufacturing security specialty are responsible for issues involving not only sales transactions, but also transport issues, ordering and purchasing of raw materials, and the protection of resources against loss or theft. Manufacturers are becoming increasingly aware of the potential for loss. Prevention of loss can be accomplished only through employing competent security directors and managers who can help integrate the security function into the total operation instead of allowing it to remain isolated. Depending on the products being manufactured, individuals in this specialty may work in a variety of environments, including exposure to varying weather conditions and involvement with chemical processing areas.

Table 2-2 Locations Requiring Security and Loss Prevention Programs

• Agriculture/Food Facilities	• Industrial
• Airport/Airline	• Library
• Campus/School	• Medical
• Commercial Buildings	• National Monument
• Cultural Properties	• Nuclear Plant
• Defense Industries and Facilities	• Park/Recreation
• Drinking Water	• Port
• Emergency Services	• Postal/Shipping
• Energy Facilities	• Retail Store/Mall
• Financial Institution	• Sports/Entertainment Facility
• Gaming/Wagering	• Telecommunications
• Government Building	• Transportation
• Hotel/Motel/Restaurant	• Wholesale/Warehouse
• Housing/Residential	• Others

Table 2-3 Security Services and Products from the Private Sector

Services	*Products*
• Armored Transportation (see Figure 2-2)	• Access Control Systems
• Business Continuity/Emergency Management	• Barriers
• Canine	• Closed-Circuit Television
• Central Alarm Station	• Doors
• Consulting	• Fire Alarm Systems
• Counterterrorism	• Glazing
• Detection of Deception (e.g., polygraph)	• Intrusion Detection Systems
• Executive Protection	• Lighting
• Honesty Shopping	• Locks/Keys
• Information Security	• Safes/Vaults
• Investigations	• Vehicles
• Risk Analysis/Security Survey	• Weapons
• Security Officers	• Others
• Technical Surveillance Countermeasures	
• Undercover Investigations	
• Others	

Table 2-4 Specialists and Consultants Who Can Assist Loss Prevention Efforts

• Accountant	• Forensic Scientist
• Auditor	• Landscape Architect
• Architect	• Lifesafety/Fire Consultant
• Business Consultant	• Lighting Consultant
• Computer/IT Consultant	• Locksmith
• Criminologist	• Marketing Consultant
• Critical Infrastructure Consultant	• Risk Management Consultant
• Education/Training Consultant	• Others
• Engineering Consultant	

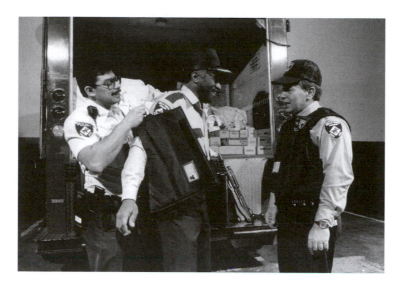

FIGURE 2-2 Employees wear bullet-resistant vests and personal hold-up alarms to help protect them as they pick up and deliver valuable shipments.

Entry-level management positions generally require at least an associate's degree and often a bachelor's degree. Most positions require two-plus years of general security experience and may require some specialty-specific training or experience. A Certified Protection Professional (CPP) designation is preferred for many positions. The salary range for most positions is $30,000 to $50,000.

Mid-level management positions generally require a bachelor's degree and five-plus years of general security experience and may require some specialty-specific training or experience. A CPP designation is required or desired for many positions.

Source: Courtesy of ASIS International (2005). "Career Opportunities in Security." www.asisonline.org.

The Limitations of the Criminal Justice System: Implications for Loss Prevention Practitioners

Federal, state, and local governments spent over $185 billion for criminal and civil justice in 2003 (U.S. Department of Justice, Bureau of Justice Statistics, 2006: 1). Despite this huge sum, many theories underpinning crime prevention and law enforcement measures have come under increased scrutiny. For example, the strategy of **deterrence** has been questioned. This criminal justice system strategy seeks to prevent crime through state-imposed punishment. This model points out that offenders rationally consider the risks and rewards of crime prior to acting. Numerous offenders simply find that "crime pays," because the certainty of punishment is a myth and the odds are in the offender's favor. John E. Conklin (2001: 466), a criminologist, writes: "People have imperfect knowledge of the maximum penalties for various crimes, but their perceptions of the severity of sanctions, the certainty with which they will be administered, and the promptness of punishment influence their choice of behavior." Since the impact of deterrence is questionable, crime prevention is a key strategy to reduce losses.

Another limitation of the criminal justice system is that tight budgets and limited resources and personnel are the main reasons why public safety agencies play a minor role in private loss prevention programs. Public police agencies cannot afford to assign personnel to patrol inside business establishments or watch for employee theft. An occasional (public) police patrol and a response to a crime are the primary forms of assistance that public police can provide to businesses. Prosecutors are unwilling to prosecute certain crimes against businesses because of heavy caseloads. Consequently, public protection is being supplemented or replaced by private security and volunteer efforts in many locales.

Law enforcement agencies expend much of their resources on street crime, traffic problems, and other issues of public safety. Although some law enforcement officers maintain an expertise in security, computer crime, accounting, fraud, intelligence, and other specializations helpful to businesses, the number of officers possessing such backgrounds is too few to assist the volume of threats facing the private sector.

Besides public police agencies, other first-responding agencies—fire departments, emergency medical services, and emergency management agencies—also have limited resources. Consequently, the private sector must develop security and loss prevention programs and hire specialists to ameliorate all-hazards.

☐ ☐ ☐ ▬▬▬▬▬▬▬▬▬▬▬▬▬▬▬▬▬▬▬▬▬▬▬▬▬▬▬▬▬▬

The United States employs an average of 2.3 full-time law enforcement officers for every 1,000 inhabitants in communities (FBI, 2006).

☐ ☐ ☐ ▬▬▬▬▬▬▬▬▬▬▬▬▬▬▬▬▬▬▬▬▬▬▬▬▬▬▬▬▬▬

The Basic Differences between Public Police and Private Security

The primary differences pertain to the *employer*, the *interests served*, *basic strategies*, and *legal authority*. Public police are employed by governments and serve the general public. Tax dollars support public police activities. On the other hand, private security personnel are employed by and serve private concerns (e.g., businesses) that provide the funds for this type of protection. There are exceptions to these general statements. For instance, government agencies sometimes contract protection needs to private security companies to cut costs. Also, public police often are involved in efforts to assist business owners in preventing crimes through security surveys and public education.

Another difference involves basic strategies. Public police devote considerable resources to **reactive strategies** to crimes. This entails rapid response to serious crimes, investigation, and apprehension of offenders. Law enforcement is a key objective. In contrast, private security personnel stress the *prevention* of crimes; arrests are often de-emphasized. These generalizations contain exceptions. For instance, public police have introduced **proactive strategies** to reduce crime through aggressive patrol methods and enhanced information systems that assist police officers on the street in identifying suspects they encounter.

The legal authority of public police and private security personnel is another distinguishing characteristic. Public police derive their authority from statutes and ordinances, whereas private security personnel function commonly as private citizens. Public police have greater arrest, search, and interrogation powers. Depending on the jurisdiction and state laws, private security personnel may be deputized or given special commissions that increase powers.

☐ ☐ ☐ ▬▬▬▬▬▬▬▬▬▬▬▬▬▬▬▬▬▬▬▬▬▬▬▬▬▬▬▬▬▬

In your opinion, what are the most serious problems of the criminal justice system, and what are your solutions?

▬▬▬▬▬▬▬▬▬▬▬▬▬▬▬▬▬▬▬▬▬▬▬▬▬▬▬▬▬▬ ☐ ☐ ☐

Challenges of the Security Industry

During the 1970s, business and government leaders increasingly viewed the growing private security industry as an ally of the criminal justice system. Both crime-fighting sectors have mutual and overlapping functions in controlling crime. With this thinking in mind, the U.S. Department of Justice provided financial support for the production of important research reports. *The Rand Report* (U.S. Department of Justice, 1972: 30) focused national attention on the problems and needs of the private security industry. This report stated, "the typical private guard is an aging white male, poorly educated, usually untrained, and very poorly paid." This conclusion has met with criticism because the research sample was small, and, thus, did not represent the entire security industry. However, with the assistance of this report and its recommendations, the professionalism of private security improved.

The Rand Report was a great aid (because of limited literature in the field) to the *Report of the Task Force on Private Security* (U.S. Department of Justice, 1976b). This report of the National Advisory Committee on Criminal Justice Standards and Goals represented the first national effort to set realistic and viable standards and goals designed to maximize the ability, competency, and effectiveness of the private security industry for its role in the prevention and reduction of crime. A major emphasis of the report was that all businesses that sell security services should be licensed and all personnel in private security work should be registered.

The task force's urging of stricter standards for the security industry reflected a need to reduce ineptitude and industry abuses, while striving toward professionalism. The task force focused on minimal hiring, training, and salary standards that are still problems today. These minimal standards enable companies to reduce costs and provide potential clients with low bids for contract service. Thus, professionalism is sacrificed to keep up with competition. The task force recommended improved hiring criteria, higher salaries (especially to reduce turnover), and better training, among other improvements. Both studies recommended state-level regulation of the security industry in general as a means of creating more uniformity.

Another major study of the security industry funded by the U.S. Department of Justice was titled *Private Security and Police in America: The Hallcrest Report* (Cunningham and Taylor, 1985). It focused research on three major areas: (1) the contributions of both public police and private security to crime control; (2) the interaction of these two forces and their level of cooperation; and (3) the characteristics of the private security industry. Several industry problems and preferred solutions were discussed in this report, as covered in subsequent pages.

The U.S. Department of Justice funded a second Hallcrest Report titled *Private Security Trends: 1970–2000, The Hallcrest Report II* (Cunningham et al., 1990). This report provided a study of security trends to the 21st century. Some of its predictions are listed next. This list can assist us in thinking critically about security today.

- Crime against business in the United States will cost $200 billion by the year 2000.
- Since the middle 1980s, companies have been less inclined to hire security managers with police and military backgrounds and more inclined to hire those with a business background.
- During the 1990s, in-house security staffs will diminish with an increased reliance on contract services and equipment.
- The negative stereotypical security personnel are being replaced with younger, better-educated officers with greater numbers of women and minority group members. However, the problems of quality, training, and compensation remain.
- The false-alarm problem is continuing. There is a massive waste of public funds when police and fire agencies must respond to current levels of false alarms. Between 97% and 99% of all alarms are false.

☐ ☐ ☐ ▬▬▬▬▬▬▬▬▬▬▬▬▬▬▬

Upon selecting at least one prediction of the *Hallcrest Report II,* is the prediction true today?

▬▬▬▬▬▬▬▬▬▬▬▬▬ ☐ ☐ ☐

Cooperation between Public Police and Private Security

The following statements are from *Law Enforcement and Private Security: Sources and Areas of Conflict* (U.S. Department of Justice, 1976a: 6):

> *A persistent problem noted by several research reports involves disrespect and even conflict between public and private police.*
>
> *Some law enforcement officers believe that being a "public servant" is of a higher moral order than serving private interests.... They then relegate private security to an inferior status.... This perceived status differential by law enforcement personnel manifests itself in lack of respect and communication, which precludes effective cooperation.*

These problems persist in the 21st century, even though many public police work part-time in the private security industry and, upon retiring, secure positions in this vocation. To reduce conflict, the *Task Force Report* and the *Hallcrest Reports* recommended liaison be implemented between public and private police. During the 1980s, the International Association of Chiefs of Police, the National Sheriffs' Association, and the American Society for Industrial Security began joint meetings to foster better cooperation between the public and private sectors (Cunningham et al., 1991). This effort continued into the 1990s. Suggested areas of increased cooperation included appointing high-ranking practitioners from both sectors to increase communication, instituting short training lessons in established training programs, and sharing expertise.

According to a 2004 national policy summit on public police and private security cooperation, only 5–10% of law enforcement chief executives participate in partnerships with private security (U.S. Department of Justice, Office of Community Oriented Policing Services, 2004). Although both groups have a lot to offer each other, they are not always comfortable working together. Police continue to criticize security over their lower standards for screening and training, and they may see security as a threat to their domain. Police often fall short of understanding the important role of private security. At the same time, some security personnel see police as elitists and claim that police are not concerned about security until they seek a position in the security field. Here are observations by participants of the 2004 national policy summit:

- Issues include respect (that is, law enforcement's lack of respect for security), trust, training differentials, and competition.
- Community policing calls on law enforcement to develop relationships with various sectors of the community. Police departments meet regularly with local clergy, business groups, neighborhood associations, and other groups. They do not seem to meet regularly with groups of corporate security directors and managers of security businesses.
- Information sharing is difficult. Corporations do not feel they receive timely information from police, and they fear that information they give to the police may end up in the newspaper. Police fear that the corporate sector may not treat law enforcement information discreetly.
- There is much role confusion between the public and private sectors, such as confusion about what will be done in an emergency. If a company's plant suffers an explosion, police may immediately declare it a crime scene, and then the company's security staff may not be able to respond as needed. Likewise, in the post-9/11 era, law enforcement officers show up to conduct risk assessments but often are not as knowledgeable about them as private security.
- A city may simultaneously have some outstanding partnerships but also some counterproductive relationships. The 9/11 attacks helped in building relationships. The true measure of success, however, is whether a partnership accomplishes something and is lasting.
- Both parties have a responsibility for improving partnerships.
- Each side should educate the other about its capabilities, before a crisis erupts, so each will know when to call on the other and what help to expect (and to offer). Integrated training may break down some barriers.

Cooperation between both groups takes many forms and occurs at many levels of government. To varying degrees, both groups share information with each other, attend each other's conferences, and plan together for protection and emergencies. They even work side-by-side at certain sites, such as downtown districts, government buildings, and special events.

An improved partnership between both groups can be beneficial to our nation by improving planning and emergency response and by sharing information, expertise, and training. At the 2004 national policy summit, public police and private security leaders recommended that both groups should make a formal commitment to cooperate. Also, the U.S. Department of Homeland Security (DHS) and/or the U.S. Department of Justice should fund relevant research and training; create an advisory council to oversee partnerships to address tactical issues and intelligence sharing, improve selection and training for private security personnel, and create a national partnership center; and organize periodic summits on relevant issues. On the local level, immediate action should be taken to improve joint response to critical incidents; coordinate infrastructure protection; improve communications and data interoperability; bolster information sharing; prevent and investigate high-tech crime; and plan responses to workplace crime (U.S. Department of Justice, Office of Community Oriented Policing Services, 2004: 3–4).

The 9/11 attacks caused the federal government to develop numerous programs and strategies to enhance homeland security. The federal government expanded its role in regulating certain aspects of private industries to protect against terrorism and other risks, especially since the private sector owns 85% of U.S. critical infrastructure. Federal law enforcement agencies are working with private sector executives, including security executives, to control terrorism. The U.S. Treasury Department, for example, has directed companies in not only the finance business, but also brokerage firms, casinos, and other businesses, to reduce terrorist financing by taking specific steps at their own expense, such as establishing or expanding anti-money-laundering programs. The U.S. Food and Drug Administration provide guidelines to the food industry to prevent terrorist attacks on the nation's food supply.

To facilitate communications and to share information on homeland security with private industry, the federal government hosts conferences and training sessions. Federal initiatives include disaster-preparedness grants involving coordination efforts of local governments and businesses.

Another initiative is the Information Sharing and Analysis Centers (ISACs). These are generally private sector networks of organizations that the federal government has helped to create to share information on threats to critical industries and coordinate efforts to identify and reduce vulnerabilities.

A variety of other public-private sector information-sharing programs is operating. For example, the Homeland Security Information Network-Critical Infrastructure (HSIN-CI) enables key executives in the public and private sectors to receive alerts and notifications from the DHS via phone (landline and wireless), e-mail, fax, or pager. It is set up on a regional basis with regional Web sites, and not every region receives the same alerts.

Regulation of the Industry

The security vocation has its share of charlatans, who tarnish the industry, and as with many types of services offered the public, government intervention has taken the form of licensing and registration. The *Task Force Report* and *Hallcrest Reports* recommend regulation of the security industry by all states. To protect consumers, the majority of states have varied laws that regulate, through licensing and registration, contract security officer services, private investigators, polygraph and other detection of deception specialists, and security alarm businesses. Security consultants are generally not regulated, but consumers should verify professional memberships and certifications. Although government regulation does not guarantee that all security practitioners will perform in a satisfactory manner, it does prevent people who have criminal records from entering the profession. Those applicants who have lived in multiple states should have their backgrounds checked for each jurisdiction. Attention to this type of background investigation varies.

Another way in which the industry is regulated is through local, state, and federal agencies that contract out private security services and mandate various contract requirements (e.g., education, training, and character) to enhance professionalism and competence. Certain industries are regulated by government and require stringent security standards. For example, the U.S. Nuclear Regulatory Commission issues rules and standards that must be followed by licensees of nuclear reactors to ensure safety and security. A variety of businesses, institutions, and other organizations also issue requirements. However, the lowest bidder on a contract may be selected and professionalism may be sacrificed.

Attempts have been made through Congress to pass a national law to regulate the security industry. Rep. Bob Barr (R-GA) introduced H.R. 2092, The Private Security Officers Quality Assurance Act of 1995. It languished in Congress in various forms when Rep. Matthew Martinez (D-CA) introduced a similar bill. Known as the Barr-Martinez Bill, if passed, it would have provided state regulators with expedited FBI criminal background checks of prospective and newly hired security officers. The minimal training standards of the bill were stricken, which would have required 8 hours of training and 4 hours of on-the-job training for unarmed officers and an additional 15 hours for armed officers. Critics argued that states are against such a national law and state regulations are sufficient. Finally, Congress passed the **Private Security Officer Employment Authorization Act of 2004** (included in the National Intelligence Reform Act of 2004) that enables security service businesses and proprietary security organizations in all 50 states to check if applicants have a criminal history record with the FBI, which may emanate from one or more states. (National training requirements were not included in the legislation.) This law is significant and it adds strength to criminal records checks of security officer applicants. Traditional name-based searches can result in false positives (i.e., an applicant's name is incorrectly matched to an offender's name or similar name) and false negatives (i.e., an applicant's name does not result in a match because the applicant is using a different name or a database was omitted from investigation). Because applicants may use different names and other bogus identifying information, fingerprints provide increased accuracy in background investigations. Security firm access to the FBI's Integrated Automated Fingerprint Identification System (IAFIS) under the act also includes access to the Violent Gangs and Terrorism Organization File. Although not all security organizations are required to check these fingerprint databases for their applicants, the effort and expense prevents litigation and the possibility that an applicant is a terrorist or other criminal. Cost is one of several factors that influence the extent of background investigations (Friedrick, 2005: 11).

□ □ □ ▬▬▬▬▬▬▬▬▬▬▬▬▬▬▬▬▬▬▬▬▬▬

Which government agency (or agencies) in your state regulates the private security industry? What are the requirements for contract security ("guard") companies, private detectives, and security alarm installers?

▬▬▬▬▬▬▬▬▬▬▬▬▬▬▬▬▬▬▬▬▬▬ □ □ □

The Need for Training

Numerous research reports and other publications have pointed to the need for more training of personnel in the security industry. Training of all security officers should be required by law *prior to assignment*. Training topics of importance include customer service, ethics, criminal law and procedure, constitutional protections, interviewing, surveillance, arrest techniques, post assignments and patrols, report writing, safety, fire protection, and specialized topics for client needs. Firearms training is also important, even though a small percentage of security officers are armed.

The harsh realities of the contract security business hinder training. Low pay and the enormous turnover of officers lead many security executives to consider costly training difficult to justify. With liability a constant threat and with insurance often unaffordable, many security firms are simply gambling by not adequately preparing their officers for the job. Security training is inconsistent and sometimes nonexistent. The *Task Force Report* and the *Hallcrest Reports* stress the need for improved recruitment, selection, pay, and training within the security industry.

Efforts in Congress and in the legislatures of many states have been aimed at increasing training. However, there has been no success in Congress for a national training mandate, and state training requirements vary. Because quality training means increases in costs in the competitive contract security business, such legislation has often been controversial.

Security Letter (McCrie, 2005: 2) reported that the United States lags behind other countries on security training. The Province of Ontario, Canada, requires 40 hours of training. Training hours required in Europe are Hungary: 350; Spain: 260; Sweden: 120; United Kingdom: 38; France: 32; and Germany: 24. In the United States, the required hours are AK: 48; CA, FL, and OK: 40; ND: 32; NY: 24; IL: 20; LA and VA: 16; MN and OR: 12; AZ, CT, GA, and UT: 8; AR: 6; NC, NV, SC, TN, and WA: 4; TX: 1; and 29 other states and DC: 0.

In essence, what we have seen following these national reports and recommendations is an industry that needs to do more to help professionalize the industry and security personnel. It is easy to forget about these reports and recommendations as a businessperson under pressure to reduce expenses and turn a profit while facing employee turnover, the pressure to ensure security officers are on client posts, and competition from low bidders. Furthermore, the security industry plays a strong role in influencing government laws and regulations that can result in added expenses for businesses. Unfortunately, we have seen changes resulting from many lawsuits claiming negligent security. Fear of such litigation motivates the industry to change. On the bright side, many security service companies are professional, set high standards for themselves, and have improved the industry. It is hoped that these companies continue to set an example to be followed by others.

ASIS International, in its effort to increase professionalism and develop guidelines for the security industry, published *Private Security Officer Selection and Training* (ASIS International, 2004). This guideline was written for proprietary and contract security and regulatory bodies. Its employment screening criteria include 18 years of age for unarmed and 21 years of age for armed security officers; high school diploma, GED, or equivalent; fingerprints; criminal history check; drug screening; and other background checks. The training requirements include 48 hours of training within the first 100 days of employment.

Ethics

A code of ethics is a partial solution to strengthen the professionalism of security practitioners. Such a code helps to guide behavior by establishing standards of ethical conduct. Twomey, Jennings, and Fox (2001: 28–31) describe **ethics** as a branch of philosophy dealing with values that relate to the nature of human conduct. They write that "conduct and values within the context of business operations become more complex because individuals are working together to maximize profit. Balancing the goal of profits with the values of individuals and society is the focus of *business ethics*." Twomey and colleagues note that capitalism succeeds because of trust; investors provide capital for a business because they believe the business will earn a profit.

Customers rely on business promises of quality and the commitment to stand behind a product or service. Having a code makes good business sense because consumers make purchasing decisions based on past experience or the experiences of others. Reliance on promises, not litigation, nurtures good business relationships.

Twomey and colleagues write of studies that show that those businesses with the strongest value systems survive and do so successfully. Citing several companies, they argue, "bankruptcy and/or free falls in the worth of shares are the fates that await firms that make poor ethical choices."

A host of other problems can develop for a business and its employees when unethical decisions are made. Besides a loss of customers, unethical decisions can result in criminal and civil liabilities. Quality ethics must be initiated and supported by top management, who must set an example without hypocrisy. All employees must be a part of the ethical environment through a code of ethics and see it spelled out in policies, procedures, and training.

International business presents special challenges when promoting ethical decision making because cultures differ on codes of ethics. Business management must take the lead and research and define guidelines for employees.

Another challenge develops when a security practitioner's employer or supervisor violates ethical standards or law. What you do not want to do is to become part of the problem and subject yourself to a tarnished reputation or criminal and civil liabilities. When faced with such difficult dilemmas, refer to your professional background and its code of ethics.

The Web is a rich source of information on ethics. The *Task Force Report* and ASIS International are sources for codes of ethics for the security profession. The former has one code for security management (as does ASIS International) and a code for security employees in general. A sample of the wording, similar in both codes, includes "to protect life and property," and "to be guided by a sense of integrity, honor, justice and morality...." (U.S. Department of Justice, 1976b: 24). Management, supervision, policies, procedures, and training help to define what these words mean.

Here are guidelines for ethical decisions:

- Does the decision violate law, a code of ethics, or company policy?
- What are the short-term and long-term consequences of your decision for your employer and yourself?
- Is there an alternative course of action that is less harmful?
- Are you making a levelheaded decision, rather than a decision based on emotions?
- Would your family support your decision?
- Would your supervisor and management support your decision?

The False Alarm Problem

Another persistent problem that causes friction between public police and the private sector is false alarms. It is generally agreed that more than 95% of all alarm response calls received by public police are false alarms. However, the definition of "false alarm" is subject to debate. It often is assumed that, if a burglar is not caught on the premises, the alarm was false. Police do not always consider that the alarm or the approaching police could have frightened away a burglar.

The *Task Force* and *Hallcrest Reports* discussed the problem of false alarms. Many police agencies nationwide continue to spend millions of dollars each year in personnel and equipment to respond to these calls. For decades, municipalities and the alarm industry have tried various solutions. Police agencies have selectively responded or not responded to alarms. City and county governments have enacted false alarm control ordinances that require a permit for an alarm system and impose fines for excessive false alarms. The industry claims that the end users cause 80% of the problems. It continues its education campaign while trying a multitude of strategies, such as offering a class for repeat offenders instead of a fine, setting standards of exit delay at no fewer than 45 seconds and entry times of at least 30 seconds, and audio and video verification of alarms. Since the industry is installing 15% more systems each year, these efforts must continue (Southerland, 2000: 1).

Martin (2005: 160–163) writes that jurisdictions across North America are adopting ordinances and policies that specify a nonresponse policy to unverified alarm activations. As an alarm industry advocate, he argues that this change places a financial burden on businesses and increases the risk of burglary. In Salt Lake City, a person must be physically present on the property to visually verify that a crime is in progress, before the police accept a call for service; CCTV confirmation is not considered sufficient. Martin sees public police as more qualified to respond to alarms than private security officers. Martin refers to the strategy of Enhanced Call Verification to reduce false alarms. This strategy requires two calls from the alarm-monitoring center to the user to determine if an error has occurred, before police are called.

Many issues affect the "false alarm" problem. Solutions include user training, proper equipment, fines, and Enhanced Call Verification. A key question is: Who will pay for alarm response—the public or the users?

☐ ☐ ☐ ▬▬▬▬▬▬▬▬▬▬▬▬▬▬▬▬▬▬▬▬▬▬▬▬

What do you think are the most serious problems facing the private security industry and what are your solutions?

☐ ☐ ☐ ▬▬▬▬▬▬▬▬▬▬▬▬▬▬▬▬▬▬▬▬▬▬▬▬

Search the Web

Several security associations exist to promote professionalism and improve the security field. Go to the Web site of ASIS International (www.asisonline.org), formerly the American Society for Industrial Security, founded in 1955. With a membership over 33,000, it is the leading general organization of protection executives and specialists. Its monthly magazine, *Security Management*, is an excellent source of information. This association offers courses and seminars. ASIS International offers three certifications: Certified Protection Professional (CPP); Physical Security Professional (PSP); and Professional Certified Investigator (PCI). For each certification, the candidate must pay a fee for administration, meet eligibility requirements, and successfully pass an examination.

Whereas ASIS International is the leading professional association of security executives and specialists, the International Foundation for Protection Officers (IFPO), founded in 1988, is the leading professional association of security officers who are on the front lines of protecting businesses, institutions, other entities, and our infrastructure. The IFPO (www.ifpo.org) has global reach and serves to help professionalize officers through training and certification. It has developed several distance delivery courses and programs: the Entry Level Protection Officer (ELPO), the Basic Protection Officer (BPO), the Certified Protection Officer (CPO) program, the Security Supervisor (SSP) program, and the Certified Security Supervisor (CSS) program. All programs are designed for self-paced home study and some are available on-line. Many corporations and institutions have included these programs in their professional development programs for security personnel. The IFPO publishes *Protection News*, a quarterly newsletter of valuable information, trends, and commentary.

How does each group promote professionalism and improve the security field?

Here are additional Web sites related to this chapter:

Bureau of Justice Statistics: www.ojp.usdoj.gov/bjs/cvict.htm

Ethics Education Resource Center: www.aacsb.edu/resource_centers/EthicsEdu/ default.asp

Federal Bureau of Investigation: www.fbi.gov/ucr/ucr.htm

International Association of Chiefs of Police: www.theiacp.org/

International Association of Security and Investigative Regulators: www.iasir.org

Markkula Center for Applied Ethics: www.scu.edu/ethics

National Association of Security Companies: www.nasco.org

National Fire Protection Association: www.nfpa.org/

Security Industry Association: www.siaonline.org/

U.S. Department of Homeland Security: www.dhs.gov/dhspublic/

▬▬▬▬▬▬▬▬▬▬▬▬▬▬▬▬▬▬▬▬▬▬▬▬ ☐ ☐ ☐

Case Problems

2A. As Manager of Loss Prevention for five retail stores, you are seeking a promotion to Regional Director of Loss Prevention. The position involves responsibilities for several more stores and subordinates. You are scheduled for an interview soon for the position, and an interview topic will be metrics. Before studying metrics related to the company and your work, you seek to go back to the basics of metrics to serve as a foundation. Prepare a list of five general questions on metrics and answer the questions to prepare for your interview. Examples of basic questions are: What are metrics? What are the purposes of metrics?

2B. As a city police detective specializing in white-collar crime, you enjoy the challenges of your work and look forward to retirement in five years to become an insurance fraud investigator. You often work with the private sector, and you are frequently in contact with corporate security investigators. As an active member of a local police-security council, you are assigned the task of developing a plan to improve police-security cooperation at all levels in the city. What are your specific plans that you will present to the council?

2C. As a uniformed security officer, how would you handle the following situations?
- Another security officer says that you can leave two hours early during second shift and she will "punch you out."
- You are assigned to a stationary post at a shipping and receiving dock, and a truck driver asks you to "look the other way" for $500 cash.
- A security officer that you work with shows you how to make the required physical inspections around the plant without leaving your seat.
- During the holidays, a group of coworkers planning a party on the premises asks you if you want to contribute to a fund to hire a stripper/ prostitute.
- You are testifying in criminal court in a shoplifting case, and the defense attorney asks you to state whether you ever lost sight of the defendant when the incident occurred. The case depends on your stating that you never lost sight of the defendant. You actually lost sight of the defendant once. How do you respond?
- Your best friend wants you to provide a positive recommendation for him when he applies for a job where you work, even though he has an arrest record.
- You see your supervisor take company items and put them in the trunk of her vehicle.

2D. As a corporate security manager, how would you handle the following situations?
- Two contract security officers fail to show up for first shift. The contract manager says that screened and trained replacements are unavailable, but two new applicants are available. You are required to make an immediate decision. Do you accept the two applicants, who lack a background investigation and state-mandated training?
- A vendor offers you a condo at the beach for a week if you support his firm's bid for an access control system. You know that the system is not the best and that it will cost your company slightly more than the best system. The condo will save you about $1,500 on your summer vacation. What is your decision?
- Your employer is violating environmental laws. You know that if the government learns of the violations, your company will be unable to survive financially criminal and civil action and pollution controls. You will certainly lose your job. What do you do?
- While reviewing CCTV video footage, you see your boss inappropriately touching a coworker who recently filed a sexual harassment suit against the boss, who vehemently denied the allegations. You placed the pinhole-lens camera in the office supply closet to catch a thief, not expecting to see your boss touching the coworker. No one knows of the placement of the camera and the video footage, except you. Your boss, who is the vice president of finance, has been especially helpful to your career, your excellent raises and bonuses, and the corporate security budget. What do you do?

- You are testifying in a case of negligent security concerning a manufacturing plant in your region of responsibility. The plaintiff's attorney asks you if any security surveys have ever been conducted at the site where the murder occurred. You know that a survey conducted prior to the murder showed the need for increased security at the site. Such information would secure a victory for the plaintiff. What is your response to the question?

References

ASIS Foundation. (2004). *The ASIS Foundation Security Report: Scope and Emerging Trends, Preliminary Findings*. www.asisonline.org, retrieved January 6, 2005.

ASIS International. (2003). *General Security Risk Assessment Guideline*. www.asisonline.org, retrieved May 10, 2006.

ASIS International. (2004). *Private Security Officer Selection and Training*. www.asisonline.org, retrieved January 3, 2005.

Barkan, S. (2006). *Criminology: A Sociological Understanding*, 3rd ed. Upper Saddle River, NJ: Pearson Prentice-Hall.

Bowman, G., et al. (1992). *Privatizing the United States Justice System*. Jefferson, NC: McFarland Pub.

Chamard, S. (2006). "Partnering with Businesses to Address Public Safety Problems." Washington, D.C.: U.S. Department of Justice, Office of Community Oriented Policing (April).

Collins, P., et al. (2005). "The ASIS Foundation Security Report: Scope and Emerging Trends." Alexandria, VA: ASIS, International.

Conklin, J. (2001). *Criminology*, 7th ed. Boston: Allyn & Bacon.

Cunningham, W., et al. (1991). *Private Security: Patterns and Trends*. Washington, D.C.: National Institute of Justice (August).

Cunningham, W., et al. (1990). *Private Security Trends: 1970–2000, The Hallcrest Report II*. Boston: Butterworth–Heinemann.

Cunningham, W., and Taylor, T. (1985). *Private Security and Police in America: The Hallcrest Report*. Portland, OR: Chancellor Press.

Fagin, J. (2005). *Criminal Justice*. Boston: Allyn & Bacon.

FBI. (2006). *Crime in the United States, 2004*. www.fbi.gov/ucr/cius_04/offenses_reported, retrieved May 8, 2006.

Flores, T., and Earl, J. (2004). "What Are Security's Lessons in Iraq?" *Security Management*, 48 (November).

Freedonia Group. (2006). "World Security Services." http://freedonia.ecnext.com/coms2/summary_0285, retrieved May 8, 2006.

Friedrick, J. (2005). "New Law Empowers Security Firms, Private Employers with Information." *Security Director News*, 2 (September).

Haddow, G., and Bullock, J. (2003). *Introduction to Emergency Management*. Boston: Butterworth-Heinemann.

Kovacich, G., and Halibozek, E. (2006). *Security Metrics Management: How to Manage the Costs of an Assets Protection Program*. Boston: Elsevier Butterworth-Heinemann.

Leimberg, S., et al. (2002). *The Tools & Techniques of Risk Management & Insurance*. Cincinnati, OH: The National Underwriter Co.

Marks, A. (2006). "Security at Military Bases: A Job for Private Firms?" *The Christian Science Monitor* (April 27). www.csmonitor.com/2006/0427/p02s01–usmi.htm, retrieved April 28, 2006.

Martin, S. (2005). "What's Best for Alarm Response Policies?" *Security Management*, 49 (March).

McCrie, R. (2005). "Training: Ontario Introduces a Bill Requiring 40 Hrs. Pre-Assignment." *Security Letter*, XXXV (January 3).

National Center for Injury Prevention and Control. (2006). "The Economic Costs of Injuries." www.cdc.gov/nipc/factsheets/Cost_of_Injury.htm, retrieved May 8, 2006.

Occupational Safety & Health Administration. (2006). "OSHA Facts." www.osha.gov, retrieved May 8, 2006.

Parfomak, P. (2004). "Guarding America: Security Guards and US Critical Infrastructure Protection" (November 12). www.fas.org/sgp/crs/RL32670.pdf, retrieved March 6, 2006.

Purpura, P. (2007). *Terrorism and Homeland Security: An Introduction with Applications*. Burlington, MA: Elsevier Butterworth-Heinemann Pub.

Quinley, K., and Schmidt, D. (2002). *Business at Risk: How to Assess, Mitigate, and Respond to Terrorist Threats*. Cincinnati, OH: The National Underwriter Co.

Southerland, R. (2000). "Dispatch to Nowhere." *Access Control & Security Systems Integration*, 1 (February).

Twomey, D., Jennings, M., and Fox, I. (2001). *Anderson's Business Law and the Regulatory Environment*, 14th ed. Cincinnati, OH: West Legal Studies.

U.S. Army. (2006). *Counterinsurgency* (FM-324). Washington, DC: Headquarters, Department of the Army.

U.S. Department of Homeland Security. (2004). *National Response Plan*. www.dhs.gov, retrieved January 12, 2005.

U.S. Department of Justice. (2000). *Critical Incident Protocol—A Public and Private Partnership*. www.ojp.usdoj.gov, retrieved November 18, 2003.

U.S. Department of Justice. (1976a). *Law Enforcement and Private Security: Sources and Areas of Conflict*. Washington, D.C.: U.S. Government Printing Office.

U.S. Department of Justice. (1976b). *Report of the Task Force on Private Security*. Washington, D.C.: U.S. Government Printing Office.

U.S. Department of Justice. (1972). *Private Police in the United States: Findings and Recommendations 1. (The Rand Report)* Washington, D.C.: U.S. Government Printing Office.

U.S. Department of Justice, Bureau of Justice Statistics. (2006). *Justice Expenditure and Employment in the United States, 2003* (April). www.ojp.usdoj.gov/bjs/pub/pdf/jeeus03.pdf, retrieved May 17, 2006.

U.S. Department of Justice, Office of Community Oriented Policing Services. (2004). *National Policy Summit: Building Private Security/Public Policing Partnerships to Prevent and Respond to Terrorism and Public Disorder*. www.cops.usdoj.gov, retrieved January 4, 2005.

U.S. Fire Administration. (2005). *Fire in the United States 1992–2001*, 13th ed. www.usfa.fema.gov/statistics/reports/pubs/fius13th.shtm, retrieved May 8, 2006.

U.S. Fire Administration. (2006). "The Overall Fire Picture, 2005." www.usfa.dhs.gov/statistics/quickstats/, retrieved November 10, 2006.

U.S. Government Accountability Office. (2006). *Contract Security Guards: Army's Guard Program Requires Greater Oversight and Reassessment of Acquisition Approach* (April). www.gao.gov/cgi-bin/getrpt?GAO-06–284, retrieved April 5, 2006.

Wagner, D. (2006). "Private Security Guards Play Key Roles Post-9/11." *The Arizona Republic* (January 22). www.azcentral.com, retrieved January 30, 2006.

Wailgum, T. (2005). "Where the Metrics Are." *CSO* (February). www.csoonline.com, retrieved February 9, 2005.

Zarate, J. (1998). "The Emergence of a New Dog of War: Private International Security Companies, International Law, and the New World Order." *Stanford Journal of International Law*, 34 (January).

Reducing the Problem of Loss

Foundations of Security and Loss Prevention

Objectives

After studying this chapter, the reader will be able to:

1. Explain precisely how the security and loss prevention field has reached the status of a profession.
2. List and explain the three-step risk analysis process.
3. Discuss planning and its importance.
4. Discuss standards and regulations.
5. Explain and illustrate how to evaluate security and loss prevention programs.
6. Describe the characteristics of proprietary security programs.

KEY TERMS
<table><tr><td><ul><li>Oscar Newman</li><li>Crime Prevention Through Environmental Design (CPTED)</li><li>situational crime prevention (SCP)</li><li>routine activities theory</li><li>Donald Cressey</li><li>risk analysis</li><li>cost/benefit analysis</li><li>annual loss exposure</li><li>planning</li><li>budgeting</li><li>value added</li><li>systems perspective</li><li>National Technology Transfer and Advancement Act</li><li>consensus standards</li><li>standard of care</li><li>code war</li><li>regulations</li><li>Code of Federal Regulations (CFR)</li><li>codes</li></ul></td><td><ul><li>recommended practices</li><li>Underwriters Laboratories (UL)</li><li>National Fire Protection Association</li><li>Security Industry Association</li><li>American Society for Testing and Materials</li><li>American National Standards Institute</li><li>International Organization for Standardization</li><li>pretest-posttest design</li><li>experimental control group design</li><li>scientific method</li><li>division of work</li><li>authority</li><li>responsibility</li><li>power</li><li>delegation of authority</li><li>chain of command</li><li>span of control</li><li>unity of command</li><li>line personnel</li></ul></td></tr></table>

• staff personnel	• policies
• formal organization	• procedures
• informal organization	• manual
• organization chart	• autocratic style
• directive system	• democratic style

The Security and Loss Prevention Profession

The security and loss prevention field has reached the status of a profession. If we look to other professions as models to emulate, we see the following in each, just as we see in the security and loss prevention profession: a history and body of knowledge recorded in books and periodicals; associations that promote advancement of knowledge, training, certification, and a code of ethics; and programs of higher education that prepare students for the profession.

Theoretical Foundations

The challenges of security and loss prevention in a complex world have created an intense search among practitioners to seek answers to protection problems. Many fields of study offer answers for the practitioner, and thus, a multidisciplinary approach to the problem of loss is best. Here we present a summary of theories and concepts to illustrate the multidisciplinary nature of security and loss prevention and its theoretical foundation.

The work of **Oscar Newman** (1972) is the bedrock of many security designs worldwide. He argued that informal control of criminal behavior could be enhanced through architectural design that creates "defensible space" and changes residents' use of public places while reducing fear. **Crime Prevention Through Environmental Design (CPTED)** evolved from Newman's concept of defensible space. CPTED consists of architectural, landscape, and urban design that promotes crime prevention and is applicable to a broad variety of businesses, institutions, and facilities.

Situational crime prevention (SCP) is closely related to CPTED. It contains the physical design characteristics of CPTED and managerial and user behaviors that impact opportunities for criminal behavior. Lab (2004) writes that instead of making changes in a community, SCP focuses on specific problems, places, people, or times. Lab (2004) sees the theoretical basis for SCP from multiple perspectives, such as **routine activities theory**. It stresses that some people engage in regular or routine activities that increase their risk of victimization (Felson, 1998). Three factors must occur for victimization under this theory: (1) an attractive target; (2) a motivated offender; and (3) the absence of "guardianship" (e.g., nearby people who can protect an intended victim).

Employee theft and embezzlement are huge problems for businesses. Criminologist **Donald Cressey** (1971) developed a formula that offers insight into causation and preventive measures. The formula is: motivation + opportunity + rationalization = theft. Cressey, in his classic study, observed that embezzlers' financial problems are "nonshareable" because of embarrassment or shame, and they rationalize their illegal behavior. Other researchers describe a form of embezzlement called "collective embezzlement," which involves groups of two or more people. Financial industries, such as banks, stock brokerages, and insurance, have been victimized by collective embezzlement (Pontell and Calavita, 1993).

Psychologist Abraham Maslow (1954) is noted for his "hierarchy of human needs." He claimed that people have a variety of needs such as basic physiological needs, safety and security needs, and societal needs. These needs can be met in the workplace through, for instance, clean lavatories, a safe working environment, and praise and rewards. The implications are that as employers do more to meet human needs, losses (e.g., internal theft) may drop. Research should focus on the relationship among types of needs met by employers and types of losses reduced.

The snapshot of theory presented here is a beginning point from which to build. Chapters 7 and 8 provide more details and greater depth on theories of crime and crime prevention. The social sciences are by no means the only disciplines helpful to security and loss prevention. In subsequent chapters, theory and concepts are drawn from law, marketing, accounting, fire science, safety, and risk management.

Security Periodicals

There are many security periodicals published by a variety of associations and organizations. Periodicals serve as a platform, not only for the theoretical foundation of the security and loss prevention profession, but also to introduce readers to new developments, security strategies and technology, research, laws, issues, professional development, and a host of other topics. What follows are noted periodicals in this discipline. The Web sites for the periodicals are located at the end of this chapter.

The *Journal of Security Administration* is the vanguard among journals in the security field. It is a semi-annual scholarly journal affiliated with the Security and Crime Prevention Section of the Academy of Criminal Justice Sciences.

The *Journal of Security Education* is the official journal of the Academy of Security Educators and Trainers, a professional group working to assist the development of degree programs and training courses. This journal reports on new or changing education and training programs and serves as a forum to discuss the professional needs of practitioners and the protection needs of organizations.

Security Journal is published by Palgrave Macmillan Journals and supported by the ASIS International Foundation. The editorial staff is from the United States and the United Kingdom. The journal publishes articles on a variety of topics on the latest developments and techniques of security management. Articles include findings and recommendations of independent research. Two other journals from this publisher are *Risk Management: An International Journal* and *Crime Prevention and Community Safety: An International Journal*.

Security Management is a monthly magazine published by ASIS International. Each issue contains a wealth of informative articles on a broad range of topics written by experienced security professionals.

Protection News, published by the International Foundation of Protection Officers, is a newsletter containing current trends of the security industry and covering topics on life safety and the protection of property.

Several periodicals focus on information technology and related threats and solutions. Examples are *Information Security* and *SC Magazine*.

By typing various security specializations in a search engine, such as "school security," "healthcare security," "transportation security," the reader can obtain a wealth of information on associations, professional development, training, certifications, and periodicals.

Security Associations

Up to this point in this book, a number of professional associations have been named and their objectives summarized. Others will follow. The private sector contains numerous associations dedicated to improving the world in which we live and promoting safety and security. These missions are accomplished by enhancing the knowledge, skills, and capabilities of members through training and education; offering certifications to demonstrate competence; conducting research; producing "best practices" and standards; disseminating information; communicating the group's goals; forming partnerships to reach common objectives; participating in community service; and advocating positions on key issues.

Professional associations typically require annual dues that pay for administrative and other expenses that are beneficial to members. Membership benefits include opportunities to network among peers; subscriptions to the group's periodicals and informative e-mails; members-only Web site privileges; discounts on national and regional educational programs and seminars; opportunities to serve on specialized committees; and career guidance and placement services.

Readers are urged to join one or more professional associations that fit their specializations and interests for a truly enriching experience for career development and service. What we invest in our membership activities impacts what we receive in return.

☐ ☐ ☐ ▬▬▬▬▬▬▬▬▬▬▬▬▬▬▬▬▬▬▬▬▬▬▬▬▬▬▬▬▬▬

If you were to begin a career in the security and loss prevention vocation, would you join a professional association? Why or why not?

▬▬▬▬▬▬▬▬▬▬▬▬▬▬▬▬▬▬▬▬▬▬▬▬▬▬▬▬▬▬ ☐ ☐ ☐

Methods for Protection Programs

Before a program of security and loss prevention is implemented, careful planning is essential. Planning should begin by identifying the threats, hazards, and risks that face an organization. These terms are defined in the preceding chapter.

Risk Analysis

There are many perspectives and methods of risk analysis from government, the private sector, researchers, and writers. Instead of engaging in a debate about the topic, we present some perspectives here, beginning with a basic three-step process of risk analysis. This simplified approach will assist the reader and provide a foundation for those who decide to enter "the jungle of risk analysis" and join the fray by studying the literature and differences in terminology, definitions, and methodology. For instance, the term *risk analysis* is used interchangeably with *risk assessment*, *risk evaluation*, and other terms.

James F. Broder (2006: 4), author of *Risk Analysis and the Security Survey*, writes: "Risk assessment analysis is a rational and orderly approach, as well as a comprehensive solution, to problem identification and probability determination. It is also a method for estimating the expected loss from the occurrence of an adverse event. The key word here is *estimating* because risk analysis will never be an exact science—we are discussing probabilities."

This chapter defines **risk analysis** as a method to estimate the expected loss from specific risks using the following three-step process: (1) conducting a loss prevention survey; (2) identifying vulnerabilities; and (3) determining probability, frequency, and cost.

Conducting a Loss Prevention Survey

The purpose of a loss prevention survey is to pinpoint threats, hazards, and vulnerabilities (e.g., weaknesses, such as inadequate access controls, unsafe conditions) and develop a foundation for improved protection. The survey should tailor its questions to the unique needs of the premises to be surveyed. Essentially, the survey involves a day-and-night, possibly multiple-day, physical examination of the location requiring a loss prevention program. *The merging of information technology (IT) specialists into the risk analysis process is vital for comprehensive protection.* For example, IT specialists can be involved in penetration testing of the IT system to identify protection needs.

The list that follows, expanded from Crawford (1995: 85–90), is a beginning point for topics for the survey.

1. Overall threats and hazards, geography, climate (possible natural disasters), and nearby hazards and potential targets that can impact the entity
2. Social, economic, and political climate surrounding the facility and in the region
3. Past events, litigation, and complaints
4. Condition of physical security, fire protection, safety measures, and business continuity plans
5. Hazardous substances and protection measures
6. Policies and procedures and their enforcement

7. Quality of security personnel (e.g., applicant screening, training, and supervision; properly registered and licensed)
8. Protection of people, assets, and operations on and off the premises
9. Protection of IT systems and information
10. Protection of communications systems (e.g., telephones, fax machines, and e-mail)
11. Protection of buildings, grounds, and utilities
12. Protection of parking lots
13. Protection of products, services, goodwill, and image

The survey document usually consists of a checklist in the form of questions that remind the practitioner or committee of what to examine. A list attached to the survey can contain the targets—for example, people, money, inventory, equipment, IT systems—that must be protected and the present strategies, if any, used to protect them. Also helpful are computer software generating three-dimensional views of the facility, geographic information systems, maps, and blueprints.

Identifying Vulnerabilities

Once the survey is completed, vulnerabilities can be isolated. For example, access controls may be weak for both the facility and IT; certain policies and procedures may be ignored; and specific people, assets, or enterprise operations may require improved protection. Vulnerabilities may also show that security, fire, and life-safety strategies are outdated and must be brought up to current codes and standards.

Determining Probability, Frequency, and Cost

The third step requires an analysis of the probability, frequency, and cost of each loss. Shoplifting and employee theft are common in retail stores, and numerous incidents can add up to serious losses. Fire and explosion are hazards at a chemical plant; even one incident can be financially devastating. The frequency of shoplifting and employee theft incidents at a retail store will likely be greater than the frequency of fires and explosions at a chemical plant. However, it is impossible to pinpoint accurately when, where, and how many times losses will occur. When the questions of probability, frequency, and cost of losses arise, practitioners can rely on their own experience, metrics, communication with fellow practitioners, information provided by trade publications, risk management or security consulting firms, and risk analysis software.

As an alternative to the preceding three-step process, the "General Security Risk Assessment Guideline" (ASIS International, 2003) offers a seven-step process to identify risks at specific locations and to begin planning to select and implement security and loss prevention strategies.

1. *Understand the organization and identify the people and assets at risk.* This includes information, reputation, and goodwill.
2. *Specify loss risk events/vulnerabilities.* Each site often has a unique history of losses and unique weaknesses.
3. *Establish the probability of loss risk and frequency of events.*
4. *Determine the impact of the events.* This includes the cost of losses from tangible or intangible assets.
5. *Develop options to mitigate risks.*
6. *Study the feasibility of implementation of options.* This focuses on practical security options that are aligned with the objectives of the enterprise.
7. *Perform a cost/benefit analysis.* This process seeks to analyze the value of the benefits from an expenditure. This is a three-step process: "identification of all direct and indirect consequences of the expenditure; assignment of a monetary value to all costs and benefits resulting from the expenditure; and discounting expected future costs and revenues accruing from the expenditure to express those costs and revenues in current monetary values."

It is argued that security directors of large, complex organizations should use quantitative, rather than qualitative, risk analysis when exposures cannot be evaluated intuitively, especially for the protection of IT and e-business (Jacobson, 2000: 142–144). The process begins with a mathematical model that can be simple or complex. A simple formula is ALE = I × F, where "ALE" is **annual loss exposure**, "I" is impact (i.e., dollar loss if the event occurs), and "F" is frequency (i.e., the number of times the event will occur each year). Software tools are available to organize and automate complex risk analyses. Debate continues over when to use quantitative risk analysis, its cost and value, how much guesswork goes into the process, and which formula and software are best. Two points are clear: (1) there are many opinions and styles of risk analysis, and (2) what works for one organization may not work for another.

The "General Security Risk Assessment Guideline" recognizes that, in certain cases, data may be lacking for a quantitative risk analysis. Consequently, a qualitative approach can be applied through multistep processes as described previously. The "Guideline" offers both qualitative and quantitative approaches.

In the preceding chapter, the importance of totaling *direct and indirect losses* was covered. Here we apply this financial strategy to exposure and potential losses to IT systems, as an illustration. Trusecure conducted research on 300 organizations following the Melissa virus catastrophe in 1999. The average victimized company had 1,120 employees and 196 infected PCs, and 8.7 infected servers (including e-mail and e-commerce) that were down for two days. Respondents claimed an average of $1,700 in losses. Total costs were probably more than sevenfold higher when consideration is given to such losses as staff time spent repairing damage, lost productivity, public relations damage, and lost business (Tippett, 2001: 36–38). Thus, when calculating loss exposure, include total potential losses.

□ □ □ ▬▬▬▬▬▬▬▬▬▬▬▬▬▬▬▬▬▬▬▬▬▬▬▬▬

Why do you think the ASIS International's "General Security Risk Assessment Guideline" offers quantitative and qualitative approaches?

▬▬▬▬▬▬▬▬▬▬▬▬▬▬▬▬▬▬▬▬▬▬▬▬▬ □ □ □

Planning

Planning results in a design used to reach objectives. It is better to know where one is going and how to get there than to adhere to a philosophy of "we'll cross that bridge when we get to it." A serious consequence of poor planning is the panic atmosphere that develops when serious losses occur; emotional decisions are made when quickly acquiring needed systems and services. This sets up an organization for unscrupulous salespeople who prey on the panic.

An integral purpose of the planning process is to fulfill organizational goals and objectives. Those who plan protection should have a clear understanding of organizational needs, corporate culture, and customer needs. Because of global competitiveness, downsizing, restructuring, and a variety of hazards and threats, today's enterprises are in a state of constant change and reengineering. To survive, a support function such as security must be a team player, adapt quickly to change, meet challenges in a positive and creative manner, and show how it is contributing to the enterprise.

Budgeting is closely related to planning because it pertains to the money required to fulfill plans. Modern practitioners state their protection plans in financial terms that justify expenditures, save the organization money, and if possible, bring in a return on investment. The concept of **value added** means that all corporate departments must demonstrate their value to the organization by translating expenditures into bottom-line impact. Corporate financial officers ask, "Is security contributing to our business and profit success, and if it is, how?" Metrics provides the opportunity to quantify performance. Illustrations of financial leverage for security include calculating total direct and indirect losses for each loss incident; conducting an undercover investigation to pinpoint not only theft, but also substance abuse and safety problems; hiring a bad check specialist who recovers several times his or her salary; purchasing an access control system that performs multiple roles, such as producing time and attendance data; and installing a closed-circuit television (CCTV) system that not only assists investigations, but helps to locate production problems to improve efficiency and cut costs.

☐ ☐ ☐ ▬▬▬▬▬▬▬▬▬▬▬▬▬▬▬▬▬▬▬▬▬▬▬▬▬▬▬▬▬▬▬▬

Modern security and loss prevention practitioners state their protection plans in financial terms that justify expenditures, save the organization money, and if possible, bring in a return on investment.

▬▬▬▬▬▬▬▬▬▬▬▬▬▬▬▬▬▬▬▬▬▬▬▬▬▬▬▬▬▬▬▬ ☐ ☐ ☐

A risk analysis provides input for planning protection. Security strategies generally take the form of personnel, systems, and policies and procedures. Some of the many factors that go into the planning process follow:

1. Has the problem been carefully and accurately identified?
2. How much will it cost to correct the problem, and what percent of the budget will be allocated to the particular strategy?
3. Is the strategy practical?
4. Is the strategy cost effective? For example, a loss prevention manager debates an increase in the staff of loss prevention officers or the purchase of a CCTV system. The staff increase will cost $40,000 per officer (three officers × $40,000 per year = $120,000 per year). CCTV will cost $150,000. After considering the costs and benefits of each, the manager decides on the CCTV system because by the second year the expense will be lower than hiring three extra officers.
5. Does the cost of the strategy exceed the potential loss? For example, it would not be cost effective to spend $5,000 to prevent theft from a $50 petty cash fund.
6. Does the strategy relate to unique needs? Often, strategies good for one location may not be appropriate for another location.
7. How will the strategy relate to the entire loss prevention program? A systems approach is wise. The interrelatedness of each strategy should be considered. For example, CCTV can be used in a retail store to prevent both shoplifting and employee theft. Security personnel are needed to respond to incidents. CCTV can also save on personnel costs and management can remotely monitor multiple sites.
8. Does the strategy conform to the goals and objectives of the organization and the loss prevention program?
9. How does the strategy compare to contract loss prevention programs? Will the strategy interfere with any contract service?
10. How will insurance carriers react?
11. If a government contract is involved, what regulations must be considered?
12. Does the strategy create the potential for losses greater than what is being prevented? For example, applying a chain and lock to the inside handles of a double door makes it more difficult for a burglar to enter; however, what if a fire takes place and employees must escape quickly?
13. Does the strategy reduce the effectiveness of other loss prevention strategies? For example, a chain-link fence with colorful plastic woven through the links and high hedges will prevent people from seeing into the property and hinder an offender's penetration, but this strategy also will cause observation problems for patrolling police.
14. Will the loss prevention strategy interfere with productivity or business operations? For example, in a high-risk environment, how much time will be necessary to search employees who leave and return at lunchtime? What if 1,000 employees

leave for lunch? As another example, if the loss prevention manager requires merchandise loaded into trucks to be counted by three separate individuals, will this strategy slow the shipping process significantly?

15. Will the strategy receive support from management, employees, customers, clients, and visitors? Can any type of adverse reaction be predicted?

16. Does the strategy have to conform to local codes, ordinances, or laws? For example, in certain jurisdictions, perimeter fences must be under a specific height and use of barbed wire is restricted.

17. Will the strategy lower employee morale or lead to a distrust of management?

18. Are there any possible problems with civil liberties violations?

19. How will the union react to the strategy?

20. Was participatory management used to aid in planning the strategy?

21. Can the strategy be effectively implemented with the present number of loss prevention personnel?

22. Will the strategy cause a strain on personnel time?

23. What are the characteristics of the area surrounding the location that will receive the loss prevention strategy? These characteristics must be considered to improve the quality of strategies. For example, if loss prevention strategies are planned for a manufacturing plant, what factors outside the plant must be considered? (Factors of consideration include crime, fire, and accident rates.) Also, certain nearby sites may be subject to disaster: nuclear plants, airports, railroads (transportation of hazardous materials), educational institutions (student unrest), forests (fire), hazardous industries (chemicals), and military installations, among others. Weather conditions are important to consider as well. Storms can activate alarms. Excessive rainfall can cause losses due to flooding. Heavy snow can result in a variety of losses. Earthquake and volcanic actions are additional factors to consider.

24. When considering loss prevention strategies such as burglar or fire alarms, what is the response time of public services such as police, fire, and emergency medical service? Where is the nearest facility housing each service?

25. Will loss prevention strategies be able to repel activity from local criminals, a gang, or organized crime?

26. Will the strategy shift crime to another target?

27. Does the strategy attempt to "loss-proof" or eliminate all losses? This often is an impossible objective to reach. Loss prevention practitioners sometimes are surprised by the failure of a strategy that was publicized as a panacea.

28. If the strategy is not implemented, what is the risk of loss?

29. Will a better, less expensive strategy accomplish the same objective?

30. Can any other present strategy be eliminated when the new strategy is implemented?

31. What other strategies are more important? Are priorities established?

32. Should a pilot program be implemented (say, at one manufacturing plant instead of at all plants) to study the strategy for problems and corrective action?

33. How will the strategy be evaluated?

◻ ◻ ◻ ▬▬▬▬▬▬▬▬▬▬▬▬▬▬▬▬▬▬▬▬▬▬▬

Incomplete Protection Plans

Andrew Smith, security manager at Tecsonics, Inc., a fast-growing electronics firm, was assigned the task of preparing a plan and one-year budget for information security. Two months later, Andrew was in front of senior executives who were eager to learn how proprietary information would be protected in such a fiercely competitive industry. At the beginning of the presentation, Andrew emphasized that the survival and growth of Tecsonics depended on its information security program. The four major strategies for protection for the first year included electronic soundproofing, also referred to as *shielding*, which would involve the use of a copper barrier throughout one conference room to cut off radio waves from a spy's bugging equipment. Cost: $250,000. The second strategy was to spend $85,000 for countermeasure "sweeps" to detect bugs in select locations on the premises. The third strategy was to upgrade the access control system at a cost of $200,000. The fourth strategy was to hire an IT security specialist for $90,000 annually.

Before Andrew was five minutes into his presentation, the rapid-fire questions began: "What is the return on investment?" "Are the plans cost effective?" "Did you perform a risk analysis?" "What are other similar businesses doing?" "Why should we spend so much money on shielding and sweeps when we can use cheaper methods, such as holding meetings in unexpected locations, preparing good policies and procedures, promoting employee education, and keeping certain sensitive information out of the IT system and locked up in a safe?" One sarcastic, hard-nosed executive quipped: "You would probably spend millions on shielding and sweeps and not realize that one of our male scientists could go out of town to a seminar, get cornered by a foxy broad, and get drunk as she pumps him for information!" Unfortunately for Andrew, everybody was laughing while he wished he had done a better job of preparing for his presentation (Purpura, 1989: 43–44).

Planning from a Systems Perspective

The **systems perspective** looks at interactions among subsystems. When actions take place in one subsystem, other subsystems are affected. For example, the criminal justice system is composed of three major subsystems: police, courts, and corrections. If, during one day, the police make 100 arrests for public intoxication, then the court and corrections subsystems must react by accommodating these arrestees. There are many other examples of systems: a loss prevention department, a business, government, a school, an automobile, the human body, and so on. All these systems have subsystems that interact and affect the whole system. In each system, subsystems are established to attain overall system objectives and goals.

Similar to other systems, a loss prevention department can be analyzed in terms of *inputs*, *processes*, *outputs*, and *feedback*. As an example, look at a loss prevention department's immediate reaction and short-term planning concerning an employee theft incident (see Figure 3-1). The loss prevention department receives a call from a supervisor who has caught an employee stealing: the *input*. The *process* is the analysis of the call, planning, and the action taken (i.e., dispatching of loss prevention personnel). The *outputs* (i.e., activity at the scene) are the arrival of the personnel, questioning, and note taking. *Feedback* involves communications from the on-site loss prevention personnel to the loss prevention department; this helps to determine if the output was proper or if corrections are necessary. For instance, suppose that an on-the-spot arrest was required. Then additional outputs might be necessary, possibly including assistance from a local public police department.

The systems perspective described in Figure 3-1 is for planning a short-term, immediate action. Figure 3-2 illustrates long-term loss prevention planning from a systems perspective.

In Figure 3-2, the *inputs* of goals and objectives relate to upper management's expectations of the loss prevention function. The resources include money, material, and human resources. Information, research, reports, risk analyses, and metrics all aid in decision making within the planning *process*. The *outputs* are the loss prevention programs and strategies evolving from the planning process that will prevent and reduce losses while increasing profits. *Feedback*, an often-overlooked activity, is essential for effective planning; and evaluation is an integral part of feedback. Ineffective programs and strategies must be eliminated. Other programs and strategies may need modification. Evaluation helps to justify programs and strategies.

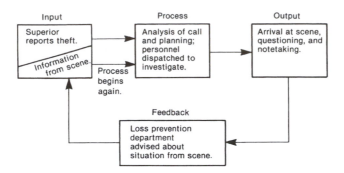

FIGURE 3-1 A systems perspective of a loss prevention department's immediate reaction and short-term planning relevant to an employee theft incident.

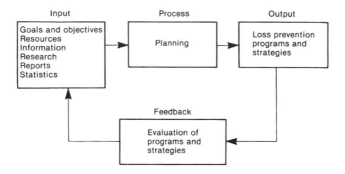

FIGURE 3-2 Long-term loss prevention planning from a systems perspective.

□ □ □ ▬▬▬▬▬▬▬▬▬▬▬▬▬▬▬

Loss prevention practitioners must be prepared when asked by senior management, "How do you know the loss prevention plans and strategies are working?"

□ □ □ ▬▬▬▬▬▬▬▬▬▬▬▬▬▬▬

Critical Thinking for Security Planning
Maxims of Security
   1. Security is never foolproof. The term *foolproof* is a misnomer. Instead of *burglarproof, bulletproof,* or *fireproof*, replace *proof* with *resistant*.
   2. State-of-the-art security has its vulnerabilities. History is filled with grand security strategies that failed.
   3. Through history, security designers have been in constant competition with adversaries seeking to devise methods to circumvent defenses. This is a "cat and mouse" cycle where one side takes the lead, often temporarily, until the other side produces a superior technique. Today, we see this competition with such areas as physical security, IT security, and counterterrorism.

4. Related to #3, the design of security plays a role in an adversary's plan of penetration and attack. Terrorists and other criminals fine-tune their plans according to how a target is protected.

5. Security often is as good as the time it takes to get through it. The longer the time delay facing the offender, the greater the protection and chances that he or she will abort the offense, be apprehended, or seek another target (i.e., displacement).

6. The "harder" the target or defensive strategy, the more likely the offender will seek weaker defenses at the same target or seek a completely new target.

7. Security must focus on not only what is leaving a facility (e.g., company assets), but also what is entering (e.g., weapons, explosives, illegal drugs, and anger).

Three Models of Security
All security strategies fall under one of the following models:

1. It protects people, assets, and/or the operations of enterprises.
2. It accomplishes nothing.
3. It helps offenders.

Illustrations of security protecting people, assets, and/or the operations of enterprises are seen when a hospital security officer escorts nurses to their vehicles at night, when a safe proves too formidable for a burglar who leaves the scene, or when a manufacturing process is protected through access controls and other security methods. Security accomplishes nothing when security officers sleep on the job or fail to make their rounds or when alarm systems remain inoperable. Sometimes unknown to security practitioners and those they serve are the security strategies that actually help offenders. This can occur when security officer applicants are poorly screened, hired, and then they commit crimes against their employer. The ordinary padlock is an example of how physical security can assist offenders. An unlocked padlock hanging on an opened gate can invite *padlock substitution,* in which the offender replaces it with his or her padlock, returns at night to gain access, and then secures the gate with the original padlock. Such cases are difficult to investigate because signs of forced entry may be absent. Fences, another example, often are built with a top rail and supports for barbed wire that are strong enough to assist and support people, rather than the fence and barbed wire. Also, attractive-looking picket fences have been knocked down by offenders and used as ladders.

Security practitioners should identify and classify all security strategies under these models to expose useful, wasteful, and harmful methods. This endeavor should be a perpetual process within risk analysis, careful planning, critical thinking, testing, and research to facilitate cost-effective, results-oriented security. Although these challenging goals require time and effort, the net result is a superior security and loss prevention program.

Using a critical thinking approach, what are your views on any of the maxims or models of security? How can they be modified or enhanced?

Standards and Regulations

Standards and regulations serve as resources for employees in the public and private sectors who seek to optimize professionalism, competence, and quality within their organizations that are reflected in the products and services they generate. There is much confusion and controversy over standards and regulations. Here we begin with a federal government perspective, basic definitions, and then information specific to security and loss prevention.

Standards

The **National Technology Transfer and Advancement Act** (NTTAA), which became law in March 1996, directs federal agencies to adopt private sector standards, wherever possible, rather than create proprietary, nonconsensus standards. The act also directs the National Institute of Standards and Technology to bring together all levels of government for the same purpose. The NTTAA cites "standard" or "technical standard" as including common and repeated use of rules, conditions, guidelines or characteristics for products or related processes and production methods, and related management systems practices.

There are many types of standards that serve a wide variety of purposes. They are classified in numerous ways. Standards based on purpose include terminology standards that standardize nomenclature, test and measurement standards that define methods to assess performance, and product and service standards that promote quality. Standards may also be classified by the intended user group. Examples are company standards that are meant for a single business, industry standards for a particular industry, international standards, and government standards. Standards may also specify requirements, such as performance standards that describe how a product is supposed to function and design standards that define how a product is to be built.

Standards are developed by hundreds of U.S., international, foreign, and regional organizations. Research on standards can be confusing and time-consuming. The end of this chapter offers federal government Web sites helpful for finding standards and regulations.

Consensus standards are accepted industry practices developed through a consensus process (i.e., open to review and modifications by experts who agree on how a specific task should be performed prior to the final standard). Consensus standards do not have the force of law unless a jurisdiction adopts them as law. Professional groups also publish "guidelines" or "guides" (also without the force of law) that offer organizations information and factors to consider when developing programs (e.g., security or fire protection).

Standards may help an industry prevent legislation that is burdensome and expensive to that industry. For instance, if an industry voluntarily produces standards that promote security and safety, then government security regulations for that industry may be averted.

Although standards may not be adopted as law by a jurisdiction, they may be used to establish a standard of care or used during litigation. Angle (2005: 22) defines **standard of care** as "the concept of what a reasonable person with similar training and equipment would do in a similar situation." In the emergency medical field, for example, a practitioner can prevent a claim of negligence if he or she performs in the same way as another reasonable person with the same training and equipment. In other words, everyone has certain expectations of performance.

An employer can face a claim of negligence by failing to adhere to policies and procedures, standards, or legal mandates (Fried, 2004: 30). Suppose employees are injured during an emergency evacuation and sue. Experts may be hired by opposite sides of the civil case to provide expertise and testimony on whether the employer provided a safe workplace and properly planned for emergencies. Comparisons may be made of what reasonable prudent management would do. If the defense side can show that management did everything "reasonable management" would have done under the same circumstances, then the employer has a good chance of showing that it acted reasonably and should not be liable for injuries.

Fried makes interesting observations about standards and litigation. He notes that if industry experts seek to develop a standard to benefit themselves or others, or to sell products or services, then the standard would not have significant weight in court. Another question sure to surface is how the standard was developed. Consensus standards often do not meet the scientific rigor of, say, how the medical profession uses multiple blind tests to determine if a drug works. Fried (2004: 30) writes: "Thus, for any standard to pass legal muster under the Daubert challenge (requiring proof that a standard or conclusion is based on scientific or sound research), the standard needs to be tested and proven to be correct. Otherwise the standard is just a suggestion."

Although the National Fire Protection Association (NFPA), for example, outlines ideal actions and what an ideal manager should achieve based on industry experts, failure to meet standards does not mean law was violated or someone is negligent. A judge may declare a standard introduced in court as not applicable in that jurisdiction because no court or legal body authorized it, even though an expert witness might argue that an unofficial standard has become an industry standard of practice. Fried writes that if over 50% of employers follow a conduct—whether or not from a standard—that conduct could be considered the reasonable industry standard that should be followed.

In reference to settling lawsuits involving negligent security, courts have ruled inconsistently. Acceptable security in one jurisdiction may be unacceptable in another. However, security standards foster uniform security. Those against standards cite costs and argue that it is impossible to standardize security because each location and business is unique.

A government jurisdiction can adopt a standard as law and enforce it. For example, this has been done by many jurisdictions with the NFPA 101 Life Safety Code. The NFPA has no enforcement authority.

Competition over Standards

There is competition among organizations over producing and publishing standards. A major issue is which organization is best suited to prepare standards in a particular field. Swope (2006: 20–23) uses the term **code war** to describe rival groups lobbying governments to accept their competing sets of standards. For instance, for many years the business community has urged governments to standardize building codes among cities and states to reduce construction costs. On one side of the competition is the International Code Council (ICC), a group supported by government building and code enforcement officials, architects, and building owners and managers. The National Fire Protection Association (NFPA) heads the other side. It is supported by fire chiefs and unions representing building specialists. Government and industry prefer one code, and they are faced with a major question: "Which code to choose?" Swope (2006: 22) writes that the code war also involves the ICC and NFPA acting as "two publishing houses engaged in a war for book sales." When a government adopts a model code or when codes change, officials, architects, engineers, construction specialists, and others must purchase up-to-date copies. Each code group earns tens of millions of dollars annually from publication sales.

A major difference between the ICC and the NFPA is how they update their codebooks. The ICC allows only building officials to vote on changes. The ICC sees this as a way to prevent special interests (e.g., trade unions, manufacturers) from influencing the codes. The NFPA permits all its members to vote, although checks and balances are applied to prevent undue influence.

Other groups are also in competition. For instance, ASIS International and the NFPA each have committees involved in the subject of security. The question is which group is most appropriate to produce security guidelines or standards? Both groups are involved in producing guidelines. ASIS International produced several excellent security guidelines (many discussed in this book) on such topics as risk assessment, chief security officer, private security officer selection and training, and business continuity.

The NFPA produced "NFPA 730, Guide for Premises Security." It is based on risk assessment principles and includes information on physical security, security personnel, and security at certain occupancies (e.g., educational, healthcare). Another publication is "NFPA 731, Installation of Electronic Premises Security Systems." It is a standard with specific requirements for the installation of various security systems. NFPA 730 was difficult to gain consensus among committee membership. The NFPA Standards Council appointed to the Premises Security Technical Committee representatives from the insurance industry, ASIS International, Underwriters Laboratories, the Security Industry Association, and other groups. It began as a code, then it became a recommended practice, and then a guide. The NFPA defines "guide" as "a document that is advisory or informative in nature and that contains only non-mandatory provisions ... the document as a whole is not suitable for adoption into law" (Moore, 2005).

□ □ □ ▬▬▬▬▬▬▬▬▬▬▬▬▬▬▬▬▬▬▬▬▬▬▬▬▬▬

Is the competition over standards beneficial or detrimental to our society and the security profession? Justify your view.

▬▬▬▬▬▬▬▬▬▬▬▬▬▬▬▬▬▬▬▬▬▬▬ □ □ □

Regulations

Regulations are rules or laws enacted at the federal, state, or local levels with the requirement to comply. These requirements may address health, product safety, environmental effects, or other matters in the public interest. A regulation may consist of agency-developed technical specifications or private sector standards. The NTTAA endorses the use of private sector standards.

Federal regulations are contained in the **Code of Federal Regulations (CFR)**. A widely known example of federal regulations is found in Title 29 CFR, Occupational Safety and Health Administration (OSHA). OSHA is a federal agency, under the U.S. Department of Labor, established to administer the law on safety and health in the workplace.

Angle (2005: 21) offers these definitions: "**Codes** are standards that cover broad subject areas, which can be adopted into law independently of other codes, or standards."

"**Recommended practices** are standards, which are similar in content to standards and codes, but are nonmandatory in compliance."

Its is important to note that the terms *regulations, standards, codes*, and *recommended practices* are used interchangeably in the literature and by the public and private sectors. OSHA, for example, uses the term *standards* in the content of *regulations*.

Post-9/11 Standards and Regulations

Prior to the 9/11 attacks, many business enterprises set their own internal security standards and policies. This still occurs; however, certain industries have been following external regulations and standards for many years. Examples include businesses involved with government contracts, or the nuclear, financial, or aviation industries. Institutions such as healthcare facilities and colleges have also been influenced by regulations and standards. OSHA has played a major role in influencing businesses and institutions in promoting a safe environment, even through crime prevention methods. And, locales have enacted ordinances to increase security at convenience stores.

The passage of the NTTAA resulted in a proliferation of standards developers and standards, and the 9/11 attacks resulted in even more growth of security standards and regulations. The federal government has spearheaded efforts to protect infrastructure and key assets through many initiatives and regulations, as described in this book. Security and loss prevention practitioners must continue to study and apply guidelines, standards, and regulations pertaining to their specific industry. These resources help to formulate internal policies and procedures. Businesses involved in transportation, for instance, refer to the U.S. Department of Transportation and the U.S. Department of Homeland Security. The banking and finance industry refers to the U.S. Department of the Treasury. Drinking water and wastewater treatment systems are guided by the Environmental Protection Agency. And, as we know, besides government regulations, many organizations publish standards of a general nature and for specific industries.

Several benefits result from adherence to guidelines, standards, and regulations. These include greater safety and security, the prevention of losses and litigation, enhanced risk management, and uniformity.

Standard-Setting Organizations

From the perspective of manufacturing and installing security and loss prevention products and systems, standards serve as written and tested guidelines that promote uniformity and quality. Additional benefits of standards include preventing people from installing unsafe systems, helping manufacturers define how their products converge with IT networks, and assisting the industry in the highly standards-oriented federal market.

Manufacturers have been producing their products in accordance with safety standards for many years. During the 1920s, for example, **Underwriters Laboratories** (**UL**), an independent testing organization, worked with insurers to establish a rating system for alarm products and installations. This system assists insurers in setting premiums for customers. An alarm company may show customers that its service is of a higher standard than a competitor's. UL has various listings, and it requires that an alarm company advertise its listing specifically. What a company has to do to obtain a listing as a central station burglar alarm company differs widely from what it has to do to be listed as a residential monitoring station; providing fire-resistant construction, backup power, access controls, and optimal response time following an alarm are a few examples.

Consumers, in general, are more familiar with UL as an organization promoting the electrical safety of thousands of retail products. Companies pay a fee to have UL test their products for safety according to UL standards. The famous UL label often is seen attached to the product. Sometimes the UL label is attached to a product without testing and authorization.

The **National Fire Protection Association** (**NFPA**) establishes standards for fire protection equipment and construction that have been adopted by government agencies, in addition to companies in the private sector. Beginning in 1898, in cooperation with the insurance industry, the NFPA has produced standards covering sprinklers, fire hoses, and fire doors, among other forms of fire protection.

The **Security Industry Association** (**SIA**) is an international trade association that promotes education, research, and technical standards. It represents manufacturers, distributors, service providers, and others in the security industry. SIA standards promote the interests of its membership by developing common, open, interoperability protocols and performance standards and through standards-related venues. SIA follows American National Standards Institute (ANSI) principles on developing standards like other standards writing bodies.

The **American Society for Testing and Materials** (**ASTM International**), organized in 1898, has grown into one of the largest voluntary standards development systems in the world. ASTM is a nonprofit organization providing a forum for producers, consumers, government, and academia to meet to write standards for materials, products, systems, and services. Among its standards-writing committees are committees that focus on security, safety, and fire protection.

The **American National Standards Institute** (**ANSI**), organized in 1918, is a nonprofit organization that coordinates U.S. voluntary national standards and represents the United States in international standards bodies such as the International Organization for Standardization. ANSI approves and accredits standards for products and personnel certification that are developed by standards-setting organizations, government agencies, consumer groups, businesses, and others. It does not develop its own standards. The ANSI Web site contains other groups' standards. ANSI serves both private and public sectors in an effort to develop standards that exist in all industries, such as safety and health, information processing, banking, and petroleum.

The **International Organization for Standardization** is a worldwide federation of national standards bodies from just about all countries. It is a nongovernmental group based in Geneva, Switzerland, established in 1947 with the purpose of promoting standardization globally to facilitate the international exchange of goods and services. Its agreements are published as International Standards, also known as ISO standards. According to Wikipedia (2006), ISO does not stand for "International Standards Organization." ISO is not an acronym; it comes from the Greek word *isos*, meaning "equal."

Evaluation of Loss Prevention Programs

How can a loss prevention program be evaluated? First, a research design can assist in the evaluation. A look at a few simplified research designs demonstrates how loss prevention programs are determined to be successful or unsuccessful.

One design is the **pretest-posttest design**. A robbery prevention program can serve as an example. First, the robbery rate is measured (by compiling statistics) before the robbery prevention program is implemented. The program then is implemented and the rate measured again. Robbery rates before and after program implementation are compared. If the robbery rate declined, then the robbery prevention program may be the causative factor.

A loss prevention training program can serve as another example. Loss prevention personnel are tested prior to the training program, and their test scores are saved. The training program is implemented. After the program is completed, another similar test is given the personnel. The pretest scores are compared to the posttest scores. Higher posttest scores may indicate that the training program was effective.

Another evaluation design or research method is called the **experimental control group design**. As an example, a crime prevention program within a corporation is subject to evaluation. Within the corporation, two plants that are characteristically similar are selected. One plant (the experimental plant) receives the crime prevention program, while the other plant (the control plant) does not. Before the program is implemented, the rate of crime at each plant is measured. After the program has been in effect for a predetermined period of time, the rate of crime is again measured at each plant. If the crime rate has declined at the "experimental" plant while remaining the same at the "control" plant, then the crime prevention program may be successful.

A good researcher should be cautious when formulating conclusions. In the crime prevention program at the plant, crime may have declined for reasons unknown to the researcher. For instance, offenders at the experimental plant may have refrained from crime because of the publicity surrounding the crime prevention program. However, after the initial impact of the program and the novelty expired, offenders could possibly continue to commit crimes. In other words, the program may have been successful in the beginning but soon became ineffective. Thus, continued evaluations are vital to strengthen research results.

Scientific Method

To assist planning and research, the **scientific method** can be used. *Four steps are involved: statement of the problem, hypothesis, testing, and conclusion.* As an example, employee theft will serve as the problem. The hypothesis is a statement whereby the problem and a possible solution (i.e., loss prevention strategy) are noted. Testing involves an attempt to learn whether the strategy reduces the problem. Several research designs are possible. Here is an example of the presentation of the problem according to the style of scientific methodology:

- *Problem*: Employee theft.
- *Hypothesis*: Employee theft can be reduced by using CCTV.
- *Testing*: Control group (plant A—no CCTV); experimental group (plant B—CCTV).
- *Conclusion*: After several months of testing, plant A maintained previous levels of employee theft, whereas plant B showed a drop in employee theft. Therefore, CCTV may be an effective loss prevention strategy to reduce employee theft.

To strengthen research results, continued testing is necessary. In the example, CCTV can be tested at other, similar locations. Further, other strategies can be combined with CCTV to see if the problem can be reduced to a greater extent.

Sources of Research Assistance

A need exists for more research to identify successful and unsuccessful loss prevention methods. Four potential sources of research assistance are in-house, university, private consulting, and insurance companies.

In-house research may be the best because proprietary personnel are familiar with the unique problems at hand. Salary costs could be a problem, but a loss prevention practitioner with a graduate degree can be an asset to loss prevention planning and programming. In-house research, however, can result in increased bias by the researcher because superiors may expect results that conform to their points of view.

University researchers usually have excellent credentials. Many educators are required to serve the community and are eager to do research that can lead to publication. The cost is minimal.

Private consulting firms often have qualified personnel to conduct research and make recommendations to enhance protection. This source can be the most expensive because these firms are in business for profit. Careful consideration and a scrutiny of the consulting staff are wise. The buyer should beware.

Insurance companies are active in studying threats, hazards, and risks. They also participate in varying degrees in research projects relevant to crime, fire, and safety. A major function of this industry is risk management, whereby strategies are recommended to reduce possible losses.

□ □ □ ▬▬▬▬▬▬▬▬▬▬▬▬▬▬▬▬▬▬▬▬▬▬▬▬▬▬▬

Performance Measures

Traditionally, public police performance has been measured by reported crime rates, overall arrests, crimes cleared by arrest, and response time to incidents. These metrics have become institutionalized, and substantial investments have been made to develop IT systems to capture such data. However, this data may tell little about police effectiveness in reducing crime and the fear of crime (U.S. Department of Justice, 1993: ix). Furthermore, do these measures reflect outmoded policing, and do they fail to account for many important contributions police make to the quality of life, such as efforts at community cohesion and crime prevention? Here is an example of performance measures for police that have implications for security:

- *Goal:* Promoting secure communities.
- *Methods and activities:* Promoting crime prevention and problem-solving initiatives.
- *Performance indicators:* Programs and resources allocated to crime prevention, public trust and confidence in police, and reduced public fear of crime (DiIulio, 1993: 113–135).

What lessons can security practitioners learn from research on performance measures in the public sector? Do security programs contain traditional systems of measuring performance that reflect outmoded security efforts, while failing to account for important contributions to protection and the business enterprise?

Performance measures do exist in security programs today, but how can they be improved? To improve security programs, research should be directed at enhancing traditional performance measures and metrics that more accurately reflect customer satisfaction, security expenditures, and return on investments.

▬▬▬▬▬▬▬▬▬▬▬▬▬▬▬▬▬▬▬▬▬▬▬▬▬▬▬ □ □ □

Proprietary Security

Proprietary security programs and organizations in general are characterized by the organizational terms and practical management tools described in the following two lists. These terms and topics also apply to contract security businesses.

Basics of Organization: The Vocabulary

- **Division of work:** Work is divided among employees according to such factors as function, clientele, time, and location.
- **Authority:** The right to act.
- **Responsibility:** An obligation to do an assigned job.
- **Power:** The ability to act.
- **Delegation of authority:** A superior delegates authority to subordinates to spread the workload. A superior can delegate authority, but a person must accept responsibility. Responsibility cannot be delegated. For example, the sergeant delegated to loss prevention officers the authority to check employee lunch boxes when employees left the plant.
- **Chain of command:** Communications go upward and downward within an organized hierarchy for the purpose of efficiency and order.
- **Span of control:** The number of subordinates that one superior can adequately supervise. An example of a broad span of control would be one senior investigator supervising 20 investigators. An example of a narrow span of control would be one senior investigator supervising five investigators. An adequate span of control depends on factors such as the amount of close supervision necessary and the difficulty of the task.
- **Unity of command:** To prevent confusion during an organized effort, no subordinate should report to more than one superior.
- **Line personnel:** Those in the organized hierarchy who have authority and function within the chain of command. Line personnel can include uniformed loss prevention officers, sergeants, lieutenants, captains, and other superiors.
- **Staff personnel:** Specialists with limited authority who advise line personnel. For example, the loss prevention specialist advised the captain about a more efficient method of reducing losses.
- **Formal organization:** An official organization designed by senior management whereby the "basics of organization" are applied to produce the most efficient organization possible.
- **Informal organization:** An unofficial organization produced by employees with specific interests. For example, several employees spend time together (during breaks and lunch) because they are active as community volunteers.
- **Organization chart:** A pictorial chart that visually represents the formal organization. Many of the "basics of organization" actually can be seen on organization charts (see Figure 3-3).

Basics of Organization: The Practical Management Tools

- **Directive system:** A formal directive system is a management tool used to communicate information within an organized group. The communications can be both verbal and written. A verbal directive can be as simple as a superior informing a subordinate of what work needs to be done. The formal verbal directive system also can include meetings in which verbal communications are exchanged.
- **Policies:** Policies are management tools that control employee decision making. Policies reflect the goals and objectives of management.
- **Procedures:** Procedures are management tools that point out a particular way of doing something; they guide action. Many procedures actually are plans that fulfill the

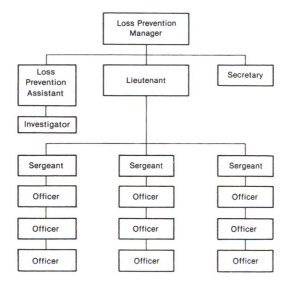

FIGURE 3-3 Small loss prevention department.

requirements of policies. The loss prevention manager must maintain an open mind when feedback evolves from policies and procedures. For instance, suppose only two security officers are assigned to search the belongings carried by 1,000 employees as they end their shift. Long lines of irritated employees may develop. Consequently, changes must be made.

- **Manual:** A manual is like a "rule book" for an organized group; it contains policies and procedures.

It is important to note that if an organization's structure is too rigid, employees may be hindered from fulfilling business objectives. Participation by subordinates in decision making and a team atmosphere of cooperation have been shown to increase morale and motivation. Leadership style will also influence success. The **autocratic style** sees managers making all decisions, whereas the **democratic style** seeks opinions from employees as input for decisions. Following decades of research, psychologists have concluded that no one style is best. Effective managers use both. For example, a manager may be autocratic with a trainee and democratic with a seasoned employee (Levy and Weitz, 2001: 534).

☐ ☐ ☐ ▬▬▬▬▬▬▬▬▬▬▬▬▬▬▬▬▬▬▬▬▬

What Are the Duties of a Security Manager?

The duties of security managers vary widely. Here, a generalization is presented.

Security managers plan, prioritize tasks, concentrate on pressing problems, and strive to stay within their budget. They delegate tasks and supervise subordinates and contractors who perform security services. Another duty is to ensure that security systems are functioning properly. Security managers may spend all day at their desks and computers sending and responding to e-mails, preparing reports, conducting research on the Web, reading, or talking on the telephone. *With modern technology, such tasks can be performed almost anywhere.* On other days they may split their time in the office or doing administrative work with visits to various locations on and off the premises for inspections or investigations. They may attend meetings, conduct or receive training, and attend a college course. Since they are interacting with people so much, they must have excellent human relations and communications skills.

Physical security and access controls are often part of their job; only authorized people should be on the premises. Security managers also realize that offenders can cause harm from remote locations by using a computer; consequently, security managers and IT specialists are increasingly working together. If an alleged crime occurs or an incident requires investigation, the manager may conduct the investigation, delegate the task, or contract the work to an outside firm. Workplace safety is another important issue, and this includes fire safety, emergency procedures, and the prevention of accidents. All security personnel and volunteers from the workforce may receive special training to prevent and suppress fires and render first aid. As risks surface, security managers prepare policies and procedures, in cooperation with other employees, in an effort to prevent losses.

A company may require the manager to spend a great deal of time providing training programs to employees on a host of topics, from employee protection to information security. Security managers may be responsible for a certain geographic area and visit corporate locations over several weeks to conduct a variety of duties as described previously. To reduce costs, businesses may add additional duties—outside traditional security duties—to the security manager's position. Examples include supervision of landscaping, parking, a fleet of vehicles, a mail system, and a cafeteria. Security managers must be flexible and available for emergencies at any hour, since the employer and employees depend on them for protection.

What is your opinion of the duties of a security manager?

Search the Web

The Web contains a wealth of information on the security and loss prevention profession. Here are Web sites relevant to this chapter:

Academy of Security Educators and Trainers: www.asetcse.org

American National Standards Institute: www.ansi.org

American Society for Testing and Materials: www.astm.org

ASIS International, *Security Management*: www.asis.com

finding regulations: http://standards.gov/standards_gov/v/Regulations/index.cfm

finding standards: http://standards.gov/standards_gov/v/Standards/index.cfm

Information Security: http://informationsecurity.techtarget.com

International Foundation of Protection Officers, *Protection News*: www.ifpo.org

International Organization for Standardization: www.iso.org

Journal of Security Administration: www.wiu.edu/users/mfkac/jsa/

National Fire Protection Association: www.nfpa.org

Palgrave Macmillan Journals, *Security Journal*: www.palgrave-journals.com/sj/index.html

SC Magazine: www.scmagazine.com

Security Industry Association: www.siaonline.org

The Haworth Press, *Journal of Security Education*: www.haworthpress.com

Underwriters Laboratories (UL): www.ul.com

Case Problems

3A. As the Chief Security Officer for a global manufacturer of a variety of products, you have in your budget only enough money to subscribe to three security periodicals. You search the Web and select three. Which ones did you choose?

3B. As a loss prevention manager, you have been asked to prepare a speech to a group of security practitioners. The topic is "Planning Security and Loss Prevention Programs and Strategies." Outline the speech or prepare notecards for your presentation.

3C. Refer to the box in this chapter titled "Incomplete Protection Plans." If you were an outside security consultant hired by Andrew Smith, what would you suggest to help him prior to his meeting with senior executives?

3D. As a security manager, you believe that the 3 P.M. meeting today with the Vice President of Finance will not bring good news. Each business quarter seems to show poor profits and the need for cutbacks in all departments. When you enter her office for the meeting, the VP, Alaine Nell, gets right to the point: "Your security budget to protect the three openings at the plant must be cut by 50%." She draws a sketch of the huge square plant and notes that the three openings are costing $500,000 annually for 24-hour-a-day security officer protection, including overtime. She states that each post requires four officers (three on and one off during each 24-hour period) at $40,000 apiece. She requests a financial plan for the next five years. Prepare such a plan, providing hypothetical information if needed.

3E. You are a security specialist at a port. Your supervisor has assigned you the task of preparing a list of the laws, regulations, standards, government agencies, and private sector organizations pertaining to security at ports. Prepare the list by conducting research on the Web.

3F. Design an organization chart for a loss prevention department of 35 people at an industrial plant. Write a one-page justification of your design to satisfy management. Provide hypothetical information about the plant if needed.

References

ASIS International. (2003). "General Security Risk Assessment Guideline." www.asisonline. org/guidelines/guidelines.htm, retrieved January 3, 2006.

Angle, J. (2005). *Occupational Safety and Health in the Emergency Services*, 2nd ed. Clifton Park, NY: Thomas Delmar Pub.

Broder, J. (2006). *Risk Analysis and the Security Survey*, 3rd ed. Burlington, MA: Elsevier Butterworth Heinemann.

Crawford, J. (1995). "Security, Heal Thyself." *Security Management* (May).

Cressey, D. (1971). *Other People's Money: A Study in the Social Psychology of Embezzlement*. Belmont, CA: Wadsworth.

DiIulio, J. (1993). *Performance Measures for the Criminal Justice System* (October). Washington, D.C.: Bureau of Justice Statistics.

Felson, M. (1998). *Crime and Everyday Life: Insights and Implications for Society*. Thousand Oaks, CA: Pine Forge Press.

Fried, G. (2004). "Ask the Expert." *Public Venue Security* (May/June).

Jacobson, R. (2000). "What Is a Rational Goal for Security?" *Security Management* 44 (December).

Lab, S. (2004). *Crime Prevention: Approaches, Practices and Evaluations*, 5th ed. www.lex-isnexis.com/anderson/criminaljustice

Levy, M., and Weitz, B. (2001). *Retailing Management*. New York: McGraw-Hill.

Maslow, A. (1954). *Motivation and Personality*. New York: Harper & Row.

Moore, W. (2005). "NFPA 730 and NFPA 731: The New NFPA Security Guide and Standard Increase the Quality and Reliability of Security System Installations." *NFPA Journal* (January/February).

Newman, O. (1972). *Defensible Space*. New York: Macmillan.

Pontell, H., and Calavita, K. (1993). "The Savings and Loan Industry." In *Beyond the Law: Crime in Complex Organizations*. M. Tonry and A. Reiss, Editors. Chicago: University of Chicago Press.

Purpura, P. (1989). *Modern Security and Loss Prevention Management*. Boston: Butterworth-Heinemann.

Swope, C. (2006). "The Code War." *Governing*, 19 (January).

Tippett, P. (2001). "Calculating Risk." *Information Security,* 4 (March).

U.S. Department of Justice. (1993). *A Police Guide to Surveying Citizens and Their Environment*. (October). Washington, D.C.: U.S. Government Printing Office.

Wikipedia. (2006). "International Organization for Standardization." http://enwikipedia.org/wiki/International_Organization_for_Standardination, retrieved June 3, 2006.

4
Law

Objectives

After studying this chapter, the reader will be able to:

1. Summarize the judicial systems of the United States.
2. Explain the origins of law.
3. List and define at least five torts.
4. Discuss the theory of premises security claims and negligence.
5. Explain contract law.
6. Outline civil justice procedures
7. Explain the relationship among administrative law, compliance auditing, and the Federal Sentencing Guidelines.
8. Summarize labor law and its relationship to private security.
9. Outline criminal justice procedures.
10. Explain the legal guidelines for arrest, use of force, searches, and questioning.

KEY TERMS

- dual court system
- limited jurisdiction courts
- courts of general jurisdiction
- appellate jurisdiction
- intermediate state appellate courts
- state supreme court
- U.S. Magistrate's Courts
- U.S. District Courts
- U.S. Courts of Appeals
- U.S. Supreme Court
- federal and state constitutions
- common law
- case law
- legislative law
- criminal law
- felonies
- misdemeanors
- civil law

- substantive law
- procedural law
- tort law
- false imprisonment
- malicious prosecution
- battery
- assault
- trespass to land
- trespass to personal property
- infliction of emotional distress
- defamation (libel and slander)
- invasion of privacy
- negligence
- legal duty
- proximate cause
- foreseeability
- prior similar incidents rule
- totality of the circumstances test

- conscious disregard
- contract
- remedies for breach of contract
- nondelegable duty
- respondeat superior
- vicarious liability
- plaintiff
- defendant
- discovery
- motion
- pretrial conference
- verdict
- administrative agencies
- administrative inspections
- administrative searches
- compliance auditing
- due diligence
- Federal Sentencing Guidelines
- Health Insurance Portability and Accountability Act of 1996 (HIPAA)
- Sarbanes-Oxley (SOX) Act of 2002
- Financial Modernization Act of 1999
- National Labor Relations Act
- Weingarten rights
- arrest
- probable cause
- booking
- initial appearance
- preliminary hearing
- arraignment
- plea bargaining
- trial
- reasonable force
- deadly force
- exclusionary rule
- Miranda warnings

Introduction

A good foundation in law is an essential prerequisite to loss prevention programming. Many crucial decisions by practitioners are circumscribed by legal parameters, and the consequences of these decisions can be serious. An arrest without the proper legal authority and evidence can result in civil and criminal action against security personnel. Negligence is a serious concern that results from the failure to exercise due care in the use of force, for example. This is why training is so important; it becomes a major issue in a lawsuit against security. Numerous lawsuits also have been directed at those responsible for security, who are claimed to be negligent for not providing a safe environment, which caused a person to become a crime victim. Consequently, security and loss prevention decisions must take into consideration the legal environment. We begin with the structure of our judicial systems.

Judicial Systems

Our nation has a **dual court system** of federal and state courts. This means that, in addition to a federal court system, each of the 50 states (as well as the District of Colombia and the territories like Guam) has its own court system (Purpura, 1997: 200–212).

State Court Systems

States commonly have a three- or four-tier court system. Keeping in mind state variation, the tiers, from lowest to highest, are

- Courts of limited or special jurisdiction
- Courts of general jurisdiction (major trial courts)
- Intermediate appellate courts
- State supreme court (the court of last resort)

Limited jurisdiction courts handle minor cases—the bulk of the judicial caseload, traffic violations, and misdemeanors. An example of this court is the justice of the peace, which in many states has been reformed or eliminated. When found, it exists more frequently in rural than urban areas. The magistrate's court resembles the justice of the peace, although there may be differences in some states. Small, medium, and large cities have established municipal courts to handle a variety of justice duties. Courts of special jurisdiction hear cases only in a single area of law, be it criminal, drug, family, juvenile, or probate (wills and transfers of assets).

State laws or constitutions define jurisdiction between lower and higher courts that may hold concurrent jurisdiction over some misdemeanors. **Courts of general jurisdiction** have jurisdiction over all cases involving civil law and criminal law. A person accused of a felony would be prosecuted in this type of court. Courts of general jurisdiction have a variety of names, which can create confusion in understanding court systems among the states. Courts of general jurisdiction may have appellate jurisdiction over lower court decisions (such as a misdemeanor tried in a court of limited jurisdiction). **Appellate jurisdiction** is the authority of a court to review and revise the decision of an inferior court.

Appeals to **intermediate state appellate courts** offer litigants a chance to change an unfavorable trial court decision by arguing that the lower court judgment was based on a reversible error. The party bringing the appeal might contend, for instance, that the trial court erred when it allowed inadmissible testimony, or that the jury was given improper instructions.

All states have a court of last resort that may be called the **state supreme court**. The highest court in the state will receive much of its caseload from the intermediate appellate court if one exists. The highest court in the state interprets the law, applies it to the case at hand, and renders a decision as the court of last resort in the state.

Each year, in the states, courts of limited jurisdiction handle about 61,000,000 cases, and courts of general jurisdiction handle about 31,000,000 cases. Most of the cases involve traffic, civil, criminal, domestic, and juvenile matters. Intermediate state appellate courts are involved in about 187,000 cases, while state supreme courts deal with about 85,000 cases (Neubauer, 2005: 82).

Federal Court System

The federal system divides into two major categories: the legislative courts and the constitutional courts. Congress established legislative courts under Article I of the U.S. Constitution. An example of these courts of special jurisdiction is the tax court, which handles disputes between taxpayers and the Internal Revenue Service. Congress also created district and appellate courts in the District of Colombia and territorial courts. Article III of the U.S. Constitution provided for the U.S. Supreme Court and authorized Congress to create the lower federal judiciary. Four constitutional courts are: U.S. Magistrate's Courts, U.S. District Courts, U.S. Courts of Appeal, and the U.S. Supreme Court.

The **U.S. Magistrate's Courts** are the lowest level of jurisdiction of the federal court system. U.S. magistrate judges conduct initial appearances and preliminary hearings, determine bail and conditions of release, conduct preliminary stages of felony cases, issue search and arrest warrants to federal law enforcement officers such as FBI agents, review cases involving prisoners, and deal with numerous civil matters. Their authority covers all tasks performed by federal district judges except trying and sentencing felony defendants. Decisions by magistrate judges can be appealed to the federal district courts.

U.S. District Courts are similar to the courts of general jurisdiction in state court systems. These courts hear criminal and civil cases.

The **U.S. Courts of Appeals**, often referred to as circuit courts, have jurisdiction over specific geographic areas and are the intermediate appellate courts of the federal system. The Courts of Appeals review cases from the district courts of each region, the U.S. Tax Court, and from certain federal administrative agencies.

The **U.S. Supreme Court** is the highest court of our nation. It receives and disposes of about 8,000 cases each year, most by a brief decision that the issue is not important enough to be heard. In that case the lower court decision is left standing. Each year the Court decides about 80 cases of great national importance.

Each year, the approximate caseload of other federal courts is as follows: U.S. Magistrate's Courts—880,000; U.S. District Courts—386,000; and U.S. Courts of Appeals—58,000. The majority of all these cases involve criminal and civil matters and prisoner petitions (Neubauer, 2005: 60).

Origins of Law

Five major sources of law are federal and state constitutions, common law, case law, legislative law, and administrative law. **Federal and state constitutions** are at the foundation of our government and legal system. The U.S. Constitution specifies powers of the federal government, powers reserved to the states, and the rights of citizens as contained in the Bill of Rights. Courts interpret the Constitution and render decisions on issues, such as whether a federal or state law is unconstitutional. State constitutions, although subordinate to the U.S. Constitution, are the supreme law within the respective state and superior to any local government constitution or charter.

English common law is the major source of law in the United States. **Common law** generally refers to law founded on principles of justice determined by reasoning according to custom and universal consent handed down from one generation to another. The development of civilization is reflected in common law. Specific acts were, and still are, deemed criminal. These acts, even today, are referred to as common law crimes: treason, murder, robbery, battery, larceny, arson, kidnapping, and rape, among others. Common law is reinforced by decisions of courts of law. After our nation gained independence from England, the common law influence remained. Nineteen states have perpetuated common law through case law (i.e., judicial precedent). Eighteen states have abolished common law and written it into statutes. The remaining states have either adopted common law via ratification or are unclear about exactly how it is reflected in the state system.

Case law, sometimes referred to as *judge-made law*, involves the interpretation of statutes or constitutional concepts by federal and state appellate courts. Previous case decisions or *precedent cases* have a strong influence on court decisions. Precedents clarify both statutes and court views to limit ambiguity. When a new case comes into existence, earlier case decisions are used as a reference for decision making. Because the justice system is adversarial in nature, opposing attorneys refer to past cases (i.e., precedents) that support their individual contentions. The court makes a decision between the opposing parties. Societal changes often are reflected in decisions. Because the meaning of legal issues evolves from case law, these court decisions are the law. Of course, later court review of previous decisions can alter legal precedent.

Legislative law from the federal government is passed by Congress under the authority of the U.S. Constitution. Likewise, individual state constitutions empower state legislatures to pass laws. Legislative laws permit both the establishment of criminal laws and a justice system to preside over criminal and civil matters. A court later may decide that a legislative law is unconstitutional; this illustrates the system of "checks and balances" that enables one government body to check on another.

Criminal law pertains to crimes against society (Table 4-1). Each state and the federal government maintains a criminal code that classifies and defines offenses. **Felonies** are considered

Table 4-1 Criminal Law and Tort Law

	Criminal Law	Tort Law
Definition:	Crime as a public wrong	A civil or private wrong
Punishment/Sanction:	Fine, probation, incarceration or death	Money damages
Who brings the action:	The State	The plaintiff
Who can appeal:	Defendant found guilty can appeal. The State usually does not appeal after losing a case.	Both parties can appeal
Standard of proof required:	Proof beyond a reasonable doubt (a higher standard of proof than is required in a civil case)	A preponderance of evidence (greater weight of facts proven)

Source: Reprinted from *Criminal Justice: An Introduction*, Philip. P. Purpura, Copyright Reed Elsevier Inc, 1997, with Permission from Elsevier.

Table 4-2 Substantive Law and Procedural Law

Criminal Law		Civil Law	
Substantive Law (Legal definitions of crimes, penalties)	Procedural Law (Law guiding the criminal justice process)	Substantive Law (Law defining rights and duties among people)	Procedural Law (Law guiding the civil justice process)
Capital crimes Felonies Misdemeanors Violations	Jurisdiction of cases Rules of evidence Other rules	Tort law Contract law Other civil law	Jurisdiction of cases Rules of evidence Other rules

Source: Reprinted from *Criminal Justice: An Introduction*, Philip. P. Purpura, Copyright Reed Elsevier Inc, 1997, with Permission from Elsevier.

more serious crimes, such as burglary and robbery. **Misdemeanors** are less serious crimes, such as trespassing and disorderly conduct.

Civil law adjusts conflicts and differences between individuals (Table 4-2). Examples of civil law cases are accidental injuries, marital disputes, breach of contract, sales that dissatisfy customers, and disputes with a government agency.

Law is also classified as substantive law and procedural law (Table 4-2). **Substantive law** defines criminal offenses (e.g., murder, embezzlement) and specifies punishments. **Procedural law** covers the formal rules for enforcing substantive law and the steps required to process a criminal case (e.g., arrest, bail).

□ □ □ ▬▬▬▬▬▬▬▬▬▬▬▬▬▬▬▬▬▬▬▬▬

Legal Quiz
Prime your mind with the following questions that are answered in this chapter.

1. Can a person be arrested and sued for the same act?
2. Do most employers monitor Internet access by employees?
3. Do employers customarily place covert closed-circuit television (CCTV) cameras in restrooms?
4. Are employers prohibited by law from installing Global Positioning System (GPS) technology in company vehicles?
5. Is it true that the vast majority of civil and criminal cases never make it to trial?
6. Do administrative searches by government regulatory agencies require a search warrant?
7. Are private security personnel required by the U.S. Supreme Court to read Miranda warnings to suspects prior to questioning?

▬▬▬▬▬▬▬▬▬▬▬▬▬▬▬▬▬▬▬▬▬ □ □ □

Tort Law and Controls Over Private Security

Public police officers have greater police powers than private security officers, who typically possess citizen's arrest powers. In conjunction with greater police powers, public officers are limited in their action by the Bill of Rights of the U.S. Constitution. On the other hand, private officers, possessing fewer powers, for the most part, are not as heavily restricted by constitutional limitations. Authority and limitations on private officers result from **tort law**, the body of state legislative statutes and court decisions that govern citizens' actions toward each other and allows lawsuits to recover damages for injury (Table 4-1). Tort law is the foundation for civil actions in which an injured party may litigate to prevent an activity or recover damages from someone who has violated his or her person or property. Most civil actions are based not on a claim of intended harm, but on a claim that the defendant was negligent. This is especially so in cases involving private security officers. Tort law requires actions that have regard for the safety and rights of others; otherwise, negligence results. *The essence of the tort law limitations on private security officers is fear of a lawsuit and the payment of damages.*

The primary torts relevant to private security are as follows:

1. **False imprisonment:** The intentional and forceful confinement or restriction of the freedom of movement of another person, also called *false arrest*. The elements necessary to create liability are detention and its unlawfulness.
2. **Malicious prosecution:** Groundless initiation of criminal proceedings against another.
3. **Battery:** Intentionally harmful or offensive touching of another.
4. **Assault:** Intentional causing of fear of harmful or offensive touching.
5. **Trespass to land:** Unauthorized entering upon another person's property.
6. **Trespass to personal property:** Taking or damaging another person's possessions.
7. **Infliction of emotional distress:** Intentionally causing emotional or mental distress in another.
8. **Defamation (libel and slander):** Injury to the reputation of another by publicly making untrue statements. *Libel* refers to the written word; *slander*, to the spoken word.
9. **Invasion of privacy:** Intruding on another's physical solitude, the disclosure of private information about another, public misrepresentation of another's actions.
10. **Negligence:** Causing injury to persons or property by failing to use reasonable care or by taking unreasonable risk.

Civil action is not the only factor that hinders abuses by the private sector. Local and state ordinances, rules, regulations, and laws establish guidelines for the private security industry. This usually pertains to licensing and registration requirements. Improper or illegal action is likely to result in suspension or revocation of a license. Criminal law presents a further deterrent against criminal action by private sector personnel. Examples are laws prohibiting impersonation of a public official, electronic surveillance, breaking and entering, and assault. *Conduct can result in both a crime and a tort: in other words, a security practitioner can be arrested and sued.*

Some court cases have applied select constitutional limitations, from the Bill of Rights, to private sector action, especially if private security is working with public police or if off-duty police are working part-time to assist private sector security efforts. Public police and private security are also subject to federal and state laws that impose civil liability. For example, 42 USC Section 1983, is a federal law that imposes civil liability for intentional violations of constitutional, civil, or statutory rights of individuals by persons "acting under color of state law" (i.e., the misuse of power by a person possessing government authority). This action is more likely against public police than private security. Nemeth (2005: 159) asks whether a private security officer who detains a suspect and who is granted authority by regulatory bodies and licensure agencies and is empowered by legislation is "acting under color of state law"? His answer to this question is that some claimants have persuaded courts that private security action falls "under color of state law," but such decisions are rare, and he notes that it is difficult to define Section 1983 liability of private security officers.

Union contracts also can limit private security. These contracts might stipulate, for instance, that employee lockers cannot be searched and that certain investigative guidelines must be followed.

Match the Tort

Suppose you are a security manager: identify the tort(s) related to each scenario.

- A retail customer was frightened by one of your security officers who hurt the customer's arm, and, in front of other customers, loudly accused the customer of shoplifting.
- You learn that an employee of a company department that is missing cash has been locked in an office by the department manager and ordered not to leave.
- An administrative assistant in the human resources department told people in the community that a specific employee is to be fired for sexual harassment, although you are only investigating allegations of such behavior.

Legal Theory of Premises Security Claims

Negligence results when a failure to exercise a reasonable amount of care in a situation causes harm to another (see Figure 4-1). For instance, management should take steps to ensure the safety of individuals on the premises. Numerous premises security claims have been directed at management for failing to provide adequate protection for employees, customers, residents, or students who were injured by a third-party criminal act (e.g., sexual assault, robbery).

The legal theory of premises security claims follows. States allow monetary damages to the plaintiff who is injured as a proximate cause of the defendant's (e.g., management's) breach of a legal duty to provide protection. The definitions of *legal duty*, *proximate cause*, and the related concept of *foreseeability* distinguish the law among the states. **Legal duty** refers to management's duty to maintain the premises in a reasonably safe condition for invitees (e.g., customers on the property of a retail store). **Proximate cause** means that the breach

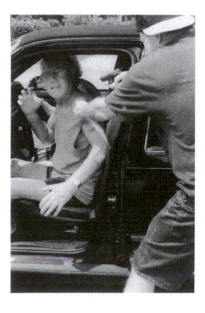

FIGURE 4-1 Assaults in parking lots have led to lawsuits alleging negligent security.
Source: Philip P. Purpura, *Criminal Justice: An Introduction* (Boston: Butterworth-Heinemann, 1997), p. 4.

of the legal duty is the actual cause of the harm. **Foreseeability** refers to whether the harm was likely to occur based on the safety history (e.g., crime metrics) of the premises and nearby property. If harm was likely, there is a duty to protect invitees.

Nemeth (2005: 136–137) writes:

> *The whole theory of negligence operates from the measure of the average man or woman—the 'reasonable person' standard. What should we expect from the average person in his or her dealings with others?... In the law of negligence, the unreasonable person is needlessly careless and even reckless and fails to take those precautions necessary to prevent injury to others.*

To succeed in a negligence case, the plaintiff must prove that the defendant (e.g., a business) owed a duty to protect the victim; the defendant breached the duty; and the breach of the duty was the proximate cause of the crime and harm to the victim. To defend the case, the defendant seeks to show that a duty was not owed to the plaintiff; that there was no breach of duty; or by refuting the argument that any breach of a duty was a proximate cause of the victimization (Kaminsky, 1995: 7–11).

The legal theory of premises security claims has evolved over the years. The **prior similar incidents rule**, for instance, means that a plaintiff must demonstrate that there had been a prior similar incident on the premises. However, courts became critical of this rule in the 1990s because it had the effect of being a "one free rape rule." At that time, the majority of jurisdictions shifted to a **totality of the circumstances test**: prior similar incidents and other factors, such as the nature of the business, its surrounding locale, security training, and whether customary security measures for the particular industry were applied (Gordon and Brill, 1996: 2–3). A third test courts place on security-related cases is **conscious disregard**: whether management or the security program knew of a problem or vulnerability but did nothing.

A lawsuit means that security faces a very big test. Management either pays for adequate protection initially to prevent a serious incident or possibly pays later, following a lawsuit. Most of these cases never make it to the trial stage and are settled out of court, which complicates research. In addition to providing basic protection for people and assets, a good security and loss prevention program becomes an investment in litigation prevention, even though premises security claims continue within our society. Apartment and condominium complexes and parking lots at a variety of locations are particularly prone to claims of inadequate security. However, many other types of sites are subject to lawsuits, such as shopping malls, retail stores, educational institutions, hotels and motels, restaurants and bars, office buildings, and healthcare facilities.

Negligence involves many types of situations pertaining to protection programs. Security personnel have been held liable for negligent use of force and firearms. Managers and supervisors have been found negligent in the areas of applicant screening and the training and supervision of employees. And such negligence is not only restricted to the security industry. Any organization and employee can be subject to negligence. A hospital, for example, may find itself in a lawsuit after a patient is sexually assaulted by an orderly because the human resources department did not check on the orderly's background.

□ □ □ ▬▬▬▬▬▬▬▬▬▬▬▬▬▬▬▬▬▬▬▬▬▬▬▬▬▬▬▬▬▬▬

Do businesses and institutions in your locale provide reasonable protection for people on the premises? Should premises security lawsuits be permitted? Why or why not?

□ □ □ ▬▬▬▬▬▬▬▬▬▬▬▬▬▬▬▬▬▬▬▬▬▬▬▬▬▬▬▬▬▬▬

You Be the Judge*

On August 1, Ken Yates and his family arrived at their motel about 6:30 P.M. While he was unloading the car, Yates was approached, threatened at gunpoint, and told to hand over his money. He resisted and was shot in the ensuing scuffle. Even though there had been a security officer on duty, no one intervened to help Yates.

Yates sued the motel, claiming that his injuries were caused by management's failure to provide an adequate number of trained security officers. Yates's expert witness supported this claim. However, he conceded that even if the motel had two officers on duty, the incident might have occurred outside the officers' direct observation. In addition, under cross-examination, the expert witness conceded that he had never developed or studied a security plan for a hotel or motel whose security needs required two security officers, so his expertise in the manner was limited.

The trial court dismissed the case, saying there was no evidence that having two officers on duty would have prevented the assault. Yates appealed, insisting that the inn could have done more to ensure his safety.

How did the appeals court rule?

Make your decision; then turn to the end of the chapter for the court's decision.

---

*Reprinted with permission from *Security Watch* (January 15, 2000), Aspen Pub.

Business Justification versus Employees' Expectation of Privacy

Technical advances have the potential to invade privacy, and there is the potential for abuse. The issues include employer monitoring of computer, Internet, e-mail, and telephone use by employees and the application of closed-circuit television (CCTV) and Global Positioning System (GPS) technology.

The American Management Association reported that 73% of major U.S. companies conduct some form of employee monitoring at work. Fifty-four percent of employers surveyed monitor Internet access and 38% monitor e-mail (Blotzer, 2000: 29–31). Courts attempt to balance business justification against employees' expectation of privacy.

When an employer electronically measures the productivity of an employee on a computer, stress can result and privacy issues can surface. Employers should communicate with employees about the monitoring and why it is being used (e.g., as a supervisory tool). For use of the Internet by employees, written policies should clearly state guidelines and the consequences of violations. Employers may choose to state that employees should assume there is no privacy, that they should reserve personal Internet access and e-mail for their home computers, and that the employer reserves the right to access employee e-mail.

Telephone monitoring is another thorny issue. Businesses are capable of generating reports on the number of calls made by telemarketers, and to improve quality, supervisors may listen to telephone conversations. Legal risks may surface. Essentially, an employer may listen to a telephone conversation when one party consents. It is best for an employer to notify employees of telephone monitoring and obtain their consent in writing. If a conversation becomes personal during monitoring, the listening must stop. Since many states require "two-party" consent to monitor, provide customers with the following message: "This call may be monitored for quality purposes."

CCTV presents additional concerns. It is a widely used method of preventing crime and conducting investigations. Cameras may be placed overtly or covertly to observe people in public areas. Employers must avoid placing cameras in restrooms, dressing rooms, locker rooms, and areas containing an expectation of privacy.

Employers are increasingly installing GPS technology in company vehicles and other items to track movements to improve efficiency and protection (McShane, 2005). GPS technology consists of satellites and receivers that allow people and devices to pinpoint their precise location on the earth. The application of this tech-nology is broad, and as the cost drops, the number of uses is increasing. Portable GPS devices are used by people to help with navigation (e.g., new cars are being equipped with GPS systems). The military uses GPS to guide cruise missiles to prespecified targets.

Employers will strengthen their position when they inform employees of the types of monitoring conducted in the workplace, post signs, and ask employees to sign a con-sent form containing policies. The enforcement of policies must be done in a uniform manner to avoid charges of unfair employment practices.

Zachary (2006) writes that employee use of e-mail and the Internet can expose employers to potential liability. Examples include confidential information inadver-tently misdirected, libelous communications, and workplace jokes that were later used against an employer in hostile environment sexual harassment cases. Zachary notes that employers have a legally protected interest in controlling employee computer usage. She emphasizes the importance of policies on employee computer use and refers to the following New Jersey appellate court decision to support her contention. The following case summary is from Zachary. In Jane Doe, individually and as guardian ad litem for Jill Doe, a minor, v. XYC Corp., 887 A.2d 1156 (Super. Ct. N.J. 2005), the court held that an employer had a legal duty to report an employee's viewing of child pornography to authorities and take effective action within the company to stop the activities. The employee was an accountant for the defendant company and worked in a cubicle that opened onto a hallway. People walking past the cubicle could see the employee's computer screen. An IT manager reviewing computer log reports learned that the employee was visiting pornographic sites. Two IT managers told the employee to stop, but they did not inform their superiors. About a year later, the employee's immediate supervisor told the senior network administrator about the recurring prob-lem, and log reports again showed that the employee was visiting pornographic sites. A senior IT manager informed the senior network administrator that he was not to access any employee logs because it was against company policy. The IT manager was wrong. The company actually had a policy providing it with the right to review, audit, access, and disclose all e-mails over the company system. And, employees were to visit only Web sites of a business nature. Violators were to be reported to the human resources department for possible disciplinary action. The policy was to be signed by each employee.

In October 2000, the employee married the plaintiff, who had a 10-year-old daughter. A few months later, a coworker of the employee complained to management about the employee visiting pornographic sites at work, but no action was taken. At home, the employee began to secretly videotape and photograph the stepdaughter in seminude positions. At work, the problem continued, the employee was confronted, and the employee agreed to stop the viewing of pornography. Later, the employee trans-mitted three photos of the stepdaughter over the Internet from his workplace. When photos of the stepdaughter were found in the company dumpster, a search warrant was executed at the employee's workspace, and e-mails showed contact with pornographic sites and others with a similar interest. The employee was terminated and later arrested. Thereafter, the employee's wife filed a suit for negligence against the employer for per-mitting the employee to use, view, and download child pornography at work without reporting him.

The trial court ruled in favor of the company, noting that the company did not have a duty to investigate private communications of the employee and did not have control over the employee's conduct at home. The appellate court disagreed. It found the following: there was no expectation of privacy on the part of the employee; the company was on notice of the activities (i.e., internal reports from coworkers); and it had a duty to investigate, report the activities to the authorities, and stop the activities. Under tort law, a company has a duty to control an employee acting outside the scope of employment in order to prevent that employee from intentionally harming others. The case was remanded to the lower court to answer the question of whether the employer's breach of duty was the proximate cause of harm to the stepdaughter.

□ □ □ ━━━━━━━━━━━━━━━━━━━━━━━━━━━━━━━━

What is your opinion of privacy issues, such as employer monitoring in the workplace?

━━━━━━━━━━━━━━━━━━━━━━━━━━━━━━━━ □ □ □

Contract Law

A **contract** is an agreement between parties to do or to abstain from doing some act. The law may enforce the agreement by requiring that a party perform its obligation or pay money equivalent to the performance. These court requirements are known as **remedies for breach of contract**. Specific circumstances may create defenses for failure to perform contract stipulations. Contracts may be express or implied. In an express contract, written or oral, the terms are stated in words. An implied contract is presumed by law to have been made from the circumstances and relations of the parties involved.

Several areas in the security and loss prevention field are relevant to the law of contracts. The company that provides a service or system to a client company may be liable for breach of contract following a dispute. A contract usually states liabilities for each party. For instance, if a third party is harmed (e.g., a person illegally arrested on the premises by a private security officer from a contract service hired by a client company), the contract will commonly establish who is responsible and who is to have insurance for each risk. However, in third-party suits, courts have held a specific party liable even though the contract stipulated that another party was to be responsible in the matter. This principle is known as **nondelegable duty**.

In the common law principle of **respondeat superior** (i.e., let the master respond), an employer (master) is liable for injuries caused by an employee (servant). This is also called **vicarious liability**. Typically, the injured party will look beyond the employee, to the employer, for compensation for damages. Proper supervision and training can prevent litigation. Businesses typically pay for liability insurance to cover this risk.

Civil Justice Procedures

The following list describes civil procedures both before a trial and during a trial (Purpura, 2003: 162–165). This list is a generalization. Civil procedures require much time, and the process can be expensive. Over 95% of civil (and criminal) cases are settled before reaching the trial stage. In other words, many civil cases are settled out of court. Many of the strategies and procedures used in civil trials are also used in criminal trials, although the rules will vary. These procedures include discovery, motions, jury selection, questioning of witnesses in court by opposing attorneys, judge's instruction to a jury, verdict, posttrial motions and many more.

1. **Plaintiff** initiates lawsuit resulting from commission of tort, breach of contract, or other event.
2. **Defendant** prepares defense after receiving summons (i.e., court order to appear in court) and complaint (i.e., a pleading of facts and claims filed in court). Failure to appear in court and defend a complaint can result in losing the lawsuit.
3. Opposing attorneys confer and communicate issues, evidence, and settlement options. This may take place anytime throughout the proceedings.

4. **Discovery** is the state in which opposing attorneys obtain all factual information (e.g., documents) in possession of the other. This stage helps to narrow the issues and saves time in dispensing justice.
5. Motions filed in court. A **motion** is a request to a judge for a decision on an issue or to take action on an issue—for example, a motion to dismiss a case.
6. Answer is the response to the lawsuit. The defendant files an answer with the court and includes denials and counterclaims.
7. **Pretrial conference** is the stage in which opposing attorneys and the judge meet to work toward settlement or face trial.
8. If a case proceeds to trial, opposing attorneys question potential jurors and a jury is selected.
9. Opening statements are comments from opposing attorneys who explain facts to the judge and jury once the trial begins.
10. Presentation of plaintiff's case is done by the plaintiff's attorney. The plaintiff's attorney presents evidence, such as witnesses and documents, to support allegations in the complaint.
11. Defendant's motion for dismissal is the stage in which the defendant's attorney moves for a dismissal if the attorney believes that the plaintiff's case failed to prove allegations. If the judge denies the motion for dismissal, the trial continues.
12. Presentation of defendant's case occurs when the defendant's attorney presents evidence to disprove (rebut) the plaintiff's case.
13. Plaintiff's rebuttal occurs when the plaintiff's attorney attempts to disprove the presentation of the defendant's attorney (from the preceding stage).
14. Defendant's rebuttal occurs when the defendant's attorney attempts to disprove newer issues argued by the plaintiff's attorney (from the preceding stage).
15. Motion for directed verdict means that either or both parties move for a directed verdict. In other words, the judge takes the decision away from the jury and informs them of what to decide. This situation results from a failure of evidence, overwhelming evidence, or the law applied to the facts favors one of the parties. If the motion is denied, the trial continues.
16. Closing arguments are summaries of the evidence presented to the jury by the plaintiff's attorney and the defendant's attorney.
17. Judge's instructions are given to the jury.
18. Jury's **verdict** occurs when the jury makes a decision.
19. Posttrial motions occur after a trial. An example is the motion for a new trial.
20. Judgment occurs when the judge declares which party prevailed at the trial (i.e., which party won the lawsuit) and the amount of recovery to be awarded.

Administrative Law

Administrative law is designed to ensure that as businesses seek profit, fairness and safety are maintained. Many federal and state agencies and executive departments influence loss prevention policies and programs. On the federal level, these include the Occupational Safety and Health Administration (OSHA), the National Labor Relations Board (NLRB), and the Equal Employment Opportunity Commission (EEOC), among others. (All three are discussed in various sections of this book.) Likewise, on the state level, similar bodies exist to regulate various activities such as the security industry. Administrative agencies are formed because legislative and executive branches of government typically lack the expertise to regulate specialized areas. Therefore, independent agencies are formed that are less susceptible to direct political influence. **Administrative agencies** are government bodies that regulate various activities, make rules, conduct investigations, perform law-enforcement functions, issue penalties, and initiate criminal and civil litigation. Federal agencies document rules in the *Federal Register*, published by the General Services Administration. State agency manuals perform a similar function. Local governments follow generally accepted fire and building codes.

Recordkeeping, Reporting, Inspections, and Searches

Although administrative agencies seek information from individuals and businesses to fulfill their mandated duties, recordkeeping is costly and a threat to privacy. Recordkeeping and reporting requirements also encounter constitutional issues as specified in the 5th Amendment of the Bill of Rights. This amendment contains the privilege against self-incrimination (i.e., a person cannot be compelled to give evidence against himself or herself). However, exceptions exist. For example, in the administrative context, a corporation may not claim the privilege. And, the privilege applies to communications that are testimonial in nature, not previously recorded records (Hall, 2006: 144–145).

Federal, state, and local administrative agency personnel visit business sites to conduct inspections and tests. An OSHA inspector may visit a workplace to ensure that safety regulations are in force to protect employees. An Environmental Protection Agency (EPA) inspector may test ground water near a facility to check on the composition of the water. Local health departments check restaurants for compliance with health codes. Inspections face issues related to invasion of privacy, even through most administrative inspections do not focus on crimes, but rather administrative violations. Inspections and tests can be considered under the 4th Amendment, which prohibits government from conducting unreasonable searches and seizures and requires warrants to be issued based on probable cause. Courts recognize that **administrative inspections** differ from searches related to criminal cases because of the following rationale: administrative inspections are not usually conducted to gather evidence for prosecution, but if prosecution is sought, the 4th Amendment applies; because society is so complex, the 4th Amendment must be relaxed to facilitate effective monitoring of compliance with administrative law; and the expectation of privacy at a business is lower than at a home. Furthermore, administrative inspections differ from **administrative searches**. The latter require 4th Amendment protections. To illustrate, an inspector may inspect the public area of a restaurant (e.g., dining room), but a demand to visit the owner's office or closed kitchen results in a search because of a greater expectation of privacy. One type of exception to the 4th Amendment requirement occurs when consent to search is provided by the business. Another exception to 4th Amendment safeguards is closely regulated businesses (e.g., nuclear plants and firearms businesses). The legal standard for obtaining an administrative search warrant, also known as an *inspection warrant*, is lower than what is required to obtain a search warrant in a criminal case (*Camera v. Municipal Court* 387 US 523, 1967). Probable cause may not be required, as long as reasonable inspection standards were established by the legislature (Hall, 2006: 146–151).

Compliance Auditing

Compliance auditing pertains to a survey of whether an organization is conforming to government regulations. A business, for example, can prepare its own checklist and conduct its own audit, based on the requirements of regulatory laws, such as the posting of laws, licenses, certificates, and policies and plans. OSHA is one of many agencies that require such compliance, subject to penalties, as described in a subsequent chapter.

Environmental protection is an especially important area of growing concern, and it serves as another example of the importance of compliance auditing. During the 1970s and 1980s, federal, state, and local governments in the United States passed hundreds of environmental statutes and regulations focusing on discharges to the air, land, and water; the manufacture, transport, storage, and disposal of goods and their by-products; and the location of facilities. The 1990s began the era of enforcement of these laws on the federal, state, and local levels. Consequently, U.S. industry spends tens of billions of dollars to comply with these laws and prevent severe criminal and civil penalties, imprisonment, and liability for personal injuries and property damage. The EPA provides audit protocols (i.e., detailed checklists that can be customized to a particular facility) to guide industry in developing programs at facilities to evaluate their compliance with requirements under federal laws (Environmental Protection Agency, 2006). The American Society for Testing and Materials (2006) standard practices E1527 (WK7383 is a revision of E1527 for compliance with new Environmental Protection Agency regulations) and E1528 on environmental site assessment often are referred to as the foundation for designing an environmental compliance audit. This type of audit often is used as part of a due diligence investigation when, for example, a company buys a plant and land. Also, it will help in the "innocent landowner defense" under federal environmental law. **Due diligence** is the attention and care legally expected in checking on the accuracy of information and omissions. Businesses that audit themselves and put forth efforts to reach compliance may receive a lighter sanction under the Federal Sentencing Guidelines and in certain states (Chilcutt, 1995: 41–43).

□ □ □ ▬▬▬▬▬▬▬▬▬▬▬▬▬▬▬▬▬▬▬▬▬▬▬

Do you believe our government is too tough on businesses? Why or why not?

▬▬▬▬▬▬▬▬▬▬▬▬▬▬▬▬▬▬▬▬▬▬▬ □ □ □

Federal Sentencing Guidelines

The federal government views incarceration of corporate executives as a strong deterrent to corporate crime. The **Federal Sentencing Guidelines**, which apply to all federal crimes, contain stiff sentencing provisions and strong economic penalties for corporate crimes such as environmental violations, fraud, and safety and health violations. In reference to environmental crimes, the FBI has about 450 pending environmental crimes cases—roughly half of which are Clean Water Act cases. Most investigations are conducted jointly with other federal agencies, such as the EPA and the U.S. Coast Guard, as well as with state regulatory agencies (Federal Bureau of Investigation, 2003). Examples of sentences include the former chairman of a Georgia chemical company who was sentenced to 9 years in prison for exposing workers to dangerous chemicals in the workplace. In another case, a Florida man received 13 years for dumping toxic waste into Tampa's sewer system. The states and state judges are taking environmental crimes more seriously (Kenworthy 2000: 3A). Examples of cases involving accounting fraud are explained in a later chapter.

The sentencing guidelines are a judicial strategy to encourage corporations to enforce compliance with legal requirements and avert ignorance of the law throughout a corporation. Communications and training are essential to corporate compliance programs. The guidelines themselves state the importance of corporate programs exercising due diligence (i.e., attention and care) in preventing, detecting, and reporting criminal conduct of employees and other agents—customary duties of security programs. Research reveals that many companies had compliance programs in place when their problems occurred, but the programs failed to penetrate the culture. Consequently, an effective ethics program must embrace the entire corporation (Edwards and Goodell, 1994: 1).

Sentencing is controversial and sentences vary. Lynch (2005) writes that although the 6th Amendment provides a right to a jury trial, the reality of the criminal justice system is that about 97% of defendants sentenced in federal court enter into plea-bargaining with prosecutor, defense attorney, and judge. He argues that we have a system of charge and sentence bargaining, and criticizes the common practice of prosecutors filing more-serious charges against defendants to exert leverage to induce a guilty plea to reduced charges. Lynch emphasizes that in the U.S. Supreme Court landmark ruling in *United States v. Booker* (2005) changes may occur to improve sentencing. This decision declared the federal sentencing guidelines to be advisory only and not legally binding standards. A judge cannot be overruled simply for a sentence that is inconsistent with the guidelines. The ruling weakens the U.S. Sentencing Commission that was established to guide judges in their sentencing.

□ □ □ ▬▬▬▬▬▬▬▬▬▬▬▬▬▬▬▬▬▬▬▬▬▬▬

What is your opinion of the impact of the U.S. Supreme Court landmark ruling in *United States v. Booker* (2005) on the sentencing of federal offenders?

▬▬▬▬▬▬▬▬▬▬▬▬▬▬▬▬▬▬▬▬▬▬▬ □ □ □

□ □ □ ▬▬▬▬▬▬▬▬▬▬▬▬▬▬▬▬▬▬▬▬

A Comprehensive Compliance Program

Whether public or private, organizations are required to maintain corporate compliance programs if they seek the benefit of prosecutorial discretion from a U.S. attorney and sentencing mitigation from a U.S. District Court (Maatman, 2004). Because compliance is such a serious issue, seven recommendations are presented here that can assist a corporation in proving it has taken steps to comply with laws. These recommendations can apply to numerous compliance programs.

1. Ensure that line management is attentive to regulatory compliance. Appoint one or more compliance officers to manage the program.
2. Communicate relevant policies, procedures, and standards to all employees.
3. Audit and monitor all relevant activities.
4. Establish a training program for all employees.
5. Establish an incentive program.
6. Avoid delegating authority to individuals that the organization should have known are likely to commit illegal acts. Discipline wrongdoers.
7. Evaluate the whole effort through an outside expert.

□ □ □ ▬▬▬▬▬▬▬▬▬▬▬▬▬▬▬▬▬▬▬▬

Impact of Legislation on Private Security Operations

ASIS International–funded research showed that legislation directly impacts not only organizations in general, but also private security operations (Collins et al., 2005). The top three acts cited in this research as having the most impact on security policies and procedures were the Health Insurance Portability and Accountability Act of 1996 (HIPAA), the Sarbanes-Oxley (SOX) Act of 2002, and the USA Patriot Act of 2001. The Patriot Act and the USA Patriot Improvement and Reauthorization Act of 2005 are covered later in this book. HIPPA, SOX, and the Financial Modernization Act of 1999 are explained here.

Health Insurance Portability and Accountability Act of 1996 (HIPAA): HIPPA is a law designed to improve healthcare services delivery, lower costs by reducing paper records and claims, enhance electronic transmission of documents, secure medical data and patient information, prevent errors in the healthcare system, and transfer funds more securely. IT systems play a major role in fostering these activities. The act establishes compliance rules to reach the objectives of this legislation. The Department of Health and Human Services is the regulatory agency for this act, and it issues various standards, such as those for information security. Typical of legislation, many questions remain unanswered and answers often develop from litigation and case law. For example, how is an organization to know when security measures are reasonable under the risk analysis and risk management sections of the law, and how to answer law enforcement demands for patient information protected by privacy laws.

Sarbanes-Oxley (SOX) Act of 2002: SOX was enacted following several high-profile accounting scandals. The act is administered by the Securities and Exchange Commission, a federal government administrative agency. The legislation seeks to prevent fraud and impacts the processes and accountability for financial reporting in publicly traded U.S. companies. SOX makes executives responsible for establishing, evaluating, and monitoring the effectiveness of internal controls over financial and operational processes. Senior executives must sign an attestation that they are responsible and that the internal controls meet the requirements of SOX. Some SOX compliance provisions are becoming standard operating procedure for all businesses, besides publicly held ones. Specifics of the law include using accounting controls, identifying how companies report financial results and disclose executive compensation, holding company executives and external auditors directly accountable for the accuracy of financial reports, and protecting employees who blow the whistle on suspected fraud. *Security and audit departments in corporations have become involved with SOX because these departments investigate internal fraud.* Chapter 11 elaborates on SOX.

Financial Modernization Act of 1999: This act, also known as the *Gramm-Leach-Bliley Act* or GLB, includes provisions to ensure security and confidentiality of customer financial information held by financial institutions. The Federal Trade Commission, an administrative agency, is the primary administrator of GLB. The act requires an assessment of internal and external risks and the sufficiency of existing security. The GLB Act applies to "financial institutions," which include banks, securities firms, insurance companies, and many other businesses providing financial products and services to consumers. The services include lending, servicing consumer loans, transferring or safeguarding money, reporting credit, preparing individual tax returns, providing financial advice or credit counseling, providing residential real estate settlement services, collecting consumer debts, and many other activities. IT security practitioners in particular are involved in the compliance requirements of GLB.

Labor Law

The NLRB controls relations between management and labor. It is essential that management and loss prevention practitioners be familiar with labor laws to avert charges of unfair labor practices. Surveillance and investigation of union activities are violations of the **National Labor Relations Act** (NLRA), which makes it an unfair labor practice to interfere with, restrain, or coerce employees in the exercise of the rights to self-organize, to assist labor organizations, and to bargain collectively through representatives. One type of surveillance, photographing activities of striking workers, is unlawful unless there is a legitimate purpose, such as gathering evidence for the prosecution of criminal acts (e.g., assault or destruction of property). In one case, a security service company took 60,000 pictures and collected thousands of hours of video that were used in court against strikers, who ended up owing $64 million in fines (Sunoo, 1995: 58).

Care must be exercised when instituting loss prevention strategies during management-labor tension. Precautions (e.g., additional officers, CCTV) to protect company property may be construed as interference with union activities. For example, courts have declared illegal the observance by officers of who is going in and out of union meetings. Also, it has been held that even "creating the impression" of surveillance (e.g., management implying that surveillance is taking place) is illegal. The NLRB found that aiming CCTV on a company building in which a union meeting was held created the impression of surveillance. Undercover investigations that conduct labor surveillance are illegal.

The National Labor Relations Board periodically changes its position on recurring and important issues for both unionized and nonunion employers. The following summaries are from the work of Bloom and Bryant (2005: 84–92) and explain how NLRB decisions guide employers. As a foundation, if an employer maintains an unlawful rule, even if it is not enforced, the NLRB views the rule as an unfair labor practice.

The NLRB has found that rules prohibiting "loud, abusive or foul language" or "using abusive or threatening language to anyone on company premises" are unlawful as written. The board's justification for this view is that without further definitions by the employer of "abusive or foul language," the rules could reasonably be interpreted by employees as prohibiting lawful activity. The NLRB reversed direction on this issue in Lutheran Heritage Village-Livonia (NLRB, No. 75, 2004). The board reasoned that an employer has a right to maintain order and a "civil and decent workplace." The board also found no support for the contention that the rule would prohibit lawful union activity. In another rule of conduct in the same case, the NLRB found no problem with a rule prohibiting "harassment of other employees, supervisors, and any other individuals in any way."

On another issue impacting all employers, regardless of the presence of a union, the NLRB has ruled that nonunion employees do not have the right to have a representative present during an interview that might lead to disciplinary action. This is a current right of unionized employees. The board found that the so-called **Weingarten rights** of unionized employees do not apply to employees not represented by a union (IBM Corporation, NLRB, No. 148, 2004). This case overruled a 2000 decision by the board and the decision is the fourth time in the past 23 years that the board has altered its position on this issue. The issue of Weingarten rights originated in 1975, when the U.S. Supreme Court (*NLRB v. J. Weingarten Inc.*, No. 251, 1975) upheld a decision by the NLRB that unionized employees have a legal right to insist on union representation during an investigatory interview conducted by their employer, provided that the employee reasonably believes that the interview might result in disciplinary action. The U.S. Supreme Court explained that this right arises from federal labor laws that are a "guarantee of the right of employees to act in concert for mutual aid and protection." The right is limited to situations when an employee specifically requests representation. An employer is not required to state this right to employees. Since this decision, the NLRB has frequently changed its position on whether Weingarten rights apply to employees who are not unionized.

Another reversal occurred in Oakwood Care Center, NLRB, No. 75, 2004. This case impacts security industry employers that either provide or use temporary security staff to supplement permanent workers. In an earlier decision (M. B. Sturgis, Inc., NLRB No. 1298, 2000), the board approved temporary workers hired through a staffing company to be included along with a company's nonunion regular workers in voting for union representation. In the Oakwood ruling, union organizers are prohibited from conducting a union election with a mix of employees unless both employers agree that the union can include both types of workers.

Criminal Justice Procedures

The following list describes procedural law for criminal cases. Because jurisdictional procedures vary, a generalization is presented here.

1. The purpose of an **arrest** is to bring a person into the criminal justice system so that he or she may be held to answer criminal charges.
2. A citation frequently is used by public police instead of a formal arrest for less serious offenses (e.g., traffic violations). If the conditions set forth in the citation are not followed, a magistrate of the appropriate court will issue a misdemeanor arrest warrant.
3. All arrests must be based on probable cause, which is stated in arrest warrants. **Probable cause** is reasonable grounds to justify legal action, more than mere suspicion. Police officers, security officers, and able witnesses and victims typically provide the foundation of probable cause through their observations of offenders.
4. **Booking** takes place when an arrestee is taken to a police department or jail so that a record can be made of the person's name, the date, time, location of offense, charge, and arresting officer's name. Fingerprinting and a photograph are part of the booking process.
5. Because our system of justice has a high regard for civil liberties as expressed in the Bill of Rights, the accused is informed of his or her *Miranda rights*, by public police, prior to questioning and when the subject is in custody.
6. After booking, and without unnecessary delay, the accused is taken before a magistrate for the **initial appearance**. At this appearance, the magistrate has the responsibility of informing the accused of constitutional rights, stating the charge, and setting bail (if necessary).
7. Also after booking, the arresting officer will meet with the prosecutor, or a representative, to review evidence. A decision is made whether to continue legal action or to drop the case. A case may be dropped by the prosecutor for

insufficient evidence or because the defendant is suffering from a problem better handled by a social service agency.

8. The prosecutor prepares an "information" when prosecution is initiated. It cites the defendant's name and the charge and is signed by the complainant (e.g., the person who witnessed the crime). Then an arrest warrant is prepared by the proper judicial officer. The defendant already may be in custody at this point.

9. At the initial appearance, the magistrate will inform the defendant about the right to have a **preliminary hearing**. The defendant and the defense attorney make this decision. This hearing is used to determine if probable cause exists for a trial. The courtroom participants in a preliminary hearing are a judge, defendant, defense attorney, and prosecutor. The prosecutor has the "burden of proof." Witnesses may be called by the prosecutor to testify.

10. Federal law and the laws of more than half the states require that probable cause to hold a person for trial must result from grand jury action. The 5th Amendment of the Bill of Rights states such a requirement. When probable cause is established in an action ordered by a judge or prosecutor, the grand jury will return an "indictment" or "true bill" against the accused. A "presentment" results from an investigation initiated by a grand jury establishing probable cause. Based on the indictment or presentment, an arrest warrant is issued.

11. At an **arraignment** the accused enters a plea to the charges. The four plea options are guilty, not guilty, nolo contendere (no contest), and not guilty by reason of insanity.

12. Few defendants reach the trial stage. **Plea bargaining** is an indispensable method to clear crowded court dockets. Essentially, it means that the prosecutor and defense attorney have worked out an agreement whereby the prosecutor reduces the charge in exchange for a guilty plea. Charges also may be dropped if the accused becomes a witness in another case.

13. Pretrial motions can be entered by the defense attorney prior to entering a plea at arraignment. Some examples are a "motion to quash" an indictment or information because the grand jury was improperly selected; a "continuance" requested by the defense attorney because more time is needed to prepare the case; or a "change of venue" requested when pretrial publicity is harmful to the defendant's case and the defense hopes to locate the trial in another jurisdiction so that an impartial jury is more likely to be selected.

14. The accused is tried by the court (judge) or a jury. The system of justice is basically adversarial, involving opponents. This is apparent in a **trial**, where the prosecutor and defense attorney make brief opening statements to the jury. The prosecutor then presents evidence. Witnesses are called to the stand to testify; they go through direct examination by the prosecutor, followed by defense cross-examination. The prosecutor attempts to show the defendant's guilt "beyond a reasonable doubt." The defense attorney strives to discredit the evidence. Redirect examination rebuilds evidence discredited by cross-examination. Recross-examination may follow. After the prosecutor presents all the evidence, the defense attorney may move for acquittal. This motion commonly is overruled by the judge. Then the defense attorney presents evidence. Defense evidence undergoes direct and redirect examination by the defense and cross- and recross-examination by the prosecutor.

15. Next, the judge will "charge the jury," which means that the jury is briefed by the judge on the charge and how a verdict is to be reached based on the evidence. In certain states, juries have a responsibility for recommending a sentence after a guilty verdict; the judge will brief the jury on this issue. Closing arguments are then presented by opposing attorneys.

16. The jury retires to the deliberation room; a verdict follows. A not guilty verdict signifies release for the defendant. A guilty verdict leads to sentencing. Motions and appeals may be initiated after the sentence.

□ □ □ ▬▬▬▬▬▬▬▬▬▬▬▬▬▬▬▬▬▬▬▬▬▬▬▬▬▬▬

How Much Power is in the Hands of Private Security Officers?
Can they

- Make an arrest without probable cause?
- Arrest for a felony?
- Arrest for a misdemeanor?
- Use force to complete an arrest?
- Search an arrestee following an arrest?
- Question a suspect or arrestee without public police being present?
- Be barred from using seized evidence as the police are under the exclusionary rule?

These questions are answered in the nearby paragraphs.

▬▬▬▬▬▬▬▬▬▬▬▬▬▬▬▬▬▬▬▬▬▬▬▬▬▬▬ □ □ □

Arrest Law

Because our justice system places a high value on the rights of the individual citizen, private security and public police personnel cannot simply arrest, search, question, and confine a person by whim. A consideration of individual rights is an important factor. The Bill of Rights of the U.S. Constitution affords citizens numerous protections against government. The 4th and 5th Amendments of the Bill of Rights demonstrate how individual rights are safeguarded during criminal investigations.

> *Amendment IV—The right of the people to be secure in their persons, houses, papers, and effects, against unreasonable searches and seizures, shall not be violated, and no Warrants shall issue, but upon probable cause, supported by Oath or affirmation; and particularly describing the place to be searched, and the person or things to be seized.*
>
> *Amendment V—… nor shall [any person] be compelled in any criminal case to be a witness against himself, nor be deprived of life, liberty, or property, without due process of law.*

The 6th, 8th, and 14th Amendments are other important amendments frequently associated with our criminal justice process. Briefly, the 6th Amendment pertains to the right to trial by jury and assistance of counsel. The 8th Amendment states that "excessive bail shall not be required, nor excessive fines imposed, nor cruel and unusual punishments inflicted." The 14th Amendment bars states from depriving any person of due process of law or equal protection of the laws.

The 4th Amendment stipulates guidelines for the issuance of warrants. Public police obtain arrest and search warrants from an impartial judicial officer. Sometimes immediate action (e.g., chasing a bank robber) does not permit time to obtain warrants before arrest and search. In such a case, an arrest warrant is obtained as soon as possible. Private security should contact public police for assistance in securing warrants and in apprehending suspects.

A knowledge of arrest powers is essential for those likely to exercise this authority. These powers differ from state to state and depend on the statutory authority of the type of individual involved. Generally, public police officers have the greatest arrest powers. They also are protected from civil liability for false arrest, as long as they had probable cause that the crime was committed. Those in the private sector usually have arrest powers equal to citizen's arrest powers, which mean that they are liable for false arrest if a crime was not, in fact, committed—regardless of the reasonableness of their belief. An exception is apparent if state statutes point out that security personnel have arrest powers equal to public police only on the protected property. If private sector personnel are deputized or given a special constabulary commission, their arrest powers are likely to equal those of public police.

Whoever makes an arrest must have the legal authority to do so. Furthermore, the distinction between felonies and misdemeanors, for those making arrests, is of tremendous importance. Generally, public police can arrest someone for a felony or a misdemeanor committed in his or her view; the viewing amounts to probable cause. Arrest for a felony not seen by public police is lawful with probable cause (e.g., a radio broadcast describing a robber). Arrest for a misdemeanor not seen by public police generally is unlawful; a warrant is needed based on probable cause. There are exceptions to this misdemeanor rule; for example, public police can arrest in domestic violence cases or cases of driving under the influence, when the offense is fresh although not observed by police. On the other hand, private security personnel have fewer powers of arrest (equal to citizen's arrest powers). Basically, citizen arrest powers permit felony arrests based on probable cause but prohibit misdemeanor arrests.

A serious situation exists when, for example, a private security officer arrests and charges a person for a felony when in fact the offense was a misdemeanor and the jurisdiction does not grant security officers such misdemeanor arrest power. Many employers in the private sector are so fearful of an illegal arrest and subsequent legal action that they prohibit their officers from making arrests without supervisory approval. It is imperative that private sector personnel know state arrest law; proper training is a necessity.

Force

During the exercise of arrest powers, force may be necessary. The key criterion is **reasonable force**. This means force should be no more than what is reasonably necessary to carry out legitimate authority. If an arrestee struggles to escape but is subdued to the ground and stops resisting, it would be unreasonable for the arrestor to strike the arrestee. **Deadly force** is reserved for life-threatening situations, never to defend property. Unreasonable force can lead to difficulties in prosecuting a case, as well as civil and criminal litigation.

Searches

Ordinarily, public police conduct a search of an arrestee right after an arrest. This has been consistently upheld by courts for the protection of the officer who may be harmed by a concealed weapon. However, *evidence obtained through an unreasonable search and seizure is not admissible in court*; this is known as the **exclusionary rule**.

The 4th Amendment prohibition against unreasonable searches and seizures applies only to government action. Searches by private citizens, including security officers, even if "unreasonable," are therefore not "unconstitutional" and the exclusionary rule does not apply, as ruled in *Burdeau v. McDowell*, 256 US 465, 1921 (Inbau, et al., 1996: 54; Nemeth, 2005: 83–104). At the same time, the law of searches by private security officers is not clear and varies widely. Even though private security may not be restrained by the 4th Amendment, a lawsuit may result following a search. A search is valid when consent is given and where, in a retail environment, a shoplifting statute permits the retrieval of merchandise. A search for weapons following an arrest may be justified through common law, which states that citizens have the right of self-defense. The recovery of stolen goods as the basis for a search is typically forbidden, except in some state shoplifting statutes. Whenever possible, private security personnel should let public police conduct searches in order to transfer potential liability.

□ □ □ ▬▬▬▬▬▬▬▬▬▬▬▬▬▬▬▬▬▬▬▬▬▬▬▬▬▬▬

Call It "Inspection," Not "Search and Seizure"
Norman M. Spain (1996: 4–7), an authority on legal issues in security, states that private security officers generally are not bound by constitutional constraints of search and seizure as are public police, unless they are "tainted by the color of law"—that is, jointly working with public police. Spain favors the term *inspection* instead of *search* for private security, because the 4th Amendment does not apply in most private settings. He cites various targets for inspections in private settings: a locker, a vehicle entering or leaving a facility, or the belongings of an employee.

Spain recommends a formal inspection policy that would be backed by common law—employers have the right to take reasonable measures to protect their property against theft. All parties (e.g., employees, contractors, and visitors) should be given notice through, for example, signs and publications. The policy should have four components:

1. A formal statement that the company reserves the right to inspect
2. Illustrations of types of inspections
3. A list of items that employees should not have in their possession (e.g., illegal drugs, weapons, company property removed without authorization)
4. A statement of penalties, including those for not cooperating

Spain cautions that a "pat-down" of a person's body or inspections of pockets may result in a civil action alleging invasion of privacy, unless the site requires intense security.

Questioning

An important clause of the 5th Amendment states that a person cannot be compelled in any criminal case to be a witness against himself or herself. Therefore, what constitutional protections does a suspect have on being approached by an investigator for questioning? Here again, the law differs with respect to public and private sector investigations.

A suspect that is in custody and about to be questioned about a crime by public police must be advised of

1. The right to remain silent
2. The fact that statements can be used against the person in a court of law
3. The right to an attorney, even if the person has no money
4. The right to stop answering questions

These rights, known as the **Miranda warnings**, evolved out of the famous 1966 U.S. Supreme Court case known as *Miranda v. Arizona*. If these rights are not read to a person (by public police) before questioning, statements or a confession will not be admissible as evidence in court.

Are private security personnel required to read a subject the Miranda warnings prior to questioning? The U.S. Supreme Court has not yet required the reading. Many private sector investigators read suspects the Miranda warnings anyway, to strengthen their case. Any type of coercion or trick during questioning is prohibited by private security as well as public police. A voluntary confession by a suspect is in the best interest of public and private investigators. If security personnel are working jointly with public police (as in a cooperative protection effort), or if a police officer is working part-time in security, then the warnings should be read.

Another topic concerning questioning of subjects pertains to disciplinary hearings. As written earlier, the NLRB extends to union employees the right of representation during an interview that might lead to disciplinary action. This is not a right of nonunion employees.

Search the Web
Here is a list of general-purpose Web sites pertaining to this chapter:
Cornell Law School: www.law.cornell.edu/
Federal Register: www.gpoaccess.gov/fr/index.html
Lawyers and the Law: http://lawyers.com
Resource on law: http://www.lexisone.com/legalresearch/legalguide/practice_areas/practice_areas_fa.htm
Washburn University School of Law: www.washlaw.edu

The rapid change brought on by computers and the Internet has been characterized as a "Wild West" legal environment (Heiser, 2000: 24). Security specialists, whether involved in IT, physical security, or other areas, should be knowledgeable of legal trends and issues pertaining to cyberlaw. What follows here are helpful Web sites.

U.S. Department of Justice Cybercrime (http://www.usdoj.gov/criminal/cybercrime/searching.html). This site contains a broad array of topics. The list includes federal codes related to cybercrime; how to report Internet-related crime; search and seizure of computers and electronic evidence; computer intrusion cases; intellectual property crime; economic espionage; privacy issues; and manuals, reports, and documents.

David Loundy's E-Law (http://www.loundy.com/). This is a personal site of an attorney and cyberlaw professor who is a leader in electronic law. The site contains a long list of links to other legal Web sites and sites helpful to security in general.

Case Problems

4A. You are a loss prevention officer with three years of experience and a newly acquired college degree. The plant manager of loss prevention has selected you for a special assignment: design and conduct an eight-hour training program on law for company loss prevention (security) officers. The grapevine indicates that success on this project could lead to a promotion to training officer, a position vacant at this time. You are required to (1) formulate an outline of topics to be covered and the hours for each topic, (2) justify in one to three sentences why each topic is important, and (3) prepare an examination of 10 (or 20) questions.

4B. You are a member of a jury on a civil case involving the question of negligent security. In this case, a young man was killed by a stray bullet at a restaurant parking lot at night during the weekend as he approached a group of rowdy people about to fight. The restaurant had a history of three gun incidents prior to the murder: one month earlier a shot was fired into the restaurant, without injury; three months earlier police arrested a subject for assault in the parking lot and confiscated a pistol; and five months earlier police found a revolver in the bushes in the parking lot following an arrest for public intoxication. Each incident occurred at night during the weekend. Following these three incidents, the restaurant maintained the same level of security on the premises—good lighting and training employees to call police when a crime occurred. Does the business owe a duty to provide a safe environment to those who enter the premises? Did the restaurant breach that duty? If the duty was breached, was it the proximate cause of the criminal act and the victimization? Is the restaurant negligent? Why or why not?

4C. As a security manager at a chemical plant, you learn that a plant executive is receiving kickbacks while dealing with a shady toxic disposal service company as a contractor for the plant. Two months earlier you learned from another source the same information, and you reported your investigative findings to your superior, who stated that he would handle the situation. You are wondering why the same executive is in the same job and the same shady toxic disposal service company is still a contractor for your employer. What do you do at this point and why?

4D. Research and prepare a report on the laws of arrest and search and seizure in your state for citizens, private security officers, private detectives, and public police.

4E. Create, in writing, situations in which each of the preceding types of individuals in case problem 4D can make a legal arrest. In each of the situations you create, describe appropriate search and seizure guidelines.

The Decision for "You Be the Judge"

The appeals court said the trial court acted properly. Yates had failed to show that another security officer would have prevented the assault. [*Walsh v. Ramada Franchise Systems, Inc. et al.*, No. 98–5040, US Ct. of App. for the 6th Circ., 1999 US App. Lexis 11281.] Comment: What methods do you use to arrive at staffing levels for your officers? How would you defend those methods in court?

The motel was lucky; Yates's expert failed to show that more security officers would have been more effective. If the expert had testified that similarly sized and located motels used more security officers, the motel would have been in the difficult position of defending its use of only one officer.

Benchmarking your practices against industry norms and against companies in your neighborhood is an excellent way to assess whether your company is doing enough to secure your grounds.

References

American Society for Testing and Materials. (2006). "Standards." www.astm.org, retrieved June 13, 2006.

Bloom, H., and Bryant, M. (2005). "Labor Law's Changing Tides." *Security Management*, 49 (August).

Blotzer, M. (2000). "Privacy in the Digital Age." *Occupational Hazards* 62 (July).

Chilcutt, D. (1995). "Making Sense of Environmental Compliance." *Risk Management* (November).

Collins, P., et al. (2005). "The ASIS Foundation Security Report: Scope and Emerging Trends." Alexandria, VA: ASIS, International.

Edwards, G., and Goodell, R. (1994). "Three Years Later: A Look at the Effectiveness of Sentencing Guidelines." *Ethics Journal* (Fall-Winter).

Environmental Protection Agency. (2006). "Compliance Incentives and Auditing." http://www.epa.gov/compliance/incentives/auditing/protocol.html, retrieved June 17, 2006.

Federal Bureau of Investigation. (2003). "Facts and Figures 2003, Environmental Crimes." http://www.fbi.gov/libref/factsfigure/enviro.htm, retrieved June 17, 2006.

Gordon, C., and Brill, W. (1996). "The Expanded Role of Crime Prevention Through Environmental Design in Premises Liability" (April). Washington, DC: National Institute of Justice.

Hall, D. (2006). *Administrative Law: Bureaucracy in a Democracy*, 3rd ed. Upper Saddle River, NJ: Pearson Education.

Heiser, J. (2000). "You'll Hear From My Lawyer." *Information Security*, 3 (October).

Inbau, F., Farber, B. and Arnold, D. (1996). *Protective Security Law*, 2nd ed. Boston: Butterworth-Heinemann.

Kaminsky, A. (1995). *A Complete Guide to Premises Security Litigation*. Chicago, IL: American Bar Association.

Kenworthy, T. (2000). "It's a New World: Polluters Go to Prison." *USA Today* (April 21).

Lynch, T. (2005). "Changing of the Gavel." *Legal Times* (January 24).

Maatman, G. (2004). "Ignoring Federal Sentencing Guidelines Is Risky: New Document Sets Criteria for Corporate Ethics and Compliance Programs." *National Underwriter Property & Casualty-Risk & Benefits Management*, 108 (November 15).

McShane, L. (2005). "GPS Technology in Workplaces Raises Privacy Concerns." *Associated Press* (November 18).

Nemeth, C. (2005). *Private Security and the Law*. Burlington, MA: Elsevier Butterworth-Heinemann.

Neubauer, D. (2005). *America's Courts and the Criminal Justice System*, 8th Ed. Belmont, CA: Thomas Wadsworth.

Purpura, P. (1997). *Criminal Justice: An Introduction*. Boston: Butterworth-Heinemann.

Purpura, P. (2003). *The Security Handbook*, 2nd Ed. Boston: Butterworth-Heinemann.

Spain, N. (1996). "Call It 'Inspection' (Not 'Search and Seizure')." *Security Management Bulletin* (May 10).

Sunoo, B. (1995). "Managing Strikes, Minimizing Loss." *Personnel Journal* (January).

Zachary, M. (2006). "Labor Law: New Source of Liability for Employee Internet Use." *Supervision*, 67 (June).

5

Internal and External Relations

Objectives

After studying this chapter, the reader will be able to:

1. Define internal and external relations.
2. Explain methods of marketing security and the value of marketing.
3. Discuss internal relations.
4. Explain how an intranet and e-mail can assist security.
5. Discuss external relations.
6. Explain how to work with the media.
7. Debate the issues of prosecution.
8. Debate the issues of loss prevention attire.

KEY TERMS	
• internal relations	• target marketing
• external relations	• return on investment
• customer driven	• intranet
• value added	• designated spokesperson
• marketing	• prosecution threshold
• market segmentation	

Internal and External Relations

This chapter explains why it is so important to recruit people and organizations to assist with security and loss prevention efforts. With practitioners being asked to handle increasingly complex problems, often with limited resources, it is vital that all possible sources of assistance be solicited. Strategies are delineated here for improving relations between the loss prevention department and those groups that loss prevention serves and works with in reducing losses. **Internal relations** refer to cooperative efforts with individuals and groups within an organization that a loss prevention department serves. **External relations** refer to cooperative efforts with external individuals and groups that assist in loss prevention objectives.

In reference to examples for the internal relations chart (clockwise, Figure 5-1), upper management dictates loss prevention goals. Information technology (IT) and loss prevention departments are increasingly working closer together because of threats and hazards facing

FIGURE 5-1 Internal relations.

IT systems. A risk management department in an organization can provide the foundation for prioritizing risks and developing broad strategies to deal with risks. Both the human resources and loss prevention departments should coordinate activities relevant to applicant screening and workplace violence. When labor problems (e.g., unrest, strike) are anticipated, losses can be minimized through cooperative efforts. In addition, labor union contracts and labor law stipulate limitations on loss prevention activities (e.g., the questioning of suspect employees). Loss prevention practitioners are wise to tune in on feedback and criticism from formal and informal employee groups. By listening to and satisfying employee needs (e.g., clean restrooms, a well-run cafeteria, and recreational programs), with other departments, an organization can reduce losses. When new facilities are being planned, architects, engineers, and loss prevention practitioners can jointly design prevention strategies into the plan and thereby save money by not having to install equipment after construction is completed. Trade secrets and other proprietary information must be under strict security, especially in research and development. Accountants and auditors can help create cooperative strategies against losses. Furthermore, the loss prevention manager should be given an opportunity to review their findings. At various times, a loss prevention department may require legal assistance. Because loss prevention personnel are the backbone of the program, the manager should do everything possible (e.g., professional development, give praise and pay raises, and institute participatory management) to satisfy their needs. Good rapport with the external relations department ensures that appropriate security and loss prevention information is released to outsiders and that this information is in the best interest of the organization. Communicating with management in general is vital for many reasons. For instance, the objectives of the loss prevention program can be transmitted to all employees via meetings with management. Feedback from management also assists in planning loss prevention strategies that do not hinder productivity or profit.

In reference to examples for the external relations chart (clockwise, Figure 5-2, beginning with law enforcement agencies), public safety agencies are an essential ingredient of private sector loss prevention programs. Good communications and cooperation are important in case crimes occur or a disaster strikes. Business continuity planning should consider a variety of resources in the community (e.g., police, fire, medical). Educational institutions can provide expertise, research assistance, and potential employees. The loss prevention manager may want to serve on a college advisory committee or speak to classes to spread the word about loss prevention. When possible, the news media should be recruited to aid in loss prevention objectives. Other businesses and loss prevention peers with similar problems

FIGURE 5-2 External relations.

can be a good source of ideas. Insurance companies can provide information to improve prevention strategies while reducing premiums. Independent auditors and certified public accountants can point out weaknesses in the loss prevention program to protect against fraud and other crimes. When people (e.g., customers) visit the premises, they should not be seriously inconvenienced by loss prevention systems (e.g., access controls), but at the same time, losses must be prevented. Friendly dialogue and cooperative efforts should be emphasized when government administrative agencies are involved in a loss prevention program. *To enhance all the preceding relations, the security and loss prevention practitioner is wise to emphasize two-way communication and understanding, and partnering for mutual benefits.*

Benefits of Good Relations

The following are reasons why good internal and external relations are important to a loss prevention program. Good relations

1. Build respect for the loss prevention department, its objectives, and its personnel.
2. Reinforce compliance with policies and procedures to prevent losses.
3. Foster assistance with loss prevention activities, such as programs and investigations.
4. Provide a united front against vulnerabilities, extend the impact of strategies, and save money.
5. Educate employees, community residents, and others.
6. Improve understanding of complex security problems.
7. Reduce rumors and false information.
8. Improve understanding of the loss prevention program.
9. Stimulate consciousness-raising relevant to loss prevention.
10. Make the loss prevention job easier.

Good internal and external relations enhance the effectiveness of security and loss prevention programs.

Internal Relations

Customer-Driven Security and Loss Prevention Programs

Like well-managed companies, security and loss prevention programs should be **customer driven** through constant contact with customers who provide feedback and direction for improvements in performance. Customers should be made aware that they are receiving value from the services provided. Corporations often use the term **value added**. It means that all corporate departments must prove their value to the business by translating expenditures into bottom-line impact. Security departments must go beyond preparing a report of security accomplishments. Examples are as follows: The investment in training security officers in first aid and CPR provided life-saving assistance in the past 12 months to three employees and one customer. The hiring of a bad check specialist recovered three times her salary. The expenditures for workers' compensation fraud investigations saved hundreds of thousands of dollars. The investment in security technology saved personnel costs.

Marketing

Marketing consists of researching a target market and the needs of customers and developing products and services to be sold at a profit. Marketing also is considered the study of consumer problems as opportunities.

The concepts of marketing are universally applicable. **Market segmentation** divides a market into distinct groups of consumers. When one or more of the market segments is chosen for a specific product or service, this is known as **target marketing**. To illustrate, for security programs, market segmentation within a corporation can yield the following groups: executives, women, salespeople, production workers, and truck drivers. Once the market is segmented, a protection program can be designed for each target market. Research and risk analyses will produce a foundation from which to satisfy the protection needs of each type of customer. For those security programs that are so general in nature that few customers find them appealing, marketing strategies may be the solution to generate interest. Loss prevention influence over a target group or groups is better than no influence at all (Purpura, 1989: 141–148).

These seven strategies contain a heavy emphasis on marketing and are designed to produce a high-quality security program (Wozniak, 1996: 25–28):

1. Identify all internal and external customers of security services and determine what the customers want and how security can tell whether they are satisfied with the quality of the services rendered.
2. Focus on the customer and his or her perspective. Security should avoid an "us versus them" viewpoint.
3. Facilitate teamwork by meeting with representatives of all internal departments to discuss security issues and to seek solutions.
4. Listen and be receptive to customer concerns. In one hospital, employees complained about the need to enter their departments outside regular business hours. In response, the security department used its technology to customize access control for each department.
5. Develop definitions. Ensure that customers and security share each group's definitions of security and loss prevention.
6. Set priorities among customers. One hospital ranked its customers as follows: patients or outside customers, employees, and employees' families.
7. Take action and be prepared to constantly adapt to new circumstances.

☐ ☐ ☐ ▬▬▬▬▬▬▬▬▬▬▬▬▬▬▬▬▬▬▬▬▬▬▬▬▬▬▬▬▬▬▬▬▬▬▬▬

Do you think marketing concepts can really assist a security manager, or does marketing consist of theories that have no practical value in the real world?

▬▬▬▬▬▬▬▬▬▬▬▬▬▬▬▬▬▬▬▬▬▬▬▬▬▬▬▬▬▬▬▬▬▬▬▬ ☐ ☐ ☐

Surveys Improve Security Services and Add Value

McCoy (2006: 44–46), a director of security, writes of how he improved security through the use of internal surveys. He notes that security departments are in a difficult position with customer relations because security must enforce policies and conduct investigations. However, he seeks positive views of security from customers by ascertaining customer needs and fulfilling these needs. McCoy recruited an outside firm to conduct surveys and collect data. The firm provided benchmarks for internal customer service because of its experience with hundreds of clients. As McCoy's department received feedback from the research, specific changes were put in place for continuous improvement that was followed by more research. Survey questions focused on access, response time, expertise, courtesy, value, and other subjects. The response rate was about 30%. Surveys often produce unexpected results, and in McCoy's case he learned that background screening generated numerous complaints because of the length of time required for the check. The average time to complete a check was 14 days, and many managers resented the delay when bringing in a new employee. The security department processed about 4,000 screenings annually, with a denial rate of 4%. To improve performance, the security department began to use a management system model for continuous improvement; background screening was reduced to 5 days by selecting a vendor that emphasized speed, besides accuracy. This accomplishment was highlighted in a security awareness letter prior to a survey. Survey data was used to justify requests for additional personnel and other resources, and to require security certification to enhance skills. In essence, through internal surveys, the security department improved performance and internal relations.

International Perspective: Market Research to Improve Crime Prevention

Crime prevention by residents in the community is not a unitary construct; it is composed of various types of preventive activities (Hope and Lab, 2001: 7–22). Research from a British crime survey revealed that citizens take part in five clear groupings of preventive activities. An understanding of the groupings, and the characteristics of citizens who choose the groupings, can assist those in the public and private sectors who market crime prevention programs. Here are the groupings:

- *Evening Precautions:* Actions taken at night to protect against attack, such as special transportation arrangements.
- *Self-Defense:* Taking self-defense classes and carrying weapons and personal alarms.
- *Neighborhood Watch:* Membership in a watch group and marking property.
- *Technological Security:* Burglar alarms and timed lights.
- *Fortress Security:* Door and window locks and grills.

This British research showed that people's use of various preventive methods represents their different perceptions of crime, their "routine activities," their aims and needs, and to a lesser extent, demographic variables. Only particular types of people will adopt certain crime prevention methods, and more extensive research is needed on this topic.

Corporate security practitioners should consider surveying employees to ascertain what is on their minds (i.e., understanding customers) as input for selecting the best possible security methods. Survey questions can focus on perceptions of security and safety on and off the premises, their "routine activities," and their needs. Such information provides a foundation for market segmentation and target marketing.

Human Relations on the Job

Getting along with others is a major part of almost everyone's job. Many say it is half of their job. The result of such effort is increased cooperation and a smoother working environment.

These suggestions can help a person develop good human relations:

1. Make getting along with others as well as possible a conscious goal. Cooperation increases productivity.
2. Say hello to as many employees as possible, even if you do not know them.
3. Smile.
4. Think before you speak.
5. Be aware that nonverbal communication such as body language, facial expression, and tone of voice may reveal messages not included in your oral statements.
6. Listen carefully.
7. Maintain a sense of humor.
8. Try to look at each person as an individual. Avoid stereotyping (i.e., applying an image of a group to an individual member of a group).
9. Personalities vary from one person to another.
10. People who are quiet may be shy, and these people should not be interpreted as being aloof.
11. Carefully consider rumors and those who gossip. Such information often is inaccurate.
12. Remember that when you speak about another person your comments often are repeated.
13. If possible, avoid people with negative attitudes. A positive attitude increases the quality of human relations and has an impact on many other activities (e.g., opportunity for advancement).
14. Do not flaunt your background.
15. Everybody makes mistakes. Maintain a positive attitude and learn from mistakes.

Management Support

Support from senior management is indispensable for an effective loss prevention program, and it can be enhanced through good human relations. Frequent dialogue between loss prevention practitioners and senior management should be a high priority. One method of gaining the interest of management is to show loss prevention has a **return on investment**. This means that money invested in security and loss prevention can generate not only savings, but also a profit. A good knowledge of business principles and practices can aid the practitioner who must speak "business management language" for effective communications. A loss prevention practitioner who does not speak "business management language" would be wise to enroll in management and accounting courses at a local college.

In one large corporation, the strategy of the security department to gain management support is to quantify its worth and prove it can provide services more efficiently than an outside contractor. This is the reality of proprietary security today as it struggles to survive and escape the outsourcing and downsizing trends. This corporation's security department tracks everything from the number of investigations conducted to the turnover rate of security officers. Such information (i.e., metrics) helps the security function evaluate and improve its services to its internal customers. Surveys are also used to measure customer satisfaction. Additionally, the department measures losses avoided because of security action. For example, the department takes credit for the annual savings from an investigation that reveals that a worker's compensation claim that the corporation has been paying for several years is fraudulent. Another avenue to gain management support is to show that a $50,000-a-year investigator can recover an average of $500,000 in lost inventory each year (Hollstein, 1995: 61–63).

Orientation and Training Programs

Beginning with a new employee's initial contact with a business, an emphasis should be placed on loss prevention. Through the employment interview, orientation, and training, an atmosphere of loss prevention impressed on the new people sets the stage for consciousness-raising about the importance of reduced losses through prevention strategies.

Specifically, orientation and training sessions should include a description of the loss prevention plan pertaining to crimes, fires, and accidents. Program objectives, benefits to employees, and how employees can help reduce losses also are topics of concern. Other topics include access controls and cards, information security, emergency procedures, and various loss prevention services, systems, policies, and procedures.

Loss Prevention Meetings

Meetings with superiors, with employees on the same level as the loss prevention manager, and with subordinates all strengthen internal relations because communication is fostered. When the loss prevention manager meets with superiors, goals and objectives often are transmitted to the manager. Essentially, the manager does a lot of listening. However, after listening, the manager usually has an opportunity to explain the needs of the loss prevention program while conforming to senior management's expectations. This two-way communication facilitates mutual understanding.

Meetings with other managers vary, depending on the type of organization. For instance, a meeting between the human resources manager and the loss prevention manager helps to resolve problem areas. One typical conflict pertains to disciplinary decisions. Another problem area between both departments evolves from applicant screening. Both departments should meet, work together, and formulate a cooperative plan.

When a loss prevention manager meets with subordinates, internal relations are enhanced further. Morale and productivity often are heightened when subordinates are given an opportunity to express opinions and ideas. A manager who is willing to listen to subordinates fosters improved internal relations.

Intranet and E-Mail

The communications technology of today offers a security and loss prevention program superb opportunities to market its services (Huneycutt, 2000: 103–107; Richardson, 2000: 24–26). This involves informing customers of available services, providing helpful information, requesting assistance from customers, seeking input on the needs of customers to improve protection, and illustrating the value of security and loss prevention to the organization.

An **intranet** is an in-house, proprietary electronic network that is similar to the Internet. To prepare an internal Web page for security, a committee can be formed composed of management, security personnel, a Web master to take a leadership role, and an employee from the internal relations department. Next, ascertain through a survey what the customers of security would like to see on the Web page. Consideration must be given to what not to post and possible external access by nonemployees. Moderation should be used with visual images so the site does not require excessive time to load to a customer's computer. Visuals of police badges and handcuffs should be avoided to favor a partnering, loss prevention approach. To help market the site, it can be placed on the home page of the organization's intranet.

An organization's security and loss prevention internal Web site can contain the following:

1. Goals, objectives, polices, and procedures
2. Services offered
3. Educational material on a host of topics such as personal protection, property protection, IT security, and information security
4. Answers to frequently asked questions
5. Links to resources and information
6. Information on how to obtain parking privileges and access cards
7. Information on how to handle various emergencies
8. An incident form for reporting and avenues to report off-line anonymously

9. A bomb threat form
10. A survey form for feedback to improve security
11. A quarterly report on incidents and accomplishments to show the value of security and security personnel
12. An e-mail feature for ease of interaction and to request information
13. A counter to record the number of "hits" at the Web site

E-mail is a convenient way to communicate. Management and other internal customers can be sent a quarterly report on vulnerabilities, incidents, direct and indirect losses, prevention strategies, and achievements. "Tooting one's own horn" should not be perceived as bragging, but a method to inform others that the past budget allocation was worthwhile. For example, achievements may include lowering shrinkage and increasing profits, foiling a criminal conspiracy, and quickly extinguishing a fire. Such a report for superiors will better prepare them for meetings, budgets, and decisions associated with loss prevention.

☐ ☐ ☐ ▬▬▬▬▬▬▬▬▬▬▬▬▬▬▬▬▬▬▬▬▬▬▬▬▬▬

As a security manager, what types of information would you avoid placing on the Internet and a company intranet?

▬▬▬▬▬▬▬▬▬▬▬▬▬▬▬▬▬▬▬▬▬▬▬▬▬▬ ☐ ☐ ☐

Involvement Programs

The essence of involvement programs is to motivate employees who are not directly associated with the loss prevention department to participate in loss prevention objectives. How can this be accomplished? Here are some suggestions: The employee responsible for the lowest shrinkage among several competing departments within a business wins $200 and a day off. The employee with the best loss prevention idea of the month wins $50. Those people who become involved should be mentioned in loss prevention reports to show others the benefits of participating in loss prevention activities. Another strategy is the use of anonymity and reward for reporting information helpful to loss prevention objectives.

External Relations

Law Enforcement

Without the assistance of public law enforcement agencies, criminal charges initiated by the private sector would not be possible. Public police and prosecutors are the main components of public law enforcement. Police frequently are guided by a prosecutor, who is often referred to as the *chief law enforcement officer*. The prosecuting attorney has broad discretion to initiate criminal cases. Community sentiment and powerful groups almost always have an influence on a prosecutor's discretion. Various alternatives are open to a prosecutor. If there is sufficient evidence, the prosecutor can charge an individual. Charges frequently are reduced after a defendant has agreed to plead guilty to a lesser offense, and this plea bargaining process avoids an expensive trial.

Unless private security officers adhere to the basic requirements within local jurisdictions, cases cannot be prosecuted successfully. An example can be seen in shoplifting cases. Depending on state law and local prosecutor requirements, a jurisdiction may require apprehension of a shoplifter after the offender leaves the store with the item instead of apprehending within the store. Many prosecutors feel that this strengthens the case.

External relations with law enforcement agencies are vital for loss prevention programs. Sharing information is a major factor in enhancing this working relationship. Law enforcement agencies often provide information that aids the private sector. Intelligence information pertaining to the presence in an area of professional criminals, bad-check violators, counterfeiters, and con artists assists the private sector in preventing losses. Because of cybercrime, police agencies are increasingly working with the private sector to investigate and prosecute hackers and other cyberoffenders.

Public Safety Agencies

In addition to law enforcement, other public safety agencies such as fire departments, emergency medical services, rescue squads, and emergency management agencies are helpful to loss prevention programs. An analysis of these services is particularly important when a new facility is being planned. Factors relevant to emergency response time, equipment, and efficiency assist in planning the extent and expense of a loss prevention program.

Very little is accomplished by overtly criticizing local public safety agencies for their deficiencies. This action results in negative attitudes and strained relations. Moreover, in the future, the severity of losses very well may depend on action taken by these agencies.

Several strategies help create good relations:

1. Do not become too aggressive when striving toward good external relations.
2. Speak on the same vocabulary level as the person with whom you are communicating.
3. Do not brag about your education and experience.
4. Do not criticize public safety practitioners, because these comments often are repeated.
5. Try to have a third party, such as a friend, introduce you to public safety personnel.
6. Join organizations to which public safety personnel belong.
7. Join volunteer public safety organizations (e.g., the local public police reserve or volunteer fire department), if possible.
8. Speak to civic groups.
9. Ask to sit in on special training programs and offer to assist in training.
10. Try to join local or regional criminal intelligence meetings, where information is shared and crimes are solved.
11. Create a softball league with private and public sector participation. Have a picnic at the end of the season. Try to obtain company funds for these activities.
12. Obtain a position on an advisory committee at a college that has a criminal justice, security and loss prevention, homeland security, or fire science program.
13. Form an external loss prevention advisory board and ask local public safety heads to volunteer a limited amount of time. Secure company funds to sponsor these as dinner meetings.
14. Accept official inspections and surveys by public safety practitioners.
15. Begin an organization, such as a local private sector–public sector cooperative association, that has common goals.

The Community

When a new industry moves to a community, external relations become especially important. Residents should be informed about safety plans. Safety is a moral obligation, as well as a necessity, to ensure limited losses and business survival. As shown in the media, over and over again, community resistance to certain industries is strong. Consequently, an industry with a history of adverse environmental impact must cultivate relations that assure residents that safety has improved to the point of causing minimal problems and an extremely low probability of accidents. Engineers, scientists, senior management, and other support personnel are needed to provide community residents, politicians, and resistance groups with a variety of information and answers. Another consideration involves reassuring the community that a proposed industry will not adversely drain public service resources while creating additional community problems.

To promote strong ties to the community, companies often become involved in community service projects. Employees volunteer time to worthy causes such as helping the needy and mentoring youth. ASIS International promotes a Security for Houses of Worship Project that offers security practitioners an opportunity to partner with college security and criminal justice academic programs to protect houses of worship (Purpura, 1999).

The Media

The media can help or hinder a loss prevention program. Efforts must be made to recruit the media. Difficulties often arise because members of the media usually are interested in information beyond that offered by interviewees. It is worthwhile to maintain positive relations; negative relations may create a vicious cycle leading to mutual harm.

In almost all large organizations, educated and experienced media relations personnel handle the media. Loss prevention practitioners should take advantage of such an organizational structure. This, in effect, insulates the loss prevention department from the media. Policy statements should point out that comments to the media are released through a **designated spokesperson**. When all loss prevention personnel clearly understand the media policy, mistakes and embarrassing situations are minimized. An example of a mistake is the story about a young police officer who was confronted by an aggressive news reporter about a homicide investigation. Investigators had one lead: clear shoe prints under the window of entry to the crime scene. It was hoped that the suspect would be discovered with the shoes that matched the prints. Unfortunately, the news reporter obtained this information from the young officer. The local newspaper printed the story and mentioned the shoes. After reading the newspaper, the offender destroyed the shoes, and the case became more difficult to solve. There had never been a clear policy statement concerning the media within the organization. Another blunder may take place if the amount of valuables (e.g., cash) stolen in a burglary or robbery is revealed to the media, or the fact that the offenders overlooked high-priced valuables during the crime. Both types of information, broadcast by the media, have been known to cause future crimes at the same location.

When working with the media and answering questions, Sewell (2007: 4) recommends projecting sincerity and credibility, keeping it simple, understanding the reporter's question before answering, and being ready to think on the spur of the moment. An article in *Security Management*, "Stress from the Press—and How to Meet It" (1980: 8–11), states many useful ideas concerning relations with the media. The article stresses the importance of preparation, knowing what you want to say, being prepared for tricky questions, and carefully phrasing answers. Numerous firms train executives in effective communication techniques. These courses vary, but most participants learn how to deal with hostile questioning and receive feedback and coaching with the assistance of videotaping. The courses generally run for one to three days and can cost thousands of dollars per participant.

The article recommends several "don'ts" for interviews with the media:

1. Don't return any hostility from the interviewer.
2. Don't lose the audience. Speak clearly and use simple words.
3. Don't say "no comment." If you can't answer the questions, at least tell the audience why.
4. Don't make up answers. If you do not know an answer, say so.
5. Don't say "off the record." If you don't want it repeated, don't say it.
6. Don't offer personal opinions. You are on the air to represent your company, and everything you say will appear to be company policy.

External Loss Prevention Peers

The practitioner who exists in a vacuum is like a student who doesn't pay attention. No knowledge is obtained. Through formal and informal associations with peers, the practitioner inevitably becomes involved in a learning experience. One of the results of relations with peers is information that can improve loss prevention programming.

No individual is an expert about everything. If a group of experts comes together, a broad spectrum of ideas results. When a loss prevention practitioner does not know the answer to a particular question, a call or e-mail to a peer can produce an answer. Peers are helpful in the selection of services and systems, budget preparation, and even presentations to management.

Many formal organizations are open to practitioners. The one organization known by almost all practitioners is ASIS International. This organization is at the forefront in upgrading the security and loss prevention field by educating members and increasing professionalism. Local chapters, national meetings, seminars, and specialized committees and councils bring peers together for mutually beneficial relations.

Special Problems

Certain select areas of concern overshadow both internal and external relations. Two important areas are prosecution decisions and loss prevention attire.

Prosecution Decisions

Prosecution decisions concerning employee–offenders, usually for theft, often are difficult for management. The difficulty arises because a wise manager considers numerous variables. No matter what decision is made, the company may suffer in some way. The situation is tantamount to "damned if we do and damned if we don't." The following are benefits of prosecuting:

1. Prosecuting deters future offenders by setting an example. This reduces the potential for future losses.
2. The company will rid itself of an employee–offender who may have committed previous offenses.
3. The company will appear strong, and this will generate greater respect from employees.
4. Morale is boosted when "rotten apple" employees are purged from the workforce.
5. If a company policy states that all offenders will be prosecuted, then after each prosecution, employees will know that the company lives up to its word and will not tolerate criminal offenses.
6. The company aids the criminal justice system and the community against crime.
7. Local law enforcement will feel that the company is part of the war against crime. This will reinforce cooperation.
8. A strong prosecution policy will become known inside and outside the company. Those seeking employment who also are thinking of committing crimes against the company will be deterred from applying for work.

The following are benefits of not prosecuting:

1. The company shows sympathy for the employee–offender. Therefore, employees say the company has a heart. Morale is boosted.
2. Not prosecuting saves the company time, money, and wages for those employees such as witnesses and the investigator, who must aid in the prosecution.
3. If the employee–offender agrees to pay back the losses to the company and he or she is not fired, the company will not lose an experienced and trained employee in whom it has invested.
4. The criminal justice system will not be burdened by another case.
5. Sometimes companies initiate prosecution, an arrest is made, and then management changes its mind. This creates friction with law enforcement agencies.
6. Possible labor trouble is avoided.
7. Possible litigation is avoided.
8. Prosecution sometimes creates friction among human resources, internal and external relations, and loss prevention departments.
9. Giving bad news to financial supporters, stockholders, customers, and the community is avoided.

To complicate the prosecution decision even more, the policy statement concerning prosecution must be carefully worded by management. There is no perfect statement that can apply to all incidents. A look at a strict policy statement illustrates this problem. Suppose a company policy states that all employees committing crimes against the business will be impartially and vigorously prosecuted. Thereafter, what if a 15-year employee, with an excellent work record and accumulated company-paid training, is caught stealing a box of envelopes? How would you handle this decision as a senior executive?

Employees Smoking Marijuana

An undercover investigation at the Southern Manufacturing Plant by public and private investigators revealed that seven experienced and well-trained employees smoke marijuana before work.

The company loss prevention and human resources managers met with senior management to decide what to do. One solution was to fire all the employees; however, these offending employees had good work records and considerable work experience, and the company had invested heavily in their training. The loss prevention and human resources managers suggested that the employees be confronted and threatened with firing unless they participated in an Employee Assistance Program through a local alcohol and drug abuse program and submitted to drug testing. The managers stated that another local business had a similar problem and a contract was formulated between the business and the government agency dealing with alcohol and drug abuse problems. Senior management at Southern favored this idea.

Later, the employees were confronted and surprised. They all admitted that they liked their jobs and were willing to participate in a drug abuse program on their own time to avoid being fired. By this time, the local alcohol and drug abuse commission had agreed to conduct a program for these employees. The local police chief and prosecutor favored the program as an innovative diversion from the criminal justice system.

Senior management was satisfied. Internal and external relations were improved. The company provided a second chance for the employees and did not lose experienced workers or the money invested in their training.

Many organizations would not choose this lenient path. Numerous organizations would terminate the substance abusing employees who were under the influence at work, especially in industries that are regulated and/or involved in public safety and security.

Much economic crime is disposed of privately (Cunningham et al., 1991: 4). The *Report of the Task Force on Private Security* (U.S. Department of Justice, 1976: 128) adds interesting perspectives to the issue:

> [I]t would appear that a large percentage of criminal violators known to private security personnel are not referred to the criminal justice system. A logical conclusion would be that there is a "private" criminal justice system wherein employer reprimands, restrictions, suspensions, demotions, job transfers, or employment terminations take the place of censure by the public system.... [I]n many instances private action is more expedient, less expensive, and less embarrassing to the company. Fear of lawsuits or protecting the offender from a criminal record may be important. However, violations of due process, right to counsel, and other individual rights are more likely to occur under such a system. The criminal justice system is established for the purpose of resolving criminal offenses and can be a viable resource for the private security sector in this regard.

Another factor affecting prosecution is the **prosecution threshold,** which is the monetary level of the alleged crime that must be met before prosecution. Trends indicate a rise in dollar amounts of individual instances of theft that are partly tied to employee perception of changes in company and prosecutor policies concerning prosecution thresholds. An article in *Security Management Bulletin* ["Finding Where the (Financial) Bodies Are Buried," 1993: 4–5] states: "In the 1970s, an employee who stole $10,000 would have been prosecuted. Today, in many places, that amount won't even produce a criminal referral."

□ □ □

Should management in companies seek to prosecute or not prosecute employee offenders?

□ □ □

Loss Prevention Attire

The appearance of loss prevention personnel has an impact on how people perceive a loss prevention program. A vital part of appearance is attire (i.e., uniforms). Wrinkled, messy uniforms send a message to observers that loss prevention objectives are not very important. A variety of people observe loss prevention personnel: employees, customers, visitors, salespeople, truck drivers, law enforcement personnel, and the community in general. What type of message to these people is desired from an effective loss prevention program? Obviously, neat, good-looking attire is an asset and shows professionalism.

Attire can project two primary images: subtlety or visibility. Subtle attire consists of blazers or sports jackets (see Figure 5-3). It is generally believed that blazers project a warmer, less threatening, and less authoritarian image. Increased visibility and a stricter image are projected through traditional uniforms. However, it is vital that traditional uniforms do not look similar to those worn by public police; this can cause mistakes by citizens needing aid, public police resent private security officers wearing such uniforms, and state regulatory authorities over the private security industry may prohibit uniforms (and vehicles) that appear as public police.

FIGURE 5-3 Security officers at a museum. *Courtesy* of Wackenhut Corporation. Photo by Ed Burns.

□ □ □

All security and loss prevention personnel must realize that they have only one opportunity to create a first, favorable impression.

□ □ □

Research on the psychological influence of the public police uniform should be considered
by those who plan uniforms for the private sector. It has been shown in psychological tests
that individuals associate the color blue with feelings of security and comfort, and the color
black with power and strength. Other research shows black and brown being perceived as
strong and passive, but also bad, and eliciting emotions of anger, hostility, and aggression.
Darker police uniforms may send negative subconscious signals to citizens. One experiment
showed that lighter-colored sheriff's uniforms were rated higher for warmth and friendliness
than darker uniforms. Furthermore, a half-dark uniform (i.e., light shirt, dark pants) sends
a better message than an all-dark uniform. Research on the traditional uniform versus the
blazer shows mixed results. The Menlo Park, California, police tried the blazer for eight
years but found that assaults on police increased and that it did not command respect. After
18 months of wearing blazers, the police of this department displayed fewer authoritarian
characteristics when compared to police from other nearby agencies (Johnson, 2001: 27–32).
For the private sector, research questions are: Do light-colored uniforms or blazers send
more positive signals than dark-colored apparel? Do blazers really create a less authoritarian
atmosphere than uniforms? What impact do blazers have on assaults and respect for private
security officers?

□ □ □

Do you favor traditional uniforms or blazers for security officers? Why?

□ □ □

Search the Web
Check out the following sites on the Web:

   American Marketing Association: www.marketingpower.com/
   Marketing virtual library: www.knowthis.com/
   Professional Associations and Institutes: http://ritim.cba.uri.edu/resources/
   Public Relations Society of America: www.prsa.org/
   Society for Industrial and Organizational Psychology: http://siop.org/

□ □ □

Case Problems

5A. As a security supervisor, you have received reports that a security officer assigned
    to the employee parking lot is having repeated verbal confrontations with
    employees. One report described the officer's use of profane language and threats.
    Specifically, what do you say to this officer, and what actions do you take? How
    do you repair internal relations?

5B. You are a loss prevention supervisor, and two company employees report to
    you that a loss prevention officer is intoxicated while on duty. You approach
    the officer, engage in conversation, and smell alcohol on his breath. What do
    you do? An added complication is that this particular officer has a brother in
    the local police department who has provided valuable aid during past loss

prevention investigations. Furthermore, the officer has had a good work record while employed by the company for five years. After you carefully study the advantages and disadvantages of various internal and external ramifications to proposed actions, what do you do?

5C. While a loss prevention officer was routinely patrolling the inner storage rooms of a manufacturing facility, he accidentally stumbled on two employees engaged in sexual intercourse. All three were shocked and surprised. The man and woman should have been selecting orders for shipment. The woman cried and begged the loss prevention officer to remain silent about this revelation. The man also pleaded for mercy, especially because both were married to other people. When the officer decided that he should report the matter, the man became violent. A fight developed between the officer and the man and woman. The officer was able to radio his location and within 10 minutes other officers arrived. The pair has been brought to the loss prevention office. What do you do as the loss prevention supervisor?

5D. You are a newly hired security manager for an electronics company of 2,000 employees. You were told by your supervisor, the vice president of human resources, "You are here to bring our security program into the 21st century." Apparently, the previous security manager did not meet management's expectations. As you speak with employees and public safety practitioners in the community, you get the impression that you need to "build many bridges." What are your ideas for improving internal and external relations?

5E. An unfortunate explosion and injuries took place at Smith Industries, and a company vice president designates you, a loss prevention supervisor, to speak to the media. It has been only one hour since the explosion, the investigation is far from complete, and you have no time to prepare for the media representatives who have arrived. As you walk to the front gate, several news people are anxiously waiting. The rapid-fire questions begin: "What is the extent of injuries and damage?" "Is it true that both high production quotas and poor safety have caused the explosion?" "What dangers will the community face due to this explosion and future ones?" "What are your comments about reports that safety inspectors have been bribed by Smith Industries executives?" How do you, as a loss prevention supervisor with the authority and responsibility to respond to media questions, answer each question?

5F. Because of your experience and college education, you are appointed manager of loss prevention at a large manufacturing facility in a small city. It is your understanding that the local police chief is introverted and uncooperative with strangers. The chief has an 11th-grade education and is extremely sensitive about this deficiency. He refuses to hire college graduates. Despite these faults, he is respected and does a good job as a police administrator. The local fire chief is the police chief's brother. Both have similar backgrounds and character traits. Furthermore, the local prosecutor is a cousin of both chiefs. A "clannish" situation is apparent. As the loss prevention manager, you know that you will have to rely on as much cooperation as possible from these public officials. What do you do to develop good relations with them?

5G. Allen Dart has worked for the Music Manufacturing Company for 14 years. He has always done above-average work and was recently promoted to production supervisor. One afternoon when Allen was leaving the facility, he dropped company tools from under his coat in front of a loss prevention officer. Allen was immediately approached by the officer, who asked Allen to step inside to the loss prevention office. At this time, Allen broke down and began crying. Before anybody could say a word, Allen stated that he was very sorry and that he would not do it again. Later, the loss prevention and human resources managers met to discuss the incident. An argument developed because the loss prevention manager wanted to seek prosecution, whereas the human resources manager did not. How do you, as a vice president in this company, resolve the situation?

References

Cunningham, W., et al. (1991). *Private Security: Patterns and Trends*. Washington, D.C.: National Institute of Justice.

"Finding Where the (Financial) Bodies Are Buried." (1993). *Security Management Bulletin* (August 25).

Hollstein, B. (1995). "Internal Security and the Corporate Customer." *Security Management* (June).

Hope, T., and Lab, S. (2001). "Variation in Crime Prevention Participation: Evidence from the British Crime Survey." *Crime Prevention and Community Safety: An International Journal*, 3.

Huneycutt, J. (2000). "Nothing But Net." *Security Management*, 44 (December).

Johnson, R. (2001). "The Psychological Influence of the Police Uniform." *FBI Law Enforcement Bulletin*, 70 (March).

McCoy, R. (2006). "Better Service Through Surveys." *Security Management*, 50 (May).

Purpura, P. (1989). *Modern Security and Loss Prevention Management*. Boston: Butterworth-Heinemann.

Purpura, P. (1999). *Security for Houses of Worship: A Community Service Manual for ASIS Chapters*. Alexandria, VA: ASIS International.

Richardson, N. (2000). "A Blueprint for Value." *Security Management* 44 (March).

Sewell, J. (2007). "Working with the Media in Times of Crisis: Key Principles for Law Enforcement." *FBI Law Enforcement Bulletin*, 76 (March).

"Stress from the Press—and How to Meet It" (1980). *Security Management* 24 (February).

U.S. Department of Justice. (1976). *Report of the Task Force on Private Security*. Washington, D.C.: U.S. Government Printing Office.

Wozniak, D. (1996). "Seven Steps to Quality Security." *Security Management* (March).

6

Applicant Screening and Employee Socialization

Objectives

After studying this chapter, the reader will be able to:

1. Define applicant screening and employee socialization.
2. Summarize the legal guidelines for applicant screening.
3. Explain each of the following and how it relates to the employment environment: equal employment opportunity, affirmative action, quotas, diversity, and sexual harassment.
4. List and explain at least four applicant screening methods.
5. Describe how to enhance employee socialization.

KEY TERMS

- applicant screening
- socialization
- Equal Pay Act of 1963
- Civil Rights Act of 1964, Title VII
- Age Discrimination in Employment Act of 1967
- Equal Employment Opportunity Act of 1972
- Rehabilitation Act of 1973
- Pregnancy Discrimination Act of 1978
- Americans with Disabilities Act of 1990
- Civil Rights Act of 1991
- disparate impact
- disparate treatment
- Family and Medical Leave Act of 1993
- *Griggs v. Duke Power*
- *Bakke v. University of California*
- equal employment opportunity (EEO)

- affirmative action (AA)
- quotas
- diversity
- sexual harassment
- quid pro quo
- hostile working environment
- negligent hiring
- diploma mills
- bona fide occupational qualification
- validity
- reliability
- Sarbanes-Oxley (SOX) Act of 2002
- Fair Credit Reporting Act of 1971
- Fair and Accurate Credit Transaction Act of 2003
- job reference immunity statutes
- Employee Polygraph Protection Act of 1988
- agent of socialization

Introduction

One of the most important assets of an organization is its personnel. The purpose of **applicant screening** is to find the most appropriate person for a particular job. Several methods are available for screening applicants, such as interviewing and testing.

The culmination of the applicant screening process results in hiring an applicant. At this stage, an organization already has invested considerable personnel, money, and time in making the best possible choice. The next step is to develop a productive employee. This can be accomplished through adequate **socialization**, which is a learning process that, it is hoped, produces an employee who will benefit the organization. Two primary methods of socialization are employee training and example setting by superiors.

Both applicant screening and employee socialization are primary loss prevention strategies. If an organization can select honest, stable, and productive people, less has to be done to protect the organization from employees and protect employees from employees. If employees can be socialized to act safely and protect company assets, security and loss prevention strategies are enhanced further.

☐ ☐ ☐ ▬▬▬▬▬▬▬▬▬▬▬▬▬▬▬▬▬▬▬▬▬▬▬▬▬▬▬▬▬▬▬▬

Applicant screening and employee socialization are primary loss prevention strategies.

▬▬▬▬▬▬▬▬▬▬▬▬▬▬▬▬▬▬▬▬▬▬▬▬▬▬▬▬▬▬▬▬ ☐ ☐ ☐

Employment Law

Government regulation affects the balance and working relationship between employers and employees in three major areas: (1) the prohibition of employment discrimination; (2) the promotion of a safe and healthy workplace; and (3) fair negotiation between management and labor concerning terms of employment (Mann and Roberts, 2001: 858). Here we begin with major federal laws prohibiting employment discrimination, followed by applicant screening methods. The laws on workplace safety and labor are covered in other chapters.

It is important to note that beyond the federal law emphasized here, and executive orders of presidents, are state and municipal laws that exceed federal legal requirements and state court decisions that interpret state laws. For instance, several states consider sexual orientation a "protected class." Also, many corporations have policies to protect employees on the basis of sexual orientation (DeCenzo and Robbins, 2005: 62).

Federal Legislation

- **Equal Pay Act of 1963:** This legislation requires that men and women be paid equally if they work at the same location at similar jobs. Exceptions include a seniority or merit system and earnings through quantity or quality of production. The act is enforced by the Equal Employment Opportunity Commission (EEOC).
- **Civil Rights Act of 1964, Title VII:** This law prohibits employment discrimination based on race, color, religion, gender, or national origin. Title VII prohibits discrimination with regard to any employment condition, including recruiting, screening, hiring, training, compensating, evaluating, promoting, disciplining, and firing. It also prohibits retaliation against an individual who files a charge of discrimination. The law impacts both public and private sectors. Title VII requires that organizations go beyond discontinuing discriminatory practices and gives preferences to minority group members in employment decisions; this is referred to as affirmative action. Congress established the EEOC to enforce Title VII.
- **Age Discrimination in Employment Act of 1967:** The ADEA prohibits employment discrimination on the basis of age in areas such as hiring, firing, and compensating.

It applies to private employers with 20 or more employees and all government units. This law protects employees between 40 and 65 years of age, but in 1978 the law was amended to afford protection to age 70, and then in 1986 the law was amended again to eliminate the upper age limit. Mandatory retirement is prohibited, absent a suitable defense. The act is enforced by the EEOC.

- **Equal Employment Opportunity Act of 1972:** The purpose of this federal law (EEO) is to strengthen Title VII by providing the EEOC with additional enforcement powers to file suits and issue cease-and-desist orders. Further, EEO expands coverage to employees of state and local governments, educational institutions, and private employers of more than 15 persons. EEO programs are implemented by employers to prevent discrimination in the workplace and to offset past employment discrimination.

- **Rehabilitation Act of 1973:** This act requires government agencies and contractors with the federal government to take affirmative action to hire those with physical or mental handicaps. The act is enforced by the Office of Federal Contract Compliance Procedures.

- **Pregnancy Discrimination Act of 1978:** This law requires pregnancy to be treated as any other type of disability. And, EEO protection is afforded to pregnant employees.

- **Americans with Disabilities Act of 1990:** The ADA prohibits discrimination against individuals with disabilities and increases their access to services and jobs. The law requires employers to make reasonable accommodations for employees with a disability if doing so would not create an undue hardship for the employer. Reasonable accommodations include making existing facilities accessible and modifying a workstation. This law has had a significant impact on the security and safety designs of buildings. Access controls, doorways, elevators, and emergency alarm systems are among the many physical features of a building that must accommodate disabled people. The act is enforced by the EEOC.

- **Civil Rights Act of 1991:** This legislation provides additional remedies to deter employment discrimination by codifying disparate impact concepts and allowing plaintiffs to demand a jury trial and seek damages. Ivancevich (2001: 74) writes: "**Disparate impact** or unintentional discrimination occurs when a facially neutral employment practice has the effect of disproportionately excluding a group based upon a protected category." (The U.S. Supreme Court expanded the definition of illegal discrimination to include disparate impact as illustrated in the *Griggs* case.) This act requires businesses to prove that the business practice that led to the charge of discrimination was not discriminatory but job related for the position and consistent with business necessity. The act is enforced by the EEOC.

  Disparate treatment is another type of discrimination whereby an applicant claims that he or she was not hired because of a discriminatory reason. Examples are asking only one applicant about age or asking only female applicants about child care.

- **Family and Medical Leave Act of 1993:** This legislation requires employers to provide 12 weeks of unpaid leave for family and medical emergencies without employees suffering job loss. The act is enforced by the Department of Labor.

U.S. Supreme Court Decisions

When laws are passed, the courts play a role in helping to define what the legislation means. Such court cases evolve, for example, when the EEOC develops and enforces guidelines based on their interpretation of legislation. Confusion over how to interpret the legislation has led to many lawsuits and some conflicting court decisions. What follows here are two famous U.S. Supreme Court cases from an historical context to illustrate the development of the issues and laws.

Griggs v. Duke Power (1971): In 1968, several employees of the Duke Power Company in North Carolina were given a pencil-and-paper aptitude test for manual labor. Willie Griggs and 12 other black workers sued their employer with the charge of job discrimination under the Civil Rights Act of 1964. Their contention was that the pencil-and-paper aptitude test had little to do with their ability to perform manual labor. The U.S. Supreme Court decided that a test is inherently discriminatory if it is not job related and differentiates on the basis of race, sex, or religion. Furthermore, employers are required to prove that their screening methods are job related.

Bakke v. University of California (1978): Reverse discrimination was the main issue of this case. Allan Bakke, a white man, sued the Davis Medical School under the "equal protection" clause of the 14th Amendment because it set aside 16 of 100 openings for minorities, who were evaluated according to different standards. The Court concluded that the racial quota system was unacceptable because it disregarded Bakke's right to equal protection of the law, and that affirmative action programs are permissible as long as applicants are considered on an individual basis and a rigid number of places has not been set aside. Race can be a key factor in the selection process; however, multiple factors must be considered.

What do all these laws and cases mean for those involved in applicant screening? Basically, all screening methods must be job related, valid, and nondiscriminatory. Included in this mandate are interviews, background investigations, and tests. Simply put, the EEOC regards all screening tools as capable of discriminating against applicants.

Equal Employment Opportunity Commission

The EEOC does not have the power to order employers to stop a discriminatory practice or to provide back pay to a victim. However, the EEOC has the power to sue an employer in federal court. The EEOC requires employers to report employment statistics annually. It investigates claims, collects facts from all parties, seeks an out-of-court settlement, and promotes mediation.

According to the Equal Employment Opportunity Commission, Office of General Counsel (2005), over 24,000 callers a month speak with EEOC customer service representatives. Another 15,000 customers a month receive answers to questions through other technology. Customers can communicate in more than 150 different languages by telephone, fax, written correspondence, e-mail, and web inquiries. During FY 2005, the agency resolved 66% of private sector charges within 180 days or fewer, 51,060 charges out of 77,441 total resolutions. Fifty-two percent of appeals were resolved within 180 days or fewer (3,899 out of 7,490 appeals received). The FY 2005 litigation workload was 944 suits, with 561 active and 383 filed. Seventy-three percent of cases involved Title VII, 12% involved the ADA, and 10% involved the ADEA. Federal District Court litigation activity resulted in about $108 million in monetary relief for FY 2005. The top five defendants versus EEOC were as follows: Abercrombie & Fitch Stores, Inc. ($50 million); Ford Motor Co. ($10.2 million); Home Depot, USA, Inc. ($5.5 million); Dial Corp. ($3.3 million); and Hamilton Sundstrand Corp. ($1.2 million).

□ □ □ ▬▬▬▬▬▬▬▬▬▬▬▬▬▬▬▬▬▬▬▬▬▬▬▬▬▬▬▬▬▬▬▬▬▬▬▬

Denial of Equal Employment Opportunities Because of Sex

Women's access to employment opportunities continues to be obstructed by sex bias in some workplaces, particularly in jobs traditionally held by men. In a case brought against a nationwide manufacturer of household products, the Commission alleged that Dial Corporation's use of a physical "work tolerance" test for production operator positions at a food processing plant in Iowa intentionally discriminated against female applicants and also had a disparate impact on women (Equal Employment Opportunity Commission, Office of General Counsel, 2005). In *EEOC v. Dial Corp* (S.D. Iowa Sept. 29, 2005), EEOC presented at trial the testimony of an expert witness that 97% of men pass the test while only 40% of women succeed, that the test is more difficult than the job, that the scoring is subjective, and that the test does not accomplish its stated objective of reducing injuries. EEOC also presented testimony from 10 of approximately 40 unsuccessful female applicants, focusing on their experience in performing jobs that require heavy lifting. The company presented two expert witnesses, who testified that the production operator job is in the 99th percentile of all jobs in the economy with respect to the physical strength required, that the test is very like the job and therefore is content valid, and that the test had in fact reduced injuries.

The jury returned a verdict for EEOC, finding that the company's continued use of the work tolerance test since April 2001 (when the company became aware of the test's disparate impact on women) constituted intentional sex discrimination against women. The court later ruled that the test had had a disparate impact on women since its inception in January 2000. The judgment provides approximately $3.38 million in back pay, benefits, prejudgment interest, and compensatory damages to 52 class members. It also prohibits the company from implementing any preemployment screening device for five years without first consulting EEOC, and provides job offers with rightful place wages to all class members.

EEO, AA, and Quotas

Equal employment opportunity, affirmative action, and quotas are important terms relevant to staffing organizations (Heneman et al., 1997: 62–64). **Equal employment opportunity (EEO)** refers to practices that are designed so that all applicants and employees are treated similarly without regard to protected characteristics such as race and sex. For example, suppose a vacant position requires applicants to undergo a written job knowledge test and an interview to assess applicants. Anyone is free to apply for the position, and all who apply will be given both the test and the interview. How well each performs on both screening methods determines who is hired. Thus, all applicants have an equal opportunity and the job will be offered following an unbiased assessment.

Affirmative action (AA) focuses on procedures employers use to correct and abolish past discriminatory employment practices against minority group members, women, and those in other groups, while setting goals for hiring and promoting persons from underrepresented groups. AA may be voluntarily undertaken by an employer or court ordered. In our previous example, AA could result if there was a failure to recruit women and minority group members or if the job knowledge test was biased. Then management would make a good faith effort to meet certain hiring goals, for instance, by improved recruiting.

Quotas are rigid hiring and promotion requirements. In our previous example, a hiring formula would be set that specifies the number or percent of women and minorities to be hired.

These concepts, as applied in the workplace, have raised considerable legal turmoil and controversy over whether in fact they have been successful in correcting discrimination. The issue of "reverse discrimination" has intensified the debate. Court decisions provide guidelines for employers.

Diversity

Diversity in the workforce encompasses many different dimensions, including sex, race, national origin, religion, age, and disability (Byars and Rue, 1997: 8). The workforce, historically dominated by white men, is being increasingly replaced with workers from diverse backgrounds. DeCenzo and Robbins (2005: 13) write that much of the workforce change is attributed to federal legislation prohibiting discrimination, and minority and female applicants are the fastest growing segments of the workforce. Projections for the workforce show that half of the new entrants into the workplace will be women, the average age of employees will climb, immigrant employees will have language and cultural differences, and as companies become more global, there will be an increasing need to respond to the unique needs of individual employees, including their languages, values, and customs. Diversity facilitates tolerance of different behavioral styles and wider views, which can lead to greater responsiveness to diverse customers. The challenge of learning to manage a diverse workforce is an investment in the future.

In August of 2000, ASIS International held a conference on "Women and Minorities in Security." The conference was noteworthy because this field has been dominated by white males since the beginning. The speakers were straightforward with the challenges facing minorities and the security industry. With an increasingly diverse society, recruitment of women and minorities is essential; however, public and media perceptions of security—often in a negative light—make recruitment difficult. Women have played an increasing role in the industry, but more needs to be done to recruit more women, African Americans, and Hispanics (Hamit, 2000: 60–62).

ASIS International is in a key position to take the lead to meet the challenges of diversity in the security industry. Solutions include a recruitment campaign; improved partnering among the ASIS, proprietary and contract security organizations, and colleges and universities; internships; and mentoring.

You Be the Judge*

Facts of the Case

When security officer Bronislav Zaleszny was passed over for promotion to supervisor, he decided that his Eastern European origin was at least one of the reasons (his English was rather thickly accented). So he went to the Equal Employment Opportunity Commission and filed a charge against his employer, Hi-Mark Home Products, alleging discrimination on the basis of national origin.

During the month after the EEOC notified the company of the charge, Zaleszny's troubles multiplied. First, Hi-Mark informed the police that products had been disappearing for months, that the disappearances evidently had occurred during Zaleszny's shift, and that Zaleszny was a reasonable suspect. Second, the company terminated him on suspicion of theft. Police arrested Zaleszny, but a preliminary hearing resulted in dismissal of the charges against him.

Zaleszny fumed with anger at his former employer. He sued, alleging that Hi-Mark had prosecuted him maliciously and had fired him in retaliation for his EEOC complaint.

Exactly Who Prosecuted, and Exactly Who Knew about the EEOC Complaint?

In court, the company argued that Zaleszny's allegations really couldn't stand up to logical analysis. "We didn't prosecute him, maliciously or otherwise," Hi-Mark noted. "We truthfully told the police everything we knew about the disappearance of our products, and we said that on the basis of the facts, Mr. Zaleszny seemed to us to be a logical suspect. Then, completely on their own discretion, the police and the district attorney initiated charges against him. We disagree that the prosecution was malicious, but whether it was or not, we're not the ones who prosecuted."

In answer to Zaleszny's retaliatory-firing allegation, Hi-Mark's director of corporate security took the stand. "I'm the company official who recommended Mr. Zaleszny's termination," she testified, "and when I made the recommendation, I didn't know about his EEOC complaint. Yes, the Commission had notified our company, and yes, our HR department knew, but I didn't! And if I didn't know about the complaint when I fired him, then the firing obviously wasn't a retaliation."

Did Zaleszny win his suit against Hi-Mark Home Products?

Make your decision; then turn to the end of the chapter for the court decision.

*Reprinted with permission from *Security Management Bulletin*, a publication of the Bureau of Business Practice, Inc., 24 Rope Ferry Road, Waterford, CT 06386.

Sexual Harassment

The EEOC defines **sexual harassment** as unwelcome sexual conduct that has the purpose or effect of unreasonably interfering with an individual's work performance or creating an intimidating, hostile, or offensive work environment. Although the Civil Rights Act was passed in 1964, only during the 1970s did courts begin to recognize sexual harassment as a form of gender discrimination under Title VII. Thereafter, the EEOC issued guidelines for determining what activity is sexual harassment, and these guidelines influence courts.

The two theories upon which an action for sexual harassment may be brought are explained here. **Quid pro quo** involves an employee who is required to engage in sexual activity in exchange for a workplace benefit. For example, a male manager tells his female assistant that he will get her a promotion and raise if she engages in sex with him. A second theory of sexual harassment is **hostile working environment**, which occurs when sexually offensive behavior by one party is unwelcome by another and creates workplace difficulties. Examples include unwelcome suggestive remarks or touching, and posted jokes or photos of a sexual nature.

Employers, who are vicariously liable for sexual harassment, must take immediate and appropriate corrective action; otherwise, civil and criminal legal action can be devastating. Besides legal action for harassment, these tort actions may be initiated: assault, battery, intentional infliction of emotional distress, and false imprisonment. In addition, these criminal charges may be filed: assault, battery, and sexual assault.

Bryant (2006: 50–58) notes that harassment claims go beyond sexual harassment and involve allegations of unlawful discrimination against members of any of the "protected classes." She writes that to file a discrimination lawsuit, most individuals obtain a right-to-sue letter from the EEOC and then contact a private attorney. However, in some cases the EEOC initiates action. Bryant categorizes actionable workplace harassment of a nonsexual nature into three groups:

- Harassment because of an individual's affiliation or association with a particular religious or ethnic group. Examples are harassing a person who is of the Islamic faith, paying an employee less because of being Hispanic, or intimidating an individual who associates with a particular religious or ethnic group.
- Harassment because of physical or cultural traits. Examples are harassment of a Muslim woman for wearing a headscarf or not hiring a man because he has an accent.
- Harassment because of perception pertains to bullying. The National Institute for Occupational Safety and Health defines bullying as "repeated intimidation, slandering, social isolation, or humiliation by one or more persons against another."

The following list offers guidance when taking action against the problem of sexual harassment and other types of workplace harassment (Bryant, 2006: 50–58; Warfel, 2005: 14–20):

1. Ensure that top management takes the lead to establish a zero tolerance policy.
2. Communicate the policy and reporting procedures to all employees, including strong prohibitions against retaliation for reporting.
3. Provide relevant training.
4. Ensure that reported incidents are taken seriously and thoroughly and promptly investigated, and that corrective action is taken if the allegations are true.
5. Ensure that the human resources department is notified about each complaint.
6. Maintain confidentiality, providing information only on a "need to know" basis.

☐ ☐ ☐ ━━━━━━━━━━━━━━━━━━━━━━━━━━━━━━

Cases of Sexual Harassment

Sexual harassment can occur in any work environment, from the fields to the factory floor to the boardroom. Teenagers are a group particularly vulnerable to sexual harassment. Many of EEOC's suits involving the harassment of young women occur in the setting of restaurants and retail establishments, typical part-time jobs for teens (Equal

Employment Opportunity Commission, Office of General Counsel, 2005). In *EEOC v. Midamerica Hotels Corp. d/b/a Burger King* (E.D. Mo. Dec. 7, 2004), at a Burger King franchise in Missouri, the EEOC found evidence that a restaurant manager subjected female employees, most of them teenagers, to repeated groping, sexual comments, and demands for sex. The women complained to their first line supervisors and to a district manager, but no action was taken until they learned how to contact the corporate office. Under a consent decree, the company will pay a total of $400,000 to seven women, and is prohibited from future sex discrimination and from rehiring the restaurant manager. In addition, the company, which operates 37 Burger King restaurants in four states, will distribute its sexual harassment policy, complaint procedure, and hotline information to all current employees and new hires at its restaurants. The company also will display in all restaurants a new poster containing information about its sexual harassment policy, place the hotline number and an explanation of the sexual harassment policy on all employee paychecks, and require managers to attend sexual harassment training.

In another case, *EEOC v. Carmike Cinemas, Inc.* (E.D.N.C. Sept. 26, 2005), teenage boys were the victims in a case against a large movie theater chain. A 29-year-old male concessions manager in the chain's Raleigh, North Carolina, theater subjected 16- and 17-year-old boys he supervised to offensive verbal and physical sexual conduct over a 9-month period. The manager had previously served more than two years in prison after being convicted of two counts of taking indecent liberties with a minor. Several of the boys complained about the manager, but the theater failed to take corrective action. The manager was finally discharged only when he violated the company's "no call/no show" rule, occasioned by his arrest for failing to register as a sex offender. Under a consent decree, 14 victims will share $765,000 and the company is prohibited from future discrimination. In addition, the company will take the following actions at 13 theaters in North Carolina and Virginia: revise its sexual harassment policy, provide a copy to all new employees, display an 11- by 17-inch poster summarizing the policy, provide sexual harassment training to all new employees at the time of hire and annually to all managers and employees, and report semiannually to the EEOC on complaints of sexual harassment by employees, including the identities of the complainant and alleged harasser and the action taken by the company.

Screening Methods

Screening methods vary among organizations and depend on such factors as regulatory requirements of certain industries, budget, the number of personnel available to investigate applicants, outsourcing to service firms, and the types of positions open. Certain employers expend minimal efforts to properly screen, using the excuse that their hands are tied because of legal barriers. Others follow legal guidelines and screen carefully. The EEOC, the Office of Personnel Management, and the Departments of Justice and Labor have adopted and published the "Uniform Guidelines on Employee Selection Procedures," which is periodically updated and serves as a guide for determining the proper use of tests and other selection procedures for any employment decision such as hiring, promotion, demotion, retention, training, and transfers. These guidelines also contain technical standards and documentation requirements for the validation of selection procedures as described in the "Standards for Educational and Psychological Tests," prepared by the American Psychological Association and other groups. Courts rely on such guidelines in deciding cases.

Negligent hiring is a serious problem resulting from an employee who was an unfit candidate for hiring and retention. The courts have established screening standards from negligence cases; awards have been made to victims who have sued, claiming the employer was negligent in not conducting a reasonable inquiry into the background of an employee who, for example, had a history of physical violence. The term *reasonable inquiry* has various definitions. The theory supporting negligent hiring involves foreseeability. It is defined as follows by Black (1991: 449): "The ability to see or know in advance; e.g. the reasonable anticipation that harm or injury is a likely result from certain acts or omissions. In tort law, the 'foreseeability' element of proximate cause is established by proof that an actor, as person of ordinary intelligence and prudence, should reasonably have anticipated danger to others created by his negligent act." An employer can take a number of steps to screen applicants and prevent negligent hiring.

First, careful planning is required. Input from a competent attorney can strengthen the legality of the screening process. *No single screening tool should be used to assess an applicant. Multiple measures always are best.*

It is important that the job duties and qualifications be clearly defined through a job analysis. Noe et al. (2006: 151–157) write that there is no "one best way" for analyzing jobs. They offer various methods of job analysis that include questionnaires focusing on topics such as work behaviors, work conditions, and job characteristics. An important point they make is that errors in the job analysis process result mostly from job descriptions (based on job analyses) being outdated because of our rapidly changing world.

Help-wanted advertisements should be worded carefully to attract only those who meet the requirements of the job. This also prevents expensive turnover and charges of discrimination.

To save money, the most expensive screening methods should be performed last. The time and labor spent reading application forms is less expensive than conducting background investigations.

An employer can be held liable for negligent hiring if an employee causes harm that could have been prevented if the employer had conducted a reasonable background check.

Resumes and Applications

Applications must be carefully studied. Job seekers are notorious for exaggerating and actually lying. The Port Authority of New York and New Jersey did a study by using a questionnaire to ask applicants if they had ever used certain equipment that really did not exist. More than one-third of the applicants said that they had experience with the nonexistent equipment ("Lying on Job Applications May Be Widespread," 1988: 13).

Diploma mills, which provide a "degree" for a fee, with little or no work, are another problem. Research in the 1990s showed not only that one-third of resumes were fraudulent, but that the problem was increasing (Bachler, 1995: 51–60). Employers then began more thorough checks of applicant backgrounds and whether the degree granting institution of applicants was accredited. Then diploma mill con artists came up with bogus accreditation associations; watermarks, holographs, and encrypting on the diplomas; and toll-free numbers so employers can "verify" the graduate. Today, the problem is compounded by on-line degree programs and the difficulty of distinguishing between quality on-line degree programs and bogus programs. Databases that list accredited schools may list only those that receive federal financial aid. There is no national accrediting body, only regional ones. Solutions include carefully studying transcripts, asking specific questions about course work, requesting samples of course work (e.g., research papers), and being cautious about credit for "life education" ("Fighting Diploma Mills by Degrees," 2005: 18).

Signs of deception on resumes and applications include inconsistencies in verbal and written statements and among background documents. Periods of "self-employment" may be used to hide institutionalization. Not signing an application may be another indicator of deception. Social Security numbers are issued by the state, and that can assist in verifying past residence. A thorough background investigation is indispensable to support information presented by the applicant.

Employers are increasingly adding clauses and disclaimers to applications. Clauses include a statement on EEO and AA, employment at will (i.e., employer's decision to terminate employees), and the resolution of grievances through arbitration rather than litigation. Disclaimers warn an applicant of refusal to hire or discharge for misstatements or omissions on the application.

Today, most companies use the Internet to recruit applicants by including a recruitment section in their Web site. The use of the Internet to solicit applications has its advantages and disadvantages. Advantages, when compared to traditional recruitment methods, include the opportunity to attract more applicants globally, lower cost, convenience, and speed. Disadvantages include the workload of possibly screening numerous applications, ignoring other means of recruiting, and hiring too quickly without screening properly.

Applicants also establish their own Web sites containing their resume and other information. Because "Googling" a name is simple, applicants may place themselves at a competitive disadvantage if they establish a Web site or blog that contains information, photographs, or art that would be offensive to an employer.

Interview

When the applicant is asked general questions about work experience and education, open-ended questions should be formulated so the interviewee can talk at length. "What were your duties at that job?" elicits more information than short-answer questions requiring "yes" or "no" responses. Answers to questions should be compared to the application and resume.

Some employers ask the applicant to complete an application at home to be mailed in before the interview. Before the interview, while the applicant is waiting in an office, he or she is asked to complete another application. Both applications are then compared before the interview for consistency. Many employers require the application to be completed on-line.

The following information concerns questions prohibited during the entire screening process, including the application form. Court rulings under EEO legislation have stressed repeatedly that questions (and tests) must be job related. This legal requirement is known as a **bona fide occupational qualification** (BFOQ).

Questions pertaining to arrest records generally are unlawful, but it depends on the position. An arrest does not signify guilt. The courts have stated that minority group members have suffered disproportionately more arrests than others. A question that asks about a conviction, however, may be solicited. It is not an absolute bar to employment. Here again, minority group members have disproportionately more convictions. Certain offenses can cause an employer to exclude an applicant, depending on the particular job. Therefore, questions of arrest and conviction must be job related (e.g., related to loss prevention) and carefully considered.

Unless a "business necessity" can be shown, questions concerning credit records, charge accounts, and owning one's own home are discriminatory because minority group applicants often are poorer than others. Unless absolutely necessary for a particular job, height, weight, and other physical requirements are discriminatory against certain minority groups (e.g., Latino, Asian, and women applicants often are physically smaller than other applicants).

Other unlawful questions, unless job related, include asking age, sex, color, or race; maiden name of applicant's wife or mother; and membership in organizations that reveal race, religion, or national origin.

The questions that can be asked of an applicant and on an application form, among others, are name, address, telephone number, Social Security number, past experience and salary, reasons for leaving past jobs, education, convictions, U.S. citizenship, military experience in U.S. forces, and hobbies.

Under the ADA, an employer may ask applicants if they need reasonable accommodations for the hiring process. If the answer is yes, the employer may ask for reasonable documentation concerning the disability. Generally, the employer may not ask whether an applicant will need reasonable accommodations to do the job; however, pre-employment inquiries can be made regarding the ability of the applicant to perform job-related functions (Twomey et al., 2001: 789).

Extensive research on the interview process shows that without proper care, it can be unreliable, low in validity, and biased against certain groups. In *Watson v. Fort Worth Bank and Trust*, 108 Supreme Court 2791 (1988), the Court ruled that subjective selection methods such as the interview must be validated by traditional criterion-related or content-validation procedures. Research has pointed to concrete steps that can be taken to increase the utility of the personnel selection interview. First, the interview should be structured, standardized, and focused on a small number of goals (e.g., interpersonal style or ability to express oneself). Second, ask questions dealing with specific situations (e.g., "As a security officer, what would you do if you saw a robbery in progress?"). Third, use multiple interviewers and ensure that women and minority group members are represented to include their perspectives on the applicants (Noe et al., 2006: 234–235).

□ □ □ ▬▬▬▬▬▬▬▬▬▬▬▬▬▬▬▬▬▬▬▬▬

Validity asks how accurately a test predicts job success. Reliability asks if a test is consistent in measuring performance.

▬▬▬▬▬▬▬▬▬▬▬▬▬▬▬▬▬▬▬▬▬ □ □ □

Tests

The testing of applicants varies considerably. Here is a summary of various types of tests (DeCenzo and Robbins, 2005: 94–96, 179–180; Noe et al., 2006: 239–244).

- *Physical ability tests* may predict performance and occupational injuries and disabilities. These tests are likely to have an adverse impact on applicants with disabilities and women. However, key questions are as follows: Is the physical ability essential for the job and is it mentioned prominently in the job description? Is there a probability that the inability to perform the job would cause risk to the safety or health of the applicant or others?
- *Cognitive ability tests* measure a person's ability (e.g., verbal, quantitative, reasoning) to learn and perform a job. Highly reliable commercial tests that measure cognitive abilities are available, and they are generally valid predictors of job performance. The predictive validity of these tests is higher for jobs that are subject to change and require adaptability. Cognitive ability tests typically have an adverse impact on the hiring of minority group members, and some have favored abandoning these tests.
- *Personality inventories* attempt to measure personality characteristics and categorize applicants by what they are like, such as agreeable and conscientious. When such tests ask job applicants to answer intimate questions, such as their sex practices, class action lawsuits can result. These tests have been criticized for questionable validity and low reliability.
- *Assessment center* is a method to test applicants on their ability to handle duties encountered on the job. Multiple raters evaluate applicant performance on exercises, such as how to respond to an e-mail from a customer who has a complaint. These tests are expensive to prepare, job content validity is high, and they are low in adverse impact.
- *Medical examinations* are given to determine whether applicants are physically capable of performing the job. The ADA requires employers to make medical inquiries directly related to the applicant's ability to perform job-related duties and requires employers to make reasonable accommodations to help handicapped individuals to perform the job. This act requires that the medical exam cannot be conducted until after the job offer has been provided to the applicant.
- *Honesty tests* are paper-and-pencil tests that measure trustworthiness and attitudes toward honesty. Thousands of companies have used this evaluation tool on millions of workers, and its use is increasing as employers deal with the legal restrictions of the polygraph. These tests have helped employers screen job candidates, and validity and reliability studies have been published in scholarly journals.

- *Drug tests* have grown dramatically in a drug-oriented world. Employers expect workers to perform their jobs free from the influence of intoxicating substances, and accidents must be prevented. The opposing view favors protection from an invasion of an individual's right to privacy. Employers in regulated or safety-sensitive industries are required by law to test for alcohol or drugs. Numerous employers conduct such tests as a loss prevention measure. Drug tests vary in terms of cost, quality, and accuracy. A drug test can result in a "false positive," showing that a person tested has used drugs when that is not so. A "false negative" can show that the individual has not used drugs when, in fact, the opposite is true. Another problem with drug testing is cheating. Simply stated, if an observer is not present when a urine sample is requested, a variety of ploys may be used by an abuser to deceive an employer. For example, "clean" urine may be substituted. Such deception is a huge problem. Another strategy of drug testing is to measure drug usage from a sample of a person's hair. Some experts view this method as more accurate than urine sampling.

Hire the Right Person, Not the Wrong One!

An error in hiring can bring crime to the workplace, loss of proprietary information, and litigation. Security managers have a duty to work with employers to avoid hiring an employee who

- Has been convicted of embezzlement, but is handling accounts payable
- Has a history of convictions for computer crimes, but is a corporate IT specialist
- Has a history of convictions for felony drug offenses, robberies, and burglaries, but is working with the cleaning crew
- Has been convicted of securities violations and insider trading, but is working in the corporate public information department
- Has a history of child molestation convictions, but is working in corporate daycare
- Is a convicted rapist, but is working as a security officer escorting female employees to their vehicles at night
- As a temporary employee is collecting trash throughout the premises and is really a news reporter seeking a story
- While working in research and development, is really an industrial spy collecting information to sell to a competitor
- Has been hired as a security officer, but is really a terrorist and the "inside person"

Background Investigations

With restrictions on the use of the polygraph, employers have turned to background investigations to verify job applicant information. This can range from inquiries made by the employer to the use of a credit reporting agency, a background investigative firm, or private investigator.

Numerous laws pertain to background investigations. The **Sarbanes-Oxley (SOX) Act of 2002** requires publicly traded companies to conduct background investigations, especially for applicants for positions involving financial matters, trade secrets, IT systems, and other sensitive areas. Employers must also adhere to privacy laws pertaining to the acquisition and protection of sensitive background information (e.g., financial, health).

The **Fair Credit Reporting Act of 1971** (FCRA), enforced by the Federal Trade Commission, is a major law that seeks to protect consumers from abuses of credit reporting agencies while controlling many aspects of background and other types of investigations. (State laws must also be considered.) If a company conducts investigations with in-house investigators, instead of contracting the work to a service firm, the impact of the FCRA may be less burdensome. However, most companies cannot afford in-house investigators.

Under the FCRA, an employer is required to notify a job applicant that a background report will be obtained from an outside firm. The employer must receive written permission from the applicant prior to seeking a report. Some states require that a free copy be provided to the applicant. An employer who takes "adverse action" (e.g., not hiring) against the applicant, based on the report (credit, criminal, or otherwise), must do the following: notify the applicant about the development, show the applicant the report, provide information on the applicant's rights under the FCRA, and allow the applicant to dispute any inaccurate information in the report with the reporting agency. Following this process, if the employer still takes adverse action, the applicant must be notified of the action, with justification.

The EEOC has issued guidelines to protect applicants against discrimination from background investigations. For example, before an employer makes an adverse decision on hiring or promoting based on the candidate's personal financial data, the information should be job related, current, and severe. An employer, for instance, may decide not to offer a financial position to a candidate who has serious, current debt. The FCRA prohibits the use of negative information that is older than seven years. Applicants can bring legal action if they are rejected because of a poor credit record but can show good reasons for their financial problems (Giles, 2000: 107–111).

In an amendment to the FCRA in 2003, ASIS International and other groups were able to lobby for a provision in the law that removes workplace misconduct investigations (e.g., theft, violence, harassment) from the notice and disclosure requirements of the act. This occurred through the **Fair and Accurate Credit Transaction Act of 2003**, also called the FACT Act. Prior to this amendment, employers who used outside investigative firms for cases of employee misconduct were required to notify the suspect prior to the investigation, which could result in evidence or witness tampering.

An applicant's criminal history, if any, is a prime concern of employers, especially when the applicant is applying for a security position. Asking about an applicant's arrest record is generally unlawful, but conviction records legally are obtainable in most jurisdictions; they usually are public records on file at court offices. If an applicant appears to have no convictions, it is possible that the background investigator did not search court records in other jurisdictions where the applicant has lived.

The FBI's National Crime Information Center (NCIC) database holds an enormous amount of information on offenders and stolen items. However, its use is restricted to criminal justice agencies. For the screening of security officers, refer to Chapter 2 for the Private Security Officer Employment Authorization Act of 2004 that enables private security organizations to check with the FBI on security applicants.

Past employment is a crucial area of inquiry because it reveals past job performance. A customary response by employers is to provide dates of employment, positions, and salary. However, human resources offices may be reluctant to supply negative information because of the potential for a defamation suit. Many states have passed **job reference immunity statutes** that shield employers from lawsuits when sharing adverse information with other employers on employee or former employee work history. For protection, employer statements must be truthful, made in good faith, and made for a legitimate purpose. In those states with such laws, a copy of the law can be attached to the release (to be signed by the applicant) authorizing the background check; this may prompt the applicant and the former employer to release more information. Also, the previous employer can be tactfully advised that withholding information could result in liability for negligent referral (Nixon, 2005).

The personal references supplied by the applicant usually are those of people who will make favorable comments about the applicant. If an investigator can obtain additional references from contacting references, more will be learned about the applicant.

Most colleges will verify an applicant's attendance and degree over the telephone. College transcripts can be checked out by mail as long as a copy of the applicant's authorization is enclosed. This conforms to privacy legislation. When educational records are received, the investigator should study characteristics and look for inconsistencies.

The private use of public records is on the increase for background investigations. As we know, conviction records are available in most jurisdictions. Records from state motor vehicle departments can reveal a history of careless driving behavior. A motor vehicle report (MVR) can serve as a cross-check for name, date of birth, and physical description. Federal court records expose violations of federal laws, civil litigation, and bankruptcy. Chapter 10 discusses online databases for acquiring information.

Nadell (2004: 108–116) offers seven steps to effective background checks to protect organizations from negligent hiring allegations while promoting a safe and secure environment:

1. Prepare and distribute to all employees a background screening policy that conforms to all state and federal laws. This lets employees know that promotions depend on background screening.
2. Communicate the policy by placing signs at select locations on the premises.
3. Place a notice about background screening and drug testing on the company Web site.
4. Disclose the screening methods to job applicants.
5. Use the job application process to ask all legally allowable questions.
6. Ensure that temporary employment agencies perform background checks and request a copy of the check.
7. Ensure that vendors and contractors perform background checks and request a copy of the check.

History and Controversy: Polygraph and PSE

Background information on the polygraph and psychological stress evaluator (PSE) will assist the reader in understanding the controversy and subsequent legal restrictions on these devices. In 1895, Cesare Lombroso used the first scientific instrument to detect deception through changes in pulse and blood pressure. In 1921, Dr. John A. Larson developed the polygraph, which measured blood pressure, respiration, and pulse. By 1949, Leonard Keeler added galvanic skin response (i.e., electrical changes on the surface of the skin).

The PSE was developed for the U.S. Army in 1964 by Robert McQuiston, Allan Bell, and Wilson Ford. After it was rejected by the Army, McQuiston patented a civilian version and marketed it to the private sector.

When questions are asked during a polygraph exam, bodily changes are recorded on graph paper or a computer. The examiner interprets these readings with reference to questions asked. Persons have been known to try to "fool" the polygraph by biting their tongues or pressing a toe into a thumbtack previously hidden in their shoes. The PSE has a few variations, but basically it records voice stress as questions are asked. There is no hookup, so it can be used covertly.

A disadvantage of the PSE is that only one factor is being recorded, as opposed to the multiple factors of the polygraph. Training for administering and interpreting the PSE is shorter than for the polygraph. The accuracy of either device is subject to considerable debate, especially concerning the PSE. University of Utah research concluded that the polygraph can be over 90% accurate (U.S. Department of Justice, 1978: 8). Gardner and Anderson (2007: 240) write that "… in 2002 a panel of leading scientists confirmed a US congressional study done in 1983, with both studies reporting that lie detector tests do a poor job of identifying spies or other national security risks and are likely in security screening to produce false accusations about innocent people." Much depends on the training and skill of the examiner behind the device. The polygraph has been responsible for eliminating undesirable job applicants, in addition to assisting with criminal and civil cases, but at the same time, abuses have occurred that resulted in the passage of the Employee Polygraph Protection Act.

☐ ☐ ☐ ▬▬▬▬▬▬▬▬▬▬▬▬▬▬▬▬▬

Employee Polygraph Protection Act of 1988

The **Employee Polygraph Protection Act of 1988** (EPPA) was passed by Congress and signed into law by then-president Ronald Reagan on June 27, 1988. It became effective on December 27. The act prohibits most private employers from using polygraph or "lie detector" tests to screen job applicants and greatly restricts the use of these instruments to test present employees. The EPPA defines the term *lie detector* to include any device that is used to render a diagnostic opinion regarding the honesty of an individual. The congressional Office of Technology Assessment estimated that 2 million polygraph exams had been conducted each year—90% by private employers.

The EPPA states that it is unlawful for an employer to directly or indirectly force an employee to submit to a polygraph test. Discrimination against those who refuse to be tested or who file a complaint under the EPPA is prohibited. Employers who violate the EPPA may be assessed a civil penalty up to $10,000 for each violation. In addition, the Secretary of Labor may seek a restraining order enjoining the employer from violating the act. The law provides individuals with the right to sue employers in federal and state courts for employment reinstatement, promotion, and payment of lost wages and benefits.

A few kinds of employees are exempt from the act and can be tested, including employees of

- National security organizations or defense industries
- Federal, state, and local governments
- Businesses involved with controlled substances
- Certain security service firms, such as armored car or security alarm firms

In addition, a limited exemption exists for any employer who is conducting an ongoing investigation involving economic loss or injury; the suspect employee must have had access to the subject of the investigation, and reasonable suspicion must be present. Considerable justification and documentation is required. Chapter 10 contains proper testing procedures under the EPPA.

☐ ☐ ☐ ▬▬▬▬▬▬▬▬▬▬▬▬▬▬▬▬▬

Should the EPPA be amended to permit more widespread use of the polygraph in the workplace to screen job applicants for honesty?

▬▬▬▬▬▬▬▬▬▬▬▬▬▬▬▬▬ ☐ ☐ ☐

Employee Socialization

Socialization, the learning process whereby an employee gains knowledge about the employer and how to become a productive worker, is broader in scope than orientation and training programs. Employers who understand the socialization process are likely to enhance the value of employees to the organization. Furthermore, losses can be reduced as employees adhere to loss prevention strategies. The following emphasizes orientation, training programs, examples set by superiors, and employee needs.

Loss Prevention Orientation for New Employees

When new employees begin to work for an organization, the orientation session plays a significant role in the socialization process. Employees learn about company policies, procedures, departments, products and services, customers, and the community (Noe et al., 2006: 314). Examples set at the beginning can go a long way in preventing future problems and losses. The orientation program should be designed to acquaint the new employees with the "big picture" of loss prevention. Such discussion can enhance the employees' understanding of the objectives of the loss prevention program, how employees can help, and the benefits to everyone.

Employee Training

In this discussion the focus is on training protection personnel, but the principles that follow can apply to a variety of training programs for a broad spectrum of employees.

Despite the training problems of the security industry, as covered in Chapter 2, increasing numbers of practitioners in the field realize the importance of training. Consequently, training standards and programs constantly are being upgraded. Although training costs money, the investment is well worth it. Training helps to prevent problems such as critical incidents and litigation. Training provides personnel with an improved understanding of what is expected of them, heightens morale and motivation, and reduces disciplinary problems. All these benefits are impossible unless there is management support for training.

Planning Training

Step 1: Training Needs
Several questions need to be answered. Who are the recipients of the training (loss prevention personnel or regular employees; new or experienced employees)? What training programs are available? What deficiencies were noted in employee evaluations? What are the suggestions from supervisors? What are the suggestions from employees? Of particular importance is to conduct a job analysis to pinpoint the skills required for the job.

Step 2: Budget
Before the training program is prepared, an estimate of money available is necessary, since one cannot spend what one does not have.

Step 3: Behavioral Objectives
Each behavioral objective consists of a statement, usually one sentence, which describes the behavioral changes that the student should undergo because of the training. For example, loss prevention officers must explain how the 5th Amendment to the Bill of Rights relates to the private sector.

Step 4: Training Program Outline
With the use of the behavioral objectives, an outline is prepared. It can be considered a step-by-step sequence for training.

Step 5: Learning Medium
The method of presentation is described. Various strategies are available, such as lecture, discussion, demonstration, case method, role playing, and e-learning (on-line learning).

Hipkiss (2006: 29) writes of learning through alternatives to the classroom. She notes that the classroom is just one way to learn and that people learn in many ways. Hipkiss argues that employers are realizing that experiential learning—by doing, reflection, and real-world application—has greater value than sitting in a classroom.

Many training programs use a mixture of techniques. Scenario training or simulations, for example, create workplace situations that trainees will encounter on the job. For this to be successful, managers must determine what types of behavior or performance are desired. Then the training is designed around such objectives. Several trainees can participate in each scripted scenario, acting as security officers, employees, customers, visitors, and evaluators. As the scenarios change, so should the roles of the trainees. Examples of scenarios are assisting a visitor who is lost and upset about being late to a meeting, assisting a handicapped person who must deal with an inoperable elevator, barring access to an estranged spouse of an employee, and responding to a report of employee theft. A variation of scenario training is written scenario testing whereby the trainee reads a script and decides what to do and why. As with all training methods, feedback by the instructor is essential so performance can be improved (Dominguez, 1999: 29–30).

Technology-based training methods involving CD-ROM, DVD, Internet, or intranet are popular and used by many organizations. Each is characterized by advantages and disadvantages. Major advantages are flexibility as to the location (i.e., globally) and time (i.e., 24/7) of training, cost savings on travel, and management's ability to track employee progress. Whereas the traditional classroom offers an instructor who can provide immediate guidance and feedback to students, technology-based training methods, such as computer-assisted, self-paced, and distance learning offer a mixture of approaches in providing guidance and feedback to students.

Step 6: Evaluation, Feedback, and Revision

After the training is completed, the students should provide valuable feedback to the instructor. An evaluation questionnaire, completed by students, can guide the instructor in revising the training program. The training is further validated through interviews of participants and supervisors a few months after the training to see if the training helped participants to perform their tasks effectively and to identify topics requiring more or less attention. Audits can be used to further assess the success of training. This can entail observing an employee on the job, checking the quality of written reports, or hiring external investigators to audit the courtesy of employees or perform access penetration tests.

Learning Principles

1. Learning results in a behavioral change. Learning objectives are stated in terms of specific behaviors. When a student is able to perform a task that he or she was unable to perform before a training program, then behavior has changed.
2. Tests are used to measure the changed behavior.
3. If the proper conditions for learning are presented to students, learning will take place. The teacher should help the student to learn by facilitating learning through effective instructional methods.
4. An instructional program should begin with basic introductory information to develop a foundation for advanced information.
5. Feedback, an instructor informing the student whether a response was correct or incorrect, is vital to learning.
6. An instructional program must consider the learner's ability to absorb information.
7. A student will be more receptive to learning if information is job related.
8. Conditioning aids the learning process. Conditioning can be perceived as a method of molding or preparing a student for something through constant practice; for example, repetitive drills so that employees know exactly what to do in case of fire.
9. Increased learning will take place if the practice is spread out over time as opposed to a single, lengthy practice session.
10. Information that is learned and understood is remembered longer than that which is learned by rote.

Wasted Training

In an article in *Administrative Management*, "How Not to Waste Your Training Dollars," Donald J. Tosti (1980: 44) declares that American businesses and government agencies spend billions of dollars annually on training, and about half of that amount is wasted. Tosti describes "Seven Deadly Sins of Training," which are still applicable today:

1. Using training to solve motivational problems.
2. Making training more complicated than is necessary.
3. Training personnel at the wrong time, such as training all of an organization's employees for a program that will be instituted in two years.
4. Overtraining, such as instructing retail clerks on the theoretical aspects of their job before explaining important procedural aspects of retailing.
5. Failing to understand the true costs of training.
6. Failing to calculate training on a cost-effective basis. Evaluations of training programs help to predict benefits. Questions of concern are as follows: Did employees learn and apply the new information? Are losses reduced? Was the training worth the money?
7. Following fads in training.

☐ ☐ ☐ ▄▄▄

Think about a training program or course you attended in the past. In what ways could it have been improved?

☐ ☐ ☐ ▄▄▄

U.S. Army Guard Program, Contractors' Training Requirements
(U.S. Government Accountability Office, 2006: 21)

1. Use of force
2. Antiterrorism, threats, definition, and identification
3. Security operations, basic functions, patrolling techniques and responsibilities
4. Response to hostage situations; initial actions prior to military police response
5. Personnel identification procedures, package and vehicle search procedures, and contraband identification/seizure procedures
6. Firearm (pistol and/or shotgun) qualification and safety
7. Unarmed self-defense
8. Oleoresin capsicum (OC) spray techniques, use, and application
9. Nightstick and police baton use and techniques
10. Clearing, securing, and protecting crime scene
11. Use of interpersonal skills, verbal skills, de-escalation, nonverbal actions
12. Techniques for searches, 4th Amendment rights, consent and seizure
13. Application of handcuffs
14. Hand and arm signals, basic traffic control techniques
15. Recording of police information and sworn statements
16. Contract security guard authority and jurisdiction
17. Prevention of sexual harassment
18. Customer service
19. Military customs and courtesies

▄▄▄ ☐ ☐ ☐

Examples Set by Superiors

Poor example setting is pervasive in many organizations. All organizations have informal rules that serve as guides to action. These rules often are transmitted to subordinates from superiors. The length of the 15-minute coffee break varies within organizations, as does the time when the 11:00 A.M. meeting begins; the amount of time allowed before an employee is considered late also varies; the number of minor safety violations permitted before strict disciplinary action differs from one organization to another as well as from one superior to another. Clearly, superiors serve as teachers and role models. The actions of superiors greatly affect subordinate performance. Poor supervision results in both low subordinate productivity and losses.

A supervisor can be perceived to be what sociologists call an **agent of socialization**, a person who plays a dominant role in the socialization of an individual. In society, parents, teachers, and clergy are agents of socialization. In a business organization, a supervisor becomes an agent of socialization after establishing a working relationship with a new employee. The superior first makes the new employee feel some degree of belonging, in calming the uneasy new worker. The superior may have to skillfully break down the old methods that the new subordinate may have carried over from a previous job.

Because first impressions are lasting, the initial part of the socialization process is important. A good example must be set in the beginning.

☐ ☐ ☐ ━━━━━━━━━━━━━━━━━━━━━━━━━━━━━━━━━

Based on your experience, can you think of any poor examples set by superiors in the workplace?

☐ ☐ ☐ ━━━━━━━━━━━━━━━━━━━━━━━━━━━━━━━━━

Poor Example Set by Ralph Marks, Loss Prevention Manager

The Locost retail store chain emphasized the importance of loss prevention procedures as an aid to increased profits. All employees were expected to adhere to these procedures. The loss prevention manager at each store was expected to reinforce the program. Each store's employees looked to the loss prevention manager for guidance.

At one particular store, Ralph Marks, the loss prevention manager, made a serious mistake. All retail employees were permitted to make purchases and receive a 15% discount. Procedures dictated that items bought were to be recorded and then stored under a designated counter until the end of the day. When Ralph Marks bought a stereo for his car, he did not follow the appropriate procedures. He installed the stereo during working hours, which also compounded the poor example. By the end of the working day, all retail employees had seen or heard of this incident. This poor example caused many employees to lose respect for the manager and the loss prevention program.

━━━━━━━━━━━━━━━━━━━━━━━━━━━━━━━━━ ☐ ☐ ☐

Employee Needs

The way an organization responds to employee needs has an impact not only on the socialization process, but also on losses. When employee needs are met, workers also learn about the employment environment. They learn that management and supervisors care; employees learn to respect and appreciate the employment environment while helping to reduce losses.

What are employee needs? Psychologist Abraham Maslow (1954) became famous for designing a "hierarchy of needs" in the early 1950s (see Figure 6-1). Maslow's view is that people are always in a state of want, but what they want depends on their level within the hierarchy of human needs.

Lower level needs must be satisfied before upper level needs. Maslow's hierarchy of needs follows:

- *Basic physiological needs.* Survival needs such as food, water, and the elimination of wastes can be satisfied with employer assistance. A well-run company cafeteria and clean lavatories are examples.

FIGURE 6-1 Maslow's hierarchy of needs.

- *Safety and security needs.* This need relates to order in one's life. A person needs to feel free from anxiety and fear. Adequate wages, medical insurance, and workplace safety help to satisfy these needs.
- *Societal needs.* The need to be loved and have friends and the need for esteem can be fulfilled by supervisors. A supervisor should praise a subordinate when appropriate. Employees should receive recognition or awards after completing a good job. Employee socials also are helpful.
- *Esteem and status needs.* A person needs to be competent, to achieve, and to gain approval and respect.
- *Self-actualization needs.* This need is at the top of the hierarchy of needs. It signifies that a person has reached his or her full potential, whether as a janitor, homemaker, doctor, or whatever. An organization and its superiors can do a lot (e.g., training, promotion) in assisting an employee to fulfill this need.

Employees learn which needs are satisfied and which are not. Suppose a workplace has a terrible cafeteria, dirty lavatories, poor wages, an inadequate safety program, authoritarian supervisors, and poor training and promotional opportunities. What level of losses would be sustained at this workplace in comparison to another that adhered to Maslow's hierarchy of human needs?

☐ ☐ ☐ ▬▬▬▬▬▬▬▬▬▬▬▬▬▬▬▬▬▬▬▬▬▬▬▬

How do you think corporate downsizing affects Maslow's hierarchy of human needs and loss prevention?

☐ ☐ ☐ ▬▬▬▬▬▬▬▬▬▬▬▬▬▬▬▬▬▬▬▬▬▬▬▬

Search the Web
Employers and job applicants are becoming increasingly knowledgeable about the validity and reliability of tests, especially because of the need to eliminate or to detect discrimination. The Buros Institute of Mental Measurement (www.unl.edu/buros/) evaluates published tests and acts as a consumers' evaluation service.

Here are additional Web sites related to this chapter:

American Psychological Association: www.apa.org/science/standards.html
ASIS International, "Preemployment Background Screening Guideline": www.asisonline.org/guidelines/guidelinespreemploy.pdf
EEOC's National Contact Center: info@ask.eeoc.gov
Federal Trade Commission: www.ftc.gov
Society for Human Resource Management: www.shrm.org/
U.S. Department of Labor: www.dol.gov/dol/allcfr/Title_41/Part_60–3/toc.htm

☐ ☐ ☐

Case Problems

6A. Plan and write a step-by-step screening process for applicants interested in uniformed loss prevention positions. Formulate an application form. Pay particularly close attention to applicable laws.

6B. You are seeking a position as a security officer at a research and development company. Officers at this site wear blazers and focus on access controls and protecting people and information. The job pays well, with opportunities for advancement, so you strive to do your best at each stage of the applicant screening process. You now must complete an assessment center "in-basket" exercise while thinking as a security officer. You are to prioritize the following items, with justification for each, upon reaching the scene of an assault in the parking lot.

- A witness to the assault approaches you to offer information.
- Someone who is scaling the perimeter fence is screaming for help because of being stuck in the razor ribbon.
- An employee approaches you for help because he locked his keys in his car.
- You receive a radio transmission from your supervisor who wants to meet with you immediately.
- The victim is down and bleeding.
- You must complete an incident report for this case.
- A car alarm has been activated.

6C. You are a candidate for the position of security manager for a large shopping mall near a major city. The number of candidates has been narrowed to six, and the mall human resources manager has decided to use an "in-basket" exercise to further narrow the list of candidates. The "in-basket" exercise consists of a series of memoranda/e-mails, telephone calls, and radio transmissions that the mall security manager would encounter in the job. Your task is to read all items, set priorities among them, and write what action you would take and the reasoning for your action for each item. The date is September 24. The time to complete this assignment is 60 minutes. It is possible that all candidates will be handed additional memoranda/e-mails, telephone messages, or radio transmissions during the exercise. A review panel (police captain, firefighter, college educator, and mall security officer) will evaluate each candidate's work without knowing the identity of the writer. [*Source*: Philip P. Purpura, *Retail Security and Shrinkage Protection* (Boston: Butterworth-Heinemann, 1993), pp. 327–329.]

Item 1

TO: Mall Security Manager

FROM: Mall Manager

SUBJECT: Security Seminar

DATE: September 20

Several merchants would like a seminar on security before the busy holiday season. Please get back to me as soon as possible.

Item 2

TO: Mall Security Manager

FROM: Human Resources Manager, Bigmart Department Store

SUBJECT: Selection of Store Detective

DATE: September 24

Please walk over to review the applications for store detective. I have no idea who would be the best one.

Item 3

TELEPHONE MESSAGE: September 21

Mr. John Poston, a mall customer, called again. He is still irate about the damage to his car window when Security Officer Mallory broke into the vehicle after Mr. Poston left his keys in the ignition. Mr. Poston is threatening to sue.

Item 4

TELEPHONE MESSAGE: September 20

Mrs. Johnson, owner of the Befit Health Store, thinks someone is entering her store at night. She is very upset and worried, and wants you to meet her at her store.

Item 5

TO: Mall Security Manager

FROM: Mall Manager

SUBJECT: Application Verification

DATE: September 22

The Westwood Mall office called to verify your application for their job opening in security. Are you planning to begin another job? Please let me know immediately. Let's talk.

Item 6

RADIO TRANSMISSION: September 24, 11:15 A.M.

"Four year old boy lost at south end of mall. We have not been able to locate for one hour."

Item 7

TELEPHONE MESSAGE: September 23

Attorney for the plaintiff who was assaulted in the parking lot last month wants you to call him right away.

Item 8

TO: Mall Security Manager

FROM: Mall Manager

SUBJECT: Emergency Plans

DATE: September 16

In speaking with other mall managers at a recent seminar, they mentioned updating their emergency plans. We probably need to do this, too. Please respond.

Item 9

RADIO TRANSMISSION: September 24, 11:20 A.M.

"Small fire in stock room of Smith's Department Store. We can put it out."

Item 10

TO: Mall Security Manager

FROM: Paula Reed, Security Officer

SUBJECT: Pay Raise

DATE: September 23

I am not pleased about my raise of only $0.15 per hour. I have been doing a good job and I really work hard when we get busy. The male security officers are making much more than my rate per hour. I believe that this difference is because I am a black woman. We have talked about this already, but you haven't done anything about it. I want something done right away or I will take legal action.

Item 11

TELEPHONE MESSAGE: September 22

The manager of Hall Stuart Clothes wants to know why it took so long for security to respond to a shoplifting incident yesterday.

6D. You are a security manager who has just been given an assignment by the vice president of human resources to obtain a copy of an e-mail containing racial jokes that has been circulating in the company. She has received complaints about the e-mail and wants you to bring it to a meeting to provide input for corrective action.

A short time later you obtain the e-mail, which contains the story of a young man named Boy. One of the sentences states: "I axed my mudder for some money. She had only too bucks so I axed my fiend, Kenya spare a quarter. He said no so Afro a chair at him." As the security manager, what do you suggest at the meeting?

The Decision for "You Be the Judge"

Ultimately, no, but the company had to run a gauntlet before breaking out into the clear. There were conflicting judgments at two lower court levels, but finally a higher court ruled in favor of Hi-Mark. In the end, Zaleszny did not win anything. This case is based on *Griffiths v. CIGN*, 988 F 2nd 457 3rd Circuit Court (1993). The names in this case have been changed to protect the privacy of those involved.

Comment

The fact that Zaleszny's company had to go through appeals can give you pause. You might suppose that simple logic should have upheld Hi-Mark from the outset. If the company didn't prosecute, how could it be guilty of malicious prosecution? If the manager who fired Zaleszny didn't know about his EEOC complaint, how could the firing have been a retaliation for the complaint? And why didn't these lines of reasoning prevail right away? Because logic doesn't always prevail in court. Often, other variables are in play, including the effectiveness with which a case is presented, a jury's understanding of a judge's instructions, the extent to which all parties understand the relevant law, and even the personalities in the courtroom.

The two questions that confronted this company can be minefields. What should you do about prosecution of a crime suspect? Can you safely fire an employee who has engaged in a protected activity, such as complaining to a federal watchdog agency? Be sure to get a qualified attorney's advice whenever you face these questions.

References

Bachler, C. (1995). "Resume Fraud: Lies, Omissions, and Exaggerations." *Personnel Journal* (June).
Black, H. (1991). *Black's Law Dictionary*, 6th ed. St. Paul, MN: West Pub.
Bryant, M. (2006). "Harassment Lawsuits and Lessons." *Security Management*, 50 (April).
Byars, L., and Rue, L., (1997). *Human Resource Management*, 5th ed. Chicago: Irwin Pub.
DeCenzo, D., and Robbins, S. (2005). *Fundamentals of Human Resource Management*, 8th ed. Hoboken, NJ: John Wiley & Sons.
Dominguez, E. (1999). "Training That Triumphs." *Security Management*, 43 (June).
Equal Employment Opportunity Commission, Office of General Counsel. (2005). "FY 2005 Annual Report." www.eeoc.gov/litigation/05annrpt/index.html, retrieved June 16, 2006.
"Fighting Diploma Mills by Degrees" (2005). *Security Management*, 49 (May).
Gardner, T., and Anderson, T. (2007). *Criminal Evidence: Principles and Cases*, 6th ed. Belmont, CA: Thomson Wadsworth.
Giles, F. (2000). "Checking Credit When It's Due." *Security Management*, 44 (June).
Hamit, F. (2000). "ASIS Confronts a Changing Demographic." *Security Technology & Design*, 10 (October).
Heneman, H., et al. (1997). *Staffing Organization*, 2nd ed. Middleton, WI: Irwin Pub.
Hipkiss, A. (2006). "Learning Moves out of the Classroom." *Personnel Today* (May 16).
Ivancevich, J. (2001). *Human Resources Management*, 8th ed. New York: McGraw-Hill Pub.
"Lying on Job Applications May Be Widespread" (1988). *Security* (February).
Mann, R., and Roberts, B. (2001). *Essentials of Business Law*, 7th ed. Cincinnati, OH: West.
Maslow, A. (1954). *Motivation and Personality*. New York: Harper & Row.
Nadell, B. (2004). "The Cut of His Jib Doesn't Jibe." *Security Management*, 48 (September).

Nixon, B. (2005). "How to Avoid Hiring Hazards." *Security Management*, 49 (February). www.securitymanagement.com/library/001706.html, retrieved February 4, 2005.

Noe, R., et al. (2006). *Human Resource Management: Gaining a Competitive Advantage*, 5th ed. Boston, MA: McGraw-Hill Irwin.

Tosti, D. (1980). "How Not to Waste Your Training Dollars." *Administrative Management*, 41 (February).

Twomey, D., et al. (2001). *Anderson's Business Law and the Regulatory Environment*, 14th ed. Cincinnati, OH: West.

U.S. Department of Justice. (1978). "Validity and Reliability of Detection of Deception." Washington, D.C.: U.S. Government Printing Office.

U.S. Government Accountability Office. (2006). *Contract Security Guards: Army's Guard Program Requires Greater Oversight and Reassessment of Acquisition Approach* (April). www.gao.gov/new.items/d06284.pdf, retrieved April 5, 2006.

Warfel, W. (2005). "SEX ED: Insulating Yourself from Sexual Harassment Litigation." *Risk Management Magazine*, 52 (February).

7

Internal Threats and Countermeasures

Objectives

After studying this chapter, the reader will be able to:

1. Describe the broad spectrum of internal threats.
2. Explain the internal theft problem.
3. Outline at least five management countermeasures to prevent internal theft.
4. List and explain the steps involved in confronting an employee suspected of internal theft.
5. Explain integration, open architecture, and convergence in reference to physical security.
6. Outline access control methods and systems, including the types of cards used for access.
7. List and describe at least three types of locks.
8. List and describe at least five types of interior intrusion detection sensors.
9. Describe CCTV technology, including IP-based network systems.
10. Explain the characteristics of safes.

KEY TERMS
• threat	• accounting
• internal loss prevention	• auditing
• theft of time	• inventory system
• telework	• marking property
• universal threats	• metal detectors
• employee theft	• integrated system
• pilferage	• open architecture
• embezzlement	• identity management system
• occupational fraud	• access controls
• Donald R. Cressey	• authentication
• employee theft formula	• authorization
• Edwin Sutherland	• cryptography
• differential association	• encryption
• accountability	• common user provisioning

- interoperable
- digital certificate systems
- tailgating
- pass back
- biometric security systems
- mechanical locks
- electromechanical locks
- deadbolt
- latches
- cylinder
- lock picking
- master key system
- intrusion detection system
- sensors
- control unit
- annunciator
- dual technologies
- digital video recorders
- network video recorder
- Internet protocol (IP)-based network cameras
- analog technology
- digital technology
- compression
- charged coupled device (CCD) or "chip" camera
- multiplex
- video motion detection
- intelligent video systems
- fire-resistive (or record) safe
- burglary-resistive (or money) safe

Introduction

A **threat** is a serious, impending or recurring event that can result in loss, and it must be dealt with immediately. **Internal loss prevention** focuses on threats from inside an organization. Crimes, fires, and accidents are major internal loss problems. Examples of internal threats include violence in the workplace, theft of proprietary information, sabotage, infiltration by gangs or organized crime, and terrorism. Losses can result from full-time, part-time, and temporary employees; contractors; vendors; and other groups who have access to the worksite both physically and remotely. Productivity losses also illustrate the range of internal losses. Such losses can result from poor plant layout or substance abuse by employees. Other productivity losses result from employees who loaf, arrive at work late, leave early, abuse coffee breaks, socialize excessively, use the Internet for nonwork-related activities, and prolong work to create overtime; these abuses are called **theft of time**. Faulty measuring devices, which may or may not be known to employees, are another cause of losses. Scales or dispensing devices that measure things ranging from truck weight to copper wire length are examples.

We can see that the spectrum of internal threats is broad. Although this chapter focuses on internal theft and associated countermeasures, the strategies covered also apply to many internal and external (e.g., burglary and robbery) threats.

□ □ □ ▬▬▬▬▬▬▬▬▬▬▬▬▬▬▬▬▬▬▬▬▬▬▬▬▬▬▬▬▬▬▬▬▬▬

Universal IT Threats

Although the media often concentrate on a few high-profile cyberattacks from outside organizations, the greatest threat to corporate information technology systems is from within (i.e., from employees). Because news of many insider attacks is not released to the public, the frequency of the following scenario is impossible to gauge: A systems administrator in one hospital learned that she was about to be fired, so she arranged for a "severance package" for herself by encrypting a critical patient database. Her supervisor feared the worst and loss of his job, so in exchange for the decryption key, the manager arranged for a termination "bonus" and an agreement that the hospital would not prosecute (Shaw et al., 2000: 62).

The dilemma facing the hospital, as to whether to meet the offender's demands or prosecute, can produce interesting debate. How long could the hospital function without the critical patient database? How much time would be required by the criminal justice system to resolve the case? As we know from previous chapters, there are several procedural steps to a criminal case, and the decision to prosecute has its advantages and disadvantages.

From a loss prevention perspective, the following methods would have placed the hospital in an improved position: maintain strict confidentiality about the impending firing of the employee, follow established policies and procedures pertaining to firing employees, exercise extreme caution, block the employee's access to the IT system and other vulnerable locations and systems, and always back up data. Technical solutions alone are not the answer because internal attacks are a "people problem" requiring personnel security solutions. The challenges include the expense of money and time for increased security. Conviction checks may be ineffective with IT personnel because their misdeeds are likely to be unrecorded and, as in the case of the hospital systems administrator, unreported. At-risk behaviors, however, can lead to exposure by supervisors and coworkers. Examples include personnel who avoid procedures and hack into a system to fix problems, curious individuals who explore the system while violating security policies, and individuals who cause outages to facilitate their own travel or advancement.

A growing threat is the insider who steals proprietary or confidential information such as customer identifying information and financial information. These losses can also result from accidental losses of data or attacks by hackers.

Two additional concerns are the growing remote workforce and the devices used to work away from the traditional worksite. Laptop and handheld computers, high-speed Internet, wireless networks, and smart cell phones have facilitated **telework** (i.e., working away from the traditional worksite by transmitting information via communication technology). Many other devices also aid the mobile workforce, including personal digital assistants (PDAs), digital cameras, and USB memory sticks—all of which are high-capacity storage devices. Because of telework, traditional internal threats are also becoming external threats. For instance, an employee working off-site may have his company laptop computer stolen from his home or while traveling. He may also be victimized by hacking while working off-site. Furthermore, because of technology, an employee can cause losses (e.g., embezzlement or theft of proprietary information) for an organization while off the premises as well as when on the premises. Differentiating internal from external threats is becoming increasingly difficult and blurred, especially because we have entered the era of **universal threats**. In other words, employees and organizations face the same threats whether work is accomplished on or off the premises.

Jordon (2006: 16) writes that both public and private sectors are increasingly embracing telework because of efforts to ensure continuity of operations when a disaster strikes. He refers to the Federal Telework Survey that showed that 41% of responding federal employees indicated that they telework, up from 19% the previous year. The research also showed that federal IT professionals expanded their support for telework initiatives. Jordan's article adds that telework is not just a technological issue, it is also an organizational and cultural change issue, and agencies must share best practices. From a security perspective, it is also a socialization issue to prevent losses.

The U.S. Department of Homeland Security, Science and Technology Directorate and the Executive Office of the President, Office of Science and Technology Policy (2004: 42) warned that the greatest threat to critical infrastructure (e.g., food, water, electricity) is from the insider who performs actions that could destroy or degrade systems and services. Insider threats develop from individuals who have authorization to access information and infrastructure resources. These threats are difficult to guard against because the offenders are on the inside and trusted. They exploit vulnerabilities and have advantages over outsiders in choosing the time, place, and method of attack. The Science and Technology Directorate and the Office of Science and Technology Policy (2004: 42–44) offer research directions for protection against insider threats:

Intent Detection: This involves examining combinations of observations, actions, relationships, and history to sense possible offending behavior. Various methods are used to support this approach, including surveillance, cataloging, pattern recognition, and computational analysis. These methods are applicable to the physical and cyber domains.

Detection and Monitoring: Detection should draw attention to early recognition of a pattern of action that is erratic or outside the norm. Computer models are necessary to distinguish between random behavior and behavior indicative of a possible internal threat. Then computer systems must monitor the possible problem.

Protection and Prevention: This includes security measures that are overt or covert. Examples are incremental access, job-specific access controls, and repetitive checking. These measures and others require research to build solutions to internal threats.

Taylor et al. (2006: 7) write that vulnerability from within an organization is the most dangerous and serious threat. They report that 73% of the risk to computer security is from internal sources, while 23% is attributable to external sources. In comparison to outsiders, Taylor et al. note that insiders find it easier to circumvent IT security because they are familiar with the system; in many instances breaches from within are not detected; an internal cybercrime can be covered up by using a special program; and detection may not surface in an audit. Computer industry research shows the average internal attack costs a company $2.7 million, compared with $57,000 for an external attack (Shaw et al., 2000: 62–66). Randazzo et al. (2004: 2) write that estimates of internal attacks are difficult to formulate because of under-reporting to law enforcement authorities and organization fear of negative publicity and increased liability. They point to statistics that vary on the prevalence of internal and external cyberattacks, the methodological problems of annual surveys and in-depth case studies, and the importance of examining incidents from both behavioral and technical perspectives simultaneously. These research problems make it difficult to gauge internal and external threats to IT systems. Examples of two surveys are the FBI (2005) *Computer Crime Survey* and the Computer Security Institute/FBI (2005) *CSI/FBI Computer Crime and Security Survey*. Both surveys depend on organizations to report their victimizations. In the former survey, 44% of respondents had experienced intrusions from within their organizations. In the latter survey, respondents compared internal and external IT security incidents in their respective organizations, and they reported that there were more security incidents from external sources; however, more respondents did not know the number of internal incidents when compared to the number of incidents from external sources (44% versus 35%). In a subsequent survey (Computer Security Institute/FBI, 2006: 11–12), *CSI/FBI Computer Crime and Security Survey*, some questions and reporting on internal versus external threats were changed from the earlier survey, which made comparisons difficult. The 2006 report stated that most respondents do not see insiders as responsible for most of their organization's cyber losses; however, a significant number of respondents believe that insiders are responsible for substantial losses. In addition, for all categories of attacks or misuse, a trend shows the detection of such attacks appears to be decreasing. Interestingly, the dollar amount of losses resulting from security breaches decreased substantially from 2004 to 2005 due to a drop in the number of respondents. Negative publicity from reporting computer crime to police is a major concern of organizations.

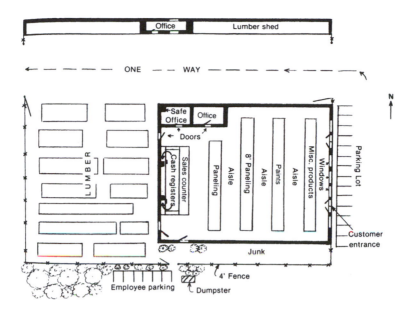

FIGURE 7-1 Woody's Lumber Company. Woody's Lumber Company has suffered declining profits in recent years. A recently hired manager quickly hired six people to replace the previous crew, which was fired for internal theft. Four additional people were quickly hired for part-time work. The process for conducting business is to have customers park their cars in the front of the store, walk to the sales counter to pay for the desired lumber, receive a pink receipt, drive to the rear of the store, pick up the lumber with the assistance of the yard crew, and then depart through the rear auto exit. At the lumber company, loss prevention is of minimal concern. An inoperable burglar alarm and two fire extinguishers are on the premises.

To personalize the information presented in this chapter, three businesses are described: a retail lumber business (see Figure 7-1), a clothing manufacturing plant (see Figure 7-2), and a research facility (see Figure 7-3). Suppose you are a loss prevention specialist working for a corporation that has just purchased these three businesses. Your supervisor informs you that you are responsible for recommending modifications at these facilities to improve internal loss prevention. First, read this chapter and then proceed to the case problem pertaining to these businesses at the end of the chapter.

Internal Theft

How Serious Is the Problem?

Internal theft also is referred to as *employee theft, pilferage, embezzlement, stealing, peculation,* and *defalcation*. **Employee theft** is stealing by employees from their employers. **Pilferage** is stealing in small quantities. **Embezzlement** occurs when a person takes money or property that has been entrusted to his or her care; a breach of trust occurs. *Peculation* and *defalcation* are synonyms for embezzlement. Whatever term is used, this problem is an insidious menace to the survival of businesses, institutions, and organizations. This threat is so severe in many workplaces that employees steal anything that is not "nailed down."

The total estimated cost of employee theft varies from one source to another, mainly because theft is defined and data are collected in so many different ways. An often-cited statistic, from The U.S. Chamber of Commerce, is that 30% of business failures result from employee theft. The National White Collar Crime Center reports that losses due to employee theft range from $20 to $90 billion annually to upwards of $240 billion annually when intellectual property theft is included (National Association of Credit Management, 2005). The Association of Certified Fraud Examiners (2006: 8) conducted research that found that the

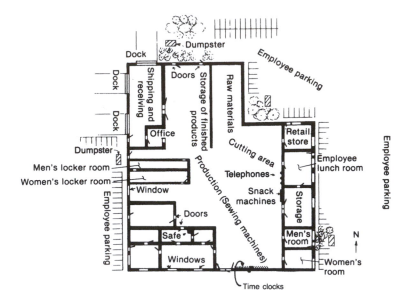

FIGURE 7-2 Smith Shirt Manufacturing Plant. In the past two years, the Smith plant has shown declining profits. During this time, managers believed that employee theft might be the cause, but they were unsure of what to do and were worried about additional costs. Employees work one shift from 8 A.M. to 5 P.M. five days per week and are permitted to go to their cars to eat lunch from noon to 1 P.M. A total of 425 employees are divided as follows: 350 sewing machine operators, 15 maintenance personnel, 20 material handlers, 20 miscellaneous workers, 2 retail salespeople, 5 managers, and 13 clerical support staff members. A contract cleanup crew works from 6 to 8 A.M. and from 5 to 7 P.M. on Monday, Wednesday, and Friday; Sunday cleanup is from 1 to 4 P.M. The crewmembers have their own keys. Garbage dumpster pickup is 7 A.M. and 7 P.M. Monday, Wednesday, and Friday. The plant contains a fire alarm system and four fire extinguishers. One physical inventory is conducted each year.

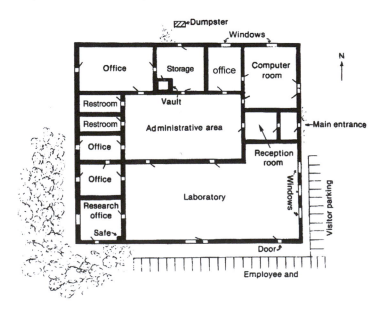

FIGURE 7-3 Compulab Corporation. Compulab Corporation is a research business with tremendous potential. However, it seems that whenever it produces innovative research results, a competitor claims similar results soon afterward. Compulab employs 33 people, including a research director, 2 assistants, 10 scientist-researchers, 8 computer specialists, and an assortment of office staff. The facility is open 24 hours a day, 7 days per week, and employees work a mixture of shifts each month and remotely from their homes and other locations. Almost every employee has his or her own key for entrance into the building.

typical organization loses 5% of its revenues to **occupational fraud**, defined as follows: "The use of one's occupation for personal enrichment through the deliberate misuse or misapplication of the employing organization's resources or assets." They claim that if this figure were multiplied by the U.S. Gross Domestic Product, which in 2006 was about $13 trillion, the losses would translate to about $652 billion in annual fraud losses. These figures may be higher when direct and indirect costs are combined. Indirect costs can include a slowing of production or an insurance premium hike after a claim. Research by Baker and Westin (1987: 12) mentions employee morale and damage to public image as expensive indirect costs following major internal crimes.

Why Do Employees Steal?

There is no one reason why employees steal from their employers. However, two major causes of employee theft are employee personal problems and the environment. Employee personal problems often affect behavior on the job. Financial troubles, domestic discord, drug abuse, and excessive gambling can contribute to theft. It is inappropriate to state that every employee who has such problems will steal, but during trying times, the pressure to steal may be greater. A wise employer should be alert to troubled employees and suggest referral to an Employee Assistance Program (see Chapter 18).

The environment is perhaps the strongest factor behind internal theft. Politicians, corporate executives, and other "pillars of society" are constantly being found guilty of some form of crime. Inadequate socialization results. In other words, poor examples are set: employees may observe managerial illegalities and then act similarly. In many businesses, because so many people are stealing, those who do not steal are the deviants and outcasts; theft becomes normal and honesty becomes abnormal. Some managers believe that employee theft improves morale and makes boring jobs exciting. In many workplaces, employees are actually instructed to be dishonest. This can be seen when receiving department workers are told by their supervisor to accept overages during truck deliveries without notifying the vendor.

"Let's Not Fire Him for Stealing—He's a Good Employee"
An undercover investigation at Smith's lumberyard #7 revealed that the yard boss, Joe Crate, was stealing. The undercover investigator, Jimmy Wilson, worked at yard #7 and found that Joe was stealing about $80 worth of building products per week. Each evening Joe would hide merchandise near the back gate, and when it was time to close up and lock the gate, he would quickly load his vehicle, which was conveniently parked nearby.

Before Jimmy was assigned to another yard, he met with a vice president and the manager of yard #7 at company headquarters. During the meeting, Jimmy asked, "Are you going to fire Joe Crate?" The VP stated, "Let's not fire him for stealing—he's a good employee." Then the VP explained: "Joe's salary is $10 per hour, which is equal to $400 per week. If Joe steals about $80 per week, then Joe's salary is about equal to $480 per week. If we hired a carpenter to build the lumber sheds that Joe is building at yard #7, it would cost us almost twice as much." Jimmy could not believe what he was hearing, especially from the VP. He did not say a word and listened to instructions for his next assignment.

What are your views of the way in which internal theft was handled at Smith's lumberyard #7 in the preceding box?

When employees steal, a hodgepodge of rationalizations (excuses) are mentally reviewed to relieve guilt feelings. Some of these rationalizations are "Everybody does it," "It's a fringe benefit," and "They aren't paying me enough."

Donald R. Cressey analyzed thousands of offenders to ascertain common factors associated with inside thievery (Lary, 1988: 81). He found three characteristics that must be present before theft would be committed. Cressey's **employee theft formula** is

Motivation + Opportunity + Rationalization = Theft

Motivation develops from a need for money to finance a debt or a drug problem or to win approval from others. Opportunity occurs at many unprotected locations, such as a loading dock. Rationalizations relieve guilt, as stated already. This formula illustrates the need for security and an honest environment.

Edwin Sutherland, a noted criminologist, offered his theory of **differential association** to explain crime. Simply put, criminal behavior is learned during interaction with others, and a person commits crime because of an excess of definitions favorable to violation of law over definitions unfavorable to violation of law. *The implication of this theory for the workplace is that superiors and colleagues in a company are probably a more important determinant of crime than is the personality of the individual.* Conklin (2001: 278–279) writes in his criminology textbook that a former head of the Securities and Exchange Commission's Division of Enforcement stated bluntly: "Our largest corporations have trained some of our brightest young people to be dishonest."

A study of college student knowledge of how to commit computer crimes found that threat of punishment had little influence on their misdeeds. In this study, the strongest predictor of computer crime was differential association with others who presented definitions favorable to violation of the law (Skinner and Fream, 1997: 495–518).

The implications for security from differential association theory point to the importance of ethical conduct by top management, who should set a good example in the socialization of all employees. In addition, since criminal laws can be impotent, preventive security strategies are essential.

How Do Employees Steal?

The methods used to steal from employers are limited by employee imagination. Typically, employees pilfer items by hiding them under their clothing before leaving the workplace. Methods that are more sophisticated involve the careful manipulation of accounting records. Collusion among several employees (and outsiders) is common. The kinds of item to be taken (e.g., tools, a piano, cash) and the obstacles (e.g., loss prevention strategies) dictate the method of theft. A tool can be hidden in a person's pocket or underwear, and a piano might be pilfered piece by piece over a year and then assembled in a home garage. Some employee theft methods follow:

1. Wearing manufactured items while leaving the workplace—for example, wearing pilfered underwear or wearing scrap lead that has been molded to one's body contours
2. Smuggling out pilfered items by placing the item in a lunchbox, pocketbook, bundle of work clothes, umbrella, newspaper, hat, or even one's hair
3. Hiding merchandise in garbage pails, dumpsters, or trash heaps to be retrieved later
4. Returning to the workplace after hours, with a pass key, and helping oneself to goods
5. Truck drivers turning in fictitious bills to employers for fuel and repairs and then splitting the money with truck stops
6. Collusion between truck drivers and receiving personnel
7. Executives padding expense accounts
8. Purchasing agents receiving kickbacks from vendors for buying high-priced goods
9. Retail employees pocketing money from cash sales and not recording the transaction
10. Padding payrolls as to hours and rate of pay

11. Maintaining nonexistent or fired employees on a payroll and then cashing the paychecks
12. Accounts payable employees paying fictitious bills to a bogus account and then cashing the checks for their own use

Possible Indicators of Theft

Certain factors *may* indicate that theft has occurred:

1. Inventory records and physical counts that differ
2. Inaccurate accounting records
3. Mistakes in the shipping and receiving of goods
4. Increasing amounts of raw materials needed to produce a specific quantity of goods
5. Merchandise missing from boxes (e.g., every pallet of 20 boxes of finished goods has at least two boxes short a few items)
6. Merchandise at inappropriate locations (e.g., finished goods hidden near exits)
7. Security devices found to be damaged or inoperable
8. Windows or doors unlocked when they should be locked
9. Workers (e.g., employees, truck drivers, repair personnel) in unauthorized areas
10. Employees who come in early and leave late
11. Employees who eat lunch at their desks and refuse to take vacations
12. Complaints by customers about not having their previous payments credited to their accounts
13. Customers who absolutely have to be served by a particular employee
14. An unsupervised, after-hours cleaning crew with their own keys
15. Employees who are sensitive about routine questions concerning their jobs
16. An employee who is living beyond his or her income level
17. Expense accounts that are outside the norm

Management Countermeasures

Management Support

Without management support, efforts to reduce losses are doomed. *A good management team sets both a foundation for strategies and an atmosphere in which theft is not tolerated.* Support for budget requests and appropriate policies and procedures are vital.

Effective Planning and Budgeting

Before measures are implemented against internal theft, a thorough analysis of the problem is necessary. What types of losses are occurring, where, by whom, when, and why?

Internal and External Relations

Good internal and external relations can play a role in preventing employee theft. Loss prevention practitioners who show appropriate courtesy, demeanor, and appearance are respected by employees. Prompt investigations of incidents indicate that losses are a major concern.

With a heightened prevention atmosphere within a workplace, an external reputation is sure to follow. Outside people with ulterior motives will think twice before applying for a job.

Job Applicant Screening and Employee Socialization

The screening of job applicants from full-time to part-time and temporary workers is a major theft-prevention technique. Whatever steps are taken, an atmosphere of loss prevention should exist from every applicant's initial contact.

Accountability, Accounting, and Auditing

Accountability defines a responsibility for and a description of something. For example, John Smith is responsible (i.e., is held accountable) for all finished products in a plant, and he maintains accurate records (i.e., a description) of what is in stock. **Accounting** is concerned with recording, sorting, summarizing, reporting, and interpreting business data. **Auditing** is an examination or check of a system to uncover deviations. Personnel audit physical security by checking intrusion alarm systems, closed-circuit television (CCTV), and so on. An auditor audits the accounting records of a company to see if the records are reliable and to make sure embezzlement has not occurred.

Policy and Procedural Controls

Policy and procedural controls coincide with accountability, accounting, and auditing. In each of these three functions, policies and procedures are communicated to employees through manuals and memos. *Policies* are management tools that control employee decision making and reflect the goals and objectives of management. *Procedures* guide action to fulfill the requirements of policies.

As an example, a company policy states that, before trash is taken to outside dumpsters, a loss prevention officer must be present to check for stolen items. Procedures point out that, to conform to this policy, the head of the cleaning crew must call the loss prevention office and wait for an officer to arrive before transporting the trash outside.

Signs

Placing messages about loss prevention on the premises is another method. The message must be brief, to the point, and in languages for diverse readers. An example of a message is "Let's all work together to reduce losses and save jobs."

Loss Reporting and Reward System

Numerous organizations have established a toll-free number to facilitate ease of loss reporting. A company Web site and intranet are other avenues to facilitate loss reporting. A reward system is a strategy to reinforce reporting. One method employed is to provide the informant with a secret number that is required to pick up reward money at a bank at a time convenient to the caller, who is encouraged to send a substitute to strengthen anonymity.

The Sarbanes-Oxley (SOX) Act of 2002 requires publicly traded companies to provide a system of reporting anonymously, with penalties for noncompliance. Research shows that the best avenue to encourage reporting is through a confidential, 24-hour hotline operated by a third party (Greene, 2004).

Research by Scicchitano et al. (2004: 7–19) found that, among the large retailers they surveyed, management encouraged employees to report dishonesty that they observed in the workplace. In addition, companies use a variety of methods (e.g., posters, announcements) to promote peer reporting. All the respondents used a toll-free hotline and one-half used financial incentives. No clearly established methods of reporting were noted from the research. The researchers emphasized that corporate climate plays an important role in facilitating peer reporting.

Investigation

Employee thieves often are familiar with the ins and outs of an organization's operation and can easily conceal theft. In addition, a thorough knowledge of the loss prevention program is common to employee thieves. Consequently, an undercover investigation is an effective method to outwit and expose crafty employee thieves and their conspirators.

Property Losses and Theft Detection

To remedy property losses within an organization, several strategies are applicable. Closed-circuit television (CCTV), both overt and covert, and Radio Frequency Identification (RFID) are popular methods discussed in other parts of this book. Here, an emphasis is placed on inventory system, marking property, and use of metal detectors. An **inventory system** maintains accountability for property and merchandise. For example, when employees borrow or use equipment or tools, a record is kept of the item, its serial number, the employee's name, and the date. On return of the item, both the clerk and the user make a notation, including the date. Inventory also refers to merchandise for sale, raw materials, and unfinished goods. This topic will be covered at greater length in Chapter 11 on accounting, accountability, and auditing.

Marking property (e.g., tools, computers, furniture) serves several useful purposes. When property is marked with a serial number or a special substance, or a firm's name is etched with an engraving tool, thieves are deterred because the property can be identified if the thief is caught. Publicizing the marking of property reinforces the deterrent effect.

Besides the popular use of a pinhole lens camera for covert surveillance to catch an offender, another investigative technique is to use fluorescent substances to mark property. An ultraviolet light (black light) is necessary to view these invisible marks, which emerge as a surprise to the offender. Organizations sometimes experience the theft of petty cash. To expose such theft, fluorescent substances, in the form of powder, crayon, or liquid, are used to mark money. The typical scenario involves a few suspects who are the only people with access to petty cash after hours. Before these after-hour employees arrive, the investigator handling the case places bills previously dusted with invisible fluorescent powder in envelopes at petty cash locations. The bills even can be written on with the invisible fluorescent crayon. Statements such as "marked money" can be used to identify the bills under ultraviolet light. Serial numbers from the bills are recorded and retained by the investigator. Before the employees are scheduled to leave, the "planted" bills are checked. If the bills are missing, then the employees' hands are checked under an ultraviolet light. Glowing hands expose the thief, and identification of the marked money carried by the individual strengthens the case. The marked money must be placed in an envelope because the fluorescent powder may transfer to other objects and onto an honest person's hands. A wrongful arrest can lead to a false-arrest suit. A check of a suspect's bills, for the marked money, helps avoid this problem. Many cleaning fluids appear orange under an ultraviolet light. The investigator should analyze all cleaning fluids on the premises and select a fluorescent color that is different from the cleaning substances. Other items that may fluoresce include lotions, plastics, body fluids, and some drugs.

Another method of marking property is by applying microdots. Microdots contain a logo or ID number, and the dots are painted or sprayed on property. A microscope is used to view the dots that identify the owner of the property. As with other methods of marking property, the purpose is to reduce losses from internal and external sources of theft. One utility company, for example, suffered millions of dollars of losses from the theft of copper wire and equipment, so it applied the dots to copper assets to help identify company property during investigations and recovery (Canada.com, 2007).

Walk-through **metal detectors**, similar to those at airports, are useful at employee access points to deter thefts of metal objects and to identify employee thieves. Such detectors also uncover weapons being brought into an area. Handheld metal detectors are also helpful. It is important to note that metal detectors may be overrated because certain firearms, knives, and other weapons are made primarily of plastic. Consequently, scanners are an expensive option to identify contraband, as covered in the next chapter.

Insurance, Bonding

If insurance is the prime bulwark against losses, premiums are likely to skyrocket and become too expensive. For this reason, *insurance is best utilized as a supplement to other methods of loss prevention that may fail*. Fidelity bonding is a type of employee honesty insurance for employees who handle cash and perform other financial activities. Bonding deters job applicants and employees with evil motives. Some companies have employees complete bonding applications but do not actually obtain the bond.

Confrontation with the Employee Suspect

Care must be exercised when confronting an employee suspect. The following recommendations, in conjunction with good legal assistance, can produce a strong case. The list of steps presents a *cautious approach*. Many locations require approval of management before an arrest.

1. Never accuse anyone unless absolutely certain of the theft.
2. Theft should be observed by a reliable person. Do not rely on hearsay.
3. Make sure you can show intent: the item stolen is owned by the organization, and it was removed from the premises by the person confronted.

In steps 4 through 14, an arrest has not been made.

4. *Ask* the suspect to come to the office for an interview. Employees do not have a right to have an attorney present during one of these employment meetings. If the suspect is a union employee and requests a union representative, comply with the request.
5. Without accusing the employee, he or she can be told: "Some disturbing information has surfaced, and we want you to provide an explanation."
6. Maintain accurate records of everything. These records may become an essential part of criminal or civil action.
7. Never threaten a suspect.
8. Never detain the suspect if the person wants to leave. Interview for less than one hour.
9. Never touch the suspect or reach into the suspect's pockets.
10. Request permission to search the suspect's belongings. If left alone in a room under surveillance, the suspect may take the item concealed on his or her person and hide it in the room. This approach avoids a search.
11. Have a witness present at all times. If the suspect is female and you are male, have another woman present.
12. If permissible under the Employee Polygraph Protection Act of 1988, ask the suspect to volunteer for a polygraph test and have the suspect sign a statement of voluntariness. Follow EPPA guidelines.
13. If a verbal admission or confession is made by the suspect, have him or her write it out, and have everyone present sign it.
14. Ask the suspect to sign a statement stipulating that no force or threats were applied.
15. For the uncooperative suspect, or if prosecution is favored, call the public police, but first be sure you have sound evidence as in step 3.
16. Do not accept payment for stolen property because it can be construed as a bribe and it may interfere with a bond. Let the court determine restitution.
17. Handle juveniles differently from adults; consult the public police.
18. When in doubt, consult an attorney.

Prosecution

Many feel strongly that prosecution is a deterrent, whereas others maintain that it hurts morale and public relations and is not cost effective. Whatever management decides, it is imperative that an incident of theft be given considerable attention so that employees realize that a serious act has taken place. Establish a written policy that is fair and applied uniformly.

Research

Although employee theft is a significant national problem, limited research is available. The Association of Certified Fraud Examiners (2006) periodically publishes a *Report to the Nation on Occupational Fraud and Abuse*. Some of its findings from research of actual cases are as follows:

1. Occupational fraud is very difficult to detect.
2. The fraud is more likely to be detected by a tip rather than an audit or internal controls.
3. Organizations that had an anonymous fraud hotline suffered lower losses.
4. Industries with the highest median losses per scheme were wholesale, construction, and manufacturing. Government and retailers were among those with the lowest median losses.

5. Small businesses suffer disproportionate fraud losses. The median loss at organizations with fewer than 100 employees was $190,000 per scheme, and the most common schemes were employees fraudulently writing company checks, skimming revenues, and processing fraudulent invoices.
6. Small businesses generally do a poor job of proactively detecting fraud.
7. The higher the position of the offender in the organization, the greater the losses.
8. Most of the cases of fraud in the study involved either employees in the accounting department or upper management.
9. Almost two-thirds of victimized organizations routinely conducted background checks on applicants; however, less than 8% of offenders had prior convictions. ACFE data show that although background checks are important, certain methods are vital for detecting fraud, such as fraud training, surprise audits, and anonymous reporting.

Another research project was conducted by the University of Minnesota and the American Management Association with funds from the U.S. Department of Justice (Clark and Hollinger, 1980: 106). Thirty-five corporations including 4,985 employee respondents anonymously provided data. Conclusions from this research report are listed next:

1. In the three industries studied (retail stores, electronic manufacturers, and hospitals), employees most likely to be involved in theft constitute a significant portion of the workforce: salespersons, engineers, and nurses.
2. The dissatisfied employee was found more frequently to be involved in theft.
3. The most consistent predictor of theft involvement was the employee's perceived chance of being caught.
4. Theft decreased when a negative reaction by management and coworkers increased.
5. Informal coworker sanctions are twice as influential in changing behavior as formal management responses.
6. Prevention measures have an effect on theft.
7. Those companies with a clearly defined antitheft policy had a lower incidence of theft.
8. Theft can be lowered by communicating antitheft policies to employees (e.g., through signs or memos).
9. A lesser degree of theft was found in businesses that had theft-prevention strategies within the inventory system.
10. Pre-employment screening deters theft.
11. Lower levels of theft can be achieved by instituting several strategies at once.

Speed (2003: 31–48) writes that employee dishonesty is a complex problem, and management encounters difficulty when planning the most appropriate strategies to combat it. He focused his research on a major retailer in the United Kingdom to learn how loss prevention could be better targeted. Speed studied company records of employee offenders and surveyed attitudes of a sample of employees. He proposed a management strategy that divides employees into four groups, based on age and length of service, and then he designed loss prevention strategies for each group. The four groups and the strategies for each are summarized next:

- *First group:* Employees 20 years of age or younger, new to the company.
- *Second group:* Employees in their 20s, employed with the company for about two years.
- *Third group:* Employees with greater length of service and experience than the first two groups.
- *Fourth group:* Employees with considerably greater length of service or are much older.

Speed's research shows that the first group presents great risk of theft because they are less likely to be deterred by disapproval by others or by losing their job. However, more of them fear being caught than the slightly more experienced employees. The first group commits the simplest types of offenses with the lowest values. Strategies for this group include restricted access to high-risk operations and ensuring they are complying with systems. The second group also presents great risk of theft because they are confident they will avoid detection. They commit high value offenses but are influenced more than the first group by the possibility of losing their job. The recommended strategy for this group is to portray the risks of criminality and the possibility of prosecution. Theft among the third group is less common, but more complex and less easy to detect. This group is more likely to be deterred by disapproval by others. Controls that remove opportunities are less likely to be successful with this group. A more successful strategy is to remind them of the status and benefits they maintain within the company and the financial impact of offending. The fourth group represents the lowest risk but the greatest confidence of not being caught. This group is similar to the third group on other characteristics.

Physical Security Countermeasures

Integration, Open Architecture, and Convergence

The physical security strategies covered in subsequent pages are being increasingly combined into what is called integrated systems. Keener (1994: 6) offers this definition: "An **integrated system** is the control and operation by a single operator of multiple systems whose perception is that only a single system is performing all functions." These computer-based systems include access controls, alarm monitoring, CCTV, electronic article surveillance, fire protection and safety systems, HVAC, environmental monitoring, radio and video media, intercom, point-of-sale transactions, and inventory control. Traditionally, these functions existed separate from each other, but increasingly they are integrated and installed within facilities worldwide, controlled and monitored by operators and management at a centralized workstation or from remote locations.

The benefits of integrated systems include lower costs, a reduction in staff, improved efficiency, centralization, and reduced travel and time costs. For example, a manufacturing executive at corporate headquarters can monitor a branch plant's operations, production, inventory, sales, and loss prevention. Likewise, a retail executive at headquarters can watch the sales floor, special displays, point-of-sale transactions, customer behavior, inventory, shrinkage, and loss prevention. *These "visits" to worldwide locations are conducted without leaving the office!*

Integration requires careful planning and clear answers to many questions, such as the following:

- Will the integrated system truly cost less and be easier to operate and maintain than separate systems? Obtain separate quotations on integrated and interconnected systems.
- Does the supplier truly have expertise across all the applications?
- Is the integration software listed or approved by a third-party testing agency such as Underwriters Laboratories?
- Do authorities prohibit integration of certain systems? Some fire departments prohibit integrating fire alarm systems with other systems.

Robert Pearson (2000: 20) writes

> *When attending a conference or trade show, it becomes obvious that every vendor and manufacturer claims to have the "total integrated solution." It would appear that one would only need to place an order at any number of display booths and all the security problems at a user's facility would simply vanish. The vendors and manufacturers freely use terms such as integrated systems, enterprise systems and digital solutions in an effort to convince end users to purchase systems and components.*

Pearson goes on to describe a typical security alarm system as composed of sensors that connect to a data-gathering panel connected to a computer at a security control center. Integration would mean that sensors, card readers, and other functions would connect to the same data-gathering panel that reports to the same computer. Which multiple functions are integrated depends on the manufacturer. Some manufacturers began with energy management and added security alarm systems in later years; others began with security alarm systems and added access control. Pearson points out that integration is not easy to define because, for example, a question surfaces as to where separate functions come together. Different data-gathering units typically do not connect to a single computer; one reason for this is that there is no standard protocol among manufacturers' data-gathering systems. Thus, integrating functions among different manufacturers via a single computer is often challenging and produces various approaches. However, integration firms exist that specialize in application-specific software that combines systems for a specific client.

Besides *integration*, another term used loosely in the security industry is **open architecture**. It refers to the building of hardware and software whose specifications are public (Webopedia, 2006). "This includes officially approved standards as well as privately designed architectures whose specifications are made public by the designers. The opposite of open is closed or proprietary. *The great advantage of open architecture is that anyone can design add-on products for it*. By making an architecture public, however, manufacturers allow others to duplicate its product." To illustrate, *Windows* is closed and many lawsuits have been filed over clones. David Swartz (1999: 24) notes that the bottom line is that field security hardware is not interchangeable from one manufacturer to the next. As a result, most systems available today preclude the customer from (1) switching to more advanced products, (2) integrating products from other vendors, or (3) choosing the best product. However, Pearson (2001: 16) adds that if security systems used open architecture, safeguards would have to be added to prevent compromise. Today, standard operating systems, proprietary application programs, and data-gathering unit protocols that are proprietary combine to provide protection for the end user.

James Coleman (2000: 38–44) describes trends that help us to understand how physical security is developing. He sees standardizing on a common operating system, something often insisted upon by IT personnel to simplify support requirements. (This relates to the convergence of IT and physical security as discussed in Chapter 1.) Microsoft NT is the choice of many organizations. Coleman notes that every major access control manufacturer has responded to this trend by developing an NT-based product. Such products are becoming increasingly feature rich with improved performance with each new release and the capability to integrate new products, such as asset tracking. Another trend is how security devices communicate with each other. For many years, dedicated wiring has been used to connect security components. With computer networks becoming standard infrastructure in offices and plants, they are being used to connect portions of security systems.

As we know, convergence is characterized by the integrated security system residing on the organization's network. Although this trend results in IT professionals asking many questions about how security systems will affect IT systems, the benefits of convergence include monitoring from almost anywhere, lower personnel costs, and less traveling.

Dean (2005: 30) provides other examples of the benefits of convergence: with the access system on the organization's network, an employee needs only one access card to enter company facilities worldwide; and to enhance information security over documents, a card is required to be inserted into a reader attached to a printer.

Another trend, serving as a foundation for convergence, is the use of Internet Protocol (IP) technology to communicate between devices. IP-based products operate on a pre-existing network. An alternative to installing coaxial cable between system components, IP-based products can be connected to the existing LAN/WAN. *LAN* refers to local area networks that involve communication within a limited area. *WAN* refers to wide area networks for internal communication on a global scale (e.g., multinational corporate units).

Bernard (2006: 28–32) refers to another aspect of convergence known as **identity management system** (IDMS). It is used to manage identities and privileges of computer systems and people. Bernard touts the benefits of IDMS by explaining, for example, the following: "Physical security can leverage the HR enrollment of employees by integrating the physical access control system with the IDMS, so the access control privileges are managed automatically along with IT privileges as HR enrolls, re-assigns and terminates employees."

Bernard notes that the federal government is aware of the importance of IDMS in its personal identity verification systems mandated by Homeland Security Presidential Directive (HSPD) 12. This mandate points to a single smart access card to be used for both physical and IT security among federal agencies. In response to HSPD-12, the National Institute of Standards and Technology (NIST) developed a new standard for secure identification: the Federal Information Processing Standard Publication 201 (FIPS 201), Personal Identity Verification (PIV) for federal employees and contractors. Examples of two requirements are a background check of individuals applying for a card, and the card must be a smart card. Besides government, the private sector is embracing the concept.

Bernard's advice to physical security practitioners is to realize that IDMS requires much planning and coordination with IT; include physical security in the initial budget; and develop strategy, policy, and procedures in concert with IT.

Hunt (2006: 57–58) offers physical security specialists guidelines for convergence and working with the IT department:

- Connecting a security device to a network increases traffic across the network, so communicate bandwidth (i.e., communications capacity) needs to the IT department.
- When planning a new wireless access point, consider the impact on existing wireless networks.
- Ensure that physical security is part of the IT plan for backing up and restoring devices on the network.
- Since organizations take network segments offline periodically for maintenance, work with the IT department to ensure continuity of physical security.
- Read the IT manual on steps for approving changes to software or computers.
- Find out if the organization complies with IT security standards, such as Generally Accepted Information Security Principles or ISO: 17799.
- If physical security changes require entrance into a network closet, take digital before and after photos of the wiring or videotape the installation.

Access Controls

Access controls regulate people, vehicles, and items during movement into, out of, and within a building or facility. With regulation, assets are easier to protect. If a truck can enter a business facility easily, back up to the shipping dock so that the truck driver can load valuable cargo illegally, and then drive away, that business cannot last long. However, if the truck has to stop at the facility's front gate, where a uniformed officer issues a pass and records the license and other information, and appropriate paperwork is exchanged at the shipping dock under the watchful eyes of another officer who restricts the driver's access into the facility, then these controls can prevent losses.

Access controls are vital for the everyday movement of employees, customers, vendors, service people, contractors, and government inspectors. Any of these people can be someone who would steal. In addition to merchandise, proprietary information must be protected.

☐ ☐ ☐ ▬▬▬▬▬▬▬▬▬▬▬▬▬▬▬▬▬▬▬▬▬▬▬

At one corporation, a security officer permitted two salespeople from another company to enter a restricted area involved in new product development. The officer was fired.

▬▬▬▬▬▬▬▬▬▬▬▬▬▬▬▬▬▬▬▬▬▬▬ ☐ ☐ ☐

Access control varies from simple to complex. A simple setup includes locks and keys, officers checking identification badges, and written logs of entries and exits. More complex systems use an access card that, when placed at a card reader, records identifying information on the card and when access was granted, and then activates an electronic unlocking device while a CCTV system observes and records the entry. A prime factor influencing the kind of system employed is need. A research laboratory developing a new product requires strict access controls, whereas a retail business would require minimal controls.

Controlling Employee Traffic
The fewest entrances and exits are best for access control and lower costs. Officers can observe people entering and departing. If possible, employees should be routed to the entrance closest to the workplace away from valuable assets.

Unauthorized exits locked from within create a hazard in case of fire or other emergency. To ensure safety yet fewer losses, emergency exit alarms on each locked door are a worthwhile investment. These devices enable quick exit, or a short delay, when pressure is placed against a horizontal bar that is secured across the door. An alarm is sounded when these doors are activated, which discourages unauthorized use.

Searching Employees
Management can provide in the contract of employment that reasonable detentions are permissible; that reasonable searches may be made to protect people and company assets; and that searches may be made at any time of desks, lockers, containers carried by employees, and vehicles (Inbau et al., 1996: 47 and 68; Nemeth, 2005: 84). Case law has permitted an employer to use a duplicate key, known to the employee, to enter a locker at will. On the other hand, an employee who uses a personal lock has a greater expectation of privacy, barring a written condition of employment to the contrary that includes forced entry. When a desk is assigned to a specific employee, an expectation of privacy exists, unless a contract states otherwise. If employees jointly have access to a desk to obtain items, no privacy exists.

Policies and procedures on searches should consider input from management, an attorney, employees, and a union if on the premises. Also, consider business necessity, what is subject to search, signed authorization from each employee, signs at the perimeter and in the workplace, and searches of visitors and others.

☐ ☐ ☐ ▬▬▬▬▬▬▬▬▬▬▬▬▬▬

Should management and security have the right to search employees and others on the premises? Why or why not?

▬▬▬▬▬▬▬▬▬▬▬▬▬▬ ☐ ☐ ☐

Visitors
Visitors include customers, salespeople, vendors, service people, contractors, and government employees. A variety of techniques are applicable to visitor access control (Figure 7-4). An appointment system enables preparation for visitors. When visitors arrive without an appointment, the person at reception should lead him or her to a waiting room. Whatever the reason for the visit, the shortest route to specific destinations, away from valuable assets and dangerous conditions, can avert theft and injuries. Lending special equipment, such as a hardhat, may be necessary. A record or log of visits is wise. Relevant information would be name of the visitor, driver's license number and state, date of visit, time entering and leaving, purpose, specific location visited, name of employee escorting visitor, and temporary badge number. These records aid investigators. Whenever possible, procedures should minimize employee–visitor contact. This is important, for instance, in the shipping and receiving department, where truck drivers may become friendly with employees and conspiracies may evolve. When telephones, restrooms, and vending machines are scattered throughout a plant, truck drivers and other visitors who are permitted easy access may actually steal the place blind. These services should be located at the shipping and receiving dock, and access to outsiders should be limited.

FIGURE 7-4 Interactive kiosk that manages a variety of visitors. *Courtesy:* Honeywell Security.

Controlling the Movement of Packages and Property

The movement of packages and property also must be subject to access controls. Some locations require precautions against packaged bombs, letter bombs, and other hazards. Clear policies and procedures are needed for incoming and outgoing items. To counter employee theft, outgoing items require both scrutiny and accountability. Uniformed officers can check outgoing items, while a property pass system serves the accountability function.

Employee Identification System

The use of an employee identification (card or badge) system will depend on the number of employees that must be accounted for and recognized by other employees. An ID system not only prevents unauthorized people from entering a facility, but also deters unauthorized employees from entering restricted areas. For the system to operate efficiently, clear policies should state the use of ID cards, where and when the cards are to be displayed on the person, who should collect cards from employees who quit or are fired, and the penalties for noncompliance. A lost or stolen card should be reported so that the proper information reaches all interested personnel. Sometimes ID systems become a joke and employees refuse to wear the badges, or they decorate them or wear them in odd locations on their persons. To sustain an ID system, proper socialization is essential.

Simple ID cards contain employer and employee names. A more complex system would include an array of information: name, signature, address, employee number, physical characteristics (e.g., height, weight, hair and eye colors), validation date, authorized signature, location of work assignment, thumbprint, and color photo. ID cards often serve as access cards.

Contractors, visitors, and other nonemployees require an ID card that should be clearly distinguishable from employee ID cards. Temporary ID badges can be printed with a chemical that causes the word *void* to appear after a set period.

Lamination discourages card tampering: if an attempt is made to alter the card, it will be disfigured. To laminate a card, a paper ID card is inserted into a plastic case and then placed in a laminating machine that bonds a clear plastic coating over the card.

Pearson (2005: 66) offers anticounterfeiting measures that include the following: holograms that are added to the clear overlay of the printed badge; ultraviolet printing that uses an ultraviolet ribbon to print UV-sensitive images or text and requires a black light to see it; invisible alphanumeric type viewed only by a laser; and secret symbols or letters on the badge.

The area where ID cards are prepared, and relevant equipment and supplies, must be secure. In addition, the equipment and software should be password protected.

Automatic Access Control

The Security Industry Association traces the development of access control systems as described next (D'Agostino, 2005: 1–2). Traditionally, access control systems have been at the center of electronic security systems at buildings that include access control, ID badges, alarm systems, and CCTV. **Authentication** (i.e., verifying identity) and **authorization** (i.e., verifying that the identified individual is allowed to enter) have typically occurred as a single-step process in access control. Depending on security needs, access control has been designed for 1-factor authentication (e.g., card or personal identification number or biometric), 2-factor authentication (e.g., card-plus-PIN or card-plus-biometric), or 3-factor authentication (e.g., card-plus-PIN and biometric).

Cryptography (i.e., the study of coded or secret writings to provide security for information) became part of access control systems with the use of **encryption** (i.e., hardware or software that scrambles data, rendering it unintelligible to an unauthorized person intercepting it) to protect passwords and other information. These methods continue in importance as Ethernet networks (i.e., a trademark for a system of communications between computers on a LAN) replace proprietary equipment connections and as security systems increasingly rely on IP messages and shared networks with other businesses. Traditionally, because no security standards existed for these systems, manufacturers applied their own designs. However, according to the Security Industry Association, change is required to establish standards because of the following drivers:

- The convergence of physical and IT security
- **Common user provisioning** that permits a single point of employee registration and dismissal (usually in a human resources system) with assignment of physical and IT privileges
- Large customers (e.g., the federal government) require their facilities to be **interoperable** (i.e., products or systems working with other products or systems)
- Enterprisewide access controls that involve technology and business processes and procedures enabling a single credential to be used across the boundaries of an enterprise (e.g., the federal government Personal Identity Verification program)
- **Digital certificate systems,** which are the electronic counterparts to driver licenses and other ID, are used to sign electronic information and serve as part of the foundation of secure e-commerce on the Web, and are essential for physical access control system integration with IT

The traditional lock-and-key method of access control has its limitations. For instance, keys are difficult to control and easy to duplicate. Because of these problems, the need for improved access control, and technological innovations, a huge market has been created for electronic card access control systems. These systems contain wired and wireless components. The benefits of these systems include the difficulty of duplicating cards and cost savings because security officers are not required at each access point. The card contains coded information "read" by the system for access or denial. These systems contain a central control enabling a variety of functions such as enrollment of ID and cards, monitoring of entry points and readers, logging of access and egress events, and voiding of lost or stolen cards. Stand-alone systems use battery power and are easy to install because there is no need for a power line or transmission of data, although the data collected at the lock can be gathered via a touring security officer or a wireless system.

Before an automatic access control system is implemented, several considerations are necessary. *Safety must be a prime factor to ensure quick exit in case of emergency.* Another consideration deals with the adaptability of the system to the type of door presently in use. Can the system accommodate all traffic requirements? How many entrances and exits must be controlled? Will there be an annoying waiting period for those who want to gain access? Are additions to the system possible? What if the system breaks down? Is a backup source of power available (e.g., generators)?

Tailgating and pass back are other concerns. **Tailgating** means an authorized user is followed by an unauthorized user. To thwart this problem, a security officer can be assigned to each access point, but this approach is expensive when compared to applying CCTV, revolving doors, and turnstiles. Revolving doors can be expensive initially, and they are not an approved fire exit. Optical turnstiles contain invisible infrared beams to count people entering and leaving to control tailgating and pass back. These sensors can be installed in a doorframe and connected to an alarm system and CCTV. **Pass back** refers to one person passing an opening and then passing back the credential so another person can pass through the opening.

A summary of cards used in card access systems follows:

- *Smart cards* contain an integrated circuit chip within the plastic that serves as a miniature computer as it records and stores information and personal identification codes in its large memory. Security is increased because information is held in the card, rather than the reader. These cards permit a host of activities from access control to making purchases, while almost eliminating the need for keys or cash. This type of card is growing in popularity as its applications expand.
- *Proximity cards* (also referred to as RFID) need not be inserted into a reader but placed in its "proximity." A code is sent via radio frequency, magnetic field, or microchip-tuned circuit. This card is in wide use today.
- *Contact Memory Buttons* are stainless steel buttons that protect an enclosed computer chip used for access. The information in the button can be downloaded or updated with a reader like other systems. These buttons are known for their durability, serve to ensure accountability of security officers on patrol, and are applied as an asset tag. The buttons are used widely.
- *Magnetic stripe cards* are plastic, laminated cards (like credit cards) that have a magnetic stripe along one edge onto which a code is printed. When the card is inserted, the magnetically encoded data are compared to data stored in a computer and access is granted on verification. This card is in wide use today.
- *Weigand cards* employ a coded pattern on a magnetized wire within the card to generate a code number. To gain access, the card is passed through a sensing reader. Other technologies have reduced the popularity of this type of card.
- *Bar-coded cards* contain an array of tiny vertical lines that can be visible and vulnerable to photocopying, or invisible and read by an infrared reader. Other technologies have reduced the popularity of this type of card.
- *Magnetic dot cards* contain magnetic material, often barium ferrite, laminated between plastic layers. The dots create a magnetic pattern that activates internal sensors in a card reader. This card is rarely used.

Access card systems vary in terms of advantages, disadvantages, and costs. Each type of card can be duplicated with a sufficient amount of knowledge, time, and equipment. A magnetic stripe is easy to duplicate. A piece of cardboard with a properly encoded magnetic stripe functions with equal efficiency. Magnetic dot cards are vulnerable to deciphering. Although bar-coded cards also are easy to duplicate, they can be made more secure by covering the code with an opaque patch, which prevents photocopying. Many software programs are available that can generate bar codes, so fully concealing the code adds more security. Weigand and proximity cards are more difficult to duplicate but higher in cost. The Weigand card has the disadvantage of wear and tear on the card that passes through a slot for access. Proximity cards have the advantage of the sensing element being concealed in a wall, and the card typically can be read without removing it from a pocket. Smart cards are expensive, but they can be combined with other card systems; also, they are convenient because of the capability of loading and updating the card applications over the Web (Barry, 1993: 75; Garcia, 2006: 156–157; Gersh, 2000: 18; Toye, 1996: 23).

Biometric security systems have been praised as a major advance in access control because such systems link the event to a particular individual, whereas a key, card, personal identification number (PIN), or password may be used by an unauthorized individual. These systems verify an individual's identity through fingerprint scan, hand scan (hand geometry) (see Figure 7-5), iris scan (the iris is the colored part around the pupil of the eye), retina scan (the retina is the sensory membrane lining the eye and receiving the image formed by the lens), voice patterns, physical action of writing, and facial scan. The biometric leaders are fingerprint, hand, iris, and face recognition (Piazza, 2005: 41–55). Research continues to improve biometrics. Voice and writing are being refined, and research is being conducted on gait, body odor, heartbeat, and inner ear bones. In the near term, we will not see facial scan pick a known terrorist out of a crowd, but the technology is evolving. Digitized photos shot at angles or in poor light can be flawed. The challenge with facial scan is identifying a person on the move (Philpott, 2005: 16–21).

Basically, biometric systems operate by storing identifying information (e.g., fingerprints, photos) in a computer to be compared with information presented by a subject requesting access. The applications are endless: doors, computers, vehicles, and so on. Although biometric systems have been touted as being invincible, no security is foolproof, as illustrated by terrorists who cut off the thumb of a bank manager to gain entry through a fingerprint-based access control system. In addition, researchers have constructed fake fingers by taking casts of real fingers and molding them into Play-Doh. The researchers developed a technique to check for moisture as a way to reduce this ploy (Aughton, 2005). Harowitz (2007: 48–50) writes that a biometric fingerprint system may also be subject to defeat by using a fingerprint from dusting a latent print with graphite powder and covering it with fingerprint tape. Again, checking for moisture reduces this problem. She also writes that although iris recognition systems are less likely to be spoofed than biometric fingerprint systems, "iris recognition systems have been spoofed with high-resolution photographs with an eyehole cut for the pupil and custom contact lenses with high-resolution iris patterns printed on them." Research is being conducted to find vulnerabilities in biometric systems and correct them.

Access controls often use multiple technologies, such as smart card and biometrics. One location may require a card and a PIN (see Figure 7-6), whereas another requires scanning a

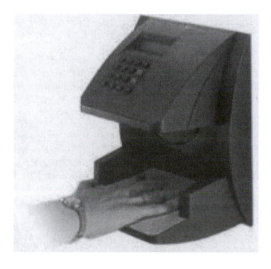

FIGURE 7-5 Verifying identity through hand geometry. *Courtesy:* HID Corporation.

FIGURE 7-6 Card reader and key pad. *Courtesy:* Diebold, Inc.

finger and a PIN. Many systems feature a distress code that can be entered if someone is being victimized. Another feature is an alarm that sounds during unauthorized attempted entry. Access systems can be programmed to allow select access according to time, day, and location. The logging capabilities are another feature to ascertain personnel location by time, date, and the resources expended (e.g., computer time, parking space, cafeteria). These features provide information during investigations and emergencies.

We are seeing an increasing merger of card access systems and biometric technology, and thus, missing or stolen cards are less of a concern. We will see more point-of-sale readers that accept biometric samples for check cashing, credit cards, and other transactions. The use of biometric systems will become universal—banking, correctional facilities, welfare control programs, and so forth.

Locks and Keys

The basic purpose of a lock-and-key system is to hinder unauthorized entry. Attempts to enter a secure location usually are made at a window or door to a building or at a door somewhere within a building. Consequently, locks deter unauthorized access from outsiders and insiders. *Many see a lock only as a delaying device that is valued by the amount of time needed to defeat it.* Zunkel (2003: 32) notes: "... it is important that designers know that a lock by itself is only part of a larger system that includes the door, the wall, the perimeter and a security plan."

Standards related to locking systems include those from American National Standards Institute (ANSI), American Society for Testing and Materials (ASTM), Underwriters Laboratories (UL), and the Builders Hardware Manufacturers Association (BHMA). Local ordinances may specify requirements for locks.

Two general ways to classify locks are mechanical and electromechanical. **Mechanical locks** include the common keyed lock and the pushbutton lock that contains a keypad to enter an access code to release the lock. **Electromechanical locks** include an electronic keypad that is connected to an electric strike, lock, or magnetic lock. When the access code is entered, the strike or lock is released to open the door (Department of Defense, 2000: D-5).

There are many types of locks and locking systems that range from those that use simple, ancient methods to those that apply modern technology, including electricity, computers, and wireless components. Here, we begin with basic information as a foundation for understanding locks. Locking devices are often operated by a key, numerical combination, card, or electricity. Many locks (except padlocks) use a deadbolt and latch. The **deadbolt** (or bolt) extends from a door lock into a bolt receptacle within the doorframe. Authorized entry is made by using an appropriate key to manually move the bolt into the door lock. **Latches** are spring loaded and less secure than a deadbolt. They are cut on an angle to permit them to slide right into the strike when the door is closed (see Figure 7-7). Unless the latch is equipped with a locking bar (deadlatch), a knife can possibly be used to push the latch back to open the door.

The **cylinder** part of a lock contains the keyway, pins, and other mechanisms that permit the deadbolt or latch to be moved by a key for access (see Figure 7-8). Double-cylinder locks, in which a cylinder is located on each side of a door, are a popular form of added security as compared to single-cylinder locks. *Double-cylinder locks require a key for both sides; however, fire codes may prohibit such locks.* With a single-cylinder lock, a thief may be able to break glass or remove a wood panel and then reach inside to turn the knob to release the lock. For safety's sake, locations that use double-cylinder locks must prepare for emergency escape by having a key readily available.

Key-in-knob locks are used universally but are being replaced by key-in-the-lever locks (see Figure 7-9) to be ADA compliant. As the name implies, the keyway is in the knob or lever. Most contain a keyway on the outside and a button on the inside for locking from within.

Entrances for Handicapped

The Internal Revenue Service offers a tax credit to eligible businesses that comply with provisions of the ADA to remove barriers and promote access for individuals with disabilities. The door hardware industry offers several products and solutions to aid the disabled (see Figure 7-10). Electrified door hardware such as magnetic locks and electromechanical locks retracts the latch when energized.

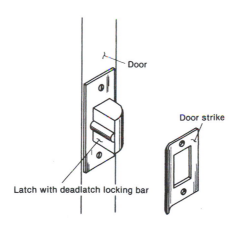

FIGURE 7-7 Latch and door strike.

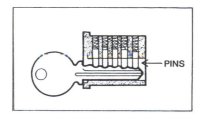

FIGURE 7-8 Cylinder.

FIGURE 7-9 Mechanical lock with lever requiring no wiring, electronics, or batteries. *Courtesy:* Ilco Unican.

Lever trim reduces force required to unlatch a door.

Push/Pull Latch

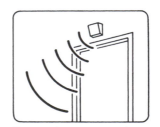

Push/Pull latches are popular on institutional doors because of ease of operation.

Proximity Card

Proximity card reader requires only close presence of the user's card to activate door's automatic opener.

Presence detectors are popular with automatic exit doors and require no physical action.

FIGURE 7-10 Entrances for handicapped. *Courtesy:* Von Duprin Division of Ingersoll-Rand Company.

Attacks and Hardware

There are several ways to attack locks. One technique, as stated earlier, is to force a knife between the doorframe (jamb) and the door near the lock to release the latch. However, when a deadlatch or deadbolt is part of the locking mechanism, more forceful methods are needed. In one method, called "springing the door," a screwdriver or crowbar is placed between the door and the doorframe so that the bolt extending from the door lock into the bolt receptacle can be pried out, enabling the door to swing open (see Figure 7-11). A 1-inch bolt will hinder this attack.

In "jamb peeling," another method of attack, a crowbar is used to peel at the doorframe near the bolt receptacle so that the door is not stopped from swinging open. Strong hardware for the doorframe is helpful. In "sawing the bolt," a hacksaw is applied between the door and the doorframe, similar to the placement of the screwdriver in Figure 7-11. Here again, strong hardware, such as a metal bolt composed of an alloy capable of withstanding a saw blade, will impede attacks. Some offenders use the cylinder-pulling technique: the cylinder on the door is actually ripped out with a set of durable pliers or tongs. A circular steel guard surrounding the cylinder (see Figure 7-11) will frustrate the attacker. Offenders also are known to use automobile jacks to pressure doorframes away from a door.

Both high-quality hardware and construction will impede attacks, but the door itself must not be forgotten. If a wood door is only 1/4-inch thick, even though a strong lock is attached, the offender may simply break through the door. A solid wood door 1 3/4 inches thick or a metal door is a worthwhile investment. Wood doorframes at least 2 inches thick provide durable protection. When a hollow steel frame is used, the hollow area can be filled with cement to resist crushing near the bolt receptacle. An L-shaped piece of iron secured with one-way screws will deter attacks near the bolt receptacle for doors swinging in (see Figure 7-12). When a padlock is used in conjunction with a safety hasp, the hasp must be installed correctly so that the screws are not exposed (see Figure 7-13).

Many attacks are by forced entry, which is easier to detect than when the use of force is minimal. Lock picking is one technique needing a minimum amount of force. It is used infrequently because of the expertise required, although picks are available on the Internet. **Lock picking** is accomplished by inserting a tension wrench (an L-shaped piece of metal) into the cylinder and applying tension while using metal picks to align the pins in the cylinder as a key would to release the lock (see Figure 7-8). The greater the number of pins, the more difficult it is to align them. A cylinder should have at least six pins.

A more difficult attack utilizes a blank key, matches, and a file. The blank key is placed over a lighted match until carbon is produced on the key. Then the key is inserted into the cylinder. The locations where the pins have scraped away the carbon signify where to file. Needless to say, this method is time-consuming and calls for repeated trials. Offenders sometimes covertly

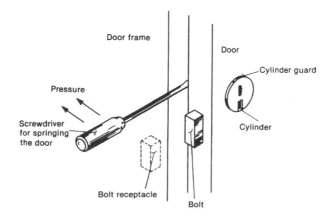

FIGURE 7-11 Deadbolt and door frame.

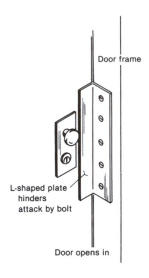

FIGURE 7-12 L-shaped plate.

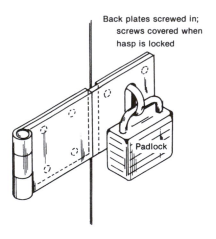

FIGURE 7-13 Safety hasp.

borrow a key, quickly press it into a bar of soap or wax, return the key, and then file a copy on a blank key. This method illustrates the importance of key control.

After gaining access, an offender may employ some tricks to make sure nobody enters while he or she is busy. This is accomplished, for instance, by inserting a pin or obstacle in the keyway and locking the door from the inside.

Whatever hardware is used, the longer it takes to attack a lock, the greater is the danger for the offender. Six or more pins and pick-resistant, impression-resistant cylinders inhibit unauthorized access. One further point: most burglary insurance policies state that there must be visible signs of forced entry to support a claim.

Other methods of entry may be used by offenders. A thief may simply use a stolen key or a key (or access card) borrowed from another person. Unfortunately, intruders often enter restricted areas because somebody forgot to use a locking device. This mistake renders the most complex locks useless.

The methods of defeating lock-and-key systems do not stop here. Innovative thieves and various kinds of locks, keys, and access systems create a hodgepodge of methods that loss prevention practitioners should understand.

Types of Locks

Volumes have been written about locks. The following briefly summarizes simple and more complex locks:

- *Warded (or skeleton key tumbler) lock:* This older kind of lock is disengaged when a skeleton key makes direct contact with a bolt and slides it back into the door. It is an easy lock to pick. A strong piece of L-shaped metal can be inserted into the keyway to move the bolt. Warded locks are in use in older buildings and are recognized by a keyway that permits seeing through. Locks on handcuffs are of the warded kind and can be defeated by a knowledgeable offender.

- *Disc tumbler (or wafer tumbler) lock:* The use of this lock, originally designed for the automobile industry, has expanded to desks, cabinets, files, and padlocks. Its operation entails spring-loaded flat metal discs, instead of pins, that align when the proper key is used. These locks are mass produced, inexpensive, and have a short life expectancy. More security is offered than warded locks can provide, but disc tumbler locks are subject to defeat by improper keys or being jimmied.

- *Pin tumbler lock:* Invented by Linus Yale in 1844, the pin tumbler lock is used widely in industry and residences (see Figure 7-8). Its security surpasses that of the warded and disc tumbler kinds.

- *Lever lock:* Lever locks vary widely. Basically, these locks disengage when tumblers are aligned by the proper key. Those found in cabinets, chests, and desks often provide minimal security, whereas those found in bank safe deposit boxes are more complex and provide greater security. The better quality lever lock offers more security than the best pin tumbler lock.

- *Combination lock:* This lock requires manipulating a numbered dial(s) to gain access. Combination locks usually have three or four dials that must be aligned in the correct order for entrance. These locks provide greater security than key locks because a limited number of people probably will know the lock combination, keys are unnecessary, and lock picking is obviated. They are used for safes, bank vaults, and high-security filing cabinets. With older combination locks, skillful burglars are able actually to listen to the locking mechanism to open the lock; more advanced mechanisms have reduced this weakness. A serious vulnerability results when an offender watches the opening of a combination lock with either binoculars or a telescope. Retailers sometimes place combination safes near the front door for viewing by patrolling police; however, unless the retailer uses his or her body to block the dial from viewing, losses may result. This same weakness exists where access is permitted by typing a secret code into a keyboard for access to a parking lot, doorway, or secure area.

- *Combination padlock:* This lock is similar in operation to a combination lock. It is used on employee or student lockers and in conjunction with safety hasps or chains. Some of these locks have a keyway so they can be opened with a key.

- *Padlock:* Requiring a key, this lock is used on lockers or in conjunction with hasps or chains. Numerous kinds of construction are possible, each affording differing levels of protection. Low-security padlocks contain warded locks, whereas more secure ones have disc tumbler, pin tumbler, or lever characteristics. Serial numbers on padlocks are a security hazard similar to combination padlocks.

Other kinds of locks include devices that have a bolt that locks vertically instead of horizontally. Emergency exit locks with alarms or "panic alarms" enable quick exit in emergencies while deterring unauthorized door use. Sequence locking devices require locking the doors in a predetermined order; this ensures that all doors are locked because the outer doors will not lock until the inner doors are locked.

The use of interchangeable core locks is a method to deal with the theft, duplication, or loss of keys. Using a special control key, one core (that part containing the keyway) is simply replaced by another. A different key then is needed to operate the lock. This system, although more expensive initially, minimizes the need for a locksmith or the complete changing of locks.

Automatic locking and unlocking devices also are a part of the broad spectrum of methods to control access. Digital locking systems open doors when a particular numbered combination is typed. If the wrong number is typed, an alarm is sounded. Combinations can be changed when necessary. Electromagnetic locks use magnetism, electricity, and a metal plate around doors to hold doors closed. When the electricity is turned off, the door can be opened. Remote locks enable opening a door electronically from a remote location. Before releasing the door lock, an officer seated in front of a console identifies an individual at a door by use of CCTV and a two-way intercom. Backup power is essential for these systems.

Trends taking place with locks and keys include increasing use of electronics and microchip technology. For example, hybrids have been developed whereby a key can serve as a standard hardware key in one door and an electronic key in another door. "Smart locks" have grown in popularity. These locks combine traditional locks with electronic access control; read various types of access cards for access; use a tiny computer to perform multiple functions, including holding data (e.g., access events); and can be connected to an access control system for uploading and downloading data. Most contain a tiny battery; others are connected to a power supply.

Wireless locking systems and RF online locking systems make use of modern technology, although care must be exercised in the evaluation and purchasing process. A pilot project helps to ensure reliability. Signals are hindered by metallic materials (e.g., steel buildings). These systems avoid the use of wire between the lock and the access control panel. Since these locks are battery operated, a backup power source is essential. In one case, during an emergency, the locks of a building became useless when the battery power in the locks ran out. The American National Standards Institute (ANSI) and Underwriters Laboratories (UL) offer standards for locks that are followed by manufacturers.

☐ ☐ ☐ ▬▬▬▬▬▬▬▬▬▬▬▬▬▬▬▬▬▬▬▬▬▬▬▬▬▬

Although card access systems are used universally, locks and keys are still used to protect a variety of assets.

▬▬▬▬▬▬▬▬▬▬▬▬▬▬▬▬▬▬▬▬▬▬▬▬▬▬ ☐ ☐ ☐

Master Key Systems

In most instances, a lock accepts only one key that has been cut to fit it. A lock that has been altered to permit access by two or more keys has been *master keyed*. The **master key system** allows a number of locks to be opened by the master key. This system should be confined to high-quality hardware utilizing pin tumbler locks. A disadvantage of the master key system is that if the master key is lost or stolen, security is compromised. A *change key* fits one lock. A *submaster key* will open all locks in, for instance, a wing of a building. The master key opens locks covered by two or more submaster systems.

Key Control

Without adequate key control, locks are useless and losses are likely to climb. Accountability and proper records are necessary, as with access cards. Computerized record-keeping programs are available for key control. Keys should be marked with a code to identify the corresponding lock; the code is interpreted via a record stored in a safe place. A key should never be marked, "Key for room XYZ." When not in use, keys should be positioned on hooks in a locked key cabinet or vault. The name of the employee, date, and key code are vital records to maintain when a key is issued. These records require continuous updating. Employee turnover is one reason why precise records are vital. Departing employees will return keys (and other valuables) if their final paycheck is withheld. Policies should state that reporting a lost key would not result in punitive action; an investigation and a report will strengthen key control. If key audits check periodically who has what key, control is further reinforced. To hinder duplication of keys, "do not duplicate" may be stamped on keys, and company policy can clearly state that key duplication will result in dismissal. Lock changes are wise every eight months and sometimes at shorter intervals on an irregular basis. Key control also is important for vehicles such as autos, trucks, and forklifts. These challenges and vulnerabilities of traditional lock and key systems have influenced organizations in switching to modern access control and biometric systems.

□ □ □ ▬▬▬▬▬▬▬▬▬▬▬▬▬▬▬▬▬▬▬▬▬▬▬▬▬▬▬▬▬

As a security manager, how do you solve the following problem? Because of employees who quit, were laid off, or fired, many keys are not being returned and remaining employees are expressing concern about their safety.

▬▬▬▬▬▬▬▬▬▬▬▬▬▬▬▬▬▬▬▬▬▬▬▬▬▬▬▬▬ □ □ □

Intrusion Detection Systems

An **intrusion detection system** detects and reports an event or stimulus within its detection area. A response to resolve the reported problem is essential. The emphasis here is on interior sensors. Sensors appropriate for perimeter protection are stressed in Chapter 8.

What are the basic components of an intrusion detection system? Three fundamental components are sensor, control unit, and annunciator. **Sensors** detect intrusion by, for example, heat or movement of a human. The **control unit** receives the alarm notification from the sensor and then activates a silent alarm or **annunciator** (e.g., a light or siren), which usually produces a human response. There are a variety of intrusion detection systems, and they can be wired or wireless. Several standards exist for intrusion detection systems from UL, ISO, the Institute of Electrical and Electronics Engineers, and other groups. Types of interior sensors are explained next (Garcia, 2006: 104–122; Honey, 2003: 48–94).

Interior Sensors

A *balanced magnetic switch* consists of a switch mounted to a door (or window) frame and a magnet mounted to a moveable door or window. When the door is closed, the magnet holds the switch closed to complete a circuit. An alarm is triggered when the door is opened and the circuit is interrupted. An ordinary magnetic switch is similar to the balanced type, except that it is simpler, is less expensive, and provides a lower level of security. Switches provide good protection against opening a door; however, an offender may cut through a door or glass. (Chapter 8 provides illustrations of switch sensors.)

Mechanical contact switches contain a pushbutton-actuated switch that is recessed into a surface. An item is placed on it that depresses the switch, completing the alarm circuit. Lifting the item interrupts the circuit and signals an alarm.

Pressure-sensitive mats contain two layers of metal strips or screen wire separated by sections of foam rubber or other flexible material. When pressure is applied, as by a person walking on the mat, both layers meet and complete an electrical contact to signal an alarm. These mats are applied as internal traps at doors, windows, and main traffic points, as well as near valuable assets. The cost is low, and these mats are difficult to detect. If the mat is detected by the offender, he or she can walk around it.

Grid wire sensors are made of fine insulated wire attached to protected surfaces in a grid pattern consisting of two circuits, one running vertical, the other horizontal, and each overlapping the other. An interruption in either circuit signals an alarm. This type of sensor is applied to grill work, screens, walls, floors, ceilings, doors, and other locations. Although these sensors are difficult for an offender to spot, they are expensive to install, and an offender can jump the circuit.

Trip wire sensors use a spring-loaded switch attached to a wire stretched across a protected area. An intruder "trips" the alarm (i.e., opens the circuit) when the wire is pulled loose from the switch. These sensors are often applied to ducts but can be applied to other locations. If the sensor is spotted by an offender, he or she may be able to circumvent it.

Vibration sensors detect low-frequency energy resulting from the force applied in an attack on a structure (see Figure 7-14). These sensors are applied to walls, floors, and ceilings. Various sensor models require proper selection.

Capacitance sensors create an electrical field around metallic objects that, when disturbed, signals an alarm (see Figure 7-15). These sensors are applied to safes, file cabinets, grills at openings (e.g., windows), and other metal objects. One sensor can protect many objects; however, it is subject to defeat by using insulation (e.g., heavy gloves).

Infrared photoelectric beam sensors activate an alarm when an invisible infrared beam of light is interrupted (see Figure 7-16). If the system is detected, an offender may jump over or crawl under the beam to defeat it. To reduce this vulnerability, tower enclosures can be used to stack sensors.

Ultrasonic motion detectors create a pattern of inaudible sound waves that are transmitted into an area and monitored by a receiver. These detectors operate on the *Doppler effect*, which is the change in frequency that results from the motion of an intruder. These detectors are installed on walls or ceilings or used covertly (i.e., disguised within another object). They are subject to nuisance alarms from high-pitched noises or air currents and can be defeated by objects blocking the sensor or by fast or slow movement. The use of this detector is limited because of false alarms.

Microwave motion detectors operate on the Doppler frequency-shift principle. An energy field is transmitted into an area and monitored for a change in its pattern and frequency, which results in an alarm. Because microwave energy penetrates a variety of construction materials, care is required for placement and aiming. However, this can be an advantage in protecting multiple rooms and large areas with one sensor. These sensors can be defeated (like ultrasonic ones) by objects blocking the sensor or by fast or slow movement.

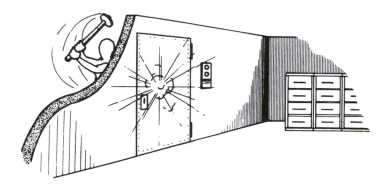

FIGURE 7-14 Vibration sensor.

FIGURE 7-15 Capacitance sensor.

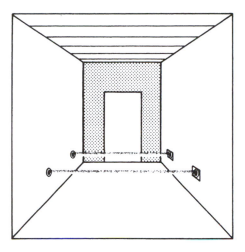

FIGURE 7-16 Infrared photoelectric beam system.

Passive infrared (PIR) intrusion sensors are passive in that they do not transmit a signal for an intruder to disturb. Rather, moving infrared radiation (from a person) is detected against the radiation environment of a room. When an intruder enters the room, the level of infrared energy changes, and an alarm is activated. Although the PIR is not subject to as many nuisance alarms as ultrasonic and microwave detectors, it should not be aimed at sources of heat or surfaces that can reflect energy. The PIR can be defeated by blocking the sensor so it cannot pick up heat.

Passive audio detectors listen for noise created by intruders. Various models filter out naturally occurring noises not indicating forced entry. These detectors can use public address system speakers in buildings, which can act as microphones to listen to intruders. The actual conversation of intruders can be picked up and recorded by these systems. To enhance this system, CCTV can provide visual verification of an alarm condition, video in real time, and still images digitally to security or police, and evidence. The audio also can be two-way, enabling security to warn the intruders. *Such audiovisual systems must be applied with extreme care to protect privacy, confidentiality, and sensitive information, and to avoid violating state and federal wiretapping and electronic surveillance laws.*

Fiber optics is used for intrusion detection and for transmission of alarm signals. It involves the transportation of information via guided light waves in an optical fiber. This sensor can be attached to or inserted in many things requiring protection. When stress is applied to the fiber optic cable, an infrared light pulsing through the cable reacts to the stress and signals an alarm.

Intrusion detection systems only detect and report an alarm condition. These systems do not stop or apprehend an intruder.

Trends

Two types of sensor technologies often are applied to a location to reduce false alarms, prevent defeat techniques, or fill unique needs. The combination of microwave and passive infrared sensors is a popular example of applying **dual technologies** (see Figure 7-17). Reporting can be

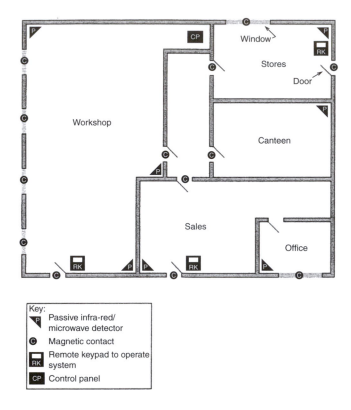

FIGURE 7-17 Commercial intrusion alarm system.

designed so an alarm is signaled when both sensors detect an intrusion (to reduce false alarms) or when either sensor detects an intrusion. Sensors are also becoming "smarter" by sending sensor data to a control panel or computer, distinguishing between humans and animals, and activating a trouble output if the sensor lens is blocked. *Supervised wireless sensors* have become a major advancement because sensors can be placed at the best location without the expense of running a wire; these sensors are constantly monitored for integrity of the radio frequency link between the sensor and panel, status of the battery, and whether the sensor is functioning normally (Garcia, 2006: 104; O'Leary, 1999: 36–48).

Operational Zoning

Operational zoning means that the building being protected has a segmented alarm system, whereby the alarm can be turned on and off within particular zones depending on usage. For example, if an early morning cleaning crew is in the north end of a plant, then that alarm is turned off while other zones still have the alarm on. Furthermore, zoning helps to pinpoint where an intrusion has occurred.

Alarm Monitoring

Today, many entities have an alarm system that is monitored by an in-house station (e.g., a console at a secure location) or from a central station (contract service) located off the premises. These services easily can supply reports of unusual openings and closings, as well as those of the regular routine. Chapter 8 covers alarm signaling systems.

Closed-Circuit Television

Closed-circuit television, or CCTV (see Figure 7-18), assists in deterrence, surveillance, apprehension, and prosecution. This technology is also helpful in civil cases to protect an

FIGURE 7-18 Closed-circuit television (CCTV) sign. Camera at top.

organization's interests. The applications go beyond security and justice. For instance, CCTV can serve as a tool to understand production problems or customer behavior. Although it may be costly initially, CCTV reduces personnel costs because it allows the viewing of multiple locations by one person. For instance, throughout a manufacturing plant, multiple cameras are installed, and one security officer in front of a console monitors the cameras. Accessories include pan (i.e., side-to-side movement), tilt (i.e., up-and-down movement), and zoom lenses, referred to as "PTZ" in the industry, which are mechanisms that permit viewing mobility and opportunities to obtain a close look at suspicious activity. Additional system capabilities include recording incidents and viewing when limited light is present. Modern technology has greatly altered CCTV capabilities, as described in subsequent paragraphs.

Standards for CCTV systems are from several sources. These include ANSI, SIA, National Electrical Manufacturers Association, American Public Transportation Association, government agencies, ISO/International Electrotechnical Commission, and the International Code Council. England and Australia are especially active preparing CCTV standards.

During the 1950s, CCTV began its development. The traditional CCTV system that came into greater use in the 1970s consisted of analog recording systems, solid-state cameras, and coaxial cable (Siemon Company, 2003; Suttell, 2006: 114). This older technology applied multiple cameras connected through cabling to a camera control unit and a multiplexer that fed several videocassette recorders (VCR) in a central control room. The images were viewed real time via several monitors. The disadvantages of this technology include the following: the control room is a single point of failure within the security infrastructure; if a camera is moved, cable is required for the connection; the use of VCRs results in numerous cassette tapes requiring storage space; and humans are necessary to change and store tapes.

Older technology, such as the VCR that could record for a limited number of hours, was followed by time-lapse recorders (i.e., single frames of video are stored at intervals over an extended period of time) with recording capabilities up to several hundred hours, plus an alarm mode in which the recorder reverts to real time when an alarm condition exists. Real-time setting records 30 frames a second; time-lapse video may record between one frame a second and one frame every eight seconds. Time-lapse recorder features included a quick search for alarm conditions during playback, the playing of recorded video frames according to the input of time by the user, and the interface with other security systems such as access controls to ensure a video record of all people entering and departing.

Advances in technology have improved the capabilities of CCTV systems. A new generation CCTV system developed with unshielded twisted-pair (UTP) cabling (i.e., a cable with multiple pairs of twisted insulated copper conductors in a single sheath) that enabled cameras to run on the existing infrastructure. **Digital video recorders** (DVR) were introduced in the mid-1990s, and with them, several advantages over analog, including recording on hard disk drives like a file is stored on a personal computer. Other advantages are avoiding tape storage, remote viewing, easy playback and searches, improved quality of images, and longer life of recordings. Another advance is digital recording in networking, which is referred to as **network video recorder** (NVR). Rather than many DVRs networked together, an NVR is the camera system. An NVR is digital cameras managed by specially designed computer operating software designed to manage video surveillance (Alten, 2005: 8).

Internet protocol (IP)-based network cameras permit IP networking of video to be shared where the network reaches, including offsite storage. IP video can be controlled and viewed from a PDA, phone, laptop computer, or other mobile device. It is also encrypted. IP-based CCTV systems, including IP cameras, IP video servers, and IP keyboards, can be located almost anywhere. In addition, the IP keyboard can control the PTZ and other management functions such as recording and searching. When the existing infrastructure in a building is used, a building can become automated on one cable system and include not only CCTV, but also access control, fire/safety systems, voice, network traffic, and other systems.

It is important to distinguish between the older **analog technology** and the newer **digital technology**. Analog signals are used in their original form and placed, for example, on a tape. Most earlier electronic devices use the analog format (e.g., televisions, record players, cassette tape recorders, and telephones). Analog technology is still applied today. With digital technology, the analog signals are sampled numerous times and turned into numbers and stored in a digital system. Today, many devices contain digital technology (e.g., high-definition TV, CDs, fiber-optic telephone lines, and digital telephones).

Even with the shift to IP-based network systems for CCTV, video is still transmitted over coaxial cable, twisted pair wire, fiber-optic cable, microwave, radio frequency, and telephone lines. What we have is the opportunity (as with other electronic security systems) for, say, an executive in New York to monitor inside a business in Hong Kong.

Wireless video transmission (e.g., RF or microwave) is an option under certain circumstances. Examples include flexible deployment whereby cameras must be moved periodically (e.g., changing exhibition hall), covert surveillance requiring quick and easy installation, at emergency sites, and historical buildings where a cable route is not possible. Careful planning is required prior to the installation of transmitters and receivers to prevent the radio signal from being blocked. *Line of sight* is an important issue. Interference can result from environmental conditions such as metallic buildings, aluminum siding, solar flares, lightning, heavy rain, snow, and high wind (Chan, 2005: 46–48).

When IT personnel are approached about including CCTV on a network, they are often concerned about how much bandwidth the video will use. To allay fears, one option at a multibuilding facility is to maintain a DVR at every building for storage of video so all video is not transmitted to the central computer.

For those end users using traditional analog technology while moving toward an IP-based retrofit, options include using "hybrid" products that accommodate both analog and IP-based signals. Lasky (2006: 38) advises against a full IP retrofit at this time because there are too many variables that are not standardized with IP cameras, a major one being the amount of bandwidth required on a network with numerous IP cameras.

Organizations that employ CCTV systems may consider streaming video surveillance from remote sites to regional centers. Although this approach can be challenging, it can also reduce plant and personnel costs. A key factor in this decision is compression because bandwidth limitations affect the amount of video that can be exchanged between transmitting and receiving sites. Similar to a roadway tunnel, only a certain number of vehicles can enter the tunnel at any one time. However, if the vehicles are made smaller, more can fit. **Compression** is the amount of redundant video that can be stripped out of an image before storage and transmission, and there are various compression techniques (Mellos, 2005: 34).

Another concern, as physical security personnel increasingly rely on a network, is access to the network for a variety of security-related information. In this case, the IT personnel have the option of placing such security information on a subnet to prevent access to the whole network.

Changing technology has brought about the **charged coupled device (CCD) or "chip" camera**, a small, photosensitive unit designed to replace the tube in the closed-circuit camera. CCD technology is found in camcorders. CCD cameras have certain advantages over tube cameras: CCD cameras are more adaptable to a variety of circumstances, they have a longer life expectancy, "ghosting" (i.e., people appearing transparent) is less of a problem, there is less intolerance to light, less power is required, and less heat is produced, thereby requiring less ventilation and permitting installation in more locations.

Another technology for capturing images digitally is the complementary metal oxide semiconductor (CMOS). This camera is less popular than the CCD camera and more complex. Both types of cameras convert light into electric charge and process it into electronic signals.

Digital cameras are replacing analog cameras. Although analog signals can be converted into digital signals for recording to a PC, quality may suffer. Digital cameras use digital signals that are saved directly to hard drive, but space on a hard drive is limited for video. Network cameras are analog or digital video cameras connected to the Internet with an IP address.

Increasing "intelligence" is being built into CCTV–computer-based systems. **Multiplex** means sending many signals over one communications channel. Video multiplex systems minimize the number of monitors security personnel must watch by allowing numerous cameras to be viewed at the same time on one video screen. The pictures are compressed, but a full view is seen of each picture. If an alarm occurs, a full screen can be brought up. The digital multiplex recorder enables users to record events directly to a hard drive, reducing storage space.

The prolonged watching of CCTV monitors (i.e., screens) by personnel, without falling asleep, has been a challenge since the origin of these systems. Personnel that are not rotated periodically become fatigued from watching too much TV. This serious problem is often overlooked. People may "test" the monitoring of the system by placing a bag or rag over a camera or even spraying the lens with paint. If people see that there is no response, CCTV becomes a hoax. The use of dummy cameras is not recommended because, when people discover the dummy, CCTV can be perceived as a deceitful farce.

Users of CCTV systems are especially interested in the recording capabilities of their systems, knowing their personnel are often occupied with multiple tasks (e.g., answering questions for customers, providing information over the telephone) and unable to watch monitors continuously. When an event does occur, these systems permit a search of recordings by date, time, location, and other variables.

CCTV capabilities can be enhanced by using **video motion detection** (VMD). A video motion detector operates by sending, from a camera, a static (i.e., having no motion) picture to a memory evaluator to analyze the image for pixel changes. Any change in the picture, such as movement, activates an alarm. These systems assist security officers in reacting to threats and reduce the burden of increasing camera usage. Tse (2006: 42) refers to a study by an Australian firm that found that after 12 minutes of continuous watching of monitors, an operator would often miss up to 45% of scene activity, and after 22 minutes, up to 95% is overlooked.

The integration of VMD and **intelligent video systems** (IVS) is a developing technology that offers a variety of promising functions that aim to precisely define alarm conditions, enhance the capabilities of CCTV systems, and reduce the problem of humans missing important events on monitors. These systems enable the user to preselect actions that are programmed into the digital video system, and this software signals an alarm when such an event takes place. Examples of events triggering an alarm include stopped or moving vehicles, objects that are abandoned or removed, and loitering of people (Duda, 2006: 48–50).

Cameras commonly are placed at public streets, access points, passageways, shipping and receiving docks, merchandise storage areas, cashier locations, parts departments, and overlooking files, safes, vaults, and production lines. In the workplace, the location of cameras requires careful planning to avoid harming employee morale. A key restriction on the placement of cameras is that they must not be applied to an area where someone has a reasonable expectation of privacy (e.g., restrooms, locations where individuals change clothes).

The extent of the use of hidden surveillance cameras is difficult to measure, especially because many individuals are unaware of the existence of these cameras in workplaces. Pinhole lenses are a popular component of hidden surveillance cameras. They get their name from the outer opening of the lens, which is 1/8 to 1/4 inch in diameter and difficult to spot. Cameras are hidden in almost any location, such as clocks, file cabinets, computers, sprinkler heads, and mannequins.

It is important to note that when the network is down, IP cameras, NVR, and other technology tied to the network are down; therefore, emergency plans are essential to maintain business continuity.

Security Officers

Security officers play an important role in countering internal losses. They must be integrated with technology, and this entails quality training and supervision. When uniformed officers patrol on foot inside a facility—through production, storage, shipping, receiving, office, and sales floor areas—an enhanced loss prevention atmosphere prevails. Unpredictable and irregular patrols deter employee theft (among other losses). A properly trained officer looks for deviations, such as merchandise stored or hidden in unusual places, and tampered devices (e.g., locks, alarms, and CCTV). Thoroughly searching trash containers deters employees from hiding items in that popular spot. Losses also are hindered when officers identify and check people, items, and vehicles at access points.

Safes, Vaults, and File Cabinets

Safes

Protective containers (see Figure 7-19) secure valuable items (e.g., cash, confidential information). These devices generally are designed to withstand losses from fire or burglary. Specifications

FIGURE 7-19 Safe with electronic lock. *Courtesy:* Sargent & Greenleaf, Inc.

vary, and an assessment of need should be carefully planned. Management frequently is shocked when a fire-resistive safe in which valuable items are "secured" enables a burglar to gain entry because the safe was designed only for fire. The classic **fire-resistive (or record) safe** often has a square (or rectangular) door and thin steel walls that contain insulation. During assembly, wet insulation is poured between the steel walls; when the mixture dries, moisture remains. During a fire, the insulation creates steam that cools the safe below 350°F (the flash point of paper) for a specified time. The FBI maintains safe insulation files to assist investigators. Record safes for computer media require better protection because damage can occur at 125°F, and these records are more vulnerable to humidity. Fire safes are able to withstand one fire; thereafter, the insulation is useless.

The classic **burglary-resistive (or money) safe** often has a thick, round door and thick walls. Round doors were thought to enhance resistance, but today many newer burglary-resistive safes have square or rectangular doors. The burglary-resistive safe is more costly than the fire-resistive safe.

Better quality safes have the Underwriters Laboratories (UL, a nonprofit testing organization) rating (see Table 7–1). This means that manufacturers have submitted safes for testing by UL. These tests determine the fire- or burglary-resistive properties of safes. For example, a fire-resistive container with a UL rating of 350–4 can withstand an external temperature to 2000°F for four hours while the internal temperature will not exceed 350°F. The UL test actually involves placing a safe in an increasingly hot furnace to simulate a fire. An explosion impact test requires another safe of the same model to be placed in a preheated (2000°F) furnace for half an hour. Then the heat is lowered slightly for another half hour before the safe is dropped 30 feet onto rubble. If the safe is still intact, it is returned to the furnace for an hour at 1700°F before it is allowed to cool so that the papers inside can be checked for damage. In reference to burglary-resistive containers, a UL rating of TL15, for example, signifies weight of at least 750 pounds and resistance to an attack on its door by common tools for a minimum of 15 minutes. UL-rated burglary-resistive safes also contain UL-listed combination locks and other UL-listed components. UL is constantly toughening its standards. When selecting a safe, consider recommendations from insurance companies and peers, whether or not safe company employees are bonded, and how long the company has been in business.

Attacks

Before a skilled burglar attacks a safe, he or she studies the methods used to protect it. Inside information (e.g., a safe's combination) is valuable, and scores of employees and former employees of attacked firms have been implicated in burglaries. Listed next are major attack techniques of two types: with force and without force.

Attack methods using force include the following:

- *Rip or peel:* Most common, this method is used on fire-resistive safes that have lightweight metal. Like opening a can of sardines, the offender rips the metal from a corner. The peel technique requires an offender to pry along the edge of the door to reach the lock.
- *Punch:* The combination dial is broken off with a hammer. A punch is placed on the exposed spindle, which is hammered back to enable breakage of the lock box. The handle then is used to open the door. This method is effective against older safes.
- *Chop:* This is an attack of a fire-resistive safe from underneath. The safe is tipped over and hit with an ax or hammer to create a hole.
- *Drill:* A skillful burglar drills into the door to expose the lock mechanism; the lock tumblers are aligned manually to open the door.
- *Torch:* This method is used against burglar-resistive safes. An oxygen-acetylene cutting torch melts the steel. The equipment is brought to the safe, or the offender uses equipment from the scene.
- *Carry away:* The offender removes the safe from the premises and attacks it in a convenient place.

Table 7-1 UL Testing of Safes

Class	Resistance to Attack	Attack Time	Description
Fire			
350-*	Not tested	N/A	For paper and document storage
150-*	Not tested	N/A	For storage of magnetic computer tapes and photographic film
125-*	Not tested	N/A	For storage of flexible disks
Burglary			
TL-15	Door or front face	15 min	Resists against entry by common mechanical and electrical tools or combination of these means, Group 2, 1, or 1R combination lock.**
TL-15X6	6 sides	15 min	Same as above
TRTL-15X6	6 sides	15 min	Resists against entry by common mechanical, electrical tools and cutting torches or combination of each, Group 1, 1R, M, 2 combination lock or, Type 1 high-security electronic lock.**
TL-30	Door or front face	30 min	Same tools as TL-15, Group 1 or 1R combination lock.**
TL-30X6	6 sides	30 min	Same tools as TL-15, Group 2, 1 or 1R combination lock.**
TRTL-30	Door or front face	30 min	Same tools as TRTL 15X6, Group 1 or 1R combination lock, encased in a minimum 3" of concrete or in a larger safe or container.**
TRTL-30X6	6 sides	30 min	Same tools as TRTL 15X6, Group 1 or 1R combination lock.**
TRTL-60X6	6 sides	60 min	Same tools as TRTL-15, Group 1 or 1R combination lock, minimum weight 750 lbs., body 1" thick solid open hearth steel.
TXTL-60X6	6 sides	60 min	Same tools as TRTL-15 + up to 8 oz. of nitroglycerine with a maximum of 4 oz., per test, Group 1 or 1R combination lock or Type 1 high-security electronic lock, minimum weight 1000 lbs., wall thickness not specified.

*Hour rating 4, 2 or 1. Before inside temperature reaches 350, 150, or 125°F as shown by class designation.
**Minimum weight 750 lbs., body 1" steel, minimum tensile strength of 50,000 PSI.
   UL 2058: new standard for Type 1 high-security electronic lock for safes.

Combination Locks (These products are tested in accordance with UL 768)
Group 1. Highly resistant to expert or professional manipulation. Used in safes designated as TRTL-15X6, TRTL-30, TRTL-30X6, TRTL-60X6, and TXTL-60X6.
Group 1R. These locks meet all of the requirements of Group 1 and are resistant against radiological methods of manipulation.
Group M. Moderate resistant to skilled manipulation, these are found in TL-15, TL-15X6, TL-30, and TL30X6 safes, ATM safes, gun safes, and fire-rated record containers.
Group 2. Resistant to semiskilled manipulation, these locks are found in non-Listed safes, insulated record containers, and residential security containers.

Source: Correspondence (June 7, 2006) with UL, 1285 Walt Whitman Rd., Melville, NY 11747.

Attack methods using no force include the following:

- *Office search*: Simply, the offender finds the safe combination in a hiding place (e.g., taped under a desk drawer).
- *Manipulation*: The offender opens a safe without knowing the combination by using sight, sound, and touch—a rare skill. Sometimes the thief is lucky and opens a safe by using numbers similar to an owner's birth date, home address, or telephone number.
- *Observation*: An offender views the opening of a safe from across the street with the assistance of binoculars or a telescope. To thwart this, one should place the numbers on the top edge of the dial, rather than on the face of the dial.
- *Day combination*: For convenience, during the day, the dial is not completely turned each time an employee finishes using the safe. This facilitates an opportunity for quick access. An offender often manipulates the dial in case the day combination is still in effect.
- *X-ray equipment*: Metallurgical X-ray equipment is used to photograph the combination of the safe. White spots appear on the picture that helps to identify the numerical combination. The equipment is cumbersome, and the technique is rare.

The following measures are recommended to fortify the security of safes and other containers:

1. Utilize alarms (e.g., capacitance and vibration), CCTV, and adequate lighting.
2. Secure the safe to the building so it is not stolen. (This also applies to cash registers that may be stolen in broad daylight.) Bolt the safe to the foundation or secure it in a cement floor. Remove any wheels or casters.
3. Do not give a burglar an opportunity to use any tools on the premises; hide or secure all potential tools (e.g., ladder or torch).
4. A time lock permits a safe to be opened only at select times. This hinders access even if the combination is known. A delayed-action lock provides an automatic waiting period (e.g., 15 minutes) from combination use to the time the lock mechanism activates. A silent signal lock triggers an alarm when a special combination is used to open a safe.
5. At the end of the day, turn the dial several times in the same direction.
6. A written combination is risky. Change the factory combination as soon as possible. When an employee who knows the combination leaves, change it.
7. Maintain limited valuables in the safe through frequent banking.
8. Select a safe with its UL rating marked on the inside. If a burglar identifies the rating on the outside, an attack is made easier.

Vaults

A walk-in vault is actually a large safe; it is subject to similar vulnerabilities from fire and attack. Because a walk-in vault is so large and expensive, typically, only the door is made of steel, and the rest of the vault is composed of reinforced concrete. Vaults are heavy enough to require special support within a building. They commonly are constructed at ground level to avoid stress on a building.

File Cabinets

Businesses that sustain loss of their records from theft, fire, flood, or other threats or hazards face serious consequences, such as the possibility of business failure and litigation. Certain types of records require protection according to law. Some vital records are customer-identifying information, accounts receivable, inventory lists, legal documents, contracts, research and development, and human resources data. Records help to support losses during insurance claims.

File cabinets that are insulated and lockable can provide fair protection against fire and burglary. The cost is substantially lower than that of a safe or vault, but valuable records demanding increased safety should be placed in a safe or vault and copies stored off-site. Special computer safes are designed to protect against forced entry, fire, and moisture that destroys computer media.

☐ ☐ ☐

Search the Web

Use your favorite search engines to see what vendors have to offer and prices for the following products: access control systems, locks, interior intrusion detection systems, closed-circuit television, and safes.

Also, check out the following sites:

American National Standards Institute: www.ansi.org
American Society for Testing and Materials: www.astm.org
Association of Certified Fraud Examiners: www.acfe.com/home-live.asp
Builders Hardware Manufacturers Association: www.buildershardware.com/
International Organization for Standardization: www.iso.org
National Fire Protection Association: www.nfpa.org
National White Collar Crime Center: www.nw3c.org/
Security Industry Association: www.siaonline.org
Underwriters Laboratories (UL): www.ul.com

☐ ☐ ☐

Case Problems

7A. Consult the floor plans for Woody's Lumber Company, the Smith Shirt manufacturing plant, and Compulab Corporation (Figures 7-1, 7-2, and 7-3). Draw up a priority list of 10 loss prevention strategies for each company that you think will reduce risks from internal losses. Why did you select as top priorities your first three strategies in each list?

7B. As a corporate security manager, you learn that an IT specialist at the same company is extremely upset because he did not receive a promotion and raise he was expecting. This very intelligent young man told his supervisor that he would get back at the company for the injustice before he quits. What do you do?

7C. You are a security officer at a manufacturing plant where an employee informs you about observing another employee hiding company property near a back door. You check the area near the door and find company property under boxes. What action do you take?

7D. As a security officer, you learn that officers on your shift and your immediate supervisor have secretly installed, without authorization, a pinhole lens camera in the women's restroom. You refuse to be involved in peeping. The officers have been your friends since high school, and you socialize with them when off duty. One day the chief security officer summons you to her office and questions you concerning the whereabouts of the pinhole lens camera. What do you say?

References

Alten, J. (2005). "Shhh…Don't tell Anyone That DVRs Are Becoming Obsolete." *Security Director News*, 2 (March).

Association of Certified Fraud Examiners. (2006). *2006 ACFE Report to the Nation on Occupational Fraud and Abuse*. www.acfe.com/documents/2006-rttn.pdf, retrieved July 13, 2006.

Aughton, S. (2005). "Researchers Crack Biometric Security with Play-Doh." *PC PRO*. www.pcpro.co.uk/news/81257, retrieved December 14, 2005.

Baker, M., and Westin, A. (1987). "Employer Perceptions of Workplace Crime." Washington, DC: US Department of Justice.

Barry, J. (1993). "Don't Always Play the Cards You Are Dealt." *Security Technology & Design* (July-August).

Bernard, R. (2006). "Web Services and Identity Management." *Security Technology & Design*, 16 (January).

Canada.com (2007). "Hydro Lost Millions from Theft, Damage Last Year." *Vancouver Sun* (February 7). www.canada.com, retrieved February 9, 2007.

Chan, H. (2005). "Overcoming the Challenges of Wireless Transmission." *Security Technology & Design*, 15 (October).

Clark, J. and Hollinger, R. (1980). "Theft by Employees." *Security Management*, 24 (September).

Coleman, J. (2000). "Trends in Security Systems Integration." *Security Technology & Design*, 10 (August).

Computer Security Institute/FBI. (2005). *CSI/FBI Computer Crime and Security Survey*. www.GoCSI.com, retrieved July 11, 2006.

Computer Security Institute/FBI. (2006). *CSI/FBI Computer Crime and Security Survey*. www.GoCSI.com, retrieved July 14, 2006.

Conklin, J. (2001). *Criminology*, 7th ed. Boston: Allyn & Bacon Pub.

D'Agostino, S., et al. (2005). "The Roles of Authentication, Authorization and Cryptography in Expanding Security Industry Technology." www.siaonline.org, retrieved May 30, 2006.

Dean, R. (2005). "Ask The Expert." *Security Products*, 9 (September).

Department of Defense. (2000). *User's Guide on Controlling Locks, Keys and Access Cards*. Port Hueneme, CA: Naval Facilities Engineering Service Center.

Duda, D. (2006). "The Ultimate Integration—Video Motion Detection." *Security Technology & Design*, 16 (June).

FBI. (2005). *FBI Computer Crime Survey*. www.fbi.gov/publications/ccs2005.pdf, retrieved January 13, 2006.

Garcia, M. (2006). *Vulnerability Assessment of Physical Protection Systems*. Burlington, MA: Butterworth-Heinemann.

Gersh, D. (2000). "Untouchable Value." *iSecurity* (November).

Greene, C. (2004). "Hang Up on Fraud with Confidential Hotlines." *Fraud Alert*. Chicago, IL: McGovern & Greene.

Honey, G. (2003). *Intruder Alarms*, 2nd ed. Oxford, UK: Newnes.

Harowitz, S. (2007). "Faking Fingerprints and Eying Solutions." *Security Management*, 51 (March).

Hunt, S. (2006). "Integrated Security Solutions: Getting to Know It." *Security Products*, 10 (February).

Inbau, F., et al. (1996). *Protective Security Law*, 2nd ed. Boston: Butterworth-Heinemann.

Jordan, B. (2006). "Telework's Growing Popularity." *Homeland Defense Journal*, 4 (June).

Keener, J. (1994). "Integrated Systems: What They Are and Where They Are Heading." *Security Technology & Design* (May).

Lary, B. (1988). "Thievery on the Inside." *Security Management* (May).

Lasky, S. (2006). "Video from the Top." *Security Technology & Design*, 16 (June).

Mellos, K. (2005). "A Choice You Can Count On." *Security Products*, 9 (October).

National Association of Credit Management. (2005). "Embezzlement/Employee Theft." *Business Credit*, 107 (February).

Nemeth, C. (2005). *Private Security and the Law*. Burlington, MA: Elsevier Butterworth-Heinemann.

O'Leary, T. (1999). "New Innovations in Motion Detectors." *Security Technology & Design*, 9 (November).

Pearson, R. (2000). "Integration vs. Interconnection: It's a Matter of Semantics," *Security Technology & Design,* 11 (November).

Pearson, R. (2001). "Open Systems Architecture: Are We There Yet." *Security Technology & Design*, 11 (January).

Pearson, R. (2005). "Well-Designed Badges Help Prevent Loss." *Security Technology & Design*, 15 (July).

Philpott, D. (2005). "Physical Security—Biometrics." *Homeland Defense Journal*, 3 (May).

Piazza, P. (2005). "The Smart Cards Are Coming ... Really." *Security Management*, 49 (January).

Randazzo, M., et al. (2004). "Insider Threat Study: Illicit Cyber Activity in the Banking and Finance Sector." Washington, D.C.: US Secret Service.

Scicchitano, M., et al. (2004). "Peer Reporting to Control Employee Theft." *Security Journal*, 17 (April).

Siemon Company. (2003). "Video over 10G *ip*™." www.siemon.com, retrieved July 24, 2006.

Shaw, E., et al., (2000). "Managing the Threat from Within." *Information Security*, 3 (July).

Skinner, W., and Fream, A. (1997). "A Social Learning Theory Analysis of Computer Crime among College Students." *Journal of Research in Crime and Delinquency*, 34 (November).

Speed, M. (2003). "Reducing Employee Dishonesty: In Search of the Right Strategy." *Security Journal*, 16 (April).

Suttell, R. (2006). "Security Monitoring." *Buildings*, 100 (May).

Swartz, D. (1999). "Open Architecture Systems: The Future of Security Management." *Security Technology & Design*, 9 (December).

Taylor, R., et al. (2006). *Digital Crime and Digital Terrorism*. Upper Saddle River, NJ: Pearson Education.

Toye, B. (1996). "Bar-Coded Security ID Cards Efficient and Easy." *Access Control* (March).

Tse, A. (2006). "The Real World of Critical Infrastructure." *Security Products*, 10 (May).

U.S. Department of Homeland Security, Science and Technology Directorate and the Executive Office of the President, Office of Science and Technology Policy. (2004). *The National Plan for Research and Development in Support of Critical Infrastructure Protection*. www.dhs.gov, retrieved June 13, 2005.

Webopedia. (2006). "Open Architecture." www.webopedia.com/TERM/O/open_architecture.html, retrieved July 16, 2006.

Zunkel, D. (2003). "A Short Course in High-Security Locks." *Security Technology & Design*, 13 (February).

8

External Threats and Countermeasures

Objectives

After studying this chapter, the reader will be able to:

1. Describe methods of unauthorized entry.
2. List and define the five "Ds" of security.
3. Explain how environmental design can enhance security.
4. Discuss perimeter security and list and define five types of barriers.
5. List and explain methods to protect buildings against terrorism.
6. Explain window and door protection.
7. Describe the application of intrusion detection systems to perimeter protection.
8. Explain lighting illumination and at least five types of lamps.
9. Describe parking lot and vehicle controls.
10. Explain the deployment and monitoring of security officers.
11. Explain the importance of communications and the control center.
12. Discuss the use of protective dogs.

KEY TERMS	
• external loss prevention	• "Broken Windows" theory
• forced entry	• situational crime prevention
• smash and grab attacks	• rational choice theory
• surreptitious entry	• routine activities theory
• aura of security	• lifestyle perspectives
• redundant security	• perimeter
• layered security	• clear zones
• environmental security design	• natural barriers
• Oscar Newman	• structural barriers
• defensible space	• human barriers
• natural surveillance	• animal barrier
• natural territorial reinforcement	• energy barriers
• Crime Prevention Through Environmental Design (CPTED)	• passive vehicle barriers
	• active vehicle barriers

- common wall
- land use controls
- target-rich environment
- stand-off distance
- blast and antiramming walls
- keep out zones
- fiber optics
- bypass
- spoofing
- point protection
- spot or object protection
- area protection
- perimeter protection

- local alarm
- central station
- remote programming
- lumens
- illuminance
- foot-candle (FC)
- lux
- color rendition
- traffic calming strategies
- stationary post
- foot or vehicle patrols
- contraband

Introduction

External loss prevention focuses on threats from outside an organization. This chapter concentrates on countermeasures to impede unauthorized access from outsiders. If unauthorized access is successful, numerous losses are possible from such crimes as assault, burglary, robbery, vandalism, arson, and espionage. Naturally, employees as well as outsiders or a conspiracy of both may commit these offenses. Furthermore, outsiders can gain legitimate access if they are customers, repair technicians, and so on.

Internal and external countermeasures play an interdependent role in minimizing losses; a clear-cut division between internal and external countermeasures is not possible because of this intertwined relationship. In addition, as explained in the preceding chapter, we are in an era of universal threats. This means that because of telework, employees and organizations face the same threats whether work is accomplished on or off the premises.

The IT perspective is important to produce comprehensive security. IT specialists use terms such as *denial of access* and *intrusion detection*, as do physical security specialists; however, IT specialists apply these terms to the protection of information systems. As IT and physical security specialists learn from each other, a host of protection methods will improve, examples being integration of systems, investigations, and business continuity planning.

□ □ □ ▬▬▬▬▬▬▬▬▬▬▬▬▬▬▬▬▬▬▬▬▬▬▬▬

Many organizations have developed formidable perimeter security to prevent unauthorized entry, while not realizing that the greatest threat is from within.

▬▬▬▬▬▬▬▬▬▬▬▬▬▬▬▬▬▬▬▬▬▬▬▬ □ □ □

Methods of Unauthorized Entry

A good way to begin thinking about how to deter unauthorized entry is to study the methods used by offenders. Both management (to hinder penetration) and offenders (to succeed in gaining access) study the characteristics of patrols, fences, sensors, locks, windows, doors, and the like. By placing yourself in the position of an offender (i.e., *think like a thief*) and then that of a loss prevention manager, you can see, while studying Woody's Lumber Company, the Smith Shirt manufacturing plant, and Compulab Corporation (discussed in Chapter 7), that a combination of both perspectives aids in the designing of defenses. (Such planning is requested in a case problem at the end of this chapter.)

Forced entry is a common method used to gain unauthorized access. Windows and doors are especially vulnerable to forced entry. Offenders repeatedly break or cut glass (with a glasscutter) on a window or door and then reach inside to release a lock or latch. To stop the glass from falling and making noise, the offender uses a suction cup or tape to remove or hold the broken glass together. Retail stores may be subject to **smash and grab attacks**: a store display window is smashed, merchandise is quickly grabbed, and the thief immediately flees. A complex lock may be rendered useless if the offender is able to go through a thin door by using a hammer, chisel, and saw. Forced entry also may be attempted through walls, floors, ceilings, roofs, skylights, utility tunnels, sewer or storm drains, and ventilation vents or ducts.

Unauthorized access also can be accomplished *without force*. Wherever a lock is supposed to be used, if it is not locked properly, access is possible. Windows or doors left unlocked are a surprisingly common occurrence. Lock picking or possession of a stolen key or access card renders force unnecessary. Dishonest employees are known to assist offenders by unlocking locks, windows, or doors and by providing keys and technical information. Offenders sometimes hide inside a building until closing and then break out following an assault or theft. Tailgating and pass back are other methods of gaining access without force, as covered in the preceding chapter. Sly methods of gaining entry are often referred to as **surreptitious entry**.

Countermeasures

Countermeasures for external (and internal) threats can be conceptualized around the five "Ds":

- *Deter*: The mere presence of physical security can dissuade offenders from committing criminal acts. The impact of physical security can be enhanced through an **aura of security**. An aura is a distinctive atmosphere surrounding something. Supportive management and security personnel should work to produce a professional security image. They should remain mum on such topics as the number and types of intrusion detection sensors on the premises and security system weaknesses. Security patrols should be unpredictable and never routine. Signs help to project an aura of security by stating, for example, PREMISES PROTECTED BY HIGH-TECH REDUNDANT SECURITY. Such signs can be placed along a perimeter and near openings to buildings. The aura of security strives to produce a strong psychological deterrent so offenders will consider the success of a crime to be unlikely. It is important to note that no guarantees come with deterrence. (Criminal justice policies are in serious trouble because deterrence is faulty; criminals continue to commit crimes even while facing long sentences.) In the security realm, deterrence must be backed up with the following four "Ds."
- *Detect*: Offenders should be detected and their location pinpointed as soon as they step onto the premises or commit a violation on the premises. This can be accomplished through observation, closed-circuit television (CCTV), intrusion sensors, duress alarms, weapons screenings, protective dogs, and hotlines.
- *Delay*: Security is often measured by the time it takes to get through it. **Redundant security** refers to two or more similar security methods (e.g., two fences; two types of intrusion sensors). **Layered security** refers to multiple security methods that follow one another and are dissimilar (e.g., perimeter fence, strong doors, a safe). Both redundant and layered security creates a time delay. Thus, the offender may become frustrated and decide to depart, or the delay may provide time for a response force to arrive to make an apprehension.
- *Deny*: Strong physical security, often called *target hardening*, can deny access. A steel door and a safe are examples. Frequent bank deposits of cash and other valuables extend the opportunity to deny the offender success.
- *Destroy*: When you believe your life or another will be taken, you are legally permitted to use deadly force. An asset (e.g., proprietary information) may require destruction before it falls into the wrong hands.

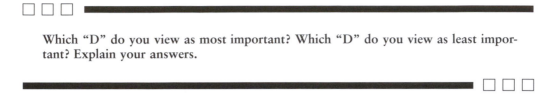

Which "D" do you view as most important? Which "D" do you view as least important? Explain your answers.

Construction and Environmental Security Design

When a new facility is being planned, the need for a coordinated effort by architects, fire protection and safety engineers, loss prevention practitioners, and local police and fire officials cannot be overstated. Further, money is saved when security and safety are planned before actual construction rather than accomplished by modifying the building later.

Years ago, when buildings were designed, loss prevention features were an even smaller part of the planning process than today. Before air conditioning came into widespread use, numerous windows were required for proper ventilation, providing thieves with many entry points. Today's buildings also present problems. For example, ceilings are constructed of suspended ceiling tiles with spaces above the tiles that enable access by simply pushing up the tiles. Once above the tiles, a person can crawl to other rooms on the same floor. Roof access from neighboring buildings is a common problem for both old and new buildings. Many of these weak points are corrected by adequate hardware such as locks on roof doors and by intrusion sensors.

Architects are playing an increasing role in designing crime prevention into building plans. **Environmental security design** includes natural and electronic surveillance of walkways and parking lots, windows and landscaping that enhance visibility, improved lighting, and other architectural designs that promote crime prevention. Additionally, dense shrubbery can be cut to reduce hiding places, and grid streets can be turned into cul-de-sacs by using barricades to reduce ease of escape.

During the late 1960s and early 1970s, **Oscar Newman** (1972), an architect, conducted innovative research into the relationship between architectural design and crime prevention that developed into the concept of **defensible space**. He focused on the built environment, studied more than 100 housing projects, and identified design elements that inhibit crime. For instance, Newman favored the creation of surveillance opportunities, called **natural surveillance**, through both windows for residents and clear lines of sight; this increases the potential to report crimes. Another strategy, known as **natural territorial reinforcement**, provides clear boundaries between public and private areas through such features as landscaping, signs, and fences. These boundaries send a message to potential intruders to avoid entering the area, and the strategy enables easier identification of intruders. He also recognized that the neighborhood surrounding the residential setting influences safety. An essential part of defensible space is to create designs that increase residents' use of public places while reducing fear of crime; this is hoped to have a snowballing effect. Oscar Newman found that physical design features of public housing affect both the rates of victimization of residents and their perception of security.

Crime Prevention Through Environmental Design (CPTED) is multidisciplinary and goes beyond the concept of defensible space. It includes psychological and sociological issues of deterring offender behavior and influencing resident behavior in preventing crime. CPTED is applicable not only to public housing but also to businesses, industries, public buildings, transportation systems, and schools, among others. In the past, the U.S. Department of Justice has funded CPTED programs in several cities.

An illustration of how CPTED is applied can be seen with the design of Marriott hotels (Murphy, 2000: 84–88). To make offenders as visible as possible, traffic is directed toward the front of hotels. Lobbies are designed so that people walking to guest rooms or elevators must pass the front desk. On the outside, hedges are emphasized to produce a psychological barrier that is more appealing than a fence. Pathways are well lit and guide guests away from isolated areas. Parking lots are characterized by lighting, clear lines of sight, and access control. Walls of the garage are painted white to enhance lighting. On the inside of hotels, the swimming pool, exercise room, and vending and laundry areas have glass doors and walls to permit maximum witness potential. One application of CCTV is to aim cameras at persons standing at the lobby desk and install the monitor in plain view. Since people can see themselves, robberies have declined. CPTED enhances traditional security methods such as patrolling officers and emergency call boxes.

Research from the United Kingdom has extended the reach of CPTED. The UK Design Against Crime (DAC) Program seeks a wide group of design professionals to develop creative and often subtle design solutions to combat crime and fear of crime. The DAC is a holistic, human-centered approach that facilitates crime prevention without inconveniencing people or creating a fortress environment. Examples include the following: a fence with a top rail that is angled to discourage young people from sitting on the fence and "hanging out"; the playing of classical music to prevent youth from congregating in certain areas; and the "antitheft handbag" that has a short strap, a carefully located zipper, thick leather, and an alarm (Davey et al., 2005: 39–51).

Since the physical environment can influence behavior, offenders may decide whether to commit a crime at a location after they determine the following (Taylor and Harrell, 1996: 1–32):

1. How easy will it be to enter?
2. How visible, attractive, or vulnerable do targets appear?
3. What are the chances of being seen?
4. If seen, will the people in the area do something about it?
5. Is there a quick, direct route from the location?

CPTED is enhanced through the **"Broken Windows" theory** of James Q. Wilson and George Kelling (1982). This theory suggests that deteriorated buildings that remain in disrepair and disorderly behavior attract offenders and crime while increasing fear among residents. If someone breaks a window and it is not repaired, more windows may be broken, and a continuation of dilapidated conditions may signal that residents do not care. Minor problems, such as vandalism, graffiti, and public intoxication, may grow into larger problems that attract offenders and destroy neighborhoods. However, residents can increase safety and security when they take pride in the conditions of their neighborhood.

Another theory related to CPTED is **situational crime prevention** (SCP). "This approach encompasses many CPTED principles; however, it focuses on managerial and user behavior factors that affect opportunities for criminal behavior in a specific setting for a specific crime, whereas CPTED focuses on changing the physical design aspects of environments to deter criminal activity" (U.S. Department of Homeland Security, 2003: 2–19).

Lab (2004: 177) writes: "Instead of attempting to make sweeping changes in an entire community or neighborhood, situational prevention is aimed at specific problems, places, people, or times. The situational approach assumes that a greater degree of problem identification and planning will take place prior to program implementation and that the impact will be more focused and, perhaps, identifiable."

Lab (2004: 177) traces SCP to the crime prevention work of the British Home Office (Clark, 1983) in the late 1970s. The goal was to successfully address different crime problems.

Lab (2004: 178–179) sees the theoretical basis for SCP from the following perspectives:

- **Rational choice theory:** Individuals make calculated decisions about crime based on many inputs, including the potential payoff, the risks, and needs.
- **Routine activities theory:** Day-to-day activities of people result in the convergence of motivated offenders with victims. Examples: Multiple-income households leave more homes unoccupied and subject to burglary. Increased mobility in society brings victims and offenders together more so than in the past.
- **Lifestyle perspectives:** This approach focuses on the activity of the victim as a contributing factor in criminal acts and victimization. Individual lifestyle and behavioral choices can lead to victimization. For example, an individual who frequents bars where fights occur often increases the risk of assault.

Perimeter Security

Perimeter means outer boundary, and it is often the property line and the first line of defense against unauthorized access (see Figure 8-1). Building access points such as doors and windows also are considered part of perimeter defenses at many locations. Typical perimeter security begins with a fence and gate and may include multiple security methods (e.g., card access, locks, sensors, lighting, CCTV, and patrols) to increase protection (see Figure 8-2). Technology can extend security surveillance beyond the perimeter, as illustrated with radar that is applied by a facility near a waterway (see Figure 8-3).

The following variables assist in the design of perimeter security:

1. Whatever perimeter security methods are planned, they should interrelate with the total loss prevention program and business objectives.
2. Perimeter security needs to be cost effective. When plans are presented, management is sure to ask: "What type of return will we have on our investment?"
3. Although the least number of entrances strengthens perimeter security, the plan must not interfere with normal business and emergency events.
4. Perimeter security has a psychological impact on potential intruders. It signals a warning to outsiders that steps have been taken to block intrusions. Offenders actually "shop" for vulnerable locations.
5. Even though a property line may be well protected, the possibility of unauthorized entry cannot be totally eliminated. For example, a fence can be breached by going over, under, or through it.
6. Penetration of a perimeter is possible from within. Merchandise may be thrown over a fence or out of a window. Various things are subject to smuggling by persons walking or using a vehicle while exiting through a perimeter.
7. The perimeter of a building, especially in urban areas, often is the building's walls. An offender may enter through a wall (or roof) from an adjoining building.
8. To permit an unobstructed view, both sides of a perimeter should be kept clear of vehicles, equipment, and vegetation. This allows for what is known as **clear zones**.
9. Consider integrating perimeter intrusion sensors with landscape sprinkler systems. Trespassers, protesters, and other intruders will be discouraged, and, when wet, they are easier to find and identify.

FIGURE 8-1 Perimeter security. *Courtesy:* Wackenhut Corporation. Photo by Ed Burns.

FIGURE 8-2 Multiple security methods increase protection.

FIGURE 8-3 Radar extends security surveillance beyond the perimeter at a facility near a waterway. *Courtesy:* Honeywell Security.

10. Perimeter security methods are exposed to a hostile outdoor environment not found indoors. Adequate clothing and shelter are necessary for security personnel. The selection of proper security systems prevents false alarms from animals, vehicle vibrations, and adverse weather.

11. Perimeter security should be inspected and tested periodically.

□ □ □

International Perspective: Physical Security Proves Its Value

Forty hooded demonstrators seemed to have appeared out of nowhere at the front gate of a breeding farm in the English countryside, where a pharmaceutical giant breeds animals for government-mandated testing of new medicines. A video recording of the incident showed protesters rocking the perimeter fence and harassing employees. What follows here is a description of how this business responded to its protection needs (Gips, 1999: 42–50).

For simplicity's sake, we will refer to this actual company as "PC" for pharmaceutical company. One threat facing the PC was the 50 or so incidents from animal activists in one year. Consequently, protection against sabotage, terrorism, and infiltration by animal rights activists became top priorities. Measures included physical security and access control, internal theft countermeasures, information safeguards, and bomb threat response. Protection was afforded not only to 2,000 scientists, support personnel, intellectual property, and physical assets, but also to the company image.

The PC favors a layered approach to physical security, which begins with strong perimeter protection. At the breeding farm, a seven-foot-high fence bounds the site and security officers monitor the farm from a gatehouse that doubles as a control room for intrusion and fire detection and CCTV. Because no police are nearby, a PC facility 12 miles away provides backup. The PC's response to protestors is low-key in part because in England simple trespass is a civil, not a criminal, matter. Protestors, even if verbally abusive, can be arrested only if they are violent; then police will make the arrests. Protestors generally want media attention, so they usually surrender to security when found on the premises. They know they will not be arrested, and no civil action will be initiated.

At another PC facility, security integration is shown through CCTV cameras, mounted every 75 yards along the perimeter, which work with video motion detection and infrared sensors. Although continuous recording occurs, when motion is detected, the action appears on a monitor for evaluation in the control room. This facility requires vehicles to pass through a raising-arm barrier. Pedestrians must register at a gatehouse, and employees use their Wiegand access control cards as they pass through a full-height antipassback turnstile. Doors are alarmed, and windows are treated with antibandit glazing to delay an offender.

To reduce internal theft from employees and contractors, personnel are reminded of their responsibility to secure valuables, vulnerable areas have restricted access, doors are kept locked, and a crime prevention day is held. Information is protected through an awareness course, security bulletins, secure fax and videoconferencing facilities, a high priority on IT security, technical surveillance sweeps, and tours under close controls.

The animal activist threat is handled through counterintelligence (i.e., a database of information), vetting (i.e., examination of all personnel to prevent infiltration or the planting of devices to collect information), and public relations (i.e., outreach to explain the importance of research with animals). To deal with bomb threats, PC facilities are too large for a dedicated team to conduct a search, so each employee is responsible for checking for anything unusual in his or her work area. Also, all incoming mail passes through an X-ray scanner. One lesson from all this protection is that losses can be much more expensive than security.

□ □ □

Barriers

Post and Kingsbury (1977: 502–503) state, "the physical security process utilizes a number of barrier systems, all of which serve specific needs. These systems include natural, structural, human, animals, and energy barriers." **Natural barriers** are rivers, hills, cliffs, mountains, foliage, and other features difficult to overcome. Fences, walls, doors, and the architectural arrangement of buildings are **structural barriers. Human barriers** include security officers who scrutinize people, vehicles, and things entering and leaving a facility. The typical **animal barrier** is a dog. **Energy barriers** include protective lighting and intrusion detection systems.

The most common type of barrier is a *chain-link fence* topped with barbed wire. A search of the Web shows many industry standards for fences from ASTM, UL, ISO, and other groups from the United States and overseas. For example, ASTM F 567 focuses on materials specifications, design requirements, and installation of chain-link fencing.

One advantage of chain-link fencing is that it allows observation from both sides: a private security officer looking out and a public police officer looking in. Foliage and decorative plastic woven through the fence can reduce visibility and aid offenders. Opposition to chain-link fencing sometimes develops because management wants to avoid an institutional-looking environment. Hedges are an alternative.

It is advisable that the chain-link fence be made of at least 9-gauge or heavier wire with 2" × 2" diamond-shaped mesh. It should be at least 7 feet high. Its posts should be set in concrete and spaced no more than 10 feet apart. The bottom should be within 2 inches of hard ground; if the ground is soft, the fence can become more secure if extended a few inches below the ground. Recommended at the top is a *top guard*—supporting arms about 1 or 2 feet long containing three or four strands of taut barbed wire 6 inches apart and facing outward at 45 degrees.

Barbed wire fences are less effective and used less frequently than chain-link fences. Each strand of barbed wire is constructed of two 12-gauge wires twisted and barbed every 4 inches. For adequate protection, vertical support posts are placed 6 feet apart, and the parallel strands of barbed wire are from 2 to 6 inches apart. A good height is 8 feet.

Concertina fences consist of coils of steel razor wire clipped together to form cylinders weighing about 55 pounds. Each cylinder is stretched to form a coil-type barrier 3 feet high and 50 feet long. The ends of each 50-foot coil need to be clipped to the next coil to obviate movement. Stakes also stabilize these fences. This fence was developed by the military to act as a quickly constructed barrier. When one coil is placed on another, they create a 6-foot-high barrier. One coil placed on two as a base provides a pyramid-like barrier that is difficult to penetrate. Concertina fences are especially helpful for quick, temporary repairs to damaged fences.

Razor ribbon and *coiled barbed tape* are increasing in popularity. They are similar to concertina fencing in many ways. Every few inches along the coil are sharp spikes, looking something like a small-sharpened bow tie.

Gates are necessary for traffic through fences. The fewer gates, the better because, like windows and doors, they are weak points along a perimeter. Gates usually are secured with a chain and padlock. Uniformed officers stationed at each gate and fence opening increase security while enabling the observation of people and vehicles.

Vehicle barriers control traffic and stop vehicles from penetrating a perimeter. The problems of vehicle bombs and drive-by shootings have resulted in greater use of vehicle barriers. These barriers are assigned government-certified ratings based on the level of protection; however, rating systems vary among government agencies. One agency, for example, tests barriers against 15,000-pound trucks traveling up to 50 miles per hour, while another agency tests 10,000-pound trucks traveling the same speed. **Passive vehicle barriers** are fixed and include decorative bollards, large concrete planters, granite fountains, specially engineered and anchored park benches, hardened fencing, fence cabling, and trees. An alternative to bollards is a *plinth wall*—a continuous low wall of reinforced concrete with a buried foundation (U.S. Department of Homeland Security, 2003: 2–33). Moore (2006) notes alternatives to bollards, including *tiger traps* (i.e., a path of paving stones over a trench of low-density concrete that will collapse under a heavy weight) and *NOGOs* (i.e., large, heavy bronze blocks). **Active vehicle barriers** are used at entrances and include gates, barrier arms, and pop-up type systems that are set underground and, when activated, spring up to block a vehicle (True, 1996: 49–53). As we know, no security method is foolproof, and careful security planning is vital, including ADA requirements. In 1997, to protest government policy, the environmental group Greenpeace penetrated government security in Washington, D.C., and dumped four tons of coal outside the Capitol building. The driver of the truck drove the wrong way up a one-way drive leading to the building!

Walls are costly and a substitute for fences when management is against the use of a wire fence. Attractive walls can be designed to produce security equal to fences while blending into surrounding architecture. Walls are made from a variety of materials: bricks, concrete blocks, stones, or cement. Depending on design, the top of walls 6 or 7 feet high may contain barbed wire, spikes, or broken glass set in cement. Offenders often avoid injury by throwing a blanket or jacket over the top of the wall (or fence) before scaling it. Many jurisdictions prohibit ominous features at the top of barriers. Check local ordinances. An advantage of a wall is that outsiders are hindered from observing inside. However, observation by public police during patrols also is hindered; this can benefit an intruder.

Hedges or shrubbery are useful as barriers. Thorny shrubs have a deterrent value. These include holly, barberry, and multiflora rose bushes, all of which require a lot of watering. The privet hedge grows almost anywhere and requires minimal care. A combination of hedge and fence is useful. Hedges should be less than 3 feet high and placed on the inside to avoid injury to those passing by and to create an added obstacle for someone attempting to scale the fence. Any plants that are large and placed too close to buildings and other locations provide a climbing tool, cover for thieves, and a hiding place for stolen goods.

Municipal codes restrict the heights of fences, walls, and hedges to maintain an attractive environment devoid of threatening-looking barriers. Certain kinds of barriers may be prohibited to ensure conformity. Planning should encompass research of local standards.

The following list can help a security manager eliminate weak points along a perimeter or barrier.

1. Utility poles, trees, boxes, pallets, forklifts, tools, and other objects outside a building can be used to scale a barrier.
2. Ladders left outside are an offender's delight. Stationary ladders are made less accessible via a steel cage with a locked door.
3. A **common wall** is shared by two separate entities. Thieves may lease and occupy or just enter the adjoining building or room and then hammer through the common wall.
4. A roof is easy to penetrate. A few tools, such as a drill and saw, enable offenders to cut through the roof. Because lighting, fences, sensors, and patrols rarely involve the roof, this weakness is attractive to thieves. A rope ladder often is employed to descend from the roof, or a forklift might be used to lift items to the roof. Vehicle keys should be hidden and other precautions taken.
5. Roof hatches, skylights, basement windows, air-conditioning and other vent and duct systems, crawl spaces between floors and under buildings, fire escapes, and utility covers may need a combination of locks, sensors, steel bars, heavy mesh, fences, and inspections. A widely favored standard is that any opening greater than 96 square inches requires increased protection.

Protecting Buildings against Terrorism

To help justify security and loss prevention expenditures, executives should refer to the *Reference Manual to Mitigate Potential Terrorist Attacks against Buildings* (U.S. Department of Homeland Security, 2003: iii), here referred to as FEMA 426. This publication notes that building designs can serve to mitigate multiple hazards. For example, hurricane window design, especially against flying debris, and seismic standards for nonstructural building components apply also to bomb explosions. Next, Purpura (2007) describes protection methods from FEMA 426.

FEMA 426 refers to site-level considerations for security that include land use controls, landscape architecture, site planning, and other strategies to mitigate risks of terrorism and other hazards. **Land use controls**, including zoning and land development regulations, can affect security because they define urban configurations that can decrease or increase risks from crime and terrorism. For instance, managing stormwater on-site can add security through water retention facilities that serve as a vehicle barrier and blast setback. This reduces the need for off-site pipes and manholes that can be used for access or to conceal weapons. FEMA 426 offers several building design suggestions to increase security (see Figure 8-4).

A **target-rich environment** is created when people, property, and operations are concentrated in a dense area. There are advantages and disadvantages to a dense cluster. An advantage is the possibility to maximize stand-off (i.e., protection when a blast occurs) from the perimeter. Additional security benefits are a reduction in the number of access and surveillance points and a shorter perimeter to protect. A dense cluster of buildings can possibly save energy costs through, for instance, heat transfer from heat-producing areas to heat-consuming areas. In addition, external lighting would not be dispersed over a large area, requiring more lights and energy. In contrast, dispersed buildings, people, and operations spread the risk. However, dispersal can increase the complexity of security (e.g., more access points), and it may require more resources (e.g., security officers, CCTV, lighting perimeter protection).

FEMA 426 recommends that designers consolidate buildings that are functionally compatible and have similar threat levels. For instance, mailrooms, shipping and receiving docks, and visitor screening areas, where people and materials are often closely monitored prior to access, should be isolated and separated from concentrations of people, operations, and key assets.

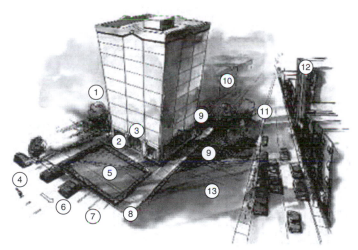

1	Locate assets stored on site but outside of the facility within view of occupied rooms in the facility	8	Minimize vehicle access points
2	Eliminate parking beneath facilities	9	Eliminate potential hiding places near facility; provide an unobstructed view around facility
3	Minimize exterior signage or other indications of asset locations	10	Site facility within view of other occupied facilities on the installation
4	Locate trash receptacles as far from the facility as possible	11	Maximize distance from facility to installation boundary
5	Eliminate lines of approach perpendicular to the building	12	Locate facility away from natural or man-made vantage points
6	Locate parking to obtain stand-off distance from facility	13	Secure access to power/heat plants, gas mains, water supplies, and electrical service
7	Illuminate building exteriors or sites where exposed assets are located		

FIGURE 8-4 Summary of site mitigation measures. *Source:* U.S. Department of Homeland Security (2003). *Reference Manual to Mitigate Potential Terrorist Attacks against Buildings*, FEMA 426 (December). Washington, D.C.: FEMA.

The design of open space with protection in mind offers several benefits: the ease with which to monitor and detect intruders, vehicles, and weapons; stand-off value from a blast; pervious open space that permits stormwater to percolate back into the ground, reducing the need for pipes, manholes, and other covert access points and weapon concealment sites; and wetland or vegetated area to improve aesthetic value while hindering vehicle intrusion.

Here are other suggestions for buildings from FEMA 426:

- Provide redundant utility systems to continue life safety, security, and rescue functions in case of an emergency.
- Since hardened glazing may cause windows not to blow out in a blast, a system for smoke removal is essential.
- When possible, elevate fresh-air intakes to reduce the potential of hazardous materials entering a building from ground level. The intakes should be sloped down and have screens in case a device is thrown toward the opening.
- Manipulation of the HVAC system could minimize the spread of a hazardous agent. Filtration systems are another option, although expensive.

Mitigation for Explosive Blasts

Stand-off distance is the distance between an asset and a threat. FEMA 426 views *distance* as the most effective and desirable strategy against a blast because other methods may vary in effectiveness, be more costly, and result in unintended consequences. A blast wall can become a part of the fragmentation if a bomb is detonated close to it. Urban environments create challenges when designing stand-off distance because land is often expensive. There is no ideal stand-off distance; numerous variables take part in planning, such as the type of threat or explosive, construction characteristics and target hardening, and desired level of protection.

Blast and antiramming walls provide an expensive option for protecting buildings, especially in urban areas where stand-off distance may be unavailable. Revel (2003: 40) writes that a test of a blast wall conducted by the U.S. Government's Technical Support Working Group (TSWG) showed the effectiveness of this security method. The blast wall sustained an explosion more powerful than the one that destroyed the Murrah Federal Building (Oklahoma City bombing) and the effects on the test building behind the blast wall were reduced by about 90%. The blast wall was constructed by first inserting in the ground 18-foot blast posts, with 9 feet extending above the ground. Then steel-jacketed concrete and rebar-filled panels were lowered between the posts in an interlocking pattern. When the explosion occurred, the posts twisted and deflected the blast above and back from the panels, directing the force up and beyond the lower structural steel of the building and around the ends of the wall. The blast wall is also capable of absorbing large vehicle impact at high speeds.

Although several building design features can mitigate explosive blasts, many factors enter into the design of buildings, including cost, purpose, occupancy, and location. A high-risk building should incorporate more mitigation features than a low-risk building. Significant changes to existing buildings may be too expensive; therefore, lower cost changes must be sought. Bollards and strong gates are less expensive than making major structural changes to a building. In addition, trees, vegetative groupings, and earth berms offer some degree of blast shielding. Examples of mitigation features from FEMA 426 are as follows:

- Avoid "U" or "L" shaped building designs that trap the shock waves of a blast. Circular buildings reduce a shock wave better than a rectangular building because of the angle of incidence of the shock wave.
- Avoid exposed structural elements (e.g., columns) on the exterior of a facility.
- Install as much glazing (i.e., windows) as possible away from the street side.
- Stagger doors located across from one another in interior hallways to limit the force of a blast through the building.
- High-security rooms should be blast- and fragment-resistant.
- Provide pitched roofs to permit deflection of launched explosives.

Keep out zones help to maintain a specific distance between vehicles or people and a building. This is accomplished by installing perimeter security (e.g., fences), access controls, bollards, and other security methods. If terrorists plan to attack a specific building, they will likely use surveillance to study security features, look for vulnerabilities, and try to penetrate access controls and defenses through creative means.

Glazing

Annealed glass, also called *plate glass*, is commonly used in buildings. It has low strength, and upon failure, it fractures into razor sharp pieces. *Fully thermally tempered glass* (TTG) is four to five times stronger than annealed glass, and upon failure, it will fracture into small cube-shaped fragments. Building codes generally require TTG anywhere the public can touch (e.g., entrance doors). *Wire-reinforced glass* is made of annealed glass with an embedded layer of wire mesh. It is applied as a fire-resistant and forced entry barrier. All three types of glass present a dangerous hazard from a blast (U.S. Department of Homeland Security, 2003).

Traditionally, window protection focused on hindering forced entry. Today, we are seeing increasing designs that mitigate the hazardous effects of flying glass from a variety of risks, besides explosion. Experts report that 75% of all damage and injury from bomb blasts results from flying and falling glass. Vendors sell *shatter-resistant film*, also called *fragment retention film* (FRF), that is applied to the glass surface to reduce this problem. Conversely, a report on the 1993 World Trade Center attack claimed that the destroyed windows permitted deadly gases to escape from the building, enabling occupants to survive. A balanced design (i.e., type of glass, glass frame, and frame to building) means that all the window components have compatible capacities and fail at the same pressure levels. The U.S. General Services Administration publishes glazing protection levels based on how far glass fragments would enter a space and cause injuries. It is important to note that the highest level of protection for glazing may not mitigate the effects from a large explosion (U.S. Department of Homeland Security, 2003).

Blast curtains are window draperies made of special fabrics designed to stop glass window shards that are caused by explosions and other hazards. Various designs serve to catch broken glass and let the gas and air pressure dissipate through the fabric mesh. The fibers of these curtains can be several times as strong as steel wire. The U.S. General Services Administration establishes criteria for these products (Owen, 2003: 143–144).

Glass can be designed to block penetration of bullets, defeat attempted forced entry, remain intact following an explosion, and protect against electronic eavesdropping. The Web shows many standards for glazing from the American Architectural Manufacturers Association (AAMA), ANSI, UL, ASTM, Consumer Product Safety Commission, ISO, and overseas groups. Security glazing should be evaluated on comparative testing to an established national consensus standard such as ASTM F1233, Standard Test Method for Security Glazing Materials and Systems. Important issues for glazing include product life cycle, durability, installation, maintenance, and framing (Saflex, Inc., 2005).

Underwriters Laboratories classifies *bullet-resistant windows* into eight protection levels, with levels 1 to 3 rated against handguns and 4 to 8 rated against rifles. Level 4 or higher windows usually are applied by government agencies and the military. Protective windows are made of either glass or plastic or mixtures of each.

Laminated glass absorbs a bullet as it passes through various glass layers. The advantage of glass is in its maintenance: it is easy to clean and less likely to scratch than plastic. It is less expensive per square foot than plastic but heavier, which requires more workers and stronger frames. Glass has a tendency to spall (i.e., chip) when hit by a bullet. UL752-listed glass holds up to three shots, and then it begins to shatter from subsequent shots.

Two types of plastic used in windows are acrylic and polycarbonate. Both vary in thickness and are lighter and more easily scratched than glass. *Acrylic windows* are clear and monolithic, whereas glass and polycarbonate windows are laminates consisting of layers of material bonded one on top of another. Acrylic will deflect bullets and hold together under sustained hits. Some spalling may occur. *Polycarbonate windows* are stronger than acrylics against high-powered weapons. Local codes may require glazing to pop out in an emergency.

In addition to protective windows, wall armor is important because employees often duck below a window during a shooting. These steel or fiberglass plates also are rated.

Burglar-resistant windows are rated (UL 972, Burglary Resisting Glazing Material); available in acrylic and polycarbonate materials; and protect against hammers, flame, "smash and grab," and other attacks. Combined bullet- and burglar-resistant windows are available. Although window protection is an expense that may be difficult to justify, insurers offer discounts on insurance premiums for such installations.

Electronic security glazing, containing metalized fabrics, can prevent electromagnetic signals inside a location from being intercepted from outside, while also protecting a facility from external electromagnetic radiation interference from outside sources. Standards for this type of glazing are from the National Security Agency, NSA 65–8.

Window Protection

Covering windows with grating or security screens is an additional step to impede entrance by an intruder or items being thrown out by a dishonest employee. *Window grating* consists of metal bars constructed across windows. These bars run horizontally and vertically to produce an effective form of protection. Although these bars are not aesthetically pleasing, they can be purchased with attractive ornamental designs. *Security screens* are composed of steel or stainless steel wire (mesh) welded to a frame. Screens have some distinct advantages over window grating. Employees can pass pilfered items through window bars more easily than through a screen. Security screens look like ordinary screens, but they are much heavier in construction and can stop rocks and other objects.

When planning window protection, one must consider the need for emergency escape and ventilation. To ensure safety, certain windows can be targeted for the dismantling of window protection during business hours.

Window Locks

Businesses and institutions often contain windows that do not open. For windows that do open, a latch or lock on the inside provides some protection. The *double-hung window*, often applied at residences, is explained here as a foundation for window protection. It consists of top and bottom windows that are raised and lowered for user convenience. When the top window is pushed up and the bottom window pushed down, a sash lock containing a curved turn knob locks both parts of the whole window in place (see Figure 8-5). By inserting a knife under the sash lock where both window sections meet, an offender can jimmy the latch out of its catch. If an offender breaks the glass, the sash lock can be unlocked by reaching inside. With such simple techniques known to offenders, more complicated defenses are necessary. Nails can be used to facilitate a quick escape while maintaining good window security: one drills a downward-sloping hole into the right and left sides of the window frame where the top and bottom window halves overlap and inserts nails that are thinner and longer than the holes. This enables the nails to be quickly removed during an emergency escape. If a burglar attacks the window, he or she cannot find or remove the nails (see Figure 8-5). Another method is to attach a window lock requiring a key (see Figure 8-5). These locks are capable of securing a window in a closed or slightly opened position. This can be done with the nail (and several holes) as well. The key should be hidden near the window in case of emergency.

Electronic Protection for Windows

Four categories of electronic protection for windows are foil, vibration, glass-breakage, and contact-switch sensors. *Window foil*, which has lost much of its popularity, consists of lead foil tape less than 1-inch wide and paper thin that is applied directly on the glass near the edges of a window. In the nonalarm state, electricity passes through the foil to form a closed circuit. When the foil is broken, an alarm is sounded. Window foil is inexpensive and easy to maintain. One disadvantage is that a burglar may cut the glass without disturbing the foil. *Vibration sensors* respond to vibration or shock. They are attached directly on the glass or window frame. These sensors are noted for their low false alarm rate and are applicable

200   REDUCING THE PROBLEM OF LOSS

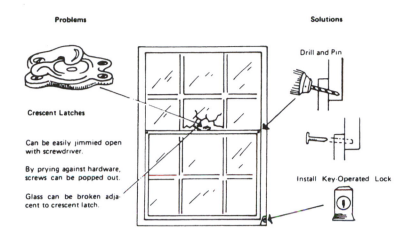

FIGURE 8-5 Double-hung window (view from inside).

to fences, walls, and valuable artwork, among other things. *Glass-breakage sensors* react to glass breaking. A sensor the size of a large coin is placed directly on the glass and can detect glass breakage several feet away. Some types operate via a tuning fork, which is tuned to the frequency produced by glass breaking. Others employ a microphone and electric amplifier. *Contact switches* activate an alarm when opening the window interrupts the contact. In Figure 8-6, this sensor protects a door and roof opening.

Additional ideas for window protection follow:

1. A strong window frame fastened to a building prevents prying and removal of the entire window.
2. First floor windows are especially vulnerable to penetration and require increased protection.
3. Consider tinting windows to hinder observation by offenders.
4. Windows (and other openings) that are no longer used can be bricked.
5. Expensive items left near windows invite trouble.
6. Cleaning windows and windowsills periodically increases the chances of obtaining clear fingerprints in the event of a crime.

Doors

Many standards apply to doors, from the AAMA, ANSI, ASTM, BHMA, National Association of Architectural Metal Manufacturers (NAAMM), NFPA, Steel Door Institute (SDI), UL, and ISO. In addition, other countries have standards.

Doors having fire ratings must meet certain frame and hardware requirements. Decisions on the type of lock and whether electronic access will be applied also affect hardware. Decisions on doors are especially crucial because of their daily use and the potential for satisfying or enraging users and management (Schumacher, 2000: 40).

Businesses and institutions generally use aluminum doors. Composed of an aluminum frame, most of the door is covered by glass. Without adequate protection, the glass is vulnerable, and prying the weak aluminum is not difficult. The all-metal door improves protection at the expense of attractiveness.

Hollow-core doors render complex locks useless because an offender can punch right through the door. Thin wood panels or glass on the door are additional weak points. More expensive, *solid-core doors* are stronger; they are made of solid wood (over an inch thick)

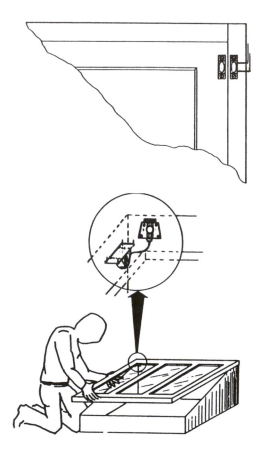

FIGURE 8-6 Switch sensors have electrical contacts that make or break an electrical circuit in response to a physical movement.

without the use of weak fillers. To reinforce hollow-core or solid-core doors, one can attach 16-gauge steel sheets, via one-way screws.

Whenever possible, door hinges should be placed on the inside. Door hinges that face outside enable easy entry. By using a screwdriver and hammer, one can raise the pins out of the hinges to enable the door to be lifted away. To protect the hinge pins, it is a good idea to weld them so they cannot be removed in this manner. Another form of protection is to remove two screws on opposite sides of the hinge, insert a pin or screw on the jamb side of the hinge so that it protrudes about half an inch, and then drill a hole in the opposite hole to fit the pin when the door is closed. With this method on both top and bottom hinges, even if the hinge pins are removed, the door will not fall off the hinges (see Figure 8-7).

Contact switches applied to doors offer electronic protection. Greater protection is provided when contact switches are recessed in the edges of the door and frame. Other kinds of electronic sensors applied at doors include vibration sensors, pressure mats, and various types of motion detectors aimed in the area of the door.

More hints for door security follow:

1. A wide-angle door viewer within a solid door permits a look at the exterior prior to opening a door.
2. Doors (and windows) are afforded extra protection at night by chain closures. These frequently are seen covering storefronts in malls and in high-crime neighborhoods.
3. To block "hide-in" burglars (those who hide in a building until after closing) from easy exit, require that openings such as doors and windows have a key-operated lock on the inside as well as on the outside.

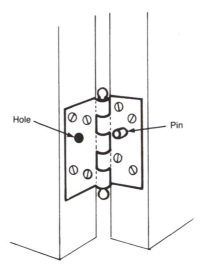

FIGURE 8-7 Pin to prevent removal of door.

4. Almost all fire departments are equipped with power saws that cut through door locks and bolts in case of fire. Many firefighters can gain easy access to local buildings because building owners have provided keys that are located in fire trucks. Although this creates a security hazard, losses can be reduced in case of fire.
5. All doors need protection, including garage, sliding, overhead, chain-operated, and electric doors.

Intruding Neighbors

The Finch Brothers Supermarket Company maintained a busy warehouse stocked with hundreds of different items for local Finch supermarkets. The company leased the large warehouse to accommodate the increasing number of supermarkets. After 18 months at this location, managers were stumped as to why shrinkage was over 4%. Several precautions were taken to avert losses: perimeter security consisted of intrusion sensors, lighting, and a security officer. A perpetual inventory was maintained.

Eventually, Finch's loss prevention manager's job was on the line, so he began a secret, painstaking, and continuous surveillance of the warehouse at night. After an agonizing week went by, he made an astonishing discovery. A printing company building next door was only 7 feet away from the warehouse, and printing company employees on the late shift were able to slide a 12′ × 16″ × 2″ board from a third-story window to a window of the same height at the warehouse. Within 30 minutes, the group of thieves hauled and threw many burlap sacks of items from one building to another. With camera equipment, the manager recorded the crime. Police were later notified and arrests made.

The thieves confessed that, when they worked the 11 P.M. to 8 A.M. shift, they stole merchandise from the warehouse. They stated that a maintenance man, who visited the warehouse each day, left the window open so the board could be slipped in. They added that dim lighting and the fact that intrusion sensors existed only on the first floor were factors that aided their crimes.

Intrusion Detection Systems

Standards for intrusion detection systems are from UL, the Institute of Electrical and Electronics Engineers (IEEE), and ISO, plus other groups in the United States and overseas. UL, for example, "lists" installation companies that are authorized to issue UL Certificates on each installation. This means that the installer conforms to maintenance and testing as required by UL, which conducts unannounced inspections.

Table 8-1 describes intrusion detection systems; these systems have gone through several generations, leading to improved performance. Not in the table is *magnetic field*, which consists of a series of buried wire loops or coils. Metal objects moving over the sensor induce a current and signal an alarm. Research shows that the vulnerability to defeat (VD) for magnetic field and infrared photo beam is high. Microwave, electric field, fence disturbance, seismic sensor cable, taut wire, and video motion systems all have a medium VD. The VD for ported coaxial cable systems is low. Visible sensors are relatively easy to defeat but cost effective for low-security applications. Multiple sensors, and especially covert sensors, provide a higher level of protection (Clifton and Vitch, 1997: 57–61; Reddick, 2005: 36–42; Shelton, 2006: 80–82).

Fiber optics is a growing choice for intrusion detection and transmission. **Fiber optics** refers to the transportation of data by way of guided light waves in an optical fiber. This differs from the conventional transmission of electrical energy in copper wires. Fiber optic applications include video, voice, and data communications. Fiber optic data transmission is more secure and less subject to interference than older methods.

Fiber optic perimeter protection can take the form of a fiber optic net installed on a fence. When an intruder applies stress on the cable, an infrared light source pulsing through the system notes the stress or break and activates an alarm. Optical fibers can be attached to or inserted within numerous items to signal an alarm, including razor ribbon, security grills, windows, and doors, and it can protect valuable assets such as computers.

Garcia (2006: 83–84) views intrusion sensor performance based on three characteristics: probability of detection of the threat, nuisance alarm rate, and vulnerability to defeat. The probability of detection depends on several factors including the desired threat to be detected (e.g., walking, tunneling), sensor design, installation, sensitivity adjustment, weather, and maintenance/testing. According to Garcia, a *nuisance alarm rate* results from a sensor interacting with the environment, and a sensor cannot distinguish between a threat and another event (e.g., vibration from a train). A *false alarm rate* results from the equipment itself, and it is caused by inadequate design, failure, or poor maintenance. Vulnerability to defeat varies among systems. **Bypass** means the adversary circumvented the intrusion detection system. **Spoofing** means the adversary traveled through the detection zone without triggering an alarm; depending on the sensor, one strategy is by moving very slowly. Garcia emphasizes the importance of proper installation and testing of intrusion detection systems.

No one technology is perfect; many protection programs rely on dual technology to strengthen intrusion detection. In the process of selecting a system, it is wise to remember that manufacturers' claims often are based on perfect weather. Security decision makers must clearly understand the advantages and disadvantages of each type of system under a variety of conditions.

Applications

Intrusion detection systems can be classified according to the kind of protection provided. There are three basic kinds of protection: point, area, and perimeter. **Point protection** (see Figure 8-8) signals an alarm when an intrusion is made at a special location. It is also referred to as **spot or object protection**. Files, safes, vaults, jewelry counters, and artwork are targets for point protection. Capacitance and vibration systems provide point protection and are installed directly on the object. These systems often are used as a backup after an offender has succeeded in gaining access. **Area protection** (see Figure 8-9) detects an intruder in a selected area such as a main aisle in a building or at a strategic passageway. Microwave and infrared systems are applicable to area protection. **Perimeter protection** (see Figure 8-10) focuses on the outer boundary of the premises. If doors and windows are part of the perimeter, then contact switches, vibration detectors, and other devices are applicable.

Table 8-1 Types of Intrusion Alarm Systems[*]

System	Graphic Idea	Concept	Advantages	Disadvantages
Motion detection				
Fence-mounted sensor		Detection depends on movement of fence	Ease of installation; early detection on interior fence; relatively inexpensive; requires little space; follows terrain easily	Frequent false alarms (weather and birds); conduit breakage; dependent on quality, rigidity of fence, and type of installation
Seismic sensor cable (buried)		Detection depends on ground movement (intruder walking over buried movement sensors, or other seismic disturbances)	Good for any site shape, uneven terrain; early warning; good in warm climate with little rain	False alarms from ground vibrations (vehicles, thunderstorms, heavy snow); not recommended for heavy snow regions; difficult installation and maintenance
Balanced capacitance		Detection depends on touching of cable, interfering with balance of cable	Few false alarms; good for selected areas of fence, rooftops, curves, corners, any terrain	Not to be used independently; for selected areas only
Taut wire		Detection depends on deflecting, stretching, or releasing the tension of wire that triggers alarming mechanism	Good for any terrain or shape; can be used as interior fence; extremely low false alarm rates adjustments	Relatively expensive; possible false alarms from snow, ice, birds, etc.; temperature changes require
Energy field				
Microwave sensor		Based on line of sight; detection depends on intrusion into volumetric area above ground between transmitter and receiver	Does not require a great deal of maintenance	Not good on hilly or heavily contoured terrain; costly installation; potential false alarms caused by weather (snow, ice, wind, and rain); vegetation must be removed

(Continued)

Table 8-1 Types of Intrusion Alarm Systems*—Cont'd

System	Graphic Idea	Concept	Advantages	Disadvantages
Energy Field				
Infrared photo beam sensor		Based on line of sight; detection depends on intrusion into beam(s) stacked vertically above ground	Good for short distances, building walls, and sally ports	Distances between transmitter and receiver must be short, requiring more intervals; potential false alarms by animals and weather conditions (fog, dust, snow); voltage surges
Ported coaxial cable		Detection depends on interruption of field in terms of mass, velocity, and length of time	Adaptable to most terrains	False alarms caused by heavy rain (pooling of water), high winds, tree roots; relatively expensive installation and maintenance
Video motion detection		Detection depends on change in video-monitor signal	Good for enhancing another system; good for covering weak spots	Lighting is a problem
Electric field sensor		Detection depends on penetration of volumetric field created by field wires and sensor wires	Good on hilly or heavily contoured terrain; can be freestanding or fence-mounted	Requires more maintenance; sensor wires must be replaced every 3 years; vegetation must be controlled

*Sources: Information from New York State Department of Corrections, Pennsylvania Department of Corrections, South Carolina Department of Corrections, and Federal Bureau of Prisons. Reproduced from U.S. Dept. of Justice, National Institute of Justice, Stopping Escapes: Perimeter Security (U.S. Government Printing Office, August 1987), p. 6.

FIGURE 8-8 Point protection.

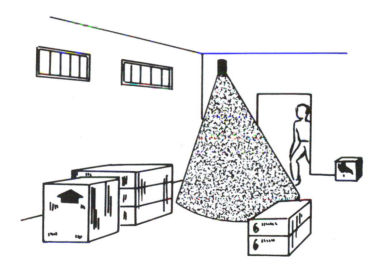

FIGURE 8-9 Area protection.

Control Unit

As described in Chapter 7, intrusion detection systems contain three major components: once a *sensor* detects an intruder, a *control unit* receives this information and activates an *annunciator* (e.g., noise or light) to summon security or police. Figure 8-11 shows a control unit with user instructions.

Alarm Signaling Systems

Alarm signaling systems transmit data from a protected area to an annunciation system. Local ordinances and codes may restrict certain systems, designate to whom the alarm may be transmitted, limit the length of time the alarm is permitted to sound, and fine the user of

FIGURE 8-10 Perimeter protection.

FIGURE 8-11 Alarm control unit with user instructions.

the system for excessive false alarms. In addition, police agencies vary on policies pertaining to their response to alarms.

Local alarm systems notify, by sound or lights, people in the hearing or seeing range of the signal. This includes the intruder, who may flee. Typically, a siren or bell is activated outside a building. Often, local alarms produce no response—in urban areas responsible action may not be taken, and in rural areas nobody may hear the alarm. These alarms are less expensive than other signaling systems but are easily defeated. If a local alarm is used during a robbery, people may be harmed. Research from the UK (Coupe and Kaur, 2005: 53–72) points to the benefits of delayed-audible alarms during a burglary that are triggered as the offender enters the premises but sound a few minutes later so CCTV cameras have an opportunity to record the offender and police still have time to respond prior to the offender's escaping if they are notified promptly. Combining these strategies with an immediate silent alarm to a central station increases the opportunity for an arrest.

A **central station** alarm system receives intrusion or fire signals or both at a computer console located and monitored a distance away from the protected location. When an alarm signal is received, central station personnel contact police, firefighters, or other responders. Central station services employ sales, installation, service, monitoring, and response personnel. Proprietary monitoring systems are similar to central station systems, except that the former does the monitoring and the system is operated by the proprietary organization. Resources for central station design are available from UL, NFPA, and the Security Industry Association (Patterson, 2000: 80).

Technology drives advances in central station capabilities. They include remote video monitoring, global positioning system (GPS), and off-site video storage. Remote video monitoring enables a central station operator to view what triggered an alarm to verify the need for a human response. GPS permits real-time tracking (e.g., location, direction, and speed) and archiving of moving assets and people. Off-site video storage, especially at a UL-listed central station, affords increased protection and backup for video recordings. It also helps to prevent the problem of offenders taking recording equipment with them as they leave the crime scene and, thus, destroy evidence (Evans, 2005: 44–46).

Various data transmission systems are utilized to signal an alarm. Here, the earlier technology is covered first before the modern technology.

Automatic telephone dialer systems are of two kinds: tape dialer and digital dialer. Tape dialer systems seldom are used today. They deliver a prerecorded or coded message to an interested party (e.g., central station, police department) after that party answers the telephone. Digital dialers do not use a recorded tape message; coded electronic pulses are transmitted, and an electronic terminal decodes the message onto a panel or teletype.

With *direct connect* systems the intrusion device is connected by wire directly to an alarm receiver located on the premises, at a police station, or some other location. Local ordinances may not permit direct reporting to police stations. A variation of this method is the "buddy" alarm system, in which the alarm signal is transmitted via direct wire to a neighbor, who calls the police. These systems usually are silent alarms.

Radio frequency (RF) and *microwave* data transmission systems often are applied where telephone lines are not available or where hardwire lines are not practical. The components include transmitter, receiver, and repeaters to extend range, battery backup, and solar power.

Fiber optic data transmission systems, as discussed earlier, transport data by way of light waves within a thin glass fiber. These cables are either underground or above ground. The components include transmitter, receiver, repeaters, battery backup, and solar power. Fiber optic systems are more secure than direct wire.

Signals should be backed up by multiple technologies. Options for off-site transmission of activity include satellite, local area network (LAN), wide area network (WAN), cellular, and the Internet. Cellular is especially useful for backup, since it is more likely to remain in operation in certain disasters. It can also be used as a primary transmission method (Zwirn, 2003: 74–83).

Among the advances in alarm monitoring is **remote programming**. Using this method, a central station can perform a variety of functions without ever visiting the site. Capabilities include arming and disarming systems, unlocking doors, performing diagnostics and corrections, and, with access systems, adding or deleting cards.

Alarm systems also may be multiplexed or integrated. *Multiplexing* is a method of transmitting multiple information signals over a single communications channel. This single communications channel reduces line requirements by allowing signal transmission from many protected facilities. Two other advantages are that information that is more detailed can be transmitted, such as telling which detector is in an alarm state, and transmission line security is enhanced with encoding. *Integrated systems*, as covered in Chapter 7, combine multiple systems (e.g., alarm monitoring, access controls, and CCTV).

CCTV

CCTV allows one person to view several locations. This is a distinct advantage when protecting the boundaries of a facility, because it reduces personnel costs.

Television programs and movies sometimes portray an intruder penetrating a perimeter barrier by breaking through when a CCTV camera had momentarily rotated to another location. Usually, the camera just misses the intruder by returning to the entry point right after the intruder gains access. Such a possibility can be averted via overlapping camera coverage. If cameras are capable of viewing other cameras, personnel can check on viewing obstructions, sabotage, vandalism, or other problems. In addition, covert CCTV surveillance should also be considered for outdoor applications in conjunction with overt CCTV surveillance.

Tamper-proof housings will impede those interested in disabling cameras. Different models are resistant to bullets, explosion, dust, and severe weather. Housings are manufactured with heaters, defrosters, windshield wipers, washers, and sun shields.

Low-light-level cameras provide the means to view outside when very little light is available. When no visible light is available, an infrared illuminator creates light, invisible to the naked eye, but visible to infrared-sensitive cameras. Another option is *thermal imaging cameras*, which sense heat from an intruder and are especially helpful to spot them in darkness, fog, smoke, and foliage (Pierce, 2006: 24–28).

An essential aspect of CCTV is proper monitoring. To reduce fatigue and ensure good-quality viewing, it is a good idea to rotate personnel every two hours if possible, limit TV monitors to fewer than 10, arrange the monitors in a curved configuration in front of the viewer, control the lighting over the console to avoid glare on the monitor screens or tilt the monitors if necessary, place the monitors in an order that permits easy recognition of camera locations, provide a swivel chair that hampers the opportunity for sleeping, and assign tasks to the viewer (e.g., communications, logging). The previous chapter covers technology that has enhanced monitoring and CCTV systems.

Lighting

From a business perspective, lighting can be justified because it improves sales by making a business and merchandise more attractive, promotes safety and prevents lawsuits, improves employee morale and productivity, and enhances the value of real estate. From a security perspective, two major purposes of lighting are *to create a psychological deterrent to intrusion* and *to enable detection.* Good lighting is considered such an effective crime control method that the law, in many locales, requires buildings to maintain adequate lighting.

A major study on the effect of lighting on the incidence of crime was conducted in England by Painter and Farrington (1999). Three residential areas were selected. One was the experimental area that contained improved lighting. The second was labeled the adjacent area. And the third served as the control area. Lighting in the adjacent and control areas remained unchanged. The research included the question of whether improved lighting might result in a reduction of crime in the adjacent area. The research results showed a marked reduction in a variety of crimes in the experimental area, whereas crime in the adjacent and control areas remained the same.

One way to analyze lighting deficiencies is to go to the building at night and study the possible methods of entry and areas where inadequate lighting will aid an offender. Before the visit, one should contact local police as a precaution against mistaken identity and to recruit their assistance in spotting weak points in lighting.

Three sources for information on lighting are the Illuminating Engineering Society of North America (IESNA), the National Lighting Bureau, and the International Association of Lighting Management Companies. The IESNA provides information on recommended lighting levels for a variety of locations.

□ □ □ ▬▬▬▬▬▬▬▬▬▬▬▬▬▬▬▬▬▬▬▬

Negligence Caused by Lighting Deficiency

Entities have an obligation to create a safe environment through lighting. In addition to moral and societal obligations, legal responsibilities are illustrated in the Illinois case of *Fancil v. Q.S.E. Foods, Inc.* In this case, a police officer's widow won a wrongful death suit because a storeowner had disconnected his backdoor light even though the location had been burglarized several times and the owner was aware that local police checked the business during the evenings. A burglar hidden in a dark area shot the officer. The court found the storeowner guilty of negligence through this failure to provide adequate lighting (U.S. Department of Justice, 1976: 183).

▬▬▬▬▬▬▬▬▬▬▬▬▬▬▬▬▬▬▬▬ □ □ □

What lighting level will aid an intruder? Most people believe that under conditions of darkness a criminal can safely commit a crime. However, this view may be faulty, in that one generally cannot work in the dark. Three possible levels of light are *bright light*, *darkness*, and *dim light*. Bright light affords an offender plenty of light to work but enables easy observation by others; it will deter crime. Without light—in darkness—a burglar finds that he or she cannot see to jimmy a door lock, release a latch, or perform whatever work is necessary to gain access. However, dim light provides just enough light to break and enter while hindering observation by authorities. Support for this view was shown in a study of crimes during full-moon phases, when dim light was produced. This study examined the records of 972 police shifts at three police agencies, for a two-year period, to compare nine different crimes during full-moon and non-full-moon phases. Only one crime, breaking and entering, was greater during full-moon phases (Purpura, 1979: 350–353). Although much case law supports lighting as an indicator of efforts to provide a safe environment, security specialists are questioning conventional wisdom about lighting (Berube, 1994: 29–33). Because so much nighttime lighting goes unused, should it be reduced or turned off? Does an offender look more suspicious under a light or in the dark with a flashlight? Should greater use be made of motion-activated lighting? How would these approaches affect safety and cost-effectiveness? These questions are ripe for research.

□ □ □ ▬▬▬▬▬▬▬▬▬▬▬▬▬▬▬▬▬▬▬▬

What are your views on nighttime lighting? Should certain locations turn it off?

▬▬▬▬▬▬▬▬▬▬▬▬▬▬▬▬▬▬▬▬ □ □ □

Illumination

Lumens (of light output) per watt (of power input) are a measure of lamp efficiency. Initial lumens-per-watt data are based on the light output of lamps when new; however, light output declines with use. **Illuminance** is the intensity of light falling on a surface, measured in foot-candles (English units) or lux (metric units). The **foot-candle (FC)** is a measure of how bright the light is when it reaches 1 foot from the source. One **lux** equals 0.0929 FC. For measures of illuminance, values not labeled as vertical are generally assumed to be horizontal FC (or lux). The light provided by direct sunlight on a clear day is about 10,000 FC; an overcast day would yield about 100 FC; and a full moon, about 0.01 FC. A sample of outdoor lighting illuminances recommended by the Illuminating Engineering Society of North America (2003) are as follows: guarded facilities, including entrances and gatehouse inspection, 10 FC (100 lux); parking facilities, garages, and covered parking spaces, 6 FC (60 lux) on pavement and 5 FC (50 lux) for stairs, elevators, and ramps; and for fast-food restaurant parking, general parking at schools and hotels/motels, and common areas of multifamily residences and dormitories, 3 FC (30 lux).

Care should be exercised when studying illuminance. Horizontal illuminance may not aid in the visibility of vertical objects such as signs and keyholes. FC vary depending on the distance from the lamp and the angle. If you hold a light meter horizontally, it often gives a different reading than if you hold it vertically. Are the FC initial or maintained? Maintenance and bulb replacement ensure high-quality lighting (National Lighting Bureau, n.d.: 1–36; Smith, 1996: 1–4).

Lamps

The following lamps are applied outdoors (National Fire Protection Association, 2005: 12–13; National Lighting Bureau, n.d.: 1–36; Smith, 1996: 1–4):

- *Incandescent* lamps are commonly found at residences. Electrical current passes through a tungsten wire enclosed in a glass tube. The wire becomes white-hot and produces light. These lamps produce 17 to 22 lumens per watt, are the least efficient and most expensive to operate, and have a short lifetime of from 500 to 4,000 hours.
- *Halogen* and *quartz halogen* lamps are incandescent bulbs filled with halogen gas (like sealed-beam auto headlights) and provide about 25% better efficiency and life than ordinary incandescent bulbs.
- *Fluorescent* lamps pass electricity through a gas enclosed in a glass tube to produce light, producing 67 to 100 lumens per watt. They create twice the light and less than half the heat of an incandescent bulb of equal wattage and cost 5 to 10 times as much. Fluorescent lamps do not provide high levels of light output. The lifetime is 9,000 to 17,000 hours. They are not used extensively outdoors, except for signage.
- *Mercury vapor* lamps also pass electricity through a gas. The yield is 31 to 63 lumens per watt, and the life is over 24,000 hours with good efficiency compared to incandescent lamps. Because of their long life, these lamps are often used in street lighting.
- *Metal halide* lamps are also of the gaseous type. The yield is 80 to 115 lumens per watt, and the efficiency is about 50% higher than mercury vapor lamps, but the lamp life is about 6,000 hours. They often are used at sports stadiums because they imitate daylight conditions, and colors appear natural. Consequently, these lamps complement CCTV systems, but they are the most expensive light to install and maintain.
- *High-pressure sodium* lamps are gaseous, yield about 80 to 140 lumens per watt, have a life of about 24,000 hours, and are energy efficient. These lamps are often applied on streets, parking lots, and building exteriors. They cut through fog and are designed to allow the eyes to see more detail at greater distances.
- *Low-pressure sodium* lamps are gaseous, produce 150 lumens per watt, have a life of about 15,000 hours, and are even more efficient than high-pressure sodium. These lamps are expensive to maintain.

Each type of lamp has a different **color rendition**, which is the way a lamp's output affects human perceptions of color. Incandescent, fluorescent, and certain types of metal halide lamps provide excellent color rendition. Mercury vapor lamps provide good color rendition but are heavy on the blue. High-pressure sodium lamps, which are used extensively outdoors, provide poor color rendition, making things look yellow. Low-pressure sodium lamps make color unrecognizable and produce a yellow-gray color on objects. People find sodium vapor lamps, sometimes called *anticrime lights*, to be harsh because they produce a strange yellow haze. Claims are made that this lighting conflicts with aesthetic values and that it affects sleeping habits. In many instances, when people park their vehicles in a parking lot during the day and return to find their vehicle at night, they are often unable to locate it because of poor color rendition from sodium lamps; some report their vehicles as being stolen. Another problem is the inability of witnesses to describe offenders accurately.

Mercury vapor, metal halide, and high-pressure sodium take several minutes to produce full light output. If they are turned off, even more time is required to reach full output because they first have to cool down. This may not be acceptable for certain security applications. Incandescent, halogen, and quartz halogen have the advantage of instant light once electricity is turned on. Manufacturers can provide information on a host of lamp characteristics including the "strike" and "restrike" time.

Lighting Equipment

Fresnel lights have a wide flat beam that is directed outward to protect a perimeter, glaring in the faces of those approaching. A floodlight "floods" an area with a beam of light, resulting in considerable glare. Floodlights are stationary, although the light beams can be aimed to select positions. The following strategies reinforce good lighting:

1. Locate perimeter lighting to allow illumination of both sides of the barrier.
2. Direct lights down and away from a facility to create glare for an intruder. Make sure the directed lighting does not hinder observation by patrolling officers.
3. Do not leave dark spaces between lighted areas for offenders to move within. Design lighting to permit overlapping illumination.
4. Protect the lighting system: locate lighting inside the barrier, install protective covers over lamps, mount lamps on high poles, bury power lines, and protect switch boxes.
5. Photoelectric cells will enable lights to go on and off automatically in response to natural light. Manual operation is helpful as a backup.
6. Consider motion-activated lighting for external and internal areas.
7. If lighting is required in the vicinity of navigable waters, contact the U.S. Coast Guard.
8. Try not to disturb neighbors by using intense lighting.
9. Maintain a supply of portable, emergency lights and auxiliary power in the event of a power failure.
10. Good interior lighting also deters offenders.
11. If necessary, join other business owners to petition local government to install improved street lighting.

Parking Lot and Vehicle Controls

In the preceding chapter, considerable attention was focused on access controls. Here, parking lot and vehicle controls are discussed as integral components of access controls.

A well-designed parking lot is a chief prerequisite to construction. Space usually is limited, and the layout of parking spaces and traffic lanes demands care. Employee access control to a building is easier when a parking lot is on one side of a building rather than surrounding the building. Vehicles should be parked away from shipping and receiving docks, garbage dumpsters, and other crime-prone locations.

Executives and other employees should have permanent parking stickers, whereas visitors, delivery people, and service groups should be given a temporary pass to be displayed on the windshield. Stickers and passes allow uniformed officers to locate unauthorized vehicles.

Parking lots are more secure when these specific strategies are applied: CPTED, access controls, signs, security patrols, training, lighting, CCTV, and panic buttons and emergency phones. Crimes often occur in parking lots, and these events can harm employee morale and result in lawsuits, unless employees (and customers) are protected. Hospitals, for example, supply an escort for nurses who walk to their vehicles after late shifts. Employee education about personal safety, locking vehicles, and additional precautions prevent losses.

Certain types of equipment can aid a parking lot security/safety program. Cushman patrol vehicles, capable of traveling through narrow passageways, increase patrol mobility.

Bicycles are another option. A guard house or security booth (unfortunately called *guard shack* at times) is useful as a command post in parking lots.

Various technologies can be applied to controlling vehicles at access points. One example is *automatic license plate recognition systems* that apply image-processing technology that reads a vehicle's license plate and uses infrared light to illuminate a plate in the dark. A high-speed camera is used to photograph a plate, and then the recorded information is compared to a database. Besides access controls, the applications include fleet management, locating stolen vehicles, and border security (National Law Enforcement and Corrections Technology Center, 2006: 1).

The threat of terrorism has influenced the design of parking lots and vehicle controls. Different types of parking lots present various security issues. Surface lots keep vehicles away from buildings, consume large amounts of land, and may add to storm water runoff volume. On-street parking provides no setback. A garage may require blast resistance. If the garage is under a building, a serious vulnerability exists, since an underground bomb blast can be devastating.

A designer can propose minimizing vehicle velocity because, for example, a bollard that can stop a 15,000-pound truck moving at 35 MPH may not be able to stop the same truck moving at 55 MPH (FEMA 426). *The road itself can become a security measure by avoiding a straight path to a building.* A straight road enables a vehicle to gather speed to ram a barrier, penetrate a building, and then detonate a bomb. Approaches should be parallel to the building and contain high curbs, trees, or berms to prevent vehicles from leaving the road. Curving roads with tight corners offer another strategy.

Traffic calming strategies are subtler and communicate appropriate speed. Examples are speed humps and raised crosswalks. A speed hump is not as rough as a speed bump. The latter is often used in parking lots. All these strategies reduce speed and liability while increasing safety. Drawbacks are that the response time of first responders increases, and snow removal may become difficult.

Security Officers

Officers normally are assigned to stationary (fixed) posts or to patrol. A **stationary post** is at a door or gate where people, vehicles, and objects are observed and inspected. Stationary posts also involve directing traffic or duty at a command post where communications, CCTV, and alarms are monitored. **Foot or vehicle patrols** conducted throughout the premises and along perimeters identify irregularities while deterring offenders. Examples of unusual or harmful conditions that should be reported are damaged security devices, holes in perimeter fences or other evidence of intrusion, hidden merchandise, unattended vehicles parked inappropriately, keys left in vehicles, employees sleeping in vehicles or using drugs, blocked fire exits, cigarette butts in no-smoking areas, accumulations of trash, and odors from fuels or other combustibles. In contrast to public police officers, private security officers act in primarily a preventive role and *observe and report*.

Before security officers are employed, far-sighted planning ensures optimum effectiveness of this service. What are the unique characteristics of the site? How many people and what assets require protection? How many hours per day is the facility open? How many employees? How many visitors and vehicles are admitted daily? What are the particular vulnerabilities? How will security officers interact with other loss prevention measures?

Security officers are expensive. Wages, insurance, uniforms, equipment, and training add up to a hefty sum per officer per year. If each officer costs $30,000 per year for a proprietary force and 5 officers are required for the premises at all times, to maintain all shifts seven days per week requires approximately 20 officers. The cost would be about $600,000 per year. To reduce costs, many companies switch to contract security services and/or consider technological solutions.

Several specific steps can be taken to improve the effectiveness of officers. Three of the most critical are *careful applicant screening*, *sound training*, and *proper supervision*. Management should ensure that officers know what is expected of them. Policies, procedures, and day-to-day duties are communicated via verbal orders, memos, and training programs.

Policies should ensure that supervisors check on officers every hour. Irregular, unpredictable patrols hinder offenders. Rotating officers reduces fatigue while familiarizing them with a variety of duties. Providing inspection lists for adverse conditions will keep them mentally alert. The formal list should be returned with a daily report. Courtesy and a sharp appearance command respect from employees and visitors.

Monitoring Officers

Historically, *watch clocks* have been used to monitor officer patrols along preplanned routes. The officer on patrol carried this older technology, consisting of a timepiece that contained a paper tape or disc divided into time segments. A watch clock was operated by an officer via keys mounted in walls at specific locations along a patrol route. These keys were often within metal boxes and chained to walls. When inserted into the watch clock, the key made an impression in the form of a number on the tape or disc. Supervisors could examine this to see whether the officer visited each key location and completed the scheduled route. Keys were located at vulnerable locations (e.g., entry points, flammable storage areas). Good supervision prevented officers from disconnecting all the keys at the beginning of the shift, bringing them to one location for use in the watch clock (and, thus, avoiding an hourly tour), and returning the keys at the end of the shift.

Automatic monitoring systems are another way to monitor patrols and keep records. Key stations are visited according to a preplanned time schedule and route. If an officer does not visit a key station within a specific time period, a central monitoring station receives a transmitted signal, and if contact cannot be made, personnel are dispatched.

Bar-code or *touch button* technology provides other avenues for monitoring patrols. A security officer carries a wand that makes contact with a bar code or touch button to record data that is later downloaded into a computer. Bar codes or buttons are affixed at vulnerable locations for a swipe by the wand to record the visit by the officer, who can also swipe bar codes or buttons that represent various conditions (e.g., fire extinguisher needs recharging). Supervision of these systems ensures that officers are patrolling properly and conditions are being reported (Arnheim, 1999: 48–58). To improve the efficiency of a security officer, the officer can use a wireless tablet PC (see Figure 8-12), which enables the officer to leave a monitoring post and take the workstation with him or her. If, for example, an officer must leave a control center to investigate an incident, the officer can bring the tablet PC and continue to watch CCTV, monitor alarms, and open doors for employee access.

Lower burglary and fire insurance premiums are possible through the use of monitored patrols. Insurance personnel may subject records to inspection.

Contraband Detection

Contraband is an item that is illegal to possess or prohibited from being brought into a specific area. Examples are weapons, illegal drugs, and explosives. *Security officers play a crucial role in spotting contraband* at businesses, schools, airports, courthouses, and many other locations. They use special devices to locate contraband, and *these devices are as good as the personnel behind them*. Here is an overview of these devices ("Scanning for Trouble," 2000: 1–3):

- *Metal detectors* transmit a magnetic field that is disturbed by a metallic object, which sets off a light or audio signal. Two types of metal detectors are handheld and walk-through. False alarms are a common problem.
- *X-ray scanners* use pulsed energy to penetrate objects that are shown on a color monitor. Drugs, plastic explosives, and firearms with plastic parts are difficult to identify with this method of detection.
- *Dual-energy systems* use X-rays at different energy levels to classify objects as organic, inorganic, or mixed. Colors are assigned to each classification to help spot contraband. When color and shape are observed, these systems are good at detecting explosives, since most are organic.

FIGURE 8-12 The tablet PC is a mobile workstation enabling a security officer to leave a post and do many things mobile that are done from a desktop PC, such as view CCTV, monitor alarms, and open doors. *Courtesy:* Hirsch Electronics, Santa Ana, CA.

- *Computed tomography scanners* are like CAT scanners used in hospitals. An X-ray source is spun around an object taking slice pictures that show on a computer. Although this device is expensive, detection of items is good.

Armed versus Unarmed Officers

The question of whether to arm officers is controversial. Probably the best way to answer this question is to study the nature of the particular officer's assignment. If violence is likely, then officers should be armed. Officers assigned to locations where violent crimes are unlikely do not need firearms, which, if worn by officers, could be offensive. The trend is toward unarmed officers because of liability issues.

If weapons are issued to officers, proper selection of officers and training are of the utmost importance. Instructions on the use of force and firearms safety, as well as practice on the firing range every four months, will reduce the chances of accidents, mistakes, and costly lawsuits.

Communications and the Control Center

As emergency personnel know, the ability to communicate over distance is indispensable. Every officer should be equipped with a portable two-way radio; this communication aid permits officers to summon assistance and notify superiors about hazards and impending disasters. Usually, officers on assignment communicate with a control center that is the hub of the loss prevention program. FEMA 426 (U.S. Department of Homeland Security 2003: 3–45) recommends redundant communications. The control center is the appropriate site for a console containing alarm indicators, CCTV monitors, door controls, the public address system, and an assortment of other components for communication and loss prevention (see Figure 8-13).

Because of the convergence of IT and physical security, the traditional security control center may be within a network operations center. Some organizations may choose to outsource a portion of operations. Since these operations are critical, they must be secure both electronically and physically (Milne, 2005).

FIGURE 8-13 Security officer at console managing access control, CCTV, alarm monitoring, and video imaging. *Courtesy:* Diebold, Inc.

Because personnel will seek guidance from a control center in the event of an emergency, that center must be secure and operational at all times. A trend today is automated response systems programmed into the control center because so many decisions and actions are required for each type of emergency (Patterson, 2000: 76–81). The control center is under increased protection against forced entry, tampering, or disasters when it contains a locked door, is located in a basement or underground, and is constructed of fire-resistant materials. An automatic, remotely operated lock, released by the console operator after identifying the caller, also enhances security. Bullet-resistant glass is wise for high-crime locations. FEMA 426 (U.S. Department of Homeland Security, 2003: 3–47) recommends a backup control center, possibly at an off-site location. Whoever designs the control center should be well versed in ergonomics, which deals with the efficient and safe partnership between people and machines.

Protective Dogs

Classified as an animal barrier, a dog can strengthen security at a protected site. An *alarm dog* patrols inside a fenced area or building and barks at the approach of a stranger, but does not attempt to attack. These dogs retreat when threatened but continue to bark. Such barking may become so alarming to an intruder that he or she will flee. A *guard or attack dog* is similar to an alarm dog, with an added feature of attacking an intruder. To minimize the possibility of a lawsuit, a business should selectively apply and adequately fence in these dogs, and should post warning signs. An experienced person on call at all times is needed to respond to emergencies. Another type of attack dog is the *sentry dog*. This dog is kept on a leash and responds to commands while patrolling with a uniformed officer. The advantages are numerous. These animals protect officers. Their keen senses of hearing and smell are tremendous assets when trying to locate a hidden offender (or explosives or drugs). Dogs can discern the slightest perspiration from people under stress, enabling the dogs to sense individuals who are afraid of them. An ingredient in stress perspiration irritates dogs, which makes frightened persons more susceptible to attack. When an "attack" command is given, a German shepherd has enough strength in its jaws to break a person's arm.

In addition to the possibility of a lawsuit if a dog attacks someone, there are other disadvantages to the use of dogs. If proprietary dogs are part of the protective team, personnel and kennel facilities are needed to care for the dogs. These costs and others include the purchase of dogs and their training, medical care, and food. Using a contract service would probably be more feasible. Another disadvantage is the possibility that dogs may be poisoned, anesthetized, or killed. An offender also may befriend a dog. Dogs should be taught to accept food only from the handler. Neighbors near the protected premises often find dogs noisy or may perceive them as offensive for other reasons.

Since the 9/11 attacks, interest in canines has increased. At the same time, there is a need for consistent standards for training, quality assurance, kenneling, selection of handlers, and presentation of evidence. Definitions also present a problem. For example, there is no consistent definition as to what constitutes an explosive detection canine. The Bureau of Alcohol, Tobacco, Firearms and Explosives has developed the National Odor Recognition Testing initiative, which could be a standard to which dogs could be certified. Research is being conducted on the possible use of chemical warfare agent detector dogs and GPS technology in conjunction with remote commands for searches, surveillance, and tracking of persons (Harowitz, 2006: 36–38).

□ □ □ ▬▬▬▬▬▬▬▬▬▬▬▬▬▬▬▬▬▬▬▬▬

Which strategies do you view as affording the best protection against unauthorized entry? Support your answer.

□ □ □ ▬▬▬▬▬▬▬▬▬▬▬▬▬▬▬▬▬▬▬▬▬

International Perspective: UN Efforts at Global Crime Prevention

In 1951, the United Nations established the Ad Hoc Advisory Committee of Experts to advise the UN on crime matters. In 1971, the group's name changed to the Committee on Crime Prevention and Control.

Several strategies are employed by the UN to prevent crime and improve justice. The UN fosters UN norms in national legislation, conducts research, and provides technical expertise to countries. Every five years since 1955, the UN has held a congress on crime issues, where successful policies and strategies are shared (United Nations, 1993: 1–19).

In light of the crime problem, the UN asked its member states to prepare an inventory of crime prevention measures so the information can be published and shared worldwide. The inventory focuses on four sections:

- *Crime prevention through social measures:* This approach tackles the root causes of crime and works to improve the family, schools, activities for youth, employment, and health.
- *Situational crime prevention:* These measures involve the management, design, or manipulation of the environment to reduce opportunities for criminal behavior and increase the risk for the offender. Specific strategies include hardening the target through security surveys, building and design codes, publicity and awareness campaigns, and insurance incentives to install physical security. Additional measures are marking property, natural surveillance (i.e., designing the inside and outside of buildings so people can more easily observe others), Neighborhood Watch, and citizen patrols.
- *Community crime prevention:* This approach recognizes that physical security should be part of a broader, community-based response to crime. Community policing and multiagency cooperation are also a part of this approach.
- *Planning, implementation, and evaluation of crime prevention:* The first step in this approach is an analysis of crime and victimization. Compiling and analyzing the location and nature of offenses and many other characteristics of a crime enhance crime prevention planning and implementation. Evaluation assesses whether preventive measures were successful (United Nations, 1990).

In essence, crime is a global problem, and many of the crime prevention methods applied in the United States are applied overseas. The UN is asking member nations to compile and share their ideas on how best to reduce crime.

When the 10th congress on crime prevention was held (United Nations, 2000), there was much concern about transnational organized crime and the need for increased global cooperation among nations. There was also continued emphasis on the preceding four categories. However, ethical concerns focused on situational crime prevention because it is seen as a more repressive approach and more harmful to society than other methods of crime prevention. This criticism included the development of a "fortress society," the erosion of civil liberties through CCTV, and inconvenient security checks. Conversely, these arguments met counterclaims, such as the success of CPTED and situational crime prevention in reducing crime, and the public's acceptance of increased security.

Search the Web

Use your favorite search engine to see what vendors have to offer and prices for the following: fences, window protection or glazing, door protection, exterior intrusion detection systems, security lighting, and protective dogs.

Check out the following sites on the Web:

American Institute of Architects, Security Resource Center: www.aia.org/security
American National Standards Institute: www.ansi.org
American Society for Testing and Materials: www.astm.org
American Society of Landscape Architects: www.asla.org
Builders Hardware Manufacturers Association: www.buildershardware.com/
Illuminating Engineering Society of North America: www.iesna.org
International Association of Lighting Management Companies: www.nalmco.org
International CPTED Association: www.cpted.net
International Organization for Standardization: www.iso.org
National Crime Prevention Council: www.ncpc.org
National Fire Protection Association: www.nfpa.org
National Lighting Bureau: www.nlb.org
Security Industry Association: www.siaonline.org
Technical Support Working Group: www.tswg.gov
Underwriters Laboratory (UL): www.ul.com
United Nations Crime and Justice Information Network: www.uncjin.org
U.S. General Services Administration: www.gsa.gov

Case Problems

8A. Study the characteristics of Woody's Lumber Company, the Smith Shirt manufacturing plant, and Compulab Corporation (refer to Figures 7-1, 7-2, and 7-3). Establish a priority list of what you think are the 10 most important countermeasures for each location to prevent unauthorized entry. Why did you select as top priorities your first three strategies in each list?

8B. As a security manager for a corporation, you made several written recommendations to management to improve perimeter security at corporate headquarters located in a suburban environment. Management rejected your plans because "headquarters will look like a prison." What measures can you include in your new plan that provide security and are aesthetically pleasing?

8C. As a newly hired security manager for an office building, a site for research and development, you are faced with three immediate challenges: (1) some employees are not wearing required ID badges from the time they first enter the building to when they depart; (2) during off-hours there are too many security system false alarms; and (3) public police are responding to about half of these alarms. What do you do?

8D. You are a physical security specialist for a corporation with locations worldwide. Your next big assignment from your supervisor, the VP of Loss Prevention, is to work with a corporate IT specialist to apply Internet technology to the integration of access controls, intrusion detection, and CCTV systems. Basically, the VP wants to "visit" all corporate locations from her office. The IT specialist that you must work with constantly complains, feels that the corporate IT infrastructure has reached its maximum capacity, and seems to be distrustful of loss prevention personnel. How do you gain his cooperation, promote harmony, and get the job done?

8E. You are a physical security specialist for a major global corporation based in the United States. Upon conducting a security survey of a large corporate building in a medium-size city in the United States, you listed the following vulnerabilities. Prepare solutions for each vulnerability and prioritize the list so the most serious items are corrected as soon as possible (Purpura, 2007).

Item A
The building contains an underground garage with minimal controls (i.e., an access gate opened by an employee access card).

Item B
The front of the building is on Main Street, close to the street, and any vehicles can park at the front on the street. The three other sides of the building contain parking lots close to the building and accessible through an access gate opened by an employee access card.

Item C
The rear lobby of the building is at ground level and at the ending point of a straight road of one-eighth mile long.

Item D
In the last 12 months, two employees were robbed at night outside the building in the parking lots.

Item E
Corporate offices, functions, assets, and utilities are clearly marked by signs inside and outside the building.

Item F
Air intakes for the building are at ground level at the rear of the building.

Item G
Although employees use a card key to access the building, tailgating is a problem.

Item H
A minimum number of security officers on the premises results in gaps in security and at access points as they are called off-post to obtain mail and conduct other errands.

Item I
Executive staff have their names on designated parking spaces.

Item J
Two garbage dumpsters are located up against the rear of the building.

Item K
The rear of the building faces nearby hills containing a variety of buildings.

References

Arnheim, L. (1999). "A Tour of Guard Patrol Systems." *Security Management* (November).

Berube, H. (1994). "New Notions of Night Light." *Security Management* (December).

Clark, R. (1983). "Situational Crime Prevention: Its Theoretical Basis and Practical Scope." In M. Tonry and N. Morris (eds.). *Crime and Justice*, 4. Chicago: University of Chicago Press.

Clifton, R., and Vitch, M. (1997). "Getting a Sense for Danger." *Security Management* (February).

Coupe, T., and Kaur, S. (2005). "The Role of Alarms and CCTV in Detecting Non-residential Burglary." *Security Journal*, 18.

Davey, C., et al. (2005). "Design Against Crime: Extending the Reach of Crime Prevention through Environmental Design." *Security Journal*, 18.

Evans, R. (2005). "Remote Monitoring." *Security Products*, 9 (March).

Garcia, M. (2006). *Vulnerability Assessment of Physical Protection Systems*. Burlington, MA: Butterworth-Heinemann.

Gips, M. (1999). "A Pharmacopoeia of Protection." *Security Management*, 43 (March).

Harowitz, S. (2006). "Dog Use Dogged by Questions." *Security Management*, 50 (January).

Illuminating Engineering Society of North America. (2003). *Guideline for Security Lighting for People, Property, and Public Spaces*. New York, NY: IESNA.

Lab, S. (2004). *Crime Prevention: Approaches, Practices and Evaluations*, 5th ed. www.lexis-nexis.com/anderson/criminaljustice

Milne, J. (2005). "Build Your Own Security Operations Center." *Secure Enterprise* (August 1). www.secureenterprisemag.com, retrieved September 26, 2005.

Moore, M. (2006). "Defensive Devices Designed to Blend In with New York." *USA Today* (July 31). www.usatoday.com/news/nation/2006-07-31-ny-security_x.htm, retrieved August 1, 2006.

Murphy, P. (2000). "Grounds for Protection." *Security Management*, 44 (October).

National Fire Protection Association. (2005). "NFPA 730, Guide for Premises Security, 2006 Edition." Quincy, MA: NFPA.

National Lighting Bureau. (n.d.). *Lighting for Safety and Security*. Washington, D.C.: National Lighting Bureau.

Newman, O. (1972). *Defensible Space*. New York: Macmillan.

National Law Enforcement and Corrections Technology Center. (2006). "No License to Steal." *TECHbeat* (Spring).

Owen, D. (2003). *Building Security: Strategies & Cost*. Kingston, MA: Reed.

Painter, K., and Farrington, D. (1999). "Street Lighting and Crime: Diffusion of Benefits in the Stoke-on-Trent Project." In K. Painter and N. Tilly (eds.), *Crime Prevention Studies*. Monsey, NY: Criminal Justice Press.

Patterson, D. (2000). "How Smart Is Your Setup?" *Security Management*, 44 (March).

Pierce, C. (2006). "Thermal Video for the Mainstream?" *Security Technology & Design*, 16 (May).

Post, R., and Kingsbury, A. (1977). *Security Administration: An Introduction*, 3rd ed. Springfield, IL: Charles C. Thomas.

Purpura, P. (1979). "Police Activity and the Full Moon." *Journal of Police Science and Administration*, 7 (September).

Purpura, P. (2007). *Terrorism and Homeland Security: An Introduction with Applications*. Burlington, MA: Elsevier Butterworth-Heinemann.

Reddick, R. (2005). "What You Should Know about Protecting a Perimeter." *Security Products*, 9 (April).

Revel, O. (2003). "Protective Blast and Anti-Ramming Wall Development." *Security Technology & Design* (November).

Saflex, Inc. (2005). "Introduction to Security Glazing." www.saflex.com, retrieved June 1, 2005.

"Scanning for Trouble." (2000). *Security Watch*, 2908 (April 15).

Schumacher, J. (2000). "How to Resolve Conflict with Proper Systems Integration." *Security Technology & Design,* 10 (October).

Shelton, D. (2006). "The New and Improved Moat." *Security Technology & Design*, 16 (March).

Smith, M. (1996). "Crime Prevention through Environmental Design in Parking Facilities" (April). Washington, D.C.: National Institute of Justice.

Taylor, R., and Harrell, A. (1996). "Physical Environment and Crime." Washington, D.C.: National Institute of Justice.

True, T. (1996). "Raising the Ramparts." *Security Management* (October).

United Nations. (2000). "Effective Crime Prevention: Keeping Pace with New Developments." Vienna, Austria: Tenth United Nations Congress on the Prevention of Crime and the Treatment of Offenders. www.uncjin.org, retrieved August 16, 2006.

United Nations. (1990). "Inventory of Comprehensive Crime Prevention Measures." Havana, Cuba: Eighth United Nations Congress on the Prevention of Crime and the Treatment of Offenders.

United Nations. (1993). "Work of the United Nations in Crime Prevention and Criminal Justice." *Crime Prevention and Criminal Justice* (June).

U.S. Department of Homeland Security. (2003). *Reference Manual to Mitigate Potential Terrorist Attacks against Buildings*, FEMA 426 (December). Washington, D.C.: FEMA.

U.S. Department of Justice (1976). *Report of the Task Force on Private Security*. Washington, D.C.: U.S. Government Printing Office.

Wilson, J., and Kelling, G. (1982). "Broken Windows: The Police and Neighborhood Safety." *Atlantic Monthly* (March).

Zwirn, J. (2003). "Alarm Design That Rings True." *Security Management*. (April).

 **9**

Services and Systems: Methods Toward Wise Purchasing Decisions

Objectives

After studying this chapter, the reader will be able to:

1. Discuss pitfalls when purchasing security/loss prevention services and systems.
2. List five specific purchasing rules and eight sources of information.
3. List guidelines and inquisitive questions that improve purchasing decisions when seeking security services.
4. List guidelines and inquisitive questions that improve purchasing decisions when seeking security systems.
5. Name and explain three types of bids in the purchasing process.
6. Explain outsourcing.

KEY TERMS

- security services
- security systems
- vendors
- key performance indicators
- competitive bid
- request for information

- request for quotation
- request for proposal
- work breakdown structure
- outsourcing
- contract lifecycle management
- due diligence

Introduction

One topic often neglected in the security literature is how to make wise purchasing decisions when obtaining security services and systems. The best security plans are useless when poor purchasing decisions are made to implement those plans. **Security services** include activities performed by personnel to further the goals of security and loss prevention. Security officers represent a large part of available security services. **Security systems** include manufactured items that protect people and assets. An example is an intrusion detection system. This chapter emphasizes security services and systems, keeping in mind the understanding that fire protection and safety are integral components of an effective loss prevention program.

Most business executives and institutional administrators do not know how to select security services or systems or even what questions to ask vendors. Frequently, money is wasted and the results after the purchases are made are disappointing. A specialist in the field who is not a salesperson can improve decision making.

During their careers, loss prevention practitioners are most likely to purchase all kinds of services and systems. Purchasing decisions have a definite impact on career opportunities and on the success of loss prevention programs. Care is required during decision making to obtain the best services and systems for the money at hand. This task is difficult when one is confronted with a multitude of salespeople and a varied market that is taking in billions of dollars per year.

Pitfalls when Purchasing Security Services and Systems

Suppliers of services and systems are not immune to the temptation of unethical and illegal activities for profit. Vendors have been known to misrepresent information, exaggerate, lie, and fail to deliver what was promised. **Vendors** are sellers or salespeople. The rotten-apple syndrome is prevalent in this industry just as it is in other facets of life—there are unscrupulous vendors as well as honest ones.

A U.S. Department of Justice (1972: 59) publication, *Private Police in the United States: Findings and Recommendations*, states

> On the basis of regulatory-agency reports of the number of complaints filed and the reasons for licenses being suspended and revoked, and on the basis of impressions gleaned from security executives, we conclude that substantial dishonesty and poor business practices exist. The former entails common crimes by some security employees and employers, including burglary, robbery, theft, and extortion. The latter include franchising licenses, operating without a license, failure to perform services paid for, misrepresenting price or service to be performed, and negligence in performing security duties.

Purchasers of security officer services may be billed for hours not worked. Because this service industry is so competitive, some companies bid very low, knowing that they will have to bill the client for phantom services (services not rendered) to make a profit. Other companies lie to clients about training and experience. Promised supervision may not take place. Liability insurance coverage may be exaggerated or nonexistent. Investigative companies that conduct overt and undercover investigations are known to deceive clients about excessive losses through scary weekly reports in order to lengthen investigations and thereby reap greater profits.

Techniques employed by people selling systems include selling unneeded equipment. Alarm systems composed of outdated technology, which are overstocked at warehouses, are pushed on buyers who do not realize that offenders can easily defeat these systems. Salespeople conveniently delete information concerning extra personnel needed, additional hardware required, software problems, and expensive maintenance. Vendors sell technology that makes customers think they are monitoring remotely, but with real-time delay, it is not so. Demo videos are sent to prospective buyers with systems operating under ideal conditions of perfect weather and lighting (Strauchs, 2001: 98). Some security system installers set sensors to detect minor intrusions during a test and then, following the test, lower the sensitivity of the sensor to reduce false alarms. *One specific tactic involves reinforcing the purchaser's fear.* Crime, fire, and accident dangers are intertwined within high-pressure sales pitches.

McCumber (2006: 55–58) notes that hype is also a problem in the IT security industry. He offers the example of an IT salesperson who exaggerated a problem that a customer would pay a high price to avoid. The salesperson demonstrated the vulnerability on his laptop and showed how his company's software solution eradicated the problem. When the salesperson offered to load the software onto the customer's IT system to show its effectiveness, and emphasizing how he could easily delete it, the salesperson was escorted to the exit.

Many vendors adhere to ethical conduct. The point of the industry criticism here is that the buyer should be aware of these practices when confronted with a purchasing decision.

The *Report of the Task Force on Private Security* (U.S. Department of Justice, 1976: 146–147) and the first Hallcrest report (U.S. Department of Justice, National Institute of Justice, 1985: 71) stated several recommendations for improving the industry with the consumer in mind. For example, both reports favor certified training for alarm service personnel.

The following five cardinal rules, designed with the consumer in mind, can put the buyer on the road toward making wise purchasing decisions:

1. Buyer beware.
2. Properly evaluate the needs of the organization to be protected.
3. Acquire information and know the state of the art.
4. Analyze the advantages and disadvantages of each service or system. Apply critical thinking skills.
5. Avoid panic buying.

A risk analysis will assist the buyer in pinpointing weaknesses and evaluating needs. If the buyer has a list of weaknesses and needs, the salesperson will be hindered from influencing the buyer into purchasing something unnecessary. To acquire information about services and systems, eight beneficial sources are the Web, standards and related organizations, peers, consultants not affiliated with any vendors, seminars, courses, trade publications, and salespeople.

Is the security industry the only industry where the buyer should beware? Support your answer.

Purchasing Security Services

Questions When Considering Contract Security Officers

1. Does the company conform to state and local regulatory law, such as registration, licensing, training, and bonding?
2. What are the contract company's liability and other insurance coverage? Request copies of policies. Are there lawsuits pending against the company?
3. Have there been any EEO complaints against the company?
4. What is the company's Dun and Bradstreet financial rating?
5. Is the company willing to customize service for client company needs?
6. Does the company have the ability to provide extra officers?
7. Can the company perform expanded services, such as investigations?
8. Have you been invited to visit the company's offices?
9. Have you read the employment application form and company publications (e.g., orders, regulations, training literature)?
10. What type of background screening is conducted on applicants? Can you set up an agreement whereby your company interviews officers before assignment? Do you require personnel folders to help you select the best candidates?
11. How often during a shift does a supervisor visit?
12. How does the company ensure the honesty of its officers?
13. How are disciplinary problems handled?
14. In general, how is morale? What is the turnover rate?
15. What is the extent of training?
16. What equipment is supplied to officers?

17. What are the pay scales and benefits?
18. What is the wage-to-rate ratio? This shows the portion of the total rate received by each officer.

Many security firms draft their contracts so that much of the risk is on the customer. An attorney should review contracts and negotiate changes. It is important that both parties know the amount of duty the security company is agreeing to. The contract should specify number of officers and hours, location of officers, and equipment. If, for example, an assault takes place on the 10th floor of a building, the security company may go back to the contract and read that an officer was assigned only to the lobby and that more services were available, but the client refused them (Finnerty, 1996: 4–7).

Heil (2006: 57–64) recommends that customers of contract security services carefully consider the low bidder before final selection. A low bidder may result in poor quality officers and increased liability. He also favors ongoing expectations for performance during the contract through metrics (also called **key performance indicators**) that can be tied to financial rewards or penalties for the vendor. These metrics include the following: no-show rates, missed tours, missed supervisory visits, complaints against officers, violations of policies and procedures, and inappropriate uniform and appearance.

When one is dealing with contract companies, it is good to know the views of these business people: a portion of the managers in contract guard companies refer to their vocation as a "nickel-and-dime-business" with a "never-ending turnover of bodies." The former comment refers to the awarding of contracts by clients based on slim differences in bids. The latter comment refers to the high turnover of officers because of low wages.

Contract Undercover Investigators

A common scenario in businesses is the panic atmosphere after the discovery of a high inventory-shrinkage statistic following an inventory. When this happens, management wants immediate action even when it is predisposed to avoid panic buying. Management often recruits an outside firm specializing in undercover investigations. The undercover investigator secretly infiltrates employee informal groups, as a regular employee, to gather information about losses.

With an understanding of how contract undercover investigation services operate, the client will obtain better results. When speaking to a service representative, the client needs to find out the cost and probable length of the investigation. These investigations last from six to eight weeks but may require months to yield success. The cost varies from $1,500 to $2,000 per week (Ferraro, 2000: 70). The client should ask the representative about the backgrounds of investigators, selection methods (for employment and assignment), training, and supervision. Are investigators bonded? Proof should be provided. Are they prepared to testify in court, if necessary? How many reports will the client receive each week? Undercover investigators send reports to their immediate supervisor, who edits them before sending a report to the client. The reporting phase of the investigation is the time when unscrupulous activity by the service company may take place. Supervisors are known to withhold from clients good information to submit later during "dry weeks," when no substantial information is uncovered. Frightening reports about losses can scare clients into paying for unnecessarily lengthy investigations. When clients become impatient and ask why the investigation is taking so long, sometimes the service company's response is that "a break in the case is right around the corner and we just need a few more weeks." If put under excessive pressure by supervisors, investigators may succumb to exaggerated reports and may even invent information. Although these practices produce a negative image of undercover investigative services, not all of these companies are unethical. Undercover investigations are a widely used and effective method to combat losses.

Consultants

Why would an executive require the services of a loss prevention consultant? Two major reasons are (1) the executive lacks knowledge about loss prevention and there is an absence of a proprietary loss prevention practitioner; or (2) the executive is a loss prevention practitioner but lacks expertise in a specialized field.

A consultant is contacted when a loss problem needs to be corrected—for instance, a baffling shrinkage problem, the loss of trade secrets, protection against terrorism, or numerous workplace accidents. Consultants also can be a tremendous asset when an organization is contemplating a loss prevention program for the first time or when an established program suffers from morale or training problems. New ideas can stimulate greater efficiency and effectiveness. Consultants can act as a company's representatives in negotiating contract services and purchasing systems.

Executives sometimes refrain from hiring a consultant because they feel that it will reflect adversely on their ability. A consultant can be a cost-effective investment, but the buyer must beware.

A client interested in a successful consulting experience will be involved in three specific phases: (1) selection, (2) direction, and (3) evaluation. The objective of the selection phase is to contact the most appropriate person for the job. The executive must first *clearly define the problem* and then search for the individual with the required background.

Select a consultant who is independent, that is, not affiliated with any particular service or system. Also, ask how much money and time are required to complete the work.

In the second phase, the client assists the consultant in becoming familiar with the business and the problem. The consultant is introduced to select personnel. A tour of the premises is another part of what is known as the startup time, which can easily consume a day. The consultant will be preoccupied with collecting information via interviews, observation, and records. The consultant will ask many questions. A previously prepared survey or checklist form is brought by the consultant as a reminder of what specific questions to ask or areas to check. Clients may request a one-day survey followed by verbal advice, whereas other assignments may last for weeks, months, or years.

When sufficient information has been collected, and the consultant has a good grasp of the problem and possible solutions, he or she presents a report of findings and recommendations to the client. Naturally, the consultant is in an advisory capacity, and the executives in charge have the authority and must accept the responsibility of instituting the recommendations.

The third and final phase for the client pertains to evaluating the consultant. A standard personnel evaluation form provides several relevant questions (e.g., works well with others, is flexible, communicates clearly). However, the primary question is this: was the problem uncovered and satisfactorily remedied?

Certifications in Security

Most states have no regulation for security and loss prevention consultants. When registration or licensing is required, it often is accomplished via the laws regulating security officers and private investigators. With such minimal controls, almost anybody can call himself or herself a consultant. Hence, charlatans appear who tarnish the field and create a bad image that reflects on competent professionals.

In light of the scarcity of regulations or standards for security and loss prevention consultants and managers, and to reinforce professionalism in this field, ASIS International created the Certified Protection Professional (CPP) program in 1972. To qualify for CPP certification, the applicant must meet certain education and experience requirements, affirm adherence to the CPP Code of Professional Responsibility, receive endorsement by a person certified as a CPP, and achieve a passing grade on the written examination. ASIS International also offers two other certifications: Physical Security Professional (PSP) and Professional Certified Investigator (PCI).

In addition to ASIS International CPPs as a source of consultants, another source, although small, is the International Association of Professional Security Consultants (IAPSC), founded in 1984. Members of this professional association are required to have education and experience, and the CPP is accepted as a component of the qualifications for membership. Like ASIS, the IAPSC requires its members to adhere to a code of ethics. The IAPSC offers the Certified Security Consultant program.

□ □ □ ▬▬▬▬▬▬▬▬▬▬▬▬▬▬▬▬▬▬▬▬▬▬▬▬▬

For you, as a practitioner, what are the benefits of obtaining certifications in security?

▬▬▬▬▬▬▬▬▬▬▬▬▬▬▬▬▬▬▬▬▬▬▬ □ □ □

Purchasing Security Systems

The National Burglar and Fire Alarm Association (NBFAA) provides consumer tips through its Web site for selecting security systems. The NBFAA is a nonprofit association that promotes professionalism and standards in the industry.

The National Fire Protection Association (NFPA, 2005) is another source of information, especially in reference to standards. For example, "NFPA 731, Standard for the Installation of Electronic Premises Security Systems, 2006 Edition" contains information on standards of other organizations (e.g., ANSI, SIA, and UL), definitions, fundamentals, and various systems.

Questions When Considering a Security System

1. What can the system do?
2. What is the *total cost* of the system, including installation, additional personnel, training, maintenance, finance charges, and so on? When the purchaser buys in large volume, the greater profit for the vendor may result in lower prices.
3. Is the total price competitive with other vendors?
4. Can the system adapt to new technological developments? What modifications are possible? Costs?
5. How long will it take for the system to be installed and become operational? If the manufacturer contracts the installation to a subcontractor, how are standards maintained and inspections conducted, and what are the related stipulations in the contract?
6. What is the system life?
7. What does the warranty cover?
8. What maintenance is required and by whom? Since a system is useless when it fails and is not repaired, are preventive maintenance and emergency maintenance part of the contract?
9. Have we checked the company's Dun and Bradstreet rating?
10. Does the vendor have appropriate business licenses? Does the vendor conform to applicable state laws requiring training or registration?
11. Is the vendor a member of trade associations that help members stay current on new technology and product developments?
12. What is the background of personnel involved with the product? Are professional engineers employed? Do licensed contractors do electrical work? Is pre-employment screening conducted? Are employees trained and certified?
13. Have we requested references from the vendor from current users of the same product? Have we followed up on those references?
14. Does the manufacturer freely release information about its systems to outsiders? (Offenders are known to pose as writers, reporters, or customers to acquire system information.)
15. Have the system and its components been evaluated by an independent testing organization? If applicable, does it meet NFPA and other standards?
16. How will the system be evaluated? Can security personnel, in a controlled test, "trip" a sensor to ensure reliability?

Rather than purchase a security system, a company may choose the option of leasing. Security vendors, manufacturers, and integrators are not only offering products, technical support, and installation, but also equipment leasing, rentals, and specialized services. For security executives on a tight budget, and for those searching for value-added services and an improved return on investment, creative avenues should be researched to acquire security systems and services. Among the benefits of leasing is the opportunity to keep up with newer technology, quicker, rather than having to retain older, purchased equipment to recoup the investment (Whittemore, 2007: 20). A financial analysis of purchasing versus leasing is best.

System Acquisition

Khairallah (2006: 159–272) provides a foundation for acquiring security systems as described next. Once a security need is established, a preliminary design is prepared, and when management approves the plan and funding, the next step is to prepare a solicitation for the market to obtain pricing and availability of the products and services. The solicitation process is referred to as a **competitive bid**. Three types of bids are explained in subsequent paragraphs: request for information (RFI), request for quotation (RFQ), and request for proposal (RFP). The type of bid to employ depends on such factors as the complexity of the project and the purchasing policies of the company. In addition, elements of multiple types of bids may be used.

A **request for information** serves to gather information for an RFQ or RFP. The RFI is especially helpful when security needs are unusual and the security practitioner is searching for guidance. The RFI is not specific as to what will be purchased; it describes mission and functions broadly. Essentially, the market helps with problem solving. One drawback to the nonspecific nature of the RFI is that vendors typically recommend products that they sell instead of meeting the customer's need.

A **request for quotation** seeks the costs of the required components of the security system. It also contains other elements including project management, scheduling and cost controls, system demonstration, freight and insurance, installation, system testing, user training, warranty, and post-installation support. The RFQ provides an opportunity to compare bidders.

A **request for proposal** contains the elements of an RFQ, plus equipment performance criteria. There are several variations of the RFP. The National Contract Management Association offers a listing of contract types and conditions. Khairallah notes that even for a trained professional it is nearly impossible to know all the features of all security products from the numerous manufacturers. He recommends that the RFP be well organized and indexed. Khairallah suggests using a technique from federal government contracting called **work breakdown structure** (WBS). This process separates parts of a project into clearly definable tasks, and it includes features and capabilities from the preliminary design. The security practitioner can use the WBS to check each bid to ensure that all components of the project are included and vendors can respond to each section. For the security practitioner, this process facilitates ease of comparison and helps with the ranking of bids.

Following the evaluation of the written proposals, the next step is to request a product demonstration from the most likely vendors that can meet the requirements of the RFP. As the evaluation of vendor proposals ends, the security practitioner prepares a written report for management to pinpoint the most favorable bidder. Once the contract is awarded, there are specific stages of installation and implementation. They include inspections, testing, and training.

___

You Be the Judge*

Carl Simpson, the security director at Southeast Tool Company, was fighting mad. The plant had been burglarized again, but that was nothing new. What had him angry was that the alarm system the company had leased recently had failed to detect the intrusion.

"Get Security Systems International on the phone," snapped Simpson at his secretary.

Once SSI came on the line, Simpson began his attack: "We had $135,000 worth of precision machine tools stolen last night, and your people are responsible. According to our contract, you're supposed to make sure this alarm system works. It doesn't, so your company had better come up with $135,000."

The manager of SSI just laughed. "Calm down and reread your contract," he said. "It has what's called an exculpatory clause, which says that SSI is not responsible for any loss caused by burglary."

"But this was your fault!" Simpson cried.

"It doesn't matter," replied the manager. "The clause covers us even if we're negligent." He chuckled, "I can tell you've never dealt with a burglar alarm company before. Almost all alarm contracts have an exculpatory clause in them."

But Simpson refused to give up without a fight. He had Southeast sue SSI for breach of contract, breach of warranty, and negligence, despite the exculpatory clause in the contract. "It's not fair," Simpson argued. "When we contracted with SSI, we put the safety of our company in their hands. They took on the responsibility, and they shouldn't be able to use a catch-all clause to escape liability for their negligence."

Did the court agree?

Make your decision; then turn to the end of the chapter for the court's decision.

---

*Reprinted with permission from *Security Management—Plant and Property Protection*, a publication of Bureau of Business Practice, Inc., 24 Rope Ferry Road, Waterford, CT 06386.

━━━━━━━━━━━━━━━━━━━━━━━━━━━━━━   ☐ ☐ ☐

Outsourcing

Outsourcing is purchasing, from outside companies, services that were previously performed in-house. In *Business at the Speed of Thought*, Bill Gates writes: "An important reengineering principle is that companies should focus on their core business and outsource everything else." Internet connectivity has produced a global economy with intense competition requiring management to concentrate on new challenges and opportunities or be left behind. For success and profit, management staff are learning that they must focus on what the company does best and outsource support functions. Outsourcing improves a company's focus, frees internal resources for other purposes, reduces costs, and shares risks. Consequently, activities that do not contribute directly to the bottom line and are part of "the cost of doing business" are ripe targets for outsourcing. Examples are human resources, risk management, environmental management, safety, and security (Caldwell, 2001: 18–20).

Here, we consider some outsourcing decisions. A frequent outsourcing decision concerns choosing between in-house and contract security officer services. Consider the following generalized advantages and disadvantages. With in-house, the advantages are lower turnover and increased control over hiring, training, and quality. In addition, officers often have greater loyalty and are familiar with unique needs. The disadvantages are higher costs and total responsibility for security. With contract services, the advantages are lower costs, fewer human resources duties, and shared responsibilities. The disadvantages are less direct control, less impact on hiring and loyalty, and higher turnover. It is not uncommon for a contract security officer to work for months without the client knowing that the officer has a felony record. One solution is for the contractor to maintain a personnel folder on-site for each officer and for it to contain a copy of the application, background check, training, and regulatory papers (Maurer, 2000: 14–18).

Another outsourcing decision involves choosing between in-house and off-site access control. For many years, central stations have serviced clients by monitoring intrusion and fire detection systems. In the late 1970s and early 1980s, central stations began to offer access control services. This avenue works well in multitenant facilities with both limited entry points and visitors, and a preference to avoid the presence of a security officer. Off-site access controls typically include audio and video systems. Conversely, facilities characterized by many visitors and exception-based entry requests can result in access delays if access is controlled off-site. Delay becomes more problematic if people must wait in adverse weather. The screening of packages presents another problem for off-site access controls; personnel on-site may be necessary for this task (Friedenfelds, 2006: 42–46).

Outsourcing may include hiring a systems integrator. Selecting the best integrator is a crucial and tricky process. Seek evidence of financial stability, insurance bonding, and a close relationship between the integrator and manufacturers. In addition, visit customers of the integrator, seek an open architecture, and get IT personnel involved.

In the IT sphere, "managed security" is a growing trend involving outsourcing of security technologies, infrastructure, and services. Many companies with in-house staff simply cannot keep up with all the pressing IT security issues (DeJesus, 2001: 34–49).

Adler et al. (2005: 61–65) write about the popularity of outsourcing and the importance of the process being well managed to meet corporate objectives. They note that the key to success is to have a plan for every step of the process of outsourcing, beyond selecting the vendor and integrating the service into company operations. They suggest a model known as **contract lifecycle management** (CLM) that contains four primary steps: (1) contract governance and oversight, (2) RFP, (3) due diligence, and (4) contract negotiation and execution. Governance consists of a council of specialists from such areas as procurement, legal, finance, operations, and IT, who participate in all phases of the CLM. The second step is the RFP. Step three, **due diligence**, is the attention and care expected in checking the accuracy of information and omissions. This step can begin with an RFI from vendors and include a variety of information. Examples are vendor operations, financial information, licensure requirements, insurance, and a list of clients. The contract negotiation and execution is the last step. It focuses on the final terms between the client and the vendor and the signing of the contract. Adler et al. add three elements to a successful transition: (1) a team to oversee and manage the change; (2) communication to affected people, with explanations of the reasons for the change and its impact; and (3) key performance indicators that are often in contracts.

☐ ☐ ☐ ━━

Is outsourcing a good or bad idea? Justify your answer.

☐ ☐ ☐ ━━

Career: Security Sales, Equipment, and Services

This security specialty can be stimulating, challenging, and financially rewarding. New security-related products and services have resulted from emerging threats and evolving high technology, and the number of companies offering various security services has grown as a result. Sales positions can range from products such as barriers, alarm systems, sophisticated biometrics, CCTV, biological detection equipment, and risk management software, to uniformed security services. Sales and service personnel may be employed by a product manufacturer to sell that particular company's products or by an independent dealer that represents a variety of products. Entry-level positions may involve making sales calls, handling advertising queries, staffing and organizing sales booths, demonstrating products, and providing input on government proposal requests. In addition to typical management functions, mid-level management responsibilities may include directing and motivating sales personnel, organizing sales and marketing campaigns, preparing and presenting proposals, conducting briefings, and managing a trade show booth.

Entry-level management positions may call for a college degree, depending on the size and nature of the employer. It is recommended that broad-based education and experience be achieved in areas such as accounting, industrial engineering, management, marketing, human resources, communications, statistics, or labor relations. The nature and extent of the desired education and experience and the entry-level salary range can vary depending on the type of product or service being provided, the size of the vendor, and other factors.

Mid-level management positions require the experience to perform a wide range of functions as indicated previously. The ability to effectively deal with a range of people and the capability to present information verbally and in writing are particularly important.

Source: Courtesy of ASIS International (2005). "Career Opportunities in Security." www.asisonline.org.

□ □ □ ▬▬▬▬▬▬▬▬▬▬▬▬▬▬▬▬▬▬▬▬▬▬▬▬▬▬▬▬

Search the Web
Use your favorite search engines to view what is on-line for "security services" and "security systems." Also, check out the following sites:

ASIS International: www.asisonline.org
International Association of Professional Security Consultants: www.iapsc.org
National Burglar and Fire Alarm Association: www.alarm.org
National Fire Protection Association: www.nfpa.org

▬▬▬▬▬▬▬▬▬▬▬▬▬▬▬▬▬▬▬▬▬▬▬▬▬▬ □ □ □

Case Problem

9A. Select a specific security service or system. Study the state of the art. Then list, in order of priority, 10 questions you would ask vendors. Explain why the first three questions are placed at the top of the list.

The Decision for "You Be the Judge"

The court did not agree with Simpson's reasoning and dismissed Southeast's lawsuit against SSI. The court held that the clause was valid and clear in totally absolving SSI from liability for the burglary. If your company has leased a burglar alarm system, check the contract to see if it has an exculpatory clause. If it does, take heart. Not all courts have upheld the validity of such clauses in all circumstances. Check with your company's lawyer to find out where your state courts stand on this issue.

This case is based on *L. Luria & Son v. Alarmtech International*, 384 So2d 947. The names in this case have been changed to protect the privacy of those involved.

References

Adler, S., et al. (2005). "The Inside Story on Outsource Planning." *Security Management*, 49 (August).
Caldwell, G. (2001). "Do It Yourself or Outsource It?" *Security Technology & Design*, 12 (March).

DeJesus, E. (2001). "Managing Managed Security." *Information Security*, 4 (January).

Ferraro, E. (2000). "End Game." *Security Management*, 44 (August).

Finnerty, J. (1996). "Who's Liable, the Security Firm or You?" *Risk Management Advisor* (May).

Friedenfelds, L. (2006). "Is Outsourcing Right for You?" *Security Technology & Design*, 16 (February).

Heil, R. (2006). "Guarding Against Poor Performance." *Security Management*, 50 (June).

Khairallah, M. (2006). *Physical Security Systems Handbook: The Design and Implementation of Electronic Security Systems*. Boston, MA: Butterworth-Heinemann.

Maurer, R. (2000). "Outsourcing: An Option or a Threat?" *Security Technology & Design*, 10 (August).

McCumber, J. (2006). "Truth in Advertising." *Security Technology & Design*, 16 (April).

National Fire Protection Association. (2005). "NFPA 731, Standard for the Installation of Electronic Premises Security Systems, 2006 Edition." Quincy, MA: NFPA.

Strauchs, J. (2001). "Which Way to Better Controls?" *Security Management*, 45 (January).

U.S. Department of Justice. (1972). *Private Police in the United States: Findings and Recommendations*. Washington, D.C.: U.S. Government Printing Office.

U.S. Department of Justice (1976). *Report of the Task Force on Private Security*. Washington, D.C.: U.S. Government Printing Office.

U.S. Department of Justice, National Institute of Justice. (1985). *Crime and Protection in America (Executive Summary of the Hallcrest Report)*. Washington, D.C.: U.S. Government Printing Office.

Whittemore, S. (2007). "Leasing Offers Attractive Benefits to Security Directors." *Security Director News*, 4 (January).

10
Investigations

Objectives

After studying this chapter, the reader will be able to:

1. List and discuss the six basic investigative questions.
2. Describe at least five types of investigations in the private sector.
3. Differentiate among proprietary and contract investigations, private and public investigations, and overt and undercover private investigations.
4. List and explain at least five subject areas important to the investigative process.
5. Explain both digital evidence and digital forensics.

KEY TERMS
• proprietary investigation   • open-ended questions

<table>
<tr><th colspan="2">KEY TERMS</th></tr>
<tr><td>• proprietary investigation</td><td>• open-ended questions</td></tr>
<tr><td>• contract investigation</td><td>• close-ended questions</td></tr>
<tr><td>• private investigations</td><td>• Freedom of Information Law</td></tr>
<tr><td>• public investigations</td><td>• identity theft</td></tr>
<tr><td>• overt investigation</td><td>• phishing</td></tr>
<tr><td>• undercover investigation</td><td>• modus operandi</td></tr>
<tr><td>• qualified privilege</td><td>• artificial intelligence</td></tr>
<tr><td>• attorney/client privilege</td><td>• data mining</td></tr>
<tr><td>• direct evidence</td><td>• link analysis</td></tr>
<tr><td>• circumstantial evidence</td><td>• Identi-Kit</td></tr>
<tr><td>• hearsay evidence</td><td>• digital evidence</td></tr>
<tr><td>• chain of custody of evidence</td><td>• digital forensics</td></tr>
<tr><td>• interview</td><td>• surveillance</td></tr>
<tr><td>• interrogation</td><td>• deposition</td></tr>
</table>

Introduction

An investigation is a search for information. Information is obtained from many sources, including the following: people, such as victims, witnesses, suspects, and informants; physical evidence, such as fingerprints, DNA, shoe prints, and tool marks; and information technology, such as the Web and databases.

There are six basic questions to ask in an investigation:

1. *Who?* Who are the individuals involved in the particular incident being investigated? Names, addresses, and telephone numbers are important.
2. *What happened?* What is the story of the incident? For instance, what happened before, during, and after a theft incident?
3. *Where?* The location of the incident and the movement of people and objects are important. For example, where exactly were witnesses and the suspect when the theft occurred?
4. *When?* A notation of the times of particular activities during an incident is necessary for a thorough investigation. If a particular theft occurred between 7 and 8 P.M. on April 9, and Joe Doe is a suspect, he later can be exonerated because he really was at another location at that time.
5. *How?* The focus of this question is how the incident was able to take place in the face of (or absence of) loss prevention measures. After a theft, investigators often attempt to find out how the thief was able to circumvent security. In the case of an industrial accident, investigators study how the accident occurred while safety equipment was supposedly in use.
6. *Why?* This question can be difficult to answer. However, the answer can lead to the discovery of a pressing problem that may not be obvious. An example is seen with numerous losses in a manufacturing plant brought about by low employee morale. In this case, theft and destruction of company property can be reduced by, for example, increasing management's concern for employees through praise, a sports program, contests, and high-quality meals in the cafeteria.

The answer to the "why" question helps to establish the motive for the loss activity. Once the motive is established, suspects can be eliminated. A recently fired employee would have a motive of retribution for setting fire to his or her former place of employment.

Investigations are not always criminal in nature, and not every investigation requires answering all six investigative questions. Once an investigator gathers sufficient information, a report is often written and submitted to a supervisor. After that, the information in the report results in action or inaction by supervisors and management. Typically, investigative reports lead to either punitive or nonpunitive action. Punitive action can include discipline or prosecution or both. Nonpunitive action can include exonerating a suspect, hiring an applicant, promoting an employee, or obtaining an insurance reimbursement. Investigations can also result in corrective action such as an improved loss prevention program.

Investigations are unique to each type of business, institution, or organization served. The varieties and depths of investigations vary; they reflect management's needs, objectives, and budget. The personnel involved also vary and may include company investigators, auditors, IT specialists, contract investigators, public police, and attorneys.

The following steps can guide the process of an investigation:

1. the decision to begin an investigation
2. selection of a supervisor and investigator
3. planning, objectives, and methods of investigation
4. gathering accurate facts
5. accurate, factual report to management
6. management decision making

As covered in Chapter 4, ASIS International–funded research showed that legislation directly affects not only organizations in general, but also private security operations (Collins et al., 2005). The top three acts cited in this research as having the most impact on security policies and procedures were the Health Insurance Portability and Accountability Act of 1996 (HIPAA), the Sarbanes-Oxley (SOX) Act of 2002, and the USA Patriot Act of 2001. Major reasons for these laws are to protect corporate assets and prevent corporate crime. SOX, for example, has forced businesses to develop internal investigation teams to comply with regulations and improve the protection of assets and stockholder investments. This includes increased attention to employee theft and fraud, workplace violence, sexual harassment, due diligence, and other issues (Daniels, 2006: 22–23).

Types of Investigations

There are several types of investigations in the private sector. The following list illustrates some of the more common ones, categorized according to the target of the investigation.

The laws or "ground rules" for each type of investigation vary. In addition, the policies of organizations guide investigations, although subservient to law. The term *workplace investigation* is a generic term focusing on a wide variety of allegations. Examples are misconduct, substance abuse, and threats and violence. An *applicant background* investigation requires adherence to the laws discussed in Chapter 6. A private investigation of an alleged *criminal offense* requires knowledge of criminal law and evidence. In a private-sector criminal investigation, the notification of public police depends on such factors as whether company investigators arrested the suspect and whether management seeks to prosecute. A *financial investigation* checks on alleged fraud or embezzlement. *Computer crime* investigations focus on a variety of acts involving computers and information systems. The Internet has expanded the scope and complexity of these investigations. In an *accident* investigation, the investigator usually is knowledgeable about safety, the Occupational Safety and Health Act, workers' compensation insurance, and applicable laws. A major objective of a *fire and arson* investigation is to determine the probable cause of the fire. Sophisticated equipment may be used to locate and identify any substance employed to accelerate the fire. A *civil or negligence and liability* investigation involves, among other things, gathering evidence to determine whether a failure to exercise reasonable care in a situation caused harm to someone or something. For example, a customer (plaintiff) may seek to show that a retail store (defendant) with poor housekeeping caused the customer's injury. Both the plaintiff initiating the suit and the defendant are likely to conduct investigations and present evidence in court. A civil court decides on both liability (who is responsible) for a negligent act and any obligation (money award to the plaintiff) enforceable by the court. *Insurance* investigations, which at times result in litigation, are conducted to determine losses and their causes, and to assist in deciding on indemnification. Both the insurer and the insured may conduct separate investigations before an insurance claim is settled. Investigations of *labor* matters (e.g., workers' activities during a strike) are often sensitive. Legal counsel is necessary to guide the investigator because of associated federal and state laws. *Due diligence* is the attention and care legally expected in checking the accuracy of information and omissions. It can range from determining a customer's financial status to assessing the desirability of acquisition targets.

Proprietary and Contract Investigations

A **proprietary investigation** is undertaken by an in-house company employee who performs investigative work. A **contract investigation** requires the contracting of an outside company (agency) to supply investigative services for a fee.

There are inadequate and varied laws regulating contract investigative employees and firms. However, several jurisdictions have effective regulation (e.g., requirements of license, residency, training, experience, no felony convictions, examination, and insurance) that protect clients.

For the most part, proprietary investigators are not subject to government regulation. Many businesses, institutions, and organizations maintain their own investigators. Large corporations, utilities, insurance companies, and banks are some of the many concerns that rely on a large staff of proprietary investigators.

Numerous firms utilize both contract and proprietary investigators. If a large corporation has a particular season when the investigative workload is heavy, some of the extra workload can be assigned to a contract investigation company. This approach frees proprietary investigators for more pressing and specialized problems.

Citizens frequently obtain a distorted picture of private investigations via television, which produces misconceptions that falsify the various kinds of investigative work—work that is interesting, exciting, and also often boring. Another misconception is that many investigators in the private sector are armed. Few are armed, and those who are rarely use their weapons.

Private and Public Investigations

Private investigations serve the private sector (e.g., businesses and private citizens). **Public investigations** feature public police agencies, for the most part, serving the public. Both investigative efforts often are entwined. This can be seen, for example, when an office building is burglarized and company investigators call local police in a joint effort to solve the crime. However, how much time and effort can the public police devote to the office building burglary in comparison to the company investigators? Public police can devote only limited resources to such a crime. Typically, a uniformed public police officer will arrive for a preliminary investigation, and an incident report will be completed. Next, the incident report is transferred to a detective unit. Within a day or two, a detective arrives at the scene of the crime and conducts a follow-up investigation that involves gathering additional information and perhaps some placation, a public relations effort that assures the citizens that the police are doing everything possible to solve the crime. Generally, public police devote more time and effort to crimes against people than crimes against property.

The inability of the criminal justice system to assist adequately in private loss prevention efforts can also be illustrated by clearance rates, which are the proportion of cases solved by an arrest. Clearance rates (Federal Bureau of Investigation, 2006) are higher for crimes against people (e.g., murder, 62%; rape, 41%; robbery, 25%) and lower for crimes against property (e.g., burglary, 13%; larceny, 18%). These 2005 clearance rates show a decline of from 1 to 9% in comparison to the clearance rates of 1998 for the same types of crimes (Federal Bureau of Investigation, 1999). The success of private-sector investigations is difficult to gauge, since many firms do not prosecute and the outcome of investigations is usually confidential and unpublished.

Overt and Undercover Private Investigations

An **overt investigation** is an obvious investigation. People coming into contact with the overt investigator know that an investigation is taking place. A common scenario would be a company investigator, dressed in a conservative suit, arriving at the scene of a loss to interview employees and collect evidence. An **undercover investigation** (UI), on the other hand, is a secret investigation. In a typical approach, an undercover investigator is hired as a regular employee, a truck driver, for example, and collects information by associating with employees who are not knowledgeable about the undercover investigation. Law prohibits such investigators from collecting information on union activities.

Each type of investigation serves many useful purposes. An overt investigation that begins immediately after a loss shows that the loss prevention staff is on the job. This in itself acts as a deterrent. An overt investigation does not have to be in response to a loss; for example, preemployment investigations prevent losses.

An example can illustrate the usefulness of a UI. The XYZ warehouse is losing thousands of dollars of merchandise every week. Management believes that employees are stealing the merchandise. In an effort to reduce losses, management decides to hire a private investigator. The investigator interviews numerous employees over a two-week period, but the case remains unsolved. An executive of the company argues to management that the private investigator idea is a waste. The executive points out that the private investigator is unfamiliar with the warehouse operations, cannot penetrate the employee informal organizations, has no informers, is wasting time during surveillance from another building, and has no substantial leads. After three weeks, the private investigator is terminated. The vocal executive argues for a UI. A loss prevention service company is contacted, and an undercover investigator is placed in the warehouse. After three weeks, the new investigator penetrates the informal employee organization. Four key employees are implicated and fired. Losses are reduced. The company decides to conduct a yearly UI as a loss prevention strategy.

□ □ □ ▬▬▬▬▬▬▬▬▬▬▬▬▬▬▬▬▬▬▬▬▬▬▬▬▬▬▬▬▬▬▬

Accident at Hardy Furniture Plant

The Hardy Furniture Plant provided more than 700 jobs to Clarkston residents as sales boomed. Most workers at the plant were satisfied with their jobs. Unfortunately, a group of young forklift drivers was becoming increasingly bored while transporting furniture throughout the plant. One day, two forklifts collided, and both drivers were hospitalized with broken arms and legs. The forklifts were damaged slightly; furniture on the forks was a total loss. Immediately, the company loss prevention staff began an investigation. The forklift drivers and witnesses were interviewed. All interviewees reported that neither forklift operator saw the other because excessive furniture on the forks obstructed their views. Investigators and a forklift mechanic inspected the forklifts and found no irregularities.

The investigators became suspicious when all of the interviewees produced identical stories during questioning. Later, another round of questioning included nonwitnesses. Finally, after two weeks of persistent interviewing, the case broke when an older employee, loyal to the company, informed investigators that several bored employees bet on forklift drivers who were "playing chicken" while racing toward each other. It was learned that five previous contests had taken place involving hundreds of dollars in cash. Also, one minor accident had occurred that resulted in damaged furniture. Two supervisors were involved in covering up the loss of the damaged furniture.

When the investigation was complete, loss prevention investigators filled out appropriate reports and presented their findings to management. The two forklift drivers and the two supervisors were fired.

□ □ □ ▬▬▬▬▬▬▬▬▬▬▬▬▬▬▬▬▬▬▬▬▬▬▬▬▬▬▬▬▬▬▬

Undercover Investigation of Missing Shirts

The Chester Garment Company, headquartered in New York City, experienced a loss of hundreds of men's shirts at its plant in North Carolina. Company executives were concerned and worried because they had no experience with such losses and no loss prevention program.

The plant manager in North Carolina had notified the New York office that 900 shirts were missing. Because of their limited knowledge of loss prevention strategies, company executives decided to contact Harmon Lorman Associates, a company specializing in loss prevention and investigations. A meeting between managers of the investigative company and the garment company decided that an undercover investigator, assigned to the North Carolina plant, would be a wise strategy. The UI would cost $1,500 per week for an unspecified time period.

One week later, the investigator, Gary Stewart, arrived at the Chester Garment Plant in North Carolina to seek employment. The plant manager, who was the only plant employee who knew about the UI, hired Gary and assigned him to shipping and receiving.

Gary was from New York and educated at a college in North Carolina. The investigative company felt that his experience, a college degree in criminal justice, and his living experience in the South would add up to a good background for this assignment. Anyway, he was the only company investigator who had lived in the South.

Harmon Lorman executives told Chester executives that Gary had been working with them for a year and a half. In addition, they told them that Gary had extensive experience and loss prevention training. The truth was that Gary had been recently hired with six months of previous investigative experience. Gary had no previous loss prevention training; he had a criminal justice degree with no loss prevention or business courses.

After two weeks at the plant, Gary had established numerous contacts. His fictitious background ("cover") pointed out that he grew up in Maryland and that he arrived at the Chester Garment plant because a friend said that he could get a job there while taking a semester off from college. Gary obtained North Carolina license plates as soon as he entered North Carolina from New York.

Gary mailed three to five reports per week to his supervisor at Harmon Lorman Associates. The first few reports contained background information on the plant, such as the plant layout and the names, addresses, telephone numbers, description of autos, and plate numbers of select employees. Thereafter, the reports contained information pertaining to loss prevention features and loss vulnerabilities. Janitorial service, employee overtime, Saturday activities, and any unusual events were also reported.

Within three months of undercover investigation, Gary had made close contacts with employees and had worked in numerous assignments throughout the plant. His findings showed numerous instances of pilferage by many employees. Women sewing-machine operators were hiding several manufactured shirts under their outer clothes immediately before the workday ended.

Gary's reports were "edited" by his superiors and then sent to the home of one of Chester Garment's executives. After three months, Chester Garment executives became impatient. They wanted better quality results and threatened to terminate the investigation.

Harmon Lorman executives assured Chester Garment executives that "a break in the case was imminent." Increased pressure was put on investigator Gary Stewart, who realized that the investigation was being prolonged for profit. He responded by withholding information from reports for dry spells when good information was unavailable. As the investigation went on, the report quality went down.

Finally, after two more weeks, Chester Garment executives ordered an inventory at the plant. Surprisingly, half of the missing shirts were accounted for and a previous inventory was criticized as inaccurate. The undercover investigation was terminated. Gary returned to New York.

□ □ □ ▬▬▬▬▬▬▬▬▬▬▬▬▬▬▬▬▬▬▬▬▬▬▬▬▬▬▬

What type of investigative work do you think you would prefer as a career?

▬▬▬▬▬▬▬▬▬▬▬▬▬▬▬▬▬▬▬▬▬▬▬▬▬▬▬ □ □ □

Important Considerations

The following considerations relate to investigations in general:

1. The supervision of investigators must be adequate to produce tangible results. Rarely will a supervisor/investigator ratio of 1 to 20 prove adequate. Investigators may require close supervision by attorneys and other specialists.
2. Sensitive and confidential information must be safeguarded.
3. Information resulting from investigations can be used to improve loss prevention efforts and reduce vulnerabilities. For example, if machine shop workers are constantly stealing company tools, then it may be a good idea to have all workers provide their own tools.
4. Investigations can support the loss prevention budget by documenting vulnerabilities and losses.
5. Investigations should be cost effective. If an investigation costs more than the loss, the expense of the investigation may not be worthwhile. For example, the loss of a box of pencils is not worth an investigator's time when losses that are more serious are occurring.

6. Although computer crimes can be committed remotely, modern technology also permits investigations to be conducted remotely. For example, instead of an investigator visiting stores to check out CCTV videos of cashier-customer transactions, a system can link CCTV with register data to be viewed together on-line.
7. The investigator's job is to collect information and facts. Supervisors and managers decide what to do with the investigative results.
8. An investigation may be required of senior management because of criminal, civil, or regulatory misconduct. Authorization and direction for such a sensitive investigation may come from the corporate board of directors.

Law

Knowledge of law is indispensable to the investigative process. For example, as explained in Chapter 6, the Fair Credit Reporting Act of 1971 and the Fair and Accurate Credit Transaction Act of 2003 guide investigations of employment applicants and incidents involving employees in the workplace.

Another important area of law pertains to electronic surveillance (electronic devices used to listen to conversations) and wiretapping (listening to telephone communications). The U.S. Supreme Court has called these techniques a "dirty business." Generally, both are prohibited unless under court authority. However, because of the difficulty of detection and the advantages in information gathering, some private (and public) sector investigators violate the law. Federal law imposes a $10,000 fine and up to five years in prison for these offenses. In addition, a lawsuit may occur. Although private conversations of two parties cannot be recorded unless under court order, if one of the parties approves, recordings are legal. Examples include one party cooperating with an investigation or serving as an UI. An employee in the workplace, using a company telephone (or computer), does not generally have an expectation of privacy, especially if the employer informs employees of monitoring.

Conflict of interest is another concern. An example of conflict of interest can be seen when a full-time public police officer works part-time for a private investigative firm. Generally, states prohibit one person from holding dual commissions (i.e., public police commission and private investigator license). The *Report of the Task Force on Private Security* (U.S. Department of Justice, 1976: 238) states that "a citizen might file a defamation-of-character suit against a city, law enforcement agency, or officer by claiming that surveillance conducted by an off-duty law enforcement officer working as a private investigator gave others the impression he was the target of a law enforcement criminal investigation." Other issues can evolve, such as a suspect's rights during questioning by a public police officer working part-time in private security. The task force recommended that public police officers should be "strictly forbidden" from performing private-sector investigative work.

Poorly executed investigations can result in liability. In one case, a bank investigator believed that a loan manager had mob connections and an investigation was conducted, resulting in termination. Police brought charges, but the judge dismissed the case on groundless charges, and the manager sued and was awarded damages. In another case, an oil company terminated an agent who was manipulating prices, but the prosecutor declined to bring charges because of insufficient evidence. When a truck driver stated to someone that the agent was a "thief," the agent sued for slander. Investigators can protect themselves from slander and libel by the use of privilege when issuing reports. **Qualified privilege** permits defamatory statements if made in the discharge of duty and without malice. At one company, an employee was fired for a security violation and sued by claiming defamation from a security report, but the court held that the investigator was responsible for reporting security breaches, that she acted within her authority, and that her report was privileged. **Attorney/client privilege** (also referred to as confidential communications) is another form of protection. It involves statements between persons who have a necessary relation of trust to help communication. The statements cannot be disclosed. To facilitate this privilege, investigators should ensure that reports are issued directly to counsel. However, the best defense is accurate reports (Ray, 2000: 94).

Roman (2005), an attorney, offers suggestions of what to avoid during workplace investigations. Failure to investigate cases of discrimination or harassment can result in liability under antidiscrimination laws. Courts have held that no investigation was evidence that the employer acted with "malice or reckless indifference." Using a biased investigator can harm a case. Examples include assigning an investigator from the accused's chain of command and following up on leads from the accused, but not from the accuser. Roman emphasizes the importance of conducting thorough, objective, and unbiased investigations. To avoid claims for defamation and invasion of privacy, the employer and investigator should disclose information only on a "need to know" basis. To prevent loss of credibility as an investigator, do not state to the accused that the accuser is a chronic complainer or whiner.

Reibold (2005: 18–29), an attorney, writes of the legal liabilities of hiring private investigators (PIs). Those who hire PIs can be held vicariously liable for torts committed by PIs, directly liable for actions of PIs, and negligent in hiring and supervising them. A lawsuit may be directed at an employer, a law firm, and a PI agency. Lawsuits against PIs and those who hire them may involve trespass, invasion of privacy, infliction of emotional distress, assault and battery, and conversion after gathering garbage from a subject's trash container. The defense argument that the PI was an independent contractor has been rejected by courts.

Reibold offers the following suggestions when screening a PI firm: ensure the PI is properly licensed; request references; determine if the PI is a member of a professional association that promotes ethics; use a Freedom of Information Act request to the state regulatory authority to check on the PI; require the PI to contractually indemnify the entity hiring the PI; and upon verifying the PI's liability insurance, request that the PI add the entity hiring the PI to the policy.

Evidence

Laws govern the introduction of evidence into judicial proceedings to ensure fairness and due process. Evidence law is contained in federal and state constitutions, statutes, and case law.

There are several classifications of evidence. **Direct evidence** directly proves or disproves a fact without drawing an inference (i.e., conclusion). Examples are a confession, an eyewitness identification of a suspect, and physical evidence (e.g., contraband in possession of the accused). **Circumstantial evidence** indirectly proves or disproves a fact and an inference must be made. Examples are a statement by the accused that he or she was with the victim right before the victim was murdered, and physical evidence, such as fingerprints and DNA found at a crime scene (Gardner and Anderson, 2007: 62–63). Another type of evidence is **hearsay evidence**. It is second-hand information or what someone heard. Courts favor first-hand information through personal observation or the use of other senses. Hearsay evidence is generally inadmissible in court, although there are exceptions, such as a dying declaration or a spontaneous declaration by an offender following a crime.

The accountability of physical evidence, especially before it reaches a court of law, can have a definite impact on a case. The **chain of custody of evidence** must be maintained. This refers to the written accountability of persons having possession of evidence from its initial discovery, through judicial proceedings, and to its final location. A loss scene should be protected, photographed, videotaped, and sketched before evidence is touched. The proper labeling, packaging, and storage of evidence is equally important. The accountability of evidence often is brought forth in court. Attorneys are sure to scrutinize the paperwork and procedures associated with the evidence. The following questions are among the many frequently asked in court. Who saw the evidence first? Who touched it first? Where was it taken? By whom? How was it stored? Was the storage area locked? Who had the keys or access code?

□ □ □ ▬▬▬▬▬▬▬▬▬▬▬▬▬▬▬▬▬▬▬▬▬▬▬▬▬▬▬▬▬▬▬▬▬▬▬▬

International Perspective: Overseas Investigations
Global business has resulted in increasing demand for overseas investigations. Such investigations are conducted for a variety of reasons, including potential locations for

investment (see the Chapter 16 box titled "International Perspective: Supply Chain Risks and Security"). The following information provides tips and guidelines for overseas investigations (Van Nostrand and Luizzo, 1995: 33–35).

Carefully plan and check with the following U.S. agencies on the Web:

- *U.S. Department of State* ensures that passports are current and valid for all countries not off limits to U.S. citizens. Some countries require a special visa. Fact sheets on-line are provided on many countries and include information on such topics as political stability and crime.
- *Central Intelligence Agency* maintains fact books on countries.
- *U.S. Department of Health and Human Services* determines whether travel to particular countries requires immunization.
- *U.S. Department of Commerce* publishes information to alert U.S. citizens to countries that may be dangerous to U.S. travelers.
- Because legal systems vary among countries, a major rule in conducting a foreign investigation is to study the legal and policing system of the respective country.
- Investigations are fundamentally about personal interaction, so another major rule is to study and understand the host culture and try to speak some of the language.
- The international investigator who travels to many countries and freely investigates is actually Hollywood fantasy. Foreign countries do not permit such activities and neither does the U.S. Department of State. Without careful research, an investigator can find himself or herself in jail in a foreign country.
- An option is to work with an official of the foreign country, such as a police official or attorney, or contract the investigation to an investigator in that country. The key is to select someone who has experience in the country, has reliable contacts, and speaks the language.
- Avoid bringing a firearm to a foreign country. Illegal possession of a firearm aboard any U.S. airline is a felony.

Another source is the Overseas Security Advisory Council (n.d.). OSAC "is a Federal Advisory Committee with a U.S. Government Charter to promote security cooperation between American business and private sector interests worldwide and the U.S. Department of State. OSAC currently encompasses the 34-member core Council, an Executive Office, over 100 Country Councils, and more than 3,500 constituent member organizations and 372 associates." The objectives of OSAC are to facilitate cooperation between State Department security functions and the private sector, exchange information on the overseas security environment and suggestions for security planning, and recommend methods to protect the competitiveness of American businesses operating worldwide.

Interviewing and Interrogation

Interviewing and interrogation are methods of gathering information from people. During an **interview**, the suspect supplies information willingly; but during an **interrogation**, the suspect is often unwilling. The investigator needs to know the techniques associated with each type of situation. Although a few recognized training programs focus on conducting interviews and interrogations, no single method holds all the answers and is applicable in all situations. Investigators often use a variety of methods.

Why are interviews or interrogations conducted? A primary reason is to learn the truth. Other reasons are to obtain evidence or a confession to aid in prosecution, eliminate suspects, recover property, and obtain information that results in corrective action. This chapter emphasizes investigations in the private sector, although many of the ideas presented are used in public-sector investigations.

The preliminaries include

1. Maintaining records
2. Planning the questioning
3. Making an appointment, if necessary
4. If a procedure or law question arises, consulting with a superior or an attorney
5. Questioning in privacy, if possible, and ensuring that the interviewee can leave when he or she chooses
6. Making sure someone of the same sex as the interviewee is present
7. Identifying yourself to the interviewee
8. Openly recording the questioning, if possible

Regarding the interviewee:

1. Consider the interviewee's background, intelligence, education, biases, and emotional state.
2. Communicate on the same level.
3. Watch for nervousness, perspiration, and fidgeting.
4. Reluctance to talk can indicate that the interviewee feels the need to protect himself or herself or others.
5. Responding freely can indicate that the interviewee may need to relieve guilt or may want to cause problems for an enemy not involved in the loss.

The objectives of the investigator include

1. Establishing good rapport (e.g., asking, "How are you?")
2. Maintaining good public relations
3. Maintaining eye contact
4. Not jumping to conclusions
5. Maintaining an open mind
6. Listening attentively
7. Being perceptive to every comment and any slips of the tongue
8. Maintaining perseverance
9. Controlling the interview
10. Carefully analyzing hearsay

Strategies by the investigator include the following:

1. Asking **open-ended questions,** those questions that require lengthy answers—for example, "What happened at the plant before the accident?" **Close-ended questions** require short yes or no answers that limit responses—for example, "Were you close to the accident?"
2. Maintaining *silence* makes many interviewees feel uncomfortable. Silence by an investigator, after an interviewee answers an open-ended question, may cause the interviewee to begin talking again.
3. Building up interviewee memory by having the interviewee relate the story of an incident from its beginning.
4. To test honesty, asking questions to which you know the answers.
5. Using trickery. For example, stating that the suspect's fingerprints were found at the crime scene. In *Frazier v. Cupp* 394 US 731 (1969), the U.S. Supreme Court upheld the use of false information to obtain a confession.

The reader probably is familiar with movies and television programs that portray the interrogation process as a "third degree," in which one bright light hangs over the seated suspect in a dark room and investigators stand around constantly asking questions and using violence when they try to "break" the suspect. Court action against police has curbed this abuse. However, because of the unpleasant connotations associated with interrogations, for the private sector, to prevent litigation, a less threatening term such as *intensive interview* is more appropriate.

During interrogation or *intensive interview* (an extension of the interview)

1. Discuss the seriousness of the incident.
2. Request the story several times. Some investigators request the story backward to catch inconsistencies.
3. Appeal to emotions; for example, "Everybody makes mistakes. You are not the first person who has been in trouble. Don't you want to clear your conscience?"
4. Point out inconsistencies in statements.
5. Confront the interviewee with some of the evidence.

Why would a private security investigator choose to "interview" rather than "interrogate"?

Polygraph: Proper Testing Procedures under the Employee Polygraph Protection Act

In the course of a workplace investigation, an employer cannot suggest to employees the possible use of a polygraph instrument until these 10 conditions are satisfied:

1. *Economic loss or injury.* The employer must administer the test as part of an investigation of a *specific incident* involving economic loss or injury to the business, such as theft or sabotage.
2. *Access.* The employee who is to be tested must have had access to the property that is the subject of the investigation.
3. *Reasonable suspicion.* The employer must have a reasonable suspicion of the worker's involvement in the incident under investigation.
4. *Before the test,* an employer's failure to adhere to guidelines can void a test and subject the employer to fines and liability. The employee who is to be tested must be notified in writing at least 48 hours, not counting weekends and holidays, prior to the test:
   • Where and when the examination will take place
   • The specific matter under investigation
   • The basis for concluding that the employee had access to the property being investigated
   • The reason the employer suspects the employee of involvement
   • The employee's right to consult with legal counsel or an employee representative before each phase of the test

   Also before the test, the employee must be provided with the following:

   • Oral and written notice explaining the nature of the polygraph, its physical operation, and the test procedure
   • Copies of all questions that will be asked during the test
   • Oral and written notice, in language understood by the employee and bearing the employee's signature, advising the worker of his or her rights under the EPPA
5. *Procedural requirements for polygraph examinations* include the following:
   • The test must last at least 90 minutes unless the examinee terminates the test.
   • Either party, employer or employee, can record the test with the other's knowledge.

- Questions cannot pertain to religious, political, or racial matters; sexual behavior; or beliefs, affiliations, or lawful activities related to unions or labor organizations; and they cannot be asked in a degrading or needlessly intrusive manner.
- A worker can be excused from a test with a physician's written advisement that the subject suffers from a medical or psychological condition or is undergoing treatment that might cause abnormal responses during the examination.
- An employee has the right to consult with counsel before, during, and after the examination but not to have counsel present during the actual examination.
- An employee must be advised that his or her confessions may be grounds for firing or demotion and that the employer may share admissions of criminal conduct with law enforcement officials.
- A worker can terminate or refuse to take a test and cannot be demoted or fired for doing so. But, the employer can demote or fire the worker if he or she has enough separate supporting evidence to justify taking that action.

6. *After the test,* the employee has a right to a written copy of the tester's opinion, copies of the questions and corresponding replies, and an opportunity to discuss the results with the employer before an employer can take action against a worker based on the test results. An employee may be disciplined, fired, or demoted on the basis of the test results if the employer has supporting evidence, which can include the evidence gathered to support the decision to administer the test, to justify such action. Test results cannot be released to the public, only to the employee or his or her designate; the employer; a court, government agency, arbitrator, or mediator (by court order); or appropriate government agency if disclosure is admission of criminal conduct (without court order). The examiner may show test results, without identifying information, to other examiners in order to obtain second opinions.

7. *Qualifications of examiners.* An employer can be liable for an examiner's failure to meet requirements, which cover licensing, bonding, or professional liability coverage; testing guidelines; and formation of opinions.

8. *Waiving employee rights.* A worker cannot be tested—even at his or her insistence—if the employer cannot meet procedural requirements and prove reasonable suspicion and access. Employees may not waive their rights under the EPPA except in connection with written settlement of a lawsuit or pending legal action.

9. *State law and collective bargaining agreements.* The EPPA does not preempt any state or local law or collective bargaining agreement that is more restrictive than the act.

10. *Record-keeping requirement.* Records of polygraph exams should be kept for at least three years by the employer and the examiner, who must make them available—within 72 hours upon request—to the Department of Labor.

Source: U.S. Chamber of Commerce. See Chapter 6 for the Employee Polygraph Protection Act of 1988.

□ □ □

Information Sources

Traditional information sources include interviewing people in person; traveling to a government agency, library, or other location to comb through records and information; obtaining information over the telephone; and conducting surveillance. Additionally, the Internet has made it easier than ever to investigate personal and business information. For a nominal fee, a variety of information can be obtained with a computer from the comfort of one's office or home, as illustrated here:

www.pimall.com/
This excellent site offers a wealth of information and links to information brokers, private investigators (PIs), a PI store, PI associations, training, and magazines.
www.ussearch.com/
This site can be used to locate someone, conduct a background check, trace phone numbers, obtain a satellite photo, and seek the following records: criminal, Department of Corrections, court, real estate, bankruptcies, divorce, and death. Business searches include due diligence and verification of professional licenses.
www.datahawk.com/
This site is similar to the preceding sites; costs are readily available.
www.teldir.com/
To check for people outside the United States, this site has links to Yellow Pages, White Pages, business directories, e-mail listings, and more from more than 150 countries.
global.lexisnexis.com/about.aspx
This site offers an extensive search of legal, news, and business sources.
www.dnb.com
Offers a variety of business information.

One problem with these databases is selecting the most appropriate information broker. Another problem is that data may not be verified. In addition, the scope of the search must be considered. What geographic area and what months or years were searched? Information brokers must adhere to legal restrictions and should provide such guidelines to clients.

Despite the problems with databases, such information sources are used in a variety of ways by security practitioners. One airport security director uses such databases to locate owners of vehicles abandoned in the airport's parking lots. Another security practitioner conducts asset searches of employees suspected of fraud; a database may show that an employee earning $45,000 per year has purchased a $600,000 house.

For those security practitioners who outsource information searches to PIs or other firms, evaluations of vendors are necessary to gauge adherence to legal and ethical standards, accuracy, completeness, timeliness, cost, and other consumer requirements.

Legal Restrictions When Collecting Information

Investigator ability to obtain usable information in today's privacy-protected environment has been reduced. In earlier years, the "old boy" network was in greater use. It consists of employees in both the public and private sectors who informally assist each other with information. For example, a retired police officer joins an investigative firm and contacts friends from the police agency where he or she was previously employed to obtain criminal history information on individuals subject to a private-sector investigation. There have been indictments against people involved in acquiring nonpublic information.

The reality of information acquisition is that no information is totally secure from unauthorized acquisition. Although difficult to measure, information is periodically obtained in an unethical or illegal manner. For example, a private-sector investigator pays money to an employee of a bank to secure nonpublic information about an individual. This activity should be condemned because it violates individual rights and laws.

Another problem for the investigator results when he or she mistakenly collects information that is not usable in court. In litigation, information improperly obtained and not authenticated or certified by the respective agency could subject a litigation team to civil or criminal action, unless the records are subpoenaed or are part of a court action (civil or criminal). Another challenge is waiting for a Freedom of Information Law request to obtain documents, which can take as long as a year. The **Freedom of Information Law** (FOIL) grants citizens access to public documents because an informed electorate is essential to safeguard democracy and because publicity is a protection against official misconduct. This law requires all federal agency documents to be publicly disclosed, unless exempted. This law also recognizes the need to restrict intrusions into a private individual's affairs.

□ □ □ ▬▬▬▬▬▬▬▬▬▬▬▬▬▬▬▬▬▬▬▬▬▬▬▬▬▬▬▬▬▬▬▬▬▬

The Internet as a Liability and an Asset

Here, we illustrate how the Internet can harm and help businesses. First, we see how a manager was scammed, and then we see how corporations can protect themselves against extremist groups.

Care should be exercised with the Internet because it contains a variety of fraudulent information. Internet fraud is rising rapidly and the Securities and Exchange Commission (SEC), a federal regulatory agency that enforces laws to reduce financial fraud, has reported many cases of individuals and companies attempting to deceive investors and others through the Internet. In one case, a credit manager tried the Internet to investigate the creditworthiness of a customer seeking a large order of computer components. The manager checked the Web site of the customer and found impressive graphics, solid financial data, multiple corporate locations across the country, impressive biographies of corporate executives, and testimonials (with links) to customers and vendors. Following this research, the manager knew that his days of spending hours on the telephone checking credit references were over, and he approved the large order. When the bill was past due, he called the customer, but the telephone had been disconnected, and he checked the Web site, but it was gone. He was victimized by a scam that set up the Web site on an Internet service provider (ISP) host instead of obtaining a domain name. The scammers paid for their ISP account with a stolen credit card number. The testimonials were e-mail links to confederates. The "ship to" address was leased space paid for by a check from a shell corporation with a bank account established with fraudulent identification. All the merchandise was gone. To prevent such victimization, obtain business credit reports, use the SEC's database (http://www.sec.gov/edgarhp.htm), enter PR Newswire (http://www.prnewswire.com/), type the company name into your favorite search engines, use the telephone to check credit and other references, and consider a thorough investigation by a specialist (Mendell, 1999: 130).

On the other hand, the Internet is a useful source of information to protect personnel and businesses against extremist groups. Activists, for example, are known to place their plans (e.g., demonstrations) on-line. Security practitioners should conduct on-line searches by entering key words such as "anticapitalism" and "socialism." Research "sucks.com" sites such as "walmart-sucks.com" that have been created to vent at companies. Through these searches, corporations will be better prepared to protect people and assets (Snow, 2000: 60–64).

▬▬▬▬▬▬▬▬▬▬▬▬▬▬▬▬▬▬▬▬▬▬▬▬▬▬▬▬▬▬▬▬▬▬ □ □ □

Identity Theft

Identity theft is the illegal acquisition of another individual's personal identifying information to be used fraudulently for illegal gain. The Bureau of Justice Statistics reported that in 2004, 3.6 million households, representing 3% of the households in the United States, discovered that at least one member of the household was victimized by identity theft during the previous 6 months (Baum, 2006: 1). The Federal Trade Commission (FTC) reported that in 2003, identity theft cost consumers $3.8 billion and businesses $32.9 billion (Federal Bureau of Investigation, Financial Crimes Section, 2005). There are many ways in which an offender can steal personal and business information, and there are many types of crimes committed by using such information.

Traditional methods of obtaining personal and business information include looking over another's shoulder at a bank or ATM; searching trash (i.e., "dumpster diving"); impersonation over the telephone; stealing a wallet or mail; fraudulently ordering a copy of a victim's credit record; or going to a cemetery to locate a deceased person whose age, if living, would approximate the offender's age and securing documents to develop the identity. The Internet has expanded the opportunities to steal identities. As we know from previous pages, various Web sites offer a wealth of personal information. In addition, hackers penetrate corporate databases and e-commerce Web sites and download credit card numbers. ChoicePoint, a huge data broker, unwittingly sold consumer ID information to offenders posing as businesspersons. Other companies, such as Bank of America, Time Warner, Wachovia, MCI, and Ameritrade, have lost data on millions of customers (Brenner, 2005: 4–5). **Phishing** is another threat; it is a word coined from the analogy that offenders use e-mail bait to fish for personal information. The technique often uses spam or pop-up messages that trick people into disclosing a variety of sensitive identification information.

An offender can use a victim's identity to secure credit cards, open bank and checking accounts, apply for a loan, purchase and sell a home or car, establish cellular service, file for bankruptcy, obtain a job, seek workers' compensation, file a lawsuit, and commit a crime in the victim's name. The possible offenses are endless, and victims often learn about the identity theft months after it occurred.

Congress passed the Identity Theft and Assumption Deterrence Act of 1998 to make identity theft a federal crime. This crime is investigated by the FBI, the U.S. Postal Service, and the U.S. Secret Service. To increase consumer awareness of identity theft, the FTC created the Identity Theft Clearinghouse. It collects complaints from victims and offers resources to restore credit.

Personal protection strategies include the following:

- Protect personal and financial information in public, over the telephone, and on-line. Carry only necessary ID.
- Closely study bills and completely destroy unneeded papers containing personal information.
- When making on-line transactions, be sure they are made over secure, encrypted connections and verify the address and telephone numbers on Web sites.
- If you have been victimized, contact creditors, the three major credit reporting agencies (Equifax, 800–525–6285; Experian, 888–397–3742; and TransUnion, 800–680–7289), and file a report (and obtain a copy) with police.

Organizational strategies that protect proprietary information also help to protect business financial information and customer information. Information security for organizations is explained later in this book.

Investigative Leads

Investigative work requires patience and perseverance, and difficult cases often tax the abilities of investigators as they search for answers. Investigative leads are aids to the investigator.

Scene of the Loss

A search of the scene of a loss can provide answers to investigative questions. Offenders at a crime scene often leave something (e.g., fingerprints) or take something with them (e.g., stolen item), either of which ties them to the crime.

Because RFID tags are increasingly being attached to consumer goods, evidence (e.g., knife) at a crime scene may contain such a tag, and the tag can possibly be traced through the supply chain to a retailer. If the item was purchased with a bankcard or other digital ID, the customer can possibly be identified. RFID tags can also be applied to chain of custody requirements of evidence.

The loss scene requires protection from unauthorized persons. Photographs, video, and sketches should be made without disturbing the characteristics of the scene and before evidence is removed.

☐ ☐ ☐

Offenders at a crime scene often leave something or take something with them, either of which ties them to the crime.

☐ ☐ ☐

Victims

Care and empathy for victims are essential in the investigative process. However, sometimes the victim is an offender. Good leads can be obtained by checking the background of the victim. The victim can be a business or organization or a person. A person owning a failing business may have perpetrated an accident, arson, or other crime to collect on an insurance policy. A male employee may falsely claim that he was attacked at work by his wife's lover. Sometimes employees are hurt off the job but are able to go to work, claim injury on the job, and hope for improved compensation. In most instances, the victim is not an offender; however, the investigator must maintain an open mind.

Motive

The motive behind a loss is an important consideration. Questions of concern include these: Who will gain from the loss? Are there any ulterior motives? What types of persons would create such a loss? Why? The investigator also must recognize that the human factor may not be involved in the loss. Equipment malfunction or weather may be the cause.

Witnesses

Investigative leads frequently are acquired from witnesses. Good interviewing is important and can turn up valuable leads.

Informants

Why do informants divulge information? Sometimes, they do so because they are seeking favors or money, because they see it as their duty, or because they want to get someone in trouble (e.g., competitor, unfaithful lover). Informants often supply misinformation to investigators. An investigator can test an informant by asking questions to which he or she knows the answers. An investigator must never become too involved with informants or perform any unethical or criminal activity to acquire information. Obviously, an informant's identity must be protected, unless a court requires otherwise. Many investigators (private and public) have money in their budgets specifically designed to pay informants for information. (Chapter 7 explains loss reporting and reward system.) A common practice of investigators is to catch an individual in violation of a rule or law but not seek punishment (e.g., prosecute) if that individual supplies the investigator with useful information.

Modus Operandi

MO stands for **modus operandi,** or method of operation. An investigator may ask, "What method was used by the burglar?" Because people differ, they commit crimes in different ways. Many police departments have MO files on offenders. When a crime takes place, investigators may check the MO files for suspects who are known to commit crimes in a certain way. A particular offender may use a specific tool during a burglary. A robber may wear a unique style of clothing during robberies. A saboteur at a manufacturing plant may be using a particular type of wire cutter. Sometimes, a rare MO is discovered—for example, a burglar who defecates at the crime scene.

Computers and Software

Computers and various types of software assist investigators. **Artificial intelligence** uses software and databases containing a variety of stored investigative information to analyze data to link crime scene evidence to a suspect. **Data mining** seeks useful information from a large amount of information or databases to develop patterns and anomalies. With enormous amounts of data (e.g., travel records, expense accounts, and telephone and e-mail records) available to investigators, data mining saves time. **Link analysis** is especially helpful with complex investigations. It also involves large amounts of information and seeks commonalties and relationships among, for example, people, organizations, and geographic locations.

Harold (2006: 66–72) emphasizes the value of data mining. He writes that an investigator, who is able to ask the right questions, and a computer programmer, who is able to translate the questions into effective code, can produce answers for investigations. He explains the case of an employee thief who stole valuables in an office building of 5,000 employees. The 10 victims had worked all hours of the day and night, weekends, and one holiday. The building could be entered only with an access card, and there were 65 access points. All entries were recorded in the access control computer. One and a half million access control records were used to form a database. Then a table was created containing the distinct dates, times, victims, and building locations of the thefts. With millions of records to review, there was only one query for the database: Who was in the building when all the thefts occurred? One employee was revealed who was targeted for further investigation and eventually prosecuted.

The **Identi-Kit,** which police have used for years, consists of hundreds of overlays of facial features (e.g., eyes, noses, chins) that a victim or witness selects to create a drawing of the suspect. Computer-aided identification software uses the same principle and stores more than 100,000 facial features.

Digital Investigations and Evidence

Digital evidence is electronically stored records or information located on a computer, server, storage network, or other media. Investigators are finding that the locations of digital evidence are varied. Besides computers, laptops, and personal digital assistants (PDAs), digital evidence may also be found in such devices as digital cameras, cell phones, MP3 players, iPods, Xboxes, DVD players that contain hard drives, and even a mouse that has features similar to a flash storage drive. Ordinary items such as watches and pens can also be suspect and hold memory cards. In addition, because of wireless technology, a wireless hard drive can be hidden almost anywhere (Bartolomie, 2005: 5).

Digital forensics is the application of investigative and scientific skills and specialized tools and software to examine digital media to collect evidence. Investigators preserve a digital crime scene by making a copy of the data and then search for evidence from such sources as e-mails and files, which may be hidden or deleted. Digital forensics is a growing field supporting investigators who seek evidence in cases involving Internet abuse, fraud, extortion, cyberattacks, theft of confidential information, intelligence, sexual harassment, child pornography, on-line defamation, breach of contract, negligence, insurance claims, and other areas.

The following list offers guidelines for digital evidence (Lang, 2005: 55–74; Mallery, 2005: 44–50):

- For the workplace, policies and procedures are important to ensure that employees know that the company owns workstations, company information, IT systems, data, and hard-copy files, and that monitoring and searches may occur.
- Avoid assigning the IT department to investigate because the investigation should be objective and the IT department should not examine its own department.
- Usually, begin cybercrime investigations internally instead of contacting public police immediately.
- Large entities often maintain a digital forensic department, separate from IT. Smaller concerns outsource.

- The International Association of Computer Investigative Specialists and the International Society of Forensic Computer Examiners both offer certifications that enhance professionalism and competence.
- Management must decide whether to contact police during the investigation. Cases involving embezzlement at a public company or child pornography are examples of cases requiring police notification.
- If an employee refuses to give up personal property (e.g., iPod) that contains evidence, seek assistance from public police. A search warrant may be the next step.
- Once items are seized, maintain a chain of custody. Company policies and procedures should ensure proper handling and preservation of digital evidence so it is not altered or destroyed. For example, special techniques can produce an exact copy of the media that is then used to conduct the examination.
- Opposing counsel in a case is sure to attack the evidence and how it was handled and examined. To comply with Federal Rules of Evidence (e.g., Rule 702), a digital forensic examiner must build case testimony from a foundation of documented science, accepted procedures, and reliability. The National Institute for Standards and Technology tests commercial forensic products, and the results can assist experts.

Donnelly (2005: 59–61) writes that iPods—those trendy music players—provide offenders with huge storage capacity as portable hard drives. These devices are becoming more frequent in the workplace and enable offenders to copy sensitive data. Donnelly describes one case in which police served a search warrant at the home of a suspect book-keeper. As police collected computers, hard drives, and other related equipment, they noticed an iPod and it was also seized. Forensic examiners at a lab examined the suspect's equipment, except the iPod, and found no evidence of embezzlement. Careful to treat the iPod as any other external hard drive and to preserve its integrity, an examiner made a complete copy of the iPod's hard drive, to be used for examination. It contained two data partitions: one held music and the other held data files of illegal financial transactions (i.e., the evidence used for prosecution).

Interestingly, an iPod can be used as a mobile forensic device once it is configured and loaded with forensic software. Such a device avoids bringing bulky equipment into the field. Add-ons include voice-recording capability and a camera connection to download photos to the iPod for storage (Donnelly, 2005: 61–62).

Rules involving cell phones, camera phones, and other personal electronic devices should be included in workplace policies and procedures and communicated to employees. Generally, security personnel cannot seize a personal device such as a cell phone that may contain evidence. Public police can be called for assistance, and they would follow such guidelines as listed next (Dunnagan and Schroader, 2006: 46–53):

- Public police must have a search warrant prior to seizing and searching a device, or obtain a signed consent form.
- Do not change the condition of evidence. If the cell phone is on or off, do not change it.
- Bring the device, power and other cables, and all accessory devices to a lab for processing. Use forensically sound software and tools and validate evidence. No one software package can examine all cell phones.
- Text messages that pass through a messaging center may remain on a server for only a few days, so process the device as soon as possible.
- Place a seized cell phone in a Faraday bag to block all wireless signals; an alternative is aluminum foil. This prevents data from being remotely erased.

Nagosky (2005:1–9), of the FBI, writes about digital photos. He notes that film-based photos can be manipulated by, for example, selection of exposure times, or by crop and splice, whereby two different negatives are combined. To counter such manipulation, a negative can be requested. Digital photos are also subject to manipulation by, for example, adding and deleting items. Detection of manipulation is through, for example, density of the image based on light exposure and splice lines. Nagosky offers these recommendations for digital photos as evidence: preserve the original; concentrate on integrity of the image (i.e., chain of custody); store it on a compact disc that can be written to only once and then is only readable; and limit access to files.

Gips (2005: 26–28) reports on the Digital Video Evidence System (DVES) that has the potential to ensure the integrity of digital video and photographs. Developed by researchers at John Hopkins University, the process is touted as easy to use, inexpensive, and invulnerable to attack. The process is described as equal to signed evidence tape for bits of data. An algorithm extracts data from digital video and creates something like a digital fingerprint of each frame, followed by encryption. These digital signatures are stored separately from the video footage. An investigator would record evidence with a camcorder and then attach the camcorder to a small computer that would generate a digital signature and store the data on a memory stick. The investigator would then enter his or her ID card and code on the small computer.

Another topic related to digital evidence is the eDiscovery amendments to the Federal Rules of Civil Procedure that became effective December 1, 2006. These rules address corporate electronically stored information (ESI) that may be subpoenaed in a civil case. Such information includes e-mail, voice mail, and data on computer drives. To avoid court sanctions and an adverse settlement, a corporate team (e.g., attorney, IT specialist, CSO) must adhere to the rules by identifying, preserving, and producing ESI. The rules require parties to meet early on discovery of ESI and allow a request for limiting ESI discovery if sufficient detail and costs are provided as to why compliance is burdensome (Plante, 2007: 20).

Surveillance

Surveillance, watching or observing, is an investigative aid used widely to acquire information. Among the kinds of cases in which surveillance is helpful are these examples: assembly line workers are suspected of stealing merchandise; an employee is suspected of passing trade secrets to another company; truck drivers, while on their routes, experience unexplainable losses between company facilities; and an employee, claiming to be unable to work because of an on-the-job accident, is observed building an extension on his home.

Two major kinds of surveillance are stationary and moving. *Stationary surveillance* requires the investigator to remain in one spot while observing—for example, an investigator sitting in an auto watching a suspect's house. This type can be tedious and frustrating. In *moving surveillance*, investigators follow a suspect—for example, tailing a truck driver whose cargo was "lost."

During surveillance, an investigator must be careful not to attract attention. The person being watched usually has the advantage and can attempt to lose the investigator through a variety of quick moves (e.g., going out a back door, jumping on a bus, driving through a red light). Therefore, the investigator must blend into the environment to prevent detection.

Another type of surveillance is audio surveillance. This includes wiretapping and eavesdropping, which are restricted by law.

Equipment used during surveillance can include binoculars, a telescope, communication equipment, cameras, listening devices, video and audio recorders, and global positioning system (GPS) tracking devices. One of the most successful methods of surveillance is the use of a concealed pinhole lens camera. If a video motion sensor is used, time will not have to be spent on reviewing many hours of tape. Investigators must keep informed about these devices and related legal restrictions on usage.

☐ ☐ ☐ ▬▬▬▬▬▬▬▬▬▬▬▬▬▬▬▬▬▬▬▬▬▬▬▬▬▬▬▬▬

Concealed pinhole lens cameras are a popular method of surveillance. What is your opinion of this technique?

▬▬▬▬▬▬▬▬▬▬▬▬▬▬▬▬▬▬▬▬▬▬▬▬▬▬▬▬▬ ☐ ☐ ☐

Information Accuracy

An investigation is essentially an information-gathering process. The accuracy of the information not only reflects on the investigator but also has a direct bearing on the consequences of the investigation. The following guidelines are helpful in obtaining accurate information:

1. Double-check information whenever possible.
2. Ask the same questions of several people. Compare the results.
3. To check on the reliability of a source, ask questions for which you know the answers.
4. Cross-check information; for example, if you have a copy of a person's employment application and college transcript, cross-check name, date of birth, and so on.
5. Read information back to a source to check for accuracy.
6. If possible, check the background of a person providing information or check the accuracy of a records system.
7. Maintain accurate notes, records, photographs, and sketches; do not depend on memory for details.
8. If you are unable to write notes or a report, for instance, while driving an auto, record the information on a tape recorder.
9. Provide adequate security for information and records to prevent tampering or loss.

Report Writing

Report writing usually begins after the investigator has invested time and energy in collecting sufficient information on the basic investigative questions. How well these reports are prepared will have a definite impact on the investigator's career. Many supervisors get to know their subordinates more through reports than from any other means of communication. Furthermore, many supervisors consider report writing a major skill when promoting investigators.

Reports have a variety of uses aside from punitive results. They are used by management to analyze critical problems (e.g., excessive thefts or accidents). Summations of many reports can assist planning and budgetary efforts. Reports also may be used in litigation.

Investigators usually record information in a small notebook before completing a report. An investigator has many thoughts in mind during an investigation that prevents the report from being written as the investigation proceeds. In addition, after appropriate information is collected, the investigator has an overall view of the incident; this assists in the development of an outline that will improve the structure of the report.

Standard reports are used by many investigators. These reports are formulated by management to guide investigators in answering important questions. A typical standard report begins with a heading that includes the type of incident, date, time, and location. Next is a list of persons involved in the incident along with their addresses, telephone numbers, ages, and occupations. Another section can include a list of evidence. The narrative, sometimes called "the story," follows, usually written in chronological order. The end of the report contains a variety of information such as the investigator's name and the status of the investigation. Diagrams and photographs may be attached. Report characteristics vary depending on need.

During report writing, the investigator should get to the point in easily understood language. An impressive vocabulary is not an asset to a report. Neatness and good grammar are important. Supervisors often complain about poor narratives written by subordinates. Let us look at some blunders that have reflected on the investigator:

- "When the employee was approached by loss prevention staff he had a switchblade he had bought in his lunch box."
- "A telephone pole of manufacturing plants within our corporation showed that 15 percent of employees were ignoring loss prevention rules."
- "The woman caused the loss because her newborn son was branded as illiterate."
- "The sick employee was honestly in bed with the doctor for two weeks even though he did not give her any relief."

□ □ □

Career: Investigations

The process of investigation is an important function in both the public and private sectors. It is a very broad field and includes many subspecialties. Investigators use a variety of tools and techniques such as interviewing, evidence collection and processing, physical and technical surveillance, computer forensics, database searches, and crime analysis algorithms. Like most security measures, an effective investigations program serves both as a deterrent to crime and a response once a crime has been committed.

Entry-level management positions generally prefer a four-year degree. Criminal justice and criminology are popular, but a business degree is acceptable. Two-year degrees can help the entry-level aspirant. Depending on the position, no experience may be required, but specialty areas usually require at least one to two years in the respective area. Experience from police or security investigations is taken into consideration. The salary range is $35,000 to $55,000, depending on many factors.

Mid-level management positions, requiring expertise in multiple investigative and business disciplines, generally require a degree in an appropriate discipline, as well as five or more years of demonstrated success in the field. Professional certifications such as the Professional Certified Investigator and the Certified Fraud Examiner are often desired as an indicator of professionalism and qualifications. Mid-level investigative managers may expect a salary range from $60,000 to $85,000.

Source: Courtesy of ASIS International (2005). "Career Opportunities in Security." www.asisonline.org.

□ □ □

Testimony

Security practitioners periodically testify in depositions or in court. A **deposition** is a pretrial discovery method whereby the opposing party in a case asks questions of the other party (e.g., victim, witness, expert) under oath, usually in an attorney's office, and while a word-for-word transcript is recorded. Depositions help to present the evidence of each side of a case and assist the justice system in settling cases before the expensive trial stage. Most civil and criminal cases never make it to trial.

Well-prepared testimony in both criminal and civil cases can be assured most readily by the following suggestions. (See Table 10-1 for additional advice.)

1. Prepare and review notes and reports. Recheck evidence that has been properly labeled and identified. Confer with an attorney.
2. Dress in a conservative manner, if not in uniform. Appear well groomed.
3. Maintain good demeanor (conduct, behavior). Do not slouch or fidget. Do not argue with anyone. Remain calm (take some deep breaths without being obvious).
4. Pause and think before speaking. Do not volunteer information beyond what is requested. Never guess. If you do not know an answer, say so.
5. If you bring notes, remember that the opposing attorney can request that the notes become part of the evidence. Recheck notes to prevent any unwanted information from entering the case.
6. Request feedback from associates to improve future performance.

Table 10-1 Brief Review of Common Tactics of Cross-Examination

Counsel's Tactic	Example	Purpose	Officer's Response
Rapid-fire questions	One question after another with little time to answer.	To confuse you; attempt to force inconsistent answers.	Take time to consider the question; be deliberate in answering, ask to have the question repeated, remain calm.
Condescending counsel	Benevolent in approach, over-sympathetic in questions to the point of ridicule.	To give the impression that you are inept, lack confidence, or may not be a reliable witness.	Firm, decisive answers, asking for the questions to be repeated if improperly phrased.
Friendly counsel	Very courteous, polite; questions tend to take you into his confidence.	To lull you into a false sense of security, where you will give answers in favor of the defense.	Stay alert; bear in mind that the purpose of defense is to discredit or diminish the effect of your testimony.
Badgering, belligerent	Counsel staring you right in the face, shouts "That is so, isn't it, officer?"	To make you angry so that you lose the sense of logic and calmness. Generally, rapid questions will also be included in this approach.	Stay calm, speak in a deliberate voice, giving prosecutor time to make appropriate objections.
Mispronouncing officer's name; using wrong rank	Your name is Jansen, counsel calls you Johnson.	To draw your attention to the error in pronunciation rather than enabling you to concentrate on the question asked, so that you will make inadvertent errors in testimony.	Ignore the mispronunciation and concentrate on the question counsel is asking.
Suggestive question (tends to be a leading question allowable on cross-examination)	"Was the color of the car blue?"	To suggest an answer to his or her question in an attempt to confuse or to lead you.	Concentrate carefully on the facts, disregard the suggestion. Answer the question.
Demanding a yes or no answer to a question that needs explanation	"Did you strike the defendant with your club?"	To prevent all pertinent and mitigating details from being considered by the jury.	Explain the answer to the question; if stopped by counsel demanding a yes or no answer, pause until the court instructs you to answer in your own words.
Reversing witness's words	You answer, "The accident occurred 27 feet from the intersection." Counsel says, "You say the accident occurred 72 feet from the intersection?"	To confuse you and demonstrate a lack of confidence in you.	Listen intently whenever counsel repeats back something you have said. If counsel makes an error, correct him or her.

Repetitious questions	The same question asked several times slightly rephrased.	To obtain inconsistent or conflicting answers from you.	Listen carefully to the question and state, "I have just answered that question."
Conflicting answers	"But Officer Smith, Detective Brown just said . . ."	To show inconsistency in the investigation. This tactic is normally used on measurements, times, and so forth.	Remain calm. Conflicting statements have a tendency to make a witness extremely nervous. Be guarded in your answers on measurements, times, and so forth. Unless you have exact knowledge, use the term "approximately." Refer to your notes.
Staring	After you have answered, counsel stares as though there were more to come.	To have a long pause that one normally feels must be filled, thus saying more than necessary. To provoke you into offering more than the question called for.	Wait for the next question.

Source: Reproduced from *The Training Keys* with permission of the International Association of Chiefs of Police, Gaithersburg, MD.

☐ ☐ ☐ ▉▉▉▉▉▉▉▉▉▉▉▉▉▉▉▉▉▉▉▉▉▉

Search the Web
Refer to the Web sites in this chapter to check the variety of personal and business information available.

Check "sucks.com" sites and search "anticapitalism" to view sites that are in contention with corporate America.

Here are additional sites relevant to this chapter:

ASIS International, Professional Certified Investigator: www.asisonline.org/
   certification/pci/pciabout.xml
International Association of Computer Investigative Specialists: www.iacis.info/
   iacisv2/pages/home.php
International Society of Forensic Computer Examiners: www.isfce.com/
Overseas Security Advisory Council (OSAC): www.osac.gov/

▉▉▉▉▉▉▉▉▉▉▉▉▉▉▉▉▉▉▉▉▉▉ ☐ ☐ ☐

Case Problems

10A. The Loreton Company, a California-based manufacturer of televisions, continuously increased profits because of high output at six company-owned plants in the United States and overseas. A recent inventory at a distribution facility located outside Los Angeles showed that more than 200 televisions were missing. The management of the Loreton Company became desperate about the losses. You are a partner at Klein and Smith Loss Prevention Associates, a consulting firm specializing in loss problems. Loreton Company executives contact you for assistance. A meeting is arranged. After competition with two other security and loss prevention firms, Loreton executives decide on a two-month contract for your firm's services. You are in charge. What are your specific plans and actions?

10B. You are senior investigator for the Bolt Corporation, which is a top 100 corporation with large holdings in electrical supplies, oil and gas exploration, and pharmaceuticals. Because you have an excellent record and 11 years of varied investigative experience with Bolt, you are selected by the director of loss prevention to train five newly hired college-educated investigators. The director stresses that you will design a 105-hour training program to span three weeks. After three weeks, the investigators will be assigned to various divisions within Bolt, where they will receive specialized training while working with experienced investigators. The director states that your typed curriculum design is due tomorrow for a 4 P.M. loss prevention meeting. She requires that you list the topics, hours for each topic, and why the particular topics and hours were chosen.

References

Bartolomie, J. (2005). "Hide and Seek." *TECHbeat* (Summer).
Baum, K. (2006). "Identity Theft, 2004." Washington, D.C.: U.S. Department of Justice, Office of Justice Programs.
Brenner, L. (2005). "How to Guard Your Identity." *Parade* (July 31).
Collins, P., et al. (2005). "The ASIS Foundation Security Report: Scope and Emerging Trends." Alexandria, VA: ASIS International.
Daniels, R. (2006). "Compliance Forcing Firms to Take Investigative Stance." *Security Director News*, 3 (March).
Donnelly, D. (2005). "iPods Sing for Investigators." *Security Management*, 49 (March).
Dunnagan, K., and Schroader, A. (2006). "Dialing for Evidence: Finding and Protecting Forensic Treasures in Mobile Phones." *Law Officer Magazine* (January/February).

Federal Bureau of Investigation. (1999). *Crime in the United States 1998*. Washington, D.C.: U.S. Government Printing Office.

Federal Bureau of Investigation. (2006). *Crime in the United States 2005*. www.fbi.gov/ucr/05cius/offenses/clearances/index.html, retrieved October 2, 2006.

Federal Bureau of Investigation, Financial Crimes Section. (2005). "Financial Crimes Report to the Public." http://www.fbi.gov/publications/financial/fcs_report052005/fcs_report052005.htm, retrieved October 4, 2006

Gardner, T., and Anderson, T. (2007). *Criminal Evidence: Principles and Cases*, 6th ed. Belmont, CA: Thomas Higher Education.

Gips, M. (2005). "Digital Video May Have Its Day in Court." *Security Management*, 49 (November).

Harold, C. (2006). "The Detective and the Database." *Security Management*, 50 (March).

Lang, D. (2005). "Dos and Don'ts for Digital Evidence." *Security Management*, 49 (June).

Mallery, J. (2005). "Cyberforensics: The Ultimate Investigative Tool." *Security Technology & Design*, 15 (December).

Mendell, R. (1999). "Is the Internet Just a Web of Misinformation?" *Security Management*, 43 (June).

Nagosky, D. (2005). "The Admissibility of Digital Photographs in Criminal Cases." *FBI Law Enforcement Bulletin*, 74 (December).

Overseas Security Advisory Council. (n.d.). "About OSAC." https://www.osac.gov/About/index.cfm, retrieved February 10. 2007.

Plante, W. (2007). "New Rules for Your Electronically Stored Information: FRCP's eDiscovery Rules." *Security Technology & Design*, 49 (April).

Ray, D. (2000). "When Bad Things Happen to Good Businesses." *Security Management*, 44 (October).

Reibold, R. (2005). "The Hidden Dangers of Using Private Investigators." *South Carolina Lawyer*, 17 (July).

Roman, G. (2005). "Ten Things to Avoid During Workplace Investigations." *RJL Newsletter*. www.rothgerber.com/newslettersarticles/le0054.asp, retrieved March 7, 2005.

Snow, E. (2000). "Adapting Technologies to the Task." *Security Management*, 44 (June).

U.S. Department of Justice. (1976). *Report of the Task Force on Private Security*. Washington, D.C.: U.S. Government Printing Office.

Van Nostrand, G., and Luizzo, A. (1995). "Investigating in a New Environment." *Security Management* (June).

11
Accounting, Accountability, and Auditing

Objectives

After studying this chapter, the reader will be able to:

1. Define and explain accounting, accountability, and auditing.
2. Describe how accountability is applied to the areas of cashier operations, purchasing, and inventory.
3. Describe the functions of auditors.
4. Explain the problem of fraud and the Sarbanes-Oxley Act of 2002.
5. Define and explain the importance of governance, risk management, and compliance.

KEY TERMS
<ul><li>accounting</li><li>accountability</li><li>auditing</li><li>purchase requisition</li><li>purchase order</li><li>invoice</li><li>receiving report</li><li>kickback</li><li>inventory</li><li>shrinkage</li><li>periodic inventory system</li><li>perpetual inventory system</li><li>attest function</li><li>American Institute of Certified Public Accountants</li></ul> <ul><li>National Association of State Boards of Accountancy</li><li>Association of Certified Fraud Examiners</li><li>forensic accounting</li><li>internal control questionnaire</li><li>fraud</li><li>Enron Corporation</li><li>Sarbanes-Oxley (SOX) Act of 2002</li><li>Public Company Accounting Oversight Board</li><li>governance</li><li>risk management</li><li>compliance</li></ul>

Introduction

Accounting, often referred to as the language of business, is concerned with recording, sorting, summarizing, reporting, and interpreting data related to business transactions. Accounting information assists executives, auditors, investors, regulators, and others in decision making. Virtually every type of concern requires accounting records. For the most part, bookkeepers perform the day-to-day recording of business data; accountants design the accounting systems and prepare and interpret reports. For example, a bookkeeper in a business, after counting cash and checking cash sales receipts, records the amount in the cash receipts journal. Or, based on accounting data—specifically, inventory reports—an accountant decides that shrinkage is too high in a particular business; the loss prevention department is notified.

☐ ☐ ☐ ▬▬▬▬▬▬▬▬▬▬▬▬▬▬▬▬▬▬▬▬▬▬▬▬▬▬▬▬▬▬▬▬▬▬▬▬

Accounting is the language of business.

▬▬▬▬▬▬▬▬▬▬▬▬▬▬▬▬▬▬▬▬▬▬▬▬▬▬▬▬▬▬▬▬▬▬▬▬ ☐ ☐ ☐

Accountability defines a responsibility for and a description of something. For example, John Smith is responsible (i.e., is held accountable) for all finished products in a plant, and he maintains accurate records (i.e., an inventory) of what is in stock. Another example would be a loss prevention officer keeping a log of people entering and leaving a restricted area. Or, while a truck is being loaded for shipment, a clerk records on a tally the number of items being shipped. In these examples, employees sign their names to the documents (inventory, log, and tally); they are responsible, and accountability is maintained.

Auditing is an examination or check of something; the major purpose of an audit is to uncover deviations. An audit can be simple or intricate. For example, a loss prevention officer audits (checks) a CCTV system to ensure that it is working properly. Or, an auditor examines the financial records of a company and reports that they are fair, reliable, and conform to company policies and procedures.

Accounting

Within a business, for example, the accounting department has control over financial matters that are vital to business operations. Common components of an accounting department are cashiering operations, accounts receivable, accounts payable, payroll, and company bank accounts. Each component of an accounting department has the responsibility for maintaining records that are scrutinized by management to ascertain the financial position of the business. Without adequate loss prevention strategies or controls in financial transactions and records, organizations could not survive.

Potential losses are possible throughout the accounting department. A cashiering operation must be protected, not only from burglary and robbery, but also from employee theft. Accounts receivable must be protected from opportunities that allow employees to destroy bills and pocket cash. Accounts payable also needs protection; employees in collusion with supply company employees have been known to alter invoices to embezzle money. A frequent scheme by some payroll clerks is to maintain fictitious employees on the payroll and cash their paychecks.

Accounting also is a system of principles and procedures that enable clerks and bookkeepers to record financial data in a logical manner. A record of an individual transaction does not have as much impact as the summation of transactions in a financial statement or business report (see Table 11–1). The accounting statements assist management in decision making.

Table 11-1 Financial Statements of Two Separate Companies

Trico Corporation Balance Sheet June 30, 20_

Assets		Liabilities		
Cash	4,000	Accounts payable	44,000	
Accounts receivable	100,300	Notes payable	100,000	
Inventory	100,000			144,000
Equipment	34,000			
Land	80,000	**Capital**		
Buildings	300,400			
	618,700	Preferred stock	74,700	
		Common stock	400,000	
				474,700
Total assets	618,700	Total liabilities and capital		618,700

Simple examples of an income statement and a capital statement follow. Note that "expenses" and "net income" are two additional major categories of accounting besides assets, liabilities, and capital.

Quality Loss Prevention Service Income Statement for month ended October 31, 20_

Sales and service		11,800
Operating expenses:		
Salary expenses	6,000	
Supplies expense	1,100	
Rent expense	1,400	
Miscellaneous expense	1,300	
		−9,800
Net income		2,000

Quality Loss Prevention Service Capital Statement for month ended October 31, 20_

Capital, October 2, 20_		10,000
Net income for the month	2,000	
Less withdrawals	−1,000	
Increase in capital		1,000
Capital, October 31, 20_		11,000

Accounting statements assist management in answering many questions:

What is the financial condition of the concern?
What is the financial value?
Was there a profit or loss?
Which part of a firm is doing well (or poorly)?
How serious are losses from hazards?

Because security and loss prevention practitioners often investigate financial matters and manage a budget, they are well advised to study accounting at the college level to prepare for their careers.

Accountability

The definition of formal accountability points to the documentation or description of something. Informal accountability usually is verbal and results in no documentation; for example, a loss prevention manager asks a subordinate if a fire extinguisher was checked (audited). The subordinate states that it was audited. Thus, a basic audit of a loss prevention device is accomplished. What if two weeks pass, a fire takes place near the particular fire extinguisher, and it is found to be inoperable? An employee who tries to extinguish the fire with the inoperable extinguisher complains to management. Superiors ask the loss prevention manager if the extinguisher was checked. The manager states that it was audited. The superiors ask for documentation to support the statements. Because of the verbal accountability, no record exists. From that point on, the loss prevention manager realizes the value of formal accountability and develops an excellent system of records.

The importance of accountability must not be underestimated. It is a key survival strategy. Documentation can result from many types of loss prevention activities. Examples are a variety of investigative reports (e.g., crimes, accidents); security surveys; security system maintenance; alarm activations; visitor logs; crime prevention, fire protection, and life safety plans; meetings; policies and procedures; and training. As well as assisting a loss prevention practitioner when supporting a contention, documentation can assist in planning, budgeting, preparing major reports, and providing general reference.

Accountability is a key survival strategy.

Cashier Operations

A detailed procedure for accountability in retailing is illustrated next (Curtis, 1980: 14):

> *The key to front end control is accountability. Each cashier must have his or her own cash register drawer. Relief cashiers should bring their own drawer, and the cashier going on relief should lock up her cash or remove her drawer during relief periods. The relief person should also sign the register tape when taking over, and the regular cashier should sign when leaving the register.*
>
> *The head cashier should periodically review register detail tapes, watching for continuity of transaction numbers. If the last transaction on the register Monday night was number 112334, then the first transaction on Tuesday morning must be 112335. If it is not, the missing chronological numbers may indicate theft of several sales by the cashier and destruction of the tape containing the missing transaction numbers.*

Retail cashier operations have been enhanced by computers. More on retail accountability and point-of-sale accounting systems in Chapter 17 regarding retail security.

Purchasing

Because procedures vary and various types of computer software are available to enhance purchasing systems, a generalized approach to purchasing is presented here. Four forms are discussed in the subsequent purchasing system: purchase requisition, purchase order, invoice, and receiving report.

When a company orders merchandise, equipment, or supplies, for example, the order should be documented to avoid any misunderstandings. Suppose a maintenance department head at a plant seeks to order an item. Generally, the documentation process begins when the order is written on a standard form known as a **purchase requisition**. This form may also be completed in the company computerized accounting information system. The purchase requisition lists, among other things, the originator (who placed the order), the date, the item, a description, justification for need, and cost. Once the originator completes the purchase requisition and makes a copy for filing, superiors approve or disapprove the purchase and sign the requisition. If it is approved, the purchasing department reviews the purchase requisition and selects the best vendor. The purchasing staff completes a prenumbered purchase order. Copies of the purchase order are sent to the originator, the receiving department, and the accounts payable department; the purchasing department retains the original purchase order. The **purchase order** contains, among other things, the originator, the item, quantity, possibly an item code number from a vendor catalog, and the cost. The purchase order is sent to the vendor. Upon fulfillment of the order, the vendor sends an **invoice** to the buyer's accounts payable department. An invoice contains the names and addresses of both the buyer and the vendor, cost, item, quantity, date, and method of shipment.

When the accounts payable department receives the invoice, it checks the invoice for accuracy by comparing it with a copy of the purchase order. Cost, type of item, proper quantity, and address of buyer are checked.

The receiving and purchasing departments of the buyer receive copies of the invoice to check it for accuracy. To decrease the possibility of mistakes (or collusion), the purchase order and invoice sent to the receiving department may have the number of items deleted. When the merchandise arrives, the receiving person records the number of items and type, and checks for irregularities (e.g., damage). This form often becomes a **receiving report**. Copies are sent to the purchasing and accounts payable departments. The purchasing department compares the receiving report with the invoice. The accounts payable department makes payment after examining the purchase order, invoice, and the receiving report. These three documents and a copy of the check constitute the inactive file for this purchase (see Figure 11–1).

This purchasing system may appear complicated; however, without such accountability, losses can increase. For example, in one company, accounting employees in collusion with outside supply company employees altered records so items paid for were never delivered, but sold on the black market for illegal gain. In another case, a mid-level accountant for a utility company submitted bogus check requests for payments to vendors. The accountant had set up accounts for phony companies at a bank, and when the utility paid the "vendors," the accountant simply transferred the money to his personal account at the same bank (Mann and Roberts, 2001: 470).

Another widespread vulnerability in purchasing results from a **kickback**. This means that the purchaser receives something of value from the seller for buying the seller's product or service. Losses occur if the product or service is inferior and overpriced in comparison to the competition. For example, in a secret deal, John Doe Forklift Company agrees to pay Richard Ring, purchaser for Fence Manufacturing, $1000 cash for each forklift purchased at an inflated cost. After the forklifts are delivered, it is discovered that the forklift tires are too smooth for the outside gravel and dirt grounds of the manufacturing company. With limited traction, the forklifts frequently get stuck, and employees are unable to work until delivery trucks return and pull the forklifts free. The losses include both cash and lost time.

Accounting controls and loss prevention strategies in purchasing include the following suggestions:

1. Centralize all purchasing through a purchasing department.
2. Maintain accountability through documents (standard forms), signatures, and carefully designed computer software.
3. Separate duties and responsibilities so that each person and department can check on the others' work.
4. Test by deliberate error.
5. Use unalterable paper to prevent alterations or erasures.
6. Prenumber purchase order forms (and other forms when needed).
7. Conduct loss prevention checks without notice.
8. Conduct periodic audits.
9. Scrutinize the purchasing department to prevent favoritism and kickbacks. Use competitive bidding.
10. Prohibit gifts or favors from vendors (sellers).
11. Screen applicants for employment.
12. Develop clear policies and procedures.

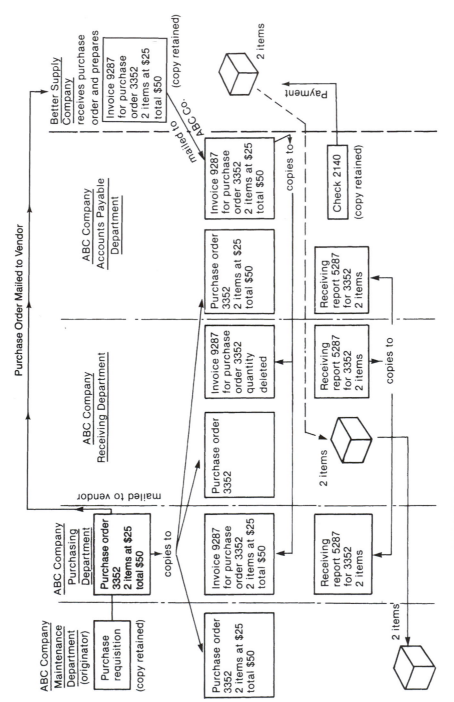

FIGURE 11-1 Accountability and paper trail for purchase of two items by ABC company.

Inventory

In a wholesale or retail business, merchandise is continuously purchased and sold. This sale of merchandise is the primary source of revenue. A substantial amount of a business's resources is invested in saleable merchandise, and this merchandise is the largest asset. Therefore, this asset must be protected. The term **inventory** includes merchandise for sale, raw materials, and unfinished goods. Inventory is reported on the balance sheet as an asset.

Shrinkage is the amount of merchandise that has disappeared through theft, has become useless because of breakage or spoilage, or is unaccounted for because of sloppy recording. It is often expressed as a percentage. Levy and Weitz (2001: 548) define shrinkage as "the difference between the recorded value of inventory (at retail prices) based on merchandise bought and received and the value of the *actual* inventory (at retail prices) in stores and distribution centers divided by retail sales during the period." For example, if accounting records indicate the inventory should be $1,500,000, the *actual* count of the inventory reveals $1,236,000, and sales were $4,225,000, the shrinkage is 6.2%, or ($1,500,000 − $1,236,000)/$4,225,000.

In many businesses, shrinkage of 3% or more is a serious loss problem. Loss prevention managers frequently express the objective of their job as lowering shrinkage. An accurate measurement of shrinkage depends on the quality of the inventory system; both have a definite impact on the loss prevention program and its manager.

Two primary inventory systems are the periodic and the perpetual systems. The **periodic inventory system** results in a physical count of merchandise only at specific intervals, usually once per year. When this system is used, daily revenue from sales is recorded in accounting records, but no transaction is recorded to adjust the inventory account to reflect the fact that a sale was made. The periodic system makes it difficult to measure shrinkage accurately. To make matters worse, when a monthly or quarterly financial statement is necessary for a particular business using the periodic inventory system, managers sometimes estimate the inventory without taking a physical count.

The **perpetual inventory system** uses accounting records that maintain an up-to-date inventory count. These systems typically are computerized. Handheld microcomputer technology and point-of-sale (POS) computers capture data through bar-code scanning. RFID is increasingly replacing bar codes. In addition to recording daily revenue from sales, an individual inventory record is maintained for each type of merchandise sold, which enables a continuous count. Thus, the accounting records reflect cost of goods sold and the inventory quantity. This information provides a better opportunity to measure shrinkage than that available with the periodic system.

To increase the accuracy of an inventory and the shrinkage statistic, these strategies are recommended:

1. Maintain a careful inventory system.
2. Establish accountability.
3. Standardize forms and procedures for the count.
4. Make sure employees can count accurately.
5. If possible, do not subject employees to extensive inventory counts at any one time.
6. Automate the process by using handheld microcomputer technology that captures data.
7. Conduct surprise counts of a sample of the merchandise at erratic time intervals. Compare manual counts with computer data.
8. If possible, require prenumbered requisition forms for merchandise taken out of inventory.
9. Prohibit unnecessary people (e.g., truck drivers, service people, and other employees) from entering merchandise storage areas.
10. Use an undercover investigator to participate in the inventory count.
11. The loss prevention manager should have an opportunity to examine the methods used to formulate the shrinkage statistic, especially because it will reflect on him or her and on the loss prevention program.

□ □ □

Radio Frequency Identification: Great Potential, But Vulnerable

RFID was applied as early as World War II when it was used to identify aircraft. Today, it has wide applications beyond protecting library books and merchandise at retail stores. The system has three basic components: tags, readers, and a host computer.

RFID tags contain tiny semiconductor chips and antennas. Many tags appear as paper labels, while others are embedded into such items as containers or wristbands. Each tag is programmed with a unique identifier that permits wireless tracking of the tag and the object holding the tag. Tags can hold a large amount of data, including serial numbers, time stamps, travel history, and technical data. Similar to television and radio, RFID uses various frequency bands. A tiny battery powers active tags, and passive tags are powered by a reader that "wakes up" the tag when it is within range of the reader.

Readers contain an antenna that communicates with tags and an electronics module networked to a computer. The reader performs security functions including encryption/decryption and user authentication. Software connects the RFID system to the IT system where supply chain management or asset management databases are located.

Supply chains benefit from RFID technology through increased efficiency and decreased labor costs and losses. To illustrate, readers installed at loading dock doors detect tags on pallets of merchandise passing by. The reader signals the tags to transmit their identities and other data to the reader that forwards the data to a computer. The computer then credits or debits the inventory depending on whether the merchandise is entering or leaving.

The applications of RFID are broad and include tracking of property, evidence, passports, visas, inmates in prison, and visitors at facilities. RFID may prove more efficient than bar codes for recording, locating, and tracking. RFID technology is also applicable to access controls (National Law Enforcement and Corrections Technology Center, 2005: 6–8).

RFID is not without vulnerabilities. Johnston and Warner (2005: 116), who conducted tests on RFID at Los Alamos National Laboratory, warn that low-end tags can be counterfeited and that readers can be tampered with, replaced, or controlled remotely. Tags can also be removed from one object and placed on another. RFID signals can be blocked or jammed. Organizations should test these systems at unpredictable times. High-end systems that use cryptography, challenge-response protocols, rotating passwords, or tamper detection technology afford increased protection but are used infrequently. Another vulnerability is that a tag could contain a software virus that, when scanned by a reader, could spread through an RFID system.

□ □ □

Auditing

Auditors

An auditor examines business accounting records to check for irregularities. These irregularities may include (1) deviations from the particular firm's accounting methods, (2) mistakes, and (3) criminal activity. During an audit of financial records by an independent auditor, known as a certified public accountant (CPA), guidance is provided by state and federal statutes, court decisions, a contract with the client, and professional standards as established by Generally Accepted Auditing Standards and Generally Accepted Accounting Practices. Because it is impossible to check every financial record and transaction, a CPA narrows an audit to certain records, such as financial reports and areas where problems are common to the particular concern. How accounting data are recorded and summarized is frequently studied.

At times, a CPA may encounter misleading financial information that attempts to make a business look better than its true financial position. The misleading information often is an attempt by management to attract investors. To counter this problem, cautious investors are more likely to favor a business that has had an audit by an outside independent CPA, as opposed to no audit or one performed by an internal auditor.

When an independent CPA completes an audit, a report is prepared. If a business's financial records are dependable and credible, then the CPA expresses this favorable opinion in the audit report. This is known as the **attest function**.

CPAs, like other skilled professionals, are liable for damages proximately caused by their negligence. A CPA is liable to a client when he or she negligently fails to detect or fraudulently conceals signs that an employee of the client is embezzling. In addition, the CPA is liable for not detecting and reporting to the client that internal audit controls are lax (Twomey et al., 2001: 926).

Requirements for becoming a CPA are found in the Board of Accountancy in each state and jurisdiction. Generally, to sit for the CPA examination developed by the **American Institute of Certified Public Accountants** (AICPA) and administered by the **National Association of State Boards of Accountancy**, a candidate must have a bachelor's or master's degree with an emphasis in accounting. For final certification, a candidate who passes the examination with only a bachelor's degree needs two years of work experience. A candidate who passes the examination with 150 credit hours needs one year of work experience for certification.

Many firms maintain internal auditors. These internal auditors audit various internal activities that independent auditors may or may not audit. For instance, in addition to studying specific accounting records, internal auditors may examine whether management's policies and procedures are being followed. An internal auditor may also conduct surprise audits.

Public (e.g., federal, state, municipal) and private investigation practitioners have expanded their competency in accounting. A major reason for this is a response to increased investigations into the white-collar crime arena.

Cross-training can be used to reduce the knowledge gap between auditor and criminal investigator. Cross-training involves the auditor being trained in criminal investigation and the criminal investigator being trained in auditing. An auditor's training could include criminal law, evidence, interviewing, and interrogation. A criminal investigator's training could include accounting principles and procedures and auditing. Both should have training in information systems and related investigative methods.

The **Association of Certified Fraud Examiners** promotes professionalism, training, and certification (CFE). Bodnar and Hopwood (2004: 105) write: "**Forensic accounting** is one of several terms that is used to describe the activities of persons who are concerned with preventing and detecting fraud. The terms 'fraud examiner,' 'fraud auditor,' and 'loss prevention professional' are also descriptive of this type of activity."

Internal Control Questionnaire

A popular and convenient way to conduct an audit is through an **internal control questionnaire**. These questionnaires are used by public accounting firms, internal audit departments, and other organizations that are involved in reviews of internal controls (Bodnar and Hopwood, 2004: 131–132). A typical questionnaire has a list of questions to remind the person conducting the audit to focus attention on specific areas of concern. Questionnaire results provide feedback that help to pinpoint and correct deviations and deficiencies. Here are sample questions from the American Institute of Certified Public Accountants (1978: 54) for a small business. Many of the questions are relevant to other organizations.

- Are accounting records kept up-to-date and balanced monthly?
- Are monthly or quarterly financial reports available to the owner?
- Are the personal funds of the owner and his or her personal income and expenses completely segregated from the business?

- Does the company practice "separation of functions" (e.g., separate check preparation from check authorization) so accountability is assigned and each employee can check on the other?
- Are employees rotated periodically among financial jobs and are they required to take vacations?
- Are over-the-counter receipts controlled by cash register tapes, counter receipts, and so on?
- Are employees who handle funds bonded?
- Do two different people reconcile the bank records and make out the deposit slip?
- Are prenumbered checks used?
- Is the owner's signature required on checks?
- Does the owner review the bank reconciliation?
- Does the owner never sign blank checks?
- Do different people reconcile the bank records and write the checks?
- Are work orders or sales invoices prenumbered and controlled?
- Is credit granted only by the owner?
- Is the person responsible for inventory someone other than the bookkeeper?
- Are periodic physical inventories taken?
- Are perpetual inventory records maintained?
- Are there detailed records available of property assets and allowances for depreciation?
- Does someone other than the bookkeeper always do the purchasing?
- Are suppliers' monthly statements compared with recorded liabilities regularly?
- Does the owner approve, sign, and distribute payroll checks?

□ □ □ ▬▬▬▬▬▬▬▬▬▬▬▬▬▬▬▬▬▬▬▬▬▬▬▬▬▬▬▬▬▬▬▬▬▬

IT Staffers Influenced to Go Bad

In what may be a trend, the U.S. Securities and Exchange Commission (SEC), which enforces laws to reduce fraudulent financial reporting, is increasingly charging IT directors with securities fraud. Sensormatic Electronics Corp., for example, was in trouble because its home security systems firm had its IT personnel roll back computer clocks so sales could be booked sooner to inflate revenue figures. In another company, Bio Clinic Corp., more than 400 invoices with a value of $6 million, which had already been paid, were added into the ledger a second time (to falsify revenue) by reprogramming the accounting software. The SEC notes that IT directors are responsible for the accuracy and integrity of the documents and data generated by a company computer system. In addition, they should know if unauthorized changes have been made in general ledger, accounts receivable, and other accounting software (Nash, 1999: 20).

▬▬▬▬▬▬▬▬▬▬▬▬▬▬▬▬▬▬▬▬▬▬▬▬▬▬▬▬▬▬▬▬▬▬ □ □ □

Fraud

Fraud is a broad term that includes a variety of offenses that share the elements of deceit or intentional misrepresentation of fact, with the intent of unlawfully depriving a person or organization of property or legal rights. It is a multibillion dollar problem. Although subsequent paragraphs emphasize fraud by top executives, fraud can occur at any level of an organization. Chapter 7 describes internal theft and fraud.

The FBI partners with many public agencies (e.g., Securities and Exchange Commission; Internal Revenue Service) and private sector organizations (e.g., AICPA; Dunn & Bradstreet) to combat fraud. Through fiscal year 2005, FBI investigations of corporate fraud resulted in 497 indictments and 317 convictions, with numerous cases pending plea agreements and trials. From July 1, 2002, through March 31, 2005, accomplishments regarding corporate fraud cases were as follows: $2.2 billion in restitution, $34.6 million in recoveries, $79.1 million in fines, and $27.9 million in seizures (Federal Bureau of Investigation, Financial Crimes Section, 2005: B2).

In 2001, one of the most infamous corporate scandals began to unfold from the Houston-based energy company known as **Enron Corporation**. It filed for bankruptcy protection with $63 billion in assets, while its stock closed under $1 a share. A year earlier one share sold for $75. Unfortunately, investors lost billions of dollars. Many company employees had received compensation in the form of company stock, and they lost billions of dollars in their retirement and life savings, besides losing their jobs.

The collapse of Enron resulted from years of "creative accounting," whereby top executives hide billions of dollars in debt and made failing ventures appear successful and profitable. In 2006, former Enron founder, Kenneth Lay, age 64, was convicted of fraud, conspiracy, and lying to banks. A month later, he died of a heart attack. Interestingly, a judge followed legal precedent and vacated Lay's conviction. Other former Enron executives were convicted and sentenced to prison. Andrew Fastow, former chief financial officer, cooperated with prosecutors and was sentenced to 6 years in prison. He helped to secure the prosecution's case against former chief executive officer, Jeffrey Skilling, who was sentenced in 2006 to 24 years in prison following his conviction for fraud, conspiracy, insider trading, and lying to auditors. The judge also approved a settlement requiring Skilling to surrender $43 million in assets for a restitution fund for Enron retirees and shareholders. Skilling's sentence was close to the 25-year sentence that former WorldCom chief executive officer Bernard Ebbers received for his involvement in an $11 billion accounting fraud. In 2002, the accounting firm that audited Enron, Arthur Andersen, was forced to surrender its CPA licenses pending prosecution by the U.S. Department of Justice.

Unfortunately, as the memory of Enron and WorldCom is still fresh in the minds of executives, some continue to falter and face indictments. Consequently, as written in Chapter 2, *the impact of deterrence is questionable and prevention is a key strategy to reduce losses.*

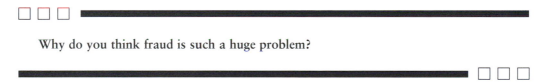

Why do you think fraud is such a huge problem?

Although the Enron case was not the only corporate scandal that created uproar over fraudulent accounting practices, it did spark legislation seeking to control the problem. As explained in Chapter 4, the **Sarbanes-Oxley (SOX) Act of 2002** seeks to prevent fraud and affects the processes and accountability for financial reporting in publicly traded U.S. companies. It redesigned the federal regulations and reporting requirements of public companies. The act makes executives responsible for establishing, evaluating, and monitoring the effectiveness of internal controls over financial and operational processes. SOX emphasizes the importance of an audit committee as an essential component of a public company's board of directors. Some SOX provisions are becoming standard operating procedure for all businesses, besides publicly held ones. The law includes accounting controls and how companies report financial results and executive compensation. It holds company executives and external auditors directly accountable for the accuracy of financial reports and protects employees who blow the whistle on suspected fraud. *Security and audit departments in corporations have become involved with SOX because these departments investigate internal fraud.*

Sox established the **Public Company Accounting Oversight Board** (PCAOB), which regulates the conduct of auditors and influences management in public companies. The PCAOB promulgates rules and imposes sanctions in conjunction with Securities and Exchange Commission (SEC) review. The SEC is a federal administrative law enforcement agency that protects investors. SOX also increased criminal sentences for fraud. It broadened the scope of violations pertaining to obstruction of justice and includes acts of knowingly destroying, altering, or falsifying documents to interfere with any federal investigation. In addition, SOX restricts nonaudit services of outside auditors, such as bookkeeping services related to financial statements, IT financial system guidance, and investment banking services.

Wilson (2004: 7) provides a view of how two security directors applied SOX in their respective corporations, as described next. In one company, the security director lobbied for and was assigned to the corporate SOX task force. It focused on SOX, section 404, on internal controls, which pertains to management's assessment of internal controls, while requiring executives and auditors to confirm the effectiveness of those controls. The task force prepared fraud policies, internal controls, and best practices. In addition, data analysis techniques were implemented to search for anomalies in a variety of departments and reporting documents. A financial integrity department was established with the following objectives: determining risk potential, improving internal controls, identifying technology solutions, communicating the code of conduct and fraud policies, and implementing prevention programs. In the other corporation, the security director played a limited role in SOX and focused on section 302. This pertains to anonymous, confidential reporting by employees of accounting and auditing irregularities and other problems.

Although privately held businesses and nonprofit organizations are not required by law to conform to SOX, increased concern over accounting irregularities is causing management in a variety of entities to consider some provisions of SOX. This concern impacts decisions of public companies planning to merge with private companies and of private companies planning to become public companies.

Another point about SOX is that compliance is expensive and time-consuming. Companies are spending millions of dollars to comply with the law.

☐ ☐ ☐ ▬▬▬▬▬▬▬▬▬▬▬▬▬▬▬▬▬▬▬▬▬▬▬▬▬▬▬▬▬▬

Do you think there is too much pressure on executives to reach business goals? Explain your answer.

▬▬▬▬▬▬▬▬▬▬▬▬▬▬▬▬▬▬▬▬▬▬▬▬▬▬▬▬▬▬ ☐ ☐ ☐

Governance, Risk Management, and Compliance

Zoellick and Frank (2005: 1) note that corporate boards of directors and senior management are generally aware of the importance of setting objectives and managing programs that involve governance, risk management, and compliance (GRC). They write about seven operational concerns, drawn from the Federal Sentencing Guidelines, to promote effective compliance and ethics programs to strengthen GRC operations. Earlier, in Chapter 4, compliance auditing and the Federal Sentencing Guidelines were explained. The next chapter includes risk management. Here, GRC is defined from the perspectives of Zoellick and Frank (2005: 3–6), followed by the seven operational concerns.

Governance is "the process by which the board sets the objectives for an organization and oversees progress toward those objectives." **Risk management** means different things in different contexts." "The old view of risk...managed by buying insurance..." "What has happened...board members and senior management are using the language and techniques of risk management to address a much broader range of organizational concerns." "...risk management is part of the process of making decisions." "...risk management supports risk taking and the organization's ability to compete." [**Compliance** refers to an organization adhering to numerous laws, regulations, and initiatives.] "Monitoring and supporting compliance is not just a matter of keeping the regulators happy; it is the way that the organization monitors and maintains its health."

Here is a list of core GRC operations (Zoellick and Frank, 2005: 13–16):

1. *Establish and support policies, procedures, and controls.* This creates the foundation to ensure that the GRC program works.
2. *Maintain centralized oversight.* The key is high-level oversight of the program from top management.
3. *Maintain decentralized administration and accountability.* Ensure accountability for every unit of the organization.
4. *Establish communication channels across all organization levels.* Communications should provide up-to-date policies, procedures, and controls.
5. *Audit, monitor, and report.* Methods must be implemented to ensure that policies and procedures are being employed.
6. *Provide uniform support, remediation, and enforcement.* Ensure consistent incentives to comply and discipline for violators.
7. *Implement continuous process improvement.* Management must respond to feedback to improve GRC.

Search the Web

To learn more about preventing and detecting fraud, embezzlement, and other white-collar crimes, check these Web sites:

American Institute of Certified Public Accountants, Anti-Fraud and Corporate Responsibility Center: http://antifraud.aicpa.org/
Association of Certified Fraud Examiners: www.cfenet.com/
Institute of Management & Administration: www.ioma.com/
National Coalition for the Prevention of Economic Crime: www.ncpec.org/
National White Collar Crime Center: www.nw3c.org/
Securities and Exchange Commission: www.sec.gov/

Case Problems

11A. With reference to the purchasing accountability section of this chapter and Figure 11-1, design an accountability system to strengthen control and prevent losses when merchandise travels from the receiving department to the originator. Look for any other weaknesses and suggest controls.

11B. You are a CSO for a medium-sized corporation that manufactures computer components. Your boss asks you to prepare a plan of antifraud strategies. Prepare a list of what you think are the top five strategies that will be the heart of your plan.

11C. As a corporate IT director, you have been asked by a top executive to program software so revenue will appear greater than it actually is because of a slowing economy. What are your choices in the matter, and how do you respond to the executive?

11D. As director of loss prevention for a corporation, you learn that the company president and the head of IT have conspired to fraudulently alter financial records to show revenue higher than what is expected. What do you do?

References

American Institute of Certified Public Accountants. (1978). "A Small Business Internal Control Questionnaire." *The Journal of Accountancy* (July).

Bodnar, G., and Hopwood, W. (2004). *Accounting Information Systems*, 9th ed. Upper Saddle River, NJ: Pearson Prentice Hall.

Curtis, B. (1980). "Executive Insights." *Security World*, 17 (February).

Federal Bureau of Investigation, Financial Crimes Section. (2005). "Financial Crimes Report to the Public." http://www.fbi.gov/publications/financial/fcs_report052005/fcs_report052005.htm, retrieved October 4, 2006.

Johnston, R., and Warner, J. (2005). "The Dr. Who Conundrum." *Security Management*, 49 (September).

Levy, M., and Weitz, B. (2001). *Retailing Management*, 4th ed. New York: McGraw-Hill Irwin.

Mann, R., and Roberts, B. (2001) *Essentials of Business Law*, 7th ed. Cincinnati, OH: West.

Nash, K. (1999). "IT Staffers Charged in Accounting Frauds." *Computerworld* (December).

National Law Enforcement and Corrections Technology Center. (2005). "Technology Primer: Radio Frequency Identification." *TECHBeat* (Summer).

Twomey, D. (2001). *Anderson's Business Law & the Regulatory Environment*, 14th ed. Cincinnati, OH: West.

Wilson, R. (2004). "Sarbanes-Oxley: Lessons from Security Directors." *Security Director News*, 1 (August).

Zoellick, B., and Frank, T. (2005). "Governance, Risk Management, and Compliance: An Operational Approach" (May 16). http://gilbane.com/publications/GRC_Operational_Approach_PD1_0_050512.pdf, retrieved October 28, 2006.

12

Risk Management, Business Continuity, and Emergency Management

Objectives

After studying this chapter, the reader will be able to:

1. Define risk management and explain its purpose.
2. Describe the role of the risk manager.
3. Explain the risk management process, risk modeling, risk management tools, and enterprise risk management.
4. List and explain at least eight types of insurance.
5. Elaborate on the insurance claims process.
6. Discuss how to establish a business continuity plan.
7. Explain the role of government in risk management, all-hazards preparedness, and emergency management.

KEY TERMS

- risk
- risk management
- risk perception theory
- risk communication theory
- insurance brokers
- risk management process
- first party risks
- third party risks
- risk financing
- risk control
- Delphi approach
- game theory
- enterprise risk management
- event risk management

- financial risk management
- insurance
- shared risk
- commercial package policy
- bond
- fidelity bond
- surety bond
- Terrorism Risk Insurance Act of 2002
- cyber insurance
- claims management
- business continuity
- NFPA 1600 Standard on Disaster/Emergency Management and Business Continuity Programs

- emergency management
- systems theory
- chaos theory
- decision theory
- management theory
- organizational behavior theory
- risk perception and communication theory
- social constructionist theory
- Weberian theory
- Marxist theory
- all-hazards preparedness concept
- generic emergency management
- specialized emergency management
- Civil Defense Programs

- community-based mitigation
- Federal Emergency Management Agency (FEMA)
- mitigation
- response
- recovery
- preparedness
- interoperability
- National Response Plan (NRP)
- National Incident Management System (NIMS)
- National Preparedness Goal
- logistics
- U.S. Northern Command (NORTH-COM)
- Posse Comitatus Act

Note: Portions of this chapter are from: Purpura, P. (2007). *Terrorism and Homeland Security: An Introduction with Applications.* Burlington, MA: Elsevier Butterworth-Heinemann.

Risk Management

As defined in Chapter 2, **risk** is the measurement of the frequency, probability, and severity of losses from exposure to threats or hazards (e.g., crime, fire, accident, and natural disaster). The wise businessperson is knowledgeable about all exposures. Business interruption, for example, results from crime, fire, accident, flood, tornado, and the like. Another exposure is liability. A customer might become injured on the premises after falling or be harmed in some way when using a product manufactured by a business.

The most productive way of handling unavoidable risks is to manage them as well as possible. Hence, the term *risk management* has evolved. **Risk management** makes the most efficient before-the-loss arrangement for an after-the-loss continuation of a business. Insurance is a major risk management tool. Leimberg et al. (2002: 6), from the insurance industry, define risk management as follows: "A preloss exercise that reflects an organization's postloss goals; a process to recognize and manage faulty and potentially dangerous operations, trends, and policies that could lead to loss and to minimize losses that do occur."

Risk management is important to not only businesses, but also our whole society. It is applicable to government, institutions, all types of organizations, the family, and individuals. The purpose of risk management is to protect people and assets.

Risk management and loss prevention are naturally intertwined. Loss prevention is another tool for risk managers to make their job easier. Insurance is made more affordable through loss prevention methods. Additional risk management tools are described in subsequent pages.

Both loss prevention and risk management originated in the insurance industry. Fire insurance companies, soon after the Civil War, formed the National Board of Fire Underwriters, which was instrumental in reducing loss of life and property through prevention measures. Today, loss prevention has spread throughout the insurance industry and into the business community. Risk management is also an old practice. The modern history of risk management is said by many insurance experts to have begun in 1931, with the establishment of the insurance section of the American Management Association. The insurance section holds conferences and workshops for those in the insurance and risk management field.

Risk management theory draws on probability and statistics, mathematics, engineering, economics, business, and the social sciences, among other disciplines. The study of risk has expanded to include the understanding of the psychological, cultural, and social context of risk. The expanding nature of the study of risk is illustrated by the two theories that follow (Borodzicz, 2005: 14–47).

- **Risk perception theory** focuses on how humans learn from their environment and react to it. Psychologists apply a cognitive research approach to understand how humans gain knowledge through perception and reasoning. For instance, risk can be researched by isolating a variable and simulating it in a laboratory with a group of subjects in an experiment involving risk decision making (e.g., gambling). The psychometric approach is another method of researching risk; it involves a survey to measure individual views of risks. Research on risk perception shows that people find unusual risks to be more terrifying than familiar ones and, interestingly, the familiar risks claim the most lives; voluntary risk (e.g., smoking) is preferred over imposed risk (e.g., a hazardous industry moving near one's home); and people have limited trust in official data.

- **Risk communication theory** concerns itself with communication perceptions of experts and lay citizens. Although experts work to simplify information for lay citizens, communication of simplified information and behavior change may not be successful. Research on this topic focuses on lay citizen perceptions of risk within the context of psychological, social, cultural, and political factors. Risk communication theory is important because it holds answers for educating and preparing citizens for emergencies.

The Role of the Risk Manager

Traditionally, businesses purchased insurance through outside **insurance brokers**. Generally, a broker brings together a buyer and a seller. Insurance brokers are especially helpful when a company seeking insurance has no proprietary risk manager to analyze risks and plan insurance coverage. Not all businesses can afford the services of a broker or a proprietary risk manager; however, risk management tools are applicable to all entities.

The risk manager's job varies with the company served. He or she may be responsible for insurance only; or for security, safety, and insurance; or for loss prevention, insurance, investments, and business continuity. *One important consideration in the implementation of a risk management (or loss prevention) program is that the program must be explained in financial terms to top executives.* Is the program cost effective? What is the return on investment? Financial benefits and financial protection are primary expectations of top executives that the risk manager must consider during decision making. Leimberg et al. (2002: 4) write

> *It is extremely difficult to measure tangible benefits against a nonevent (i.e., the catastrophic loss did not occur due to our highly effective risk management program). Yet this is the challenge facing all risk managers. Ultimately, the metrics that senior management uses to gauge success—for example, earnings growth and return on invested capital—must also serve as the yardsticks used to measure the effectiveness of risk management.*

Research in England of the activities of risk managers in 30 different organizations showed five major factors influenced risk managers' roles. *Top management* had a major influence on the risk manager in the form of direct instruction on primary tasks. *External influences* included recommendations from outside groups to increase attention to risk management within businesses and requirements for risk reporting. The *nature of the business, corporate developments* (e.g., expansion and exposures), and *characteristics of the risk management department* (e.g., resources available) also influenced the role of the risk manager (Ward, 2001: 7–25).

Among the many activities of the traditional risk manager are to develop specifications for insurance coverage wanted, meet with insurance company representatives, study various policies, and decide on the most appropriate coverage at the best possible price. Coverage may be required by law or contract, such as workers' compensation insurance and vehicle liability insurance. Plant and equipment should be reappraised periodically to maintain adequate insurance coverage. In addition, the changing value of buildings and other assets, as well as replacement costs, must be considered in the face of depreciation and inflation (Bieber, 1987: 23–30).

It is of tremendous importance that the expectations of insurance coverage be clearly understood. The risk manager's job could be in jeopardy if false impressions are communicated to top executives, who believe a loss is covered when it is not. Certain things may be excluded from a specific policy that might require special policies or endorsements. Insurance policies state what incidents are covered and to what degree. Incidents not covered are also stated. An understanding of stipulations concerning insurance claims, when to report a loss, to whom, and supporting documentation is essential in order not to invalidate a claim.

During this planning process, loss prevention measures are appraised in an effort to reduce insurance costs. Because premium reductions through loss prevention are a strong motivating force, risk managers may view strategies, such as security officers, as a necessary annoyance.

Deductibles are another risk management tool to cut insurance expenses. There are several forms of deductibles, but generally the policyholder pays for small losses up to a specified amount (e.g., $1,000, $10,000), while the insurance carrier pays for losses above the specified amount, less the deductible.

A major concern for the risk manager in the planning process is *what amount of risk is to be assumed by the business beyond that covered by insurance and loss prevention strategies*. A delicate balance should be maintained between excessive protection and excessive exposure.

Today, the risk manager's job has become more complicated, and executives throughout corporations—from finance to human resources to corporate boards of directors—are increasingly concerned about risks. Financial failures and corporate scandals (e.g., Enron and WorldCom) illustrate the variety of risks businesses face. Regulatory laws, such as the Sarbanes-Oxley (SOX) Act of 2002, reinforce the legal obligations of businesses to properly identify, assess, and manage risks. In addition, country-specific risks are becoming more important as international business operations and the global economy grow (Moody, 2006).

The Risk Management Process

As the risk management discipline developed, a need arose for a systematic approach for evaluating risk. Leimberg et al. (2002: 2–3) describe what is known as the **risk management process**.

> *Step 1, Risk Identification:* Risks must be identified prior to being managed. Risks are divided into various categories. For example, **first party risks** involve owned assets. Damage to a company truck is a first party risk. **Third party risks** pertain to liability resulting from business operations. If a company truck is involved in a traffic accident, the company may be liable for property damage and injury to others not connected to the company. Risk identification is challenging because many threats and hazards face organizations, as listed in Chapter 2.
>
> *Step 2, Quantitative Analysis:* Risk quantification applies probability, statistics, tools, and software to anticipate the maximum and expected financial loss from each identified risk. If a fire destroys a building costing $10 million to replace, the maximum loss is $10 million. However, loss prevention methods (e.g., fire-resistive construction and a sprinkler system) can reduce the loss significantly. Risk quantification for physical assets is usually easier than for public liability and worker safety.
>
> *Step 3, Evaluate Treatment Options:* This step uses identified risks and quantitative analysis as a foundation to prepare measures to reduce exposure. Two methods included in this step are risk financing and risk control. **Risk financing** is very broad and can be categorized as "on-balance sheet" and "off-balance sheet." The former includes insurance policy deductibles and self-insured loss exposures; essentially, a business absorbs losses. The latter includes insurance policies and contractual transfers

of risk. Transferring risks "off-balance sheet" is not free, and costs can increase. For instance, if insured losses increase in frequency, insurance premiums and deductibles are likely to rise. **Risk control**, also known as loss prevention, involves precautions (e.g., security and safety methods) to reduce risk.

Step 4, Implementation: Once the treatment options are studied and planned, the next step is to put the selected options into practice.

Step 5, Monitoring and Adjusting: The risk management process concludes with program oversight, analysis, and modifications.

Risk Modeling

The process of selecting which exposures deserve increased attention is difficult. Although no person or technology can predict the future, methodologies are available to help estimate risk, while serving as a foundation for prioritizing and planning. Risk modeling offers various methodologies to estimate risk; however, it is not a "crystal ball." The Rand Corporation, for example, developed the **Delphi approach**, during World War II. It consists of sending a structured questionnaire to a group of experts and then conducting a statistical analysis to generate probabilistic forecasts. To enhance the process, the experts may play the role of an adversary making decisions. Another type of risk modeling is **game theory**. In reference to the problem of terrorism, Starner (2003: 32) states: "Game theory suggests that the likelihood—and targets—of a future terrorist attack can be modeled by understanding the operational and behavioral characteristics of the terrorist organization." It involves the concept that adversaries are rational and make choices based on their information and rules. Game theory is a method to get inside the minds of terrorists. The key is to know adversaries and their rules to anticipate their actions.

Modeling helps insurance companies understand risks and set premiums. Since the 9/11 attacks, for example, insurers have been asking specific questions about the number of employees at individual buildings at specific geographic locations so they can compute the risk they are accepting. For instance, if 3,000 employees are at one location, it represents a $3 billion workers' compensation exposure in a state that puts a $1 million price tag on a life (Stoneman, 2003: 18).

Risk Management Tools

Within the risk management process, and before a final decision is made on risk management measures, the practitioner should consider the following tools for dealing with risk:

- *Risk avoidance:* This approach asks whether to avoid the risk. For example, the production of a proposed product is canceled because the danger inherent in the manufacturing process creates a risk that outweighs potential profits. Or, a bank avoids opening a branch in a country subject to political instability or terrorism.
- *Risk transfer:* Risk can be transferred to insurance. The risk manager works with an insurance company to tailor a coverage program for the risk. This approach should not be used in lieu of loss prevention measures but rather to support them. *Insurance should be last in a series of defenses.* Another method of transferring risk is to lease equipment rather than own it. This would transfer the risk of obsolescence.
- *Risk abatement:* In abatement, a risk is decreased through a loss prevention measure. Risks are not eliminated, but the severity of loss is reduced. Sprinklers, for example, reduce losses from fire. Sand bags assist in delaying erosion (Figure 12-1).
- *Risk spreading:* Potential losses are reduced by spreading the risk among multiple locations. For example, a copy of vital records is stored at a remote, secure location. In another example, following the 9/11 attacks, companies have spread operations among multiple locations to facilitate business continuity and survivability.
- *Risk assumption:* In the assumption approach, a company makes itself liable for losses. In one path, no action is taken and no insurance is obtained. This may result because the chance for loss is minute. Another path, self-insurance, provides for

FIGURE 12-1 Florida hotel faces risk of beach erosion from Hurricane Irene. *Courtesy:* Ty Harrington/FEMA.

periodic payments to a reserve fund in case of loss. Risk assumption may be the only choice for a company if insurance cannot be obtained. With risk assumption, prevention strategies become essential.

Enterprise Risk Management

A trend today in the risk management field is known as **enterprise risk management** (ERM). Leimberg et al. (2002: 6) define it as "a management process that identifies, defines, quantifies, compares, prioritizes, and treats all of the material risks facing an organization, whether or not it is insurable." It refers to a comprehensive risk management program that addresses a variety of business risks. Examples are risk of profit or loss; uncertainty regarding the organization's goals as it faces its strengths, weaknesses, opportunities, and threats; and risk of accident, fire, crime, and disasters. When all of these risks are packaged into one program, planning is improved and overall risk can be reduced. Because risks frequently are uncorrelated (i.e., all of them causing loss in the same year), insurance costs are lower. For instance, the following risks are unlikely to occur in the same year: fire, adverse movement in a foreign currency, and homicide in the workplace (Rejda, 2001: 64–66).

Leimberg et al. (2002: 6) describe the trend of two separate and distinct forms of risk management. **Event risk management** focuses on traditional risks (e.g., fire) that insurance covers. **Financial risk management** protects the financial assets of a business from risks that insurers generally avoid. Examples are foreign currency exchange risk, credit risk, and interest rate movements. Various capital risk transfer tools are available to protect financial assets. ERM seeks to combine event and financial risk for a comprehensive approach to business risks.

Since ERM is interdisciplinary in nature, corporations are forming committees for planning. At Hallmark Cards, Inc., the enterprise risk management oversight committee consists of personnel from finance, risk management, legal, human resources, IT, and internal audit (Conley, 2000: 43–50).

□ □ □ ▬▬▬▬▬▬▬▬▬▬▬▬▬▬▬▬▬▬▬▬▬▬▬▬

Should a security and loss prevention executive or a CSO be part of an enterprise risk management committee? Why or why not?

▬▬▬▬▬▬▬▬▬▬▬▬▬▬▬▬▬▬▬▬▬▬▬▬ □ □ □

□ □ □

International Perspective: Risk Management in a Multinational Business
Morris (2001: 22–30) writes about overseas business operations and the need for answers to specific questions about each country in which business will be conducted. She begins with the following questions: How is business conducted in comparison to the United States? How strong is the currency? How vulnerable is the area to natural disasters, fire, and crime? What are the potential employment practices liability issues? What is the record of accomplishment of shipments to and from the area?

Political risks are especially challenging in overseas operations. Are terrorist groups or the government hostile to foreign companies and their employees? Does the host government have a record of instability and war, seizing foreign assets, capping increases in the price of products or adding taxes to undermine foreign investments, and imposing barriers to control the movement of capital out of the country?

Eighty percent of the terrorist acts committed against U.S. interests abroad target U.S. businesses, rather than governmental or military posts. These threats include kidnapping, extortion, product contamination, workplace violence, and IT sabotage.

The concept of enterprise risk management can be especially helpful with multinational businesses because of a multitude of threats. A key challenge for the risk manager is to bring together a full range of resources and network in the United States and overseas prior to potential losses so, if a loss occurs, a speedy and aggressive response helps the business to rebound.

Options for insurance include buying it in the home country and arranging coverage for overseas operations; however, this may be illegal in some countries that require admitted insurance. Another approach is to let the firm's management in each country make the insurance decision, but this means that the corporate headquarters has less control of risk management. A third avenue is to work with a global insurer who has subsidiaries or partner insurers in each country; this approach offers uniform coverage globally. A key question in these approaches: *Is the insurer financially solvent to pay the insured following a covered loss?*

□ □ □

Insurance

Insurance is the transfer of risk from one party (the insured) to another party (the insurer), in which the insurer is obligated to indemnify (compensate) the insured for economic loss caused from an unexpected event during a period of time for which the insured makes a premium payment to the insurer. This permits the insured to avoid holding a large amount of liquid capital (cash) in reserve to pay for huge losses; the liquid capital can be invested. The essence of insurance is the sharing of risks; insurance permits the insured to substitute a small cost (the premium) for a large loss under an arrangement whereby the fortunate many who escape loss will indirectly assist in the compensation of the unfortunate few who experience loss. For an insurance company to function properly, a large number of policyholders are required. This creates a **shared risk**.

The technical aspects of the insurance industry involve the skills of statisticians, economists, financial analysts, engineers, attorneys, physicians, and, of course, risk managers and loss prevention specialists, among others. Insurance companies must carefully set rates, meticulously draft contracts, establish underwriting guidelines (i.e., accepting or rejecting risks for an insurance company), and invest funds prudently.

Insurance rates are dependent on two primary variables: the frequency of claims and the cost of each claim. When insurance companies periodically review rates, the "loss experience" of the immediate past is studied.

The insurance industry is subject to two forms of control: competition among insurance companies and government regulation. Competition enables the consumer to compare rates and coverage for the best possible buy. Government regulatory authorities in each state or jurisdiction have a responsibility to the public to assure the solvency of each insurance company so policyholders will be indemnified when appropriate. Furthermore, rates should be neither excessive nor unfairly discriminatory. Problems with the state system of regulation came to light following the case of Martin Frankel, who looted $200 million from insurance companies he owned during the 1990s (Gurwitt, 2001: 18–24). Since the case affected insurers in five states, Congress asked the U.S. General Accounting Office (GAO) to investigate. A fall 2000 report by the GAO blamed the states for inadequate regulatory policies, procedures, practices, and investigations, and a lack of information sharing. There are calls for a federal regulatory system, but the states will fight for the revenue—$10.2 billion in insurer premium taxes and fees while spending $839 million to regulate the industry. Insurance industry executives argue that "50 monkeys are better than one gorilla."

To check on the financial health of an insurer, contact an insurance company rating service and look for a rating of A+ or better. Examples of these firms are A.M. Best and Standard & Poor's.

Types of Insurance

Insurance can be divided into two broad categories: government and private. Government insurance programs include Social Security, Medicare, unemployment insurance, workers' compensation, retirement, insurance on checking and savings accounts in banks, flood insurance, and numerous other programs on the federal and state levels.

In the United States, the private insurance industry is divided into property and liability (casualty) insurance and life and health insurance. This industry employs millions in the United States, among thousands of insurance companies, while administering trillions of dollars in assets. Outside the United States, the private insurance industry is divided into life and nonlife (or general) insurance. In 2005, world insurance premium volume totaled $3.4 trillion, and the United States wrote about one-third of this volume (Insurance Information Institute, 2006).

Property and liability insurance covers fire, ocean marine, inland marine (i.e., goods shipped on land), and liability insurance, which is a broad field such as general liability (e.g., from sales of products, professional services), automobile, crime, workers' compensation, boiler and machinery, glass, and nuclear, among other types. The property and liability field also includes multiple-line insurance (i.e., two or more perils covered under one policy) and fidelity and surety bonds.

Advisory organizations have been established in the property and liability field to offer a variety of research services to insurance companies, develop policy forms, and pool loss statistics among insurance companies to increase the accuracy of rates. Two major advisory organizations are the Insurance Services Office (ISO) and the American Association of Insurance Services (AAIS).

Because types of insurance are numerous, varied and confusing, groups such as the ISO develop insurance contracts and forms and seek standardization. This group's effort is illustrated through the **commercial package policy** (CPP) that contains multiple coverage in a single policy, fewer gaps in coverage, lower premiums because individual policies are not purchased, and convenience. The CPP is used by retail stores, office buildings, manufacturers, motels, hotels, apartments, schools, churches, and many other organizations. CPP coverage commonly contains two or more coverage parts. A business may select, for example, coverage focusing on commercial property, general liability, auto, and crime (Rejda, 2001: 266–268).

Crime Insurance and Bonds

Two basic kinds of protection against crime losses are (1) fidelity and surety bonds and (2) burglary, robbery, and theft insurance. The first covers losses caused by dishonesty or incapacitation from persons entrusted with money or other property that violate this trust. The second type of protection covers theft by persons who are not in a position of trust.

Various crime coverage forms, which describe what is covered, are currently in use. These forms can be issued as a monoline policy or as part of a CPP. Malecki (2006) notes that, in 2006, there was a general "tightening" of coverage conditions of commercial crime forms. For instance, courts have strengthened the exclusion that commercial crime insurance is not intended to cover employees who committed theft or dishonesty prior to issuance of a policy.

The Surety Association of America has developed forms pertaining to employee dishonesty and loss from forgery. Examples include Form A, Employee Dishonesty; Form B, Forgery or Alteration; and Forms O and P, Public Employee Dishonesty. The coverage of Form A, a bond, includes embezzlement of funds by a company's treasurer or stealing by a cashier.

What are the differences between insurance and a bond? A **bond** is a legal instrument whereby one party (the surety) agrees to indemnify another party (the obligee) if the obligee incurs a loss from the person bonded (the principal or obligor). Although a bond may seem like insurance, there are differences between them. Generally, a bonding contract involves three parties, whereas an insurance contract involves two. With a bond, the surety has the legal right to attempt collection from the principal after indemnifying the obligee; collection would be absurd by an insurer against an insured party, unless fraud was evident. Another difference is that insurance is easier to cancel than a bond. The insured can cancel insurance by simply notifying the insurer or by nonpayment of premium. Breach of the insurance contract by the insured or nonpayment of premium are the insurer's frequent reasons for cancellation and a legal defense by the insurer to avoid liability. On the other hand, with a bond, the surety is liable to the beneficiary even though breach of contract or fraud occurred by the principal.

Fidelity Bond

Generally, a **fidelity bond** requires that an employee(s) be investigated to limit the risk of dishonesty for the insured. If the bonded employee violates the trust, the insurer (bonding company) indemnifies the employer (insured) for the amount of the policy.

Fidelity bonds may be of two kinds: (1) those in which an individual is specifically bonded, by name or by position, and (2) "blanket bonds," which cover a whole category of employees.

Surety Bond

A **surety bond** essentially is an agreement providing for compensation if there is a failure to perform specified acts within a certain period of time. One of the more common surety bonds is called a *contract construction bond*. It guarantees that the contractor(s) involved in construction will complete the work that is stipulated in the construction contract, free from debts or encumbrances.

Several types of surety bonds are used in the judiciary system. A *fiduciary bond* ensures that persons appointed by the court to supervise the property of others will be trustworthy. A *litigation bond* ensures specific conduct by defendants and plaintiffs. A *bail bond* ensures that a person will appear in court; otherwise, the entire bond is forfeited.

Burglary, Robbery, and Theft Insurance

Understanding the definitions for burglary, robbery, and theft is important when studying insurance contracts. In reference to businesses, a valid *burglary* insurance claim requires the unlawful taking of property from a closed business that was entered by force. In the absence of visible marks showing forced entry, a burglary policy is inapplicable. *Robbery* is the unlawful taking of property from another by force or threat of force. Without force or threat of force, robbery has not occurred. *Theft* is a broad, catchall term that includes all crimes of stealing, plus burglary and robbery.

Despite the availability of insurance, crime against property is one of the most underinsured perils. Estimates are that less than 10% of loss to property from ordinary crime is insured. Risk assumption remains the often-used tool to handle the crime peril.

Federal Crime Insurance

The *Federal Crime Insurance Program*, established by Congress, began operation in 1971 to counter the difficulty of obtaining adequate burglary and robbery insurance, particularly in urban areas. The program was discontinued in 1995. Private insurers and their agents administered the coverage, and the federal government, through the *Federal Insurance Administration*, was the bearer of the risk.

Kidnapping and Extortion Insurance

Another form of crime insurance covers losses from a ransom paid in a kidnapping or through extortion. During the 1970s, an upsurge in domestic and international kidnappings and terrorism created a need for this form of insurance. U.S. banks and corporations with overseas executives are especially interested in this coverage. These policies cover executives, their families, ransom money during delivery to extortionists, and corporate negligence during negotiations, among other areas of coverage.

Higgins and Cullison (2005) report that the number of reported kidnappings worldwide is growing, although many of these crimes are unreported. In 2004, there were about 14,500 reported cases. What was once a problem concentrated in Latin America has become a global criminal enterprise. Unfortunately, in certain regions, a portion of ransom payments goes to police or security officials. Government no-ransom pronouncements are often followed by denials that a ransom was paid to free a hostage. The U.S. government has a policy of not paying ransom. However, American companies and individuals produce ransom and negotiate through intermediaries hired by insurers.

Terrorism Insurance

The **Terrorism Risk Insurance Act of 2002** (TRIA) was passed by Congress to calm the insurance industry that faced claims resulting from the 9/11 attacks and concern over subsequent attacks. The act requires insurance companies to provide terrorism coverage to businesses willing to purchase it. Participating insurance companies pay out a claim (a deductible) before TRIA pays for the loss. TRIA losses are capped at $100 billion. The act is viewed as important to the U.S. economy to support recovery in the event of attacks. TRIA was set to expire at the end of 2005; however, President Bush signed a two-year extension. The extension raised industry deductibles and copayments to increase the insurance industry role in the program (BOMA Files, 2006: 20).

Cyber Insurance

Traditional insurance products often do not cover cyber risks. Thus, more and more insurers are offering businesses **cyber insurance** against risks such as viruses, denial of service attacks, theft of customer and proprietary information, and intellectual property disputes (France, 2006). Because this insurance field is developing as technology advances, the insured must be careful in selecting an insurer and understanding the definitions, terms, and limitations of these policies.

▢ ▢ ▢ ▬▬

You Be the Judge #1*

Cliff Hawkins, the newest member of Conway Excavation's repair crew, pulled his rolling tool chest to a stop and extended his hand to his new supervisor.

"Well," said Dave Greco, smiling and shaking Hawkins's hand, "it looks like you brought everything but the kitchen sink."

"A good mechanic can't do much without a good set of tools," replied Hawkins, patting the chest gently. "It took me five years and almost $3,000 to build up this set. Which reminds me"—he glanced around the garage—"if you expect me to leave these tools here, you'd better have some kind of security."

"You've got nothing to worry about," replied Greco. "We lock up at night, and nothing has ever been stolen yet."

However, there is a first time for everything. A short time after Hawkins started working for Conway Excavation, the garage was broken into. Hawkins's tools were stolen.

"I thought you said my tools would be safe here," Hawkins fumed when he faced Greco.

"I never said that," Greco corrected him. "I said this garage had never been broken into. And it hadn't."

"Yeah, well, I hope this company is prepared to reimburse me," Hawkins said.

Greco sat up in his chair, surprised. "Reimburse you?" he echoed. "No way! You knew our security wasn't very extensive, but you chose to leave your tools here anyway."

"I had to leave my tools here," Hawkins said angrily.

Greco shrugged. "Still, they were your tools and their loss isn't this company's responsibility."

"We'll see about that," Hawkins said as he stormed out of the office.

Hawkins went to court to try to force Conway Excavation to reimburse him for his stolen tools. Did Hawkins get his money?

Make your decision; then turn to the end of the chapter for the court's decision.

---

*Reprinted with permission from *Security Management—Plant and Property Protection*, a publication of Bureau of Business Practice, Inc., 24 Rope Ferry Road, Waterford, CT 06386.

Fire Insurance

Historically, the fire policy was one of the first kinds of insurance developed. For many years, it has played a significant role in assisting society against the fire peril. Prior to 1873, fire insurance contracts were not standardized. Each insurer developed its own contract. Omissions in coverage, misinterpretations, and conflicts between insurer and insured resulted in considerable problems. These individualized contracts and resultant ambiguities caused the state of Massachusetts, in 1873, to establish a standard contract. Seven years later, the standard contract became mandatory for all insurance companies in the state. Today, except for minor variations in certain states, the wording of fire insurance contracts is very similar. However, in recent years, these standard fire policies have diminished in importance as broad coverage policies have increased in number.

An understanding of insurance rating procedures provides risk managers and loss prevention managers with the knowledge to propose investments in fire protection that can show a return on investment. Factors that influence fire insurance rates include the ability of the community's fire alarm, fire department, and water system to minimize property damage once a fire begins. Class 1 communities have the greatest suppression ability, whereas Class 10 has the least. Strategies such as convincing the community to take steps to improve its grade and installing sprinkler systems in buildings can produce a return on investment (Williams et al., 1995: 341–345).

Property and Liability Insurance

Business Property Insurance

The building and personal property coverage form is one of several property forms developed by the ISO program. It covers physical damage loss to commercial buildings, business personal property (e.g., furniture, machinery, inventory), and personal property of others in the control of the insured. Additional coverage includes debris removal, pollutant removal, and fire department service charge. A cause-of-loss form is added to the policy to have a complete contract. A basic cause-of-loss form covers fire, lightning, explosion, windstorm or hail, smoke, aircraft or vehicles, riot, vandalism, sprinkler leakage, and other perils. A broader form can be selected to expand coverage to, for example, glass breakage and earthquake (Rejda, 2001: 268–274).

Another important kind of insurance is business income insurance (formerly called *business interruption insurance*). It indemnifies the insured for profits and expenses lost because of damage to property from an insured peril.

Liability Insurance

Legal liability for harm caused to others is one of the most serious risks. Negligence can result in a substantial court judgment against the responsible party. There are several kinds of exposures in the liability area for businesses. Relevant factors are the functions performed, relationships involved, and care for others required, such as the employee–employer relationship, a contract situation, consumers of manufactured products, and professional acts. Examples of liability exposures are bodily injury or death of customers, product liability, completed operations (i.e., faulty work away from the premises), environmental pollution, personal injury (e.g., false arrest, violation of right of privacy), sexual harassment, and employment discrimination.

In many jurisdictions, the law views the failure to obtain liability insurance against the consequences of negligence as irresponsible financial behavior. Mandatory liability insurance for automobile operators in all states is a familiar example.

Several kinds of business liability insurance are available. The commercial general liability (CGL) policy, developed by ISO, is widely used and can be written alone or as part of a CPP.

Workers' Compensation Insurance

Workers' compensation coverage includes loss of income and medical and rehabilitation expenses that result from work-related accidents and occupational diseases. An employer can obtain the coverage required by law through three possible avenues: (1) commercial insurance companies, (2) a state fund or a federal agency, or (3) self-insurance (i.e., risk assumption).

□ □ □ ▬▬▬▬▬▬▬▬▬▬▬▬▬▬▬▬▬▬▬▬▬▬▬▬▬▬▬▬▬▬▬▬▬▬

Risk and Insurance Management Society, Benchmark Survey

The Risk and Insurance Management Society (RIMS) publishes an annual *Benchmark Survey* (formerly called *Cost of Risk Survey*). The purpose of the survey is to provide an opportunity for risk managers to measure their organization's risk management performance. The survey provides data to assist risk managers in structuring insurance programs, making cost comparisons to others in the same industry, and preparing recommendations to senior executives.

A major gauge in the survey is the cost of risk (COR) per $1,000 of revenue. The 2005 survey showed that the total cost of risk (TCOR) was down for the first time since 2001. Almost every industry showed a decrease in the median premium per $1,000 of revenue for 2005. Following the 9/11 attacks, insurance costs increased through 2003. In 2004, insurance costs fell in most lines, except for workers' compensation, which caused a slight increase in TCOR. In 2005, the median TCOR fell about 11%. Despite Hurricanes Rita, Wilma, and Katrina, the property and casualty insurance industry earned about $55 billion in 2005 (Insurance Newsnet, 2006).

▬▬ □ □ □

You Be the Judge #2*

A vice president had been embezzling money from the Michigan Mining Corporation for several years, but Security Director Steve Douglas finally caught him. It was something of a Pyrrhic victory, however—the culprit was nabbed, but the company was out $135,000. Luckily, MMC had comprehensive business insurance that Douglas was sure would cover most of the loss.

The security director looked over the two policies, but they were poorly written and very confusing, so he called Lester Blank, the agent who handled the policies.

"I limped through the policies," Douglas explained, "and I think I get the gist of them. MMC's covered for $100,000, right?"

"Wrong," Blank said. "The second policy replaced the first. You're only covered for $50,000."

Douglas was stunned, but he recovered quickly. "Now, wait a minute," he said. "I may not have caught every mixed-up word in these policies, but the second one says we can collect on the first one for up to a year after its expiration date, provided the loss occurred during the time the first policy was in effect."

"But the total limit is still $50,000," insisted the insurance agent. "You'll find a clause to that effect in the second policy, if you read carefully."

"If I read carefully!" Douglas cried. "This second policy is so full of spelling and clerical errors that it's anybody's guess what it means. One look at this piece of slipshod writing and any court will side with us."

Therefore, MMC went to court, claiming that because the policy was so complicated and poorly written, it should be interpreted in the company's favor.

Did the court agree with MMC?

Make your decision; then turn to the end of the chapter for the court's decision.

---

*Reprinted with permission from *Security Management—Plant and Property Protection*, a publication of Bureau of Business Practice, Inc., 24 Rope Ferry Road, Waterford, CT 06386.

Claims

When an insured party incurs a loss, a claim is made to the insurer to cover the loss as stipulated in the insurance contract. For an insurance company, the settling of losses and adjusting differences between itself and the policyholder is known as **claims management**. Care is necessary by the insurer because underpayments can lead to lost customers, yet overpayments can lead to bankruptcy.

An insurance company investigation of a claim commonly includes (1) a determination that there has been a loss, (2) a determination that the insured has not invalidated the insurance contract, (3) an evaluation of the proof of loss, and (4) an estimate of the amount of loss. An example of item 2 occurs when the insured has not fulfilled obligations under the insurance contract, such as not protecting property from further damage after a fire or not adequately maintaining loss prevention measures.

Furthermore, most insurance contracts specify that the insured party must give immediate notice of loss. The purpose is to give the insurer an opportunity to study the loss before evidence to support the claim has been damaged. Failure to provide immediate notice may render the insurance invalid. The insured usually has 60 to 90 days to produce proof of loss. The insured is expected to provide accounting records, bills, and so on that might help in establishing the loss.

Before a settlement is reached, the insurer checks the coverage, the claim is investigated, and loss reports and claim papers are prepared. Then the insurance company claims department studies the loss, the policy is interpreted and applied to the loss, and a payment is approved or disapproved.

Insurance companies employ different classifications of adjusters to settle claims. An *insurance agent* (i.e. salesperson) may serve as an adjuster for small claims up to a certain amount. A *company adjuster* is more experienced about claims and handles larger losses. *Independent adjusters* offer services to insurance companies for a fee. *Public adjusters* represent the insured party for a fee.

From the insurance industry's perspective, the work of an adjuster is demanding. A high priority is to satisfy claimants in order to retain customers. At the same time, the interests and assets of the insurance company must be protected. Some claimants make honest mistakes in estimating losses. They may place a value on destroyed property that is above the market value. Exaggerations are common. Confusion may arise when claimants have not carefully read their insurance policy. Consequently, a process of education and negotiation often takes place between the adjuster and the claimant. Once the claimant signs the proof of loss papers or cashes the settlement check, this signifies that the claimant is satisfied and that further rights to pursue the claim are waived. In a certain number of claims, an agreement is not reached initially. The policy states the terms for settling claims. Typically, arbitration results. Each party appoints a disinterested party to act as arbitrator. The two arbitrators then select a third disinterested party. Agreements between two of the three arbitrators are binding. In liability cases, the court takes the place of arbitrators.

Dishonest claimants are a serious problem for the insurance industry, and for society. Insurance fraud is pervasive and costly. Policyholders are the ultimate group that pays for these crimes through increased premiums.

Arson is unfortunately a popular way of defrauding insurance companies. Generally, a property owner sets a fire to collect on an insurance policy. A professional arsonist may be recruited. Law enforcement agencies and the insurance industry have increased efforts to combat arson through additional arson investigators, improved training, better detection equipment, and computers that search data for patterns of those who defraud insurance companies.

Claims for Crime Losses

A loss prevention practitioner or risk manager may be confronted with important decisions in a claim in an attempt to minimize losses for his or her employer. Although crime claims are emphasized here, several points are applicable to other types of claims.

When a person or business takes out an insurance policy to cover valuables, the insurance agent may not require proof that the valuables exist. However, when a claim is filed, the insurer becomes very interested in not only evidence to prove that the valuables were stolen (e.g., police report), but also evidence that the valuables in fact existed. Without proof, indemnification may become difficult. To avoid this problem, several steps are useful. First, the insured should prepare an inventory of all valuables. Accounting records and receipts are good sources for the inventory list. The list should include the item name, serial number, date it was purchased, price, and a receipt. Photographs and video of valuables are also useful. Copies should be located in two separate safe places.

Bonding Claims

Numerous insurance companies have found the fidelity bond business to be generally unprofitable. To compound the situation, businesspeople have attempted to used fidelity bond claims to cover losses from mysterious disappearance and general inventory shortages, rather than for their intended purpose—coverage for internal theft. For these reasons, when a claim takes place, the insurer and insured have a tendency to enter negotiations as adversaries. The strength of the loss prevention practitioner's case will definitely affect the settlement. Care must be exercised throughout the interaction with the insurer so as not to in any way invalidate the contract. Furthermore, the burden of proof for losses rests entirely on the insured.

Before 1970, the insurer investigated applicants and notified the insured of any criminal history of the applicant that would bar coverage. Because of economy measures and the difficulty of checking into a person's background, many insurers have made a shift to the insured for verifying the applicant's past. Bonds stipulate that past dishonesty by the employee justifies an exclusion from bonding from the day the information is discovered; if a loss occurs and the insurer can prove that this information was known to the insured company but not reported to the insurer, the bond is likely to be invalid.

Another way to invalidate a bond is through restitution by the employee to the employer without notifying the insurer. In many cases, the employee is eager to pay back what was stolen but makes only a few payments before absconding. Thereafter, if a claim is made, the bond is useless.

In reference to the burden of proof, the loss prevention practitioner should have considerable expertise when dealing with the insurer on behalf of his or her employer. Confusion often arises from the "exclusionary clause" of the fidelity bond policy. This clause essentially states that the bond does not cover losses that are dependent on proof from inventory records or a profit and loss computation. Prior to 1970, these records were not even allowed to establish the extent of losses even though employees had confessed. However, in the early 1970s, courts began to be more flexible in limiting the exclusionary clause and thus allowing inventory records and associated computations to establish the amount of loss when independent proof also was introduced to establish that there was loss due to employee theft.

A confession is of prime importance to bonding claims. A guilty verdict in a criminal court or a favorable labor arbitration ruling are additional assets for the claimant.

□ □ □

What do you think are the most difficult challenges of a risk manager's job?

□ □ □

Business Continuity

As we know, businesses and government face an enormous number of exposures to threats and hazards, and risk refers to the measurement of the frequency, probability, and severity of these exposures. *Risk management* helps business and government executives study and manage risks so they can prioritize risks and then plan and take action under limited budgets. *Risk management* is at the foundation of planning and action against risks. *Business continuity* is the term applied in the private sector (business) for planning and action against risks. *Emergency management* is the term applied in the public sector (government) for planning and action against risks. Here, we begin with a discussion of business continuity, and then we turn to emergency management to understand the role of government in emergencies.

Business continuity is defined by ASIS International (2004: 7) as follows: "A comprehensive managed effort to prioritize key business processes, identify significant threats to normal operation, and plan mitigation strategies to ensure effective and efficient organizational response to the challenges that surface during and after a crisis."

The essence of business continuity is an up-to-date, comprehensive plan to increase the survivability of a business when it faces an emergency. Examples of topics in the plan are employee safety; IT backup; customer support; and limited, if any, recovery time. *There is a lack of consistency in the private sector with business continuity planning.* Top executives view and support it differently among businesses.

Many factors influence the success of business continuity. Examples are local infrastructure and the resources of public safety agencies. Because of recovery challenges following the 9/11 attacks, increased public-private sector cooperation has occurred.

Garris (2005: 28–32) writes that in our litigious society, organizations that fail to plan for emergencies could be held liable for injuries or deaths. He recommends learning about codes, regulations, and laws that are an essential foundation of plans. Sources include the Occupational Safety and Health Administration, the National Fire Protection Association, the Environmental Protection Agency, the Americans with Disabilities Act, as well as city and state authorities. Garris writes that 44% of all businesses that suffer a disaster never reopen.

Guidance for Business Continuity Planning

The **NFPA 1600 Standard on Disaster/Emergency Management and Business Continuity Programs** has been acknowledged by the U.S. Congress, American National Standards Institute (ANSI), and the 9/11 Commission. It has been endorsed by the Federal Emergency Management Agency, the National Emergency Management Association, and others. *This standard has been referred to as the "National Preparedness Standard" for all organizations, including government and business.* NFPA 1600 serves as a benchmark of basic criteria for a comprehensive program, and it contains elements from emergency management and business continuity. There has been a convergence of these fields and a convergence of public and private sector efforts. Disasters (e.g., the 9/11 attacks) are showing the vital interdependencies of the public and private sectors.

The NFPA 1600 includes standards on program management, risk assessment, mitigation, training, and logistics, among other standards. It also contains definitions of terms and lists of resources and organizations.

The NFPA 1600 is not without its detractors (Davis, 2005). The Business Continuity Institute, located in the United Kingdom, claims that there is no business continuity document, and in NFPA 1600, business continuity is buried within emergency management. In addition, there are groups (e.g., ANSI) looking to the International Organization for Standardization (ISO) for enhanced business continuity standards.

The *Business Continuity Guideline* (ASIS International, 2004) offers an in-depth, multistep process for business continuity planning. It includes interrelated processes and activities that help in creating, testing, and maintaining an organizationwide plan for emergencies. Here is a sample of questions from the appendix of the guideline:

- Has your organization planned for survival?
- Is the business continuity plan up-to-date?
- Have the internal audit, security, and insurance units reviewed the plan?
- Has a planning team been appointed?
- Has a risk assessment been conducted?
- Are people protected?
- Have critical business processes been identified and ranked?
- Is technology (i.e., data, systems) protected?
- Have resources required for recovery been identified?
- Have personnel been trained and exercises conducted?
- Has a crisis management center been identified?
- Have alternative worksites been identified?

Another source for business continuity planning, especially for small and medium-sized businesses, is the Department of Homeland Security Web site www.ready.gov. It offers guidelines, sample emergency plans, tips for mail safety, security suggestions, and it uses an all-hazards approach.

Methodology for Business Continuity

Moskal (2006: 56–62), with an IT background, offers a business continuity management methodology to sort, summarize, and organize business requirements in a methodical manner.

He writes that one barrier to planning and preparation is lack of support and funding from management. Citing a list of real world events that cost businesses billions of dollars, Moskal also supports his arguments for business continuity planning by referring to business survivability, cost of downtime (e.g., lost revenue, lost customers), penalties from contract stipulations on deadlines, and legal requirements (especially as a public company). His seven-step methodology is as follows:

1. *Risk assessment report* containing the identification of critical functions; business process threats and vulnerabilities, ranked by risk level; and risk-mitigating safeguards and costs.
2. *Business impact analysis report* containing critical business functions and workflow, qualitative and quantitative impacts of disruption, and recovery time objectives.
3. *Disaster recovery plan* containing resources, actions, and tasks to manage the recovery.
4. *Business recovery plan* containing advance plans, arrangements, and procedures for the complete recovery of business processes, including employees, workspace, equipment, and facilities.
5. *Business resumption plan* containing plans for continued availability of essential business processes and operations. It includes facility and operations management, as well as IT systems.
6. *Contingency planning* containing plans to respond to specific system or operation failures. Resources may include alternate work areas, reciprocal agreements, workaround procedures, and replacement resources.
7. *Crisis management* focuses on overall coordination of organizational response to a crisis to protect people and minimize damage to profitability, reputation, or ability to operate.

Persson (2005) sees the need for increased effort to provide quantitative, accurate, empirical reporting on how business continuity planning is working. He favors the use of metrics and lists the following benefits:

- They present activities in objective terms.
- Metrics help focus on issues. For example, if recovery time objective (RTO) is 6 hours on paper, but testing shows it is 24 hours, this issue needs to be addressed.
- It can be included in personnel objectives (i.e., responsibilities) and measured.

Here is a sample of metrics applicable to continuity planning from Persson's IT perspective:

- Disaster recovery planning (DRP) as a percentage of total IT budget. This may be between 2% and 8%.
- Percentage of mission-critical applications covered. The goal should be to recover 100%.
- Anticipated recovery time.
- Total number of outages per year by category (e.g., power, network, virus).

Drawing on Persson's IT work, metrics can be applied more broadly. Examples include the business continuity budget as a percentage of assets or revenue; the number of full-time employees (may be less than 1.0) who work on business continuity per $10 million of assets or revenue; and metrics can be compared within and among industries.

☐ ☐ ☐ ▬▬▬▬▬▬▬▬▬▬▬▬▬▬▬▬▬▬▬▬▬▬

What do you think influences senior executive interest in business continuity planning?

▬▬▬▬▬▬▬▬▬▬▬▬▬▬▬▬▬▬▬▬▬▬ ☐ ☐ ☐

Emergency Management

Bullock et al. (2006: 1–2) write that there is no single definition of emergency management because the discipline "has expanded and contracted in response to events, the desires of Congress, and leadership styles." They note that emergency management "has clearly become an essential role of government" and the "Constitution entrusted the states with responsibility for public health and safety—hence, responsibility for public risks—and assigns the federal government to a secondary, supportive role. The federal role was originally conceived such that it intervenes when the state, local, or individual entities are overwhelmed."

Bullock et al. (2006: 2) define emergency management as "the discipline dealing with risk and risk avoidance." Here, we define **emergency management** as preparation for potential emergencies and disasters and the coordination of response and resources during such events.

McEntire (2004: 14–18) writes that the discipline of emergency management is going through a massive transformation. He refers to issues such as definitions of terms, what hazards to focus on, what variables to explore (e.g., location of buildings, building construction, politics, critical incident stress), and what disciplines should contribute to emergency management. McEntire notes that there is no single overarching theory of emergency management because it would be impossible to develop a theory that would contain every single variable and issue involving disasters. He sees systems or chaos theory as gaining recognition because they incorporate many causative variables. McEntire also offers other theories and concepts (below), that he views as relevant to emergency management. Notice the similarities in some of the following theories to those explained under risk management (i.e., risk perception theory; risk communication theory):

- **Systems theory** involves diverse systems that interact in complicated ways and impact vulnerability. These systems include natural, built, technological, social, political, economic, and cultural environments.
- **Chaos theory** has similarities to systems theory in that many variables interact and affect vulnerability. This theory points to the difficulty of detecting simple linear cause-and-effect relationships and it seeks to address multiple variables simultaneously to mitigate vulnerability.
- **Decision theory** views disasters as characterized by uncertainty and limited information that results in increased vulnerability to causalities, disruption, and other negative consequences. This theory focuses on perceptions, communications, bureaucracy, politics, and other variables that impact the aftermath of disasters.
- **Management theory** explains disasters as political and organizational problems. Vulnerability to disasters can be reduced through effective leadership and improved planning. Leaders have the responsibility to partner with a wide variety of players to reach objectives that reduce vulnerability.
- **Organizational behavior theory** sees agencies concerned about their own interests and turf, without understanding how their action or inaction affects others. Cultural barriers, a lack of communications, and other variables limit partnering to increase efficiency and effectiveness. Improved communications during the 9/11 attacks in New York City would have saved some of the lives of firefighters, police, and others.
- **Risk perception and communication theory** focuses on the apathy of citizens prior to disasters. Vulnerability can increase if citizens do not understand the consequences of disasters and do not take action for self-protection (e.g., evacuation). Citizens may be more likely to reduce their vulnerability if authorities communicate risk accurately and convincingly.
- **Social constructionist theory** shifts from hazards that we cannot control to the role of humans in disasters, who determine through decisions the degree of vulnerability; for example, citizen decisions to reside in areas subject to mudslides.

- **Weberian theory** looks to culture—including values, attitudes, practices, and socialization—as contributing to increased vulnerability. Other factors under this theory resulting in greater vulnerability are weak emergency management institutions and a lack of professionalization among emergency managers.
- **Marxist theory** explains economic conditions and political powerlessness as playing roles in disaster vulnerability. The poor and minorities are more likely to reside in vulnerable areas and are often unable to act to protect themselves. The Hurricane Katrina disaster serves as an example; thousands of citizens were trapped in flooded New Orleans, which was built below sea level.

Risk Management in Government

Risk management is as important in the public sector as it is in the private sector. Risk management helps government executives study and manage risks so they can prioritize risks and then plan and take action under limited budgets. For government, exposures and risks are enormous and broad—affecting local, state, national, and global levels. Examples include liability, crime, workers' compensation, fire, war, terrorism, proliferation of weapons of mass destruction (WMD), disease and pandemics, natural disasters, conflicts over natural resources, and issues of migration.

Although the private sector, especially the insurance industry, has played a lead role in advancing the discipline of risk management, local and state governments are increasingly employing risk management methods. The Public Risk Management Association (PRIMA), the largest network of public risk management practitioners, states: "Risk management in the public sector finds itself at a challenging moment in time." "... [T]here is a very high level of interest in the subject, but a lack of clarity and consistency as to its meaning, form and purpose." The group sees pockets of advanced risk management practice in the United States; however, most small government entities do not have a formal risk management unit. PRIMA sees various segments of the discipline spread among departments in government (e.g., insurance, purchasing, finance) and efforts to unify the function under the emerging concept of enterprise risk management have just begun in the public sector (Public Risk Management Association, 2003).

On the federal government level, the U.S. Government Accountability Office (GAO), a federal "watchdog," is a strong proponent of risk management. It has argued for risk management to be applied at all levels of government, including the Departments of Homeland Security and Defense and the FBI. The U.S. Government Accountability Office (2005: 124–125) stated: "... [A] vacuum exists in which benefits of homeland security investments are often not quantified and are almost never valued in monetary terms." The GAO argues for criteria for quantifiable and nonquantifiable benefits of homeland security spending so analysts can develop information to inform management.

The U.S. Department of Homeland Security (2004c: 54) stated: "We will guide our actions with sound risk management principles that take a global perspective and are forward-looking. Risks must be well understood, and risk management approaches developed, before solutions can be implemented."

All-Hazards Preparedness Concept

"All hazards" include natural disasters (e.g., hurricanes, earthquakes) and human-made events (e.g., inadvertent accidents, such as an aircraft crash, and deliberate events, such as the terrorist bombing of an aircraft). Another category is technological events (e.g., an electric service blackout resulting from a variety of possible causes). FEMA (2004) states: "The all-hazards preparedness concept is simple in that how you prepare for one disaster or emergency situation is the same for any other disaster." *The all-hazards approach is important because it plays a role in preventing our nation from over-preparing for one type of disaster at the expense of other disasters* (Figure 12-2).

It is argued here that the all-hazards approach seeks to maximize the efficiency and cost effectiveness of emergency management efforts through a realization that different

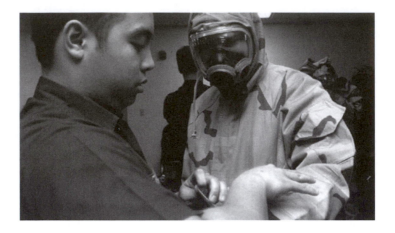

FIGURE 12-2 The U.S. government is working to provide an all-hazards response capability. *Courtesy:* U.S. Department of Homeland Security.

disasters contain similarities that can benefit, to a certain degree, from generic approaches to emergency management. This includes generally similar emergency services, equipment, and products. Conversely, there is a point at which **generic emergency management** must divide into **specialized emergency management**. For example, the detonation of a "dirty-bomb" or an approaching hurricane necessitates evacuation; however, the victims and the scene of these disasters require markedly different expertise, treatment, and equipment.

The History of Emergency Management

Haddow and Bullock (2003: 1–13) traced the development of emergency management as described next. The first example of the federal government becoming involved in a disaster was when, in 1803, a Congressional Act was passed to provide financial assistance to a New Hampshire town that was destroyed by fire. During the Great Depression (1930s), President Franklin D. Roosevelt spent enormous federal funds on projects to put people to work and to stimulate the economy. Such projects had relevance to emergency management. The Tennessee Valley Authority was created to not only produce hydroelectric power, but to reduce flooding.

During the 1950s, as the Cold War brought with it the threat of nuclear war, **Civil Defense Programs** grew. These programs were characterized by communities and families building bomb shelters as a defense against attack from the Soviet Union. Air raid drills became common at schools; children practiced going under their desks or kneeling down in the hall while covering their heads. Civil defense directors, often-retired military personnel, were appointed at the local and state levels, and these individuals represent the beginning of emergency management in the United States. The Federal Civil Defense Administration (FCDA) provided technical assistance to local and state governments. Another agency, the Office of Defense Mobilization (ODM), was established in the Department of Defense (DOD) to quickly amass materials and production in the event of war. In 1958, both the FCDA and the ODM were merged into the Office of Civil and Defense Mobilization.

A series of destructive hurricanes in the 1950s resulted in ad hoc Congressional legislation to fund assistance to the affected states. The 1960s also saw its share of natural disasters that resulted in President John F. Kennedy's administration, in 1961, creating the Office of Emergency Preparedness to deal with natural disasters. The absence of flood insurance on the standard homeowner policy prompted Congress to enact the National Flood Insurance Act of 1968, which created the National Flood Insurance Program (NFIP). This noteworthy act included the concept of **community-based mitigation**, whereby action was taken against the risk prior to the disaster. When a community joined the NFIP, the program offered federally subsidized, low-cost flood insurance to citizens in exchange for the community enacting an ordinance banning future development in its floodplains. As a voluntary program, the NFIP was not successful. The Flood Insurance Act of 1972 created an incentive for communities to join the NFIP. This act required mandatory purchase of flood insurance for homeowner loans backed by federal mortgages, and a significant number of mortgages were federally backed.

The 1970s brought to light the fragmentation of federal, state, and local agencies responsible for risk and disasters. Over 100 federal agencies added to the confusion and turf wars. Unfortunately, the problems were compounded during disasters. The administration of President Jimmy Carter sought reform and consolidation of federal emergency management. The **Federal Emergency Management Agency (FEMA)** was established by Executive Order 12127 on March 31, 1979. The goal of this effort was to consolidate emergency preparedness, mitigation, and response into one agency, with a director who would report directly to the president. John Macy, who was in the Carter cabinet, became the director of FEMA. He emphasized similarities between natural hazards preparedness and civil defense and developed an "all-hazards" approach containing direction, control, and warning as goals common to all emergencies.

Through the 1980s, FEMA experienced numerous troubles and criticism. The top priority of FEMA became preparation for nuclear attack, at the expense of other risks. Environmental cleanup (e.g., Love Canal) became another priority. States saw their funding for emergency management decline. By the end of the 1980s, FEMA was in need of serious reform. FEMA's problems included tension with its partners at the state and local level over priorities and funding, and difficulty in responding to natural disasters. In 1989, Hurricane Hugo became the worst hurricane in a decade and caused 85 deaths and damage of more than $15 billion as it slammed into South Carolina, North Carolina, and other locations. The FEMA response was so poor that Senator Ernest Hollings (D-SC) called the agency the "sorriest bunch of bureaucratic jackasses." The FEMA problems with Hurricane Andrew, in 1992, in Florida, further eroded confidence in the agency.

Reform in FEMA finally occurred in 1993 when President William Clinton nominated James L. Witt, of Arkansas, to be director. Witt was the first director with emergency management experience, and he was skilled at building partnerships and serving customers. Inside FEMA, Witt fostered ties to employees, reorganized the agency, and supported new technologies to deliver disaster services. Externally, he improved relationships with state and local governments, Congress, and the media. Subsequent disasters, such as the Midwest floods in 1993 that resulted in nine states being declared disaster areas and the Northridge, California, earthquake in 1994, tested the reforms FEMA had made. Witt was elevated to be a member of President Clinton's cabinet, illustrating the importance of emergency management. Witt then sought to influence the nation's governors in elevating state emergency management directors to cabinet posts.

The World Trade Center bombing in 1993 and the Oklahoma City bombing in 1995 brought the issue of terrorism to the forefront of emergency management. A major question surfaced: Which agency would be in charge following a terrorist attack? Prior to the 9/11 attacks, several federal agencies sought leadership against terrorism. Major agencies included FEMA, the Department of Justice (DOJ) (it contains the FBI), the DOD, the National Guard, and the Department of Health and Human Services (HHS). Coordination was poor as agencies pursued their own agendas. The DOD and the DOJ received the most funds. State and local governments felt unprepared and complained about their vulnerabilities and needs. The 9/11 attacks resulted in a massive reorganization of the federal government and the creation of the Department of Homeland Security (DHS) to better coordinate both actions against terrorism and homeland security.

In September of 2005, FEMA experienced another setback when its director, Michael Brown, was relieved as commander of Hurricane Katrina (Figure 12–3) relief efforts along the Gulf Coast, and he was sent back to Washington, D.C. Three days later, he resigned. Critics argued that he was the former head of an Arabian horse association and that he had no background in disaster relief when his friend and then-FEMA Director, Joe Allbaugh, hired him in 2001 to serve as FEMA's general counsel. Although "finger-pointing" occurred by politicians at all levels of government as the relief effort became overwhelmed, Michael Brown became the classic scapegoat. Following the Katrina disaster, there were calls for reform of FEMA.

FIGURE 12-3 In 2005, Hurricane Katrina flooded sections of New Orleans, left hundreds of thousands of people homeless, and overwhelmed government response. *Courtesy:* Gary Nichols, DOD.

Emergency Management Disciplines

Haddow and Bullock (2003) divide emergency management into the disciplines of mitigation, response, recovery, preparedness, and communications. Although they emphasize natural hazards, their writing provides a foundation for multiple risks.

Mitigation

Haddow and Bullock (2003: 37) define **mitigation** as "a sustained action to reduce or eliminate risk to people and property from hazards and their effects." It looks at long-term solutions to reduce risk, as opposed to preparedness for emergencies and disasters.

Mitigation programs require partners outside traditional emergency management. Examples are land-use planners, construction and building officials, and community leaders. The tools of mitigation include hazard identification and mapping and building codes.

Response

Response includes activities that address the short-term, direct effects of an incident, and it seeks to save lives, protect property, and meet basic human needs. Depending on the emergency, response can entail applying intelligence to lessen the effects or consequences of an incident; increased security; investigations; public health and agricultural surveillance and testing processes; immunizations, isolation, or quarantine; operations to disrupt illegal activity; and arresting offenders. First responders at emergencies and disasters are usually local police, fire, emergency medical specialists, and not state or federal personnel. Besides local, state, and federal responses, volunteer organizations and the business community respond to emergencies and disasters.

All 50 states and six territories of the United States operate an office of emergency management. The names of these offices vary, as does the placement in the organizational structure of each jurisdiction. National Guard Adjutant Generals lead these offices in most states, followed by leadership by civilian employees. Governors rely primarily on their state National Guard for responding to disasters. National Guard resources include personnel, communications systems, air and road transport, heavy construction equipment, mass care and feeding equipment, and assorted supplies (e.g., tents, beds, blankets, medical). When a state is overwhelmed by a disaster, the governor may request federal assistance under a presidential disaster or emergency declaration.

The Homeland Security Act of 2002 established the DHS to reduce our nation's vulnerability to terrorism, natural disasters, and other emergencies, and to assist in recovery. The Secretary of Homeland Security is responsible for coordinating federal operations in response to emergencies and disasters.

Recovery

Recovery involves actions to help individuals and communities return to normal. It serves to restore infrastructure, basic services, government, housing, businesses, and other functions in a community. Haddow and Bullock (2003: 95) view the goal of effective recovery as bringing all the players together to plan, finance, and prepare a recovery strategy. Besides action by all levels of government, recovery includes the role of the insurance industry, which provides financial support. However, the federal government plays the largest role in technical and financial support for recovery. The range of grant and assistance programs that the federal government has been involved in over the years, especially through FEMA, has been enormous and cost tens of billions of dollars.

Preparedness

Before a disaster strikes, preparation is vital. **Preparedness** includes risk management to identify threats, hazards, and vulnerabilities. Then all levels of government and the private sector plan and prepare for disasters through planning, training, exercises, and identifying resources to prevent, protect against, respond to, and recover from disasters. Preparedness is the job of everyone and all sectors of our society.

Communications

The U.S. Department of Homeland Security emphasizes the importance of communications, information management, and information and intelligence sharing. Also important are a common operating picture and systems interoperability to disseminate warnings, communicate operational decisions, prepare for requests, and maintain overall awareness across jurisdictions. Jurisdictional systems must be able to work together and not interfere with one another (U.S. Department of Homeland Security, 2004a: 49).

During the 9/11 attacks at the World Trade Center, an unforeseen enemy of first responders was their own communications systems. During the months following the attacks, a serious flaw was found in the police and fire radio systems: they were incompatible. When the first WTC tower collapsed, police were notified to evacuate the second tower, but firefighters (on a different system) did not hear the warning and hundreds of first responders died. This serious problem can be solved by what has been called **interoperability**—the ability of multiple agencies to communicate using technology.

□ □ □ ▬▬▬▬▬▬▬▬▬▬▬▬▬▬▬▬▬▬▬▬▬▬▬▬▬▬▬▬▬▬

National Response Plan, National Incident Management System, and National Preparedness Goal

The 9/11 attacks changed dramatically emergency response plans in the United States. Besides a host of manmade and natural hazards—such as accidents, earthquakes, hurricanes, and floods—the United States faces creative, asymmetrical attacks by terrorists who resort to WMD. This range of hazards and threats has resulted in the need for a unified and coordinated national approach to emergency management. This need is met through the **National Response Plan (NRP)** (U.S. Department of Homeland Security, 2004b), the **National Incident Management System (NIMS)** (U.S. Department of Homeland Security, 2004a), and the **National Preparedness Goal (the Goal)**. Both the NRP and the NIMS are national, rather than federal plans, and aim to align the patchwork of federal emergency management plans into an effective and efficient structure, while coordinating the capabilities and resources of all levels of government and the private sector.

According to the Department of Homeland Security, the NRP is an all-hazards approach incorporating best practices and procedures from many incident management disciplines. It ties together emergency management activities to include prevention, mitigation, preparedness, response, and recovery.

The NRP is designed to coordinate structures, roles, and responsibilities among federal, state, and local levels of government. It requires cooperation, collaboration, and information sharing among jurisdictions, as well as between the public and private sectors. It groups capabilities and resources that are most likely to be needed during an incident. Examples are firefighting, search and rescue, and mass care. It outlines core responsibilities and expertise for specific contingencies (e.g., radiological, biological, cyber). The NRP describes common processes and specific administrative requirements (e.g., fiscal, worker safety and health). It also includes a glossary, acronyms, and authorities.

The NRP priorities are to save lives, protect health and safety, secure the homeland, protect and restore critical infrastructure, conduct investigations to resolve incidents, protect property, and facilitate recovery.

The NRP multiagency coordination structure includes the responsibilities of the president and a flexible national capability that addresses local, regional, and national issues. It is a signed and binding agreement among 32 federal departments and agencies, the American Red Cross, and the National Voluntary Organizations Active in Disasters. The Department of Homeland Security maintains the NRP.

The principal authorities that guide the structure and implementation of the NRP are numerous federal laws, executive orders, and presidential directives. The NRP lists 42 laws. An example is the Homeland Security Act of 2002. Another example is the Robert T. Stafford Disaster Relief and Emergency Assistance Act of 1974. Amended in 2002, and known as the Stafford Act, this federal law establishes the programs and processes for the federal government to provide disaster and emergency assistance to states, local governments, tribal nations, individuals, and nonprofit organizations. It covers all hazards, including terrorism. This act includes the process for governors to request federal assistance from the president.

The Homeland Security Presidential Directive (HSPD)-5, Management of Domestic Incidents, February 28, 2003, is intended to establish a single, comprehensive NRP and NIMS. This directive designates the Secretary of Homeland Security to administer these programs.

The NIMS was developed with input from many groups in the public and private sectors. It represents best practices; strives for standardization; and contains a core set of doctrines, concepts, principles, terminology, and organizational processes. HSPD-5 requires all federal agencies and departments to adopt the NIMS and make it a requirement for state and local organizations to receive federal preparedness assistance. The NIMS Integration Center publishes standards, guidelines, and compliance protocols. The DHS offers no-cost, on-line training for the NIMS, and thousands have completed the training.

NIMS emphasizes standardization. Examples include standardization in incident command structure, planning, training, exercises, personnel qualifications and certification, equipment, resource management, forms, and information management.

On December 17, 2003, the president issued Homeland Security Presidential Directive 8 "National Preparedness" (HSPD-8). The purpose of HSPD-8 is to "establish policies to strengthen the preparedness of the United States to prevent and respond to threatened or actual domestic terrorist attacks, major disasters, and other emergencies by requiring a national domestic all-hazards preparedness goal, establishing mechanisms for improved delivery of Federal preparedness assistance to State and local governments, and outlining actions to strengthen preparedness capabilities of Federal, State, and local entities." The *goal* will guide federal departments and agencies, state, territorial, local and tribal officials, the private sector, nongovernment organizations, and the public in determining how to most effectively and efficiently strengthen preparedness for terrorist attacks, major disasters, and other emergencies. The *goal* utilizes a Capabilities-Based Planning approach: planning, under uncertainty, to provide capabilities suitable for a wide range of threats and hazards, within an economic framework that necessitates prioritization and choice. Capabilities-Based Planning addresses uncertainty by analyzing a wide range of possible scenarios (e.g., WMD, natural disasters, cyber, pandemic influenza) to identify required capabilities. The purpose of the *goal* is to develop readiness priorities, targets, and metrics. It focuses on three key questions: How prepared do we need to be? How prepared are we? How do we prioritize efforts to close the gap?

The Military

The military has the capability to provide significant resources to civilian authorities in the event of a disaster (Figures 12-4 and 12-5). Federal troops can provide communications, transportation, food, water, shelter, and other assets under what is referred to as **logistics**. Specifically, **U.S. Northern Command** (**NORTH-COM**), in the DOD, is charged with protecting the United States from foreign attacks and is responsible for supplying military resources to emergency responders. The DOD emphasizes that it understands its role in assisting civilian authorities—serve to support, not take the lead.

A state's governor is responsible for disaster response, with the option of requesting assistance from FEMA. Then, if necessary, FEMA can contact the DOD for assistance. Once the request arrives, DOD officials must determine whether the request is legal under the **Posse Comitatus Act** (PCA), a post-Civil War–era act that generally prohibits the military from engaging in civilian law enforcement. The PCA does not apply to the U.S. Coast Guard in peacetime or to the National Guard in Title 32 (United States Code) or State Active Duty status.

Prohibiting direct military involvement in civilian law enforcement is in keeping with long-standing U.S. law and policy limiting the military's role in domestic affairs. However, this law has been labeled as archaic because it limits the military from responding to disasters. Consequently, a modification of the law is an option.

Congress enacted a number of exceptions to the PCA that allow the military, in certain situations, to assist civilian law enforcement agencies in enforcing the laws of the United States. The most common example is counterdrug assistance (Title 10 USC, Sections 371–381). Other examples include

- **The Insurrection Act** (Title 10 USC, Sections 331–335). This act, passed in 1807, allows the president to use U.S. military personnel at the request of a state legislature or governor to suppress insurrections. It also allows the president to use federal troops to enforce federal laws when rebellion against the authority of the United States makes it impracticable to enforce the laws of the United States. This law was invoked in 1992 when California Governor Pete Wilson requested federal troops to quell race riots in Los Angeles. President George H.W. Bush dispatched 4,000 active-duty troops.
- Assistance in the case of crimes involving nuclear materials (Title 18 USC, Section 831). This statute permits DOD personnel to assist the Justice Department in enforcing prohibitions regarding nuclear materials, when the attorney general and the secretary of defense jointly determine that an "emergency situation" exists that poses a serious threat to U.S. interests and is beyond the capability of civilian law enforcement agencies.
- Emergency situations involving chemical or biological weapons of mass destruction (Title 10 USC, Section 382). When the attorney general and the secretary of defense jointly determine that an "emergency situation" exists that poses a serious threat to U.S. interests and is beyond the capability of civilian law enforcement agencies. DOD personnel may assist the Justice Department in enforcing prohibitions regarding biological or chemical weapons of mass destruction.

FIGURE 12-4 U.S. Navy Search and Rescue specialist prepares to bring a Hurricane Katrina Victim onboard a helicopter. *Courtesy:* Jay C. Pugh, USN.

FIGURE 12-5 U.S. Army soldier directs Hurricane Katrina victims away from helicopter following rescue. *Courtesy:* Robert McRill, USN.

An example of the DOD assisting in past disasters includes Hurricane Katrina, in August of 2005, when New Orleans was flooded and city residents were forced to evacuate. Because Gulf-state and FEMA resources were overwhelmed, the DOD provided massive aid to assist victims, conduct search-and-rescue missions, maintain order, and deal with the flooding.

□ □ □ ▬▬▬▬▬▬▬▬▬▬▬▬▬▬▬▬▬▬▬▬▬▬▬▬▬▬▬▬▬▬▬

The Katrina Disaster

Despite the best intentions and efforts of the specialists who formulated the "all-hazards" National Response Plan, the National Incident Management System, and the National Preparedness Goal, Hurricane Katrina, in 2005, showed the difficulty of planning for disasters. The hurricane caused about 1,300 deaths, the flooding of New Orleans, and enormous destruction along Gulf-coast states. The media, reporting from New Orleans, offered vivid coverage of looters, snipers, fires, bloated corpses, victims sitting on rooftops or swimming through toxic water, and the awful conditions at the Superdome where people sought shelter and help from the government. Today, many victims of Hurricane Katrina are living in cities across the United States and are unable or unwilling to return to their communities while rebuilding goes on.

One major lesson from the Hurricane Katrina disaster was the collapse of intergovernmental relations. The NRP calls for an immediate activation of a joint operations center to bring together all levels of government. Why did this NRP requirement occur so slowly? Why did each level of government appear inept with its authority? Why were the resources inadequate? Did the federal government place too much emphasis on the threat of terrorism at the expense of emergency management? Local, state, and federal officials blamed each other for the response failures, and the issues were politicized. Interestingly, officials received warning of the approaching hurricane. A WMD attack is unlikely to be preceded by a warning. If a warning preceded Hurricane Katrina and government reacted so inadequately, what type of government reaction can citizens expect from a surprise WMD attack?

Another major lesson was the chaos that can result from a serious disaster, whether from a WMD attack, pandemic, or other cause. Leaders should learn from the Katrina disaster and enhance planning at all levels of government.

In 2006, following congressional hearings that exposed the shortcomings of government response to Hurricane Katrina, a revised NRP was formulated to react more quickly with improved resources. U.S. Government Accountability Office (2006) staff visited the affected areas, interviewed officials, and analyzed a variety of information. It found widespread dissatisfaction with the preparedness and response, and many of the lessons that emerged from Hurricane Katrina were similar to those the GAO identified more than a decade ago with Hurricane Andrew. For example, the president should designate a senior official in the White House to oversee federal preparedness and response to major disasters. Again, in 2006, the GAO recommended that, prior to disasters, the leadership roles, responsibilities, and lines of authority for all levels of government must be clearly defined prior to disasters. The GAO also emphasized the need for strong advance planning among responding organizations, as well as robust training and exercises to test plans in advance of disasters. Changes are inevitable for all future plans, because disasters are often unpredictable and public and private sector plans typically fall short of need during major disasters.

Following Hurricanes Katrina and Rita, as of mid-December 2005, FEMA had distributed nearly $5.4 billion in assistance to more than 1.4 million registrants under the Individuals and Households Program (IHP) to meet necessary expenses and serious needs, such as temporary housing and property repair. Because of the devastation, FEMA also activated expedited assistance to provide fast-track money to victims. GAO investigators found rampant fraud with expedited assistance. FEMA made millions of dollars in payments to thousands of registrants who used Social Security numbers that were never issued or belonged to deceased or other individuals, and several hundred registrants used bogus damaged property addresses. FEMA made duplicate expedited assistance payments of $2,000 to about 5,000 of the 11,000 debit card recipients—once through the distribution of debit cards and again through a check or electronic funds transfer. Although most of the payments were applied to necessities, some funds were used for adult entertainment, to purchase bail bond services, to pay traffic tickets, and to purchase weapons. The GAO recommended improvements by FEMA to automate the validation of identities and damaged properties (U.S. Government Accountability Office, 2006).

☐ ☐ ☐ ▬▬▬▬▬▬▬▬▬▬▬▬▬▬▬▬▬▬▬▬▬▬

What are your suggestions to improve government response to disasters?

☐ ☐ ☐ ▬▬▬▬▬▬▬▬▬▬▬▬▬▬▬▬▬▬▬▬▬▬

Search the Web
Here are Web sites relevant to this chapter:
Insurance and Risk Management:

American Association of Insurance Services: www.aaisonline.com/
American Insurance Association: www.aiadc.org
A.M. Best: www.ambest.com/
American Risk and Insurance Association: www.aria.org
Coalition Against Insurance Fraud: www.insurancefraud.org/
General advice: FREEADVICE.com
Insurance Committee for Arson Control: www.arsoncontrol.org/
Insurance Services Office: www.iso.com
International Risk Management Institute: www.irmi.com
National Alliance for Insurance Education & Research: www.TheNational
    Alliance.com
Public Risk Management Association: www.primacentral.org
Risk and Insurance Management Society: www.rims.org
Risk World: www.riskworld.com
Society for Risk Analysis: www.sra.org
Standard & Poor's: www.standardandpoors.com
State Risk and Insurance Management Association: www.strima.org
Surety & Fidelity Association of America: www.surety.org/

Business Continuity and Emergency Management:

Business Continuity Institute: www.thebci.org
Centers for Disease Control and Prevention: www.bt.cdc.gov
DRI International: www.drii.org
Emergency Management Accreditation Program: www.emaponline.org/index.cfm
Federal Emergency Management Agency: www.fema.org
International Association of Emergency Managers: www.iaem.com
National Emergency Management Association: www.nemaweb.org
Office for Domestic Preparedness: www.ojp.usdoj.gov/odp/
The International Emergency Management Society: www.tiems.org

U.S. Department of Homeland Security: www.dhs.gov/odp

U.S. Department of Homeland Security: www.ready.gov (Site for business continuity planning.)

U.S. Northern Command: http://www.northcom.mil

Case Problems

12A. As a loss prevention manager, you will soon explain to top management why they should provide support and funds to initiate a risk management program by hiring a risk manager. Research and answer the following questions to prepare for your meeting.

(a) How will a risk manager help to perpetuate the business?

(b) How can a risk manager produce a return on investment?

(c) How are five risk management tools applied?

(d) How will the risk manager and loss prevention manager work together, and what will each do for the company?

12B. You are a corporate risk management executive responsible for insurance, business continuity, and the corporate safety and security departments for all corporate locations. You are challenged by the following list of tasks upon returning to your office. Prioritize these tasks and explain why you placed them in your particular order of importance.

Item A

E-mail message. At your request, an insurance company representative replies that she can meet with you at your convenience to explain why the corporate liability insurance premium will rise by 10% next year.

Item B

Telephone voice message. An accident on the premises between a truck and a forklift has resulted in two injured employees. The director of human resources wants to meet with you immediately.

Item C

E-mail message. As treasurer of a regional risk management association, you are assigned to arrange the next meeting, including location, meal, and speaker.

Item D

Your "to do list" states that you need to re-evaluate the risks facing the corporation and implement an improved risk management plan that maximizes risk management tools and is more financially sound.

Item E

Telephone call. A security officer on the premises calls and states: he cannot locate a security supervisor; there is a fire in the warehouse; he can extinguish it; and you do not have to call the fire department.

Item F

Telephone voice message. Your boss wants to meet with you immediately because insurance covered only 50% of losses from an accident at another corporate plant.

Item G

Telephone voice message. An attorney representing a plaintiff/employee in a sexual harassment suit against the corporation wants to speak with you.

Item H
Telephone voice message. The emergency management director for the local county wants to meet with you about cooperation on joint planning and training.

Item I
E-mail message. The information technology (IT) director needs to meet with you as soon as possible. The corporate IT business continuity plan was rejected by one of the insurers of the corporation.

The Decision for "You Be the Judge #1"

Hawkins was reimbursed for the stolen tools. The court held that when Hawkins left his tools in the work area overnight with the knowledge and consent of his employer, his employer accepted temporary custody of the property. This situation is known as a *bailment*, and in such a situation, the party accepting custody of the property usually is responsible for its care and safekeeping. Under the laws of the state in which this case was tried, Conway Excavation might have escaped liability for the theft of Hawkins's tools if it had taken more extensive steps to make the garage secure. Instead, it had to pay him some $3,000.

     This case is based on *Harper v. Brown & Root* 398 Sa2d 94. The names in this case have been changed to protect the privacy of those involved.

The Decision for "You Be the Judge #2"

The court disagreed with MMC, concluding that, although the policy was complicated and full of errors, it was not ambiguous in spelling out the limits of its liability—$50,000. MMC would have to absorb the rest of the loss itself. Security Director Douglas *could have saved his company a lot of money if he had taken the time to read the insurance policy when it was first issued.* That's the time to ask questions and demand clarification. If you can't understand the policy, find someone who can; the insurance agent or your company's attorney are two of the best people to ask. After the company puts in a claim, it may be too late to clear up the ambiguities.

     This case is based on *Davenport Peters v. Royal Globe Ins.*, 490 FSupp 286. The names in this case have been changed to protect the privacy of those involved.

References

ASIS International. (2004). *Business Continuity Guideline*. www.asisonline.org, retrieved November 15, 2006.

Bieber, R. (1987). "The Making of a Risk Manager—Part One." *Risk Management* (September).

BOMA Files. (2006). "Terrorism Insurance Program Extended in Final Days of Session." *Buildings*, 100 (February).

Borodzicz, E. (2005). *Risk, Crisis & Security Management*. West Sussex, England: John Wiley & Sons.

Bullock, J., et al. (2006). *Introduction to Homeland Security*, 2nd ed. Burlington, MA: Elsevier Butterworth-Heinemann.

Conley, J. (2000). "Leaders of the Evolution." *Risk Management*, 47 (December).

Davis, S. (2005). "NFPA 1600." www.davislogic.com, retrieved March 17, 2005.

FEMA. (2004). "All-Hazards Preparedness." www.fema.gov/preparedness/hazards_prepare. shtm, retrieved March 1, 2005.

France, L. (2006). "Cyber Liability." *Rough Notes* (March). http://www.roughnotes.com/ rnmagazine/03cdindex06.htm, retrieved May 8, 2006.

Garris, L. (2005). "Make-or-Break Steps for Disaster Preparation." *Buildings*, 99 (February).

Gurwitt, R. (2001). "The Riskiest Business." *Governing*, 14 (March).

Haddow, G., and Bullock, J. (2003). *Introduction to Emergency Management*. Boston: Butterworth-Heinemann.

Higgins, A., and Cullison, A. (2005). "Dutch Court Fight Lays Bare Reality of Kidnap Industry." *The Wall Street Journal Online* (September 22). http://online.wsj.com/article/0, SB112735374607948223,00.html, retrieved September 22, 2005.

Insurance Information Institute. (2006). "International Insurance Fact Book." www.internationalinsurance.org/international/overview/, retrieved November 13, 2006.

Insurance Newsnet. (2006). "RIMS Benchmark Survey Book Records Total Cost of Risk Down in 2005" (May 25). www.insurancenewsnet.com, retrieved November 14, 2006.

Leimberg, S., et al. (2002). *The Tools & Techniques of Risk Management & Insurance*. Cincinnati, OH: The National Underwriter Co.

Malecki, D. (2006). "Who Knew What When?" *Rough Notes* (March). http://www.rough-notes.com/rnmagazine/03cdindex06.htm, retrieved May 8, 2006.

McEntire, D. (2004). "The Status of Emergency Management Theory: Issues, Barriers, and Recommendations for Improved Scholarship." Paper presented at the FEMA Higher Education Conference, Emmitsburg, MD, June 8. www.training.fema.gov/EMIWeb/edu/highpapers.asp, retrieved February 14, 2006.

Moody, M. (2006). "Risk Management: A Board Issue Yet?" *Rough Notes* (April). www.roughnotes.com/rnmagazine/2006/april06/04p034.htm, retrieved May 8, 2006.

Morris, B. (2001). "Risk Takes on the World." *Risk & Insurance*, 12 (April 16).

Moskal, E. (2006). "Business Continuity Management: Post 9/11 Disaster Recovery Methodology." *Disaster Recovery Journal*, 19 (Spring).

Persson, J. (2005). "The Time Has Come for DRP Metrics." *Disaster Recovery Journal*, 18 (Winter). www.drj.com, retrieved January 28, 2005.

Public Risk Management Association. (2003). *Core Competency Statement: A Framework for Public Risk Management*, www.primacentral.org, retrieved February 18, 2005.

Rejda, G. (2001). *Principles of Risk Management and Insurance*, 7th ed. Boston, MA: Addison Wesley.

Starner, T. (2003). "Modeling for Terrorism." *Risk & Insurance* (April 1).

Stoneman, B. (2003). "An Aversion to Dispersion." *Risk & Insurance* (September 15).

U.S. Department of Homeland Security. (2004a). *National Incident Management System*. www.dhs.gov, retrieved February 10, 2005.

U.S. Department of Homeland Security. (2004b). *National Response Plan*. www.dhs.gov, retrieved January 12, 2005.

U.S. Department of Homeland Security. (2004c). *Securing Our Homeland: U.S. Department of Homeland Security Strategic Plan*. www.dhs.gov, retrieved October 1, 2004.

U.S. Government Accountability Office. (2005). *Agency Plans, Implementation, and Challenges Regarding the National Strategy for Homeland Security* (January). www.gao.gov/cgi-bin/getrpt?GAO-05-33, retrieved February 15, 2005.

U.S. Government Accountability Office. (2006). "Statement by Comptroller General David M. Walker on GAO's Preliminary Observations Regarding Preparedness and Response to Hurricanes Katrina and Rita" (February 1). www.gao.gov/new.items/d06365r.pdf, retrieved February 3, 2006.

Ward, S. (2001). "Exploring the Role of the Corporate Risk Manager." *Risk Management: An International Journal*, 3.

Williams, C., et al. (1995). *Risk Management and Insurance*, 7th ed. New York: McGraw-Hill.

13

Life Safety, Fire Protection, and Emergencies

Objectives

After studying this chapter, the reader will be able to:

1. Explain the significance of life safety and name two sources for life safety planning.
2. Discuss the problem posed by fire.
3. Describe the roles of private organizations and public fire departments in fire protection.
4. List and explain five fire prevention strategies.
5. List and explain five fire suppression strategies.
6. Describe the roles of public police and emergency medical services in public safety.
7. List and describe three human-made emergencies and three natural disasters.

KEY TERMS
<table><tr><td>• life safety</td><td>• sheltering-in-place</td></tr><tr><td>• Occupational Safety and Health Administration (OSHA)</td><td>• integrated fire suppression systems</td></tr><tr><td>• NFPA 101 Life Safety Code</td><td>• standpipes</td></tr><tr><td>• authority having jurisdiction</td><td>• fire brigade</td></tr><tr><td>• building codes</td><td>• performance-based fire protection</td></tr><tr><td>• fire codes</td><td>• public safety</td></tr><tr><td>• fire prevention</td><td>• personal protective equipment</td></tr><tr><td>• fire suppression</td><td>• triage</td></tr><tr><td>• HAZMAT</td><td>• weapon of mass destruction (WMD)</td></tr><tr><td>• floor wardens</td><td>• pandemic</td></tr><tr><td>• areas of refuge</td><td>• zoonotic diseases</td></tr><tr><td></td><td>• quarantine enforcement</td></tr></table>

Note: Portions of this chapter are from: Purpura, P. (2007). *Terrorism and Homeland Security: An Introduction with Applications.* Burlington, MA: Elsevier Butterworth-Heinemann.

Life Safety

Life safety pertains to building construction design that increases safety, what organizations and employees can do in preparation for emergencies, and what they can do once an emergency occurs. *Citizens cannot depend on government during the initial stages of an emergency*. Citizens facing emergencies—in their home, workplace, and in public—must take steps to protect themselves for a duration that may last from a few minutes to possibly days until government, first responders, and assistance arrive. Although this chapter focuses on life safety in the workplace, protection methods for a variety of emergencies, at home or in public, are available from numerous sources (see "Search the Web" at the end of the chapter).

Standards, Regulations, and Codes

Standards, regulations, and codes (explained in Chapter 3) provide a foundation for professionals involved in life safety programs. Here, we provide a brief overview. *Consensus standards* are accepted industry practices developed by experts who agree on how a specific task should be performed. Consensus standards do not have the force of law unless a jurisdiction adopts them as law, as done by many jurisdictions with the National Fire Protection Association (NFPA) 101 Life Safety Code. Although standards may not be adopted as law by a jurisdiction, they may be used to establish a standard of care or used during litigation. *Regulations* are rules or laws enacted at the federal, state, or local levels with the requirement to comply. *Codes* are standards that cover broad subject areas that can be adopted into law.

OSHA Regulations

The **Occupational Safety and Health Administration (OSHA)** is a federal agency established to administer the law on safety and health in the workplace. Its regulations, as are other federal regulations, are contained in the Code of Federal Regulations (CFR). A widely known example of federal regulations is found in Title 29 CFR, OSHA.

An example of an OSHA regulation that promotes life safety is 1910.38 Emergency Action Plans. It includes these minimum elements:

- An emergency action plan must be in writing, kept in the workplace, and available to employees for review.
- Procedures for reporting a fire or other emergency.
- Procedures for emergency evacuation, including type of evacuation and exit route assignments.
- Procedures to account for all employees after evacuation.
- Procedures to be followed by employees performing rescue or medical duties.
- An employer must have and maintain an employee alarm system that uses a distinctive signal for each purpose.
- An employer must designate and train employees to assist in a safe and orderly evacuation of other employees.
- An employer must review the emergency action plan with each employee.

Another OSHA regulation oriented toward life safety is 1910.39 Fire Protection Plans. It includes these minimum elements:

- A fire protection plan must be in writing, kept in the workplace, and available to employees for review.
- A list of all major five hazards, proper handling and storage procedures for hazardous materials, potential ignition sources and their control, and the type of fire protection equipment necessary to control each major hazard.
- Procedures to control accumulations of flammable and combustible waste materials.
- Procedures for regular maintenance of safeguards installed on heat-producing equipment to prevent the accidental ignition of combustible materials.
- The name or job title of employees responsible for maintaining equipment to prevent or control sources of ignition or fires and for control of fuel source hazards.
- An employer must inform employees upon initial assignment to a job of the fire hazards to which they are exposed and review with each employee those parts of the fire protection plan necessary for self-protection.

NFPA 101 Life Safety Code

The **NFPA 101 Life Safety Code** is used in every state and adopted statewide in 38 states. It is also used by numerous federal agencies. The state fire marshal's office serves as a resource if one seeks to find out if the code has been adopted in a particular locale and which edition is being used. The code is published every three years.

The state fire marshal often serves as the **authority having jurisdiction** (AHJ), meaning the person or office charged with enforcing the code. In some jurisdictions, the AHJ is the fire department or building department. For some occupancy, there is more than one AHJ. A hospital, for example, may require approval for life safety from multiple authorities having jurisdictions.

The NFPA 101 Life Safety Code publication begins with a disclaimer of liability as paraphrased next. NFPA codes, standards, recommended practices, and guides are developed through a consensus standards development process approved by the American National Standards Institute (ANSI). This process recruits volunteers with varied expertise and viewpoints to achieve consensus on fire and other safety issues. The NFPA does not independently test, evaluate, or verify the accuracy of information contained in its codes and standards. It does not list, certify, test, or inspect products, designs, or installations. The NFPA disclaims liability for any personal injury or property damage resulting from the use of its documents. Its documents are not released to render professional or other services, and the NFPA has no enforcement powers.

The history of NFPA 101 began with a presentation by R. H. Newbern at the 1911 Annual Meeting of the NFPA. The following year, his presentation resulted in the Committee on Safety to Life publishing "Exit Drills in Factories, Schools, Department Stores and Theaters." This committee studied notable fires and causes of loss of life, and prepared standards for the construction of stairways, fire escapes, and egress routes. The publication of additional pamphlets, which were widely circulated and put into general use, provided the foundation for the NFPA 101 Life Safety Code. New material and revisions to the code continued through the 20th century. National attention focused on the importance of adequate exits and fire safety following the Cocoanut Grove Night Club Fire in Boston in 1942, resulting in 492 deaths. The code was increasingly being used for regulatory purposes.

The 1991 edition contained numerous new requirements for mandatory sprinklers in a variety of facilities. The 1994 edition contained new requirements for egress, areas of refuge, and ramps to conform to the Americans with Disabilities Act Accessibility Guidelines.

In the 2003 edition, the first part consists of Chapters 1 through 11 (except Chapter 5) and is called the *base chapters* or *fundamental chapters*. Chapter 5 explains the performance-based option (i.e., building design features meeting specific Life Safety Code performance objectives). Many of the provisions of the first part are mandatory for specific occupancies. Some provisions are mandated only when referenced by a specific occupancy, whereas other provisions are exempted for specific occupancy. The statement "where permitted by Chapters 12 through 42" refers to provisions that can be used only where specifically permitted by an occupancy chapter (e.g., educational, healthcare, lodging, and industrial). One can find an example in Chapter 7, 7.2.1.6.1 on delayed egress locks that are allowed only when permitted by Chapters 12 through 42. If the permission is not found in an occupancy chapter, the delayed egress lock cannot be used in that type of facility. Other types of restricted permission are found for such features as double cylinder locks, security grills, and revolving doors.

Here are samples from the NFPA 101 Life Safety Code:

Chapter 1 Administration
1.1.2 Danger to Life from Fire. The Code addresses those construction, protection, and occupancy features necessary to minimize danger to life from fire, including smoke, fumes, or panic.

1.1.3 Egress Facilities. The Code establishes minimum criteria for the design of egress facilities so as to allow prompt escape of occupants from buildings or, where desirable, into safe areas within buildings.

Chapter 3 Definitions

3.2.4 Labeled. Equipment or materials to which has been attached a label, symbol, or other identifying mark of an organization that is acceptable to the authority having jurisdiction and concerned with product evaluation, that maintains periodic inspection of production of labeled equipment or materials, and by whose labeling the manufacturer indicates compliance with appropriate standards or performance in a specified manner.

3.2.5 Listed. Equipment, materials, or services included in a list published by an organization that is acceptable to the authority having jurisdiction and concerned with evaluation of products or services, that maintains periodic inspection of production of listed equipment or materials or periodic evaluation of services, and whose listing states that either the equipment, material, or service meets appropriate designated standards or has been tested and found suitable for a specified purpose.

Chapter 7 Means of Egress

7.1.10 Means of Egress Reliability.

7.1.10.1 Means of egress shall be continuously maintained free of all obstructions or impediments to full instant use in the case of fire or other emergency.

7.2.1.5 Locks, Latches, and Alarm Devices.

7.2.1.5.1 Doors shall be arranged to be opened readily from the egress side whenever the building is occupied.

7.2.1.5.2 Locks, if provided, shall not require the use of a key, a tool, or special knowledge or effort for operation from the egress side.

7.2.1.6 Special Locking Arrangements.

7.2.1.6.1 Delayed-Egress Locks. Approved, listed, delayed egress locks shall be permitted to be installed on doors serving low and ordinary hazard contents in buildings protected throughout by an approved, supervised automatic fire detection system in accordance with Section 9.6 or an approved, supervised automatic sprinkler system in accordance with Section 9.7, and where permitted in Chapter 12 through Chapter 42, provided that the following criteria be met:

(1) The doors shall unlock upon actuation of one of the following:

(a) An approved, supervised automatic sprinkler system in accordance with Section 9.7

(b) Any heat detector

(c) Not more than two smoke detectors of an approved, supervised automatic fire detection system in accordance with Section 9.6

(2) The doors shall unlock upon loss of power controlling the lock or locking mechanism.

(3) An irreversible process shall release the lock within 15 seconds, or 30 seconds where approved by the authority having jurisdiction, upon application of a force to the release device required in 7.2.1.5.9 under the following conditions:

(a) The force shall not be required to exceed 67 N (15 lbf).

(b) The force shall not be required to be continuously applied for more than 3 seconds.

(c) The initiation of the release process shall activate an audible signal in the vicinity of the door.

(d) Once the door lock has been released by the application of force to the releasing device, relocking shall be by manual means only.

(4) A readily visible, durable sign in letters not less than 25 mm (1 in.) high and not less than 3.2 mm (1/8 in.) in stroke width on a contrasting background that reads as follows shall be located on the door adjacent to the release device:

PUSH UNTIL ALARM SOUNDS

DOOR CAN BE OPENED IN 15 SECONDS

7.2.1.7 Panic Hardware and Fire Exit Hardware.

7.2.1.7.1 Where a door is required to be equipped with panic or fire exit hard-ware, such hardware shall meet the following criteria:

(1) *It shall consist of a cross bar or a push pad, the actuating portion of which extends across not less than one-half of the width of the door leaf.*

(2) *It shall be mounted as follows:*

   (a) *New installations shall be not less than 865 mm (34 in.), nor more than 1220 mm (48 in.), above the floor.*

   (b) *Existing installations shall be not less than 760 mm (30 in.), nor more than 1220 mm (48 in.), above the floor.*

(3) *It shall be constructed so that a horizontal force not to exceed 66 N (15 lbf) actuates the cross bar or push pad and latches.*

7.2.1.7.3 Required panic hardware and fire exit hardware, in other than deten-tion and correctional occupancies as otherwise provided in Chapter 22 and Chapter 23, shall not be equipped with any locking device, set screw, or other arrangement that prevents the release of the latch when pressure is applied to the releasing device.

7.9 Emergency Lighting.

7.9.1.1 Emergency lighting facilities for means of egress shall be provided in accordance with Section 7.9 for the following:

(1) *Buildings or structures where required in Chapter 11 through Chapter 42*

(2) *Underground and limited access structures as addressed in Section 11.7*

(3) *High-rise buildings as required by other sections of this Code*

(4) *Doors equipped with delayed-egress locks*

(5) *Stair shaft and vestibule of smokeproof enclosures, for which the following also apply:*

   (a) *The stair shaft and vestibule shall be permitted to include a standby generator that is installed for the smokeproof enclosure mechanical ventilation equipment.*

   (b) *The standby generator shall be permitted to be used for the stair shaft and vestibule emergency lighting power supply.*

Chapter 9 Building Service and Fire Protection Equipment

9.7.1 Automatic Sprinklers.

9.7.1.1 Each automatic sprinkler system required by another section of this Code shall be in accordance with one of the following:

(1) *NFPA 13, Standard for the Installation of Sprinkler Systems*

(2) *NFPA 13R, Standard for the Installation of Sprinkler Systems in Residential Occupancies up to and Including Four Stories in Height*

(3) *NFPA 13D, Standard for the Installation of Sprinkler Systems in One- and Two-Family Dwellings and Manufactured Homes*

9.7.1.2 Sprinkler piping serving not more than six sprinklers for any isolated hazardous area shall be permitted to be connected directly to a domestic water supply system having a capacity sufficient to provide 6.1 mm/min (0.15 gpm/ft2) throughout the entire enclosed area. An indicating shutoff valve, supervised in accordance with 9.7.2 or NFPA 13, Standard for the Installation of Sprinkler Systems, shall be installed in an accessible, visible, location between the sprinklers and the connection to the domestic water supply.

Chapter 11 Special Structures and High-Rise Buildings

11.8.2 Extinguishing Requirements.

11.8.2.1 High-rise buildings shall be protected throughout by an approved, super-vised automatic sprinkler system in accordance with Section 9.7. A sprinkler con-trol valve and a waterflow device shall be provided for each floor.

11.8.4 Emergency Lighting and Standby Power.

11.8.4.1 Emergency lighting in accordance with Section 7.9 shall be provided.

9/11 Transcripts Released

The following is from a *USA TODAY* (Cauchon, et al., 2003) news story on the radio transmissions and telephone calls during the 9/11 attacks:

> *A man on the 92ⁿᵈ floor called the police with what was—though he did not know it—the question of his life. "We need to know if we need to get out of here, because we know there's an explosion," said the caller, who was in the south tower of the World Trade Center. A jet had just crashed into the Trade Center's north tower. "Should we stay or should we not?" The officer on the line asked whether there was smoke on the floor. Told no, he replied: "I would wait 'til further notice." "All right," the caller said. "Don't evacuate." He then hung up. Almost all the roughly 600 people in the top floors of the south tower died after a second hijacked airliner crashed into the 80ᵗʰ floor shortly after 9 a.m. The failure to evacuate the building was one of the day's great tragedies. The exchange between the office worker and the policeman was one of many revealed when the Port Authority of New York and New Jersey, which owned and patrolled the office complex, released transcripts of 260 hours of radio transmissions and telephone calls on 9/11.*

Morgan Stanley

The following is from the U.S. Department of Homeland Security, READYBusiness (n.d.):

> *In 1993, when terrorists attacked the World Trade Center for the first time, financial services company Morgan Stanley learned a life-saving lesson. It took the company 4 hours that day to evacuate its employees, some of whom had to walk down 60 or more flights of stairs to safety. While none of Morgan Stanley's employees was killed in the attack, the company's management decided its disaster plan just wasn't good enough. Morgan Stanley took a close look at its operation, analyzed the potential disaster risk and developed a multi-faceted disaster plan. Perhaps just as importantly, it practiced the plan frequently to provide for employee safety in the event of another disaster. On September 11, 2001, the planning and practice paid off. Immediately after the first hijacked plane struck One World Trade Center, Morgan Stanley security executives ordered the company's 3800 employees to evacuate from World Trade Center buildings Two and Five. This time, it took them just 45 minutes to get out to safety!*
>
> *The crisis management did not stop at that point, however. Morgan Stanley offered grief counseling to workers and increased its security presence. It also used effective communications strategies to provide timely, appropriate information to management and employees, investors and clients, and regulators and the media. Morgan Stanley still lost 13 people on September 11th, but many more could have died if the company had not had a solid disaster plan that was practiced repeatedly. In making a commitment to prepare its most valuable asset, its people, Morgan Stanley ensured the firm's future.*

□ □ □ ▬▬▬▬▬▬▬▬▬▬▬▬▬▬▬▬▬▬▬▬▬▬▬▬

Does the U.S. Department of Homeland Security Place Enough Emphasis on Protecting Civilian Facilities?

Sternberg and Lee (2006: 1–19) write that when disasters strike, people's safety often depends on the buildings they occupy. They argue that the U.S. Department of Homeland Security is misdirected by placing too much emphasis on protecting infrastructures (e.g., transportation, utilities, and government buildings) at the expense of improving protection at civilian facilities (e.g., apartment and office buildings). Sternberg and Lee offer specific suggestions to improve the protection of civilian facilities:

- The protection of civilian facilities necessitates a category of homeland security that deserves discrete federal, state, and local attention.
- The federal government should do more to facilitate incentives, support, information, training, technology, and research to protect civilian facilities.
- The challenge is not for government to find a central solution for protecting civilian facilities, but rather to find policy solutions that motivate more managers in civilian facilities to assess risks and search for solutions.
- Governments at all levels must work to improve and clarify regulations so that investments in protection at civilian facilities increase.

▬▬▬▬▬▬▬▬▬▬▬▬▬▬▬▬▬▬▬▬▬▬▬▬ □ □ □

Building Design and Building Codes

Making changes in building design and building codes is a slow process, and new codes often do not apply to existing buildings. Experts (e.g., structural engineers), industry groups (e.g., real estate), and government leaders frequently disagree over what changes, if any, should be made. The following information on trends in building design and building codes since the 9/11 attacks is from Gips (2005: 43–49), the National Institute of Standards and Technology (2005), and the International Code Council (2004):

- Guidance for local governments for building codes is found with the International Code Council (ICC) or the NFPA. The ICC's International Building Code (IBC) has been widely adopted in the United States. The NFPA writes the Life Safety Code (LSC) and the Building Construction and Safety Code (BCSC). The LSC has been adopted by far more jurisdictions than the BCSC.
- The IBC establishes minimum standards for the design and installation of building systems, and it addresses issues of occupancy, safety, and technology. It plays a major role in transforming lessons from the 9/11 attacks into updated building codes, and it relies on research from the U.S. Department of Commerce, National Institute of Standards and Technology (NIST). The NIST detailed reports on the collapse of the World Trade Center (WTC) towers, and its reports also include the impact of natural hazards (e.g., hurricanes) on tall buildings.
- NIST research found the following factors in the collapse sequence of the WTC towers: each aircraft severed perimeter columns, damaged interior core columns, and knocked off fireproofing from steel; jet fuel initially fed the fires, followed by building contents, and air from destroyed walls and windows; and floor sagging and exposure to high temperatures caused the perimeter columns to bow inward and buckle.
- NIST recommendations that could have improved the WTC structural performance on 9/11 are as follows: fireproofing less susceptible to being dislodged; perimeter columns and floor framing with greater mass to enhance thermal and buckling performance; compartmentation to retard spread of fire; windows with improved thermal performance; fire-protected and hardened elevators; and redundant water supply for standpipes.

- One successful code change of the IBC is that buildings 420 feet and higher (about 42 floors) must have a minimum three-hour structural fire-resistance rating, whether sprinklers are present or not. The earlier rating was for two hours, with sprinklers. The reasoning for the change is that fire departments are generally not capable of supplying adequate water pressure and flow to floors above 420 feet, and the building must be able to stand on its own.

- IBC proposals that were rejected: widen stairs from 44 inches to 72 inches in buildings 20 stories and higher and encasing stairwells in either concrete or masonry in buildings 25 stories and higher.

- Both the ICC and the NFPA have committees that focus on NIST research that may serve to support changes in their respective building codes. Issues drawing attention include evacuation procedures, fire resistance, collapse, redundant water supplies, and how to prevent metal-detection equipment from hindering emergency egress.

- Although the NFPA is hesitant about endorsing alternative escape systems, it does acknowledge the following that need further study: use of elevators during emergencies, platforms that move along the outside of a building, high-wire escape to nearby buildings, and parachutes.

- The new Seven World Trade Center (WTC) building at "ground zero" has gone beyond building code requirements. It is protected against progressive collapse by, for example, spray-on fireproofing that is five times more adhesive that what is required by existing standards. Stairs and elevators are fully encased in reinforced concrete. (FEMA found that at the WTC, during the attacks, plasterboard that was designed to provide fire resistance to the stairways was knocked off by the impact of the jets.) In the new WTC, fire stairs are located at opposite ends of the building. (FEMA noted that the jets were able to destroy two sets of emergency stairways because they were close together.) In the new WTC, stairs have triple redundancy for light: emergency lighting, battery power, and photoluminescent paint.

- Chicago is another city enhancing building safety following the 9/11 attacks. The emphasis is more on planning than building designs, and like other locales, it ties building height to safety requirements. For instance, buildings 540 feet or higher must file an emergency evacuation plan with the city's office of emergency communications. The plan includes evacuation procedures, posting of a floor plan, a list of occupants needing assistance, drills, marked stairwells to identify floor number, and the site of re-entry locations.

- Innovations and changes in buildings for safety include sensors in HVAC systems to detect WMD, multiple HVAC systems to isolate fire and other hazards, HVAC "nanofilters" to capture harmful agents, stairway pressurization to reduce smoke, and wider stairs for evacuation and emergency response.

- ICC (2004) research of the building departments of the 15 most populated cities in the United States found that officials varied in their reporting of top concerns. The most often cited concern was inadequate resources during the building boom for permitting and plan inspection services.

- Eight of the 15 building departments in the ICC research stated that they were involved in some form of response program concerning the risk of terrorism.

- All 15 cities expressed concerns about weather and natural disasters, and emergency plans are in place, drills are conducted, and supplies (e.g., cots, water, and generators) are stockpiled.

- Dr. W. Gene Corley (2004), team leader of the WTC Building Performance Study, writes that NFPA data from a 10-year study of 8,000 commercial fires showed that sprinklers do not operate about 16% of the time. He notes that despite this risk of failure, model codes increasingly rely on sprinklers, while reducing fire-resistant construction. In addition, although many view fire barriers as costly excess, first responders see them as lifesavers and another method to prevent building collapse.

- Local governments have been slow to make changes in building or life safety codes since the 9/11 attacks. However, insurance companies can raise premiums on coverage for buildings not meeting recommended criteria. Such insurer action can lead to stricter building codes.

- Although terrorism may appear as a remote threat to building owners, an "all hazard" approach brings to light numerous risks. This broader perspective impacts building codes, the standard of care that courts might impose for building protection, and liability issues.

Fire Protection

The Problem of Fire

As written in Chapter 2, the U.S. Fire Administration (2005b) reported that the U.S. fire problem is one of the worst in the industrial world. In 2005, the fire problem resulted in the following losses: 3,675 civilian deaths and 17,925 injuries; 115 firefighter deaths while on duty; 1.6 million fires reported and many went unreported; property loss at about $10.7 billion; and there were 31,500 intentionally set structure fires resulting in 315 civilian deaths. Furthermore, fire killed more Americans than all natural disasters combined, and 83% of all civilian fire deaths occurred in residences (U.S. Fire Administration, 2006). Most human casualties in fires result from smoke and the toxic fumes or gases within it.

The U.S. Fire Administration (2002) reported that each year there are about 15,500 high-rise structural fires, and three-quarters of these fires are in residential structures. The challenges posed by high-rise fires include the following:

- Smoke and flame movement in high-rise structures is very different from other structures.
- High-rises often contain multiple types of occupancies such as residential, commercial, restaurant, and underground parking. Each type presents challenges that must be approached differently.
- Exits from high-rises are limited, and emergency evacuation is difficult.
- High-rise fires require significantly more personnel and equipment to extinguish than do other types of fires.

Private Organizations Involved in Fire Protection

As explained in Chapter 3, a number of private organizations assist public and private sector efforts at security, safety, and fire protection. This assistance is through research, standards, and publications. Examples of these private organizations include NFPA and UL. Another related private organization is Factory Mutual Global. This organization works to improve the effectiveness of fire protection systems and new fire suppression chemicals, as well as cost evaluation of fire protection systems. It tests materials and equipment submitted by manufacturers. An approval guide is published, and like UL, it issues labels to indicate that specific products have passed its tests.

Fire Departments

Fire departments are local institutions. There are about 31,000 local fire departments in the United States and over one million firefighters, of which about 750,000 are volunteers. Over half of firefighters protect small, rural communities of fewer than 5,000 residents, and these locales rely on volunteer departments with scarce resources. One of the best strategies for these locales, outside major metropolitan areas, is to develop mutual aid agreements to share resources. This approach improves preparation and response to fires and emergencies (U.S. Department of Homeland Security, n.d.).

Historically, fire departments have focused on fire prevention and fire suppression. However, in the past 30 years, fire departments have expanded services to include emergency medical needs, hazardous material incidents, terrorism response, natural disasters, specialized rescue, and other community needs. Because of these additional community requirements and the need for research on the changing nature of the fire service, the U.S. Fire Administration (USFA) and the International Association of Fire Fighters (IAFF) are working together to enhance risk management capabilities of local fire departments. The goals of this initiative are to design risk management programs based on community vulnerabilities and service commitments, improve firefighter safety, and provide evaluative tools for response systems. One avenue of research in this initiative is to employ geographic information system (GIS) computer simulation to develop staffing and deployment models that will be recommended for departments of various sizes serving different communities. The research results will be available to fire service standards setting committees such as the NFPA (U.S. Fire Administration, 2005a).

The "Firefighting Annex," within the *National Response Plan* (U.S. Department of Homeland Security, 2004), states that the primary agency for coordination during a significant fire is the U.S. Department of Agriculture/Forest Service, with support from the Departments of Commerce, Defense, Homeland Security, Interior, and the Environmental Protection Agency. The function is to detect and suppress wildland, rural, and urban fires resulting from an Incident of National Significance and to provide personnel and equipment to supplement all levels of government in firefighting.

Fire Department Protection Efforts

Public fire protection tasks often involve private-sector loss prevention practitioners. These tasks include facility planning, prefire planning, codes, and inspections.

Facility Planning

In many locales, it is legally mandatory that public fire personnel review construction plans for new facilities. This may entail consultation with architects, engineers, and loss prevention practitioners on a number of subjects ranging from fire codes to water supplies for sprinkler systems. On-site inspections by fire personnel ensure compliance with plans. Fire and water department officials often prepare recommendations to local government bodies concerning improvements in water supply systems for new industrial plants to ensure an adequate water supply in the event of a fire. Cooperation and planning with interested parties can create an improved atmosphere for preventing and suppressing fires.

Prefire Planning

Preparatory plans assist fire personnel in case of fire. An on-site survey is made of a particular building with the aid of a checklist. Then the actual prefire plans are formulated for that structure. Drawings and computer-aided designs are used to identify the location of exits, stairs, firefighting equipment, hazards, and anything else of importance. Additional information is helpful: construction characteristics and that of adjacent buildings, types of roofs, number of employees, and the best response route to the building. Prefire plans also serve as an aid to training. Naturally, firefighting personnel do not have the time to prepare prefire plans for all structures in their jurisdiction. One- and two-family residential structures are omitted in favor of more complex structures where greater losses can occur, such as schools, hospitals, theaters, hotels, and manufacturing plants.

Public Education

This strategy involves educating the public about the fire problem and how to prevent it. The public can become a great aid in reducing fires if people are properly recruited through education campaigns. Public education programs utilize mass media, contests, lectures, and tours of firehouses. Building inspections also educate the public by pointing out fire hazards.

Codes

Years ago, as the United States was evolving into an industrial giant, buildings were constructed without proper concern for fire prevention. Building codes in urban areas either did not exist or were inadequate to ensure construction designed to prevent fire-related losses.

In fact, a year before the Great Chicago Fire in 1871, Lloyd's Insurance Company of London halted the writing of policies in that city because of fire-prone construction practices.

Prompted by the difficulty in selling insurance because of higher rates for hazardous buildings and the losses incurred by some spectacular fires, insurance companies became increasingly interested in fire prevention strategies. Improvements in building construction and fire departments slowly followed.

Although insurance associations played an important role in establishing fire standards, government support was necessary to enforce fire codes. Today, local governments enforce state regulations and local ordinances that support fire codes. Fire department personnel inspect structures to ensure conformance to codes. To strengthen compliance by owners of buildings, penalties are meted out for violations so that fire hazards are reduced. Penalties usually are in the form of fines.

Codes can be in the form of fire codes and building codes. Frequently, there is disagreement about what should be contained in each and what responsibility and authority should be given to fire inspectors as opposed to building inspectors.

Generally, construction requirements go into **building codes**, and these codes are enforced by building inspectors. Model building codes are from the Building Officials Code Administrators, Southern Building Code Congress International and the International Conference of Building Officials, the new International Building Code, and NFPA 101. The building codes contain fire resistance ratings of floors, walls, ceilings and other construction features that affect code requirements for electrical installations, sprinkler systems, exits, vents, and the like (Bangor and Faust, 2001: 68–71).

Fire codes, enforced by firefighting personnel, deal with the maintenance and condition of various fire prevention and suppression features of buildings (e.g., sprinkler systems). In addition, fire codes cover hazardous substances, hazardous occupancies, and general precautions against fire.

Codes have afforded buildings greater fire protection, especially when compared to earlier days. However, in some localities codes are of poor quality. A prime factor is construction costs. Interest group (e.g., the construction industry) pressure on government officials who stipulate codes has been known to weaken codes. It is a sad case when a high-rise building catches fire and people perish because no sprinklers were installed on upper floors, and the fire department was ill equipped to suppress a fire so high up. Later, the media broadcasts the tragedy, and government officials meet to satisfy the public outcry. Stronger fire codes often emerge. A similar scenario occurs with weak building codes following natural disasters (e.g., a hurricane).

Inspections

The primary purpose of building inspections by firefighting personnel is to uncover deviations from the fire code. The frequency and intensity of these inspections vary. Because of budget constraints and a shortage of personnel, many fire departments are not able to conduct enough inspections to equal national standards of several inspections per year for hazardous buildings. The *NFPA Inspection Manual* outlines methods for conducting inspections.

Legal Implications

Fire marshals are provided with broad powers to ensure public safety. This is especially evident in fire inspections and investigations, in rights to subpoena records, and in fire marshal's hearings. Most courts have upheld these powers.

In almost all local jurisdictions, the state has delegated police powers so that local officials regulate safety conditions through ordinances. Fire ordinances stipulate inspection procedures, number of inspections, violations, and penalties. When differences of opinion develop over individual rights (e.g., of a building owner) versus fire department police powers, the issue is often resolved by the courts. Chapter 4 differentiates administrative inspection and administrative search warrant. It also notes that the legal standard for obtaining an administrative search warrant, also known as an inspection warrant, is lower than what is required to obtain a search warrant in a criminal case (Hall, 2006: 146–151).

Fire Prevention and Fire Suppression Strategies

Businesses and institutions can do a lot to protect against fire. **Fire prevention** focuses on strategies that help to avoid the inception of fires. **Fire suppression** applies personnel, equipment, and other resources to suppress fires.

The following strategies are emphasized in subsequent pages:

Fire Prevention	*Fire Suppression*
Inspections	Integrated systems
Planning	Detection of smoke and fire
Safety	Contact the fire department
Good housekeeping	Extinguishers
Storage and transportation of hazardous substances and materials	Sprinklers
	Standpipe and hose systems
Evacuation	Fire-resistive buildings
Training	Training and fire brigades

The fire triangle (see Figure 13-1) symbolizes the elements necessary for a fire. Fire requires heat, fuel, oxygen, and then a chemical chain reaction. When all three characteristics, plus a chemical chain reaction, are present, there will be fire. If any one is missing, either through prevention strategies (e.g., good housekeeping, safety) or suppression (i.e., extinguishment), fire will not occur. Heat often is considered the ignition source. A smoldering cigarette, sparks from a welder's torch, or friction from a machine can produce enough heat to begin a fire.

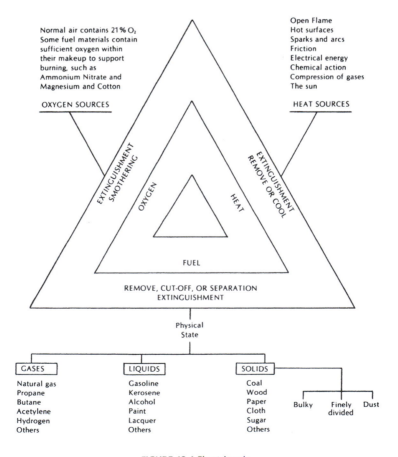

FIGURE 13-1 Fire triangle.

Almost every working environment has fuels, heat, and oxygen. Loss prevention practitioners, and all employees in general, must take steps to reduce the chances for fire by isolating fuels and controlling heat. Not much can be done about pervasive oxygen, but fuels such as gasoline and kerosene should be stored properly away from sources of heat.

Fire Prevention Strategies

Inspections

Inspections or audits to check on fire hazards are the mainstay of any organization's strategy against fires (Breisch, 1989: 40–44). Checklist questions include the following: Are new facility designs and manufacturing processes being submitted to appropriate personnel for fire protection review? Do employees receive periodic training on fire prevention and suppression systems, polices, and procedures (see Figure 13-2)? What is the condition of fire suppression equipment? Are plant wastes and other combustibles disposed of properly? The basic purpose of inspections is to uncover deficiencies. Then corrective action becomes the heart of the inspection prevention strategy.

Planning

Feedback from inspections helps to plan strategies against fire losses. An interdisciplinary planning group often is an excellent source for plans. Fire department personnel, architects, engineers, insurance specialists, loss prevention practitioners, and others can provide a multitude of ideas. Management support is an important ingredient in the planning process. By supplying adequate personnel, funding, and policies and procedures, management can strengthen the fire protection program. Earlier, OSHA regulations pertaining to fire protection plans were explained.

Safety

Some safety strategies for a fire prevention program follow:

1. Set up smoking and no smoking areas that are supervised, safe, and clearly marked with signs.
2. In smoking areas, provide cigarette butt and match receptacles or sand urns.
3. When fire protection equipment or systems are planned, select those that have been approved by a reputable testing organization (e.g., UL).

FIGURE 13-2 Training and inspections improve fire protection.

4. In the use of heating systems, such as boilers, maintain safety when lighting up, during usage, and when shutting down.
5. Examine motors frequently to ensure safe operation and to prevent overheating.
6. Never overload electrical circuits.
7. Maintain lightning protective devices (e.g., lightning rods).
8. Employ an electrician who is safety conscious.
9. Prohibit the use of welding equipment near flammable substances or hazardous materials.
10. Watch sparks during and after welding.
11. Train employees to create an atmosphere of safety.
12. Conduct inspections and correct deficiencies.
13. Ensure fire protection standby for hazardous operations.

Good Housekeeping

Good housekeeping is another fire prevention strategy. It consists of building care, maintenance, cleanliness, proper placement of materials, careful waste and garbage disposal, and other general housekeeping activities.

Hazardous Materials (HAZMAT) Incidents

HAZMAT refers to substances that are toxic, poisonous, radioactive, flammable, or explosive and can cause injury or death from exposure (Schottke, 2007: 450). The prevention of disasters from hazardous substances and materials is extremely important. Such materials are used in every community and transported by trucks, railcars, ships, barges, and planes. Examples of hazardous substances and materials are plastics, fuels, and corrosive chemicals (e.g., acids). A tremendous amount of information exists concerning their physical and chemical properties, methods for storage and transportation, and the most appropriate strategies in the event of fire or accident. Numerous federal (e.g., OSHA and U.S. Department of Transportation) and state agencies and laws and regulations promote HAZMAT safety.

HAZMAT responses require *caution* because the effects can be deadly and first responders do not want to become victims themselves. Approaches, with proper protective clothing, should be made from upwind, uphill, and upstream, and vehicles should be parked facing out for quick escape. Top priorities during a HAZMAT incident are to protect yourself and others from exposure and contamination, isolate the area, identify the substance for subsequent action, and deny entry to reduce exposure.

Evacuation and Medical Services

Whatever fire prevention strategies are planned, a key factor must be to prevent injuries and deaths. Two vital considerations are *evacuation* and *medical services*. Evacuation plans and drills help people prepare for the risk of fire and other emergencies (Figure 13-3). Smoke and fire alarms often provide warning for escape. Emergency exit maps and properly identified emergency doors also prevent injuries and deaths. Employees should turn off all equipment, utilize designated escape routes, avoid elevators, and report to a predetermined point on the outside to be counted. While employees are evacuating, firefighters may be entering the premises. At this point, a coordinated traffic flow is crucial. Firefighting equipment and personnel need to be directed to the fire location. Personnel should also be assigned to crowd control.

If injuries do take place, the quickness and quality of emergency medical services can save lives and unnecessary suffering. Preplanning will improve services. Specific employees should be trained to administer first aid while waiting for public emergency medical services.

Here is a list of suggestions to promote safety and fire protection in buildings (Azano and Gilbertie, 2003; Carter et al., 2004; Quinley and Schmidt, 2002; U.S. Fire Administration, 2004). An emphasis is placed on evacuation.

- A committee should be formed to plan life safety.
- Life safety plans should be coordinated with public safety agencies and a variety of groups on the premises (e.g., management, employees in general, safety and security officers, and others).

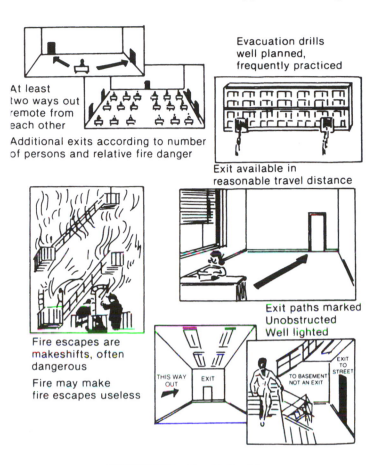

FIGURE 13-3 Principles of exit safety.

- Training, education, drills, and exercises are an investment in life safety. Records should be maintained of such activities for regulators, insurers, and others. The records should be secured in multiple locations.
- A chain of command and hierarchy of life safety volunteers should be maintained. For example, a building executive can choose **floor wardens** who can choose assistant floor wardens and searchers. Floor wardens and assistants are trained, and then they train occupants and lead drills. Searchers ensure no one is left behind.
- Training for floor wardens and assistants should include these topics: the variety of risks (e.g., fire, workplace violence), the evacuation plan, escape routes, safety, means of communication, what to do if someone is injured, where to assemble outside the building, and counts.
- Wardens can be supplied with evacuation kits containing flashlight, reflective vest, clipboard for recording employees outside the building, and a flag to mark the rendezvous point.
- Evacuation plans should include occupants with special needs, and employees should be assigned to assist them.
- Evacuation of high-rise buildings is complicated because of the number of occupants and the time needed to evacuate, especially those in upper floors. A minor fire may require evacuation of the floor containing the fire and two floors both above and below the fire. A serious fire would require a total evacuation.
- Evacuation plans should include **areas of refuge** (e.g., oversized landing at a stairwell or sealed smoke or fire compartments on a floor) and how they will be used. A method of communication should be installed at the area of refuge.

- Before opening a door during a fire emergency, feel the door with the back of your hand to gauge temperature. If it is warm, opening it may cause smoke and fire to enter. This means you may be forced to stay in your office or apartment. Stuff the cracks around the door with towels. Telephone the fire department to inform them about your location and go to the window with a flashlight or wave a sheet.
- If the door is not warm, brace your body against it, stay low, and slowly open it. If there is no smoke or fire, evacuate.
- If smoke is around you, stay low because smoke rises. Place a cloth over your mouth and nose.
- Employee information is crucial during an emergency, and it should be up-to-date. Also important is a contact list of public safety agencies, medical services, regulators, government officials, critical suppliers, and others.
- Building and site maps are important to indicate such features as utility shutoffs, water lines, electrical and other utilities, floor plans, exits, stairways, hazards, and high-value assets.
- Practitioners responsible for safety and fire protection programs should seek feedback to improve performance. Feedback can be gathered from training, drills, and exercises. Also, audits can expose deficiencies in the expertise of personnel, equipment, systems, communications, and coordination with others.
- An airborne hazard (e.g., WMD) outside a building may necessitate **sheltering-in-place**. For example, a plume of hazardous material may be approaching a high-rise building with no time to evacuate, and traffic would block escape. Ideal rooms to shelter-in-place would be on the opposite side of the approaching plume, above the first floor, windowless, and with a minimum number of vents and doors. Duct tape or other materials can be used to seal the room, and the HVAC system should be turned off. Because many hazardous agents are heavier than air, occupants should shelter-in-place in upper floors.

Training

Through training, fire prevention becomes everybody's responsibility. Employees must first understand the disastrous effects of serious fire losses. This includes not only harm to humans, but also lost productivity and jobs. Topics within training can include safety, good housekeeping, hazardous substances and materials, evacuation, and first aid. Knowledge is transmitted via on-line courses, lectures, videos, demonstrations, drills, visits by public fire prevention personnel, pamphlets, and posted fire prevention signs. Incentive programs, whereby employees compete for prizes (e.g., the best fire prevention poster) also can increase fire prevention awareness.

☐ ☐ ☐ ▬▬▬▬▬▬▬▬▬▬▬▬▬▬▬▬▬▬▬▬▬▬▬▬

Haphazard Fire Protection at Bestbuy Service Company

The Bestbuy Service Company was a unique and rapidly growing business that sold numerous consumer items similar to those in department stores. Bestbuy's success was due to a no-frills store design and customer self-service. Each store essentially was a warehouse located away from main roads. Loss prevention was of minimal concern to management. Strategies against crime, fire, and accidents were haphazard.

One store, which also served as a distribution center, had an unfortunate experience. Late one afternoon, before closing, a salesperson threw a lighted cigarette butt into a trash container. The trash and then some boxes nearby caught fire. When store personnel were surprised by the spreading fire, they panicked. The first thing they all did was to run out of the warehouse with the customers. While the employees watched the burning warehouse in amazement, the manager asked if anybody had called the fire department. Nobody responded, so he used his cell phone to call the fire department.

The manager continued to watch the fire and remembered that the automatic sprinklers were turned off because of freezing temperatures. Also in his thoughts were the thousands of dollars' worth of merchandise burning up.

For the Bestbuy Company, the store and its contents were a tremendous loss. Insurance covered only a small part of the losses, especially because many insurance company recommendations went unheeded: the local fire department was never contacted for prefire plans, and employees were never trained for simple fire procedures. Senior management was clearly at fault.

☐ ☐ ☐ ▬▬▬▬▬▬▬▬▬▬▬▬▬▬▬▬▬▬▬▬▬

What do you think can improve fire prevention in the United States?

▬▬▬▬▬▬▬▬▬▬▬▬▬▬▬▬▬▬▬▬▬ ☐ ☐ ☐

Fire Suppression Strategies

The success of fire suppression strategies depends primarily on preplanning, preparation, equipment quality, and the readiness of personnel.

Integrated Systems

Integrated fire suppression systems perform a variety of functions (Suttell, 2006: 78–80). Detectors can measure smoke and the rate of temperature rise. If danger is evident, an alarm is sounded at the earliest stages of a fire. The fire can be extinguished automatically by water from sprinklers. Other functions include displaying CCTV video or AutoCAD floorplans on a computer screen to pinpoint the fire, notifying the fire department of the fire and its exact location, activating a public address (PA) system to provide life safety messages to occupants, starting up emergency generators for emergency lights and other equipment, detecting changes in sprinkler system water pressure, turning off certain electrical devices and equipment (e.g., shutting down fans that spread fire and smoke), venting specific areas, closing doors, creating safe zones for occupants, and returning elevators to ground level to encourage the use of emergency stairways. If a human being were to analyze the fire threat and make these decisions, the time factor would obviously be greater than the split second needed by a computer.

Because buildings often contain integrated fire and security systems, it is important that engineers with verified skills design such systems. In addition, the local fire department can be contacted for their input. It is often recommended that the fire alarm system be planned as the first priority because of the need to deal with the fire authority's jurisdiction and codes and standards.

Detection of Smoke and Fire

Many businesses utilize a combination of the following detectors for increased protection:

- *Smoke detectors* are widely used, especially since most human casualties in fires result from smoke and the toxic fumes or gases within smoke. These detectors operate with photoelectric light beams and react when smoke either blocks the beam of light or enters a refraction chamber where the smoke reflects the light into the photo cell.
- *Ionization detectors* are sensitive to invisible products of combustion created during the early stages of a fire. These detectors are noted for their early warning capabilities.
- *Thermal detectors* respond to heat either when the temperature reaches a certain degree or when the temperature rises too quickly. The latter is known as a *rate-of-rise detector*. Thermal detectors are made with either feature or a combination of both.
- *Flame detectors* detect flame and glowing embers. These detectors are sensitive to flames not visible to the human eye. The infrared kind is responsive to radiant energy that humans cannot see.

- *Sprinkler water flow detectors* contain a seal that melts when heat rises to a specific temperature. Then water flows from the sprinkler system. An alarm is activated when the water flow closes pressure switches.
- *Carbon monoxide detectors* protect against what is often called the "silent killer," because carbon monoxide is difficult to detect. In fact, victims, in their drowsy state, may be wrongly diagnosed as being substance abusers.
- *Gas detectors* monitor flammable gases or vapors. These devices are especially valuable in petroleum, chemical, and other industries where dangerous gases or vapors are generated.
- *Combination detectors* respond to more than one fire-producing cause or employ multiple operating principles. Examples include smoke/heat detector or rate-of-rise/fixed temperature heat detector.

Contact the fire department. Sometimes simple steps are overlooked. When a serious fire begins, the local fire department must be contacted as soon as possible to reduce losses. The best strategy to prevent a situation in which everybody thought somebody else had contacted the fire department is to ask: "Who called the fire department?" Another problem develops when *people think that they can extinguish a fire without outside assistance*. It is not until precious time has elapsed and serious danger exists that the fire department is contacted.

Alarm signaling systems are automatic or manual. With *automatic systems*, an attachment of a siren or a bell to a smoke or fire detection device or sprinkler system will notify people in the immediate area of a smoke or fire problem. This type of alarm is called a *local alarm*. Unless incorporated into this system, a local alarm will not notify a fire department. Automatic systems also consist of a local alarm and an alarm that notifies a central station or a fire department. Many large industries have a central, proprietary monitoring station that checks smoke, fire, burglar, and other sensors. *Manual fire alarm signaling systems* use a pull station fixed to a wall. This is a local alarm unless an alarm signal is transmitted to a central station or fire department.

Portable Extinguishers

The following classes of fires provide a foundation for firefighting and use of portable extinguishers:

- *Class A* fires consist of ordinary combustible materials such as trash, paper, fibers, wood, drapes, and furniture.
- *Class B* fires are fueled by a flammable liquid, such as gasoline, oil, alcohol, or cleaning solvents.
- *Class C* fires occur in live electrical circuits or equipment such as generators, motors, fuse boxes, computers, or copying machines.
- *Class D* fires, the rarest of the four types of fires, are fueled by combustible metals such as sodium, magnesium, and potassium.
- *Class K* fires involve combustible cooking fuels such as vegetable or animal oils or fats (Carter, 2004: 186).

Portable fire extinguishers are used to douse a small fire by directing onto it a substance that cools the burning material, deprives the flame of oxygen, or interferes with the chemical reactions occurring in the flame. Ratings and effectiveness of these extinguishers are in NFPA 10, Standard for Portable Fire Extinguishers (Nolan, 2001: 83–85).

Employees and loss prevention practitioners must be knowledgeable about the proper use of extinguishers. If the wrong extinguisher is used, a fire may become more serious. Water must not be used on a flammable liquid such as gasoline (Class B fire) because the gasoline may float on the water and spread the fire. Neither should one spray water on electrical fires (Class C fires) because water conducts electricity, and electrocution may result. Many locations use multipurpose dry chemical extinguishers that can be applied to A, B, or C fires. This approach reduces confusion during a fire. Class D fires are extinguished with dry powder extinguishers. Class B extinguishers have been used on Class K fires with limited effectiveness.

Class K extinguishing agents are usually wet chemicals—water-based solutions of potassium carbonate, potassium acetate, or potassium citrate (Carter, 2004: 187).

Fire extinguishers should be checked at least every week during a loss prevention officer's patrol. Systems are available whereby extinguishers are connected to a control panel via an electrical cable. If the extinguisher is removed from its bracket, a signal is sent to the control panel. In addition, this system provides a reading of whether the extinguisher is pressurized to the correct level. Service companies recharge extinguishers when necessary. A seal is attached to the extinguisher that certifies its readiness. For those servicing fire extinguishers, 2008 is the year certification requirements begin, and it is based on NFPA 10 (Conroy, 2006).

An Angry Ex-Employee's Revenge

Albert Drucker had been warned numerous times about pilfering small tools from the maintenance department at Bearing Industries. When he was caught for the third time, via a strict inventory system, management decided to fire him. When Drucker was informed, he went into a rage and stormed out of the plant. While leaving, he vowed, "I'm gonna get you back for this." Management maintained that it made the right decision.

Two weeks later, Drucker was ready with his vindictive plan. At 2:00 one morning, he entered the Bearing plant by using a previously stolen master key. No loss prevention systems or services hindered his entrance. Within 15 minutes, he collected three strategically located fire extinguishers. When Drucker arrived home, he quickly emptied the contents of the extinguishers and then filled each one with gasoline. By 5:30 a.m., Drucker had replaced the three extinguishers and he was home sleeping.

At 2:00 p.m., two days later, when the Bearing plant was in full production, Drucker sneaked into the plant unnoticed and placed, on a pile of old rags, a book of matches with a lighted cigarette underneath the match heads. By the time Drucker was a few miles away, the old rags and some cardboard boxes were on fire. When employees discovered the fire, they were confident that they could extinguish it. They reached for the nearest extinguishers and approached the fire. To their surprise, the fire grew as they supplied it with gasoline. Their first reaction was to drop the extinguishers and run; one extinguisher exploded while the fire intensified. The fire caused extensive damage but no injuries or deaths. The police and management suspected arson. When police investigators asked management if there was anybody who held a grudge against the company, Albert Drucker's name was mentioned. He was arrested a week later and charged with arson.

Sprinklers

A sprinkler system consists of pipes along a ceiling that contain water under pressure, with an additional source of water for a constant flow. Attached to the pipes, automatic sprinklers are placed at select locations. When a fire occurs, a seal in the sprinkler head ruptures at a pre-established temperature, and a steady stream of water flows.

Sprinklers are an effective fire suppression strategy. Angle et al. (2001: 199) note that the NFPA has kept records of automatic sprinkler performance for more than 80 years; that organization reports: "These remarkably comprehensive records show that in 95 percent of the some 117,770 fires in sprinklered buildings (where the Association has reliable data), the sprinklers have performed satisfactorily." The failure of a sprinkler system most often is due to human error—the water supply was turned off at the time of the fire.

A sprinkler system is a worthwhile investment for reducing fire losses. Lower insurance premiums actually can pay for the system over time.

There are several kinds of automatic sprinkler systems. Two popular ones are the wet-pipe and dry-pipe systems. With the *wet-pipe system* (Figure 13-4), water is in the pipes at all times and is released when heat ruptures the seal in the sprinkler head. This is the most common system and is applicable where freezing is no threat to its operation. Where freezing temperatures and broken pipes are a problem, the *dry-pipe system* is useful. Air pressure is maintained in the pipes until a sprinkler head ruptures. Then the air escapes, and water enters the pipes and exits through the opened sprinklers.

Older buildings may have pipes that apply fire-suppressant chemicals such as *carbon dioxide* or *Halon*. Fire codes now prohibit these chemicals. The former absorbs oxygen, creating a danger to humans, whereas the latter depletes the earth's ozone layer.

Standpipe and Hose Systems

Standpipe and hose systems enable people to manually apply water to fires in buildings. **Standpipes** are vertical pipes that allow a water supply to reach an outlet on each floor of a building. In multiple-story structures, standpipes often are constructed within fire-resistant fire stairs as an added defense for the standpipes, hoses, and firefighting personnel. The typical setup is a folded or rolled 2 1/2–inch hose enclosed in a wall cabinet and identified with fire emergency information (Figure 13-5). A control valve, which looks like a small spoked wheel, enables water to flow. Automatic extinguishing systems (e.g., sprinklers) often are the preferred system; however, the standpipe and hose systems are advantageous when the automatic system fails or is not present, when sections of a building are not accessible to outside hose lines and hydrants, and when properly trained employees are capable of fire suppression.

Training is essential for employees if they are to have the responsibility of fighting a fire. With hoses, two people are required: one to stretch the hose to its full length and another to turn the water flow valve. Without training, employees may be injured if they do not understand the danger of turning the valve before the hose is stretched. This could cause the coiled section of the hose to react to the water pressure by acting like a whip and possibly striking someone.

Fire Walls and Doors

Fire walls are constructed in buildings to prevent the spread of fire. These walls are made of materials that resist fire and are designed to withstand fire for several hours. Fire walls are weakened by openings such as doorways. Therefore, fire doors at openings help to strengthen the fire wall

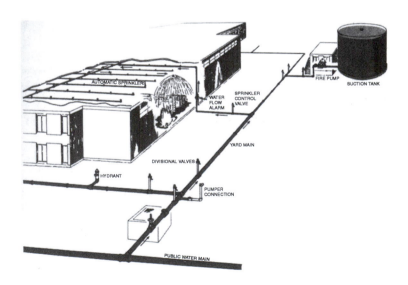

FIGURE 13-4 Total concept of the wet-pipe automatic sprinkler system.

FIGURE 13-5 Standpipe system including wall cabinet, hose with nozzle, and valves. A portable fire extinguisher is also contained in the cabinet.

when resisting fire. Fire doors often are designed to close automatically in case of fire. Nationally recognized testing laboratories study the reliability of these doors.

Stairwells

During evacuation, stairwells (made of masonry construction) provide a fire-resistant path for escape. Fire codes often require stairwells to withstand a fire for at least two hours. Stairwells may be equipped with fans to reduce smoke during evacuation.

Access Control

During an emergency, electronically controlled doors should be connected to the life safety system to permit escape. From a security perspective, this presents a problem because an alarm condition may provide an opportunity for an offender to enter or exit with ease. To deal with such a vulnerability, CCTV and security officers can be applied to select locations.

Codes mandate the use of exit devices that enable quick escape during emergencies. A door locked from the outside may be easily unlocked from the inside to allow theft or unauthorized passage. Therefore, the door needs to be secured from both sides while permitting quick escape in case of an emergency. Often, the solution is a controlled exit device (Figure 13-6). One type of controlled exit device stays locked for a fixed time, usually 15 seconds, after being pushed, while sounding an alarm. Signage and Braille are required to alert people of the delay as it provides time for security to respond. In a true emergency, such a device should be unlocked immediately through a tie-in with the building's fire protection system as specified in NFPA 101 (Zunkel, 2000: 34–38).

The Las Vegas MGM Grand Hotel fire in 1985 provides a graphic example of security (locked exit doors) being one of the major reasons for a large loss of life. All the exit doors to the stairwell had a controlled exit device (panic hardware). However, once the occupants were in the stairwell, they encountered smoke. Unfortunately, the doors were locked on the stairwell side to ensure security for each floor. A person had to exit the building on the first floor to regain access. With heavy smoke rising in the stairwell, and no access to any of the upper floors, the occupants were trapped and died (Moore, 1997: 61–62).

Fire-Resistive Buildings

If a person stops to think about the tons of combustible materials transported into a building during construction and as it becomes operational, he or she may be hesitant to enter. Wood

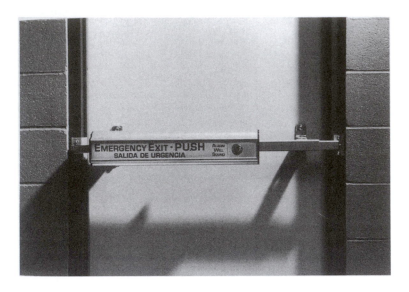

FIGURE 13-6 Emergency exit. *Courtesy:* Sargent & Greenleaf, Inc.

in construction and furnishings, cloth and fibers in curtains and carpets, paper, cleaning fluids, and other combustibles are hazardous. However, reinforced concrete or protected steel construction and fire-resistive roofs, floors, ceilings, walls, doors, windows, carpets, furniture, and so on all help to produce greater fire protection.

Training and Fire Brigades

With the threat of fire, employee training is of tremendous importance. Of top priority during a fire is to safeguard lives and then to secure valuable assets. If specific employees are responsible for fire suppression, thorough training is necessary. This is especially true when local public firefighting capabilities are incompatible with the type of fire that may develop at a site. In this case, a private fire department at the site is appropriate and referred to as a **fire brigade**. OSHA 1910.156 contains requirements for organizing, operating, training, and equipping industrial fire brigades when established by an employer. Although fire brigades are expensive, all brigade members must be trained and equipped as professional firefighters.

Inspection, Testing, and Maintenance

NFPA 25 establishes minimum requirements for inspecting, testing, and maintenance of water-based fire protection systems. The types of systems contained in this standard include sprinklers, standpipe and hose systems, and water supplies. Of particular concern during inspecting, testing, and maintenance is whether changes in a building impact fire protection and codes. Documentation of the process is essential to reinforce corrective action and for the AHJ.

☐ ☐ ☐ ▬▬▬▬▬▬▬▬▬▬▬▬▬▬▬▬▬▬▬▬▬▬▬▬▬▬▬▬▬▬▬▬▬

Performance-Based Design

A **performance-based fire protection** approach is an alternative to following a rigid set of guidelines by evaluating hazards and planning the most appropriate protection in innovative ways to meet performance goals. Supported by codes, this approach is also driven by computer software that runs fire models, technical analysis that is less subjective than traditional planning, and performance-based design that offers comparisons of products. Chapter 5 of NFPA 101 explains the performance-based option: "Performance-based design is an engineering approach to fire protection that is based on a specific design goal as opposed to the normal prescriptive code requirements based on occupancies." For example, a fire code might require exit travel distance at 250 feet. This requirement may not be appropriate in all cases. Performance-based design would seek fire safety through a goal, such as evacuation of the building within 4 minutes (Jelenewicz, 2006: 34).

☐ ☐ ☐ ▬▬▬▬▬▬▬▬▬▬▬▬▬▬▬▬▬▬▬▬▬▬▬▬▬▬▬▬▬▬▬▬▬▬▬▬

What do you think can improve fire suppression in the United States?

▬▬▬▬▬▬▬▬▬▬▬▬▬▬▬▬▬▬▬▬▬▬▬▬▬▬▬▬▬▬▬▬▬▬▬▬ ☐ ☐ ☐

Public Safety Agencies

Public safety involves primarily government employees who plan, train, and equip themselves for emergencies. They respond as quickly as possible to the scene of an emergency to save lives, care for the injured, protect people and property, and restore order. During an emergency at a corporation or institution, when proprietary life safety specialists (e.g., security officers, floor wardens, and employees trained in fire fighting and first aid) perform their duties, their work will "merge" with the duties of arriving first responders (e.g., police, firefighters). Because of this interrelationship, joint planning and training prior to an emergency can improve coordination, life safety, and public safety.

All first responders face serious safety issues. Examples are traffic accidents, disease, emotionally upset family members, violent offenders, and hazardous materials. **Personal protective equipment** (PPE) is essential; it depends on the type of incident. At a minimum, PPE must include universal precautions (e.g., gloves, mask, protective eyewear) to prevent disease transmission, but it can range to a bullet-resistant vest for high-risk incidents or locations.

Thus far in this chapter, emphasis has been placed on public fire departments within public safety. However, other agencies of government play an important role in public safety and responding to emergencies. They include emergency management (see the preceding chapter), police, and emergency medical services.

Police

In the United States, there are 13,524 municipal police agencies, 3,070 sheriff's departments, plus state police agencies and dozens of federal law enforcement agencies. Employees of these agencies, divided into sworn/not sworn, are as follows: local police, 440,920/124,995; sheriff's departments, 164,711/129,112; state, 56,384/30,680; and federal, 88,000/72,000 (Bureau of Justice Statistics, 2003).

Public police play a crucial role in responding to "all hazard" emergencies. At the scene of an emergency, police direct traffic, maintain order, keep crowds back, assist victims, protect potential crime scenes, and conduct investigations.

As with public fire departments, public police are also involved in the integration of life safety and public safety prior to emergencies. They may meet with private security management to coordinate efforts at protecting people and assets. Police often maintain floor plans of banks and other high-risk locations to assist them when responding to crimes, such as robberies and hostage incidents. Violence in the workplace has caused public police to plan, train, and drill with institutions (e.g., schools) and businesses.

Emergency Medical Service (EMS)

The U.S. Department of Homeland Security (n.d.) reports that there are over 155,000 nationally registered emergency medical technicians (EMTs). Houser et al. (2004), researchers for the RAND Corporation, list 500,000 emergency medical service responders. Carter et al. (2004: 691) write: "Emergency medical responses constitute more than 50 percent of total emergency responses for many fire departments across the country. In some jurisdictions, emergency medical calls make up 70 to 80 percent of the fire department's total emergency responses per year."

Firefighters are increasingly improving their skills at emergency medical services, and they can deliver lifesaving techniques to stabilize patients while waiting for EMTs and paramedics. Some firefighters are also EMT qualified. In comparison to EMTs, paramedics receive more training and perform more procedures during a medical emergency. States vary on training and qualification for these positions.

During a medical emergency, numerous critical, time-sensitive decisions must be made (Angle, 2005: 118). Examples are the safest and quickest route to the scene; medical treatment techniques; drug dosages; and the most appropriate method of transporting the patient. **Triage** (Figure 13-7) is a term relevant to sites of medical emergencies, and it is defined as follows: "A quick and systematic method of identifying which patients are in serious condition and which patients are not, so that the more seriously injured patients can be treated first" (Carter, 2004: 954).

FIGURE 13-7 U.S. Air Force firefighter triages victims during mass casualty exercise at Jacksonville International Airport, FL. *Courtesy:* U.S. Air Force photo by Staff Sgt. Shelley Gill.

Emergencies

Planning and training are two key strategies to mitigate losses when emergencies occur. Employees must know what to do to protect lives and assets. Business continuity plans are essential for business survival. Businesses must apply risk management and risk analysis tools to identify vulnerabilities and dependencies. "What if" scenarios help businesses plan. What if a major supplier is destroyed by a natural disaster? What if an electric service blackout occurs? What if IT service is interrupted? What if a pandemic necessitates restricted travel? How would these events affect business, and what can be done to strengthen business continuity?

Human-Made Emergencies

Accidents

Although many accidents are caused by human error, other factors, such as weather conditions or poor equipment design, may cause accidents. An accident at, for example, a manufacturing plant has the potential for serious injury, death, and production slowdown. Thousands of lives, hundreds of thousands of injuries, and billions of dollars of losses are sustained each year because of accidents. Safety and related issues are explained in the next chapter.

Bomb Threats, Explosions, and Terrorism Hoaxes

Because of past bombings and terrorism, bomb threats and the possibility of bombings are taken very seriously today. Even the commonly circulated statistic that 98% of bomb threats are hoaxes makes decision makers more concerned than ever about the other 2%. The Bureau of Alcohol, Tobacco and Firearms (ATF) reports hundreds of bombing incidents in the United States each year. Pipe bombs and Molotov cocktails are often encountered in these incidents (Office of Justice Programs, 2000: 2–3). Accurate statistics are difficult to gather on bomb threats, attempts, and actual bombings. Organizations may not report threats. Police agencies may "play down incidents" to prevent copycat threats and bombings (Estenson, 1995: 120).

Here are basic strategies for protection against bomb threats and explosions:

1. Seek management support and prepare a plan and procedures.
2. Ensure that employees know what to ask if a bomb threat is made (Figure 13-8).
3. Establish criteria and procedures for evacuation. Post routes. The evacuation decision can be especially difficult for management because of safety concerns versus the thousands of dollars in productivity lost due to evacuation of large numbers of employees.
4. Recruit and train *all* employees to observe and report suspicious behavior, items, or vehicles. In addition, never approach or touch something suspicious.
5. Control parking and access according to the unique characteristics and requirements of the facility.
6. Control and verify outsiders (e.g., service personnel) prior to access.
7. Screen mail and deliveries. Route mail and deliveries to a specific location or building for screening instead of permitting direct access to employees (see Figure 13-9).
8. Maintain unpredictable patrols to avoid patterns that can be studied by offenders.
9. Inspect the exterior and interior of buildings.
10. Ensure that emergency plans, response teams (e.g., fire brigades), and public safety agencies are coordinated for action. What are the qualifications, experience, and response time of the nearest bomb squad?

Terrorism hoaxes, like bomb threats, are a serious problem for police and homeland security agencies and the private sector. Hoaxes result in an expensive drain on personnel and first responder resources, while hindering worker productivity during evacuations. Authorities

```
Date of Threat: _____

Time: _____    Number of minutes on telephone: ___

Exact words of caller: _____
_____
_____
_____
_____
_____
_____

Ask the caller these questions: _____
When will the bomb explode? _____
Where is bomb? _____
What type of bomb? _____
What does it look like? _____
Why did you place bomb? _____
_____

Description of caller's voice: Age: _____ Accent: _____
Sex: _____ Background noise: _____
Tone of voice: _____
Additional comments: _____
_____
Employee receiving call: _____ Telephone number: _____
```

FIGURE 13-8 Smith Corporation bomb threat form.

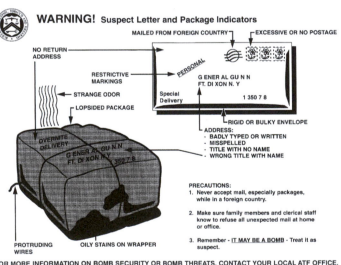

FIGURE 13-9 Suspect letter and package indicators.

must take threats seriously because it is difficult to distinguish between a real threat and a hoax. Disruption of our daily lives results when a threat is received and an evacuation and search is required at, say, a building, bridge, tunnel, or cruise ship. Congress has increased penalties to deter hoaxes, and judges can sentence offenders to prison for five years. Skilled investigators and their techniques and technology have produced positive results in apprehending offenders. For example, a "dirty bomb" threat was made against seven football stadiums on several Internet sites in October 2006. A grocery store clerk, named Jake Brahm of Wauwatosa, Wisconsin, was arrested. In another case, Jose Quinonez called into San Diego's 9-1-1 center in January 2005 and stated he had smuggled foreign chemists across the Mexican border and they were traveling to Boston with nuclear material. He was subsequently arrested (Hall, 2007).

Weapon of Mass Destruction (WMD)

A **weapon of mass destruction (WMD)** is something capable of inflicting mass casualties and/or destroying or rendering high-value assets as useless. Although chemical, biological, nuclear, and radiological weapons often serve as examples of WMD, many things can be used as a WMD. This became painfully true from the September 11, 2001, attacks when airliners, loaded with fuel, became missiles, killed thousands of people, leveled the 110-story Twin Towers of the World Trade Center, and hit the Pentagon. The range of potential WMD attacks depends on the creativity of the enemy. Examples include blowing up a train filled with toxic chemicals as it travels near a town while the wind is blowing toward the town; driving a fuel truck loaded with explosives into a corporate headquarters' underground garage; placing a radiological device, disguised as HVAC equipment, near the intake vents of a crowded building during its peak business hours; and attacking key electrical substations and high-voltage transmission lines to cause a cascade of power failures that disrupt almost all aspects of life, and then exploit the crisis by attacking other targets. The number of "soft" targets capable of being targeted is astounding. The threat of WMD and response are explained in Chapter 15.

Strikes

The direct and indirect costs of a strike are astronomical. Major losses include productivity, profits, employees and customers who never return, vandalism, additional loss prevention services, and legal fees.

The best defense for a strike is early preparation. When a labor contract is close to expiring, a strike is possible. A company that anticipates a strike should build up inventory and oversupply customers. Management should contact local law enforcement agencies to ensure that peace is maintained and property protected. Security is likely to focus on perimeter protection for the facility, the protection of key executives and their families, and evidence gathering. Both public police and security should work together to maintain order. Chapter 4 covers labor law and issues relevant to security.

Civil Disturbances

Demonstrations and precipitating incidents have evolved into destructive riots. Demon-strations are common as groups display their views. A typical precipitating incident is a public police arrest of a minority group member for a minor charge. Sometimes, all it takes for a crowd to go into a contagious frenzy is a rock thrown into the crowd. Deaths, injuries, and extensive property damage can result from a civil disturbance. Public police may not be able to contain rioters, and the private sector must be prepared for the worst. Summer months and high temperatures, when people gather out of doors, may precede a civil disturbance. Rumors also are dangerous. The social and political climate can be analyzed for possible predicting indicators.

Technological Emergencies

A technological emergency is the interruption of a vital service such as a utility (e.g., electric service blackout). These events have varied causes. A prolonged electric service blackout results in extreme hardship in communities. For businesses, it affects not only production, but also security and loss prevention measures. Without a source of electric power, alarms, CCTV, access control, electrically activated extinguishing systems, and other systems are useless. Secondary power sources (e.g., generators) should be in place for all vital services.

Natural Disasters

Windstorms

Hurricanes, typhoons, tornadoes, and cyclones are regionally specific names characterized by extremely violent and destructive winds. In the United States, the Atlantic and Gulf coasts are more susceptible to hurricanes, whereas tornadoes occur in many parts of the country. Loss prevention efforts should concentrate on studying local climate conditions and then preparing contingency plans. The following measures are useful:

1. Design buildings for maximum wind velocity expected.
2. Closely follow weather reports.
3. Close down business if necessary.
4. Establish a safe area for people.
5. Instruct people to stay away from windows.
6. Open doors and windows on the side of the building away from the storm. This will help to equalize pressure and prevent building collapse.
7. Acquire emergency power sources.
8. Set up a communications system.
9. Anchor and protect company property from being damaged or blown away.
10. Cooperate with local officials.
11. Take steps to hinder looting.

Floods

Lowlands along bodies of water are subject to flooding. Dams and dikes have reduced this problem, but flooding is still a threat to many locales. Some practical remedies are these:

1. Work with the U.S. Army Corps of Engineers, which provides assistance to those areas subject to frequent flooding.
2. Work with local officials to enhance safety and to hinder looting.
3. Provide a safe place for valuable assets.
4. Exit from the flood area in time to avoid being marooned. Secure adequate gasoline for vehicles.
5. If a team remains at a business site, ensure adequate supplies, such as food, blankets, a boat, life preservers, rope, communications equipment, first-aid kit, sandbags, and pumps.
6. Store valuable records, equipment, tools, and chemicals above the expected flood level. Shut off utilities.

Blizzards

Blizzards are snowstorms accompanied by high winds and very cold temperatures. Sufficient warning usually is obtained from weather forecasts. Injuries and deaths occur because people do not reach proper shelter. If a blizzard is forecast, employees should be sent home. Preplanning is essential if employees have a chance of being stranded at work. Food, bedding, a heat supply, radios, communications equipment, and televisions will aid those stranded.

Earthquakes

Stringent building codes and adequate building design in suspect areas (e.g., California) are vital for reduced losses. Building collapse, damage to bridges, and falling debris are major causes of injuries and deaths. If indoors, one should take cover in a basement or under reinforced floors or doorways. If outdoors, one should watch out for falling objects and electrical wires.

The December 2004 Sumatra-Andaman earthquake caused a series of tsunamis (i.e., large destructive waves) that killed almost 300,000 people and affected 18 countries around the Indian Ocean. The human and financial strain on nations to prepare and respond to such natural disasters is overwhelming (Figure 13-10). The challenges require global cooperation.

FIGURE 13-10 U.S. Navy helicopter arrives with supplies for tsunami survivors on Sumatra, Indonesia, in 2005. *Courtesy:* Jacob J. Kirk, USN.

International Perspective: The U.S. View of Hazards: Thoughts from Europe
Here is a critical thinking perspective of the U.S.-driven paradigm that social and technological approaches to mitigation can act, overall, to reduce the incidence or severity of disastrous events. Rockett (2001: 71–74) counters the U.S. paradigm by arguing that disasters are not the result of external forces, but rather the way we live our lives. Social, political, and economic forces are as much the cause of disasters as the natural environment. We already know where earthquakes, hurricanes, and flooding are likely to occur. Furthermore, we also know that many technologies (e.g., automobiles, which cause pollution) carry with them the power of mass disruption. Consequently, disaster reduction will result only from fundamental changes in political and social mores.

Rockett's viewpoint is illustrated when people, businesses, and organizations insist on congregating on a well-known tectonic fault when predictable earthquakes cause multibillion-dollar losses. Yes, we are speaking of Los Angeles as one example. However, this is a global problem. Other types of predictable disasters occur when, for example, a Yangtze or Bangladesh flood kills tens of thousands of people. Such hazards of the environment are impossible to eliminate, and continuing to have children and building in these areas load the costs of disasters.

What Rockett suggests is to change social structure, and not social reaction. "Progress in disaster reduction will occur when we accept that we are the creators of disaster rather than its victims." Rockett argues that as we build stronger structures and invent more efficient mitigation systems, we run the risk of engendering a false sense of safety and security that will, when the bigger event arrives, lead to an even greater catastrophe.

☐ ☐ ☐ ━━━

What is your opinion of Rockett's contentions?

━━━ ☐ ☐ ☐

Pandemics

A **pandemic** is an outbreak of an infectious disease that affects humans over a large geographic area. Pandemics have occurred throughout history, with many from zoonotic diseases resulting from the domestication of animals. **Zoonotic diseases** are diseases transmitted from animals to humans. Examples are the West Nile virus that can cause encephalitis, avian influenza, and human monkeypox. One type of avian influenza is the "bird flu" strain that is causing a great deal of concern worldwide.

Examples of pandemics occurring through history include the bubonic plague, also called the "Black Death," that killed about 20 million Europeans during the 1300s, seven cholera pandemics through the 1800s and 1900s, and numerous influenza pandemics. The 1918–1919 "Spanish flu" caused the highest number of known influenza deaths. Over 500,000 people died in the United States, and up to 50 million may have died worldwide. Many people died within the first few days of infection, and nearly half of those who died were young, healthy adults (Centers for Disease Control and Prevention, Department of Health and Human Services, 2006).

The CDC and the World Health Organization (WHO) have extensive surveillance programs to monitor and detect influenza activity worldwide. The CDC is involved in preparedness activities through vaccine development and production, stockpiling of medications, research, risk communications, and unified initiatives with other organizations.

A vaccine is unlikely to be available in the early stages of a pandemic. Scientists must select the virus strain that will provide the best protection. Then manufacturers use the strain to produce a vaccine. Antiviral medications are available, but they may not work because virus strains can become resistant to the medications.

According to the CDC, the severity of the next influenza pandemic cannot be predicted. Modeling studies suggest that the impact could be substantial. Between 15% and 35% of the U.S. population could be affected, and the economic impact could range between $71 and $166 billion (Centers for Disease Control and Prevention, Department of Health and Human Services, 2006).

Reissman et al. (2006: 2) write that pandemic influenza preparedness plans from the United States and WHO focus on (1) surveillance and early detection, (2) community containment (e.g., movement restrictions and facility closure), and (3) vaccines and antiviral medication. However, they note that "relatively little attention has been paid to identifying and managing psychological and social factors likely to influence human behavior during a pandemic." Examples are numerous and include how citizens will respond to containment, the need for healthcare and mental health services, and the impact on religious and cultural rituals surrounding burial and grieving.

Pandemics present numerous issues for businesses, besides homeland security and emergency management. *How will businesses function when large numbers of customers stay home and employees call in sick?*

A pandemic is likely to last longer than most emergencies and may include "waves" separated by months. The number of healthcare workers and first responders available to work may be reduced because of exposure and the need to care for ill family members. In addition, resources, vaccines, and medications in many locations could be limited (Centers for Disease Control and Prevention, Department of Health and Human Services, 2006).

During a pandemic, people who have had contact with symptomatic persons may be asked to voluntarily quarantine themselves. Those with and without symptoms may wear facemasks to control the spread of disease. Government may decide to close schools and other locations of mass gatherings. If a pandemic is particularly lethal, healthcare workers would implement corpse-management procedures to safely destroy infected human remains, and government would apply emergency powers to enforce measures such as rationing and curfews (Tucker, 2006).

A serious pandemic can result in **quarantine enforcement**. It is the use of government authorities, such as police, healthcare specialists, or the military, to restrict the movement of people, by force, if necessary, for purposes of public health and safety. Quarantine enforcement can create controversy over protection of public health versus civil liberties.

Employers should prepare plans for the risk of a pandemic. Here are ideas to begin a checklist.

- Prepare a business impact study.
- Support vaccination.
- Use infection control measures (e.g., cough etiquette, hand washing, facemasks, and sick leave).
- Cross-train so healthy employees can perform the duties of sick employees.
- Plan for teleworking.
- Maintain contact with customers through various technologies.

What do you think is the most serious potential emergency facing your community or organization? What protection methods do you recommend?

Search the Web
Here are Web sites relevant to this chapter:

American National Standards Institute: www.ansi.org
American Society for Testing and Materials: www.astm.org
Centers for Disease Control and Prevention: www.cdc.gov
Factory Mutual Global: www.fmglobal.com/
Federal Emergency Management Agency: www.fema.gov
Federal Register: http://fr.cos.com/
finding regulations: http://standards.gov/standards_gov/v/Regulations/index.cfm
finding standards: http://standards.gov/standards_gov/v/Standards/index.cfm
International Association of Chiefs of Police: www.theiacp.org
International Association of Fire Chiefs: www.iafc.org
International Association of Fire Fighters: www.iaff.org/
International Organization for Standardization: www.iso.org
National Association of Emergency Medical Technicians: www.naemt.org
National Fire Protection Association: www.nfpa.org
National Oceanic & Atmospheric Administration: www.noaa.gov/index.html
OSHA: www.osha.gov
Underwriters Laboratories (UL): www.ul.com
U.S. Department of Homeland Security: www.dhs.gov
U.S. Department of Transportation, Office of Hazardous Materials Safety: http://hazmat.dot.gov/
U.S. Fire Administration: www.usfa.dhs.gov/

Case Problems

13A. You are a loss prevention manager at company headquarters. Your superior tells you to design a fire protection program for a new window and door manufacturing plant. A lot of woodcutting with electric circular saws will take place at this plant.

Workers then will assemble the windows and doors using electric drills. A large stock of wood products will be stored in the plant. What will you recommend to the architects who will design the building? What are your fire prevention plans? What are your fire suppression plans?

13B. You are a loss prevention manager at an office building containing 800 employees. Your supervisor requests that you prepare criteria for evacuation of the building in case of a bomb threat. List criteria for management to consider and estimate the cost of a two-hour evacuation if the average employee earns $40,000 annually.

13C. As a corporate loss prevention manager, you have been assigned the task of designing a protection plan against windstorms for manufacturing plants located along the coast of Florida and those located in Kansas. What general plans do you have in mind?

References

Angle, J. (2005). *Occupational Safety and Health in the Emergency Services*, 2nd ed. Clifton Park, NY: Thomas Delmar.

Angle, J., et al. (2001). *Firefighting Strategies and Tactics*. Albany, NY: Delmar.

Azano, H., and Gilbertie, M. (2003). "Making Planning a Priority." *Security Management* (May).

Bangor, T., and Faust, J. (2001). "Basic Fire Protection Strategies." *Security Technology & Design*, 11 (April).

Breisch, S. (1989). "Is Your Workplace Fireproof?" *Safety and Health* (July).

Bureau of Justice Statistics. (2003). *Law Enforcement Statistics*. www.ojp.usdoj.gov/bjs, retrieved December 4, 2006.

Carter, W., et al. (2004). *Firefighter's Handbook: Essentials of Firefighting and Emergency Response*, 2nd ed. Clifton Park, NY: Thomas Delmar.

Cauchon, D., et al. (2003). "Just-Released Transcripts Give Voice to the Horror." *USA TODAY* (August 28). www.usatoday.com, retrieved August 29, 2003.

Centers for Disease Control and Prevention, Department of Health and Human Services. (2006). "Key Facts about Pandemic Influenza." www.cdc.gov/flu/pandemic/keyfacts.htm, retrieved January 24, 2006.

Conroy, M. (2006). "NFPA 10, 2007—What's New?" *NFPA Journal* (November/December). www.nfpa.org/publicJournalDetail.asp?categoryID=1340&itemID=30734&src=NFPAJournal, retrieved December 2, 2006.

Corley, W. (2004). "A Call for Balanced Fire Protection." *Buildings*, 98 (June).

Estenson, D. (1995). "Should Bomb Blasts Be Kept Quiet?" *Security Management* (November).

Gips, M. (2005). "The Challenge of Making Safer Structures." *Security Management*, 49 (March).

Hall, D. (2006). *Administrative Law: Bureaucracy in a Democracy*, 3rd ed. Upper Saddle River, NJ: Pearson Education.

Hall, M. (2007). "Terrorism Hoaxes Still Plaguing Law Agencies." *USA Today* (January 18). http://usatoday.com, retrieved January 19, 2007.

Houser, A., et al. (2004). *Emergency Responder Injuries and Fatalities*. Santa Monica, CA: RAND Corp.

International Code Council. (2004). "Resources Top Building Official Concerns." *Building Safety Bulletin*, II (July).

Jelenewicz, C. (2006). "Performance-Based Design." *Buildings*, 100 (May).

Moore, W. (1997). "Balancing Life Safety and Security Needs." *Security Technology and Design* (January-February).

National Institute of Standards and Technology. (2005). "Latest Findings from NIST World Trade Center Investigation." www.nist.gov, retrieved April 8, 2005.

Nolan, D. (2001). *Encyclopedia of Fire Prevention*. Albany, NY: Delmar.

Office of Justice Programs. (2000). *A Guide for Explosion and Bombing Scene Investigation*. Washington, D.C.: U.S. Department of Justice.

Quinley, K., and Schmidt, D. (2002). *Businesses at Risk: How to Assess, Mitigate, and Respond to Terrorist Threats*. Cincinnati, OH: The National Underwriter Co.

Reissman, D., et al. (2006). "Pandemic Influenza Preparedness: Adaptive Responses to an Evolving Challenge." *Journal of Homeland Security and Emergency Management*, 3.

Rockett, J. (2001). "The U.S. View of Hazards and Sustainable Development: A Few Thoughts from Europe." *Risk Management: An International Journal*, 3.

Schottke, D. (2007). *First Responder: Your First Response in Emergency Care*. Sudbury, MA: Jones and Bartlett.

Sternberg, E., and Lee, G. (2006). "Meeting the Challenge of Facility Protection for Homeland Security." *Journal of Homeland Security and Emergency Management*, 3.

Suttell, R. (2006). "Fire Protection System Design." *Buildings*, 100 (June).

Tucker, P. (2006). "Preparing for Pandemic." *The Futurist* (January-February).

U.S. Department of Homeland Security. (n.d.). "About First Responders." www.dhs.gov/dhspublic, retrieved February 11, 2005.

U.S. Department of Homeland Security. (2004). *National Response Plan*. www.dhs.gov, retrieved January 12, 2005.

U.S. Department of Homeland Security, READYBusiness. (n.d.). Testimonials. www.ready.gov/business/testimonials.html, retrieved January 3, 2005.

U.S. Fire Administration. (2004). "Danger Above: A Factsheet on High-Rise Safety." (November 23). http://usfa.fema.gov/safety/atrisk/high-rise/high-rise.shtm, retrieved April 4, 2005.

U.S. Fire Administration. (2005a). "Enhancing Risk Management Capabilities of Local Fire Departments." http://www.usfa.dhs.gov/about/media/2005releases/060705.shtm, retrieved November 10, 2006.

U.S. Fire Administration. (2005b). *Fire in the United States 1992–2001*, 13th ed. www.usfa.fema.gov/statistics/reports/pubs/fius13th.shtm, retrieved May 8, 2006.

U.S. Fire Administration. (2002). "Highrise Fires." www.usfa.dhs.gov/downloads/pdf/tfrs/v2i18.pdf, retrieved November 10, 2006.

U.S. Fire Administration. (2006). "The Overall Fire Picture, 2005." www.usfa.dhs.gov/statistics/quickstats/, retrieved November 10, 2006.

Zunkel, D. (2000). "Delayed Egress Magnetic Locks Are a Technology Standard." *Security Technology & Design*, 10 (February).

14
Safety in the Workplace

Objectives

After studying this chapter, the reader will be able to:

1. Explain the importance of safety.
2. Discuss the history of safety legislation and workers' compensation.
3. Explain OSHA's development, goals, jurisdiction, standards, recordkeeping requirements, and inspections.
4. Describe at least four strategies for improving safety in the workplace.

KEY TERMS
<table><tr><td>• safety in the workplace • safety • accident • injury • workers' compensation laws • Occupational Safety and Health Administration (OSHA) • William Steiger Occupational Safety and Health Act of 1970 • National Institute for Occupational Safety and Health (NIOSH) • hazard communication standard</td><td>• Globally Harmonized System of Classification and Labeling of Chemicals • Hazardous Waste Operations and Emergency Response Standard • bloodborne pathogens standard • lockout/tagout • OSHA Whistleblower Program • willful violation • serious violation • accident proneness theory • safety performance assessment</td></tr></table>

Introduction

Safety in the workplace is a broad concept that includes a host of methods that aim to reduce risks from a variety of threats and hazards to the workplace such as accidents, violence, and natural disasters. This chapter focuses on workplace accidents and related safety methods.

Safety is a major loss prevention measure to reduce the likelihood of accidents and injuries. When accidents and injuries occur, both losses and a drain on profits inevitably result. Webster's *New Collegiate Dictionary* defines **safety** as "the condition of being safe from undergoing or causing hurt, injury, or loss" and "to protect against failure, breakage, or accident." **Accident** is "an unfortunate event resulting from carelessness, unawareness, ignorance, or a combination of causes." **Injury** is "hurt, damage, or loss sustained."

Examples of hazards in the workplace are as follows:

- Inadequate training (Figure 14-1)
- Noncompliance with safety policies and procedures
- Failure to use safety devices or equipment
- Dangerous storage of toxic or flammable substances
- Poorly supported ladders and scaffold
- Electrical malfunctions
- Blocked aisles, exits, and stairways
- Poor ventilation
- Insufficient lighting
- Excessive noise
- Horseplay; running

Accident Statistics and Costs

Since the early 1900s, great strides have been made to increase safety in the workplace. Safer machines, improved supervision, and training all have helped to prevent accidents. If one were to apply the industrial fatality rate that existed in 1910 to the present workforce in the United States, more than 1.3 million workers would lose their lives each year from industrial accidents. In the past, a manual worker's welfare was of minimal concern to management; the loss of life or limb was "part of the job" and "a normal business risk." In the construction of tall buildings, it was expected that one life would be lost for each floor. A 20-story building would yield 20 lost lives. During tunnel construction, two worker deaths per mile was the norm. Coal mining experienced exceedingly high death rates (Anderson, 1975: 5–6).

As written in Chapter 2, the Occupational Safety & Health Administration (2006a) reported 4.4 million injuries and illnesses among private sector firms in 2003, with about 32% of work-related injuries occurring in goods-producing industries and 68% in services. The same year recorded 5,559 worker deaths, including 114 additional deaths from the previous year among self-employed workers and 61 more from workplace violence. The National Center for Injury Prevention and Control (2006) reported that society-wide there are about 160,000 deaths each year from injuries and millions more are injured and survive. In 2000, the 50 million injuries that required medical treatment will ultimately cost $406 billion, including $80.2 billion in medical care costs and $326 billion in productivity losses.

Direct and indirect losses are costly; for example, the death of a worker in a manufacturing plant immediately creates a tremendous direct loss to family and friends. Direct losses also involve an immediate loss of productivity, medical costs, and insurance administration. Indirect costs include continued grief by family and friends, continued loss of productivity, profit loss, selection and training of a new employee, overtime for lost production, and possible litigation. In addition, internal and external relations may suffer. The lowering of employee morale can result from the belief that management is incompetent or does not care. Rumors frequently follow. In the eyes of the community, the company may appear to have failed.

History of Safety Legislation

In 18th century England, as the Industrial Revolution progressed, a number of statutes governing working conditions were passed. One of the first statutes for safety resulted from a serious outbreak of fever at cotton mills near Manchester in 1784. Because child labor was involved, widespread attention added to public concern and government pressure to improve the dangerous and unsanitary conditions in factories. A few years later, additional legislation dealt with hours, conditions of labor, prevention of injury, and government inspectors. In 1842, the *Mines Act* provided for punitive compensation for preventable injuries caused by unguarded mining machinery. Subsequent to this law, a series of mining accidents caused more laws to be passed for miner safety. During this time, "strong evidence" pointed to incompetent management and

U.S. Department of Labor
Occupational Safety & Health Administration

www.osha.gov   MyOSHA   Search   GO Advanced Search

ACCIDENT SUMMARY No. 15

Accident Type:	Crushed by Dump Truck Body
Weather Conditions:	Clear, Warm
Type of Operation:	General Contractor
Size of Work Crew :	N/ A
Collective Bargaining	Yes
Competent Safety Monitor on Site:	Yes
Safety and Health Program in Effect:	Yes
Was the Worksite Inspected Regularly:	Yes
Training and Education Provided:	No
Employee Job Title:	Truck Driver
Age & Sex:	25-Male
Experience at this Type of Work:	2 Months
Time on Project:	2 Weeks at Site

BRIEF DESCRIPTION OF ACCIDENT

A truck driver was crushed and killed between the frame and dump box of a dump truck. Apparently a safety "overtravel" cable attached between the truck frame and the dump box malfunctioned by catching on a protruding nut of an air brake cylinder. This prevented the dump box from being fully raised, halting its progress at a point where about 20 inches of space remained between it and the truck frame. The employee, apparently assuming that releasing the cable would allow the dump box to continue up-ward, reached between the rear dual wheels and over the frame, and disengaged the cable with his right hand. The dump box then dropped suddenly, crushing his head. The employee had not received training or instruction in proper operating procedures and was not made aware of all potential hazards in his work.

INSPECTION RESULTS

Following its inspection, OSHA issued one citation for one alleged serious violation of its construction standards. Had the required training been provided to the employee, this fatality might have been prevented.

ACCIDENT PREVENTION RECOMMENDATIONS

Employees must be instructed to recognize and avoid unsafe conditions associated with their work (29 CFT 1926.21 (b)(2)).

SOURCES OF HELP

- Construction Safety and Health Standards (OSHA 2207) which contains all OSHA job safety and health rules and regulations (1926 and 1910) covering construction. OSHA-funded free consultation services.
- Consult your telephone directory for the number of your local OSHA area or regional office for further assistance and advice (listed under U.S. Labor Department or under the state government section where states administer their own OSHA programs).

NOTE: The case here described was selected as being representative of fatalities caused by improper work practices. No special emphasis or priority is implied nor is the cases necessarily a recent occurrence. The legal aspects of the incident have been resolved, and the case is now closed.

FIGURE 14-1 Accident Report, Crushed by Dump Truck Body. *Courtesy:* OSHA.

the neglect of safety rules. Laws relating to factory safety also were expanded. More and more trades were brought under the scope of the law.

In the United States, textile factories increased in number between 1820 and 1840. Massachusetts, first of the United States to follow England's example, passed laws in 1876 and 1877 that related to working children and inspection of factories. Important features pertained to dangerous machinery and necessary safety guards. As years passed, some industries increasingly realized that hazards were potentially harmful to workers, production, and profits. Consequently, more and more industrialists became safety conscious. However, serious hazards still existed in the workplace through the 20th century (Grimaldi and Simmonds, 1975: 33–43).

Workers' Compensation

Increasing concern for workers led to **workers' compensation laws**. In essence, these laws require employers to compensate injured employees. England passed such laws in 1897, and the United States followed in 1902, when Maryland passed this country's first workers' compensation law—although, essentially, the Maryland law was so restrictive that it was almost useless. In 1911, Wisconsin passed the first effective workers' compensation law. Seven other states passed similar legislation during that year. Amid controversy between businesspeople and groups interested in the welfare of laborers, the Supreme Court upheld the constitutionality of these laws in 1916. Businesspeople argued that they could never bear such compensation costs nor could they control accidents. They predicted that the cost of goods would rise considerably. Those who favored workers' compensation laws believed that these laws would provide the impetus for greater safety, because business owners and managers would want to control losses.

Workers' compensation laws provided insurance companies with a new opportunity. As states enacted these laws, business owners became concerned about their ability to pay for workers' compensation. Therefore, insurance companies sold casualty insurance policies to businesses that needed the security from a possible workers' compensation burden. *A concurrent benefit of such insurance was that insurance companies were willing to reduce premiums if a company instituted accident prevention measures.* To remain competitive, insurance companies provided safety specialists who would survey a business and recommend prevention strategies (e.g., safeguards on machines). Businesspeople became increasingly interested in safety; insurance companies developed safety expertise.

Today, all states have workers' compensation laws. These laws vary from state to state, but each requires the reporting of injures that are compensable. Private insurance companies insure most employers for workers' compensation judgments. Other employers are self-insured (insurance provided by the employer and not purchased through a private insurance company; it is regulated by a state insurance commissioner) or place this insurance with state insurance funds. When an employee is injured, medical benefits usually are granted, and benefits for wages lost are granted when an employee is incapacitated and cannot work.

The workers' compensation system of today has its problems. Because dealings with the insurance industry are frequently adversarial, injured employees often believe that the system helps them only when they obtain the services of an attorney. Insurers, on the other hand, claim that they must protect their interests and that fraud (i.e., worker malingering) is a very serious problem.

☐ ☐ ☐ ▬▬▬▬▬▬▬▬▬▬▬▬▬▬▬▬▬▬▬▬▬▬▬▬

Are workers' compensation laws necessary today? Support your viewpoint.

▬▬▬▬▬▬▬▬▬▬▬▬▬▬▬▬▬▬▬▬▬▬▬▬ ☐ ☐ ☐

The Development of OSHA

With the advent of improved safety conditions, accidents and injuries declined until the 1950s. In the late 1950s, rates leveled off until the late 1960s, when accidents and injuries began to increase. This upward turn caused the federal government to become increasingly concerned about safety. Several safety-related laws were passed during the 1960s, but none was as monumental as the federal law creating OSHA. OSHA stands for the **Occupational Safety and Health Administration**, a federal agency, under the U.S. Department of Labor, established to administer the law on safety and health resulting from the **William Steiger Occupational Safety and Health Act of 1970**. This federal legislation was signed into law by then-president Richard Nixon and became effective on April 28, 1971. The basic purpose of the OSHA legislation was to provide a safe working environment for employees engaged in a variety of occupations.

The OSHA act was significant because it was the first national safety legislation applying to every business connected with interstate commerce. Mason (1976: 21) notes: "The need for such legislation was clear. Between 1969 and 1973 [in the United States] more persons were killed at work than in the Vietnam war."

The Secretary of Labor via ten regional offices administers OSHA. The secretary has the authority and responsibility to establish occupational safety and health standards. Workplace inspections can result in citations issued to employers who violate standards (Occupational Safety and Health Administration, 2006b: 15).

The **National Institute for Occupational Safety and Health** (NIOSH) performs numerous functions that aid OSHA and those striving for worker safety. These functions relate to research, the development of criteria and standards for occupational safety and health, training OSHA personnel and others (e.g., employers and employees), and providing publications dealing with both toxic substances and strategies on how to prevent occupational injuries and illnesses. NIOSH is under the Centers for Disease Control and Prevention (CDC), U.S. Department of Health and Human Services.

Occupational Safety and Health Administration

OSHA's Strategic Management Plan

The OSHA act of 1970 states that it is "to assure so far as possible every working man and woman in the Nation safe and healthful working conditions and to preserve our human resources." OSHA's 2003–2008 strategic management plan contains three overarching goals (Occupational Safety and Health Administration, 2003a):

- Reduce occupational hazards through direct intervention (e.g., consultation)
- Promote a safety and health culture through compliance assistance, cooperative programs and strong leadership
- Maximize OSHA's effectiveness and efficiency by strengthening its capabilities and infrastructure

"OSHA's strategic management plan also covers issues not traditionally addressed by the agency but that account for many work-related injuries, illnesses and deaths, such as workplace violence and work-related motor vehicle accidents. OSHA intends to use a variety of cooperative programs and outreach efforts to assist employers and employees in addressing these problems. In addition, the agency will focus on emergency preparedness, helping workplaces get ready to respond to workplace emergencies such as natural disasters or terrorist attacks."

The Act's Jurisdiction

OSHA rules extend to all employers and their employees in the 50 states, the District of Colombia, Puerto Rico, and other U.S. possessions. An employer is anyone who maintains employees and engages in a business affecting commerce. This broad coverage involves a multitude of fields: manufacturing, construction, agriculture, warehousing, retailing, longshoring, education, and so on. The act does not cover self-employed persons, family-owned and operated farms, and workplaces protected by other federal agencies. Although federal agencies are not covered by OSHA, agencies are required to maintain a safe working environment equal to those groups under OSHA's jurisdiction. OSHA affects state and local government employees (Occupational Safety and Health Administration, 2006b: 6–7).

OSHA Standards

OSHA promulgates legally enforceable standards to protect employees in the workplace. *Since OSHA standards are constantly being updated and reviewed, it is the employer's responsibility to keep up-to-date.* Two sources for standards and changes are the Web sites of OSHA and the *Federal Register*.

There are actually thousands of OSHA standards. Some pertain to specific industries and workers, whereas others are general and practiced by most industries. Examples include safety requirements for machines, equipment, and employees, such as requiring face shields or safety glasses during the use of certain machines; prevention of electrical hazards (Figure 14-2); adequate fire protection; adequate lunchrooms, lavatories, and drinking water; precautions against infectious diseases; and monitoring of employee exposure to chemical or toxic hazards.

The following standards demonstrate OSHA's concern for worker safety and health.

Subpart 1—Personal Protective Equipment
1910.132 General requirements.
(a) Application. Protective equipment, including personal protective equipment for eyes, face, head, and extremities, protective clothing, respiratory devices, and protective shields and barriers, shall be provided, used, and maintained in a sanitary and reliable condition wherever it is necessary by reason of hazards of processes or environment, chemical hazards, radiological hazards, or mechanical irritants encountered in a manner capable of causing injury or impairment in the function of any part of the body through absorption, inhalation or physical contact.

Subpart K—Medical and First Aid
1910.151 Medical services and first aid.
(a) The employer shall ensure the ready availability of medical personnel for advice and consultation of matters of plant health.
(b) In the absence of an infirmary, clinic, or hospital in near proximity to the workplace which is used for the treatment of all injured employees, a person or persons shall be adequately trained to render first aid. Adequate first aid supplies shall be readily available.
(c) Where the eyes or body of any person may be exposed to injurious corrosive materials, suitable facilities for quick drenching or flushing of the eyes and body shall be provided within the work area for immediate emergency use.

OSHA Hazard Communication Standard
The Hazard Communication Standard (1910.1200) covers over 7 million workplaces, more than 100 million employees, and some 945,000 hazardous chemical products, with hundreds of new ones being introduced annually. The **Hazard Communication Standard** (HCS), also known as a "right to know law," requires all employers who have employees who may be exposed to hazardous substances on the job to inform them about such substances and how to deal with them. Employers are required to write and implement a hazard communication program, conduct a chemical inventory, ensure that a *Material Safety Data Sheet* (MSDS) is available for each chemical, label chemical containers, and train employees on the safe use of chemicals (e.g., protective equipment, procedures). The information shared under the HCS requirements provides the foundation for a chemical safety and health program in the workplace (Occupational Safety & Health Administration, 2006c).

OSHA is involved in the development of the **Globally Harmonized System of Classification and Labeling of Chemicals** (GHS). It includes uniform provisions for classification of chemicals, labels, and safety data sheets. The GHS has been adopted by the United Nations and an international goal is to recruit as many countries as possible to participate in the GHS (Occupational Safety & Health Administration, 2006c).

U.S. Department of Labor
Occupational Safety & Health Administration

www.osha.gov MyOSHA Search [GO] Advanced Search | /

ACCIDENT REPORT

ACCIDENT SUMMARY No. 57

Accident Type:	Electrocution
Weather Conditions:	Clear/Hot/Humid
Type of Operation:	Window Shutter Installers
Size of Work Crew:	2
Collective Bargaining	N/A
Competent Safety Monitor on Site:	No
Safety and Health Program in Effect:	Partial
Was the Worksite Inspected Regularly:	No
Training and Education Provided:	Some
Employee Job Title:	Helper
Age & Sex:	17-Male
Experience at this Type of Work:	One Month
Time on Project:	One Month

BRIEF DESCRIPTION OF ACCIDENT

One employee was climbing a metal ladder to hand an electric drill to the journeyman installer on a scaffold about five feet above him. When the victim reached the third rung from the bottom of the ladder he received an electric shock that killed him.

The investigation revealed that the extension cord had a missing grounding prong and that a conductor on the green grounding wire was making intermittent contact with the energizing black wire thereby energizing the entire length of the grounding wire and the drill's frame. The drill was not double insulated.

INSPECTION RESULTS

As a result of its investigation, OSHA issued citations for violations of construction standards.

ACCIDENT PREVENTION RECOMMENDATIONS

1. Use approved ground fault circuit interrupters or an assured equipment grounding conductor program to protect employees on construction sites [29 CFR 1926.404(b)(1)].
2. Use equipment that provides a permanent and continuous path from circuits, equipment, structures, conduit or enclosures to ground [29 CFR 1926.404(d)(6)].
3. Inspect electrical tools and equipment daily and remove damaged or defective equipment from use until it is repaired [29 CFR 1926.404(b)(iii)(c)].

SOURCES OF HELP

- OSHA General Industry Standards [CFR parts 1900-1910] and OSHA Construction Standards [CFR Part 1926] which together include all OSHA job safety and health rules and regulations covering construction.
- OSHA-funded free consultation services listed in telephone directories under U.S. Labor Department or under the state government section where states administer their own OSHA programs.
- OSHA Safety and Health Training Guidelines for Construction (Available from the National Technical Information Service, 5285 Port Royal Road, Springfield, VA 22161; 703/487-4650; Order No. PB-239-312/AS): a set of 15 guidelines to help construction employers establish a training program in the safe use of equipment, tools, and machinery on the job.
- Courses in construction safety are offered by the OSHA Training Institute, 1555 Times Drive, Des Plaines, IL 60018, 708/297-4810.

NOTE: The case here described was selected as being representative of fatalities caused by improper work practices. No special emphasis or priority is implied nor is the case necessarily a recent occurrence. The legal aspects of the incident have been resolved, and the case is now closed.

FIGURE 14-2 Accident Report, Electrocution. *Courtesy:* OSHA.

OSHA HAZWOPER Standard

The **Hazardous Waste Operations and Emergency Response Standard (HAZWOPER)** (1910.120 and 1926.65) applies to a variety of public and private employers and employees engaged in operations that include clean-up of hazardous substances required by a government body; voluntary clean-up operations at hazardous waste sites; operations involving hazardous wastes that are conducted at treatment, storage, and disposal facilities; and emergency response operations related to hazardous substances. Training is essential to comply with this standard. It must focus on the duties employees perform without endangering themselves or others. The planning of training must also include consideration of hazards to the community and what capabilities personnel need to respond to the hazards, including a worst-case scenario. Training and equipment may include first responder capabilities and use of PPE (Occupational Safety & Health Administration, 2006d). These issues are serious, as illustrated by the multi-billion dollar lawsuits filed by New York City firefighters who claimed lung damage due to inadequate PPE during their response to the collapse of the Twin Towers. One further note is that hazmat events are regulated by not only OSHA, but also the Environmental Protection Agency (EPA).

OSHA Bloodborne Pathogens Standard

The **bloodborne pathogens standard** (1910.1030) limits exposure to blood and other potentially infectious materials, which could lead to disease or death. The standard covers all employees facing potential exposure. Employers are required to establish an exposure control plan covering safety procedures, protective equipment, and the control of waste. The hepatitis B vaccination is to be made available to all employees who have occupational exposure to blood. Postexposure evaluation and follow-up is to be made available to all employees who have had an exposure incident, including laboratory tests at no cost to the employee. Exposure records must be confidential and kept for the duration of employment plus 30 years. Training is required on all aspects of this standard, and the training records must be maintained for three years (Occupational Safety & Health Administration, 2006e).

Lockout/ Tagout

OSHA standard 1910.147 is designed to control hazardous energy. Better known as **lockout/ tagout,** the aim is to prevent the accidental startup of machines or other equipment during maintenance and servicing. The rule requires that hazardous energy sources must be isolated and rendered inoperative before work can begin. Elements of a lockout/tagout program are written procedures, training, and audits (Occupational Safety & Health Administration, 2006f).

Examples of OSHA citations involving this standard include Lifetime Doors, for 37 alleged violations after employees suffered finger amputations at the door manufacturing plant. OSHA proposed penalties of $1.1 million. In another case, an employee of Hanna Paper Recycling entered a baler to dislodge a jammed cardboard bale and was crushed to death between the bale and the gathering ram. OSHA cited Hanna for 19 alleged violations and proposed penalties of $59,200 ("Lockout/Tagout," 2001: 17).

OSHA Recordkeeping and Reporting

Before the development of OSHA's centralized recordkeeping system, workplace statistics on injuries and illnesses were kept by some states and private organizations. No uniform, standardized system existed. Today, with the help of OSHA's comprehensive statistics, it is easier to pinpoint serious hazards and work toward improvements. In addition, employee awareness and safety precautions are enhanced through knowledge about injuries, illnesses, and hazards.

In 2006, the OSHA Web site offered the following guideline for recordkeeping. All employers covered by the OSHA act must report to OSHA any incident on the premises resulting in a fatality or the in-patient hospitalization of three or more employees within 8 hours. The *Log of Work-Related Injuries and Illnesses* (Form 300) is used to list injuries and illnesses and track days away from work, restrictions, or transfers. The *Injury and Illness*

Report (Form 301) serves to record supplementary information about cases; a workers' compensation or insurance form can be used as an alternative document if it contains the same information. The *Summary* (Form 300A) shows totals for the year in each category. The employer is responsible for keeping the records up-to-date and available to OSHA inspectors. Employers with 10 or fewer employees, or those employers classified in a low-hazard industry (e.g., insurance or real estate), do not have to keep injury and illness records unless informed to do so by OSHA or the Bureau of Labor Statistics (Occupational Safety & Health Administration, 2001).

□ □ □ ▬▬▬▬▬▬▬▬▬▬▬▬▬▬▬▬▬▬▬▬▬▬▬▬▬▬▬▬▬▬▬▬

Confined Area Entry

Hazards that are not easily seen, smelled, or felt can be deadly risks to people who work in confined areas. For instance, storage tanks may reduce oxygen or leak combustible or toxic gases. The cardinal rule for entry into a confined area is, "Never trust your senses!" A harmless-looking situation may indeed be a potential threat. Some of the deadliest gases and vapors have no odor. Before entry, the following safety strategies are recommended: proper training, equipment to identify hazards, and an entry permit issued by a safety specialist. Schroll (2006: 44) emphasizes the importance of equipment. He writes that personnel should be able to select appropriate monitoring equipment and know how to use it. He also refers to personal protective equipment (PPE), especially respiratory protection. In addition, personnel should know the operation of harnesses and retrieval devices. OSHA's standard for confined spaces, Title 29 Code of Federal Regulations (CFR), Part 1910.146, contains the requirements for practices and procedures to protect employees from the hazards of entry into permit-required confined spaces.

In the petroleum industry, for example, a storage tank had been rinsed and vented for several days. When it was checked with gas detection equipment, no flammable gases were measured. However, after workers removed loose rust, scale, and sediment, the percentage of flammable gas rose, and the gas ignited.

As another example, two employees of a fertilizer company descended into an old 35-foot well to repair a pump. The well was covered with a concrete slab and entry was made through a covered manhole. About 6 feet below the opening was a plank platform. When the first worker dropped to the platform, he was immediately overcome and fell unconscious into the water below. His partner sought help quickly. When two helpers entered the well, they, too, fell unconscious into the water below. A passerby, in an attempt to save the drowning men, jumped into the water and drowned also. By this time, the fire department had arrived. The fire chief, wearing a self-contained breathing apparatus, went to rescue the victims. On the platform, he removed his facemask to give instructions to those above and was overcome. Subsequent tests revealed that the well atmosphere contained a lethal concentration of hydrogen sulfide. Five men died from pulmonary paralysis (Chacanaca, 1996: 61–65).

□ □ □ ▬▬▬▬▬▬▬▬▬▬▬▬▬▬▬▬▬▬▬▬▬▬▬▬▬▬▬▬▬▬▬▬

What would you say and do if your supervisor ordered you to enter a confined area without first taking safety precautions?

▬▬▬▬▬▬▬▬▬▬▬▬▬▬▬▬▬▬▬▬▬▬▬▬▬▬▬▬▬▬▬▬ □ □ □

Additional Employer Responsibilities

An employer is required to post specific OSHA-related material for employee review. The OSHA poster "Job Safety and Health Protection" informs employees about their rights and responsibilities and must be displayed in an appropriate location for employees. Copies of the OSHA act and relevant rules and regulations must be available if requested by employees.

If an employer receives a Citation and Notification of Penalty, the employer must post the citation, or a copy, near the place where each violation occurred to inform employees of hazards. The citation must remain posted for three working days or until the violation is corrected, whichever is longer. These requirements are mandatory even if the citation is contested (Occupational Safety and Health Administration, 2005a: 7).

The **OSHA Whistleblower Program** helps to ensure that employees are free to report safety and health violations. The OSHA act prohibits any person from discharging, retaliating, or discriminating against any employee because the employee exercised rights under the Act (Occupational Safety & Health Administration, 2006b: 16).

OSHA Inspections

An important priority of OSHA compliance inspectors was to view the workplace as it functions on a typical day. To attain this goal and to prevent an employer from altering typical workplace characteristics by concealing unsafe conditions, inspections frequently were made unannounced. However, only a few years after this practice began, it was challenged in the courts. In 1975, the president of a utility installation company, who posted a copy of the Bill of Rights on his office wall, sued while claiming that the Fourth Amendment restricts warrantless searches. The federal appellate court upheld the employer's contention. The case was appealed, and in May 1978 the Supreme Court, in *Marshall v. Barlow*, ruled that the Fourth Amendment protection against unreasonable searches protects commercial establishments as well as private homes. Therefore, OSHA inspectors must obtain a warrant before making an inspection, unless employers consent. Such a warrant is to be based on administrative probable cause: the inspector is required to show a judicial officer that the inspection is part of OSHA's general administrative plan to enforce safety and health laws, or upon evidence of a violation (Hall, 2006: 146–151; Dreux, 1995: 53).

When an inspection takes place, the employer and even employee representatives may join the inspector. The inspector is obligated to show credentials that contain a photograph and serial number. The number can be verified via the nearest OSHA office. Typically, machinery, equipment, and other workplace characteristics are examined. The inspector can interview the employer and employees in public or in private. Any interference with the inspector's duties can result in stiff penalties. The employer is wise to document the inspection and comments by the inspector through note taking. This information may become useful if a disagreement or a dispute of a citation or penalty evolves.

Because millions of workplaces are subject to inspections, OSHA has established priorities. Obviously, workplaces with serious accidents will be subject to inspections.

During the 2005–2006 fiscal year, OSHA targeted about 4,400 high-hazard worksites for unannounced comprehensive inspections. This site-specific inspection program was based on a survey of injuries and illnesses from approximately 80,000 employers. OSHA also inspected some establishments that did not respond to the survey and 400 workplaces that reported low injury and illness rates to review the actual degree of compliance with OSHA requirements (Occupational Safety and Health Administration, Office of Communications, 2005).

OSHA has a staff of about 2,300, including 1,300 compliance safety and health officers. Twenty-six states operate their own OSHA State Programs with about 3,000 state employees, including 1,300 compliance safety and health officers. Federal OSHA conducts about 38,000 inspections each fiscal year. The state programs conduct about 58,000 inspections each fiscal year (Occupational Safety and Health Administration, 2003b).

The National Federation of Independent Business recommends the following strategies during an OSHA inspection (Gaudio, 2005):

- *Manage the inspection process to minimize operational disruptions;*
- *Control the flow of information to OSHA so that when the inspection has ended, the employer understands the significance of the evidence OSHA has gathered;*
- *Present the worksite in the best possible light; and*

- *Be proactive by addressing OSHA's compliance concerns during the inspection so OSHA does not issue citations.*

As expected, the atmosphere at the worksite might be chaotic and an OSHA inspector can receive conflicting information from different sources. Thus, an employer should designate one principal contact person to act as OSHA's main contact during every inspection to control the flow of information.

By understanding OSHA's concerns early in the inspection process, the employer can provide information that refutes OSHA's factual findings or interpretation of the OSHA standard or regulations. This information may ultimately convince OSHA not to issue citations or at least to minimize penalties.

Each inspection is different, so the need for counsel will depend on individual circumstances. On one hand, a routine inspection that does not stem from a significant injury or fatality may be handled without an attorney. On the other hand, an employer is strongly advised to have counsel directly involved during an OSHA inspection when a major accident or event such as a catastrophic accident, serious injury or employee fatality has occurred. If the inspection results from a fatality or serious injuries and/or you decide that you would like a lawyer during the inspection process, the compliance officer will typically delay for a short period. The best strategy is often to allow OSHA to perform the walk-around inspection and review documents and then to have an attorney present later in the inspection when OSHA wants to begin interviews.

OSHA Fines Two Businesses

The following information is from news releases that describe OSHA investigations and fines.

OSHA National News Release 06–1961–NAT (Occupational Safety and Health Administration, Office of Communications, 2006):

> *OSHA cited Thomas Industrial Coatings Inc. of Pevely, Mo., for 33 willful, including "instance-by-instance" willful [i.e., each violation of a standard], and eight serious alleged violations of job safety and health standards. Proposed penalties total $2,362,500. OSHA's citations resulted from the investigation of two fatal workplace accidents within two months involving the painting contractor. Both accidents occurred at the same bridge painting worksite in Kansas City and the same suspended scaffold. One employee died when he fell through a hole in the platform while he was painting. The other employee fell to his death while dismantling the scaffold. The instance-by-instance willful violations alleged the lack of fall protection and training for employees, especially in the use of fall protection and the safe dismantling of the scaffold. The single willful citations alleged the lack of safe scaffold access; that a qualified person did not design the scaffold; and that there were no competent persons to supervise the work. The citations also alleged the employer failed to inspect the scaffold and its components and to secure the suspension cables properly. The serious citations addressed other unsafe practices including the employer's permitting debris that employees could trip over in front of the large platform holes and overloading the personnel lift.*

OSHA Regional News Release, OSHA-06–1937–DAL (U.S. Department of Labor, Office of Public Affairs, 2006):

> *A Wynnewood [OK] employer's alleged failure to protect employees from safety and health hazards has resulted in citations for 22*

alleged violations of standards from the U.S. Department of Labor's Occupational Safety and Health Administration (OSHA). Proposed penalties total $154,800. Wynnewood Refining Co. was cited following an initial inspection that began May 9 and again on May 12 following a fire and explosion at the refinery plant in Wynnewood. The facility, which produces gasoline, propane, propylene, butane, fuel oils, asphalts, distillates and solvents, is a subsidiary of Gary-Williams Energy Corp. based in Denver. There are about 184 employees at the Wynnewood site. The willful violation was for failing to properly maintain processing equipment relating to the operation of the hydrofluoric acid alkylation unit when it was evident that flare line leaks were occurring, exposing employees to hydrocarbons and hydrofluoric acid. A **willful violation** *is issued for intentional disregard of or plain indifference to the OSHA law and regulations. Serious violations include failure to provide required fall protection, properly maintain electrical equipment, provide adequate respiratory protection and provide the required machine guarding. A* **serious violation** *is one in which there is a substantial probability that death or serious physical harm could result from a hazardous condition about which the employer knew or should have known. One other-than-serious citation was issued for failing to maintain required employee injury and illness recordkeeping.*

For cases as above, the employer has 15 working days from receipt of the citations and proposed penalties to comply and pay the penalties, to request and participate in an informal conference with the OSHA area director, or to contest the citations before the independent Occupational Safety and Health Review Commission.

OSHA: Criticism and Controversy

Through the years since its inception, OSHA has been the target of considerable criticism and controversy. Most of the OSHA battles have taken place on Capitol Hill, when different interest groups pressure legislators either to maintain and expand OSHA or to reduce or eliminate it. The forces in favor of OSHA are primarily OSHA itself, the AFL-CIO labor organization, and select legislators. Those opposed to OSHA consist mainly of businesspeople, business organizations, and select legislators. Some say the controversy essentially is between "big labor" and "big business."

The main arguments against OSHA are the following:

1. "Regulatory overkill" is a major theme of those against OSHA. Many business organizations believe that OSHA has gone beyond what is necessary for fostering a safe and healthy workplace. Businesspeople and employers often rate OSHA as the prime example of excessive government regulation; they state that the agency's overzealous inspectors afflict employers with rules.
2. OSHA is not cost effective. It provides limited benefits.
3. The costs of OSHA, reduced productivity, lost jobs, and higher prices for goods add to inflation and are a threat to companies' competitive position.
4. OSHA and other government bureaucrats, who are appointed rather than elected and thus are not accountable to the people, are making decisions that businesspeople should be making for themselves.
5. OSHA has had an impact on the labor-management process that has compounded labor troubles. Many unions have become involved in worker safety and employees' rights under OSHA to the point where productivity is hindered.
6. Numerous employers have become paranoid due to adverse publicity and labor disputes arising from unnecessary OSHA citations.

The major arguments in favor of OSHA are these:

1. OSHA is essential to reinforce a safe and healthy workplace for employees.
2. Many deaths and injuries have been prevented because of OSHA.
3. In today's technologically complex business world, employees need protection that only government regulation can provide.
4. Employers who oppose OSHA are too interested in the costs of safety and health, and in productivity and profits, and they are not concerned enough about employees.
5. There are employers who have a favorable attitude toward OSHA and benefit from its existence. These employers actively work with OSHA in a joint effort to prevent and reduce safety and health problems. To these businesspeople, OSHA compliance is cost effective.

Assistance with Problems

There are many sources of assistance for employers concerned about workplace safety or health problems:

1. Many insurance companies provide specialists who visit, inspect, and recommend stategies for preventing and eliminating hazards at client workplaces.
2. Trade associations and employer groups have become more conscious about safety and health.
3. Trade unions and employee groups are often interested in coordinated activities for preventing and eliminating hazards.
4. The National Safety Council has an extensive information service.
5. Local doctors may be willing to provide information on a consulting basis about workplace medical matters. The Red Cross is a source of first-aid training. An employer who is not able to locate a local chapter should contact the American National Red Cross.
6. The Web and libraries contain a wealth of information on safety and health matters.
7. Local colleges and universities may have educational programs in the field of occupational safety and health. If an employer contacts the relevant departments, educators may provide useful information.
8. Free on-site consultation is offered in many states through agreements between OSHA and either a state or private contractor. These consultants do not write citations but expect cooperation or OSHA will be contacted. Enforcement action is rare, especially because the employer requested the consultant and showed a concern for safety and health.

☐ ☐ ☐ ▬▬▬▬▬▬▬▬▬▬▬▬▬▬▬▬▬▬▬▬▬▬▬

Although this chapter emphasizes accidents in the workplace, other safety issues should be considered for a comprehensive loss prevention program. Examples include workplace violence and natural disasters. Furthermore, OSHA guidelines go beyond preventing accidents. For instance, in cooperation with the U.S. Department of Homeland Security, OSHA has published guidelines for emergencies, including terrorist events.

▬▬▬▬▬▬▬▬▬▬▬▬▬▬▬▬▬▬▬▬▬▬▬ ☐ ☐ ☐

Safety Strategies

The OSHA *Small Business Handbook* states four basic elements to all good safety and health programs (Occupational Safety and Health Administration, 2005b: 6–7):

1. Management commitment and employee involvement.
2. Worksite analysis to identify all hazards.
3. Hazard prevention and control methods are put in place and maintained.
4. Managers, supervisors, and employees are trained to understand and deal with worksite hazards.

Safety and Health Committee

A safety and health committee can be an important part of an effective loss prevention program. When employees jointly communicate about and work toward increased safety and health, employees develop a greater awareness of associated problems and solutions. At meetings, topics to discuss can include past accidents and illnesses, OSHA standards and inspections, and cases of accidents, illnesses, and remedies that occurred at similar facilities.

Socialization and Incentive Programs

Training is a prime strategy for accident prevention. The objective of training is to change the behavior of the employee. He or she should think and act in a safe manner. Training is useless unless employees are motivated to continually act in a safe manner. Even if familiar with safety procedures and other relevant information, an employee will not necessarily "practice what is preached." A method for stimulating the employee to act safely and to use safety knowledge is necessary. This objective is accomplished through incentive programs. Businesses may develop such programs on their own or outsource the work to a service firm. Examples of incentives are as follows: Every time a manufacturing plant reaches a million hours without a lost-time accident, every employee receives a gift. Another approach is safety bingo: Numbers are drawn every workday for a week and posted on a sign in the employee parking lot. If an employee completes a row, $25 is awarded. If the whole card is filled, $1,000 is won. When lost-time accidents occur, the game is halted until a month later. Companies often set safety goals for individual departments, which facilitate a competitive spirit to win prizes. Safety, rewarded by merit pay increases for employees, will also reduce accidents.

What are the results of such incentive programs? Safety incentives provide a powerful, cost-effective management tool to prevent accidents. Enthusiasm and safety awareness increase. Employees are more vigilant about other workers' safety. Incentive programs provide fun in the workplace, which results in higher morale. As accidents decline, so do insurance premiums for workers' compensation. Money is saved. Fewer accidents mean fewer production interruptions and greater profits. It is feasible to use incentives for a comprehensive loss prevention effort involving not only safety but also crime and fire prevention.

The Dangers of Safety Incentive Programs

There are three basic types of safety incentive/reward programs as described here, along with concerns (Atkinson, 2000: 32–38).

Traditional programs offer rewards to employees for going a certain period without a recordable injury. The focus is on results. OSHA, labor unions, and some employers argue that these programs may be used by employers to take the place of formal programs. In addition, employees may feel pressured not to report injuries because coworkers would be upset about not winning incentives, and so a serious workplace hazard might go undetected by management.

Behavior-based programs offer rewards to employees for behaviors (e.g., wearing personal protective equipment) that promote safety. Labor groups say that this approach places safety on the shoulders of employees and then management blames them when accidents occur. Furthermore, employers watch actions and may ignore hazards that can be corrected.

Safety activities offer rewards to employees for suggestions to improve safety, identifying and correcting hazards, participating in inspections, and serving on a committee, among other activities.

Whereas the first two programs often involve a greater level of participation, safety activities are frequently voluntary; however, everyone should be involved in safety. Since each type of program can create concern, the employer and employees should seek to understand each one and capitalize on the beneficial aspects of each.

Investigations

After an accident, an investigation is vital to prevent future accidents; the cause of an accident can be pinpointed so that corrections can follow. Established procedures important for well-planned accident investigations include the following:

1. Respond quickly to reinforce that loss prevention personnel are "on the job." This will also show employees that management cares. Ensure that the injured receive proper medical attention.
2. Protect the scene of the accident to prevent unintentional or intentional harm to evidence.
3. If required, contact appropriate regulatory agencies and insurers.
4. Find out the following: who was involved, where did it occur, when did it happen, who was injured, what occurred, what was damaged, and how did the accident take place?
5. Try to pinpoint the cause. Investigate possible direct and indirect causes. Study equipment, work procedures, the environment, and the employees involved. Is a drug test required?
6. Estimate injuries and direct and indirect costs.
7. Use a standard accident report that fits management's requirements and aids the investigative inquiry.
8. Maintain an open mind, remaining aware that some employees attempt fraudulent workers' compensation claims by staging an accident or by providing false information.
9. If necessary, complete appropriate forms (e.g., workers' compensation, OSHA).
10. Prepare a presentation for the safety and health committee concerning the accident. Solicit feedback from the committee to solve problems.
11. Follow up on corrective action to ensure safety.

One of the most difficult questions to answer during an accident investigation is the *cause*; often considerable controversy is generated. Opinions vary, but facts are necessary. *There are two primary causes of accidents: unsafe conditions and unsafe acts by people.* Frequently, unsafe conditions (e.g., unguarded moving parts, poor lighting) are known, but corrections are not made because of inaction or costs. Unsafe acts by people can result from ignorance, poor training, negligence, drugs, fatigue, emotional upset, poor attitude, and high production demands. Other circumstances also can cause accidents. One of the oldest and most controversial theories of accident causation is the **accident proneness theory**. This theory suggests that people who repeatedly have accidents are accident prone. Many experts agree that about 20% of the people have most of the accidents, whereas the remaining 80% have virtually no accidents.

Haaland (2005: 51–57) writes that the literature in the discipline of safety shows that 90% of accidents are attributed to *human error*. He notes specific human traits that have been linked through empirical research to accident proneness. One of these traits is *conscientiousness* and Haaland defines it as "an individual's degree of organization, persistence, and motivation in goal-directed behavior." Those who are low in this trait tend to ignore safety rules and get into more accidents. *Extreme extroversion* and *extreme introversion* are other traits linked to accident proneness. The former is characterized by being sociable and outgoing, but also easily distracted and having a shorter attention span. The latter is characterized by limited interpersonal interactions and possibly hesitation before seeking assistance. Haaland adds that unsafe employees are also characterized by other behaviors harmful to the bottom line, such as arriving late to work, more absences, and poorer levels of productivity and quality. Consequently, employers can systematically hire applicants who are less likely to become involved in accidents and injuries. A **safety performance assessment** measures personality traits that influence safety in the workplace. It consists of written statements and an applicant can complete the assessment at a kiosk or through a Web site.

Harry Nash, Machinist, Is Injured Again

As Harry Nash was cutting a piece of metal on a band saw, he accidentally cut off his thumb. Workers in the surrounding area rushed to his aid. The foreman and the loss prevention manager coordinated efforts to get him and his thumb to the hospital as quickly as possible. After Harry was in the care of doctors, the foreman and the loss prevention manager began an investigation. A look at Harry's record showed that he had been working for the company for eight years. During the first year, he slipped on some oil on the workplace floor and was hospitalized for three weeks with a sprained back. The third year showed that he accidentally drilled into his finger with a drill press. The report stated that Harry did not receive any training from a now-retired foreman, who should have instructed Harry on drill press safety techniques. By the fifth year, Harry had had another accident. While carrying some metal rods, he fell and broke his ankle because he forgot about climbing one step to enter a newly constructed adjoining building.

Even though Harry had had no training in operating the band saw, the loss prevention manager and the foreman believed that Harry was accident prone. The foreman, angry with Harry spoiling the department's safety record and incentive gifts, wanted Harry fired. The loss prevention manager was undecided about the matter.

Later, management, the foreman, and the loss prevention manager decided to assign Harry to a clerical position in the shipping department. Harry eventually collected workers' compensation for his lost thumb.

Additional Safety Measures

Other safety measures are to display safety posters, create a safety-by-objectives program, and recognize employees with excessive accident records and reassign or retrain those workers. Safety posters or signs are effective if certain guidelines are used. Research indicates that if the safety message is in negative terms (e.g., "Don't let this happen to you," followed by a picture of a person with a physical injury), it causes fear, resentment, and sometimes anger. Posters with positive messages (e.g., "Let's all pitch in for safety") produce better results. Posters and signs (see Figure 14.3) are more potent when they reflect the diversity of employees (e.g., multiple languages), are located in appropriate places, are not too numerous, and have attractive colors. A safety-by-objectives program is a derivative of management by objectives. In a manufacturing plant, department heads formulate safety objectives for their departments. Management makes sure that objectives are neither too high nor too low. Incentives are used to motivate employees. After a year, the objectives are studied to see if the objectives were reached. Future objectives are modified or increased.

Search the Web

Here are Web sites relevant to this chapter:

American Red Cross: www.redcross.org/
Federal Register: http://fr.cos.com/
National Institute for Occupational Safety and Health (NIOSH): www.cdc.gov/niosh/homepage.html
National Safety Council: www.nsc.org/
Occupational Safety and Health Administration (OSHA): www.osha.gov

FIGURE 14-3 Safety signs.

Case Problems

14A. As a loss prevention practitioner for a large corporation, you are asked by a local college professor to lecture on the pros and cons of OSHA. What will your comments be to the class?

14B. If you were a company safety and loss prevention manager, how would you react to an OSHA inspection? What conditions in your company do you think would influence your reaction?

14C. In reference to the case describing Harry Nash, do you feel that the loss prevention manager and the foreman were justified in labeling Harry as accident prone? Support your answer.

References

Anderson, C. (1975). *OSHA and Accident Control Through Training*. New York, NY: Industrial Press.

Atkinson, W. (2000). "The Dangers of Safety Incentive Programs." *Risk Management*, 47 (August).

Chacanaca, M. (1996). "Specialty-Confined-Space Rescues." *Emergency* (February).

Dreux, M. (1995). "When OSHA Knocks, Should an Employer Demand a Warrant?" *Occupational Hazards* (April).

Gaudio, B. (2005). "OSHA Inspection … Can It Happen to You?" *NFIB Business Toolbox* (January 21). http://www.nfib.com/object/IO_19802.html, retrieved December 17, 2006.

Grimaldi, J., and Simmonds, R. (1975). *Safety Management*. Homewood, IL: Richard D. Irwin.

Haaland, D. (2005). "Who's the Safest Bet for the Job?" *Security Management*, 49 (February).

Hall, D. (2006). *Administrative Law: Bureaucracy in a Democracy*, 3rd Ed. Upper Saddle River, NJ: Pearson Education.

"Lockout/Tagout" (2001). *Occupational Hazards*, 63 (January).

Mason, J. (1976). "OSHA: Problems and Prospects." *California Management Review*, 19 (Fall).

National Center for Injury Prevention and Control (2006). "The Economic Costs of Injuries." www.cdc.gov/nipc/factsheets/Cost_of_Injury.htm, retrieved May 8, 2006.

Occupational Safety and Health Administration (2005a). "Employer Rights and Responsibilities Following an OSHA Inspection." http://www.osha.gov/Publications/osha3000.pdf, retrieved November 9, 2006.

Occupational Safety and Health Administration (2005b). *Small Business Handbook.* http://www.osha.gov/Publications/smallbusiness/small-business.pdf, retrieved November 9, 2006.

Occupational Safety and Health Administration (2003a). "OSHA's 2003–2008 Strategic Management Plan Goals: 15% Drop in Fatality Rates, 20% Drop in Injury and Illness Rates by 2008." http://www.osha.gov/pls/oshaweb/owadisp.show_document?p_table=NEWS_RELEASES&p_id=10214, retrieved December 14, 2006.

Occupational Safety and Health Administration (2003b). "Frequently Asked Questions." http://www.osha.gov/as/opa/osha-faq.html, retrieved December 17, 2006.

Occupational Safety & Health Administration (2006a). "OSHA Facts." www.osha.gov, retrieved May 8, 2006.

Occupational Safety & Health Administration (2006b). "All About OSHA." http://www.osha.gov/Publications/all_about_OSHA.pdf, retrieved November 9, 2006.

Occupational Safety & Health Administration (2006c). "Hazard Communication." http://www.osha.gov/pls/oshaweb/owadisp.show_document?p_table=FEDERAL_REGISTER&p_id=18890, retrieved December 15, 2006.

Occupational Safety & Health Administration (2006d). "Frequently Asked Questions: HAZWOPER." http://www.osha.gov/html/faq-hazwoper.html, retrieved November 10, 2006.

Occupational Safety & Health Administration (2006e). "Bloodborne pathogens—1910.1030." http://www.osha.gov/pls/oshaweb/owadisp.show_document?p_table=STANDARDS&p_id=10051, retrieved December 15, 2006.

Occupational Safety & Health Administration (2006f). "The control of hazardous energy (lock-out/tagout)—1910.147." http://www.osha.gov/pls/oshaweb/owadisp.show_document?p_table=STANDARDS&p_id=9804, retrieved December 15, 2006.

Occupational Safety & Health Administration (2001). "Recordkeeping." http://www.osha.gov/Publications/osha3169.pdf, retrieved November 9, 2006.

Occupational Safety and Health Administration, Office of Communications (2005). "OSHA Announces Targeted Inspection Plan for 2005" (August 9). www.osha.gov, retrieved December 17, 2006.

Occupational Safety and Health Administration, Office of Communications (2006). "U.S. Department of Labor's OSHA Fines Thomas Industrial Coatings Following Two Worker Fatalities in Kansas City" (National News Release 06–1961–NAT, October 30). www.osha.gov, retrieved December 20, 2006.

U.S. Department of Labor, Office of Public Affairs (2006). "Serious Violations of Health and Safety Standards Bring Wynnewood Refining Co. $154,800 in Fines from U.S. Department of Labor's OSHA" (OSHA Regional News Release: OSHA-06–1937–DAL, November 9). www.osha.gov, retrieved December 20, 2006.

Schroll, C. (2006). "Confined space training: follow these 17 key steps." *Industrial Safety & Hygiene News*, 40 (April).

PART

III

Special Problems and Countermeasures

15

Terrorism and Homeland Security

Objectives

After studying this chapter, the reader will be able to:

1. Explain the definition, history, and causes of terrorism.
2. Describe international terrorism and domestic terrorism.
3. Discuss terrorist methods and weapons.
4. List and describe weapons of mass destruction and response.
5. Describe homeland security.
6. Examine the measurement of terrorism.
7. Differentiate national security and homeland security.
8. Describe government action against terrorism.
9. Discuss the role of the private sector in homeland security.

KEY TERMS
<table><tr><td>• terrorism</td><td>• rational choice causes of terrorism</td></tr><tr><td>• Sicarii</td><td>• structural causes of terrorism</td></tr><tr><td>• Zealots</td><td>• international terrorism</td></tr><tr><td>• Assassins</td><td>• globalization</td></tr><tr><td>• French Revolution</td><td>• asymmetrical warfare</td></tr><tr><td>• "Reign of Terror"</td><td>• 9/11 attacks</td></tr><tr><td>• Ku Klux Klan</td><td>• al-Qaida</td></tr><tr><td>• state terrorism</td><td>• domestic terrorism</td></tr><tr><td>• guerilla warfare</td><td>• anarchism</td></tr><tr><td>• Palestinian Liberation Organization</td><td>• ecoterrorism</td></tr><tr><td>• Crusades</td><td>• Animal Liberation Front (ALF)</td></tr><tr><td>• Islam</td><td>• Earth Liberation Front (ELF)</td></tr><tr><td>• Prophet Muhammad</td><td>• extremism</td></tr><tr><td>• Muslims</td><td>• Ruby Ridge incident</td></tr><tr><td>• Sunni</td><td>• Christian Identity</td></tr><tr><td>• Shiite</td><td>• Waco incident</td></tr><tr><td>• fundamentalism</td><td>• Oklahoma City bombing</td></tr><tr><td>• psychological causes of terrorism</td><td>• Patriot movement</td></tr></table>

- cellular model of organization
- leaderless resistance
- secondary explosion
- improvised explosive device (IED)
- weapon of mass destruction (WMD)
- weapon of mass effect (WME)
- Anthrax
- Aum Shinrikyo cult
- radiological dispersion device
- homeland security
- National Security Strategy of the United States
- National Strategy for Homeland Security
- U.S. Northern Command (NORTH-COM)
- Defense Against Weapons of Mass Destruction Act of 1996
- Antiterrorism and Effective Death Penalty Act of 1996
- USA Patriot Act of 2001
- USA Patriot Improvement and Reauthorization Act of 2005
- Homeland Security Act of 2002
- Department of Homeland Security (DHS)
- first responders
- Homeland Security Advisory System
- business interruption
- Information Sharing and Analysis Centers (ISACs)
- Overseas Security Advisory Council (OSAC)
- American Red Cross
- Salvation Army
- National Volunteer Organizations Against Disasters
- Citizen Corps
- USA Freedom Corps

Note: Major portions of this chapter are from: Purpura, P. (2007). *Terrorism and Homeland Security: An Introduction with Applications*. Burlington, MA: Elsevier Butterworth-Heinemann Pub.

Terrorism

Terrorism Defined

Poland (2005: 2–5) writes of the complexity of defining terrorism. Many definitions exist and there is no international agreement on how to define the term. This results in methodological problems for both research and data collection and conflicts over efforts at international counterterrorism.

The United Nations has struggled with the term for many years. It has been argued that one state's "terrorism" is another state's "freedom fighter." Or, simply put, terrorism is a "dirty word" drenched in emotion, and it describes what the "other guy" has done.

The FBI (n.d.) defines **terrorism** as "the unlawful use of force or violence against persons or property to intimidate or coerce a government, the civilian population, or any segment thereof, in furtherance of political or social objectives." The United States Department of State (2006: 9) chooses the definition of terrorism contained in Title 22 of the U.S. Code, Section 2656f(d): "The term 'terrorism' means premeditated, politically motivated violence perpetrated against noncombatant targets [e.g., civilians; military personnel who are unarmed and/or not on duty] by subnational groups or clandestine agents."

History

Terrorism has existed for centuries. Ancient terrorists were "holy warriors" as we see with certain terrorists today. During the first century in the Middle East, the **Sicarii** and the **Zealots**, Jewish groups in ancient Palestine, fomented revolution against the occupying forces of Rome. The Sicarii instilled fear by using a dagger to stab Romans and Roman sympathizers during the day at crowded holiday festivities. The throngs provided cover for the killers and heightened terror because people never knew when an attacker would strike. The Zealots-Sicarii believed that by confronting the Romans, the Messiah would intervene and save the Jewish people. Between 66 and 70 A.D., revolution became a reality. However, it ended in disaster for the Zealots-Sicarii. With thousands of Jews killed and the Jewish state in shambles, the survivors fled to the top of Masada where their abhorrence to being subjected to control by the Romans, who surrounded them, resulted in mass suicide. Today, we have the term "zealot," meaning fanatical partisan.

In analyzing the methods of the Zealot-Sicarii, and drawing parallels to modern-day terrorism, Poland (2005: 26–27) writes that "the primary purpose of the Sicarii terrorist strategy, like so many terrorist groups today, seems to be the provocation of indiscriminate countermeasures by the established political system and to deliberately provoke repression, reprisals, and counterterrorism." Poland refers to Northern Ireland where, for hundreds of years, Catholics have battled Protestants. Simonsen and Spindlove (2004: 70–75) explain that during the 16th century, James I, King of England, offered land in Ireland to Scottish settlers for the purpose of establishing the Protestant church in Ireland. Conflict ensued with Catholics, but the Protestant landowners prevailed. Catholics were regulated to a life of poverty. Poland cites incidents during the twentieth century when Catholics, protesting peacefully against Protestants and British rule, were killed and wounded when police and British Security Forces overreacted.

Poland draws another parallel from the Zealot-Sicarii movement to recent times. The Irgun Zvai Leumi-al-Israel, led by Menachem Begin, terrorized the British military government of Palestine between 1942 and 1948 in an effort to establish a Jewish state. The Irgun perpetrated many bombings and assassinations, leading to a cycle of terror and counterterror. Manifestos of the Irgun argued "No Masada." Irgun fighters had actually studied terrorist methods of the Sicarii and the Irish Republican Army. Eventually, the British turned the problem over to the United Nations, and in 1948, the country of Israel was born.

The **Assassins** were another religious sect that used terrorism to pursue their goals (Weinzierl, 2004: 31–32). This group gave us the term "assassin" that literally means "hashish-eater," a reference to the drug taking that allegedly occurred (perhaps rumor) prior to murdering someone. During the 11th and 12th centuries, this group evolved from the Shiites of the present-day Mideast and they believed that the Muslim community needed the purified version of Islam to prepare for the arrival of the Inman, the Chosen of God and leader of humanity. The Assassins waged a war against the majority Sunni Muslim population. Their terror strategies consisted of using unconventional means, establishing mountain fortifications from which terror attacks were launched, and using daggers like the Sicarii. *Although the Assassins were not successful in reforming the Islamic faith or in recruiting many converts, they are remembered for their innovations in terrorist strategies, namely the suicide mission and using disguise and deception.* Acting under God, they were promised a place in paradise for their ultimate sacrifice as they sought out and killed Sunni religious and political leaders. Even today, we see conflict between Shiites and Sunni, as in Iraq.

□ □ □ ▬▬▬▬▬▬▬▬▬▬▬▬▬▬▬▬▬▬▬▬▬▬▬▬▬▬▬▬▬

Through history and today, we see the deep roots of religion within terrorism.

▬▬▬▬▬▬▬▬▬▬▬▬▬▬▬▬▬▬▬▬▬▬▬▬▬▬▬▬▬ □ □ □

Secular motivations for terrorism were within the **French Revolution**, a major historic milestone in the history of terrorism. The French Revolution ended absolute rule by French kings and strengthened the middle class. The **"Reign of Terror"** (1793–1794), from which the word "terrorism" evolved, saw leadership from Maximilien Robespierre, who led the Jacobin government in executing, by guillotine, 12,000 people declared enemies of the Revolution. During the "Reign of Terror," terrorism was viewed in a positive light and Robespierre declared that terrorism is prompt justice and a consequence of democracy applied during a time of urgent need. In 1794, when Robespierre prepared a new list of traitors of the revolution, those fearing their names were on the list, executed him at the guillotine, and thus, the "Reign of Terror" ended. By this time, terrorism was beginning to be characterized in a negative light. Edmund Burke, a British political leader and writer, criticized the French Revolution and popularized the term "terrorism" in the English language as a repulsive action. This state terrorism of the French government was significant in the history of terrorism because the terror was not justified by religion or God, but by the masses to promote a political ideology (Weinberg and Davis, 1989: 24–25). Greenberg (2001:1) writes: "Over the next century the Jacobin spirit infected Russia, Europe and the United States." Anarchist terrorist groups worked to foment revolution. In Russia, the Narodnaya Volya (meaning "people's will") was born in 1878 to destroy the Tsarist regime. They assassinated Alexander II in 1881, but the success sealed their fate because they were crushed by the Tsarist regime. This group did inspire other anarchists. During an anarchist-led labor protest at Chicago's Haymarket Square in 1886, a bomb was thrown into the crowd as police intervened. A riot ensued and several police and demonstrators were killed or injured. This incident hurt the labor movement. The anarchists were tried and sentenced to be hanged or imprisoned. Because there had been insufficient evidence, a few years later the Governor of Illinois pardoned the surviving anarchists.

As the 19th century gave way to the 20th century, anarchists and others dissatisfied with established order adopted terrorism as a strategy to reach their goals (Laqueur, 1999). Terrorist attacks and assassinations occurred in France, Italy, Spain, Germany, Ireland, India, Japan, the Balkans, and the Ottoman Empire, among other areas. Bombs were detonated in cafes, theaters, and during parades. In the United States, two Presidents were assassinated—Garfield (1881) and McKinley (1901). This era also saw an increase in nationalism and struggles for statehood as native groups revolted and used terrorism to free themselves from imperial control and European colonialism. The assassination of Austrian heir Archduke Ferdinand in 1914 is a famous illustration of how terrorism was used for nationalistic goals. Gavrilo Princip, a member of the Pan-Serbian secret group called the Black Hand planned to kill Ferdinand to help southern Slavs. The assassination actually became the precipitating incident that triggered World War I and doomed the Austrian Empire. We can see that terrorism can sometimes have a profound impact on world affairs.

Although global terrorism was primarily left-wing oriented through history, during the late 18th century and early 20th century, conservative, right-wing groups formed to maintain the status quo and prevent change. In the United States, the **Ku Klux Klan** (KKK), a right-wing group, was formed in 1865 by Confederate Army veterans who believed in the superiority of whites (Chalmers, 1981). The major goal of the KKK is to hinder the advancement of blacks, Catholics, Jews, and other minority groups. Klan methods include wearing white robes and hoods, burning crosses (at meetings and to frighten nonmembers), intimidation, tar-and-feathering, lynching, and murder. The KKK evolved through periods of strength and weakness. During the mid-20th century, it was revived to oppose racial integration and it applied terrorist strategies, such as murder and bombing. Because of infighting, splits, court cases, FBI infiltration, and imprisonment, membership has declined.

Because of the spread of communism, especially the Bolshevik Revolution of 1917 in Russia that overthrew the Czar, many political leaders worldwide became fearful and took brutal steps to eliminate communists, socialists, and other left-wing activists within their own countries. Repressive regimes included the Nazis led by Adolph Hitler in Germany and the fascists led by Benito Mussolini in Italy, both becoming allies during World War II. Violence by a government to repress dissidence among its own population, or supporting such violence in another country, is called **state terrorism**. Following the end of World War II in 1945, a resurgence of nationalism among European colonies in the Middle East, Asia, and Africa resulted in violent uprisings. A combination of **guerilla warfare** and terrorism occurred. The former was characterized by larger units resembling the military and operating from a geographic area over which they controlled, and the latter involving smaller groups blending into the population and planning spectacular attacks for maximum media attention.

According to Greenberg (2001), it was Algeria's Front de Liberation Nationale (FLN), fighting for independence from France in the 1950s, that set the tone for terrorism to come. The FLN raised the cost to France for its colonialism by bombing coastal tourist resorts, thereby randomly killing French families on vacation. By the 1960s, this precedent was copied world-wide by Palestinian and Irish nationalists, Marxists in Africa and Latin America, the Weather Underground in the United States, the Marxist Baader-Meinhoff Gang in the former West Germany, and the Red Brigades in Italy. Terrorist methods were being applied by not only nationalists seeking independence, but also by those with ethnic and ideological agendas.

It was during the 1970s, that Yasser Arafat's **Palestinian Liberation Organization** (PLO), and its splinter groups, while locked in a cycle of shocking violence with Israel, pioneered the hijacking of jet airlines to publicize their goal of Palestinian statehood. Black September, as one splinter group was known, staged an outrageous attack at the 1972 Munich Olympics in Germany and murdered 11 Israeli athletes. This attack became a major, global media event and inspired other terrorists.

During the mid-1980s, state-sponsored terrorism grew again and supported terrorist attacks against Western targets in the Middle East. Sponsors of terrorism included Syria, Libya, Iran, Iraq, and North Korea.

Religion and Politics

Confusion may arise over whether a terrorist group has a religious agenda, a political agenda, or both. Religious conflict has a long history and it characterizes several groups today. At the same time, religious conflict may be used as a front for a hidden political agenda.

The **Crusades** helps us to understand the long history of religion and violence. These eight major military expeditions originated in Western Europe between 1096 and 1270 (during the Middle Ages) with the purpose of recapturing Palestine from the Muslims because it was the area where Jesus had lived. In fact, Jerusalem is considered Holy Land to Muslims, Christians, and Jews. This was an era when Western Europe was expanding its economy and Christianity. Kings, nobles, knights, and peasants joined the Crusades and fought, not only for Christianity, but also for territory and wealth. Battles were won and lost, Jerusalem changed hands multiple times, and there was no significant impact, except for expanded trade. Subsequent attempts at organizing crusades failed as Europe turned its attention westward to the Atlantic Ocean toward the New World. The Holy Land was left to the Muslims (Queller, 1989).

The violence between the Israelis and the Palestinians is an example of religious and political conflict. Several wars have been fought between Israel and its Arab neighbors. Israeli military superiority resulted in the capture of land from its Arab neighbors. Because the PLO saw that Arab allies were unable to drive Israeli armed forces from occupied lands, the PLO began a campaign of terrorism, as did other groups. The goals are to destroy Israel and form an Arab state in Palestine. Today, a political solution is slowly developing as Israeli forces continue to withdraw from occupied lands, although the withdrawals are marred by violence from both sides.

Wilkinson (2003: 124) writes that the al-Qaida network portray themselves as fighting a holy war and use religious language to legitimize their terrorist attacks. However, their political agenda is to force the U.S. military to withdraw from the Middle East, they want to overthrow regimes that side with the West and fail to follow "true" Islam, and they seek to unite all Muslims. Al-Qaida uses the Muslim communities and mosques in the West to recruit, seek aid, and conduct covert operations, even though the majority of Muslims who live in the West reject terrorism.

The conflict among some worshippers of Islam helps us to understand some of the religious violence today. **Islam** is one of the world's largest religions and it refers to the religious doctrine preached by the **Prophet Muhammad** during the A.D. 600s. Those who believe in this doctrine are called **Muslims**. Over one-fifth of the global population is Muslim and they reside in countries throughout the world. Conflicts among Muslims over the rightful succession of Muslim rulers led to disputes within Islam. Civil war resulted in two Muslim sects that remain today, along with a history of conflict. The **Sunni** branch is the larger of the two sects and members dominate the Middle East. They are followers of the teachings of Muhammad. Al-Qaida is primarily Sunni. **Shiite** is the minority sect. They believe that Ali, cousin and son-in-law of Muhammad, is the Prophet of Islam. Shiite activism promoted the Iranian revolution of 1979 and emphasized that Islam should be lived as a tool of the oppressed, besides being a religious doctrine. Although Iraq is mostly Shiite, as is Iran, Iraq was ruled by the Sunni minority in Iraq under Saddam Hussein, until his regime was toppled by U.S.-led forces in 2003. The conflict that followed pitted the formerly oppressed Shiites (supported by coalition forces to establish a new government) against Sunnis.

Ford (2001) writes about opinions and perceptions of the United States by Arabs and others. Many Arabs see the carnage of 9/11 (Figure 15-1) as retribution for unjust policies by America. The Israeli-Palestinian conflict is a primary topic of contention. The perception is that Israel can get away with murder and the United States will turn a blind eye. Arab media shows countless photos of Israeli soldiers killing and wounding Palestinians and Israeli tanks plowing through Palestinian neighborhoods. Ford refers to the dominance of state-run media in the Middle East and how it often fans the flames of anti-American and anti-Israeli feelings because it helps to divert citizens away from the shortcomings of their own government.

Ford notes that the United States has provided billions of dollars of military and economic aid to Israel and other regional allies to strengthen U.S. interests in the oil-rich region. He writes: "It is this double standard that creates hatred." According to Ford, Middle Easterners argue that if the United States does not rethink the policies that cause anti-American sentiment, trying to root out terrorism will fail.

Greenberg (2001) writes about **fundamentalism** that refers to a strict adherence to the basic tenants of a belief system to reach purity in that belief system as defined by its leaders; it fosters intolerance of others' beliefs and it can generate terrorism. Greenberg points out that the causes of the growth of fundamentalism include the 1979 Israel-Egypt peace agreement, the Iranian revolution, and the Soviet invasion of Afghanistan. He adds that Islamic fundamentalists fear the spread of satanic Western values and influence and they believe that "to destroy America is to do God's work." Of great concern is how dangerous this mixture of religion and terrorism has become, as evidenced by the al-Qaida attacks of September 11, 2001. Future attacks might be more devastating and include weapons of mass destruction. Although al-Qaida has received a lot of attention, we should not lose sight of the "big picture" of global terrorism and the need for broad solutions.

FIGURE 15-1 Destruction of the World Trade Center in New York City following the September 11, 2001 terrorist attack.

Causes of Terrorism

An understanding of the causes of terrorism is an important foundation for planning success-ful solutions. Roach, et al. (2005: 7–25) have developed a rough framework that diagnoses terrorism through an analysis of immediate causes and prior causes from individual, group, societal, or national history. Then, each family of causes can be tackled by an equivalent family of intervention principles, using specific targeted methods. Examples include target hardening, disrupting financing, attempting to resolve ethnic conflict, and socialization (e.g., working with institutions to promote diversity and tolerance).

Kegley (2003: 10–11) writes that while one perspective of terrorism sees it like a disease requiring a remedy, an opposing view sees it as a legitimate response to unjustified repression. The causes include perceived political, social, and economic inequities, as well as the intrusion of one culture on another. The explanations and causes of terrorism are offered from many perspectives. Three major categories are psychological, rational choice, and structural. What follows here is a summary of research, including the work of Clayton et al., (2003).

Psychological Causes of Terrorism

Psychological causes of terrorism look to factors within an individual that influence acts of terrorism. Researchers often note that terrorists are not mentally disturbed. In fact, the recruiting process to obtain new recruits is selective since psychopathology can result in fric-tion within a terrorist group and when completing missions (Hudson, 1999). In addition, it is not valid to apply one set of generalized psychological characteristics to all terrorists. The research on the personal backgrounds of terrorists shows conflicting results. Research shows that terrorists were unsuccessful in their personal lives, jobs, and educations. At the same time, research shows terrorists from middle-class or upper-class backgrounds with university educa-tion (Clayton et al., 2003). Palestinian suicide bombers who terrorized Israel were often poor, with limited education and hope for the future. Their salvation was paradise after killing Jews. Conversely, the 9/11 terrorists were well-educated professionals living middle-class lives.

Silke (1998: 51–69) writes that most terrorists feel that they are doing nothing wrong when they kill, injure, and destroy property. He claims that terrorists are not mentally ill, but they share a psychological condition known as psychopathic personality disorder (also called anti-social personality disorder), which is the absence of empathy for others. He cites the case of Nezar Hindawi, who in 1986, sent his pregnant Irish girlfriend on an El Al flight to Israel, claiming that he would marry her soon. She apparently was not aware that Hindawi had hid a bomb from the Abu Nidal Organization in her belongings.

Terrorists typically rationalize and minimize their actions by referring to historical events and injustices. They plan carefully and are patient until everything is in place. Violent behavior develops through a process of gradual moral disengagement. Previously abhorrent violence is eventually accomplished callously.

Social learning models offer explanations for terrorism. Bandura (1977) emphasizes learning through observing and modeling the behaviors of others. Many terrorists grow up in locations where violence is both the norm and a daily event. The repeated success of aggres-sive behavior encourages groups to engage in violence.

Rational Choice Causes of Terrorism

Rational choice causes of terrorism view terrorism as a logical political choice among alterna-tive actions (Crenshaw, 1990). Rational choice explanations help us to understand the circum-stances surrounding terrorist decisions to choose violence. For instance, global media exposure of terrorist violence and its aims can be beneficial to the terrorist group.

Another aspect of rational choice is the timing of terrorist attacks. Terrorists may attack on an anniversary of a significant event or on an enemy's holy day or national holiday. Timothy McVeigh blew up the Alfred P. Murrah Federal Building in Oklahoma City on the second anniversary of the deaths of the Branch Davidians in Waco, Texas, a clash he blamed on the FBI.

Structural Causes of Terrorism

Structural causes of terrorism explain terrorism as a response to social-structural conditions (i.e., stable, enduring patterns of social relationship or social positions) that groups are powerless to deal with through conventional political or military methods. These conditions include citizen access to services, rights, and protection. The social structures include the laws and policies of government, the role of police and military forces, and the geographic location of the group. Social and political oppression in an environment of weak social structures may result in terrorism and revolution.

Relative deprivation theory helps us to understand terrorism (Barken and Snowden, 2001: 17). Basically, a group's rising expectations and disappointments lead to feelings of deprivation and frustration. When group members compare their plight with more fortunate groups, the ill feelings are compounded. Violence is seen as a viable option. The living conditions of Palestinians in and near Israel serve as an example.

Terrorism may also be shaped by efforts to maintain cultural identity and autonomy. An example of this is the past violence between Catholics and Protestants in Northern Ireland.

The U.S. Government (2003), in the *National Strategy for Combating Terrorism*, describes a building process from which terrorism emerges. Underlying conditions include poverty, corruption, and religious and ethnic conflict. Although these conditions may be real or manufactured, terrorists use these problems to legitimize violence and gain support.

The international environment can facilitate terrorism through, for example, open borders that enable terrorists to seek havens and travel to targets. States around the world—either through ignorance or intent—offer safe houses, training, communications systems, and financial opportunities that support terrorist operations. A terrorist organization can then thrive in a stable environment. Leadership links the components of the building process and provides direction for goals. Because leaders may be apprehended or killed, certain terrorist groups have opted for a decentralized and autonomous cell structure.

☐ ☐ ☐ ▬▬▬▬▬▬▬▬▬▬▬▬▬▬▬▬▬▬▬▬▬▬▬▬

An understanding of the root causes of terrorism is an important foundation for planning successful solutions.

▬▬▬▬▬▬▬▬▬▬▬▬▬▬▬▬▬▬▬▬▬▬▬▬ ☐ ☐ ☐

International Terrorism

The FBI (n.d.) defines **international terrorism** as "the unlawful use of force or violence committed by a group or individual, who has some connection to a foreign power or whose activities transcend national boundaries, against persons or property to intimidate or coerce a government, the civilian population, or any segment thereof, in furtherance of political or social objectives." According to the U.S. Department of State (2004: xii), "the term international terrorism means terrorism involving citizens or the territory of more than one country."

Martin (2003: 228) seeks objectivity by comparing perceptions of international terrorism by those from the West and those from developing nations. Western governments are critical of international terrorism because (1) democratic justice is the norm and terrorism is seen as criminal behavior, (2) the West is often a target of terrorism, and (3) the West finds specific methods of warfare to be acceptable and terrorism is not one of them. Developing nations may find terrorism to be acceptable because (1) anticolonial revolutionaries (also called terrorists) have become national leaders, (2) terrorism was the best choice to freedom from colonialism, and (3) many revolutionaries crafted an effective fusion of ideology and terrorism that became justified and legitimate.

The concept of globalization helps us to understand international terrorism. **Globalization** is a process of worldwide changes that are increasingly integrating and remolding the lives of the people of the world (Bailey, 2003: 75). Economic changes are the driving force behind globalization. Citizens of countries throughout the world are seeing their products and services sold globally, and they are buying from other countries. Modern technology and communications have enabled American movies, television programs, and music to reach almost anywhere in the world. McDonald's hamburgers and Kentucky Fried Chicken are sold in cities throughout the world. Likewise, the United States is a huge market for other countries. The ideology of capitalism and its goal of wealth are often seen as the driving forces behind the global economy. This ideology originated from Western (European) cultural beliefs and values. The process of globalization involves not only economic changes, but also political, social, and cultural changes. The United States is at the forefront of globalization through its military might, huge economy, power, and influence. Citizens of less developed nations perceive threats to their native culture and society from Western ideas, democratic values, and differences in religion. People in conservative cultures are angered by inequities, injustice, and the age-old problem of the "haves and the have-nots." Western industrialized nations are a ripe target for discontent. Samuel Huntington (1996), who wrote *The Clash of Civilizations and the Remaking of the World Order*, has often been quoted following the 9/11 attacks. He predicted that in the 21st century, wars would be fought, not between nations, but between different cultures and religions.

International Terrorists

When terrorists stage an attack domestically that has domestic implications, the attention they receive for their cause may not be as intense as a cross-border attack in another country. Terrorists may also select domestic targets that have international connections to enhance global attention to their cause. Examples of international targets include diplomats, tourists, foreign business people, and the locations they inhabit or visit. By bringing their struggle into the international arena, a low-budget, spectacular attack, on a symbolic or well-known target, can reap enormous, immediate publicity. Such political violence has been termed **asymmetrical warfare**, "a term used to describe tactics, organizational configurations, and methods of conflict that do not use previously accepted or predictable rules of engagement" (Martin, 2003: 216). This means that terrorists, who have an arsenal that is no match to, say, a superpower, can be successful when they apply imaginative, well-planned, low-budget, surprise attacks against a much stronger enemy. This occurred with the **9/11 attacks** on September 11, 2001, when al-Qaida suicide operatives, using box cutters, commandeered airliners and transformed them into missiles that totally destroyed the Twin Towers in New York City and damaged the Pentagon, while killing almost 3,000 people. Many countries, especially the United States, were forced to re-think their war fighting and counterterrorism capabilities because, clearly, the "wake-up call" is that conventional methods of deterrence, security, and war are no match against creative, determined terrorists.

In past decades, international terrorists (Figure 15-2) targeted U.S. citizens and interests overseas. The most memorable attacks include the suicide truck bombings of the U.S. Marine barracks in Beirut, in 1983, killing 241 military service personnel; the 1988 bombing of Pan American Flight 103 over Lockerbie, Scotland, which killed 189 Americans; the 1996 bombing of Al-Khobar Towers in Dhahran, Saudi Arabia, resulting in the deaths of 19 U.S. military personnel; the 1998 bombing of the U.S. embassies in Kenya and Tanzania, which killed 12 Americans and many others; and the attack on the USS Cole in the port of Aden, Yemen, in 2000, killing 17 U.S. Navy members.

The true number of terrorist organizations is difficult to gauge because these groups are dynamic, splinter groups form, and groups change their names. The U.S. Department of State (2006), in *Country Reports on Terrorism 2005*, lists 42 foreign terrorist organizations, followed by "a list of other groups of concern." The annual *Country Reports* contain a variety of information, including descriptions of terrorist groups, countries containing terrorist groups, and U.S. counterterrorism strategies.

FIGURE 15-2 The Faces of Global Terrorism, Wanted Poster. *Courtesy*: U.S. Department of State.

□ □ □

Al-Qaida (a.k.a. International Front for Fighting Jews and Crusaders)

Description

Al-Qaida was established by Osama bin Laden in 1988 with Arabs who fought in Afghanistan against the Soviet Union. The group helped finance, recruit, transport, and train Sunni Islamic extremists for the Afghan resistance. The goals of **al-Qaida** are to unite Muslims to fight the United States as a means of defeating Israel, overthrowing regimes it deems "non-Islamic," and expelling Westerners and non-Muslims from Muslim countries. Its eventual goal would be establishment of a pan-Islamic caliphate throughout the world. Al-Qaida leaders issued a statement in February 1998 under the banner of "The World Islamic Front for Jihad Against the Jews and Crusaders" saying it was the duty of all Muslims to kill U.S. citizens, civilian and military, and their allies everywhere. Al-Qaida merged with al-Jihad (Egyptian Islamic Jihad) in June 2001, renaming itself "Qaidat al-Jihad."

Activities

Even as al-Qaida's top leaders continue to plot and direct terror attacks worldwide, terrorists affiliated with al-Qaida but not necessarily controlled by bin Laden have increasingly carried out high-profile attacks. In 2005, bin Laden's deputy Ayman al-Zawahiri appeared to say that al-Qaida was responsible for multiple attacks against the London public transportation system. The extent of leadership involvement in planning the attack is unclear, and homegrown United Kingdom-based extremists may have been inspired rather than directed by al-Qaida. Over the past four years, al-Qaida, its affiliates and those inspired by the group were also involved in many anti-U.S. or anti-Coalition attacks in Africa, Europe, the Middle East, Afghanistan, Pakistan, and Iraq, including suicide bombings and vehicle-borne improvised explosive devices.

In 2003 and 2004, Saudi-based al-Qaida operatives and associated extremists launched more than a dozen attacks, killing at least 90 people, including 14 Americans in Saudi Arabia. Al-Qaida may have been connected to the suicide bombers and planners of the November 2003 attacks in Istanbul that targeted two synagogues, the British Consulate, and the HSBC Bank, resulting in more than 60 dead. Pakistani President Musharraf blames al-Qaida for two attempts on his life in December 2003.

In October 2002, al-Qaida directed a suicide attack on the French tanker MV Limburg off the coast of Yemen that killed one and injured four. The group also carried out the November 2002 suicide bombing of a hotel in Mombasa, Kenya, which killed 15. Al-Qaida probably provided financing for the October 2002 Bali bombings by Jemaah Islamiya that killed more than 200. On September 11, 2001, 19 al-Qaida suicide attackers hijacked and crashed four U.S. commercial jets—two into the World Trade Center in New York City, one into the Pentagon near Washington, D.C., and a fourth into a field in Shanksville, Pennsylvania—leaving nearly 3,000 individuals dead or missing. In October 2000, al-Qaida conducted a suicide attack on the USS Cole in the port of Aden, Yemen, with an explosive-laden boat, killing 17 U.S. Navy sailors and injuring 39.

Al-Qaida also carried out the August 1998 bombings of the U.S. embassies in Nairobi and Dar es Salaam killing at least 301 individuals and injuring more than 5,000 others. Al-Qaida and its supporters claim to have shot down U.S. helicopters and killed U.S. service members in Somalia in 1993, and to have conducted three bombings that targeted U.S. troops in Aden in December 1992.

Strength

Al-Qaida's organizational strength is difficult to determine in the aftermath of extensive counterterrorist efforts since 9/11. The arrests and killing of mid-level and senior al-Qaida operatives have disrupted some communication, financial, and facilitation nodes and disrupted some terrorist plots. Additionally, supporters and associates worldwide who are inspired by the group's ideology may be operating without direction from al-Qaida's central leadership, though it is impossible to estimate their numbers. Al-Qaida also serves as a focal point of inspiration or imitation for a worldwide network that is comprised of many Sunni Islamic extremist groups.

Location/Area of Operation

Al-Qaida's worldwide networks are augmented by ties to local Sunni extremists. The group was based in Afghanistan until Coalition forces removed the Taliban from power in late 2001. While the largest concentration of senior al-Qaida members now resides in Pakistan, the network incorporates members of al-Qaida in Iraq and other associates throughout the Middle East, Southeast Asia, Africa, and Europe who continue working to carry out future attacks against U.S. interests.

External Aid

Al-Qaida primarily depends on donations from like-minded supporters and individuals who believe that their money is supporting a humanitarian or other cause. Some funds are diverted from Islamic charitable organizations. Additionally, parts of the organization raise funds through criminal activities; for example, al-Qaida in Iraq raises funds through hostage-taking for ransom, and members in Europe have engaged in credit card fraud. United States and international efforts to block al-Qaida funding have hampered the group's ability to raise money.

Source: U.S. Department of State (2006).

Domestic Terrorism

The FBI (n.d.) defines **domestic terrorism** as "groups or individuals who are based and operate entirely within the United States and Puerto Rico without foreign direction and whose acts are directed at elements of the U.S. government or population."

Domestic terrorism, also called "homegrown terrorism," is difficult to define, categorize, and research. White (2003: 207–208) offers an analysis of the problems of conceptualizing domestic terrorism. He notes that law enforcement in the United States has historically labeled terrorism or political violence under various crime labels (e.g., arson, homicide). White also writes that the United States has had a long history of political violence, but only recently have more than a few scholars studied the problem under the label of "terrorism."

White refers to three early authors who pioneered publications on domestic (U.S.) terrorism. He praised H. Cooper and coauthors who wrote the *Report of the Task Force on Disorders and Terrorism* in 1976. This publication focused on the civil disorders of the time, the political context of domestic terrorism, and the need for emergency planning.

Two other pioneers are J. Bell and Ted Gurr (1979) who emphasized the historical context of terrorism and how it has been applied by the strong to control the weak, and by the weak to fight the strong. Examples in American history include the genocide against American Indians by Europeans, industrialists versus unions, and vigilantism (e.g., KKK).

Domestic Terrorists

Griset and Mahan (2003: 85–93) divide homegrown terrorism into five categories based on ideology. These researchers state that their categories may overlap. The categories are explained next with additional historical information from several sources.

State-Sponsored Terrorism

Government authorities, including Congress and the president, have passed laws and supported policies that have intimidated Americans and fostered violence. The Removal Act of 1830 required the forced march of Indian tribes from the east coast to Oklahoma; many Indians died during the march, and upon reaching reservations, the conditions were poor. In another example, during the late 1800s and early 1900s, many city and state police agencies were formed or expanded to serve as strikebreakers (Holden, 1986: 23).

Leftist Class Struggles

Identifying with Marxism, the 1960s and 1970s saw leftist groups embroiled in antiwar and civil rights struggles. The Students for a Democratic Society (SDS) began in 1960 to support the "liberal" policies of the Democratic Party. It called for an alliance of blacks, students, peace groups, and liberal organizations. As with many other leftist groups of the time, an "anti-establishment" theme prevailed (i.e., government and business were corrupt and change was needed to help the less fortunate). In 1965, the SDS organized the first anti-Vietnam War march in Washington, D.C., which resulted in increased popularity for the

SDS among students. The SDS led many campus disturbances and sit-down demonstrations in building. Military draft resistance became a top priority. As the Vietnam War intensified, the SDS divided into competing groups, each supporting violence and terrorism. One of the most noted splinter groups was the Weather Underground Organization (WUO.) This group advocated revolution against capitalism. It was responsible for almost 40 bombings, including those inside the U.S. Capitol and the Pentagon. When the war ended, interest in the WUO waned (Poland, 1988: 91–92).

Violence against nonviolent civil rights workers sparked the Black Power movement during the 1960s. It advocated political, economic, and cultural awakening. One splinter group of this movement was the Black Panthers, formed in 1966, in Oakland, California. A tactic of the Black Panthers was to dispatch members to police stops to observe. The Panthers would arrive carrying law books and an open display of shotguns and rifles (legal at the time). This paramilitary movement grew and Panthers wore black berets and black leather jackets as they marched and chanted slogans. The FBI viewed the Panthers as a threat to domestic security; gun battles and arrests occurred, and by the late 1970s, the group began its decline (Martin, 2003: 311 and 318).

During the 1980s, the May 19 Communist Organization (M19CO) emerged from members of the SDS, Black Panthers, and other groups. The group's name came from the birthdays of Ho Chi Minh (North Vietnamese Communist leader) and Malcolm X (American Black Muslim leader). This group sought links to radical black, Hispanic, and women's movements. The overall goal was violent revolution. By the end of the decade, the group split apart and members were imprisoned for crimes such as bombings, murders, and robberies (Poland, 1988: 90).

Following the Spanish-American War in 1898, Puerto Rico was ceded to the United States by the Treaty of Paris. The resolve of Puerto Rican nationalists in seeking independence from the United States was illustrated in 1950 following an uprising that was quickly suppressed by government troops. On November 1, 1950, nationalists tried to assassinate President Truman while he was at Blair House, across from the White House. A gun battle erupted, one police officer was killed, Truman was unharmed, and the independence movement gained national attention. The next attack occurred on March 1, 1954, again in Washington, D.C., when several nationalists fired shots at legislators while Congress was in session, wounding five. In 1974, the Armed Forces for National Liberation (FALN) was formed. Its agenda for independence leaned to the far left. The FALN introductory attack consisted of bombing five banks in New York City. Over 200 bombings followed, targeting federal and local government buildings, the military (especially in Puerto Rico), and businesses. The FALN was also known for ambushing and shooting U.S. armed services personnel (Poland, 1988: 72–76).

Anarchists/Ecoterrorists

Anarchism is a political ideology that reached America from 19th century Europe, opposed centralization by government, and favored the poor and working class. Martin (2003: 38–39) argues that anarchists were among the first anti-establishment radicals who opposed both capitalism and Marxism and advocated revolution; although they never offered a plan for replacing a central government. Anarchism in the United States was linked to the labor movement and the advocacy of a bombing campaign against industry and government (Combs, 2003: 163).

The Ecoterror movement in the United States focuses on both the dangers of humans encroaching on nature and preserving wilderness. The FBI (2002) defines **ecoterrorism** as the use or threatened use of violence of a criminal nature against innocent victims or property by an environmentally oriented, subnational group for environmental-political reasons or aimed at an audience beyond the target, often of a symbolic nature.

Ted Kaczynski (A.K.A. the Unabomber) was a modern day ecoterrorist. He was an anti-industrialist who targeted scientists and engineers. In 1996 he was arrested after a 17-year investigation that involved 16 bombings, including three deaths and many injuries. Upon pleading guilty in federal court, he is now serving a life sentence without the possibility of release.

Two major, domestic ecoterrorist groups are the **Animal Liberation Front (ALF)** and the **Earth Liberation Front (ELF)**. The FBI (2002) estimates that ALF and ELF have committed over 600 criminal acts in the United States since 1996, resulting in damage exceeding $43 million. Arson is the most destructive practice of ALF and ELF.

ALF is committed to ending the abuse and exploitation of animals. They seek to cause economic loss or destruction of the victim company's property. Victims include fur companies, mink farms, restaurants, and animal research laboratories.

ELF promotes "monkeywrenching," a euphemism for acts of sabotage and vandalism against companies that are perceived to be harming the environment. An example is "tree spiking," in which metal spikes are hammered into trees to damage logging saws.

Racial Supremacy
Continuing with the Griset and Mahan (2003: 86) typology of domestic terrorism, they view the racial supremacy and religious extremists classifications as right wing, but separate them based on their aims. Their research from multiple sources shows that "these two categories often overlap, but they have also developed separately—white supremacists without religion, and religious extremists without racism." The KKK, as covered earlier, has advocated hate for over a century. Griset and Mahan add that there are also black separatist groups in the United States calling themselves the "Nation of Islam" and they are followers of the Messenger Elijah Muhammad.

White supremacists are often critical of the U.S. Constitution and our government. These right-wing groups are diversified and include Skinheads, neo-Nazi Aryan Nations, militant gun advocates, antitax protesters, and survivalists.

Religious Extremists
This is the fifth typology of domestic terrorism according to Griset and Mahan (2003: 91–92). As covered earlier in this chapter, global religious terrorism has had a significant impact on terrorism in many countries. Domestically, White (2004: 11) refers to the Christian Identity movement and their claims that Jews are descendents of the devil, nonwhite people evolved from animals, and Caucasians are created in the image of God. Hoffman (1998) claims that Christian Patriot influence played a role in the Oklahoma City bombing, and those religious extremists, not necessarily of the Islamic faith, are involved in terrorism.

□ □ □ ▬▬▬▬▬▬▬▬▬▬▬▬▬▬▬▬▬▬▬▬▬

Although a lot of attention and resources are focused on international terrorists, domestic terrorists are also a serious threat.

□ □ □ ▬▬▬▬▬▬▬▬▬▬▬▬▬▬▬▬▬▬▬▬▬

Ruby Ridge, Waco, and Oklahoma City
The decade of the 1990s provides an excellent example of how citizen confrontations with the federal government can foment hate and violence from extremists. Martin (2003: G-8) defines **extremism** as follows: "Political opinions that are intolerant toward opposing interests and divergent opinions. Extremism forms the ideological foundation for political violence. Radical and reactionary extremists often rationalize and justify acts of violence committed on behalf of their cause."

The **Ruby Ridge** (Idaho) **incident** occurred in 1992 when U.S. Marshals tried to arrest Randy Weaver for failing to appear in court on charges of trying to sell illegal firearms to federal agents. Weaver was a white supremacist and believer in Christian Identity. Martin (2003: G-5) offers this definition for **Christian Identity:** "The American adaptation of

Anglo-Israelism. A racial supremacist mystical belief that holds that Aryans are the chosen people of God, the United States is the Aryan 'Promised Land,' non-Whites are soulless beasts, and Jews are biologically descended from the devil." During the siege of Weaver's mountain cabin by federal agents, a U.S. Marshal was killed, as well as Weaver's son. An FBI sniper fatally shot Weaver's pregnant wife as she stood in the cabin doorway prior to Randy Weaver's surrender. The Ruby Ridge incident became a symbol and inspiration for the struggle of right-wing extremists.

Another symbolic incident that inflamed right-wing extremists was the **Waco incident**, although it had nothing to do with right-wing extremism. On February 28, 1993, the Bureau of Alcohol, Tobacco, and Firearms (ATF), with numerous agents, tried to serve arrest and search warrants for illegal firearms on Vernon Howell, A.K.A. David Koresh. Koresh led the Branch Davidians at the Mount Carmel compound outside of Waco, Texas. He claimed that the end was near and that he was the second coming of Christ who would save the world. The ATF assault and gun battle involved thousands of rounds being fired from both sides. The media captured the fierce battle and showed, on television, ATF agents on an A-frame roof being hit by rounds fired through the wall from inside the compound as the agents attempted, but failed, to enter a window. Four ATF agents were killed and another 20 were injured, plus an unknown number of casualties on the Branch Davidian side.

Following the failed assault, the FBI was enlisted and a 51-day siege began. Continuous negotiations were unable to resolve the standoff as the Branch Davidians waited for a message from God. The FBI stopped electricity and water to the compound and bright lights and loud music were aimed at the compound at night to force members to leave. Some members did leave. Finally, on April 19, 1993, following unsuccessful negotiations, tear gas was pumped and fired into the compound. Fires began and then explosions from ammunition and combustibles created a huge fire. Seventy-five people, mostly women and children, perished; nine survived. The FBI, and especially the ATF, received an enormous amount of criticism, from many quarters, over the Waco incident (Combs, 2003: 178–179).

The **Oklahoma City bombing** was a major terrorist incident in the United States that occurred on April 19, 1995, when a powerful truck bomb exploded in front of the Alfred P. Murrah Federal Building (Figure 15-3). The attack killed 168 people and injured more than 500. The nine-story downtown building contained offices of the ATF, Secret Service, Drug Enforcement Administration, among other federal offices, and a day-care center. A rented Ryder truck served as the delivery weapon and it was converted into a mobile bomb containing ammonium nitrate, fuel oil, and Tovex (i.e., a high explosive that acted as a booster). The truck exploded near supporting columns at the front of the building, and then from the bottom up, floor slabs broke off in a "progressive collapse." The force of the explosion caused damage over several blocks in all directions (Poland, 2005: 184–186).

Initially, it was thought that a Middle East terrorist group targeted the building, but this was not the case. A clean-cut white male named Timothy McVeigh was arrested by authorities and prosecuted, convicted, and sentenced to death. In 2001, he was executed by lethal injection at the U.S. penitentiary in Terre Haute, Indiana.

McVeigh was a member of the **Patriot movement** that developed in the early 1990s. This group believes in "true" American ideals of individualism, armed citizens, and minimum interference from government. They distrust government and view it as no longer reflecting the will of the people, intrusive, and violently oppressive (Martin, 2003: 313).

Besides McVeigh, Terry Nichols, a friend from their service in the U.S. Army, was also arrested and convicted for the bombing. Interestingly, April 19, 1995, the day of the Oklahoma City attack, was the second anniversary of the law enforcement disaster at Waco.

FIGURE 15-3 Bombed Alfred P. Murrah Federal Building, Oklahoma City. *Courtesy:* DOD photo by Sgt. Preston Chasteen.

Terrorist Methods

Because of the loose, flexible, transnational network structure of modern terrorist organizations, facilitated by modern technology, terrorists can work together on funding, sharing intelligence, training, planning, and executing attacks (U.S. Government, 2003).

The **cellular model of organization** has helped transnational and homegrown terrorist groups adapt to threats from law enforcement and the military. This model is decentralized, rather than centralized. A decentralized cell is characterized by more discretion, very little, if any, communication within a larger chain of command, more self-sufficiency, and greater pressure to be creative and resourceful. This approach has also been referred to as **leaderless resistance.** Because a cell consists of a few members, and they know each other well, infiltration by government agents is very difficult. Since communication within a centralized chain of command or between cells in unnecessary, the interception of telephone calls, e-mails, and other forms of communication are less of a risk. Examples of successful cells with leaderless resistance are the al-Qaida network and the McVeigh-Nichols group.

Prior to the 9/11 attacks, the Taliban in Afghanistan permitted Osama bin Laden to operate al-Qaida training camps until the Taliban fell to U.S. forces. Because of global concern about terrorism and the efforts of many nations in combating it, there has been a shift by many terrorist to "home schooling," on-line training, and on-the-job training, as in Iraq. The Web offers a huge volume of information on political groups, terrorist groups, targets, methods and tactics of terrorism, bomb making, homeland security, policing, the military, and so forth.

The list that follows illustrates the range of methods terrorists employ and their cunning and creativity.

- Terrorists often falsify their identity, carry forged documents, and practice deception. They may change their appearance to deceive (e.g., shave a beard, wear a religious cross, carry a bible, and dress as the enemy).
- Terrorists, such as al-Qaida, are characterized by long-range planning, intense intelligence gathering, meticulous surveillance of potential targets, and the ability to conduct simultaneous attacks.
- They may communicate an anonymous threat to a potential target to monitor response and procedures.
- Terrorists often emulate military methods as they plan, train, and execute their attacks. They have a high level of concern for security of operations and they are in need of funds, weapons, communications equipment, and vehicles.
- They may use the identification, uniforms, or vehicles of delivery, utility, emergency or other type of service to access a target. Or, dress as females to lower the perceived threat.
- A terrorist may be planted in an organization as an employee to obtain information. The terrorist may work for a service or consulting firm to access many locations.
- Terrorists may attempt to detect surveillance by conducting dry runs of planned activities, using secondary roads and public transportation, employing neighborhood lookouts and tail vehicles, and establishing prearranged signals.
- Terrorists are keenly aware that counterterrorism analysts study terrorist groups, seek intelligence, and piece together information to anticipate terrorist plans and attacks. Studies of terrorist groups and their methods are available from many sources. Terrorists study these resources and, in a "cat and mouse game," seek to mislead analysts by releasing bogus information to disrupt the intelligence process. Terrorists maintain an advantage over analysts because terrorists plot and analysts must seek to uncover the plot.
- Domestic right-wing terrorists are less organized than terrorists with links to the Middle East. The Christian Identify movement, with connections to the KKK, and World Church of the Creator members, are noted for limited planning and random violence by lone wolves.
- ALF and ELF commit arson through the use of improvised incendiary devices equipped with crude timing components. Members develop intelligence through surveillance of targets and reviews of industry publications. They may post details of their bombing devices and targets on their Web sites.
- ALF and ELF, like al-Qaida, have a decentralized structure and operate in cells. ALF and ELF carry out direct action according to Web-posted guidelines. Each cell is autonomous and anonymous.

Methods of Violence

Terrorists favor certain types of violent acts. These include bombings, suicide bombings, assassinations, assaults, kidnappings, and hijacking. Terrorists have tremendous advantages over authorities as they secretly plan their surprise attacks with discretion and flexibility over target location, victims, time of attack, weapons, and creative methods.

Bombings are a favored method of violence chosen by terrorists because of the potential for high casualties and severe property damage. The terrorist can remain at a distance from a detonated bomb and avoid injury and initial capture. The **secondary explosion** is a horrible terrorist ploy: an initial explosion draws first responders, assets, bystanders, and the media; then, a second, larger bomb is detonated for more devastating losses. Suicide bombings are especially effective, inexpensive, shock society and government, and guarantee media coverage. The terrorist can precisely deliver the bomb and there is no need for an escape plan or concern about interrogation by authorities.

Terrorist Weapons

Terrorists employ a variety of small arms, grenades, mortars, and explosives. Four weapons used by terrorists are the AK-47, RPG-7, Stinger missile, and SA-7. These are explained next.

AK-47 (Soviet rifle). This weapon was invented by Mikhail Kalashnikov and it became the standard rifle for the Soviet Army in 1949 until it was succeeded by the AKM. During the Cold War, the AK-47 (Figure 15-4) was supplied by the former Soviet Union to anti-Western armed forces and insurgent terrorists. It became a symbol of left-wing revolution and it is still in the arsenal of armies, guerrillas, and terrorists. Between 30 and 50 million copies and variations of the AK-47 were distributed globally to make it the most widely used rifle in the world.

RPG-7 (Rocket Propelled Grenade). Issued by the former Soviet Union, China, and North Korea, this simple weapon is effective against a variety of targets within a range of about 500 meters for a fixed target (e.g., building) and about 300 meters when fired at a moving target. The RPG-7 (Figure 15-5) is a shoulder-fired, muzzle-loaded, antitank and antipersonnel grenade launcher. It can also bring down a helicopter. The RPG-7 fires a fin-stabilized, oversized grenade from a tube. The launcher weighs 15.9 pounds and has an optical sight. Upon firing, it leaves a telltale blue-gray smoke and flash signature that helps to identify the firer. U.S. forces in Vietnam used sandbags and chicken wire on vehicles to cause the RPG-7 grenade to explode before meeting the skin of vehicles. This technique continues to be applied, as in Iraq. Additional protection methods include avoiding the same route, pushing through ambush positions to avoid setting up a target, smoke grenades, and aerial surveillance (Mordica, 2003). The RPG is widely available in illegal international arms markets and is in the arsenal of many terrorists groups, such as those in the Middle East and Latin America.

Stinger. The U.S.-made stinger is a single person, portable, heat seeking, shoulder-fired surface-to-air missile (SAM). It proved its value when the Afghan Mujahedeen forced the Soviets out of Afghanistan during the late 1980s. The Stinger has targeted jets, helicopters, and commercial airliners.

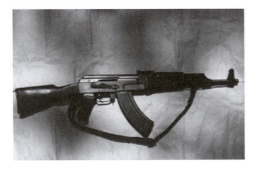

FIGURE 15-4 AK-47, Soviet Assault Rifle.

FIGURE 15-5 Rocket propelled grenade and launcher. *Source:* www.hamasonline.com

SA-7. When the Soviet Union collapsed, thousands of SAMs were sold and found their way into the arsenals of several terrorist and guerrilla groups. The SA-7, also called the Grail, uses an optical sight and tracking system with an infrared (i.e., heat-seeking) device to reach aircraft.

Bombs and Other Explosives

A bomb can be placed in almost anything—a pipe, letter, book, package, cell phone, radio, vehicle, bicycle, podium, pillow, and so forth. Terrorist bombs are mostly improvised. In other words, they construct bombs from readily available materials or the misappropriation of military or commercial blasting supplies. The Web or terrorist training and manuals provide instructions. **Improvised explosive device (IED)** is the name for such assembled bombs that kill or maim. In an IED, the trigger activates the fuse that ignites the explosive. These three components are integrated in various ways in IEDs. Nails and other materials may be added to the IED to increase lethality. An IED may contain an anti-handling device that causes it to detonate when it is handled or moved. Coalition personnel in Iraq have been repeatedly killed when IEDs—hidden along roads in trash containers, light poles, dead people (including Americans) and animals, and other locations—were detonated while convoys and patrols passed nearby.

Weapons of Mass Destruction

A **weapon of mass destruction (WMD)** is something capable of inflicting mass casualties and/or destroying or rendering high-value assets as useless. Although chemical, biological, nuclear, and radiological weapons often serve as examples of WMD, many things can be used as a WMD. This became painfully true from the 9/11 attacks.

The term **weapon of mass effect (WME)** describes the human reactions and events surrounding the use of a WMD that may result in limited or no casualties or physical damage. The mass effect may be sensationalized media reporting, panic, and social and political change.

Biological Weapons

The use of biological weapons has a long history. The United States, England, the former Soviet Union, and many other countries have developed biological weapons over many decades. Treaties attempt to eliminate production of such weapons and destroy current inventories.

Like chemical weapons, biological weapons may be perceived as a "poor person's atomic bomb" and developing countries may look to these WMD as an avenue to deter enemies. A biological weapons program is easy to disguise because the same biotechnology equipment is used in pharmaceutical manufacturing.

Biological weapons cause flu-like symptoms and then death. Detection and containment are difficult because the onset of symptoms and then the identification of the agent are delayed.

The delivery methods for biological agents vary and include sprayer, artillery shell, and missile. The strategy for respiratory infections is to create a cloud of suspended microscopic droplets containing bacterial or virus particles.

The Centers for Disease Control Web site offers extensive information on WMD. Five common types of biological agents are bacteria, rickettsiae, viruses, fungi, and toxins.

Anthrax is emphasized here because it was used to attack the United States in 2001. It is a deadly infectious disease caused by the bacterium called *Bacillus anthracis*. Its occurrence is rare in the United States, it is not contagious, and the victims must be directly exposed to it. Infection occurs in three forms: cutaneous (i.e., from a cut on the skin), inhalation, and intestinal (i.e., eating tainted meat). Symptoms: for cutaneous anthrax, a skin ulcer; for inhalation anthrax, respiratory failure; and for intestinal anthrax, nausea, vomiting, and diarrhea. Treatment includes antibiotics administered early on and a vaccine exists.

During the fall of 2001, following the 9/11 attacks, letters containing anthrax spores were mailed to news media personnel and congressional officials, leading to the first case of intentional release of anthrax in the United States (U.S. General Accounting Office, 2003). Several states and Washington, D.C., were affected. Eleven people were victimized by the cutaneous form and 11 from the inhalation form. Five people died, all from inhalation anthrax.

The anthrax was in the form of white powder placed in envelopes. During mail processing at post offices, other government offices, and businesses, it was released and it contaminated air, equipment, buildings and people who touched and inhaled the spores. Besides the unfortunate casualties, the attacks caused enormous disruptions and expenses to organizations. At about the same time, other countries reported similar attacks.

Chemical Weapons

Chemical weapons evolved more recently in history than biological weapons. World War I became the first battleground noted for massive casualties from chemical weapons. Compared to other major WMD, chemical agents such as pulmonary, blood, and blister are relatively easy to manufacture. Nerve agents are more difficult to produce. These substances are also commercially available, examples being cleaning fluids and insecticides.

Chemical agents may work immediately or cause delayed reactions. Some are difficult to detect because they are odorless and tasteless. Most chemical agents are in a liquid form that must be aerosolized into droplets to be inhaled to be effective.

As with other WMD, dual use equipment and technology help terrorists disguise their intentions. Imagine the casualties from a chemical attack by a crop duster over a sports stadium, or by use of the Global Positioning System (GPS) to guide planes (manned or unmanned drones) to a target, or by backing up a truck to a building HVAC system.

Terrorists have employed chemical weapons in the past. The **Aum Shinrikyo cult**, established in 1987, aimed to take over Japan and then the world to purify everyone. On March 20, 1995, Aum members pierced bags of the chemical nerve agent sarin on five separate subway trains as they converged on central Tokyo. The attack killed twelve passengers and injured up to 6,000 as they fled while sickened and bleeding. The cult had previously tried, but failed, to use biological agents. Interestingly, Japanese police were scheduled to raid the cult's headquarters in Tokyo on March 22nd to seize WMD. However, the cult had infiltrated the Japanese police, were tipped off about the impending raid, and they hastily launched the attack. The casualties would have been worse, but the sarin was not pure and the method of release was primitive.

Nuclear Weapons

To end World War II in the Pacific against the Japanese, and to avoid massive U.S. casualties from an invasion of the Japanese mainland, President Harry Truman approved the dropping of atomic bombs on Hiroshima and Nagasaki in 1945. Both cities were obliterated and sustained massive casualties. Then, an arms race began that continues today. The "nuclear club" has expanded from the United States to the United Kingdom, France, Russia, the People's Republic of China, India, Pakistan, Israel, South Africa, North Korea, and other countries that possess covert development programs (e.g., Iran).

According to the United Nations, Office on Drugs and Crime (n.d.), when the Cold War ended, a black market in Soviet-era weapons began to flourish. Former Soviet citizens participated in smuggling nuclear materials from poorly secured facilities to unknown buyers and transnational criminal organizations. The market for nuclear materials includes "rogue states," desperate national liberation movements, and suppressed ethnic groups. What makes matters worse is that there are 280-armed conflicts of varying intensity occurring in the world.

The explosion of a nuclear weapon creates a large fireball. Everything in the fireball vaporizes, including soil and water, and the fireball goes upward creating a large mushroom cloud. Radioactive material from the weapon mixes with the particles in the cloud and then the mixture falls to earth in what is called fallout. Because fallout is composed of particles, it may be carried by wind for long distances. Since the fallout is radioactive, it can contaminate anything it lands on, such as water resources and crops (Centers for Disease Control, n.d.).

Radiological Weapons

Radiological weapons contain radioactive material that, although not exploding itself, is scattered by a conventional explosive. These weapons are often called "dirty bombs" and consist of radioactive material attached to a conventional bomb. The technical name for "dirty bomb" is **radiological dispersion device** (RDD). It may contain radioactive material that is sealed in metal to prevent dispersal when handling it. Upon explosion, initial fatalities may be low, but climb over time due to cancer. However, the actual harm will depend on the grade of the radioactive material and the amount released. This weapon can make buildings and land unusable for many years. Its use can cause enormous expenses, fear, panic, and sensationalized media coverage.

Because terrorists are known to be creative, we can only surmise as to how they would construct a RDD and where it would be applied. It may become part of a vehicle bomb, detonated in a school, or introduced into food or water supplies.

Commercially available radiological materials are used in many industries to, as examples, sterilize food, detect flaws in metal, and to treat cancer. Many sources are not secure.

The detonation of a RDD is a serious possibility in the future. In November of 1995, Chechen rebels placed a RDD, using dynamite and cesium 137, in Moscow's Izmailovo Park. It was not detonated. In 2002, suspected al-Qaida member Jose Padilla, trained in terrorist camps in Afghanistan, was arrested in Chicago for his role in a plot to explode a RDD in the United States.

□ □ □ ▬▬▬▬▬▬▬▬▬▬▬▬▬▬▬▬▬▬▬▬▬▬▬▬▬

Do you think terrorists will use Weapons of Mass Destruction (WMD) in the future? Why or why not?

▬▬▬▬▬▬▬▬▬▬▬▬▬▬▬▬▬▬▬▬▬▬▬▬▬ □ □ □

Homeland Security

Homeland Security Defined

Homeland security is an evolving concept. The U.S. Department of Homeland Security (DHS) is continuously developing its mission under changing circumstances and events. Numerous variables influence the DHS, such as terrorist incidents, natural disasters, public opinion, and politics.

The Office of Homeland Security (2002) provides the following definition: "**Homeland security (HS)** is a concerted national effort to prevent terrorist attacks within the United States, reduce America's vulnerability to terrorism, and minimize the damage and recover from attacks that do occur." How this definition evolves is subject to debate. Will HS become more responsive to "all hazards," such as hurricanes and pandemics? Will it increase its emphasis on emergency management? Will it expand its cooperation with the private sector? HS is in its infancy and its evolution remains to be seen. At the same time, numerous publications help to define the problem of terrorism and the strategies of homeland security and national security (Figure 15-6).

The Measurement of Terrorism

Data collected on terrorism influence not only government action against it—such as laws, plans, policies, budgets, and strategies—but also evaluations of government action. Measurements of terrorism also impact the business of counterterrorism, decisions on the geographic locations of business investment, and tourism.

Disagreement exists over the methodology applied to the measurement of terrorism, and methodological differences influence both conclusions on terrorism and policy. Ideally, measurements of terrorism should be value free, providing an objective foundation for government policy. Official government data has been a major source of information on terrorism. *Do measurements of terrorism really reflect the administration of counterterrorism (e.g., how terrorism is defined; number of intelligence analysts and enforcement officers; number of investigations and arrests; and data collection and software), rather than actual terrorism?*

FIGURE 15-6 Numerous publications help to define the problem of terrorism and the strategies of homeland security and national security.

Besides government measurements of terrorism, other sources of research on terrorism are universities and the private sector. The topics of research on terrorism that influence policy are varied and include surveys of citizens' perceptions of terrorism and their fear of terrorism, and the role of the media in influencing perceptions of terrorism and terrorism itself.

The methodological problems of measuring terrorism include inconsistency in terminology, varied criteria of what acts to include and exclude from data, researcher bias, difficulty in making comparisons among different sources of data, political interference, and excessive delay in publishing data.

Grosskopf (2006) writes that "although terrorist attacks are often measured in loss of life and destruction, the immeasurable toll and intended consequence of terrorism is fear. The power of terror lies not only in attacks themselves, but also in the expectation and unpredictability of an attack." Grosskopf calls for more attention to fear and its consequences.

The U.S. Department of State (DOS), Office of Inspector General (OIG) (2005), reported that in April of 2005, less than one month before the DOS was to issue its 2004 mandated annual report, *Patterns of Global Terrorism*, the DOS ceased publishing it and instead published the first of its *Country Reports on Terrorism* (CRT). This new report excluded the statistical data on significant international terrorist incidents that were found in the *Patterns* reports. Simultaneously, the National Counterterrorism Center (NCTC) published a separate report entitled *A Chronology of Significant International Terrorism 2004* that included statistical data that previously had been in the *Patterns* reports. The NCTC's 2004 report showed an increase in the number of reported significant international terrorist incidents between 2003 and 2004. The NCTC stated that the increase was "primarily the result of a modified reporting methodology as well as an increase in staff devoted to identifying terrorist incidents."

National Counterterrorism Center

The NCTC was established by The Intelligence Reform and Terrorism Prevention Act of 2004. The Director of the Center is appointed by the President with advice and consent of the Senate. The purpose of the Center is detection, prevention, disruption, preemption, and mitigation of transnational terrorism against the people and interests of the United States. The Center analyzes and integrates global intelligence, excluding purely domestic information, and it facilitates the exchange of information among government agencies. It conducts strategic operational planning for counterterrorism activities, including diplomatic, financial, military, homeland security, and law enforcement. The Center does not direct the execution of operations. The Center works with the CIA to prepare an annual report to the President.

The NCTC's 2004 report indicated about 9,300 individuals wounded or killed in significant international terrorist incidents as compared to 4,271 a year earlier. Of those, 1,907 were killed in 2004 in comparison to 625 deaths in 2003. Of the 68 Americans killed in 2004, all but eight were killed in Iraq and Afghanistan. The overwhelming number of victims were non-U.S. citizens, and many were Muslims. In 2004, there were 651 significant attacks, compared to 208 in 2003, about a threefold increase. Ten percent of the total (64 attacks) were against U.S. interests, down from over one-third from the previous year. The NCTC contends that terrorist attacks are becoming more deadly. The top five attacks in 2004 resulted in over 4,000 wounded and dead. Also, terrorism is becoming less U.S. focused and more global in scope (Perl, 2006: 4).

National Memorial Institute for the Prevention of Terrorism

The National Memorial Institute for the Prevention of Terrorism (MIPT) is a non-profit institution focused on deterring and preventing terrorism on U.S. soil and mitigating its consequences. It was formed following the 1995 Oklahoma City bombing and is funded through the Department of Homeland Security. The MIPT sponsors research on procedures, training, and equipment relevant to emergency responders.

The MIPT Terrorism Knowledge Base (TKB) is a team effort of the MIPT, DFI International, the Rand Corporation, and university professors. This user-friendly Web resource provides information on domestic and international terrorism, terrorist incidents, and terrorist groups. It contains research, interactive maps, data, and links to other resources.

The TKB methodologies include data that is integrated from multiple terrorism incident resources, including both the RAND and NCTC incident tracking systems. Terrorism group and leader profiles are from DFI International. An indictment database is also contained in the TKB.

The following TKB data is from the National Memorial Institute for the Prevention of Terrorism (2006). For *domestic terrorism* (i.e., defined as incidents by local nationals against a purely domestic target), between January 1, 2003, and December 31, 2005, the TKB reported 33 attacks in North America, primarily by ALF and ELF, with most labeled as "attacked business target," "attacked private citizens and property target," and "attacked government target." No injuries or fatalities were reported. For domestic terrorism during the same period, the TKB reported that the Middle East/Persian Gulf region had the highest numbers in three categories at 1,882 incidents, 6,671 injuries, and 3,313 fatalities. The regions of North America and East and Central Asia showed the lowest numbers among other regions for domestic terrorism.

For *international terrorism* (i.e., defined as incidents when terrorists go abroad to attack, or choose a domestic target with links to other countries, or attack an aircraft), between January 1, 2003, and December 31, 2005, the TKB reported that the Middle East/Persian Gulf region had the highest numbers in the three categories at 458 incidents, 2,029 injuries, and 774 fatalities.

MIPT data comparing 2004 with 2005 show the following: Global incidents overall increased about 50%. Whereas the Middle East and South Asia (i.e., includes Pakistan, Afghanistan, and India) account for this increase, terrorist incidents in other regions of the world decreased by an average of almost 40%. Domestic incidents increased more than international incidents, pointing to an increase in internal conflicts among nations. There was also a 35% increase in fatalities and a 15% increase in injuries. As the measurement of terrorism is being refined, we are seeing a sharing of the same data among organizations.

National Security and Homeland Security

Here we look at the "big picture" of security for the United States. The Office of Homeland Security (2002) discussed the link between the National Security Strategy of the United States (NSSUS) and the National Strategy for Homeland Security (NSHS). The Preamble to the U.S. Constitution defines the federal government's basic purpose as "… to form a more perfect Union, establish justice, insure domestic Tranquility, provide for the common defense, promote the general Welfare, and secure the Blessings of Liberty to ourselves and our Posterity." The **National Security Strategy of the United States** aims to ensure the sovereignty and independence of the United States, with our values and institutions intact. It includes the application of political, economic, and military power (Figure 15-7) to ensure the survival of our nation. Both the NSSUS and the NSHS complement each other by addressing the challenge of terrorism. This link between both major strategies is important because "America has sought to protect its own sovereignty and independence through a strategy of global presence and engagement. In so doing, America has helped many other countries and peoples advance along the path of democracy, open markets, individual liberty, and peace with their neighbors." At the same time, there are enemies who disagree with America's role in the world and use violence to express their views. Because the United States is a great power, terrorists must use unconventional methods and weapons. They also take advantage of America's free society and openness to covertly insert terrorists into the United States.

According to the White House under President George W. Bush, the Office of Homeland Security (2002) released the **National Strategy for Homeland Security** as a comprehensive and shared vision of how best to protect America from terrorist attacks. This strategy was compiled with the assistance of many people in a variety of occupations in the public and private sectors. A major goal was to facilitate shared responsibility and cooperation.

Publication of the NSHS preceded Congressional approval of the DHS. The intent of the executive branch of government in publishing the NSHS was to provide a strategic vision for the proposed DHS that was eventually supported by Congress through the Homeland Security Act of 2002.

The NSHS concentrates on six critical mission areas:

- Intelligence and Warning
- Border and Transportation Security
- Domestic Counterterrorism
- Protecting Critical Infrastructure and Key Assets
- Defending Against Catastrophic Threats
- Emergency Preparedness and Response

FIGURE 15-7 U.S. Air Force F-16C fighter jet. Military power is an option to ensure the survival of the United States. However, other options, such as diplomacy, are available to settle differences among nations. *Courtesy*: Senior Airman Sean Sides.

Homeland security and national security are intertwined because of the global scope of terrorism and the interdependencies of the United States with other countries. Whether we are referring to aviation security, border security, security of containerized cargo entering ports, intelligence, or other aspects of security, international cooperation is essential to integrate domestic and international security strategies to avoid gaps that could be exploited by terrorists.

The Rand Corporation (Larson and Peters, 2001) provides additional insight into the relationship between national security and homeland security. When the prevention of terrorist attacks fail, government must respond through five missions:

- *Assist civilians:* First responders and local agencies and resources are the backbone of this effort.
- *Ensure continuity of government:* The 9/11 attacks illustrated the need for the protection of government leaders.
- *Ensure continuity of military operations:* Terrorist attacks could require domestic assistance from the military, besides an armed response to terrorists. Defense planners must protect military personnel and resources. The 9/11 attack on the Pentagon serves as an example.
- *Border and coastal defense:* The border of the United States includes thousands of miles along the Canadian border, the Mexican border, and the east and west coasts. Access controls and inspections are necessary for people, vehicles, and goods reaching the United States. This overwhelming workload falls on a variety of federal, state, and local agencies.
- *National air defense:* For many years, the Air Force operated the North American Air Defense Command (NORAD) to detect and provide warning of missile or bomber attacks, especially during the Cold War. Following the 9/11 attacks, the Department of Defense formed the **U.S. Northern Command (NORTH-COM)** to provide air and other types of defense for the United States.

Besides the NSSUS and the NSHS, which together take precedence over all other national strategies, there are other, more specific, strategies of the United States that are subsumed within the twin concepts of national security and homeland security. They are

- National Defense Strategy
- National Strategy for Combating Terrorism
- National Strategy to Combat Weapons of Mass Destruction
- National Strategy to Secure Cyberspace
- National Drug Control Strategy
- National Money Laundering Strategy

U. S. Government Action Against Terrorism

The U.S. Government (2003) issued a *National Strategy for Combating Terrorism* that focused on four fronts as explained next.

Defeat. This goal of the 4D strategy aims to defeat terrorist organizations of global reach through diplomatic, economic, information, law enforcement, military, financial, intelligence, and other instruments of power. The United States cannot wait for terrorists to attack and then respond. Thus, the United States will attack terrorist sanctuaries, leadership, command, communications, material support, and finances. Then, the United States will work with regional partners to squeeze and isolate terrorists. Terrorists who seek WMD will be high priority targets.

Deny. All nations must accept responsibility for taking action against terrorists within their borders. This means denying terrorists sanctuary and the opportunity to exist, train, plan, and execute attacks. Nations will be held accountable for the actions of their "guests."

Diminish. This goal seeks to reduce political, social, and economic conditions that terrorists exploit. "While we recognize that there are many countries and people living with poverty, deprivation, social disenfranchisement, and unresolved political and regional disputes, those conditions do not justify the use of terror." The United States works with other nations to reduce unfortunate conditions and to win the "war of ideas" in support of democratic values and to promote economic freedom. Furthermore, finding a solution to the Israeli-Palestinian conflict is vital.

Defend. Terrorists are an adaptive enemy who are empowered by modern technology and emboldened by success, while avoiding the strengths of the United States and exploiting its vulnerabilities. The United States will defend its people, territory, national interests, and democratic principles. Within this strategy is the adage that the best defense is a good offense. The plan includes a focused effort from the entire U.S. society—federal, state, and local governments, the private sector, and the American people. A major component of defense is the National Strategy for Homeland Security.

In September of 2006, the executive branch of government updated the National Strategy for Combating Terrorism (U.S. Government, 2006). Although the strategy remains primarily the same, the update noted successes in degrading al-Qaida and the need to adjust counterterrorism measures as terrorists change their methods. Challenges that remain include terrorists that are more dispersed, the impossibility of preventing all attacks, the threat of WMD, nations such as Syria and Iran that support terrorists, and the use of modern technology (e.g., the Internet) by terrorists.

The U.S. Department of State (2004) reiterates the *National Strategy for Combating Terrorism* and also emphasizes five "tools."

- *Diplomacy:* Through diplomacy, the U.S. Department of State promotes *allies for mutual benefit.*
- *Law Enforcement:* International law enforcement cooperation increased following the 9/11 attacks and it continues to expand.
- *Intelligence:* Quality intelligence shared among nations helps to track down terrorists and expose their plans.
- *Financial:* Countries throughout the world are waging a campaign to investigate, identify, and interdict the flow of money to terrorists groups. Recommendations have been developed among nations to protect their financial systems from terrorist financiers.
- *Military:* In Iraq, Afghanistan, and other locations, military forces are combating terrorists.

Legislative Action Against Terrorism

Laws, executive orders, and presidential directives provided the legal foundation for the war against terrorism prior to and following the 9/11 attacks. Here is a list of relevant laws enacted by Congress.

The **Defense Against Weapons of Mass Destruction Act of 1996**, also called Nunn-Lugar, was influenced by three major terrorist attacks: the World Trade Center bombing in 1993, the Oklahoma City bombing in 1995, and the Tokyo subway sarin gas attack in 1995. This Act provided the impetus for increased federal government preparedness activities, and funding for training and equipment for first responders to respond to terrorism and WMD.

The **Antiterrorism and Effective Death Penalty Act of 1996** was designed to prevent terrorist acts, enhance counterterrorism methods, and increase punishments. It provided funding for antiterrorism measures by federal and state authorities and includes the death penalty under Federal law when a death results from a terrorist act.

The **USA Patriot Act of 2001** includes a broad array of measures to protect the United States. It focuses on counterterrorism funding, enhanced police surveillance, anti-money laundering programs, border protection, victim compensation, information sharing, strengthening criminal laws against terrorism, and improved intelligence.

The Act expanded police powers to investigate and apprehend terrorist suspects. It authorizes roving wiretaps. This means that police can obtain a warrant for a wiretap on *any* telephone used by a suspected terrorist. Prior to the Act, judicial authorization was required for each telephone. In addition, federal law enforcement officers can obtain search warrants that can be used nationwide and their subpoena powers were increased to obtain e-mail records of terrorists.

The Act relaxed restrictions on sharing information among U.S. law enforcement agencies and the intelligence community. The Treasury Department was provided with greater authority to force foreign banks dealing with U.S. banks to release information on large accounts suspected of money laundering.

Under the Act, immigrant terrorist suspects can be held up to seven days for questioning without specific charges. Criminal penalties were enhanced for terrorist acts, financing and harboring terrorists, and possession of WMD.

An erosion of civil liberties became a major concern of those critical of the Patriot Act. To allay some of these fears, lawmakers included sunset provisions in this law so that expanded police powers would expire in four years.

The **USA Patriot Improvement and Reauthorization Act of 2005** extended the Patriot Act, although it will face debate in four years on certain provisions. According to the White House, since the Patriot Act was first enacted, it has been vital to the war against terrorism and protecting the American people, while breaking up terror cells and prosecuting terrorist operatives in several states (U.S. Government, White House, 2006).

The **Homeland Security Act of 2002** began the largest single reorganization of the federal government since 1947 when President Truman created the Department of Defense. President George W. Bush signed it into law on November 25, 2002. The Act was created primarily because of criticism that the 9/11 attacks could have been prevented if federal agencies had an improved system of cooperating with each other and sharing intelligence. The Act

- Established the **Department of Homeland Security (DHS)**, as an agency of the executive branch of government, with a DHS secretary who reports to the president. The DHS consolidated 22 agencies, with about 170,000 employees, under one unified organization with the aim of improving defenses against terrorism, coordinating intelligence, and minimizing the damage from attacks and natural disasters.
- Established within the office of the president the Homeland Security Council to advise the president.
- Detailed an organization chart and management structure for the DHS.
- Listed agencies and programs to be transferred to the DHS.
- Stated the responsibilities of the five directorates of the DHS: Information Analysis and Infrastructure Protection; Science and Technology; Border and Transportation Security; Emergency Preparedness and Response; and Management.

Hogue and Bea (2006: 4) write that homeland security is an outgrowth of decades of debate and organizing by government for emergency preparedness and civil defense. Major issues at the center of this debate include: the boundaries and limitations of jurisdiction among federal government departments and agencies and between federal and state governments; requirements for a response from the Department of Defense; and the sufficiency of federal statutory policies for unforeseen emergencies.

□ □ □ ▬▬▬▬▬▬▬▬▬▬▬▬▬▬▬▬▬▬▬▬▬▬▬▬▬▬▬▬▬▬

DHS does not have overarching authority for directing all aspects of the homeland security mission. As examples, the Department of Justice, the Department of Health and Human Services, and the Department of Defense are still major players in homeland security.

Gilmore Commission, 2003

□ □ □ ▬▬▬▬▬▬▬▬▬▬▬▬▬▬▬▬▬▬▬▬▬▬▬▬▬▬▬▬▬▬

The 9/11 Commission Report

The 9/11 Commission Report was prepared by the National Commission on Terrorist Attacks Upon the United States (2004). This Commission was an independent, bipartisan group created by congressional legislation and President George W. Bush in late

2002 to prepare an account of the 9/11 attacks, the U.S. response, and recommendations to guard against future attacks. This document of over 400 pages is summarized
next from the *Executive Summary*.

Findings
- U.S. air defense on 9–11–01 depended on close interaction between the Federal
  Aviation Administration (FAA) and the North American Aerospace Defense
  Command (NORAD). At the time of the attacks, protocols were unsuited for
  hijacked planes being used as WMD. NORAD planning focused on hijacked
  planes coming from overseas. Senior military and FAA leaders had no effective
  communication with each other. Even the President could not reach some senior
  officials.
- None of the measures adopted by the U.S. government from 1998 to 2001
  disturbed or even delayed the progress of the al-Qaida 9/11 plot. The terrorists
  located and exploited a broad array of weaknesses in security. They studied publicly
  available materials on aviation security and used weapons with less metal content
  than a handgun. Airline personnel were trained to be nonconfrontational in the
  event of a hijacking.
- Operational failures included not sharing information linking individuals in the
  USS Cole attack to the 9/11 terrorists, not discovering fraud on visa applications
  and passports, and not expanding no fly lists to include names from terrorist watch
  lists.
- "The most important failure was one of imagination." Leaders did not understand
  the gravity of the threat from al-Qaida.
- Terrorism was not the overriding national security concern under the Clinton or
  pre-9/11 Bush administrations. The attention Congress gave terrorism was "episodic
  and splintered across several committees."
- The FBI was not able to link intelligence from agents in the field to national
  priorities.
- The U.S. government failed at pooling and efficiently using intelligence from the
  CIA, FBI, State Department, and military.
- U.S. diplomatic efforts were unsuccessful at persuading the Taliban regime in
  Afghanistan to stop offering sanctuary to al-Qaida and to expel bin Laden to a
  country where he could face justice.
- "Protecting borders was not a national security issue before 9/11."
- Following the attacks, first responders performed well and saved many lives. In
  New York, decision-making was hampered by problems in command and control.
  Radios were unable to assist multiple commands in responding in a unified
  fashion.

Recommendations
- Because of action by our government, we are safer today than on September 11,
  2001. "But we are not safe." Therefore, we make the following recommendations.
- "The enemy is not just 'terrorism.' It is the threat posed specifically by Islamist
  terrorism, by bin Laden and others who draw on a long tradition of extreme
  intolerance within a minority strain of Islam that does not distinguish politics from
  religion, and distorts both. The enemy is not Islam, the great world faith, but a
  perversion of Islam."
- Post-9/11 efforts rightly included military action to topple the Taliban and pursue
  al-Qaida. A broad array of methods must be continued for success: diplomacy,
  intelligence, covert action, law enforcement, economic policy, foreign aid, and
  homeland defense.
- A strategy of three dimensions is proposed: attack terrorists and their organizations;
  prevent the continued growth of Islamist terrorism through coalition efforts, a
  vision for a better future, and support for public education and economic openness;

and protect against and prepare for terrorist attacks by applying biometric identifiers, improving transportation security, sharing information, improving federal funding to high risk cities, enhancing first responder capabilities and communications, and cooperating with the private sector that controls 85% of the nation's infrastructure.

- Establish a National Counterterrorism Center (NCTC) to build unity of effort across the U.S. government, including the CIA, FBI, DOD, and Homeland Security. The NCTC would not make policy, which would be the work of the President and the National Security Council.
- Appoint a National Intelligence Director (NID) to oversee the NCTC. The NID should report to the President, yet be confirmed by the Senate. The system of "need to know" should be replaced by a system of "need to share."

The 9/11 Commission officially ended in August of 2004 after issuing its recommendations. However, it continued operating with private funds as the 9/11 Public Discourse Project to monitor federal government progress on the recommendations. In December 2005, the Commission met for the last time to provide a "report card" on government action. The Commission gave the government several "Fs" and "Ds" and one "A." It characterized the failures as "shocking" and "scandalous" because of a lack of urgency by the government. The government received an "F" on such issues as allocating funds to cities based upon risk, improving radio communications for first responders, and prescreening airline passengers. The only "A" was for controlling terrorist financing.

State and Local Governments

Security and loss prevention practitioners should understand the roles, capabilities, and limitations of state and local governments in homeland security. Such information serves as input for business continuity planning.

The United States has over 87,000 jurisdictions of overlapping federal, state, and local governments. This system presents challenges as HS is increased through enhanced coordination and communications, law enforcement and prevention, emergency response, and policy development and implementation. All states and many local jurisdictions have established a homeland security office in the executive branch to deal with terrorist attacks and a variety of other risks. Coordination is vital to avoid duplication and to produce the best possible multiagency emergency response to serious events.

Every day, minor or major disasters strike in American and it is the local agencies that respond. Fire fighters, police, and emergency medical technicians are the **first responders** who rush to the scene to preserve life and to reduce property damage. Consequently, a terrorist attack or natural disaster becomes a local event, and the FBI, DHS, and FEMA do not arrive until later. A U.S. Conference of Mayors report noted in 2003, "When you dial 9–1–1, the phone doesn't ring in the White House ... those calls come in to your city's police, fire, and emergency medical personnel ... our domestic troops."

In its fifth and final annual report to the President and Congress, the *Gilmore Commission* released several critical statements pertaining to the federal role in leading state and local jurisdictions to improve HS. The full name of the Commission is: Advisory Panel to Assess Domestic Response Capabilities for Terrorism Involving Weapons of Mass Destruction (2003). A major question asked by the Commission was: "If local responders are in fact our first line of defense, have we succeeded in effectively empowering and enhancing State and local capabilities?" The Commission's extensive research included the following: States feel the federal government is giving them some support, although areas for improvement still exist; the deficit in intelligence and information sharing requires continued improvement; and inequality in funding is another problem.

☐ ☐ ☐ ▬▬▬▬▬▬▬▬▬▬▬▬▬▬▬▬▬▬▬▬▬▬▬▬▬

Homeland Security Advisory System

The DHS established the **Homeland Security Advisory System** (HSAS) to assist the Nation in remaining vigilant, prepared, and ready to deter terrorist attacks. The following threat conditions each represent an increasing risk of attack and some suggested protective measures are listed for federal departments and agencies.

- *Low Condition (Green)* is declared when there is a low risk of attack. Protective measures should include: training, assessment of vulnerabilities, and mitigation of vulnerabilities.
- *Guarded Condition (Blue)* results when there is a general risk of attack. In addition to the measures taken in the previous level, the following measures should be considered: checking communications with designated emergency response or command locations, reviewing and updating emergency response procedures, and providing the public with protective information.
- *Elevated Condition (Yellow)* is declared when there is significant risk of terrorist attacks. This level builds upon measures taken in lower threat conditions and adds increasing surveillance of critical locations, coordinating emergency plans among jurisdictions, refining protective measures according to the threat, and implementing appropriate contingency and emergency response plans.
- *High Condition (Orange)* reflects a high risk of attack. In addition to protective measures in the previous threat conditions, the following measures should be considered: coordinating security efforts with federal, state, and local law enforcement agencies or any National Guard or other armed forces organizations; enhancing protection at public events and considering alternative venues or even cancellation; preparing to execute contingency procedures, such as dispersing a workforce; and restricting threatened facility access to essential personnel only.
- *Severe Condition (Red)* is declared when there is a severe risk of attack. Under most circumstances, during this condition, the intense protective measures are not intended to be sustained for substantial periods of time. In addition to the protective measures in previous threat conditions, the following measures should be considered: increasing and directing personnel to address critical emergency needs; assigning emergency response personnel and prepositioning and mobilizing specially trained teams or resources; monitoring, redirecting, or constraining transportation systems; and closing public and government facilities.

Since the HSAS was implemented following 9/11, it has been subjected to much criticism and even ignored by the governments and citizens it was supposed to assist. It has been labeled a "damned if you do, damned if you don't" system. When a heightened level of alert is declared and an attack does not occur, complaints surface about the cost, waste of resources, and unnecessarily frightening the public and desensitizing them to alerts. Too many alerts can cause "alert fatigue" and a nonchalant attitude during subsequent alerts. If a warning is not issued when intelligence indicates a possible attack, and an attack does occur, authorities face serious repercussions (Bannon, 2004).

States and localities actually do not have to follow the HSAS. However, facilities under federal jurisdiction, such as nuclear power plants and airports, must follow specific procedures. Also, no standards are set for each alert level for state and local governments.

The effectiveness of the HSAS is difficult to ascertain. An elevated risk may cause terrorists to abort an attack. Or, the intense vigilance of authorities and citizens may uncover and disrupt terrorist plans.

Despite the criticism of the HSAS, it is an important system to provide warning of the possibility of attack and it serves to help us to remain vigilant, prepared, and ready. A major difficulty surrounding the HSAS is *when* and *where* to declare a heightened level of alert.

━━━━━━━━━━━━━━━━━━━━━━━━━━━━ □ □ □

Response to Weapons of Mass Destruction

Although the following information is aimed primarily at first responders facing WMD, security practitioners in the private sector can benefit from these guidelines and recommendations.

Chemical Attack

The U.S. Department of Homeland Security, Office for Domestic Preparedness (2004) distributed a video on guidelines for first responders facing WMD incidents. A summary of this program, that emphasizes a chemical attack, follows.

A WMD attack has potential to incapacitate first responders, by direct or secondary contact (e.g., contaminated victims). The scene must be controlled and large numbers of victims may require decontamination. In the Tokyo sarin attack, some first responders and hospital staff were contaminated by victims' clothing, shoes, and skin. *It is important to remember that responders cannot help others if they become victims themselves.*

Steps for First Responders

Recognize the danger. Pay close attention to the dispatcher's report. For example, multiple victims leaving a building, falling to the ground, coughing and complaining of dizziness. Upon approaching the scene, be aware of wind direction, weather conditions, type of building, occupancy, and number of victims. The victims of a chemical attack may experience SLUDGE:

Salivation
Lacrimation (tearing)
Urination
Defecation
Gastrointestinal distress
Emesis (vomiting)

Protect yourself. Do not rush into an area if you see multiple people down. You may become part of the problem. Warn others about the situation and report the facts and dangers. Be aware that a secondary explosion or sniper may be next. Emergency vehicles should be at least 300 feet away from the victims or dangerous area. Anyone entering the "hot zone" should wear the highest level of protection (i.e., vapor tight, fully-encapsulated suit with self-contained breathing apparatus).

Control the scene. Access controls should be maintained at 360 degrees around the scene and only authorized, properly trained and equipped personnel, should be admitted. When HAZMAT personnel arrive, they will identify the "hot zones" based upon readings from detection equipment. Public address systems can keep victims informed on procedures while responders maintain safe distances. At the same time, remember to preserve evidence, since the incident location is also a crime scene.

Rescue and decontaminate the victims. As soon as possible, victims should be brought to a shower area that can be established with fire trucks and related equipment. The outer layer of clothing should be removed and the victims should be flushed and then covered. Up to 80% of contaminants can be removed by taking off the outer layer of clothing. Kits are available that permit privacy curtains for the decontamination corridor. Runoff of the water should be controlled. Further decontamination may be necessary prior to sending patients to hospitals and triage areas.

Call for additional help. Establish a command post at 700 to 2,000 feet away to coordinate operations. Ensure space is available to expand the command post as other agencies respond. A variety of agencies may respond such as more local units, state units, FEMA, the FBI, public health, and the DOD.

Biological Attack

Bioterrorism is difficult to detect. Indications of an attack are likely to surface when victims visit hospitals and a trend is discovered through centralized reporting to local and state health agencies. The CDC is the agency that monitors public health threats. At hospitals, victims would be treated. The federal government has a "rapid response team" of medical personnel who have been vaccinated from a variety of biological threats and can enter infected locales. Vaccines do not exist for all biological threats. During an outbreak, an area (e.g., city) may require quarantine, backed by the military.

Radiation Attack

The Council on Foreign Relations (2004) and the Central Intelligence Agency (1998) offer the following information on responding to radiation attacks:

- Specialized equipment is required to determine the size of the affected area and if the level of radioactivity presents long-term hazards. Radiological materials are not recognized by senses, and are colorless and odorless.
- To reduce exposure to radiation, victims would need to be decontaminated by removing irradiated clothing, washing the body, and purging inhaled or ingested materials. These methods do not protect against "penetrating radiation" (e.g., gamma rays or neutrons).
- People endangered by "penetrating radiation" should go as far as possible from the source and maximize the amount of shielding between themselves and the source.
- Potassium iodide is recommended to prevent medical problems and cancer of the thyroid gland, but it offers no protection against other types of radiation problems.
- The onset of symptoms requires days to weeks.
- The incident area would require evacuation, and decontamination to remove radioactive material and keep radioactive dust from spreading. Contaminated buildings, roads, and soil may have to be removed.
- Many communities have neglected plans for a radiation attack since the Cold War ended. Since the 9/11 attacks, first responders have improved their response capabilities that vary.
- The federal response would come from several departments, namely the Departments of Homeland Security, Energy, and Defense. Federal agencies responding would include the FBI and EPA.

Nuclear Attack

Although a nuclear weapon is difficult to construct, deliver, and detonate, worst case scenarios must be considered. Depending on the type of bomb, casualties could be enormous, along with an awful impact on physical and mental health, the economy, and society. If a warning occurs, people should take shelter in basements and subways, unless time is available for an evacuation of the area to several miles away.

First responders must be properly trained and equipped to perform their duties following a nuclear explosion. Enormous numbers of victims would need treatment and hospitals may be destroyed. Medical problems would include thermal radiation burns, wounds, fractures, and infection. Potassium iodide is recommended. The radioactive fallout from the blast requires people to be decontaminated. Refer to the above "radiation attack" discussion for additional information applicable to nuclear attack.

Precautions for Organizational Mail Systems

Businesses, institutions, and other organizations should take precautions for mail as it enters the premises. Here is a list of protection measures to be applied depending on the threat.

- Prepare emergency plans, policies, and procedures for suspect mail.
- Isolate the mail area and limit access. Isolate the ventilation system of the mail area. Consider handling mail at a separate, isolated building.
- If necessary, use gloves (see Figure 15-8) and protective masks.
- Do not touch or smell anything suspicious.
- Be suspicious of mail. See the following guidelines on anthrax and the Chapter 13 figure on suspect letter and package indicators.
- Consider technology: X-ray for bombs, use letter and package tracking systems and automatic letter openers, and scan letters and send them electronically.

Official Centers for Disease Control (CDC) Health Advisory Distributed via Health Alert Network, October 12, 2001: HOW TO HANDLE ANTHRAX AND OTHER BIOLOGICAL AGENT THREATS

Many facilities in communities around the country have received anthrax threat letters. Most were empty envelopes; some have contained powdery substances. The purpose of these guidelines is to recommend procedures for handling such incidents.

Do Not Panic
1. Anthrax organisms can cause infection in the skin, gastrointestinal system, or the lungs. To do so, the organism must be rubbed into abraded skin, swallowed, or inhaled as a fine, aerosolized mist. Disease can be prevented after exposure to the anthrax spores by early treatment with the appropriate antibiotics. Anthrax is not spread from one person to another person.
2. For anthrax to be effective as a covert agent, it must be aerosolized into very small particles. This is difficult to do, and requires a great deal of technical

FIGURE 15-8 The September 11, 2001 terrorist attacks on the United States was followed by bioterrorism in which anthrax was spread through the mail system, necessitating precautions.

skill and special equipment. If these small particles are inhaled, life-threatening lung infection can occur, but prompt recognition and treatment are effective.

Suspicious Unopened Letter or Package Marked with Threatening Message Such as "Anthrax":
1. Do not shake or empty the contents of any suspicious envelope or package.
2. PLACE the envelope or package in a plastic bag or some other type of container to prevent leakage of contents.
3. If you do not have any container, then COVER the envelope or package with anything (e.g., clothing, paper, trash can, etc.) and do not remove this cover.
4. Then LEAVE the room and CLOSE the door, or section off the area to prevent others from entering (i.e., keep others away).
5. WASH your hands with soap and water to prevent spreading any powder to your face.
6. What to do next ...
   • If you are at HOME, then report the incident to local police.
   • If you are at WORK, then report the incident to local police, and notify your building security official or an available supervisor.
7. LIST all people who were in the room or area when this suspicious letter or package was recognized. Give this list to both the local public health authorities and law enforcement officials for follow-up investigations and advice.

Envelope with Powder and Powder Spills Out Onto Surface:
1. DO NOT try to CLEAN UP the powder. COVER the spilled contents immediately with anything (e.g., clothing, paper, trash can, etc.) and do not remove this cover!
2. Then LEAVE the room and CLOSE the door, or section off the area to prevent others from entering (i.e., keep others away).
3. WASH your hands with soap and water to prevent spreading any powder to your face.
4. What to do next ...
   • If you are at HOME, then report the incident to local police.
   • If you are at WORK, then report the incident to local police, and notify your building security official or an available supervisor.
5. REMOVE heavily contaminated clothing as soon as possible and place in a plastic bag, or some other container that can be sealed. This clothing bag should be given to the emergency responders for proper handling.
6. SHOWER with soap and water as soon as possible. Do Not Use Bleach Or Other Disinfectant On Your Skin.
7. If possible, list all people who were in the room or area, especially those who had actual contact with the powder. Give this list to both the local public health authorities so that proper instructions can be given for medical follow-up, and to law enforcement officials for further investigation.

Question of Room Contamination by Aerosolization
For example: small device triggered, warning that air handling system is contaminated, or warning that a biological agent released in a public space.

1. Turn off local fans or ventilation units in the area.
2. LEAVE area immediately.
3. CLOSE the door, or section off the area to prevent others from entering (i.e., keep others away).
4. What to do next ...
   • If you are at HOME, then dial "911" to report the incident to local police and the local FBI field office.

- If you are at WORK, then dial "911" to report the incident to local police and the local FBI field office, and notify your building security official or an available supervisor.
5. SHUT down air handling system in the building, if possible.
6. If possible, list all people who were in the room or area. Give this list to both the local public health authorities so that proper instructions can be given for medical follow-up, and to law enforcement officials for further investigation.

□ □ □

Private Sector

In addition to government action against terrorism, there is a vast community of private sector businesses, organizations, associations, and volunteers that also play a major role in homeland security and the protection of American interests. Furthermore, joint public/private sector initiatives exist.

Losses and Costs from the 9/11 Attacks

About 3,000 persons were killed in the 9/11 attacks, including those at the Pentagon. Thousands were injured, and others, including rescue workers, were affected by respiratory problems from the lingering smoke and dust at the WTC site. Direct costs from casualties included medical expenses, workers compensation payments, accidental death and dismemberment claims, and life insurance payments. Thousands of people needed counseling to deal with personal losses.

Although the U.S. economy was in a recession beginning in March 2001, the 9/11 attacks did cause a temporary disruption of the nation's economy. Specifically, airlines suffered, consumer spending and business investment fell, and hundreds of thousands of layoffs occurred, mainly in the travel and leisure sectors.

Business interruption occurred following the 9/11 attacks, although it can result from many other risks (e.g., natural disaster, accident) besides terrorism. It is defined as "the loss of profits of a business that suffers an indemnified loss when it is unable to manufacture its product(s) or provide its service" (Quinley and Schmidt, 2002: 33). Interdependencies within a business's operations or between separate businesses (e.g., a supplier to another business) can broader the interruption.

The Homeland Security Market

The homeland security market is a multi-billion dollar industry of products and services. Many companies have made handsome profits and have seen their stock prices rise considerably because of the need to enhance homeland security. Examples of products include luggage screening systems, WMD sensors, systems to track foreigners visiting the United States, and physical security. Services include the privatization of counterterrorism.

Public-Private Sector Partnerships

Reimer (2004: 10–12) sees the national system of preparedness for terrorism as a work in progress requiring a series of partnerships among the various levels of government, the public and private sectors, and the military. He notes that the strength of these partnerships will determine our level of preparedness. With the private sector owning 85% of U.S. critical infrastructure, Reimer emphasizes that private sector cooperation is essential. However, Reimer writes of the need for a common definition of "critical infrastructure" and the importance of defining the responsibilities of the public and private sectors.

Weidenbaum (2004: 189) argues that "the multifaceted national response to the September 11 terrorist attacks are altering the balance between the public and private sectors in the U.S." He describes the federal government effort against terrorism as a "mega priority" of programs and activities. This includes increased spending on the military and homeland security, special assistance and funding to companies heavily affected, and an expansion of government regulation of private activity, especially business. Weidenbaum notes that terrorism results in a hidden tax on businesses in the United States and overseas, in the form of added costs of operation. In a business, security is an expense that raises the cost of production. Security expenses include security officers, security systems, and personnel investigations. Other costs are higher insurance premiums and larger inventories (to protect against delays).

To facilitate communications and to share information on homeland security with private industry, the federal government hosts conferences and training sessions. Another initiative is the **Information Sharing and Analysis Centers (ISACs)**. These are generally private sector networks of organizations that the federal government has helped to create to share information on threats to critical industries and coordinate efforts to identify and reduce vulnerabilities. For example, the North American Electric Reliability Council (NERC) shares threat indications and analyses to help participants in the electricity sector take protective action.

The **Overseas Security Advisory Council (OSAC)** promotes security cooperation between the U.S. Department of State and businesses with interests overseas. OSAC objectives include sharing information, promoting methods for security planning, and publishing a variety of helpful guides.

According to a 2004 national policy summit on public police and private security cooperation, only 5% to 10% of law enforcement chief executives participate in partnerships with private security (U.S. Department of Justice, Office of Community Oriented Policing Services, 2004: 2). At the same time, cooperation between both groups takes many forms and occurs at many levels of government. To varying degrees, both groups share information with each other, attend each other's conferences, and plan together for protection and emergencies. They even work side-by-side at certain sites, such as downtown districts, government buildings, and special events. Plus, many off-duty police officers work part-time in security and retire to assume a security position. An improved partnership between both groups can be beneficial to our nation.

Business and Organizational Countermeasures Against Terrorism

As a security practitioner considering countermeasures against terrorism, numerous factors come into play as a foundation for planning. These factors include employees and their families, facilities and assets, the type of products and/or services offered to customers, domestic and/or international operations, and terrorist groups that may target the entity and their methods and weapons. Businesses should plan for a variety of possible scenarios. Examples include mass casualties, the loss of manufacturing capacity or a major supplier, an extended power outage, the disruption of shipping at a port, or fear that causes employees and customers to stay home. Planning to counter terrorism must be integrated with business continuity planning. Numerous sources of information are available to assist planning. These include the Web (see the end of this chapter), publications, government agencies, and private firms. Here is a list of suggestions to protect against terrorism.

- Terrorists have tremendous advantages over defenses because they search for vulnerabilities and strike almost anywhere with surprise. A British terrorism expert, Paul Wilkinson, stated, "Fighting terrorism is like a goalkeeper. You can make a hundred brilliant saves, but the only shot people remember is the one that gets past you" (Leader, 1997). Creative and astute security planning is essential.
- Maintain awareness of controversies that may increase exposure to terrorism.
- Reevaluate security, safety, and emergency plans. Seek cooperation with public safety agencies.
- Select a diverse committee for input for security and safety plans. Permit committee members to use their imaginations to anticipate weaknesses in protection.
- Increase employee awareness of terrorism and terrorist methods and tricks. Stifle and trick potential terrorists through creativity (e.g., avoid signs on the premises that identify departments, people, and job duties; periodically alter security methods).

- Know the business of tenants and whether they would be possible targets for violence.
- Consider the security and safety of childcare facilities used by employees.
- Intensify access controls by using a comprehensive approach covering people, vehicles, mail, deliveries, services, and any person or thing seeking access.
- Carefully screen employment applicants, vendors, and others seeking work.
- Secure and place under surveillance HVAC systems (e.g., air intake systems) and utilities.
- Once the best possible security and safety plans are implemented, remember that an offender (internal or external or both) may be studying your defenses to look for weaknesses to exploit.

Citizen Volunteers

The *National Strategy for Homeland Security* (Office of Homeland Security 2002: 12) makes the following statements concerning the importance of citizens becoming involved in homeland security.

> *All of us have a key role to play in America's war on terrorism. Terrorists may live and travel among us and attack our homes and our places of business, governance, and recreation. In order to defeat an enemy who uses our very way of life as a weapon—who takes advantage of our freedoms and liberties—every American must be willing to do his or her part to protect our homeland.*

Brian Jenkins, a noted authority on terrorism, points out that although public and private sectors maintain contingency plans to put into effect during heightened states of alert and emergencies, citizens must "learn to take care of themselves, to be mentally tough and self-reliant. Those who expect the government to protect them from everything are in for a lot of disappointments." He writes that for homeland security to succeed, citizens must be involved in the defense of their communities, and with quality training, "the entire United States can be turned into a vast neighborhood watch—a difficult environment for terrorists." Jenkins goes on to note that there will never be enough police and firefighters to protect all citizens. And, the first people at the scene of an attack are the unfortunate people who are there at the time of the attack. They need to learn how to protect themselves and others until first responders arrive (Jenkins, 2003).

Volunteer organizations also play a vital role of assistance in homeland security. Two noteworthy, national groups are the **American Red Cross** and the **Salvation Army**. Red Cross chapters have been involved in a variety of community-based programs for many years. These include services for seniors, volunteers for hospitals and nursing homes, food pantry and hot lunch programs, homeless shelters, and youth programs. The Salvation Army also has a long history of helping people. It is an evangelical organization dedicated to helping needy people through free temporary shelter and meals. The Salvation Army's thrift stores receive donated clothes and household goods that are sold to generate revenue. Both the Red Cross and the Salvation Army partner with all levels of government to support the immediate, critical needs of disaster victims. These needs include food, shelter, and clothing.

Many other volunteer groups assist disaster victims. The **National Volunteer Organizations Against Disasters** (NVOAD) consists of several national groups that rely on NVOAD to coordinate disaster response for increased efficiency.

In 2002, the federal government launched **Citizen Corps** to coordinate and channel citizen volunteers to help with homeland security and disaster preparedness efforts. Citizen Corps is a part of **USA Freedom Corps**—a federal government program that facilitates a partnership of nonprofit, business, educational, faith-based, and other sectors to increase citizen involvement in their communities. USA Freedom Corps seeks to create a culture of service, citizenship, and responsibility, while increasing civic awareness and community involvement.

☐ ☐ ☐

Get Ready Now

The U.S. Department of Homeland Security publishes a concise brochure entitled, "Get Ready Now," to help individuals and families prepare for terrorist attacks or other emergencies. The brochure describes what to include in an emergency supply kit, a family communications plan, and emergency plans.

Are You Ready?

The Federal Emergency Management Agency (FEMA) publishes *Are You Ready? An In-depth Guide to Citizen Preparedness.* This publication presents disaster survival techniques and how to prepare for and respond to both natural and man-made disasters. It is a comprehensive guide to personal emergency preparedness that includes information on how to prepare a disaster supply kit, how to locate and evacuate to a shelter, emergency planning for people with disabilities, and care for pets during an emergency. The guide covers natural hazards (e.g., hurricanes and earthquakes), technological hazards (e.g., hazardous materials), and terrorism.

☐ ☐ ☐

Search the Web

Here are Web sites relevant to this chapter:

Center for Defense Information: www.cdi.org
Centers for Disease Control (CDC): www.bt.cdc.gov
Center for the Study of Terrorism and Political Violence: www.st-andrews.ac.uk/
    intrel/research/cstpv/
Central Intelligence Agency: www.odci.gov
CIA World Factbook: www.odci.gov/cia/publications/factbook
Federal Bureau of Investigation: www.fbi.gov
Federal Emergency Management Agency: www.fema.gov
Government Accountability Office: www.gao.gov
International Policy Institute for Counterterrorism: www.ict.org.il/
MIPT Terrorism Knowledge Base: www.tkb.org
National Commission on Terrorist Attacks Upon the United States: www.9-
    11commission.gov
National Counterintelligence Center: www.ncix.gov
National Counterterrorism Center: www.nctc.gov
Office of the President: www.whitehouse.gov
Overseas Security Advisory Council (OSAC): www.ds-osac.org/
Stockholm International Peace Research Institute: web.sipri.org
United Kingdom Security Service (MI5): www.mi5.gov.uk
United Nations: www.un.org
UN International Court of Justice: www.icj-cij.org
U.S. Department of Defense: www.defenselink.mil
U.S. Department of Homeland Security: www.dhs.gov
U.S. Department of State: www.state.gov
Animal Liberation Front: www.animalliberationfront.com/
Earth Liberation Front: www.earthliberationfront.com/
Hezbollah: www.hizbollah.org/

Islamic Resistance Movement-HAMAS: www.hamasonline.com
People for the Ethical Treatment of Animals: www.peta.org/
White Aryan Resistance: www.resist.com/

□ □ □

Case Problems

15A. As a Chief Security Officer for a major international corporation, prepare a prioritized list of five general items about terrorism and homeland security that you would consider and apply in business continuity planning for domestic operations. In addition, prepare a prioritized list of five general items about terrorism and security for international operations. Compare the lists and study the findings.

15B. As a security executive for a corporation based in the U.S., your superior appoints you to a committee involved in strategic business planning. Business plans are being prepared for operations in Venezuela and Thailand. Your assignment is to research these countries and prepare reports on political stability, safety, security, and health issues. What resources do you use? What are your findings and recommendations?

15C. As a security executive for a corporation based in the U.S., what private and public sector groups would you seek partnerships with to enhance the survivability of your organization in case of a serious emergency?

References

Advisory Panel to Assess Domestic Response Capabilities for Terrorism Involving Weapons of Mass Destruction. (2003). *Forging America's New Normalcy: Securing Our Homeland, Preserving Our Liberty*, www.rand.org, retrieved March 5, 2004.

Bailey,G. (2003). "Globalization." In A. del Carmen (Ed.), *Terrorism: An Interdisciplinary Perspective*, 2nd ed. Toronto: Thomas Learning, Inc.

Bandura, A. (1977). *Social Learning Theory*. NY: General Learning Press.

Bannon, A. (2004). "Color-coding—or just color-confusing?" *Homeland Protection Professional*, 3 (September).

Barkan, S., and Snowden, L. (2001). *Collective Violence*. Boston: Allyn and Bacon.

Bell, J., and Gurr, T. (1979). "Terrorism and Revolution in American." In H. Graham and T. Gurr (Eds.), *Violence in America*. Newbury Park, CA: Sage.

Centers for Disease Control. (n.d.). *Frequently Asked Questions About a Nuclear Blast*. www.bt.cdc.gov/radiation, retrieved August 5, 2004.

Central Intelligence Agency. (1998). *Chemical/Biological/Radiological Incident Handbook* (October). www.fas.org, retrieved June 4, 2004.

Chalmers, D. (1987). *Hooded Americanism: The History of the Ku Klux Klan*, 3rd ed. Durham, NC: Duke University Press.

Clayton, C., et al. (2003). "Terrorism as Group Violence." In H. Hall (Ed.), *Terrorism: Strategies for Intervention*. Binghamton, NY: The Haworth Press.

Combs, C. (2003). *Terrorism in the Twenty-First Century*, 3rd ed. Upper Saddle River, NJ: Prentice-Hall.

Council on Foreign Relations. (2004). "Responding to Radiation Attacks." www.terrorismanswers.org, retrieved October 6, 2004.

Crenshaw, M. (1990). "The Logic of Terrorism: Terrorist Behavior as a Product of Strategic Choice." In H. Hall (Ed.), *Terrorism: Strategies for Intervention*.

FBI. (n.d.). *Counterterrorism*. http://denver.fbi.gov/inteterr.htm, retrieved January 14, 2004.

FBI. (2002). "The Threat of Ecoterrorism." http://www,fbi.gov/congress/congress02/jar-boe021202.htm, retrieved May, 3 2004.

Ford, P. (2001). "Why Do They Hate Us?" *The Christian Science Monitor*. September 27.

Greenberg, D. (2001). "Is Terrorism New?" *Slate.com*. http://historynewsnetwork.org, retrieved March 15, 2004.

Griset, P., and Mahan, S. (2003). *Terrorism in Perspective*. Thousand Oaks, CA: Sage Pub.

Grosskopf, K. (2006). "Evaluating the Societal Response to Antiterrorism Measures." *Journal of Homeland Security and Emergency Management*, 3.

Hoffman, B. (1998). *Inside Terrorism*. NY: Colombia University Press.

Hogue, H., and Bea, K. (2006). "Federal Emergency Management and Homeland Security Organization: Historical Developments and Legislative Options." *CRS Report for Congress* (June 1). www.fas.org/sgp/crs/homesec/RL33369.pdf, retrieved June 22, 2006.

Holden, R. (1986). *Modern Police Management*. Englewood Cliffs, NJ: Prentice-Hall.

Hudson, R. (1999). *The Sociology and Psychology of Terrorism: Who Becomes a Terrorist and Why?* Washington, D.C.: Federal Research Division, Library of Congress. In H. Hall (Ed.), *Terrorism: Strategies for Intervention*.

Huntington, S. (1996). *The Clash of Civilizations and the Remaking of the World Order*. NY: Simon & Schuster.

Jenkins, B. (2003). "All Citizens Now First Responders." *USA Today*. (March 23).

Kegley, C. (2003). *The New Global Terrorism: Characteristics, Causes, Controls*. Upper Saddle River, NJ: Prentice Hall.

Laqueur, W. (1999). *The New Terrorism: Fanaticism and the Arms of Mass Destruction*. NY: Oxford University Press.

Larson, E., and Peters, J. (2001). *Preparing the US Army for Homeland Security: Concepts, Issues, and Options*. Santa Monica, CA: RAND. In Kettl, D. (2004). *System Under Stress: Homeland Security and American Politics*. Washington, D.C.: CQ Press.

Leader, S. (1997). "The Rise of Terrorism." *Security Management* (April).

Martin, G. (2003). *Understanding Terrorism: Challenges, Perspectives, and Issues*. Thousand Oaks, CA: Sage Pub.

Mordica, G. (2003). "Phase Four Operations in Iraq and the RPG-7." *News from the Front*. (November-December).

National Commission on Terrorist Attacks Upon the United States. (2004). *The 9/11 Commission Report*. www.9–11commission.gov/, retrieved July 26, 2004.

National Memorial Institute for the Prevention of Terrorism. (2006). "MIPT Terrorism Knowledge Base." www.tkb.org, retrieved March 18, 2006.

Office of Homeland Security. (2002). *National Strategy for Homeland Security*. Washington, D.C.: The White House. (July).

Perl, R. (2006). "Terrorism and National Security: Issues and Trends." *CRS Issue Brief for Congress* (February 21). www.hsdl.org/homesec/docs/crs/nps21–022806–05.pdf, retrieved March 13, 2006.

Poland, J. (2005). *Understanding Terrorism: Groups, Strategies, and Responses*, 2nd Ed. Englewood Cliffs, NJ: Prentice Hall.

Poland, J. (1988). *Understanding Terrorism: Groups, Strategies, and Responses*. Englewood Cliffs, NJ: Prentice Hall.

Queller, D. (1989). "Crusades." *World Book*, Vol. 4. Chicago: World Book, Inc.

Quinley, K. and Schmidt, D. (2002). *Business At Risk: How to Assess, Mitigate, and Respond to Terrorist Threats*. Cincinnati, OH: The National Underwriter Co.

Reimer, D. (2004). "The Private Sector Must Be a Partner in Homeland Security." *Homeland Security*, 1 (September).

Roach, J., et al. (2005). "The Conjunction of Terrorist Opportunity: A Framework for Diagnosing and Preventing Acts of Terrorism." *Security Journal*, 18.

Silke, A. (1998). "Terrorism." *The Psychologist*, 14.

Simonsen, C., and Spindlove, J. (2004). *Terrorism Today*, 2nd ed. Upper Saddle River, NJ: Prentice-Hall.

United Nations, Office on Drugs and Crime. (n.d.). *Terrorism and Weapons of Mass Destruction*. www.unodc.org/unodc/terrorism_weapons_mass_destruction, retrieved April 21, 2004.

U.S. Department of Homeland Security, Office for Domestic Preparedness. (2004). *Weapons of Mass Destruction and the First Responder* (Video) (January).

U.S. Department of Justice, Office of Community Oriented Policing Services. (2004). *National Policy Summit: Building Private Security/Public Policing Partnerships to Prevent and Respond to Terrorism and Public Disorder*. www.cops.usdoj.gov, retrieved January 4, 2005.

U.S. Department of State. (2006). *Country Reports on Terrorism 2005*. http://www.state.gov/s/ct/rls/crt/c17689.htm, retrieved January 4, 2007.

U.S. Department of State, Office of Inspector General. (2005). "Review of the Department of State's *Country Reports on Terrorism-2005.*" http://oig.state.gov/documents/organization/58021.pdf, retrieved Mach 15, 2006.

U.S. Department of State. (2004). *Patterns of Global Terrorism 2003*. www.state.gov, retrieved August 31, 2005.

U.S. General Accounting Office. (2003). "Public Health Response to Anthrax Incidents of 2001." www.gao.gov, retrieved January 16, 2004.

U.S. Government. (2003). *National Strategy for Combating Terrorism*. www.whitehouse.gov/, retrieved March 5, 2004.

U.S. Government. (2006). *National Strategy for Combating Terrorism*. www.whitehouse.gov/, retrieved September 5, 2006.

U.S. Government, White House. (2006). "Fact Sheet: Safeguarding America: President Bush Signs Patriot Act Reauthorization." www.whitehouse.gov/, retrieved March 11, 2006.

Weidenbaum, M. (2004). "Government, Business, and the Response to Terrorism." In T. Badey (Ed.) *Homeland Security*. Guilford, CT: McGraw-Hill/Dushkin.

Weinberg, L., and Davis, P. (1989). *Introduction to Political Terrorism*. NY: McGraw Hill.

Weinzierl, J. (2004). "Terrorism: Its Origin and History." In A. Nyatepe-Coo and D. Zeisler-Vralsted (Eds.) *Understanding Terrorism: Threats in an Uncertain World*. Upper Saddle River, NJ: Pearson Prentice Hall.

White, J. (2004). *Defending the Homeland: Domestic Intelligence, Law Enforcement, and Security*. Belmont, CA: Wadsworth/ Thomson Learning.

White, J. (2003). *Terrorism: An Introduction*, 4th ed. Belmont, CA: Wadsworth/ Thomson Learning.

Wilkinson, P. (2003). "Why Modern Terrorism? Differentiating Types and Distinguishing Ideological Motivations." In C. Kegley (Ed.), *The New Global Terrorism: Characteristics,*

16

Protecting Critical Infrastructures, Key Assets, and Borders

Objectives

After studying this chapter, the reader will be able to:

1. Define critical infrastructure and key assets.
2. Explain the role of the federal government in protecting critical infrastructures and key assets.
3. Describe at least 10 recommendations from the National Infrastructure Protection Plan for the private sector.
4. Name and describe vulnerabilities and protection measures for at least five infrastructure sectors.
5. Explain the threats to cyberspace and information technology and protection measures.
6. Name and explain the roles of the government agencies involved in border and transportation security.
7. Name and describe vulnerabilities and protection measures for at least four transportation sectors.

KEY TERMS	
• cascade effect	• bioterrorism
• critical infrastructure (CI)	• agroterrorism
• critical infrastructure protection (CIP)	• Public Health Security and Bioterrorism Preparedness and Response Act of 2002
• sector-specific agencies	
• sector-specific plans	• Project BioShield Act of 2004
• *National Infrastructure Protection Plan* (NIPP)	• penetration test
	• Chernobyl
• key resources	• Three-Mile Island
• key assets	• Bhopal, India
• Homeland Security Operations Center	• Texas City, Texas
• Information Sharing and Analysis Centers (ISACs)	• Exxon Valdez

- Emergency Planning and Community Right-to-Know Act of 1986
- Cybersecurity
- denial-of-service attack
- Trojan horse
- virus
- worm
- logic bomb
- dumpster diving
- social engineering
- spam
- phishing
- keylogging programs
- spyware
- malware
- blended cyber threats
- blended cyber-physical attack
- cyberwarfare
- encryption
- National Industrial Security Program
- General Services Administration (GSA)
- Federal Protective Service
- U.S. Marshals Service
- U.S. Visitor and Immigrant Status Indicator Technology (US-VISIT)
- critical layers of defense
- U.S. Customs and Border Protection
- Container Security Initiative
- Advanced Manifest Rule
- Customs-Trade Partnership Against Terrorism (C-TPAT)
- U.S. Immigration and Customs Enforcement (ICE)
- U.S. Citizenship and Immigration Services
- Transportation Security Administration (TSA)
- Aviation and Transportation Security Act of 2001
- Intelligence Reform and Terrorism Prevention Act of 2004
- Federal Aviation Administration (FAA)
- Federal Air Marshal Service
- Man-Portable Air Defense Systems (MANPADS)
- transportation choke points
- Maritime Transportation Security Act of 2002
- Security and Accountability For Every (SAFE) Port Act of 2006
- supply chain
- anthrax attacks

Note: Major portions of this chapter are from: Purpura, P. (2007). *Terrorism and Homeland Security: An Introduction with Applications*. Burlington, MA: Elsevier Butterworth-Heinemann.

Critical Infrastructure

Following the 9/11 attacks, concern increased over the vulnerability of essential services and products that sustain our nation and its business. Several vital services and products, if harmed by an attack or subject to a natural disaster, can result in a disruption of the economy and daily activities of citizens. We all depend on such systems as water, food, energy, transportation, and communications. In addition, our modern society depends on a complex network of interdependencies among services and products. If one essential service or product is attacked or subject to a natural disaster, other services and products may be affected. This is known as the **cascade effect**. For instance, if a power failure occurs, businesses, institutions, and many daily activities would be hindered. The creativity and patience of terrorists make the protection of critical infrastructure essential. Imagine the chaos in a locale from simultaneous bombings of a high-rise building, electrical power, the 9-1-1 emergency communications system, and the water supply for fighting fires.

Critical Infrastructure Defined

The Patriot Act, Section 1016(e), defines **critical infrastructure** (CI) as "the systems and assets, whether physical or virtual, so vital to the United States that the incapacity or destruction of such systems and assets would have a debilitating impact on security, national economic security, national public health or safety, or any combination of those matters." A generally accepted estimate is that 85% of the U.S. critical infrastructure is owned by the private sector.

The *National Strategy for Homeland Security* (Office of Homeland Security, 2002: ix) states

> *Our society and modern way of life are dependent on networks of infrastructure—both physical networks such as our energy and transportation systems and virtual networks such as the Internet. If terrorists attack one or more pieces of our critical infrastructure, they may disrupt entire systems and cause significant damage to the Nation. We must therefore improve protection of the individual pieces and interconnecting systems that make up our critical infrastructure. Protecting America's critical infrastructure and key assets will not only make us more secure from terrorist attack, but will also reduce our vulnerability to natural disasters, organized crime, and computer hackers. America's critical infrastructure encompasses a large number of sectors. The U.S. government will seek to deny terrorists the opportunity to inflict lasting harm to our Nation by protecting the assets, systems, and functions vital to our national security, governance, public health and safety, economy, and national morale.*

This strategy identifies eight major **critical infrastructure protection (CIP)** initiatives:

- Unify America's infrastructure protection effort in the Department of Homeland Security (DHS).
- Build and maintain a complete and accurate assessment of America's critical infrastructure and key assets.
- Enable effective partnership with state and local governments and the private sector.
- Develop a national infrastructure protection plan.
- Secure cyberspace.
- Harness the best analytic and modeling tools to develop effective protective solutions.
- Guard America's critical infrastructure and key assets against "inside" threats.
- Partner with the international community to protect our transnational infrastructure.

The National Strategy for the Physical Protection of Critical Infrastructures and Key Assets (White House, 2003a: 9) identifies the following CI sectors and key assets for protection:

Agriculture and Food: 1,912,000 farms; 87,000 food-processing plants
Water: 1,800 federal reservoirs; 1,600 municipal wastewater facilities
Public Health: 5,800 registered hospitals
Emergency Services: 87,000 U.S. localities
Defense Industrial Base: 250,000 firms in 215 distinct industries
Telecommunications: 2 billion miles of cable
Energy
    Electricity: 2,800 power plants
    Oil and Natural Gas: 300,000 producing sites
Transportation (Figure 16-1)
    Aviation: 5,000 public airports
    Passenger Rail and Railroads: 120,000 miles of major railroads
    Highways, Trucking, and Busing: 590,000 highway bridges
    Pipelines: 2 million miles of pipelines
    Maritime: 300 inland/coastal ports
    Mass Transit: 500 major urban public transit operators
Banking and Finance: 26,600 FDIC-insured institutions
Chemical Industry and Hazardous Materials: 66,000 chemical plants
Postal and Shipping: 137 million delivery sites
Key Assets
    National Monuments and Icons: 5,800 historic buildings
    Nuclear Power Plants: 104 commercial nuclear power plants
    Dams: 80,000 dams
    Government Facilities: 3,000 government-owned/operated facilities
    Commercial Assets: 460 skyscrapers

FIGURE 16-1 The transportation system is one of several critical infrastructure sectors. Containerized cargo arriving in port to be unloaded.

The Role of Government in Protecting Critical Infrastructure and Key Resources (CI/KR)

A major mission area stated in the *National Strategy for Homeland Security* is protecting critical infrastructure. In December 2003, President George W. Bush issued Homeland Security Presidential Directive 7 (HSPD-7), establishing a policy for federal departments and agencies to identify and prioritize CI and protect them from terrorist attacks. HSPD-7 designates a sector-specific department or agency for each sector to coordinate and collaborate with relevant agencies, state and local government, and the private sector. The DHS is responsible for (1) developing a national CIP plan consistent with the Homeland Security Act of 2002, (2) recommending CIP measures in coordination with public and private sector partners, and (3) disseminating information.

The term **sector-specific agencies** (SSAs) has been used to identify federal departments and agencies with protection responsibilities for specific sectors of CI. SSAs are required to develop **sector-specific plans** (SSPs). SSAs are listed next (U.S. Department of Homeland Security, 2005a: 3; U.S. Department of Homeland Security, 2006a: 20; U.S. Government Accountability Office 2005c: 75–76).

- *Department of Homeland Security (DHS):* Responsible for emergency services; government facilities; information and telecommunications; transportation systems (with Department of Transportation); chemicals; postal and shipping sectors; dams; commercial facilities; and nuclear reactors, materials, and waste (with the Department of Energy and the Nuclear Regulatory Commission). Examples of specific functions include protection of federal property throughout the country by the Federal Protective Service, the Secret Service's role in coordinating site security at designated special events, and the National Cyber Response Coordination Group's role in coordinating national cyber emergencies.
- *Department of Defense (DOD):* Responsible for defense industrial base and physical security of military installations, activities, and personnel.
- *Department of Energy (DOE):* Responsible for developing and implementing policies and procedures for safeguarding power plants (except for commercial nuclear power facilities), oil, gas, research labs, and weapons production facilities.
- *Department of Justice (DOJ):* Through its Criminal Division and the FBI, the DOJ works to prevent the exploitation of the Internet, computer systems, or networks.

- *Department of State (DOS):* Responsible for matters of international CIP, given its overseas mission.
- *Department of Health and Human Services (DHHS):* Responsible for public health, healthcare, and food (other than meat, poultry, and egg products).
- *Environmental Protection Agency (EPA):* Responsible for drinking water and wastewater treatment systems.
- *Department of Agriculture:* Responsible for agriculture and food (meat, poultry, and egg products).
- *Department of the Treasury:* Responsible for banking and finance.
- *Department of the Interior:* Responsible for national monuments and icons.

According to the U.S. Government Accountability Office (2005c: 78), all eight CIP initiatives are being addressed by federal agencies. The DHS, DOD, and HHS cited activity in each of the eight initiatives. Specific examples cited by the GAO include the following: DHS began the Transportation Worker Identification Credential Program to enhance access security in the nation's transportation system; the Food and Drug Administration, within HHS, issued security guidance to the food industry, including employee background checks; the DOS developed diplomatic agreements with Mexico and Canada to permit background checks of truck drivers; and the DOE conducted polygraph examinations and financial disclosures of employees in the energy field.

The U.S. Government Accountability Office (2005c: 81) reported challenges to CIP efforts and noted an almost infinite number of potential terrorist targets. A major challenge is the federal government's management and planning of CIP. This entails delineating the roles and responsibilities of federal and nonfederal entities, establishing objectives and milestones, setting time frames for reaching objectives, and preparing performance measures. Other concerns included the need for better training and procedures to detect counterfeit documents and identity fraud.

In June 2006, following interim plans and feedback from the public and private sectors, the **National Infrastructure Protection Plan** (NIPP) (U.S. Department of Homeland Security, 2006a) was released by the DHS pursuant to HSPD-7. It takes the *National Strategy for Homeland Security* to the next level through an identification of assets, assessment of vulnerabilities, and prioritization of assets to guide protection programs.

The term *critical infrastructure/key resources* has replaced the term *critical infrastructure/key assets* in the NIPP. As defined in the Homeland Security Act of 2002, **key resources** are publicly or privately controlled resources essential to the minimal operations of the economy and government. **Key assets** are individual targets (Figure 16-2) whose destruction could cause large-scale injury, death, or destruction of property, and/or profoundly damage national prestige, and confidence (U.S. Department of Homeland Security, 2006b).

NIPP objectives include protecting critical infrastructure and key resources (CI/KR); managing long-term risk; assessing vulnerability; prioritizing; maintaining a national inventory of CI/KR; mapping interdependencies among assets; articulating security partner roles and responsibilities; identifying incentives for voluntary action by the private sector; facilitating best practices, information exchange, training, and metrics; strengthening linkages between physical and cyber efforts; and promoting CI/KR cooperation among international partners.

HSPD-7 requires that the NIPP be integrated with other national plans. The NIPP states that it will support the Nation Response Plan (NRP) during the prevention phase by providing information on CI/KR, vulnerabilities, and protection programs. During incident response, NIPP information will be shared through the National Incident Management System (NIMS) established communications mechanisms.

Kochems (2005: 3) describes the responsibilities of the federal government and the private sector to protect against terrorism:

> *The federal government—not the private sector—is responsible for preventing terrorist acts through intelligence gathering, early warning, and domestic counterterrorism. The private sector is responsible for taking reasonable precautions, much as it is expected to take reasonable safety and environmental precautions.*

FIGURE 16-2 The Statue of Liberty National Monument is a key asset of national pride requiring protection. *Courtesy:* DOD photo by Petty Officer 3rd class Kelly Newlin, U.S. Coast Guard.

> *The federal government also has a role in defining what is "reasonable" as a performance-based metric and facilitating information sharing to enable the private sector to perform due diligence (e.g., protection, mitigation, and recovery) in an efficient, fair, and effective manner.*

NIPP Risk Management Framework

The U.S. Government Accountability Office (2007a) notes that "risk management, a strategy for helping policymakers make decisions about assessing risk, allocating resources, and taking actions under conditions of uncertainty, has been endorsed by Congress, the President, and the Secretary of DHS as a way to strengthen the nation against possible terrorist attacks." The NIPP risk management framework includes the following activities (U.S. Department of Homeland Security, 2006a: 29–30):

- *Set security goals:* Define specific outcomes, conditions, end points, or performance targets that collectively constitute an effective protective posture.
- *Identify assets, systems, networks, and functions:* Develop an inventory of the assets, systems, and networks, including those located outside the United States, that comprise the nation's CI/KR and the critical functionality therein; collect information pertinent to risk management that takes into account the fundamental characteristics of each sector.
- *Assess risks:* Determine risk by combining potential direct and indirect consequences of a terrorist attack or other hazard.
- *Prioritize:* Aggregate and analyze risk assessment results to develop a comprehensive picture of asset, system, and network risk; establish priorities based on risk; and determine protection and business continuity initiatives that provide the greatest mitigation of risk.
- *Implement protective programs:* Select sector-appropriate protective actions or programs to reduce or manage the risk identified; secure the resources needed to address priorities.
- *Measure effectiveness:* Use metrics and other evaluation procedures at the national and sector levels to measure progress and assess the effectiveness of the national CI/KR protection program in improving protection, managing risk, and increasing resiliency.

Both output and outcome metrics will be used by SSAs and the DHS to track progress on specific activities outlined in the SSPs. Output metrics include the number of vulnerability assessments performed by a certain date. Outcome metrics include a reduced number of facilities assessed as high risk, following the implementation of protective measures. The DHS notes that selecting outcome metrics for protection programs is challenging because risk reduction is not directly observable. For example, it is difficult to measure the prevention of a terrorist attack or the extent of mitigation from a potential attack.

Examples of metrics include the total number of assets in each sector; the percent of high-consequence assets to total assets (to determine which sectors should receive a higher priority); and the percent of high-consequence assets that have been assessed for readiness, response, and recovery capability.

□ □ □ ▬▬▬▬▬▬▬▬▬▬▬▬▬▬▬▬▬▬▬▬▬▬▬▬

Incidents by Target

One source of data on terrorism that is categorized by target (e.g., critical infrastructures) is the National Memorial Institute for the Prevention of Terrorism (MIPT) Terrorism Knowledge Base (TKB), as discussed in the preceding chapter under "The Measurement of Terrorism." The TKB is a user-friendly Web resource on domestic and international terrorism. Among the site's tools, its page on "Incidents by Target" lists critical infrastructure sectors along with number of incidents, injuries, and fatalities for the years specified by the user.

▬▬▬▬▬▬▬▬▬▬▬▬▬▬▬▬▬▬▬▬▬▬▬▬ □ □ □

NIPP Recommendations for the Private Sector

The following recommended homeland security practices for the private sector are from the NIPP (U.S. Department of Homeland Security, 2006a: 171–173). The recommendations are based on best practices in use by various sectors and other groupings.

- *Asset, System, Network, and Function Identification:*
  - Incorporate the NIPP framework for the assets, systems, and networks under their control; and
  - Voluntarily provide CI/KR-related data to DHS to facilitate national CI/KR protection program implementation with appropriate information protections.
- *Assessment, Monitoring, and Reduction of Risks/Vulnerabilities:*
  - Conduct appropriate risk and vulnerability assessment activities using tools or methods that are rigorous, well documented, and based on accepted practices in industry or government;
  - Implement measures to reduce risk and mitigate deficiencies and vulnerabilities corresponding to the physical, cyber, and human security elements of CI/KR protection;
  - Maintain the tools, capabilities, and protocols necessary to provide an appropriate level of monitoring of networks, systems, or a facility and its immediate surroundings to detect possible insider and external threats;
  - Develop and implement personnel screening programs to the extent feasible for personnel working in sensitive positions; and
  - Manage the security of computer and information systems while maintaining awareness of vulnerabilities and consequences to ensure that systems are not used to enable attacks against CI/KR.
- *Information Sharing:*
  - Connect with and participate in the appropriate national, State, regional, local, and sector information-sharing mechanisms;
  - Develop and maintain close working relationships with local (and, as appropriate, Federal, State, Territorial, and tribal) law enforcement and first-responder organizations relevant to the company's facilities to promote communications, with appropriate protections, and cooperation related to prevention, remediation, and response to a natural disaster or terrorist event;

- Provide applicable information on threats, assets, and vulnerabilities to appropriate government authorities, with appropriate information protections;
- Share threat and other appropriate information with other CI/KR owners and operators;
- Participate in activities or initiatives developed and sponsored by relevant NIPP Sector Coordinating Council or entity that provides the sector coordinating function;
- Participate in, share information with (with appropriate protections), and support State and local CI/KR protection programs, including coordinating and planning with Local Emergency Planning Committees;
- Collaborate with other CI/KR owners and operators on security issues of mutual concern; and
- Use appropriate measures to safeguard information that could pose a threat and maintain open and effective communications regarding security measures and issues, as appropriate, with employees, suppliers, customers, government officials, and others.

- *Planning and Awareness:*
  - Develop and exercise appropriate emergency response, mitigation, and business continuity-of-operations plans;
  - Participate in Federal, State, local, or company exercises and other activities to enhance individual, organization, and sector preparedness;
  - Demonstrate continuous commitment to security and resilience across the entire company;
  - Develop an appropriate security protocol corresponding to each level of the Homeland Security Advisory System. These plans and protocols are additive so that as the threat level increases for company facilities, the company can quickly implement its plans to enhance physical or cybersecurity measures in operation at those facilities and modify them as the threat level decreases;
  - Utilize NFPA 1600 Standard on Disaster/Emergency Management and Business Continuity Programs, endorsed by DHS and Congress, when developing Emergency Response and Business Continuity-of-Operations Plans if the sector has not developed its own standard;
  - Document the key elements of security programs, actions, and periodic reviews as part of a commitment to sustain a consistent, reliable, and comprehensive program over time;
  - Enhance security awareness and capabilities through periodic training, drills, and guidance that involve all employees annually to some extent and, when appropriate, involve others such as emergency response agencies or neighboring facilities;
  - Perform periodic assessments or audits to measure the effectiveness of planned physical and cybersecurity measures. These audits and verifications should be reported directly to the CEO or his/her designee for review and action;
  - Promote emergency response training, such as the Community Emergency Response Team training offered by the U.S. Citizen Corps, for employees;
  - Consider including programs for developing highly secure and trustworthy operating systems in near-term acquisition or R&D priorities;
  - Create a culture of preparedness, reaching every level of the organization's workforce, which ingrains in each employee the importance of awareness and empowers those with responsibilities as first-line defenders within the organization and community;
  - As the organization performs R&D or acquires new or upgraded systems, consider only those that are highly secure and trustworthy;
  - Encourage employee participation in community preparedness efforts, such as Citizen Corps, schools, Red Cross, Second Harvest, etc.;
  - Work with others locally, including government, nongovernmental organizations, and private sector entities, both within and outside its sector, to identify and resolve gaps that could occur in the context of a terrorist incident, natural disaster, or other emergency;
  - Work with the DHS to improve cooperation regarding personnel screening and information protection; and
  - Identify supply chain and "neighbor" issues that could cause workforce or production disruptions for the company.

□ □ □

Sharing Information on Critical Infrastructure

A variety of information-sharing programs has been established. The **Homeland Security Operations Center (HSOC)** serves as a central, national information-sharing and domestic incident management system. It increases coordination among all levels of government and the private sector. The HSOC operates 24 hours a day, provides real-time situational awareness and monitoring of the homeland, coordinates incidents and response, and issues advisories and bulletins on threats and protective measures. The HSOC communicates with its partners through the Homeland Security Information Network (HSIN), an Internet-based counterterrorism tool that uses encryption and a secure network. Another tool, the HSIN-Critical Infrastructure, is designed to communicate real-time information (e.g., alerts and notifications) to CI owners and operators.

The DHS/Information Analysis and Infrastructure Protection Daily Open Source Report is a Monday through Friday e-mail report divided by CI sectors. It is intended to educate and inform personnel engaged in the protection of CI. The content includes a variety of news reports on CI from many media outlets and information bulletins.

The DHS has established **Information Sharing and Analysis Centers (ISACs)** to promote the sharing of information and work among CI sectors. These are voluntary organizations among CI sectors, such as food, electricity, and financial services. Industry associations (e.g., American Chemistry Council) often take the lead in forming ISACs and arrange meetings, establish Web sites, provide technical assistance, and issue warnings. The level of activity of ISACs varies.

Congress has promoted information sharing through the Intelligence Reform and Terrorism Protection Act of 2004, also known as the 9/11 Reform Bill. It requires the president to facilitate an "information sharing environment" (ISE) with appropriate levels of government and private entities. An ISE Council manages and promotes this effort.

The Infrastructure Security Partnership (TISP) is a private sector group organized to bring together a variety of public and private sector organizations to collaborate on all-hazards facing the nation's built environment. TISP facilitates dialogue among those in the design and construction industries. A major goal of TISP is to improve security in the nation's CI. It promotes the transfer of research to codes, standards, and public policy.

Within the states, approaches vary on protecting CI and sharing information. One private sector concern is the possibility of a leak of sensitive information from the information-sharing process. For example, if a company reports a cyberattack and the information is reported in the media, profits may suffer. Also, private sector proprietary information must be protected because it is valuable.

□ □ □

Do you think businesses are reluctant to share critical infrastructure information with government? Why or why not?

□ □ □

Critical Infrastructure Sectors

Agriculture and Food

The U.S. agriculture and food industry accounts for almost one-fifth of the gross domestic product (GDP) and a significant percentage of that figure contributes to the U.S. export economy. National and international confidence in the safety of the products of this industry is important. The greatest threats to this industry are disease and contamination. There is an urgent need to improve and validate methods for detecting bioterrorist agents in food products. The White House (2003a: 37) states that although rapid use of threat information could prevent an attack from spreading, serious institutional barriers and disincentives (e.g., economic harm) for sharing such information exist.

"The use of natural agents in attacks on agriculture or directly on people is commonly described as **bioterrorism**" (Congressional Budget Office, 2004: 39). Chalk (2003: 2) defines **agroterrorism** as "the deliberate introduction of a disease agent, either against livestock or into the food chain, to undermine socioeconomic stability and/or generate fear." Terrorism, disease, and disasters in this sector of CI can cause serious health problems, economic losses, and panic.

An attack on the food supply can take place at numerous points between the farm and human consumption. Examples are farms, processing plants, retail stores, and restaurants. Whether domestic or imported, food could be subject to biological or chemical agents. An illustration of a terrorist attack on food occurred in 1984 when members of an Oregon religious group, who followed an Indian-born guru named Bhagwan Shree Rajneesh, secretly applied salmonella bacteria to a restaurant salad bar to poison residents of a community to influence an election. Over 750 people became ill. Disgruntled employees have caused other incidents of food sabotage.

The Centers for Disease Control (CDC) estimates that 76 million illnesses, 325,000 hospitalizations, and 5,000 deaths occur annually due to food contaminated from various causes (Mead, et al., 1999). Although unintentional, the 2001 outbreak of foot-and-mouth disease in Britain showed the high expense from disease in the food chain. About four million cattle were destroyed, and the cost to the British economy (primarily agriculture and tourism) was about $48 billion (Gewin, 2003).

The primary federal regulatory agencies responsible for food safety are the Food and Drug Administration (FDA), the U.S. Department of Agriculture (USDA), and the Environmental Protection Agency (EPA). Inspectors from the DHS's Bureau of Customs and Border Protection assist other agencies with inspecting imports. States also conduct inspections.

The FDA has regulatory authority over about 80% of the nation's food supply. The USDA's Food Safety and Inspection Service regulates the safety, quality, and labeling of most meats, as well as poultry and egg products. The EPA's role is to protect public health and the environment from pesticides and promote safer pest management (Congressional Budget Office, 2004: 42–43).

Laws that defend the agriculture and food system against terrorism, disasters, and emergencies include the Homeland Security Act of 2002. It created the DHS that is responsible for consolidating federal response to emergencies, including agroterrorism, into a single plan called the National Response Plan. Another law, the **Public Health Security and Bioterrorism Preparedness and Response Act of 2002**, also called the Bioterrorism Act, bolstered the FDA's ability to identify domestic and foreign facilities that provide food, inspect food imports, and notify food businesses that become involved in the contamination of food supplies. Regulations under the authority of this law require food businesses in the chain of supply to maintain records to identify the immediate previous sources and subsequent recipients of food. HSPD-9, of January 2004, directed HHS, USDA, and EPA to increase their efforts in prevention, surveillance, emergency response, and recovery. The **Project BioShield Act of 2004** requires action to expand and expedite the distribution of vaccines and treatments to combat potential bioterrorism agents (Congressional Budget Office, 2004: 43).

Protection issues and strategies for the agriculture and food industry include the following (Chalk, 2003; Congressional Budget Office, 2004: 44):

- Use risk management methods.
- Establish more extensive labeling and tracking systems for animals and food products to help pinpoint sources of contamination.
- Establish full tracking of ownership of the most hazardous materials (e.g., nitrates) that can be used as weapons.
- Establish enhanced incentives and protections for reporting new incidents of food contamination, improper sales of hazardous materials, unsafe processing and handling procedures, and incomplete inspections.

- Modify vulnerable practices in the industry.
- Increase the number of inspectors in the food chain and strengthen the capabilities of forensic investigations for early detection and containment.
- Foster improved links among the agriculture, food, and intelligence communities.
- Continue research on vaccinations.
- The FDA established the Office of Food Safety, Defense, and Outreach (OFSDO) to consolidate its educational services with its counterterrorism and chief medical officer responsibilities.
- The USDA Food Safety and Inspection Service (FSIS) offers training and a variety of information including notices, regulations, emergency resources, and security guidelines. It offers Model Food Security Plans that are voluntary for egg, meat, and poultry facilities. These plans are risk-based and include how to identify threats, such as disgruntled employees or terrorists. The *FSIS Security Guidelines for Food Processors* contains information on food security management; access controls; internal security; and security for slaughter and processing, storage, water and ice, and mail.
- The Food Products Association (FPA) is the largest trade association serving the food and beverage industry worldwide. It operates a Center for Food Security & Emergency Preparedness (CFSEP), offering on-site vulnerability assessments, training, security plan development, awareness training, and crisis management to members and nonmembers.

Water

As we know, water is essential to our lives, and its protection is vital. The water sector has two major components: fresh water supply and wastewater collection and treatment. The United States has 170,000 public water systems that depend on reservoirs, dams, wells, aquifers, treatment systems, pumping stations, and pipelines. There are 19,500 municipal sanitary sewer systems in the United States, including 800,000 miles of sewer lines. This sector also includes storm water systems that collect storm water runoff (White House, 2003a: 39).

To prioritize protection, the water sector is studying four primary areas of possible attack (White House, 2003a: 39):

- Physical damage to assets and release of toxic chemicals used in water treatment
- Contamination of the water supply
- Cyberattack on water information systems
- Interruption of service from another CI sector

The U.S. Government Accountability Office (2005c: 87–88) reported similar vulnerabilities. It noted the challenges of protection include a lack of redundancy in vital systems; this increases the probability that an attack will render a water system inoperable. The GAO recommended that federal funds for utilities focus on high-density areas and those areas serving critical assets (e.g., military bases). Recommendations also included technological upgrades in physical security and monitoring of water systems.

Threats to water systems are varied. In one community, security was increased when vandals victimized a water reservoir. The offenders broke into a control room, opened two valves, and began to drain the water out of the reservoir. Making matters worse, they opened another valve and flooded the control room. A sensor signaled the drop in the water level of the reservoir. Following this event, an intrusion alarm system was installed at access points. Another threat is the disgruntled employee. This may be a more serious threat than outsiders because employees are knowledgeable of system weaknesses and security measures. However, almost anybody has access to thousands of miles of pipe, and an offender can patch into a neighborhood line and introduce a poison after the water has been treated and tested for safety. This type of attack could sicken a neighborhood or people in an office building. Experts argue that to poison a reservoir or other large water source would require truckloads of poisons or biological agents. If an airplane containing anthrax crashed into a water source, this attack is likely to fail because of fire or the inability of the anthrax to diffuse effectively (Winter and Broad, 2001).

HSPD-7, of December 2003, confirmed the Environmental Protection Agency (EPA) as the lead agency for identifying, prioritizing, and coordinating the protection of drinking water and water treatment systems. Under HSPD-7, the Water Security Division of the EPA has been assigned the responsibility of preparing a water sector plan for the NIPP that the DHS must produce. The plan must identify assets, prioritize vulnerabilities, develop protection programs, and measure effectiveness. Other HSPDs relevant to the EPA are HSPD-8 (strengthens preparedness), HSPD-9 (surveillance program and laboratory network for early warning of an attack), HSPD-10 (a classified document on decontamination), and HSPD-10: Biodefense for the 21st Century (strengthens biodefense).

The Public Health Security and Bioterrorism Preparedness and Response Act of 2002 addresses, in Title IV, drinking water protection. It requires water systems serving over 3,300 persons to conduct an assessment of vulnerabilities and prepare response measures. Other federal laws support safe drinking water.

Protection issues and strategies for the water sector include the following (White House, 2003a: 39–40):

- Several methodologies are available to conduct a vulnerability assessment of water utilities. These are available from the EPA, Sandia National Laboratories, the Association of Metropolitan Sewerage Agencies, and other groups.
- As with all sectors, improve protection of digital control systems and supervisory control and data acquisition systems.
- Consider new technology, such as small robots placed in pipes to detect tainted water.
- Secure openings (e.g., manhole covers) to prevent the dumping of substances into systems.
- Properly store and secure chemicals.
- Use redundancy to increase the reliability of systems.
- Increase training and awareness.
- The EPA provides helpful information on security at its Web site.
- The DHS and EPA work with the water ISAC to coordinate information on threats and other topics of interest to this sector.
- The American Water Works Association (AWWA) is the largest organization of water supply professionals in the world. It is an international scientific and educational society dedicated to improving drinking water. The group offers training and education opportunities, conferences, and publications on security. Two other related groups are the National Rural Water Association (NRWA) and the Association of State Drinking Water Administrators (ASDWA).

In late December 2006, the nation's first guidelines for the physical protection of water and wastewater systems were released. These voluntary guidelines were jointly developed by the American Society of Civil Engineers, the AWWA, and the Water Environment Federation, with a grant from the EPA. The guidelines are part of a program to address physical infrastructure security needs for water supply, wastewater and stormwater, and online contaminant monitoring systems. The program includes guidelines to improve security, the development of voluntary standards, and training materials.

□ □ □ ▬▬▬▬▬▬▬▬▬▬▬▬▬▬▬▬▬▬▬▬▬▬▬▬▬▬▬▬▬▬▬▬▬▬

Protecting Digital Control Systems and Supervisory Control and Data Acquisition Systems

Many industries in the United States have transformed the way in which they control and monitor equipment by using digital control systems (DCSs) and supervisory control and data acquisition systems (SCADAs). These systems are computer-based and are capable of remotely controlling sensitive processes that were once controlled only manually on-site. The Internet is used to transmit data, a change from the closed networks of the past. Many sectors use this technology, including water, chemical, transportation, energy, and manufacturing.

In one case, an engineer used radio telemetry to access a waste management system to dump raw sewage into public waterways and the grounds of a hotel. The offender worked for the contractor who supplied the remote equipment to the waste management system. In another case, during a **penetration test** (i.e., an authorized test of defenses), service firm personnel were able to access the DCS/SCADA of a utility within minutes. Personnel drove to a remote substation, noticed a wireless network antenna, and without leaving their vehicle, they used their wireless radios and connected to the network in 5 minutes. Within 20 minutes, they had mapped the network, including SCADA equipment, and accessed the business network and data. CI sectors must understand the risks of wireless communication (U.S. Environmental Protection Agency, Office of Inspector General, 2005). Methods to protect these systems include computer access controls, encryption of communications, virus protection, data recovery capabilities, and manual overrides.

The National Strategy to Secure Cyberspace (White House, 2003b: 32) emphasizes the importance of protecting DCS/SCADA as a national priority because disruption of these systems can result in problems for public health and safety. Security is challenging for several reasons, including the requirement of research and development to implement effective security systems, and the possibility that security could affect the performance of processes. The DHS is working with the U.S. Department of Energy to partner with private industry to increase awareness of vulnerabilities, foster training, promote certification of software and hardware, and develop best practices and new technology.

Energy

Energy is another critical infrastructure sector (White House, 2003a: 50–53). It supports our quality of life, economy, and national defense. Presidential Decision Directive 63 (PDD 63) and HSPD-3 called for cooperation between government and individual infrastructures for increased protection, and the Department of Energy (DOE) was designated as the lead agency for the energy sectors. The energy sector is often divided into two industries: (1) electricity and (2) oil and natural gas.

Electricity

The physical system of electricity consists of three major parts. Generation facilities include fossil fuel plants, hydroelectric dams, and nuclear power plants. Transmission and distribution systems link the national electricity grid while controlling electricity as customers use it. Control and communication systems maintain and monitor critical components. PDD 63 identified the electrical grid as CI.

The electricity industry is highly regulated. Regulators include the Federal Energy Regulatory Commission (FERC) and state utility regulatory commissions. The Nuclear Regulatory Commission (NRC) regulates nuclear plants and related activities.

The DOE designated the North American Electric Reliability Council (NERC) as the sector coordinator for electricity. Following the serious power blackout in New York in 1965, the electric industry established NERC consisting of public and private utilities from the United States and Canada. The aim of this group is to develop guidelines and procedures to prevent disruptions of power. This group also coordinates guidelines on physical and cybersecurity.

Serious vulnerabilities exist with the equipment used in the production and transmission of electricity, and electronic monitoring devices, because these assets are outdoors and have minimal protection. The National Research Council reported that an assault on any individual segment of a network would likely result in minimal local disruption, but a coordinated attack on key assets could cause a long-term, multistate blackout.

In December 2004, the DHS reported that power company employees in Nevada were on routine patrol when they found that nuts, bolts, and supporting cross members had been removed from five transmission line towers. The company noted that if one tower fell, eight more could be brought down at the same time; however, because of redundancy in the transmission system, loss of electricity would not occur.

An example of a broad, regional disruption is the Northeast-Midwest blackout of August 14, 2003. It affected about 50 million people and took five days to fully restore service, although most customers had power within 24 hours. The DOE estimated the total cost of this blackout at $6 billion, mostly from lost income and earnings. This emergency illustrated the importance of preparation. For example, in New York City, many high-rise buildings had no backup generators, traffic lights did not work (causing gridlock), service stations were unable to sell gas (causing vehicles to stop and block traffic), and clean water was in jeopardy because no backup power existed at water facilities. These problems were repeated throughout the region of the blackout, and it has been suggested that codes should be established for emergency backup generators (Congressional Budget Office, 2004: 37).

Protection issues and strategies for the electricity sector include the following (Congressional Budget Office, 2004: 32–37; White House, 2003a: 50–53):

- Many of the assets present unique protection challenges. Examples are power generation facilities and substations.
- The owners and operators of the electric system are a heterogeneous group, and data are needed to conduct analyses of this sector's interdependencies. Such data would help to plan protection priorities and strategies.
- One serious issue is the lack of metrics to determine and justify security investments. In the case of natural disasters or accidents, such metrics are more readily available.
- To increase reliability, this sector is seeking to build a less vulnerable grid, while looking to redundancy in its transmission and distribution facilities.
- To improve recovery from equipment failure (e.g., transformers), utilities should maintain adequate inventories of spare parts, and the design of parts should be standardized.
- This sector has initiated intra-industry working groups to address security issues and an ISAC to gather incident information and relay alert notices.
- The FERC and the DOE have worked together to enhance physical and cybersecurity.
- Power management control rooms are perhaps the most protected component of this sector. NERC guidelines require a backup system, and security requirements are being formulated.

Oil and Natural Gas

Oil and natural gas businesses are closely integrated. The oil industry includes crude oil transport, pipelines, refining, storage, terminals, ports, ships, trucks, trains, and retail stores. The natural gas industry includes production, transmission, and distribution. There are 278,000 miles of natural gas pipelines and 1,119,000 miles of natural gas distribution lines in the United States (White House, 2003a: 52). The oil and natural gas industries face similar challenges as the electric industry. Examples are issues of reliability, redundancy, risk management, and security.

Dams

According to the *National Strategy for the Physical Protection of Critical Infrastructures and Key Assets* (White House, 2003a: 76), dams are a key asset and vital to our economy and communities. The Congressional Budget Office (2004: 30–31) reported that about 80,000 dams were listed in the National Inventory of Dams. These structures are major components of CI sectors that provide not only electricity, but also water to population and agricultural areas. Failure of a dam can cause loss of life, property damage, serious economic loss, and the lost value of services (e.g., power, water, irrigation, and recreation). Locations downstream are most vulnerable, as in the Johnstown Flood of 1889 that caused 2,200 deaths. In 1976, the failure of the newly built Teton Dam, in Idaho, resulted in 11 deaths, 20,000 homes evacuated, and about $800 million in damages (more costly than the dam itself).

Most dams are small and the federal government is responsible for roughly 10% of dams. The remaining ones belong to state and local governments, utilities, and the private sector. Under current law, owners are responsible for safety and security. Because of the need to improve the management of risks pertaining to dams, the DHS (i.e., FEMA's National Dam Safety Program) is focusing on the following: (1) partnering on a host of issues (e.g., risk assessment methodologies) with owners, government agencies, the Association of State Dam Safety Officials, and the United States Society of Dams; (2) prioritizing dams for protection; (3) studying security technology (e.g., sensors and barriers to prevent an attack by watercraft); and (4) improving emergency management (White House, 2003a: 76).

□ □ □ ▬▬▬▬▬▬▬▬▬▬▬▬▬▬▬▬▬▬▬▬▬▬▬▬▬▬▬▬▬▬▬

Besides the risks of terrorism, other criminal acts, natural disasters, and accidents, critical infrastructure sectors also face the risk of equipment failure that can disrupt vital services.

▬▬▬▬▬▬▬▬▬▬▬▬▬▬▬▬▬▬▬▬▬▬▬▬▬▬▬▬▬▬▬ □ □ □

Nuclear Power Plants

The *National Strategy for the Physical Protection of Critical Infrastructures and Key Assets* (White House, 2003a: 74–75) views nuclear power plants as key assets that represent U.S. economic power and technological advancement. A disruption of these facilities could have significant impact on the safety and health of citizens and harm the economy.

Nuclear power supplies about 20% of U.S. electricity from 103 commercial nuclear reactors in 31 states. This source of power has created much controversy (Congressional Budget Office, 2004: 9–19; Hebert, 2005). It has been touted as an option to reduce dependence on fossil fuels (i.e., oil, natural gas, and coal) and Middle East oil. Some environmentalists have favored nuclear power to reduce "greenhouse" gases caused by fossil fuels. Opponents refer to nuclear plant disasters. In 1986, the **Chernobyl** nuclear plant, in Ukraine, exploded due to design deficiencies and safety problems not present in U.S. reactors. This disaster spread radioactive substances across northern Europe. Residents of Chernobyl had to permanently relocate, and agricultural lands were permanently contaminated. Thirty-one people died in the fire and meltdown, and cancer rates climbed in the area. The 1979 **Three-Mile Island** partial nuclear meltdown in Pennsylvania resulted in some radioactive material escaping into the atmosphere before the reactor could be shut down. The accident was blamed on feed water pumps that stopped, followed by pressure that began to build, and a safety valve that became stuck. About 150,000 people were forced to evacuate, and litigation resulted in damages of about $70 million (mainly from the evacuation). The biggest cost was from the loss of Three Mile Island's Unit 2 that cost ratepayers $700 million to build and $1 billion to defuel and decontaminate. This incident resulted in a halt to nuclear reactor construction in the United States.

Another controversy over nuclear power resulted from a report from the public interest group Riverkeeper (Welch, 2006: 96). The report focused on the Indian Point nuclear plant located 24 miles north of New York City. The group asserts that a successful terrorist attack could kill 44,000 people, increase cancer deaths, and cost over $2 trillion. In addition, evacuation of 17–20 million people would be very difficult. The report asks why a nuclear plant is located so close to the city. The NRC disputed the contents of the report and accused the group of sensationalism, especially because of the report title, "Chernobyl on the Hudson?"

Construction costs have been another criticism of nuclear reactors. For example, in 1976 the Seabrook plant in New Hampshire was projected to cost $850 million for two reactors and be completed in six years. Fourteen years later the project was finished at a cost of $7 billion, and the second reactor was canceled.

Terrorists find nuclear plants attractive targets because of the potential for mass casualties and long-term environmental damage. Attacks may involve a 9/11 type of strike using an airliner, internal sabotage by an employee, a truck or boat bomb, an assault by a team aiming to plant an explosive, or a combination of these methods. Alternatives to attacking a reactor consist of planting explosives at nuclear waste or fuel locations to spread radioactive materials. Assaults of nuclear plants have occurred in Spain by Basque separatists, in Russia by Chechens, in South Africa during the apartheid era, and a rocket attack targeted a French nuclear plant. Captured al-Qaida documents in Afghanistan contained diagrams of U.S. nuclear plants.

Debate continues over whether the concrete containment structure of a reactor could withstand a crash by a wide-bodied, fully fueled airliner. Reactors have walls 3.5 to 6 feet thick.

The Nuclear Regulatory Commission (NRC), an independent agency created by Congress through the Energy Reorganization Act of 1974, regulates and licenses nuclear plants. It also regulates security and safety at the plants. NRC responsibilities include storage, transportation, and disposal of high-level waste.

The NRC, in conjunction with other federal agencies, develops physical security criteria or standards for nuclear operations. These standards involve defenses against both internal and external threats. A possible internal threat is someone on the inside, with or without cooperation from others, who commits sabotage or theft of special nuclear materials (SNM). SNM can be used to manufacture a nuclear weapon. An external threat could be posed by several people who are dedicated to their objectives, are well trained in military skills, and possess weaponry and explosives. An insider may be part of this threat. Radiological sabotage of nuclear materials, during shipment or at the plant site, can endanger the public by exposure to radiation. Theft or diversion of SNM could be used for extortion, terrorism, publicity, or financial gain.

NRC security criteria stress *redundancy* and *in-depth protection*. Examples are two barriers and two intrusion alarm systems. A backup is required for every sensor, transmitter, processor, and alarm so terrorists cannot simply cut a line and catch a facility off-guard. Separate monitoring systems operate at nuclear plants. Three specific monitoring systems are security, fire, and safety. The security system is similar to a proprietary central station. A recordkeeping function is essential, especially to comply with stringent NRC recordkeeping regulations.

Title 10, Code of Federal Regulations, Part 73, explains elements of an acceptable nuclear security program. It includes physical security organization, supervision, training, physical barriers, intrusion detection, access requirements, communications, testing, maintenance, armed response requirements, and secure transportation of nuclear materials.

NRC regulations require an armed response force present at a nuclear facility at all times (Figure 16-3). Criteria established by the NRC reinforce adequate selection, training, and weapons. Sufficient power is expected from the response force to counter an adversary. This entails the use of deadly force in self-defense or in the defense of others. Local law enforcement assistance is to be called in the event of an attack. However, because of a response time delay from local authorities, the primary armed defense is expected from the on-site nuclear security force.

The U.S. Government Accountability Office (2006c) refers to the design basis threat (DBT), which describes the threat that plants must be prepared to defend against in terms of the number of attackers and their training, weapons, and tactics. The revised DBT requires plants to defend against a large number of attackers, expanded weapons, and an increase in the size of a vehicle bomb. At the same time, the DBT does not include the threat of an airborne attack. In addition, NRC regulations do not require plants to protect against attacks directed against sites by an enemy of the United States.

The Congressional Budget Office (2004: 16) stated: "Despite the many efforts by nuclear plants since September 11, emergency preparedness that would help to contain losses may not

FIGURE 16-3 Security officers at a nuclear generating plant. *Courtesy:* Wackenhut Corporation. Photo by Ed Burns.

fully reflect the realities of the current terrorist threat." The U.S. Government Accountability Office (2005c: 91–92) noted challenges for the NRC. For example, the NRC does not have a system for better utilizing information from security inspections to identify problems that may be common to all plants. Another challenge involves weaknesses in the force-on-force exercises, such as using more defenders than what would be available during an actual attack, not training forces in terrorist tactics, and using unrealistic weapons (rubber guns) that do not simulate actual gunfire. Other issues pertain to the use of automatic weapons, deadly force, and arrest authority.

Protection issues and strategies for nuclear facilities include the following (Congressional Budget Office, 2004: 13–17; White House, 2003a; 74–75):

- The DOE and the EPA maintain programs for the safe disposal of high-level radioactive waste.
- Under agreement with the NRC, states may regulate low-level radioactive materials, such as those used by medical, research, and food irradiation facilities. These locations are sources for a "dirty bomb," and thus, security is vital.
- The NRC requires strict security and emergency plans at nuclear facilities and for nuclear materials in transit. Information security is also a top priority.
- Security has been enhanced since the 9/11 attacks, including more restricted site access and improved coordination with law enforcement and military authorities.
- The NRC, the DHS, and other organizations are working together to improve security.
- Options to improve protection include the following: increasing security against both ground and air assaults; adding physical features to better shield containment structures against heavy arms or aircraft; constructing safer storage facilities for spent nuclear materials; and improving protection during transportation of related materials.
- The Price-Anderson Act, a 1957 amendment to the Atomic Energy Act of 1954, provides financial support for the nuclear power industry. It creates insurance limits beyond what is available through commercial insurers. Other sources of federal assistance are available in an emergency.

Nuclear security also entails protection at four nuclear weapons production sites and three national laboratories that design nuclear weapons. The DOE and its National Nuclear Security Administration (NNSA) are responsible for these facilities.

□ □ □

Do you think security at nuclear power plants is weakened when U.S. Government Accountability Office reports and other reports are available for public access on the Web and describe general security vulnerabilities and protection methods, even though classified versions of reports have limited circulation? Explain your answer.

□ □ □

Chemical Industry

The chemical sector provides another illustration of interdependencies among infrastructures and the ways a disruption in one sector can have a cascading affect (Congressional Budget Office, 2004: 21–28; White House, 2003a: 65–66). Chemical products depend on raw materials, electricity, and transportation, among other needs. The products from this industry include fertilizer for agriculture, chlorine for water purification, polymers that create plastics from petroleum for many household and industrial products, and a variety of medicines and other healthcare products. This industry also includes oil and gas production. The chemical sector is the top exporter in the United States, totaling 10 cents out of every dollar. As with other sectors, timely delivery of products is essential for customers. Businesses with "just-in-time" delivery systems maintain a small inventory of chemicals. Municipal water systems often hold only a few days' supply of chlorine for disinfecting drinking water.

Protection of the chemical industry is important not only because of our dependence on its products and for economic reasons, but also because of its flammable and toxic substances and the risks of fire, explosion, theft, and pollution. The EPA is the primary federal agency responsible for protecting the public and the environment from chemical accidents. It lists over 300 chemicals as "extremely hazardous," meaning that harm could result in humans from exposure for only a short time.

The EPA Risk Management Program monitors facilities that handle hazardous substances beyond a threshold limit. Nearly 15,000 facilities are in the program, and many smaller facilities and retailers (e.g., gasoline stations) are excluded. The DHS is concerned about all potential targets and the smaller ones that are dispersed, more difficult to defend, and possibly attractive to terrorists.

A chemical accident that caused widespread losses occurred in 1984 in **Bhopal, India**, where a fatal pesticide was released from a Union Carbide Corporation plant. Nearly 4,000 people were killed, and India's courts ordered the company to pay $470 million in compensation to more than 566,000 survivors and dependents, including thousands of victims who were permanently disabled. When the accident occurred, there was no emergency response, atmospheric conditions were at their worst, building standards were inadequate, and there was no zoning to limit housing near the plant. In the United States, the greatest loss of life from a chemical accident came in 1947 from a ship containing fertilizer that exploded in **Texas City, Texas**, and spread fire to other ships and to industrial facilities. About 600 lives were lost. Another U.S. disaster was the **Exxon Valdez** oil spill in 1989 in Alaska. When this ship ran aground, 240,000 barrels of crude oil, with a value of $25 million, spilled. Exxon paid about $3 billion for mostly cleanup activities.

Safety in the chemical industry has been strengthened through federal laws. The **Emergency Planning and Community Right-to-Know Act of 1986** resulted from the Bhopal accident and was the first federal initiative to promote safety specifically in chemical facilities. It requires plant operators to participate in community emergency planning, provide information to local planners about chemicals on-site, and notify local authorities of a release. The Clean Air Act Amendments of 1990 mandated a role for the EPA in risk management planning for the chemical industry. Operators must have programs to prevent, detect, and mitigate releases of chemicals. The Maritime Transportation Security Act of 2002 requires vulnerability assessments for chemical facilities along U.S. waterways. State and local governments are heavily involved in chemical safety through emergency preparedness, and FEMA has provided technical support and training.

The U.S. Government Accountability Office (2005c: 90) noted security challenges facing the chemical industry. It wrote that the federal government has not comprehensively assessed the industry's vulnerability to terrorist attacks, and the extent of voluntary efforts by the industry is unclear. In 2006, the U.S. Government Accountability Office (2006a) reiterated the same points and added the following: while the EPA formerly led federal efforts to ensure chemical facility security, the DHS is now the lead agency to protect these facilities from terrorist attacks; the DHS is developing a Chemical Sector-Specific Plan to coordinate all sectors, assess vulnerabilities, and develop protection programs; and Congress should provide the DHS with the authority to *require* the chemical industry to address plant security.

The fiscal 2007 Homeland Security spending bill, signed into law by President Bush, provides the DHS with the authority to set rules for chemical plant security for the first time. However, controversy developed in the Senate over a provision in the law that prohibits states from maintaining stricter laws than the federal government. Senators argued that the provision reduces community safety (Strohm, 2007).

In June of 2007, the DHS gained the authority to enforce, for the first time ever, national chemical facility security standards. Recognizing that not all facilities face the same risk, DHS will determine which plants are "high risk" and require vulnerability assessments and site security plans with an emphasis on access controls and the prevention of theft and sabotage. A comprehensive approach will include chemicals in transit and a reduction in standstill time (e.g., unattended cars) for rails cars holding toxic substances. The DHS will inspect, audit, and penalize to ensure compliance (U.S. Department of Homeland Security, 2007).

Telecommunications

The telecommunications sector has consistently provided reliable and vital communications and processes to meet the needs of businesses and governments, while subject to technological advances, business and competitive pressures, and changes in government regulations. This sector's cyber and physical assets have faced a challenging threat environment (White House, 2003a: 47–49).

The telecommunications sector provides voice and data service to public and private customers through the Public Switched Telecommunications Network (PSTN), the Internet, and private enterprise networks. The PSTN includes switched circuits for telephone, data, and leased point-to-point services. Components of the system are connected by nearly two billion miles of fiber-optic and copper cable. The physical PSTN is the backbone of this sector, with cellular, microwave, and satellite technologies extending service to mobile customers. Advances in data network technology and increasing demand for data services have helped to create the rapid growth of the Internet. Internet service providers (ISPs) enable customers to access the Internet. International PSTN and Internet traffic travels by underwater cables. Enterprise networks support the voice and data needs and operations of large enterprises.

The PSTN and the Internet are becoming increasingly interconnected, software driven, and remotely managed, while the physical assets of this industry are increasingly concentrated in shared facilities. Wireless telecommunications is growing through an infrastructure of base stations and radio-cell towers.

The telecommunications sector is vulnerable to a variety of risks, including adverse weather, unintentional cable cuts, and crime. The 9/11 attacks resulted in significant collateral damage to this sector. However, the damage was offset by diverse and redundant communications capabilities.

As in other sectors, government and business leaders may have different perspectives on risks, security, and reliability. In the telecommunications sector, agreement on these issues remains a challenge. Protection issues and strategies in this sector include the following (White House, 2003a: 48–49):

- As with other sectors, because interdependencies could result in a cascading effect, redundancy and diversity are major concerns.

- Government and industry continue to work together to understand vulnerabilities, develop countermeasures, and raise awareness about physical and cyber threats.
- The DHS works with this industry to define an appropriate security threshold and develop requirements.
- The DHS works with other nations to consider innovative communications paths to strengthen the reliability of this sector globally.
- Public-private partnerships that influence telecommunications security and reliability include the President's National Security Telecommunications Advisory Committee and Critical Infrastructure Protection Board (PCIPB), the Government Network Security Information Exchanges, the Telecommunications ISAC, and the Network Reliability and Interoperability Council of the FCC.

Cyberspace and Information Technology

Cyberspace and information technology (IT) are essential components of the telecommunications sector, our economy, and society. The *National Strategy to Secure Cyberspace* (White House, 2003b: iii-vii) states

> *"The way business is transacted, government operates, and national defense is conducted have changed. These activities now rely on an independent network of information technology infrastructures called cyberspace.... Cyberspace is composed of hundreds of thousands of interconnected computers, servers, routers, switches, and fiber optic cables that allow our critical infrastructures to work.*
>
> *This* National Strategy to Secure Cyberspace *is part of our overall effort to protect the Nation. It is an implementing component of the* National Strategy for Homeland Security *and is complemented by a* National Strategy for the Physical Protection of Critical Infrastructures and Key Assets.

In October 2001, President Bush issued Executive Order 13231, authorizing a protection program for cyberspace and the physical assets that support such systems. This order was complemented by the Federal Information Security Management Act (FISMA) and the Cyber Security Enhancement Act of 2002. A combination of acts, relevant presidential directives, and statutory authorities provides the legal foundation for action to secure cyberspace. The FISMA, for example, requires each federal agency to develop, document, and implement an agencywide information security program (U.S. Government Accountability Office, 2006b: 4).

The following list provides a summary of the *National Strategy to Secure Cyberspace* (White House, 2003b: vii-60):

- The economy is fully dependent on IT and the information infrastructure. The Internet is at the core of these systems. Many components of infrastructure sectors are controlled by these information systems. Examples are water treatment plants, electrical transformers, trains, and stock markets. Of primary concern is the threat of attacks to disrupt CI, the economy, and national security.
- Attack tools and methodologies are becoming widely available, and the sophistication of users is improving. Enhanced cyber threat analysis is needed to address trends related to threats and vulnerabilities.
- In peacetime, our enemies may conduct espionage on our government, university research centers, and private companies. They may seek to prepare for cyber strikes by mapping U.S. IT, identifying key targets, and lacing IT with back doors and other means of access.
- The strategy provides direction for the federal government, and it identifies steps that can be taken by state and local governments and the private sector to improve collective cybersecurity.
- Strategic objectives are to prevent cyberattacks, reduce national vulnerability, and minimize damage and recovery time from attacks that do occur.

- The Secretary of the DHS will have responsibility to develop a comprehensive plan for securing cyberspace, provide crisis management and technical assistance, coordinate with other government agencies and the private sector, and support research.
- Five national priorities are (1) a national cyberspace security response system, (2) a national cyberspace security threat and vulnerability reduction program, (3) a national cyberspace security awareness and training program, (4) securing government's cyberspace, and (5) national security and international cyberspace security cooperation.

In June 2003, the DHS established the National Cyber Security Division (NCSD) to address cybersecurity issues and to coordinate a cybersecurity strategy. The NCSD also serves to coordinate a public/private partnership supporting the U.S. Computer Emergency Response Team (US-CERT), ISAC partnerships, and the Cyber Warning Information Network, among other initiatives.

Cyber Threats

There are many threats to cyberspace and information technology, and an "all-hazards" approach is best for protection. We often think about hackers attacking computer systems; however, the threats are broad and include criminals, spies, disgruntled employees, natural disasters, accidents, and errors.

The beginning of Chapter 7, under "Universal IT Threats," offers a variety of information on cyber threats, such as the insider threat, the vulnerability of telework, the costs of losses, and the difficulty of measuring computer crime.

Cyberattacks offer several advantages to offenders. They include no physical intrusion, safety for the offender, profit, no significant funding, usually no state sponsor, immense challenges for IT specialists and investigators, and enormous potential harm to victims. **Cybersecurity** focuses on methods to counter threats from a host of offenders and others who harm cyberspace and information technology and create losses.

Computer crimes can be divided into four categories according to Taylor et al. (2006: 9–15). These categories are as follows:

- *Computer as a target:* This includes the attacker who alters data. A business can be harmed, if say, decisions are made based on the altered data. Another example is denying use of the system by legitimate individuals. Among the variations of this example is the **denial-of-service attack**. This networking prank initiates many requests for information to clog the system, slow performance, and crash the site. It may be used to cover up another cybercrime. Defacement of a Web site is another example in this category, which may be referred to as malicious acts.
- *Computer as instrument of a crime:* In this category, the offender uses the computer to commit a crime. Examples are theft, fraud, and threats.
- *Computer as incidental to a crime:* This category involves the use of a computer to facilitate and enhance crimes. For example, computers that speed transactions aid money laundering. In addition, offenders use computers to maintain records of their illegal enterprises.
- *Crimes associated with the prevalence of computers:* This category includes crimes against the computer-related industry and its customers. An example is software piracy.

Common terms associated with cyber threats are as follows. A **Trojan horse** is a program, unknown to the user, which contains instructions that exploit a known vulnerability in software. A **virus** or **worm** seeks to cause damage to an application or network and delete files. A worm is similar to a virus except it can self-replicate (i.e., spread itself across networks and the Internet). Defenses include behavior blockers that stop suspicious code based on behavior patterns, not signatures, and applications that quarantine viruses in shielded areas. A **logic bomb** contains instructions in a program that creates a malicious act at a predetermined time. Programs are available that monitor applications seeking to change other applications or files when such a bomb goes off.

Dumpster diving involves searching garbage for information, sometimes used to support **social engineering** (i.e., using human interaction or social skills to trick a person into revealing sensitive information). An example of social engineering is a person being convinced to open an e-mail attachment or visit a malicious Web site. Another example is a hacker telephoning a corporate employee and claiming to be a corporate IT technician needing an access code to repair the system.

The U.S. Government Accountability Office (2005e) studied spam, phishing, and spyware threats to federal IT systems, and its findings have relevance to state and local governments and the private sector. The three threats are among the top emerging cyber threats. Explanations of each follow.

Spam is the distribution of unsolicited commercial e-mail. It has been a nuisance to individuals and organizations by inundating them with e-mail advertisements for services, products, and offensive subject matter. Spammers can forge an e-mail header so the message disguises the actual source. The spam problem is made worse because it is a profitable business. Sending spam is inexpensive and sales do result.

As with other security methods through history, adversaries constantly seek methods to circumvent defenses. This is an ongoing "cat and mouse" competition. Antispam measures have caused spammers to design techniques to bypass detection and filtration. Spammer techniques include using alternate spelling, disguising the addresses in e-mails, and inserting the text as an image so a filter cannot read it. Compromised systems are regularly being used to send spam, making it difficult to track the source of spam.

Phishing is a word coined from the analogy that offenders use e-mail bait to fish for personal information. The origin of the word is from 1996 when hackers were stealing America Online (AOL) accounts by scamming passwords from unsuspecting AOL customers. Hackers often replace *f* with *ph*, and thus, the name *phishing* developed.

Phishing often uses spam or pop-up messages that trick people into disclosing a variety of sensitive identification information (e.g., credit card and Social Security numbers and passwords). For example, one ploy is for a phisher to send e-mails appearing as a legitimate business to potential victims. The e-mail requests an "update" of ID information or even participation in "enhanced protection against hackers, spyware, etc." Phishing applies a combination of technical methods and social engineering.

Zeller (2006) reports that keylogging programs are gaining in popularity and replacing phishing by groups of global cybercriminals. **Keylogging programs** copy the keystrokes of computer users and send the information to offenders. These programs exploit security weaknesses and examine the path that carries information from the keyboard to other parts of the computer. Sources of the keylogging programs include Web pages, software downloads, and e-mail attachments. Since these programs are often hidden inside other software and infect computers, they are under the category of Trojan horses.

Spyware lacks an accepted definition by experts and even proposed legislation (U.S. Government Accountability Office, 2005e: 31). The definitions vary depending on whether the user consented to the downloading of the software, the types of information the spyware collects, and the nature of the harm. Spyware is grouped into two major purposes: advertising and surveillance. Often in exchange for a free service (e.g., allegedly scanning for threats), spyware can deliver advertisements. It can collect Web surfing history and online buying habits, among other information. Other types of software are used for surveillance and to steal information. Consumers find it difficult to distinguish between helpful and harmful spyware.

Spyware is difficult to detect, and users may not know their system contains it. Spyware typically does not have its own uninstall program, and users must remove it manually or use a separate tool. Some types of spyware install multiple copies, and it can disable antispyware and antivirus applications and firewalls.

Malware (malicious software) is programs that create annoying or harmful actions. Often masquerading as useful programs or embedded into useful programs so users activate them, malware can include spyware, viruses, and worms.

The potential for financial gain has caused spammers, malware writers, and hackers to combine their methods into blended cyber threats. Security analysts are seeing an increase in blended threats and destructive payloads. **Blended cyber threats** combine the characteristics of different types of malicious code to bypass security controls. According to the U.S. Government Accountability Office (2005e: 44–45), several federal agencies found that current enterprise tools from vendors that protect against cyber threats are inadequate and impede efforts to detect, prevent, remove and analyze incidents. In the DOJ, for example, IT specialists, without employing certain tools from vendors, could gain greater control over systems by implementing tighter security controls, such as limiting users' rights to modify and change certain features on their computers. The GAO and the National Institute of Standards and Technology have advised agencies to *use a layered security (defense-in-depth) approach, including strong passwords, patches, antivirus software, firewalls, software security settings, backup files, vulnerability assessments, and intrusion detection systems.*

Not only could a blended cyberattack cause harm, but also a **blended cyber-physical attack** can aggravate damage and hamper recovery. Probable targets are CI, companies supporting U.S. policies, response and recovery assets, and security systems. An example of a blended cyber-physical attack is penetrating a digital control system and supervisory control and data acquisition system (DCS/SCADA) to alter a manufacturing process to cause a fire and then physically attacking a fire brigade and their equipment.

The U.S. Government Accountability Office (2005e) further describes cyber threats as follows:

- *Terrorists* may use phishing scams or spyware/malware in order to generate funds or gather sensitive information.
- *Criminal groups* are increasingly using cyber intrusions that attack systems for monetary gain; further, organized crime groups are using spam, phishing, and spyware/malware to commit identity theft and online fraud.
- *Foreign intelligence services* use cyber tools as part of their information-gathering and espionage activities.
- *Hackers* sometimes break into networks for the thrill of the challenge or for bragging rights in the hacker community. While remote cracking once required a fair amount of skill or computer knowledge, hackers can now download attack scripts and protocols from the Internet and launch them against victim sites. Thus, while attack tools have become more sophisticated, they have also become easier to use.
- *Insider threats* include the disgruntled organization insider as a principal source of computer crimes. Insiders may not need a great deal of knowledge about computer intrusions because their knowledge of a target system often allows them to gain unrestricted access to cause damage to the system or to steal system data. The insider threat also includes outsourcing vendors. Employees who accidentally introduce malware into systems also fall into this category.
- *Botnet operators* are hackers; however, instead of breaking into systems for the challenge or bragging rights, they take over multiple systems to enable them to coordinate attacks and distribute malware, spam, and phishing scams. The services of these networks are sometimes made available on underground markets (e.g., purchasing a denial-of-service attack; servers to relay spam or phishing scams).

□ □ □ ▬▬▬▬▬▬▬▬▬▬▬▬▬▬▬▬▬▬▬▬

"Bots"

Cybercrime through the use of networks of bots is a serious and growing threat. "Networks of bots" refers to personal computers (PCs) infected with malicious software that enables the hacker to control the PCs.

"Bots," also known as "Internet Bots," are software applications that operate automated tasks over the Internet. Bots perform repetitive tasks at a much higher rate than humans perform and use automated script to fetch, analyze, and file information from Web servers (Wikipedia, 2007).

Acohido and Swartz (2006) write about hackers who use networks of bots as described next. From his home in Downey, California, Jeanson Ancheta, a 19-year-old high school dropout, controlled thousands of compromised PCs, or bots, which earned him enough cash to purchase a BMW and spend hundreds of dollars a week on clothes and car parts. However, he was caught by authorities and pleaded guilty to federal charges of hijacking thousands of PCs and selling access to others to spread spam and attack Web sites. The threat is global, as evidenced by the arrest of Farid Essebar, an 18-year-old resident of Morocco, who was involved in Internet bots. Tim Cranton, director of Microsoft's Internet Safety Enforcement Team, refers to bot networks as the tool of choice for those using the Internet to commit crimes. Authorities note that young men make up the majority of "bot herders," and they assemble networks of infected PCs to acquire cash by spreading adware (i.e., pop-up advertisements for dating, porn, gambling and other activities). The offenders are paid for each PC they attack with ads. Although neophytes are slack about covering their tracks, they provide authorities with insight about their methods. In contrast, more sophisticated offenders work with organized crime groups who are more difficult to apprehend. Researchers estimate a 7% infection rate for PCs. That translates to about 48 million of the 681 million PCs connected to the Internet globally may be controlled by a bot network. McAfee, the large cybersecurity firm, detected 28,000 distinct bot networks in 2005, triple the number from the year before. The security firm nCircle noted $197 billion in annual losses to U.S. businesses from computer crimes.

Cyberwarfare

Billo and Chang (2004) describe **cyberwarfare** as follows:

> [U]nits organized along nation-state boundaries, in offensive and defensive operations, using computers to attack other computers or networks through electronic means. Hackers and other individuals trained in software programming and exploiting the intricacies of computer networks are the primary executors of these attacks. These individuals often operate under the auspices and possibly the support of nation-state actors. In the future, if not already common practice, individual cyber warfare units will execute attacks against targets in a cooperative and simultaneous manner.

The objectives of such attacks include the acquisition of classified information, the defacement of Web pages, denial of service, and the disruption of equipment. The United States has faced attacks by China, Russia, and several other countries.

Information Technology Security

Information technology security is complex, and those who work in this field face enormous challenges. Chittister and Haimes (2006: 1–20) write that the emphasis in IT security is tilted toward short-term tactical measures—such as firewalls and patches—rather than long-term, strategic approaches. They cite the work of Wulf and Jones (2004): "The truth is that we don't know how to build secure information systems." Chittister and Haimes argue that this is a global problem, losses in the United States alone from cyberattacks are estimated to surpass $100 billion annually, security breaches continue unabated, and security cannot be achieved on an ad hoc basis through piecemeal and uncoordinated responses. They emphasize enhanced security through the following principles: (1) cybersecurity must be a high priority of top management; (2) an emphasis on risk management throughout the entire development of cybersecurity; and (3) a realization that "risk of software intrusion must be assessed and managed throughout the lifecycle of software development, focusing on both the functionality of software development and on the people involved in the process, knowing that hackers will exploit every weakness in the system."

Croy (2005) writes that more entities understand the business value of IT, and once IT is better integrated into the organization, the next step is the integration of IT security, physical security, business continuity planning, and insurance into comprehensive risk management planning. To justify security expenditures, Croy notes: "Executives are also becoming more directly involved because of government regulations such as Gramm-Leach-Bliley, Sarbanes-Oxley, and HIPAA that hold them personally and legally liable for business issues including access to critical information, financial controls, customer privacy, and physical security."

Kiyota (2000: 104) refers to an *integrated information security architecture* (IISA) as a well-reasoned and thoroughly researched plan for developing and implementing an effective security program to serve an enterprise's goals and needs. An IISA is an avenue to build a security infrastructure from the ground up. It consists of these steps: (1) evaluating an organization's internal and external risks; (2) determining what defensive tools and protocols are needed; and (3) planning for the implementation of a defense of new and legacy systems for today's "virtual perimeter" environment. The IISA provides a base for policies, procedures, and contingency plans. Furthermore, by adopting security standards, an organization can monitor its performance. Standards provide a baseline for measuring effectiveness that can result in improvements.

Best practices for IT security are varied and helpful to enhance security. However, it is important to note that "best practices" are an ideal state, and reality means that such practices are not universally applicable; each entity is different, and management must make organization-specific decisions (Landoll, 2005: 110).

One source for best practices is ISO 17799. It is an internationally recognized generic standard for IT security and covers 10 sections:

- Security Policy
- System Access Control
- Computer and Operations Management
- System Development and Maintenance
- Physical and Environmental Security
- Compliance
- Personnel Security
- Security Organization
- Asset Classification and Control
- Business Continuity Management

ISO/IEC 27001 is another IT security standard. It is from ISO and the International Electrotechnical Commission. ISO/IEC 27001 is a *certification standard* specifying certain requirements and can be used in conjunction with ISO 17799.

Another international standard is the Control Objectives for Information and Related Technology (COBIT) produced by the Information Systems Audit and Control Association and the IT Governance Institute. COBIT provides IT specialists with best practices to maximize IT resources and develop security and control.

Here is a list of basic strategies from a variety of sources to enhance IT security (Computer Security Institute/FBI, 2006; Sager, 2000: 40; Savage, 2006: 23–28; and Thompson, 1997: 25–30):

1. Establish an *IT security committee* to plan and lead through a *risk management approach*.
2. Conduct an *economic evaluation* of security expenditures (e.g., return on investment).
3. Invest in quality *training* because IT security changes rapidly and it is important to ensure that all employees are involved in security.
4. Monitor and track *alert bulletins* and *best practices*.

5. Consider efforts to establish generally accepted benchmarks for securing computer networks. Such standards define levels of security that an organization can measure itself against.

6. Use a *layered approach to security*. This creates multiple "roadblocks" for offenders.

7. Ensure that *IT security and information security* are well coordinated and integrated. Remember that a variety of devices can hold data, including flash storage devices, personal digital assistants (PDA), digital cameras, cell phones, MP3 players, iPods, Xboxes, and DVD players. In addition, ordinary items such as watches and pens can hold memory cards. And, because of wireless technology, a wireless hard drive can be hidden almost anywhere.

8. Use *policies and procedures* to strengthen security.

9. Provide *physical security* for computer facilities and include servers, desktops, laptops, and other equipment.

10. When designing a computer facility, avoid glass walls or doors, single paths for power to communications lines, uncontrolled parking, underground locations (because of flooding), multitenant buildings, signs describing the facility, and information about the facility on the Web.

11. Automatic *access control systems* for a computer facility are popular in combination with limited entrances; the double-door entry concept; visual verification; badge identification systems; and access control according to time, place, and specific personnel. Access controls are required not only for a computer facility, but also for all computers. This includes protection against unauthorized remote access. Biometric access control systems enable identification by fingerprints and so forth. Access to sensitive data must be safeguarded on the premises and from remote locations, even by legitimate computer users.

12. *Passwords* or *codes* are identification procedures that permit access only after the proper code is entered into the computer. The code should be changed periodically. Alarms to signal attempts at unauthorized access should be incorporated into software.

13. *Firewalls* are software and hardware controls that permit system access only to users who are registered with a computer. Attempts to gain access are challenged by the use of passwords. These challenges are "layers" that data must go through before reaching its destination. A firewall sits between a company's internal computer network and outside communications. Firewall products offer a range of features such as file or virus checking, log and activity reports, encryption, security and authentication schemes, and monitoring and alarm mechanisms for suspicious events or network intruders. Putting up a firewall is similar in certain respects to implementing physical security—assess the vulnerability, determine need, and after understanding the technology, decide on a proper level of protection.

14. Use *intrusion detection software* that is like a physical intrusion detection system, only for the network.

15. Be proactive and conduct searches for hacker programs that may be used in an attack. Hackers tend to brag about their successes to the hacker community, so check out sites that attract hackers.

16. Carefully evaluate new techniques, such as those that purport to filter and trace malicious software sent over the Web.

17. Disable unused services. Most software programs include services that are installed by default. These unused services can be a path for hackers.

18. Update software for improved security. Quickly install *security patches*. Software firms develop "patches" for protection when hackers attack their programs. Thus, when a patch is offered to a client, it should be installed as quickly as possible.

19. Use decoy programs that trick hackers into attacking certain sites where they can be observed and tracked while the important sites remain secure.

20. Because wireless networks increase the range of wired networks (by using radio waves to transmit data to other wireless devices), "signal leakage" is a security risk. Protection methods include policies, firewalls, and encryption.
21. *Audit* IT security through frequent, rigorous *vulnerability testing*. Use monitoring software to gauge attacks and misuse. Such tools are available from many commercial sources.
22. Because of the trend of companies concentrating on their core business and outsourcing everything else, "managed security services" is an option. Essentially, the work contracted to an outside firm can be as broad as surrendering "enterprise security" to the contractor. This includes security technologies, infrastructure, services, and management. Many questions evolve from this concept. Examples: What is to be retained, and what is to be outsourced? How will proprietary information be protected? Who is to be responsible for losses?
23. Refer to publication guides of the National Institute of Standards and Technology, U.S. Department of Commerce. Examples are "Computer Security Incident Handling Guide," "Guide to Selecting Information Technology Security Services," and "Guide to Selecting Information Technology Security Products."

Encryption

Many practitioners in the computer field consider encryption to be the best protection measure for data within a computer or while it is being transmitted. Once the domain of government, encryption has traditionally been used to protect military or diplomatic secrets. During the 1970s, the private sector began marketing encryption products, and with the growth of computers and the Internet, encryption likewise grew.

Encryption consists of hardware or software that scrambles (encrypts) data, rendering it unintelligible to an unauthorized person intercepting it. The coding procedure involves rules or mathematical steps, called an *algorithm,* that convert plain data into coded data. This transformation of data is accomplished through what is called a *key*, which is a sequence of numbers or characters or both. The key is used in both transmitting and receiving equipment. Key security is vital because it is loaded into both ends of the data link. Furthermore, encryption tools should be changed periodically because breaches have become something of a game. Developers of encryption systems are finding that their estimates of how long it would take to crack the codes are too long. Rapidly evolving technology has shortened the life of promising encryption systems. Another point is noted by computer expert John M. Carroll (1996: 249), who adds that, when you become mesmerized by the wonder of some promising crypto device, ask yourself one question: "How much do I trust the person who sold me this gadget?" He extends this question to the international level by claiming that it would be unlikely for any country, even an ally, to provide an encryption system to another without retaining the keys.

Controversy has developed over whether the U.S. government should have the power to tap into every telephone, fax, and computer transmission by controlling keys. From the law enforcement perspective, such control is necessary to investigate criminals, terrorists, and spies. Opponents claim violations of privacy and damage to the ability of American businesses to compete internationally.

The growth of the Internet and business on the Internet has created the need for encryption to secure electronic interactions. Internet users are seeking privacy, confidentiality, and verification of individuals and businesses they are dealing with. The public key infrastructure (PKI) and its authentication and encryption capabilities have evolved as a solution to these needs. Whereas the handshake or handwritten agreement has been tradition for centuries, a modern trend is the digital handshake and signature through the PKI. The PKI addresses three primary security needs: authentication, nonrepudiation, and encryption. The first need verifies an individual's identity. The second need means that an individual cannot deny he or she has provided a digital signature for a document or transaction.

Today, encryption products are used widely to protect public and private information. Modern encryption technology can secure data on mobile devices and encrypt and decrypt e-mail. To protect data on laptops or other computers, an option is full-disk encryption with token-based authentication. In one case, a hospital IT security director was concerned that physicians were using PDAs containing patient information without proper safeguards to protect data if the device was lost or stolen. Encryption served as the solution to protect the hospital from embarrassment and legal liability. Businesses and government are typically interested in encryption for mobile devices and storage. Financial services organizations are especially concerned about financial transactions, besides storage. The retail and hospitality sectors are concerned about point-of-sale and payment information security (Piazza, 2007: 66–73; Smith, 2006: 10–13).

□ □ □ ▬▬▬▬▬▬▬▬▬▬▬▬▬▬▬▬▬▬▬▬▬▬▬

Inside the Mind of an IT Security Professional

Critical thinking skills are essential to "think securely" while exposing IT security hype. Jay Heiser (2001: 106), an IT security specialist, notes that the ability to make intuitive, quick, and useful decisions about IT security is a learned skill that improves with practice and time. This does not mean that the security specialist is a good guesser; it means that the specialist has enough experience, judgment, and "sense" to make intelligent guesstimates based on relatively small amounts of information. Heiser states "determine the relevance of a vulnerability to your systems, evaluate the source of the warning, and then analyze its historical context and exploitability within your computing environment. If you can't do that, you'll be constantly blown by the wind, and you'll have no credibility with your employer." Heiser recommends the following:

1. Do not accept a security warning at face value. Vendors want your money and are notorious for exaggerating risks.
2. Know where to go for proven analysis, but remember that the experts are often wrong. Find multiple sources.
3. Recognize that no attack is ever completely new. Each attack is a variation of something old. Understand what happened before to develop present solutions.
4. Most vulnerabilities are never exploited because most do not offer attackers something useful. Attackers have consistent goals and methods. Vulnerabilities that are inconsistent with the needs of cybercriminals are rarely a problem.

▬▬▬▬▬▬▬▬▬▬▬▬▬▬▬▬▬▬▬▬▬▬▬ □ □ □

Defense Industry Base

Private sector defense industries play a crucial role in supporting the U.S. military (White House, 2003a: 45–46). These industries manufacture a wide variety of weapons (e.g., fighter jets, tanks, ships, and small arms), support equipment, and supplies essential to national defense and military operations (Figure 16-4). Also, many companies provide important services (e.g., IT, maintenance, security, and meals) to the military.

For several decades, the Department of Defense has identified its own critical assets and those it depends on in the private sector. For example, private utilities service many military bases. The U.S. Government Accountability Office (2005c: 93) acknowledged that the DOD has taken steps to protect military installations. However, the GAO claims the DOD lacks a single organization with authority to manage and integrate installation preparedness and prepare a comprehensive plan.

Because of market competition and attrition, the DOD now relies on a single or limited number of private sector suppliers to fulfill essential needs. These circumstances require enhanced risk management and security.

The DOD, the DHS, and the private sector work to identify CI and protection requirements. These groups, and the intelligence and law enforcement communities, are working to establish policies and mechanisms to improve the exchange of security-related information.

FIGURE 16-4 Defense industries are a component of critical infrastructure and supply weapons, vehicles, uniforms, and other products and services to support the U.S. military. *Courtesy:* DOD photo by Petty Officer 2ⁿᵈ Class Erik A. Wehnes, U.S. Navy.

The DOD is also working with defense industry contractors to address national emergency situation requirements, such as response time and supply and labor availability.

The DOD operates the **National Industrial Security Program** (NISP). This program integrates information, personnel, and physical security to protect classified information entrusted to contractors. The goal is to ensure that contractors' security programs deter and detect espionage and counter the threat posed by adversaries seeking classified information. According to DOD's Defense Security Service (DSS), which administers the NISP, attempts by foreign agents to obtain information from contractors have increased over the last several years and are expected to increase further. The U.S. General Accounting Office (2004: 2–4) found that the DSS cannot provide adequate assurances to federal government agencies that its oversight of contractors reduces the risk of information compromise, and it is unable to provide this assurance because its performance goals and measures do not relate directly to the protection of classified information. Furthermore, the DSS maintains files on contractor facilities' security programs and their security violations, but it does not analyze this information. By not analyzing information on security violations and how well classified information is being protected across all facilities, DSS cannot identify systemic vulnerabilities and make corrective changes to increase protection. As a result, government agencies are not being kept informed of possible compromises of their information. Remedies include establishing results-oriented performance goals and measures to assess whether DSS is achieving its mission and identifying information that needs to be analyzed to spot trends regarding how contractors are protecting classified information.

Outsourcing and complex mergers and acquisitions of domestic and foreign companies have produced challenges for the DOD in ensuring that its prime contractors' second-, third-, and fourth-tier subcontractors fulfill supply and security requirements in a national emergency and during peacetime. The U.S. Government Accountability Office (2005d: 3) noted that the DSS oversight of contractors under foreign ownership, control, or influence (FOCI) depends on contractors self-reporting. DSS then verifies the extent of the foreign relationship and works with the contractor on protective measures. The GAO found that the DSS cannot ensure that its approach under FOCI is sufficient to reduce the risk of a foreign nation gaining unauthorized access to U.S. classified information. Violations of FOCI policies were found by the GAO. Remedies include central collection and analysis of information, use of counterintelligence data, research tools, training for DSS staff, and lower turnover.

☐ ☐ ☐

Career: Government/Industrial Security

Government/industrial security professionals protect a variety of special categories of classified information in accordance with the National Industrial Security Program (NISP). Personnel within this specialty must meet the requirements, restrictions, and other safeguards within the constraints of applicable law and the Code of Federal Regulations necessary to prevent unauthorized disclosure of classified information released by U.S. government departments and agencies to their contractors.

Entry-level management positions require an academic degree from an accredited institution and 3 to 5 years of experience in the government or an industrial security field, preferably in a supervisory role. Necessary specialty-specific training or experience includes successful application of security regulations and some exposure to security budgetary issues. Professional certifications or a document record of involvement in professional security activities or training and education are a plus. Other prerequisites include a proven, positive track record in problem solving and customer relations. The salary range is from $55,000 to $75,000, depending on a variety of factors.

Mid-level management positions require a baccalaureate or advanced degree from an accredited institution and 5 to 10 years experience in the government or industrial security field with supervisory or previous managerial experience. Necessary specialty-specific training or experience includes professional certification (CPP, PCI, PSP, ISP, CFE, etc.) preferred, or a documented record of professional security training from U.S. government-sponsored training sessions. Other preferred prerequisites include a proven track record in problem solving, policy development, customer relations, successful application of security regulations, and budgetary development.

Source: Courtesy of ASIS International. (2005). "Career Opportunities in Security." www. asisonline.org.

☐ ☐ ☐

Government is a critical infrastructure sector. It is broad based and includes the defense industrial base, emergency services, public healthcare, public utilities, public transportation, and the postal system. It also includes government buildings, national monuments, and dams.

☐ ☐ ☐

Key Assets

As written and defined at the beginning of this chapter, the term *critical infrastructure/key resources* has replaced the term *critical infrastructure/key assets* in the NIPP. Again, *key resources* are publicly or privately controlled resources essential to the minimal operations of the economy and government. *Key assets* are individual targets whose destruction could cause large-scale injury, death, or destruction of property, and/or profoundly damage national prestige, and confidence (U.S. Department of Homeland Security, 2006b). For simplicity's sake, and because we are discussing individual targets, we will emphasize the term *key assets* here.

In contrast to CI, key assets represent a variety of unique facilities, sites, and structures that require protection (White House, 2003a: 71). One category of key assets consists of facilities and structures of technological and economic power. Examples of these key assets are nuclear power plants and dams.

Another category of key assets includes national monuments and symbols that have historical significance and represent U.S. traditions, values, and political power. These sites attract tourists and media attention. The U.S. Department of the Interior (DOI) is the lead agency responsible for the security and safety of 70,000 employees, 200,000 volunteers, 1.3 million daily visitors, and over 507 million acres of public land that includes several national monuments (U.S. Government Accountability Office, 2005b: 5). Protection challenges for the DOI are balancing security and public access; securing assets in remote areas; and addressing jurisdictional issues among federal, state, and local jurisdictions, and in some cases, private foundations. The DOI has improved security at high-profile sites, created a central security office, and developed a risk management and ranking methodology as a foundation for security spending priorities. The DOI works with numerous law enforcement agencies, including the DHS, especially during high-profile events. State and local governments are also involved in the protection of monuments, symbols, and icons.

Government facilities are categorized as key assets (White House, 2003a: 77). This category includes buildings owned and leased by the federal government for use by federal entities. Government buildings—whether federal, state, or local—are subject to a variety of serious internal and external threats, similar to commercial high-rise buildings, and they require comprehensive protection.

In the federal system, the **General Services Administration (GSA)** is a primary agency charged with managing federal facilities; however, other government organizations are involved in protecting facilities (e.g., DOD). The GSA controls over 8,000 buildings, including office buildings, courthouses, and border stations. It owns most of the major departmental headquarters in Washington, D.C. (e.g., Departments of State, Justice, and Interior) and most of the key multiagency federal office buildings in major cities. The GSA has developed security standards and works with other groups (e.g., DHS) to enhance protection. It faces similar challenges as the DOI, namely balancing security and public access. The **Federal Protective Service** (FPS), transferred from the GSA to the DHS, serves as a law-enforcement and security service to federal buildings. The FPS offers a broad range of services, such as patrol, security, investigative, canine, and WMD response. The FPS and the **U.S. Marshals Service** (USMS) provide law enforcement and security services to federal buildings that house court functions. Both of these groups have worked together to enhance protection. Numerous private security companies also protect federal facilities. Privately owned buildings that house federal tenants present unique challenges that may create friction between the government and nonfederal occupants. The GSA must work with lessors to implement security enhancements. In federally owned buildings, federal laws and regulations are enforced. In buildings shared by federal and nonfederal tenants, federal laws and regulations that, for example, prohibit weapons apply only to those spaces occupied by federal tenants.

The 1995 Oklahoma City bombing led former President Clinton to direct the U.S. Department of Justice (1995) to assess the vulnerability of federal office buildings in the United States. Prior to the study and publication, "Vulnerability Assessment of Federal Facilities," there were no governmentwide standards for security at federal facilities and no central database of the security in place at such facilities. Because of its expertise in court security, the U.S. Marshals Service coordinated the study that focused on the approximately 1,330 federal office buildings housing about 750,000 federal civilian employees. One major result of the study was the development of standards focusing on perimeter security, entry security, interior security, and security planning. Another result of the study was the division of federal buildings into five security levels, based on staffing size, use, and the need for public access. A Level I building has 10 or fewer federal employees and is a "storefront" type of operation, such as a military recruiting office. A Level V building is critical to national security, such as the Pentagon. Recommended minimum security standards apply to each security level.

The Oklahoma City bombing also led to Executive Order 12977, establishing the Interagency Security Committee (ISC) to address the quality and effectiveness of physical security requirements for federal facilities. In 2003, Executive Order 13286 transferred the leadership of the ISC from the Administrator of General Services to the Secretary of Homeland

FIGURE 16-5 Government facilities, such as courts, are key assets requiring protection. Walk-through metal detector, left; X-ray scanner, right. *Courtesy:* Wackenhut Corporation. Photo by Ed Burns.

Security. In July 2004, based on Homeland Security Presidential Directive/HSPD-7, the ISC began reviewing federal agencies' physical security plans to better protect the nation's critical infrastructure and key resources. The ISC issued its updated "Security Design Criteria" on September 29, 2004, which set forth enhanced physical security requirements for the construction of new federal buildings, as well as for major renovations of existing buildings.

State and local government institutions also are involved in security efforts to protect government buildings, especially at criminal justice facilities. Jails and prisons have traditionally maintained tight security for obvious reasons. Police agencies, especially following the unrest of the 1960s, have strengthened security in and around police buildings, including communications centers, evidence and weapons storage rooms, and crime labs. Following violence in the judicial system, courts have also increased security (Figure 16-5). Because of the 6th Amendment right of defendants to a public trial, court security is especially challenging. Each major component of the criminal justice system—police, courts, and corrections—is connected with organizations that promote either accreditation or performance measures containing security enhancements.

Commercial centers, office buildings, sports stadiums, and theme parks comprise another category of key assets (White House, 2003a: 78–79). A large number of people congregate at these locations to conduct business, shop, and enjoy restaurants and entertainment. Life safety and public safety are important objectives at these sites for protection against all hazards, besides terrorist attacks. Day-to-day protection is the responsibility of private sector proprietary and contract security personnel with the assistance of physical security and fire protection technology. Public safety agencies provide emergency response. The federal government, especially the DHS, provides assistance through advisories and alerts; efforts to bring groups together to enhance protection; and designation of an event (e.g., Superbowl) as a National Security Special Event, resulting in federal law enforcement participation and aid. Various guidelines, standards, codes, and regulations involving private sector organizations and government agencies also play an important role in protecting people and assets.

Border and Transportation Security

Border and transportation security are intertwined because various transportation modes and travelers continuously seek access through border entry and exit points. Government agencies, transportation systems, and travelers must comply with specific legal requirements to increase security and safety along borders and within borders. The legal issues are complex, considering the borders of the United States include a 5,525-mile border with Canada, a 1,989-mile border with Mexico, and 95,000 miles of shoreline and navigable waterways. All people and goods legally entering the United States must be processed through an air, land, or seaport point of entry. Over 500 million people legally enter the United States each year, and 330 million are noncitizens. Eight-five percent enter via land, often as a daily commute. The trade across U.S. borders amounted to $1.35 trillion in imports and $1 trillion in exports in 2001 (Office of Homeland Security, 2002: 21).

As we know, terrorists are elusive, crafty, and patient as they search for vulnerabilities in potential targets. The proliferation of WMD has created opportunities for terrorists to become more lethal and inflict mass casualties and severe economic harm. Consequently, the global transportation system that crosses borders and has access to all communities must be protected against terrorists who may use this system as a means of delivering WMD. The *National Strategy for Homeland Security* (Office of Homeland Security, 2002: 22–23 and 59–61) promotes the following major initiatives to improve border and transportation security:

- Consolidate principal border and transportation security agencies in the DHS.
- Create "smart borders" through improvements in management systems, databases, coordination, intelligence, and international cooperation. Increase the information available on inbound goods and passengers so border agencies can apply risk-based management tools.
- Increase the security of shipping containers that move about 90% of the world's cargo. This initiative includes identifying high-risk containers, prescreening containers, using technology to inspect, designing containers with security features, and, when possible, placing inspectors at foreign ports to screen U.S.-bound containers.
- Implement the Aviation and Transportation Security Act of 2001 (ATSA). The goals of this act are to secure the air travel systems; recognize the importance of security for all forms of transportation; strengthen partnerships among federal, state, and local governments and the private sector; and protect critical transportation assets such as ports, pipelines, rail, and highway bridges.
- Recapitalize the U.S. Coast Guard. Increase funding to improve the aging fleet, command and control systems, shore facilities, and multiple missions.
- Reform immigration services within the DHS to improve administration and enforcement of laws.
- Pursue a sustained international agenda to counter global terrorism and improve homeland security.
- Work with key trading partners to create systems to verify the legitimacy of people and goods entering the United States.
- Seek international support on many fronts such as intensified law enforcement cooperation and improved security standards for travel documents (e.g., passports and visas).

A major federal government initiative of border security is **U.S. Visitor and Immigrant Status Indicator Technology (US-VISIT)**. This is a system for integrating data on the entry and exit of certain foreign nationals into and out of the United States. The process begins overseas and continues through a visitor's arrival and departure from the United States. The program involves entrance eligibility determinations by the Departments of Homeland Security and State. In 2001, the USA PATRIOT Act provided that, in developing this entry and exit data system, the Attorney General (now the Secretary of Homeland Security has this responsibility) and Secretary of State were to focus particularly on the utilization of biometric technology (e.g., digital fingerprints) and the development of tamper-resistant documents readable at ports of entry. It also required that the system be able to interface with law enforcement databases to identify and detain individuals who pose a threat to national security. The ultimate goal of this challenging, multibillion dollar program is to check all people entering and departing the United States (U.S. Government Accountability Office, 2007b).

The U.S. Government Accountability Office (2007b: 3), in its role studying federal programs and expenditures for Congress, notes

*[W]e focus on the progress the nation has made in strengthening or enhancing the **critical layers of defense** that either were penetrated by the terrorist hijackers of 9/11, or which our work or that of the Inspectors General shows are vulnerable to terrorist exploitation.... These layers provide a series of independent, overlapping and reinforcing redundancies—domestically, for example, at airports as well as land and sea ports of entry, or outside the country, at consular offices—designed to raise the odds that terrorist activity can be identified and intercepted.*

[I]t is important that TSA continue to invest in and develop technologies for better detecting existing and emerging threats involving explosives. This is especially important in light of the alleged August 2006 plot to detonate liquid explosives on board multiple commercial aircraft bound for the United States from the United Kingdom.

Government Agencies with Roles in Border and Transportation Security

U.S. Customs and Border Protection

U.S. Customs and Border Protection (CBP), established in 2003, is the unified border agency of the DHS (U.S. Customs and Border Protection, n.d.). The CBP contains the inspectional workforce and border authorities of legacy (i.e., predecessor agency) U.S. Customs, legacy Immigration and Naturalization Service (INS), legacy USDA Animal and Plant Health Inspection Service (APHIS), and the entire U.S. Border Patrol. This united force consists of over 40,000 employees.

The priority mission of CBP is homeland security. It is charged with managing, securing, and controlling the U.S. borders. CBP goals include facilitating the efficient movement of legitimate cargo and people while maintaining security and detecting and preventing contraband (i.e., anything illegal) from entering the country.

The CBP is involved in numerous initiatives, some of which are described next. The **Container Security Initiative** (CSI) extends the zone of security outward so that U.S. borders are the last line of defense, not the first. Maritime containers that present a risk for terrorism are identified and inspected at foreign ports before they are shipped to the United States. This initiative involves using intelligence and automated advance information to identify and target high-risk containers; detection technology; and smarter, tamper-evident containers. Teams of CBP officials work with host nations in the screening process. This initiative is important because 90% of global trade is transported in cargo containers, half of incoming trade to the United States arrives by containers onboard ships, and nine million cargo containers arrive on ships and are offloaded at U.S. seaports annually.

The CBP receives electronic information on over 95% of all U.S.-bound sea cargo before it arrives. Under the **Advanced Manifest Rule**, all sea carriers, with few exceptions (e.g., bulk carriers), must provide cargo descriptions and valid consignee addresses 24 hours before cargo is loaded at the foreign port for shipment to the United States. Under the Sea Automated Manifest System, the data include cargo type, manufacturer, shipper, country of origin, routing, and the terms of payment. Using computer systems to analyze the data, the CBP assigns a numeric score to each shipment indicating its level of risk. High-risk containers are flagged to receive a security inspection.

Because CBP resources are limited, industry partnership programs bring the trade community into the process of homeland security to prevent terrorism and focus on other threats such as money laundering and smuggling contraband. An example of an industry partnership is the **Customs-Trade Partnership Against Terrorism (C-TPAT)**. This initiative is part of the extended border strategy and entails Customs working with importers, carriers, brokers, and other businesses to improve supply chain security. America's Counter Smuggling Initiative (ACSI) is a component of C-TPAT and designed to counter the smuggling of drugs and the possible introduction of WMD in cargo and conveyances. The Business Anti-Smuggling Coalition (BASC) is a private-sector-led coalition, without government mandates, that focuses on the challenges of preventing the concealment of contraband in trade. Businesses follow BASC security standards. The Carrier Initiative Program (CIP) offers CBP antidrug smuggling training to air, sea, and land transport companies. Carriers sign agreements with the CBP that offer benefits to both groups. Carriers agree to prevent smuggling by securing their facilities and conveyances, and the CBP conducts security surveys followed by recommendations to improve security. A carrier's cooperation and compliance may become a mitigating factor if narcotics are found on board a conveyance and authorities are assessing a fine. The Free and Secure Trade (FAST) initiative offers expedited clearance of low-risk shipments to carriers and importers enrolled in C-TPAT.

C-TPAT has been criticized because it is a voluntary government-business initiative. Hoffer (2006: 30) writes that import traders and their supply chain partners evaluate their own supply chain security methods and provide proof of conforming to security guidelines to gain "trusted" status to receive less screening of their imported cargo. He argues that C-TPAT is preventive theory without effectiveness due to no specific government mandate for compliance.

The CBP continues to rely on technology as an important component of border security. It does not rely on any single technology or inspection process. Instead, it applies multiple technologies in different combinations to increase the likelihood that a WMD will be detected. The technology includes large-scale X-ray and gamma-imaging systems, mobile truck X-ray, and a variety of portable and handheld radiation detection technologies. A variety of technologies is used for surveillance. Examples are outdoor sensors, CCTV, night-vision equipment, and aircraft, including Unmanned Aerial Vehicles (UAVs). Biometric verification is another helpful and growing technology. For example, both the Mexican border and the Canadian border contain entry points that are equipped with the Biometric Verification System. It is designed to read the fingerprint encoded on a border-crossing card and compare it to the fingerprint of the person presenting the card to detect imposters.

U.S. Immigration and Customs Enforcement

The **U.S. Immigration and Customs Enforcement (ICE)** is the largest investigative arm of the DHS, and it focuses on immigration and customs law enforcement *within* the United States (U.S. Immigration and Customs Enforcement, 2005). The Office of Detention and Removal (DRO) is a division of ICE that removes unauthorized aliens from the United States. DRO resources and expertise transport aliens, manage them while they are in custody and their cases are pending, and remove aliens from the United States when ordered. DRO's primary customers are the CBP and the U.S. Citizenship and Immigration Services.

DRO established the National Fugitive Operations Program (NFOP) to apprehend, process, and remove from the United States those aliens who have failed to surrender for removal or to comply with a removal order. NFOP teams focus on fugitive cases, especially cases involving criminal aliens. The "ICE Most Wanted" program publicizes the names, faces, and other ID features of the 10 most wanted fugitive criminals sought by ICE.

ICE contains an Office of Investigations that concentrates on many types of violations, including those pertaining to national security, the transfer of WMD and arms, critical technology, commercial fraud, human trafficking, illegal drugs, child pornography/exploitation, and immigration fraud. In addition, ICE special agents conduct investigations involving the protection of critical infrastructure industries that may be victimized by attack, sabotage, exploitation, or fraud. In the financial sector, for example, ICE investigates illegal money laundering, insurance schemes, bulk cash smuggling, intellectual property rights, counterfeit goods smuggling, and other crimes.

U.S. Citizenship and Immigration Services

The **U.S. Citizenship and Immigration Services (CIS)**, within the DHS, grants immigration and citizenship benefits, promotes awareness and understanding of citizenship, ensures the integrity of the U.S. immigration system, and contributes to the security of the United States. This agency works with the U.S. Department of State, CBP, and ICE. The CIS, with its thousands of federal employees and contractors working worldwide, are responsible for establishing policies and procedures, and immigration and naturalization adjudication, such as the adjudication of immigrant visa petitions.

Transportation Security Administration

Following the 9/11 attacks, the **Transportation Security Administration (TSA)** was created under the **Aviation and Transportation Security Act of 2001** (ATSA) (U.S. Transportation Security Administration, n.d.). Originally, the TSA was in the Department of Transportation, but it was transferred to the DHS in March 2003. The mission of the TSA is to protect the U.S. transportation system while facilitating freedom of movement of people and commerce. The ATSA gave the TSA regulatory authority over all transportation modes. Although the 9/11 attacks resulted in the airline industry being a top priority for protection by the TSA, this agency recognizes the importance of securing all forms of transportation.

The TSA issues and administers Transportation Security Regulations (TSRs), which are codified in Title 49 of the Code of Federal Regulations (CFR), Chapter XII. Many TSRs are former rules of the Federal Aviation Administration (FAA) that were transferred to TSA when it assumed the FAA's civil aviation security role in 2002.

The TSA has developed numerous initiatives to increase protection in the transportation sector. TSA programs and strategies are discussed in subsequent pages under the various transportation modes.

The U.S. Government Accountability Office (2007a) notes the difficulty of protecting the transportation system:

> *DHS and the components of DHS responsible for transportation and port security have taken steps to apply risk management principles with varying degrees of progress. The Transportation Security Administration has not completed a methodology for assessing risk, and until the overall risk to the entire transportation sector is identified, it will be difficult to determine where and how to target limited resources to achieve the greatest security gains.*

Transportation Sectors

The National Strategy for the Physical Protection of Critical Infrastructures and Key Assets (White House, 2003a) identifies transportation as one of several critical infrastructure sectors. Interdependencies exist between the transportation sector and nearly every other sector, and a disruption of this sector can have a cascading affect on other sectors. For example, the agriculture and food sector is dependent on the transportation sector to ship goods to customers. The transportation sector is vital to our economy and national security, including mobilization and deployment. The lead agencies for the transportation sector are the DHS in collaboration with the U.S. Department of Transportation (DOT).

The **Intelligence Reform and Terrorism Prevention Act of 2004** directly affects the security of public transportation. It requires the DHS to develop a National Strategy for Transportation Security. This act contains provisions designed to address many of the transportation and border security vulnerabilities identified and recommendations made by the 9/11 Commission. It includes provisions designed to strengthen aviation security, information sharing, visa issuance, border security, and other areas. The focus of the act includes the identification of the transportation infrastructure, risk-based security priorities, protection strategies, and research and development.

Aviation

The aviation system is vast and made up of thousands of entry points. In the United States, it consists of two main parts: (1) airports, aircraft, and supporting personnel and assets; and (2) aviation command, control, communications, and IT systems to support and maintain safe use of airspace.

There are 19,000 General Aviation airports, 453 commercial airports, 211,000 active aircraft, and 550,000 active pilots and instructors. General Aviation airports involve primarily recreational flying but also include such activities as medical services, aerial advertising, and aerial application of chemicals (U.S. Government Accountability Office, 2004: 57).

The **Federal Aviation Administration (FAA)**, within the DOT, regulates civil aviation to promote safety and air traffic control. It issues airport operating certifications depending on the type of aircraft served. The FAA also issues certifications for aviation employees, aircraft, airlines, and other purposes.

Security varies at airports and it depends on the type of airport and aircraft (Figures 16–6 and 16–7). *General Aviation airports present a serious security vulnerability*. Here, the emphasis is on commercial airports.

Prior to the 9/11 attacks, security at airports was the responsibility of private carriers and state and local airport owners. Following the attack, Congress passed the ATSA, establishing the TSA as the responsible authority for aviation security. In other words, the TSA is charged with federalizing security at commercial airports in the United States and replacing private screeners with federal screeners. The TSA applies several layers of security to protect the air transportation sector.

FIGURE 16-6 Commercial airports maintain extensive security.

FIGURE 16-7 Security varies at General Aviation airports.

TSA Programs

The TSA operates various screening programs to increase aviation security. *Secure Flight* involves prescreening passengers through a comparison of Passenger Name Records (PNRs) from domestic flights to names in the Terrorist Screening Database (TSDB) established by the Terrorist Screening Center (TSC). Another challenge is effective and efficient screening of passengers and baggage arriving at airports for flights. The GAO has published several reports on aviation security and screening. It has repeatedly stated that challenges remain, such as hiring, training and deploying screeners and measuring performance of screeners and detection equipment.

Various technologies are applied to detect explosives, weapons, metals, and plastics. Examples include X-ray systems, metal detectors, biometrics, explosive trace detection (ETD) systems, and body scanning.

The screening of cargo transported on commercial passenger aircraft is another serious concern and vulnerability that does not receive enough attention. Calls to eliminate this practice face opposition from the passenger airline business that sees it as a source of income in an industry confronted with tight profit margins. A major issue is the source of funding for a thorough screening system for such cargo.

Another program focuses on explosive detection through canine teams. On March 9, 1972, a Trans World Airlines jet took off from JFK International airport in New York bound for Los Angeles. Initially, the flight was normal, but then the airline received an anonymous telephone call warning of a bomb on the flight. The aircraft returned to JFK, passengers were evacuated, and a bomb-sniffing dog named Brandy conducted a search of the aircraft. Brandy found the bomb 12 minutes before it was set to explode. This successful conclusion of a dangerous situation resulted in the establishment of the FAA *Explosives Detection Canine Team Program*, designed to place certified teams at strategic locations in the United States so aircraft with a possible bomb can be diverted quickly to an airport with such a program.

Airlines are required to provide basic security training for all aircrew members. The TSA is required by law to provide optional, hands-on self-defense training if crew members request it. Under the *Federal Flight Deck Officer Program*, a pilot, flight engineer, or navigator is authorized to use firearms to defend the aircraft. Crew members are trained in the use of force and firearms, defensive tactics, psychology of survival, and legal issues.

The **Federal Air Marshal Service** (FAMS) began in 1968 as the FAA Sky Marshal Program. This was a time when the Palestine Liberation Organization (PLO)-affiliated Popular Front for the Liberation of Palestine (PFLP) attracted world attention by introducing the hijacking of aircraft, which spawned subsequent hijackings (Poland, 1988: 103–104). The mission of the FAMS is to detect, deter, and defeat hostile acts targeting U.S. air carriers, passengers, and crews. The training requirements are stringent and include behavioral observation, intimidation tactics, close quarters self-defense, and a higher standard for handgun accuracy than officers of any other federal law enforcement agency. The number of Federal Air Marshals is classified information. During the Fall 2005 reorganization of the DHS, FAMS was transferred from ICE to TSA to improve coordination of aviation security.

Another TSA measure of protection is the *Alien Flight Student Program*. This program began in 2001 with the ATSA. Specific aviation training entities are prohibited from offering flight training to aliens and other individuals in the operation of certain aircraft.

The TSA partners with the private sector through various initiatives. For example, the Aviation Security Advisory Committee partnered with the TSA to develop General Aviation security recommendations titled *Security Guidelines for General Aviation Airports* (Publication A-001). Another initiative is the Airport Watch program, which includes a "hotline" in coordination with the Aircraft Owners and Pilots Association (AOPA).

The ATSA also mandates improvements in airport perimeter security and access controls. Compliance inspections and vulnerability assessments serve as a foundation for funding priorities, planning new technologies, and reducing the security threats of airport employees.

The 9/11 attacks resulted in improvements in physical security inside aircraft. For example, commercial airlines contain reinforced cockpit doors that remain locked during flight. Directly outside the door, CCTV cameras are installed in some aircraft.

Another concern, specifically against aircraft, is **Man-Portable Air Defense Systems (MANPADS)**. These handheld missile systems have been fired by terrorists against commercial aircraft in the past. A counter-system faces the establishment of system requirements, the development of technology, cost-effectiveness, and funding.

☐ ☐ ☐ ▬▬▬▬▬▬▬▬▬▬▬▬▬▬▬▬▬▬▬▬▬▬▬▬

TSA Revokes Air Cargo Security Program Approval for Two Shipping Businesses

In 2006, the TSA, in its effort to be vigilant in maintaining the integrity of air cargo security, revoked the security program approval for Professional Export Services (PES) and J.H. World Express, Inc., because these businesses did not meet TSA security standards. Among other violations, PSE tendered at least 48 shipments from unknown shippers to passenger air carriers and failed to provide cargo security training to their employees. Passenger air carriers are notified not to accept cargo from non–TSA-approved indirect air carriers. Acceptance of cargo from violating carriers can result in a civil fine up to $25,000 per violation. Firms that have their air carrier certification revoked can apply for recertification in 90 days (Transportation Security Administration, 2006).

☐ ☐ ☐ ▬▬▬▬▬▬▬▬▬▬▬▬▬▬▬▬▬▬▬▬▬▬▬▬

Self-Defense on Airliners

Self-defense in an aircraft is extremely important for not only crew members, but also passengers. As we know from the 9/11 attacks, terrorists may try to deceive passengers into thinking that they will not be harmed if they follow terrorist demands. Crew members and passengers must consider the option of being creative with available items to be used as weapons and using force to survive.

▬▬▬▬▬▬▬▬▬▬▬▬▬▬▬▬▬▬▬▬▬▬▬▬ ☐ ☐ ☐

Passenger Rail and Railroads

Trains play an important role in our economy by linking raw materials to manufacturers and carrying a wide variety of fuels and finished goods. Over 20 million intercity travelers ride the rail system annually, and 45 million passengers ride trains and subways operated by local transit authorities. Securing the rail sector is important to ensure the safety of passengers and to protect U.S. commerce (White House, 2003a: 56).

The vast U.S. rail system contains numerous entry points. It is complex because of differences in design, structure, and purpose. The differences result in disadvantages and advantages for security. For example, the size of the rail system makes responding to various threat scenarios difficult. At the same time, trains must follow specific routes, so if one were hijacked, for example, it could be diverted off a mainline. Similarly, if a bridge or tunnel were destroyed, the rail line would suffer disruption; however, national-level disruptions would be limited. A serious risk in this sector is the transportation of hazardous materials, especially through populated areas; therefore, industry and government coordination is necessary for decision making. Security and safety of containerized cargo are other challenges. Controversy has developed over the markings of containers to indicate the type of hazardous materials being transported. Although placards on rail cars provide helpful information to first responders during an emergency, the information can also assist terrorists planning an attack. Another concern of the rail sector is the cost of security. The increased threat environment means expenses for additional security personnel and overtime (White House, 2003a: 56).

Rail mode protection initiatives include the following (White House, 2003a: 57):

- The rail mode has been working with the DOT to assess risk.
- A surface transportation Information Sharing and Analysis Center (ISAC) has been formed to exchange information related to both cyber and physical threats.
- The DHS and the DOT are coordinating with other federal agencies, state and local governments, and industry to improve the security and safety of hazardous materials.
- The DHS and the DOT are working with the rail sector to identify and explore technologies and processes to efficiently screen rail passengers and baggage and to secure containers and detect threatening content.
- The DHS and the DOT are working with industry to delineate infrastructure protection roles and responsibilities for surge requirements during emergencies.

The railroad industry works with all levels of government and maintains police and security forces for its individual railroad entities. The Association of American Railroads (n.d.) uses a multistage alert system and open lines of communications with DHS and DOD officials. This group's Railroad Security Task Force applied national intelligence community "best practices" to develop a security plan consisting of the following strategies:

- A focus on hazardous materials, operations, infrastructure, IT and communications, and military movements
- A database on critical assets
- Risk management
- Increased security and random inspections
- Improved protective housings, valves, and fittings to increase security in the transportation of hazardous materials and to prevent sabotage
- Protection against signal tampering

□ □ □ ▬▬▬▬▬▬▬▬▬▬▬▬▬▬▬▬▬▬▬▬▬▬▬▬▬▬▬

Are Rail Cars Containing Toxic Cargo "Sitting Ducks"?

Authorities face an enormous number of potential terrorist targets. Risks must be prioritized, since resources are limited. Toxic substances within rail cars that are in transit or at a standstill present attractive targets to terrorists and other criminals. This is a serious vulnerability. Unfortunately, as public safety agencies are doing their best to protect citizens from a variety of threats, inside their jurisdiction or nearby are toxic substances, necessary for our everyday lives, that are unprotected. In one case, a reporter and photographer gained easy access to an unguarded rail facility close to New York City and observed rail cars filled with deadly chlorine, ammonia, and other chemicals. They also spotted unlocked switching devices that could be used to cause an accident (Kocieniewski, 2006).

Imagine the carnage from a bomb placed on one of these rail cars, or a bomb placed on such a rail car sitting near fuel storage tanks or other target to facilitate a cascading effect. Although chemical plant security is improving, the shipments linking these plants to suppliers and customers must also be improved.

The U.S. Naval Research Lab reports that each year railroads transport 105,000 rail cars of toxic chemicals and 1.6 million rail cars of other hazardous materials. They estimate that an attack on such a rail car could kill 100,000 people. The TSA is working with railroads to reduce the time such rail cars are sitting unprotected. In early 2007, the TSA began monitoring rail cars containing toxic substances. Specifically, the TSA is recording how long these rail cars are stopped on tracks or sitting in unprotected storage yards in urban areas. Rerouting to reduce the danger to cities is an option; however, this would force transporting the toxic substances in trucks, which could be more dangerous (Frank, 2007).

▬▬▬▬▬▬▬▬▬▬▬▬▬▬▬▬▬▬▬▬▬▬▬▬▬▬▬ □ □ □

Mass Transit Systems

About 9.5 billion trips are made on mass transit systems (e.g., urban subway and rail; buses) in the United States each year. Mass transit carries more passengers each day than air or rail (i.e., between cities) transportation (White House, 2003a: 61).

Mass transit systems are open and convenient to the public with minimal access controls (Figure 16-8). This makes protection difficult, challenging, and expensive.

The DHS, the DOT, and all levels of government seek to improve guidelines and standards to protect mass transit systems. Initiatives include design and engineering standards for rail and bus vehicles, improved screening and training for operators, security standards, and emergency and continuity of operations planning.

The U.S. Government Accountability Office (2005f) reports that the numerous stakeholders involved in securing rail transportation can lead to communication challenges, duplication of effort, and confusion of roles and responsibilities. Key federal stakeholders include the TSA and the Office for Domestic Preparedness (ODP), both within the DHS. The ODP provides grants to rail operations and conducts risk assessments for passenger rail agencies. Two other federal agencies, both within the DOT, are the Federal Transit Administration (FTA) and the Federal Railroad Administration (FRA). The FTA conducts nonregulatory safety and security activities, such as training, research, technical assistance, and demonstration projects. The FRA has regulatory authority over rail safety for commuter rail lines and Amtrak; it employs over 400 rail inspectors. Other important stakeholders are state and local agencies and rail operators.

The U.S. Government Accountability Office (2005c: 58) notes that whereas the aviation system is housed in a closed and controlled system, mass transit systems are open so large numbers of people can be moved quickly. Security features that limit access, cause delays, increase fares, or result in inconvenience, could make automobiles more attractive. At the same time, those mass transit systems located in large urban areas or tourist spots make them attractive targets because of the potential for mass casualties and economic damage.

Jenkins (2004: 2) writes: "For those determined to kill in quantity and willing to kill indiscriminately, trains, subways and buses are ideal targets. They offer terrorists easy access and escape." He notes that an analysis of nearly 1,000 terrorist attacks on transportation found that the percentage of fatalities was much higher than the percentage for terrorist attacks in general.

In 2004, following the Madrid rail attacks, the TSA issued directives containing required security measures for passenger rail operators and Amtrak. The security measures

FIGURE 16-8 Mass transit systems maintain limited access controls and are a challenge to protect.

produced controversy over limited dialogue to ensure industry "best practices" were included in the measures. Examples of the TSA security measures are as follows (U.S. Government Accountability Office, 2005f: 22):

- Designate coordinators to enhance security-related communication.
- Provide TSA with access to security assessments and plans.
- Reinforce employee watch programs.
- Ask passengers to report unattended property and suspicious behavior.
- Use clear plastic or bomb-resistant containers.
- Use canine explosive detection teams to screen passenger baggage, terminals, and trains.
- Allow TSA canine teams access to rail operations.
- Conduct frequent inspections of facilities and assets.
- Use surveillance systems.
- Ensure appropriate levels of policing and security that correlate with DHS threat levels.
- Lock all doors that allow access to train operators.
- Require Amtrak to request that adult passengers provide ID at the initial point where tickets are checked.

Additional measures from a variety of sources are emergency planning and drills, quality intelligence systems, visible and undercover patrols, behavioral observation skills of police and security, emergency call boxes, research and testing of WMD detection equipment, ventilation systems that remove toxic smoke, and windows that blow out to reduce both the destructive force of a blast and smoke.

Many security methods applied to trains are also applicable to buses (Figure 16-9).

Highways, Trucking, and Intercity Busing

Trucking and intercity busing are essential components of the transportation infrastructure to move people, goods, and services. Related components include highways and roads. The White House (2003a: 57–58) notes that the trucking and intercity busing industries present several protection challenges because these industries are heterogeneous in size and operations, span numerous government jurisdictions, and operate under many owners.

FIGURE 16-9 Buses are among other mass transit targets attractive to terrorists. Several security methods are applicable to all mass transit modes.

Transportation choke points (TCPs) are another challenge. These points include bridges, tunnels, highway interchanges, terminals, and border crossings that are crucial to transportation routes. TCPs are vulnerabilities in the transportation sector because they connect roads and modes of transportation. If subject to attack and destruction, traffic could be blocked at TCPs, and the vulnerabilities of people, vehicles, and vehicle contents would be compounded.

Initiatives aimed at improving the protection of highways, trucking, and intercity busing include cooperation among the DHS, the DOT, and sector stakeholders on

- Risk management
- Development of criteria for identifying and mitigating TCPs
- Technological solutions for increased protection
- National operator security education and awareness

Additional recommendations can be found through The American Association of State Highway and Transportation Officials. The American Trucking Association (ATA) also promotes security issues. For example, with cooperation and funding from the DHS, the ATA promotes a "watch" program that seeks to include the millions of drivers of commercial and public trucks, buses, and other vehicles to recognize safety and security threats. The ATA supports the North American Transportation Management Institute's Certified Cargo Security Professional designation.

Maritime

The maritime shipping infrastructure is another vital component of the economy. It consists of ports, ships that carry cargo and passengers, waterways, locks, dams, canals, and a network of transportation modes, such as railroads and pipelines that connect to ships in port. The 361 seaports in the United States are diverse in size and characteristics. They are owned and operated by either private corporations or state and local governments. Ships are primarily owned and operated by the private sector. The DOD has designated certain seaports as strategic seaports for military purposes (White House, 2003a: 60).

Annually, the U.S. maritime industry manages over 2 billion tons of freight, 3 billion tons of oil, more than 134 million ferry passengers, and about 7 million cruise ship travelers. Furthermore, about 7,500 foreign ships, operated by 200,000 sailors, enter U.S. ports each year (Maxwell and Blanda, 2005: 22).

The delivery and activation of a WMD on a ship near a port, in port, or in transit from a port would be a catastrophe. And, knowing the creativity and patience of terrorists, one possible scenario is the use of a fuel-laden supertanker as a WMD.

As with other transportation systems, maritime shipping faces the huge challenge of access controls. The inspection of all vessels and cargo that enter ports is impossible, and security concerns must be balanced with efficient access to ports by passengers and cargo. Compounding the need for improved security are international agreements and multinational authorities. The U.S. Department of State, the diplomatic arm of the U.S. government, is responsible for the negotiation of maritime rules and practices with other countries.

The *International Ship and Port Facility Security Code* takes a risk management approach and seeks global standardization of security of port facilities and ships. Similar to U.S. Coast Guard rules, the code requires minimal requirements, such as port security plans, a port security officer, ship security plans, a ship security officer, and training. Failure to comply with the code has resulted in ships being detained or denied entry by the U.S. Coast Guard.

Various government agencies work to improve protection in this industry. The DHS and the DOT work with other government agencies, the private sector, foreign governments, and international organizations to improve maritime security.

The DOT is working with the CBP to ensure security in the shipping supply chain. Those shippers who are unable to comply with rules and regulations are subject to increased attention and delay when seeking entrance to U.S. ports.

Besides the CBP, the U.S. Coast Guard is another primary agency involved in port security. It was transferred to the DHS intact in 2003. Because the 9/11 attacks hit the U.S.

mainland, the Coast Guard has had its missions expanded and its capabilities strained. Three major priorities of the Coast Guard are (1) implementing a maritime strategy for homeland security, (2) enhancing performance, and (3) recapitalizing the Coast Guard. This third priority includes the Deepwater Program that replaces or upgrades cutters and aircraft that are capable of performing missions far out at sea (U.S. Government Accountability Office, 2005a). The **Maritime Transportation Security Act of 2002** (MTSA) charged the Coast Guard with numerous responsibilities, such as assessing port vulnerabilities, ensuring that vessels and ports have security plans, and promoting uniform standards of security. Homeland security missions also include waterways and coastal security, drug interdiction, migrant interdiction, and defense readiness to assist the U.S. Navy. Non-homeland security missions include marine safety, search and rescue, aids to navigation (e.g., buoys), marine resources (e.g., fishing treaties), environmental protection, and ice operations (Office of Inspector General, 2004). Critics argue that increased security tasks by the Coast Guard hinder their traditional duties such as boating safety and rescue.

The MTSA is a major law promoting maritime security. The act mandates a National Maritime Transportation Security Plan and contingency plans in response to terrorist attacks; an increase in security personnel and screening equipment; a grant program to support security upgrades; security regulations to be developed through the DOT, such as access controls and identification cards; training and certification; a maritime intelligence system; and the establishment of local port security committees to coordinate federal, state, and local law enforcement agencies and private security.

In September 2005, the Departments of Homeland Security, Defense, and State collaborated to approve *The National Strategy for Maritime Security* (U.S. Department of Homeland Security, 2005b). This first-ever national maritime security plan, with contributors from over 20 government agencies and the private sector, contains supporting plans on awareness, intelligence, layered security, threat response, domestic and international outreach, and recovery. This national strategy considers threats from WMD, transnational crime and piracy, and environmental destruction.

Additional legislation that helps to protect ports and improve supply chain security is the **Security and Accountability For Every (SAFE) Port Act of 2006**. This act establishes a Domestic Nuclear Detection Office within the DHS, appropriates funds toward the Coast Guard modernization program, and enhances port security training.

□ □ □ ▬▬▬▬▬▬▬▬▬▬▬▬▬▬▬▬▬▬▬▬▬▬▬▬▬▬

International Perspective: Supply Chain Risks and Security
Supply chain refers to a system of businesses, transportation modes, information technology, and employees that move a product or service from supplier to customer. Business executives planning to seek new markets and operate supply lines from around the globe should incorporate security risks and countermeasures in the planning process. Purtell and Rice (2006: 78–87) write that supply chain risk assessments may include the study of the manufacturing region and site, roads, trucking operations, freight forwarders, logistic warehouses, seaports, and airports. Corruption and anti-American or anti-Western sentiments are other factors to consider.

Numerous Web sites offer basic information on conditions in various countries. U.S. Department of State Travel Warnings on countries offer a variety of information on such topics as crime, security, medical services, roads, and traffic conditions and safety. Another source is the Overseas Security Advisory Council (refer to the Chapter 10 box titled "International Perspective: Overseas Investigations"). Sources of information on supply chain security include the U.S. Customs and Border Protection.

Research by Purtell and Rice (2006) produced interesting findings. "For example, Russia and Brazil are among two of the highest risk countries in terms of supply chain theft. Incidents commonly involve government representatives including police, military, and customs officials. However, in terms of C-TPAT, these countries are given a 'low' threat rating because the governments and residents are on amicable terms with the United States and are not hostile to Western culture." They also found that a "cookie-cutter" approach to security has caused companies to overspend in low-risk countries, such as China, and underspend in high-risk countries, such as Malaysia and Indonesia. Purtell and Rice note that terrorism is not the only risk. Organized crime and piracy are other concerns, depending on the location.

Laden and Rogers (2006: 62–68) offer suggestions for supply chain security:

- Security, supply chain, and logistics practitioners should work together.
- The company should identify supply chain vulnerabilities prior to risk-based mitigation.
- The company must know its vendors and suppliers and communicate security expectations.
- The company should vet vendors and suppliers. The Internet and software tools can assist this process. Once a list and data are generated, the company should ensure that firms are not on the government's restricted lists, as published by the Departments of Commerce and Treasury and the U.S. Customs and Border Protection.
- Importers should consider restrictive language in orders so that they can control the use of subcontractors in manufacturing and shipping products.
- The company should use technology to improve supply chain visibility, so managers can see what is in the supply chain at all times. Examples of applicable technology are Radio Frequency ID (RFID) and Global Positioning Systems (GPS).

Postal and Shipping

The U.S. Postal System (USPS) handles about two-thirds of a billion pieces of mail each day as more than 300,000 postal carriers deliver mail to more than 137 million delivery addresses nationwide. Total employment in the USPS is about 749,000. The USPS consists of a headquarters in Washington, D.C., tens of thousands of postal facilities (Figure 16-10), and hundreds of thousands of official drop-boxes. The system is dependent on the transportation infrastructure and its trucks, aircraft, railroads, and ships. Annual revenue from the USPS is over $60 billion. Private industry mailing and shipping revenues exceed $140 billion (White House, 2003a: 67).

The networks of the USPS and private shipping companies present complex protection challenges. The Fall 2001 **anthrax attacks** through the USPS illustrate the impact of a serious disruption to this system. This attack resulted in five deaths and contamination at postal facilities and equipment, other government offices, and businesses.

The USPS has developed six core initiatives in its emergency preparedness plans: prevention, protection and health-risk reduction, detection and identification, intervention, decontamination, and investigation. The USPS and the DHS seek to work with all levels of government for coordinated emergency response, increase stockpiles of equipment and materials for contamination events, conduct risk analyses of high-risk facilities, and coordinate the security of mail transiting U.S. borders with the U.S. Customs Service.

Pipelines

According to *The National Strategy for the Physical Protection of Critical Infrastructures and Key Assets* (White House, 2003a: 58), pipelines are considered part of the transportation CI sector. The pipeline industry moves a variety of substances such as crude oil, refined petroleum products, and natural gas within many hundreds of thousands of miles of pipelines that are mostly underground. This industry has a commendable record of safety, contingency plans, and the capabilities to repair or bypass localized disruptions. However, protection is an important issue because of the volatile nature of the products that pipelines deliver. Pipelines

FIGURE 16-10 The U.S. Postal System is dependent on the transportation infrastructure, as are private carriers of mail and packages. Attacks of the mail system are extremely challenging for authorities.

cross local, state, and international jurisdictions, and numerous businesses and other entities depend on a reliable flow of fuel. The problem of cascading is evident with pipelines, as it is with other CI sectors. The Departments of Homeland Security, Energy and Transportation; state and local governments; and the private sector collaborate to improve protection measures and emergency response plans.

Search the Web
Here are Web sites relevant to this chapter:

American Association of Airport Executives: www.aaae.org
American Association of State Highway and Transportation Officials: www. transportation.org
American Bus Association: www.buses.org
American Chemistry Council: www.americanchemistry.com
Airports Council International: www.airports.org
American Public Transportation Association: www.apta.com
ASIS International: www.asisonline.org
American Trucking Associations: www.truckline.com/index
American Water Works Association: www.awwa.org
Association of American Railroads: www.aar.org/
Food Products Association: www.fpa-food.org
Government Web sites on food safety: www.foodsafety.gov
Information Systems Audit Control Association: www.isaca.org
Information Systems Security Association: www.issa.org
IT Governance Institute: www.itgi.org/
International Council of Cruise Lines: www.iccl.org

International Information Systems Security Certifications Consortium: www.isc2.org

International Organization for Standardization (ISO): www.iso.org

Metropolitan Transportation Authority, State of New York: www.mta.nyc.ny.us/

National Infrastructure Protection Plan: www.dhs.gov/nipp

National Institute of Standards and Technology, Computer Security Resource Center: http://csrc.nist.gov/

National Security Agency, Information Assurance Directorate: www.nsa.gov/ia/

NetLingo: www.netlingo.com/

North American Transportation Management Institute: www.natmi.org/index.cfm

Overseas Security Advisory Council (OSAC): www.osac.gov/

The Infrastructure Security Partnership: www.tisp.org

United Motorcoach Association: www.uma.org

U.S. Citizenship and Immigration Services: www.uscis.gov

U.S. Coast Guard: www.uscg.mil/USCG.shtm

U.S. Customs and Border Protection: www.cbp.gov

U.S. Department of Agriculture, Food Safety and Inspection Service: www.fsis.usda.gov

U.S. Department of Defense: www.defenselink.mil/

U.S. Department of Energy: www.energy.gov

U.S. Department of Homeland Security: www.dhs.gov

U.S. Department of Homeland Security, Critical Infrastructure Daily Report: dhsdailyadmin@mail.dhs.osis.gov

U.S. Department of Transportation: www.dot.gov

U.S. Department of Transportation, Maritime Administration: www.marad.dot.gov/

U.S. Environmental Protection Agency: www.epa.gov

U.S. Food and Drug Administration, Food Safety, Defense, and Outreach: www.cfsan.fda.gov

U.S. Immigration and Customs Enforcement: www.ice.gov

U.S. Transportation Security Administration: www.tsa.gov

Case Problems

16A. Suppose you are a terrorist leader in the U.S. planning to attack the food industry. What is your plan?

16B. Suppose you are a disgruntled employee working in the chemical industry at a plant that produces chlorine. Your anger at your employer is so intense that you do not care about yourself or anyone else. All you can think about is your plan to get back at your employer. Besides what you know from your job, you conduct research on the Web to find out everything you can about chlorine. What is your plan?

16C. As the Security and Safety Director of a company involved in the food industry, how would you prevent the attack planned in 16A? How would you respond if the plan were executed?

16D. As the Security and Safety Director of the chlorine plant in 16B, how would you prevent the crime(s) planned in 16B? How would you respond if the disgruntled employee executed the vindictive plan?

16E. As the Chief Security Officer (CSO) of a manufacturing company with multiple plants in the United States, how do you protect the company from the cascade effect from all hazards?

16F. As the security director for a city mass transit bus system, what are your top seven (prioritized) strategies for protecting passengers, employees, and assets associated with this system?

References

Acohido, B., and Swartz, J. (2006). "Malicious-Software Spreaders Get Sneakier, More Prevalent." *USA Today* (April 23). http://www.usatoday.com/tech/news/computersecurity/infotheft/2006-04-23-bot-herders_x.htm, retrieved April 24, 2006.

Association of American Railroads. (n.d.). "Freight Railroad Security Plan." www.aar.org, retrieved October 23, 2005.

Billo, C., and Chang, W. (2004). "Cyber Warfare: An Analysis of the Means and Motivations of Selected Nations." http://www.ists.dartmouth.edu/directors-office/cyberwarfare.pdf, retrieved January 24, 2007.

Carroll, J. (1996). *Computer Security*, 3rd ed. Boston: Butterworth-Heinemann.

Chalk, P. (2003). "Agroterrorism: What Is the Threat and What Can Be Done about It?" Santa Monica, CA: Rand Corp.

Chittister, C., and Haimes, Y. (2006). "Cybersecurity: From Ad Hoc Patching to Lifecycle of Software Engineering." *Journal of Homeland Security and Emergency Management*, 3.

Computer Security Institute/FBI. (2006). *CSI/FBI Computer Crime and Security Survey*. www.GoCSI.com, retrieved July 14, 2006.

Congressional Budget Office. (2004). *Homeland Security and the Private Sector* (December). Washington, D.C.: Congress of the United States.

Croy, M. (2005). "Current and Emerging Trends in Business Continuity." *Disaster Recovery Journal*, 18 (Winter).

Frank, T. (2007). "TSA to Track Rail Shipments with Toxic Cargo." *USA Today* (January 21).

Gewin, V. (2003). "Agriculture Shock." *Nature* (January).

Hebert, H. (2005). "Interest Rises in Nuclear Plants for First Time since Disasters." Associated Press (June 12).

Heiser, J. (2001). "Think Securely." *Information Security*, 4 (February).

Hoffer, E. (2006). "Cargo at Risk." *Security Technology & Design*, 16 (July).

Jenkins, B. (2004). "Terrorism and the Security of Public Surface Transportation" (April). Santa Monica, CA: RAND. Testimony presented to the Senate Committee on Judiciary on April 8, 2004.

Kiyota, S. (2000). "Planning Makes Perfect." *Information Security*, 3 (November).

Kochems, A. (2005). "Who's on First? A Strategy for Protecting Critical Infrastructure." *Backgrounder*, 1851 (May 9). www.heritage.org, retrieved June 20, 2005.

Kocieniewski, D. (2006). "Despite 9/11 Effect, Railyards Are Still Vulnerable." *The New York Times*. www.nytimes.com/2006/03/27/nyregion, retrieved March 28, 2006.

Laden, M., and Rogers, K. (2006). "Visualizing Supply-Chain Security: Why LP Professionals Should Get on Board." *Loss Prevention*, 5 (May-June).

Landoll, D. (2005). "Does IT Security Myth the Point?" *Security Management*, 49 (January).

Maxwell, C., and Blanda, T. (2005). "Terror by Sea: The Unique Challenges of Port Security." *FBI Law Enforcement Bulletin*, 74 (September).

Mead, P., et al. (1999). "Food-Related Illness and Death in the United States: Reply to Dr. Halberg." *Emergency Infectious Diseases*, 5 (November-December).

Office of Homeland Security. (2002). *National Strategy for Homeland Security* (July). www.whitehouse.gov, retrieved September 14, 2004.

Office of Inspector General. (2004). *FY 2003 Mission Performance United States Coast Guard* (September). Washington, DC: DHS.

Piazza, P. (2007). "Keys to Encryption." *Security Management*, 51 (January).

Poland, J. (1988). *Understanding Terrorism: Groups, Strategies, and Responses*. Englewood Cliffs, NJ: Prentice Hall.

Purtell, D., and Rice, J. (2006). "Assessing Cargo Supply Risk." *Security Management*, 50 (November).

Sager, I. (2000). "Cybercrime." *Business Week* (February 21).

Savage, M. (2006). "Protect What's Precious." *Information Security*, 9 (December).

Smith, D. (2006). "Encryption, Once for the Few, Now an Option for All." *IT Security*, 2 (October).

Strohm, C. (2007). "Senators Fight Pre-emption of Chemical Security Laws." *GOVEXEC.COM* (January 11). www.govexec.com, retrieved January 17, 2007.

Taylor, R., et al. (2006). *Digital Crime and Digital Terrorism*. Upper Saddle River, NJ: Pearson Prentice Hall.

Thompson, A. (1997). "Smoking Out the Facts on Firewalls." *Security Management* (January).

Transportation Security Administration. (2006). "TSA Revokes Air Cargo Security Program Approval for Minneapolis-Based Professional Export Services" (August 7). www.tsa.gov/press/releases/2006/press_release_08072006b.shtm, retrieved February 3, 2007.

U.S. Customs and Border Protection. (n.d.). "Combating the Threat of Nuclear Smuggling at Home and Abroad." www.customs.gov, retrieved October 5, 2005.

U.S. Department of Homeland Security (2007). "Fact Sheet: Securing Our Nation's Chemical Facilities." www.dhs.gov/xnews/releases/pr_1181745031563.shtm, retrieved June 15, 2007.

U.S. Department of Homeland Security, Information Analysis and Infrastructure Protection Directorate. (2005). *Fact Sheet: Protecting America's Critical Infrastructure—Chemical Security* (June 15). www.dhs.gov/dhspublic/display?content=4543, retrieved June 20, 2005.

U.S. Department of Homeland Security. (2005a). *Interim National Infrastructure Protection Plan* (February). www.dhs.gov, retrieved February 11, 2005.

U.S. Department of Homeland Security. (2006a). *National Infrastructure Protection Plan*. www.dhs.gov/interweb/assetlibrary/NIPP_Plan.pdf, retrieved June 30, 2006.

U.S. Department of Homeland Security. (2006b). *National Infrastructure Protection Plan* (revised draft). E-mail, January 20, 2006.

U.S. Department of Homeland Security. (2005b). *National Strategy for Maritime Security* (September). www.dhs.gov/interweb/assetlibrary/HSPD13_MaritimeSecurityStrategy.pdf, retrieved October 25, 2005.

U.S. Department of Justice. (1995). "Vulnerability Assessment of Federal Facilities." Washington, D.C.: U.S. Marshals Service.

U.S. Environmental Protection Agency, Office of Inspector General. (2005). *EPA Needs to Determine What Barriers Prevent Water Systems from Securing Known Supervisory Control and Data Acquisition (SCADA) Vulnerabilities* (January 6). www.epa.gov/oig, retrieved January 13, 2005.

U.S. General Accounting Office. (2004). *Industrial Security: DOD Cannot Provide Adequate Assurances That Its Oversight Ensures the Protection of Classified Information* (March). www.gao.gov/cgi-bin/getrpt?GAO-04-332, retrieved July 20, 2005.

U.S. Government Accountability Office. (2005a). *Coast Guard: Observations on Agency Priorities in Fiscal Year 2006 Budget Request* (March 17). www.gao.gov/cgi-bin/getrpt?GAO-05-364T, retrieved March 18, 2005.

U.S. Government Accountability Office. (2004). *General Aviation Security: Increased Federal Oversight Is Needed, but Continued Partnership with the Private Sector Is Critical to Long-Term Success* (September). www.gao.gov/cgi-bin/getrpt?GAO-05-144, retrieved December 13, 2004.

U.S. Government Accountability Office. (2005b). *Homeland Security: Actions Needed to Better Protect National Icons and Federal Office Buildings from Terrorism* (June). www.gao.gov/cgi-bin/getrpt?GAO-05-681, retrieved July 12, 2005.

U.S. Government Accountability Office. (2005c). *Homeland Security: Agency Plans, Implementation, and Challenges Regarding the National Strategy for Homeland Security* (January). www.gao.gov/cgi-bin/getrpt?GAO 05 213, retrieved February 15, 2005.

U.S. Government Accountability Office. (2007a). *Homeland Security: Applying Risk Management Principles to Guide Federal Investments* (February 7). http://www.gao.gov/cgi-bin/getrpt?CAO-07-386T, retrieved February 8, 2007.

U.S. Government Accountability Office. (2006a). *Homeland Security: DHS Is Taking Steps to Enhance Security at Chemical Facilities, but Additional Authority Is Needed* (January). www.gao.gov/new.items/d06150.pdf, retrieved March 1, 2006.

U.S. Government Accountability Office. (2007b). *Homeland Security: Progress Has Been Made to Address the Vulnerabilities Exposed by 9/11, but Continued Federal Action Is Needed to Further Mitigate Security Risks* (January). http://www.gao.gov/new.items/d07375.pdf, retrieved January 26, 2007.

U.S. Government Accountability Office. (2005d). *Industrial Security: DOD Cannot Ensure Its Oversight of Contractors under Foreign Influence Is Sufficient* (July). www.gao.gov/cgi-bin/getrpt?GAO-05-681, retrieved July 18, 2005.

U.S. Government Accountability Office. (2006b). *Information Security: Agencies Need to Develop and Implement Adequate Policies for Periodic Testing* (October). www.gao.gov/new.items.d0765.pdf, retrieved November 21, 2006.

U.S. Government Accountability Office. (2005e). *Information Security: Emerging Cybersecurity Issues Threaten Federal Information Systems* (May). www.gao.gov/new.items.do5231.pdf, retrieved May 16, 2005.

U.S. Government Accountability Office. (2005f). *Passenger Rail Security: Enhanced Federal Leadership Needed to Prioritize and Guide Security Efforts* (October). www.gao.gov/cgi-bin/getrpt?GAO-06-181T, retrieved October 21, 2005.

U.S. Government Accountability Office. (2006c). Nuclear Power Plants: Efforts Made to Upgrade Security, but the Nuclear Regulatory Commission's Design Basis Threat Process Should Be Improved (March). www.gao.gov/new.items.d06388.pdf, retrieved April 5, 2006.

U.S. Immigration and Customs Enforcement. (2005). "About ICE." (October 4). www.ice.gov, retrieved October 5, 2005.

U.S. Transportation Security Administration. (n.d.). "About TSA." www.tsa.gov/public/display?theme=7, retrieved September 30, 2005.

Welch, M. (2006). "Seeking a Safer Society: America's Anxiety in the War on Terror." *Security Journal*, 19.

White House. (2003a). *The National Strategy for the Physical Protection of Critical Infrastructures and Key Assets* (February). www.whitehouse.gov, retrieved September 14, 2004.

White House. (2003b). *The National Strategy to Secure Cyberspace* (February). www.whitehouse.gov, retrieved July 17, 2003.

Wikipedia. (2007). "Internet bot." http://en.wikipedia.org/wiki/Internet_bot, retrieved January 27, 2007.

Winter, G., and Broad, W. (2001). "Added Security for Dams, Reservoirs and Aqueducts." www.waterindustry.org, retrieved April 25, 2002.

Wulf, W., and Jones, A. (2004). "A Perspective on Cybersecurity Research in the United States." In *Terrorism: Reducing Vulnerabilities and Improving Response*. Washington, D.C.: National Research Council of the National Academies.

Zeller, T. (2006). "Cyberthieves Silently Copy Keystrokes." *News.Com.* (February 27). http://news.com, retrieved February 28, 2006.

17

Loss Prevention at Businesses and Institutions

Objectives

After studying this chapter, the reader will be able to:

1. Discuss the problem of inventory shrinkage in retailing.
2. Outline the crime losses incurred by retail businesses and countermeasures.
3. Discuss the shoplifting problem and countermeasures.
4. Explain robbery and burglary countermeasures for retail businesses.
5. Discuss the threats and hazards facing banks and financial businesses and countermeasures.
6. Discuss the threats and hazards facing educational institutions and countermeasures.
7. Discuss the threats and hazards facing healthcare institutions and countermeasures.

KEY TERMS
• shrinkage • shopping service • checkout counters • counterfeiting • kleptomania • organized retail theft • Violence Against Women and Department of Justice Reauthorization Act of 2005 • source tagging • robbery • burglary • substitutability • U.S. Department of the Treasury • Bank Protection Act (BPA) of 1968 • Bank Secrecy Act of 1986 • Anti-Drug Abuse Act of 1988	• The Antiterrorism and Effective Death Penalty Act of 1996 • Gramm-Leach-Bliley Act of 1999 • USA Patriot Act of 2001 • Sarbanes-Oxley (SOX) Act of 2002 • Regulation H, Code of Federal Regulations • savings and loan (S&L) scandal • suspicious activity reports • money laundering • tear-gas/dye packs • Global Positioning System (GPS) • fraud for property • fraud for profit • Gun-Free Schools Act of 1994 • zero-tolerance policy • Gang Resistance Education and Training (GREAT)

- "hard" targets
- "soft" targets
- Columbine High School massacre
- Beslan Elementary School massacre
- Virginia Tech massacre
- Student-Right-to-Know and Campus Security Act of 1990
- Campus Sexual Assault Victim's Bill of Rights
- community policing
- immune buildings
- Emergency Medical Treatment and Active Labor Act

- Health Insurance Portability and Accountability Act of 1996 (HIPAA)
- National Center for Missing and Exploited Children
- Controlled Substances Act of 1970
- Joint Commission on Accreditation of Healthcare Organizations (JCAHO)
- first receivers
- personal protective equipment (PPE)
- Public Health Security and Bioterrorism Preparedness and Response Act of 2002
- Centers for Disease Control and Prevention (CDC)

Introduction

This chapter focuses on security and loss prevention for retail businesses, banks and financial businesses, educational institutions, and healthcare institutions. *The National Strategy for The Physical Protection of Critical Infrastructures and Key Assets* (White House, 2003) includes banks and financial businesses and healthcare institutions; however, it offers limited, if any, security strategies for retail businesses or educational institutions. *The National Strategy* does refer to commercial centers, as discussed in the following section. With limited resources, the federal government must prioritize what it views as "critical infrastructures and key assets." At the same time, retail businesses expend enormous resources on security and loss prevention programs. In addition, federal, state, and local governments and the private sector are involved in numerous programs to protect students and educational institutions.

Do you think *The National Strategy for The Physical Protection of Critical Infrastructures and Key Assets* should include retail businesses and/or educational institutions? Why or why not? Do you know of other entities, not contained in *The National Strategy,* that should be included in it?

Loss Prevention at Retail Businesses

As mentioned in the preceding chapter, *The National Strategy* states that commercial centers, office buildings, sports stadiums, and theme parks comprise another category of key assets. These facilities contain retail businesses where many people conduct business, shop, and enjoy restaurants and entertainment. Loss prevention is vital at these locations to protect people and assets. Daily protection is the responsibility of private sector proprietary and contract security programs. Public safety agencies provide emergency response. The federal government, especially the DHS, provides assistance through advisories and alerts; efforts to bring groups together to enhance protection; and designation of an event (e.g., Superbowl) as a National Security Special Event, resulting in federal law enforcement participation and aid (White House, 2003: 78–79).

The National Strategy (White House, 2003: 78–79) states that to facilitate the protection of prominent commercial sites and facilities against terrorist attack, the federal government will take action to

> Share federal building security standards and practices with the private sector. *DHS, together with GSA, NIST and other federal departments and agencies will develop a program to share federal building protection standards.*
>
> Facilitate efficient dissemination of threat information. *DHS, in concert with the intelligence and law enforcement communities, will explore processes and systems to enable the timely dissemination of threat indications and warning information to commercial facility owners and operators.*
>
> Implement the Homeland Security Advisory System. *DHS will collaborate with commercial facility owners and operators to align the Homeland Security Advisory System with specific measures and procedures pertinent to commercial facility security.*
>
> Explore options for incentives for the implementation of enhanced design features or security measures. *DHS will explore options to facilitate incentives for commercial owners and operators who incorporate specific security and safety features into their facility design, or who adopt specific processes, procedures, and technologies that serve to deter, prevent, or mitigate the consequences of terrorist attacks.*
>
> Improve building codes for privately owned facilities. *NIST will develop a comprehensive set of building codes for privately owned facilities designed to better assure structural integrity, minimize probability of collapse, and increase resistance to high-temperature fires."*

Although terrorism is a serious concern for retail businesses, many other threats and hazards face these businesses, and numerous factors can be attributed to business failure. Poor management, unwise store location, noncompetitive marketing (selling) techniques, and consumer dissatisfaction with merchandise can all hinder profits.

Another important factor that can make or break a retail business is the quality of the loss prevention program. With a very small profit margin in many retail businesses, loss prevention is a necessity for survival. Vulnerability to employee theft, shoplifting, burglary, robbery, fire, and poor safety can cause extensive losses.

Shrinkage

As defined in Chapter 11, **shrinkage** is the amount of merchandise that has disappeared through theft, has become useless because of breakage or spoilage, or is unaccounted for because of sloppy recording. It is often expressed as a percentage. In retail businesses, guidelines are often in place to hold managers of stores, departments, and loss prevention responsible for shrinkage. When shrinkage becomes a measurable objective in annual reviews and bonus programs, an increased commitment to loss prevention can be expected (Kelly, 2000: 37–38). In addition, the reality of retailing is that those who fail to meet shrinkage goals are likely to be dismissed (Purpura, 1993: ix). Consequently, shrinkage must be kept as low as possible; it is gauged after an inventory, and an accurate inventory is vital (Levy and Weitz, 2001: 548).

The University of Florida, noted for its *National Retail Security Survey* (NRSS), found that, in 2005, 156 responding retail chains reported an average shrinkage of 1.59% of total annual sales. The rate in 1994 was 1.83%. The 2005 shrinkage translates into about $37.4 billion annual loss to retailers from a base of $2.334 trillion in annual sales for the retail sector as estimated in the 2005 U.S. Department of Commerce Retail Industry Census. Consistent with earlier NRSS studies, 2005 showed employee theft to be the single most significant source of shrinkage at 47%; shoplifting was reported at 33%, paperwork errors at 15%, and vendor fraud at 5.2%. The same year showed some of the lowest loss prevention budgets as a percent of sales in the history of the survey. Less than one-half of 1% of retail sales (0.46%) was budgeted for loss prevention. Hollinger (2006: 94), director of the NRSS, noted "With decreasing LP budgets and even less money for high-tech countermeasures, more of the day-to-day responsibility for loss prevention is being shifted to overworked managers and untrained sales associates, not specially schooled LP personnel."

Human Resources Problems in Retailing

Because retail loss prevention is highly dependent on the efforts of all employees, it is important to discuss the realities of human resources problems in retailing. This includes many part-time or temporary employees, inexperienced workers, employees dissatisfied with working conditions (e.g., low wages and long hours), and high turnover.

Loss can become a by-product of each of these personnel factors. For instance, some part-time employees may be working during holiday seasons to make extra money and may be stealing to support gift expenses. An inexperienced worker may unknowingly undercharge customers for merchandise. A dissatisfied employee may perform a variety of vindictive activities. A high rate of turnover creates additional training expenses and many inexperienced employees. These problems, coupled with poor performance, are especially troublesome to retailers because such employees are in direct contact with customers and this can have a negative impact on sales and customer loyalty. Research by Langton and Hollinger (2005: 27), of 103 retail companies, found that low-shrinkage retailers retain a significantly lower average percentage of part-time employees, a higher average percentage of full-time employees, and substantially lower turnover (for managers and sales associates) than high-shrinkage retailers.

Losses caused by part-time or temporary employees can be reduced by cost-effective screening, adequate socialization, and good methods for accountability of inventory. Another possible measure would be to assign part-time and temporary employees to be supervised by and work with permanent, experienced employees. Additionally, part-time and temporary employees could be barred from performing certain tasks and entering specific areas. Although the potential exists for losses from part-time and temporary employees, potential losses from full-time regular employees must not be underestimated.

Screening

The quality of job applicant screening is dependent on numerous factors. In a small store, the owner may interview the applicant; record pertinent information, such as the address, telephone number, and Social Security number; and ask for a few references. In large multistore organizations, however, employment procedures commonly are more structured and controlled. The NRSS (Hollinger and Langton, 2006: 15) found the following pre-employment screening measures based on 156 responding retail chains: verification of employment history (85%), criminal conviction checks (85%), multiple interviews (84%), reference checks (70%), drug testing (52%), credit history checks (48%), education verification (37%), and honesty testing (36%).

Socialization

Various training programs can be instituted to assist in adequately socializing an employee toward business objectives. Training can reduce employee mistakes, raise productivity, create customer satisfaction, and reduce turnover. A loss prevention training program can reinforce attitudes that result in decreased losses.

Some retail businesses require employees to sign a statement that they understand the loss prevention program. This procedure reinforces loss prevention programming. Furthermore, as models of appropriate work attitudes and behavior, executives should *set a good example* and *practice what is preached*.

The NRSS (Hollinger and Langton, 2006: 19–20) found numerous loss prevention awareness programs among respondents. These programs included anonymous telephone hot lines, discussions about shrinkage during new hire orientation, bulletin board notices and posters, employee code of conduct, honesty incentives, and a variety of training programs.

Internal Loss Prevention Strategies

Theft is a major factor in internal losses. There are numerous targets for internal theft: merchandise, damaged items, cash, repair service, office supplies and tools, parts, time, samples for customers, food and beverages, and personal property.

Although internal theft is a major part of the internal loss problem, there are other categories of internal losses. Examples are accidents, fire, unproductive employees, unintentional and intentional mistakes, and excessive absenteeism and lateness.

Here are strategies used by companies to address the problem of internal loss:

- *Motivation, morale, and rewards:* Management must attempt to help employees feel as if they are an integral part of the business organization. Praise for an employee's accomplishment can go a long way in improving morale. Other methods of increasing morale and motivation are clean working conditions, participative management, and a company sports team. Contest and reward programs also reinforce improved morale and motivation. The employee with the best loss prevention idea of the month could be rewarded with $50 and recognition in a company newspaper.
- *Employee discounts:* Employee discounts usually range between 15% and 25%. These discounts are an obvious benefit to employee morale even though employees sometimes abuse this discount by making purchases for relatives and friends.
- *Shopping service:* A **shopping service** is a business that assists retail loss prevention efforts by supplying investigators who pose as customers to test retail associates (i.e., cashiers and other retail employees) for honesty, accuracy, and demeanor. One common test of associates involves two shoppers who enter a store separately, acting as customers. One buys an item, pays for it with the exact amount of money needed, and leaves, while the second shopper, pretending to be a customer, observes whether the associate rings up the sale or pockets the money. Theft of cash is not the only source of loss; revenues are lost because of the curt or even abrasive behavior of some sales personnel.
- *Undercover investigations:* Investigations can be used as a last resort when other controls fail. By penetrating employee informal organizations, investigators are able to obtain considerable information that may expose collusion and weaknesses in controls.

Preventing Losses at Checkout Counters

Checkout counters are also called point-of-sale (POS) areas and point-of-purchase (POP) areas (Figure 17-1). These locations in a retail business accommodate customer payments, refunds, and service. Although most cashiers are honest, and bar codes and scanning technology prevent losses, the following activities hinder profits:

1. Stealing money from the cash drawer
2. Failing to key in the sale and then stealing the money (this is especially tempting when no customer change is required)
3. Failing to key in the sale, leaving the cash drawer open for the customer's change, and then stealing the money
4. Overcharging customers, keeping a mental record, and stealing the money at a later time
5. Presenting the customer with the wrong change
6. Accepting bad checks, bad charge cards, and counterfeit money
7. Making pricing mistakes
8. Undercharging for relatives and friends
9. Failing to notice an altered price tag
10. Failing to notice shoplifted items secreted in legitimate purchases

FIGURE 17-1 Checkout counter, CCTV camera domes, and electric article surveillance (EAS) system (portals at exit). *Courtesy:* Sensormatic, Inc.

Cashier Socialization of Procedures

The quality of training will have a direct bearing on accountability at checkout counters. Procedural training can include, but is not limited to, the following:

1. Assign each cashier to a particular cash drawer and register/computer.
2. Have each transaction recorded separately and the cash drawer closed afterward.
3. Establish a system for giving receipts to customers.
4. Train cashiers to count change carefully.
5. Show cashiers how to spot irregularities (e.g., altered price tags or bar codes).
6. Encourage cashiers to seek supervision when appropriate (e.g., to check price of item, question about customer credit).

Accountability of Voids

Voids are used to eradicate and record mistakes by cashiers at the checkouts. Theft occurs when, for instance, a cashier voids a legitimate no-mistake sale and pockets the money. Fraudulent voids can be prevented by limiting void access or keys to supervisors. Specialized software and records help to pinpoint irregularities.

Point-of-Sale Accounting Systems

Retailers are increasingly making use of point-of-sale (POS) accounting systems with bar code and Radio Frequency Identification (RFID) technologies to produce vital business information. (See Chapter 11 for the applications of RFID technology.) Merchandise contains a bar code that is read by a scanner during inventory or at the checkout counters. This stored information provides a perpetual inventory, helpful in ascertaining what is in stock and in ordering merchandise. In addition to shrinkage figures, POS systems can also be designed to produce a variety of loss prevention reports, exposing cashiers who repeatedly have cash shortages, voids, bad checks, and so forth. Ratios are also helpful to spot losses. Examples include cash to charge sales and sales to refunds.

Closed-Circuit Television (CCTV)

CCTV can be integrated with POS systems to give a loss prevention practitioner an opportunity to view a cash register total and compare it with the merchandise sold. System capabilities enable the total to appear on the TV monitor with the date and time. Furthermore, "exceptions" (e.g., voids) noted by the POS system can also trigger CCTV and a recording for later reference. Certain retailers are recording every transaction on every register. Today's technology permits the viewing of video images on personal digital assistants and cell phones.

The Internet is enhancing the capabilities of CCTV systems. At one retail store chain, the plan is to keep an eye on widely dispersed stores, avoid the expense of a central station, and reduce time and travel costs of loss prevention personnel. The installed system permits real-time video through the Internet from a PC or laptop. Video is accessed through a secure, password-protected Web site. The digital video is archived on a secure server at a remote location without the need for loss prevention personnel to maintain files. Optional features helped to sell the system to senior executives. Examples are customer traffic counting, time and attendance of employees, and the transmission of in-house commercials to store TV screens. CCTV cameras are placed at front and back doors, the POS, and the back hallway. The cameras at the doors are linked to contact alarms so that each time a door is opened, loss prevention personnel receive an e-mail. In one case, a manager was caught improperly opening a back door by not following strict procedures. The manager was called on the telephone immediately for corrective action. Eventually, this retail chain will have one central data-gathering system for security and administrative information (Anderson, 2001: 22–23).

Refunds

The retailer may sustain losses during refunds. Such losses can be attributed to activities of employees, customers, or both.

In loosely controlled businesses, employees have an opportunity to retain a customer receipt (or hope that the customer leaves one) and use it to substantiate a fraudulent customer refund (merchandise supposedly returned for money). With the receipt used to support the phony refund slip, the employee is "covered" and can pocket the cash.

Especially bold offenders might enter a store, pick up an item, and then go directly to the refund desk and demand a cash refund without a receipt. Offenders may also purchase merchandise with a bad check and then seek a refund before the check clears. In such cases, wait for the check to clear before issuing a refund. Another ploy is to use a stolen credit card to purchase merchandise and then obtain a refund at another branch store. In other instances, collusion may take place between employees and customers. Employees simply issue refunds to family and friends.

Refund fraud is minimized through well-controlled supervision and accountability. Consider requesting photo identification and writing a check for refunds over a certain amount. A supervisor should account for returned merchandise before it is returned to the sales floor and sign and date the sales receipt after writing *refund*. Some retailers guarantee money (e.g., $5) to customers if the customer does not receive a receipt.

Electronic Payments

Electronic payments, such as the use of credit and debit cards, are more popular than payments by cash or check. New technologies are assisting retailers as they seek innovations to speed payment transactions and save on fees. In addition, as we know, new technologies bring vulnerabilities.

Credit and debit cards have a magnetic stripe that contains information on the account, such as customer name and account number. The customer's card is "swiped" for electronic authorization to ensure that the account is valid and the purchase is within the account limit. Then the transaction is completed with the user's signature. In many locales throughout the world, a conversion is occurring from magnetic stripe to the "chip-and-PIN" card to speed transactions, especially for low-value payments (e.g., a cup of coffee), and to increase security. In the "chip-and-PIN" card, information is stored in a small computer chip. The customer places the card near a proximity reader, similar to an access card, and enters a personal identification number (PIN) instead of providing a signature. This newer type of card is less likely to be copied than the magnetic stripe card (DiLonardo, 2006: 116). A variation of this technology is referred to as "contactless payment systems," and a PIN is not required. Both the "chip-and-PIN" and "contactless" methods use a proximity reader to obtain information from the RFID computer chip imbedded in the card. Proponents claim that encryption protects the information. Critics argue that an offender nearby, armed with a specialized reader, might capture information on cards held by the customer.

Since U.S. retailers pay finance companies almost $40 billion each year for credit and debit card transaction fees, they are interested in technologies to reduce such costs. Retailers pay a fixed fee and a percentage of the transaction amount. A new type of technology to save retailers money and provide quicker customer payment is known as "pay-by-finger." This biometric fingerprint technology requires customers to place a finger on a scanner to register the transaction with their bank account to debit their account without using a card, entering a PIN, or writing a check. Customers enroll at a kiosk by providing identification, bank information, and a finger scan. The information is encrypted, and store employees do not have access to the information. Opponents of this technology claim that retailers should consider the operational impact on the business, data center issues, setup costs, and customer security (Gaur and Gilliland, 2006).

Card fraud is a huge problem costing billions of dollars. The three major groups involved in card usage are *card issuers* (banks, oil companies, retail businesses, travel, and entertainment groups), *acceptors* (merchants), and *users*. All of these groups are susceptible to losses due to fraud. Lost or stolen cards can cause monetary loss to users. Acceptors who are careless may become financially responsible for fraud under certain circumstances and could even be placed at a competitive disadvantage if no longer authorized to accept the issuer's card. Card issuers absorb billions of dollars in losses annually. Crime involving cards is varied and compounded because of identity theft. Vulnerabilities include theft of cards from the postal system and counterfeiting of cards.

Gift Card Losses

Gift cards, also known as store value cards, generate profits for retailers and the use of these cards is increasing. The methods of gift card fraud, committed mostly by employees, includes card swapping by cashiers at the POS, "skimming" gift cards to produce duplicates, and using fraudulent credit cards to purchase gift cards. Fraudulent gift cards are used by employees, traded, or sold to local residents or on-line (Hollinger and Langton, 2006: 29–30). Countermeasures focus on inventories of cards, sales data, exception reports that show trends and anomalies, employee purchases, and packaging of cards that prevents the magnetic bar from being swiped without snapping the package at the POS (Cogswell, 2006: 63–68).

Checks

Personal checks and a variety of other types of checks continue to be a source of loss for retailers. *A check is nothing more than a piece of paper until the money is collected*. It may be worthless. Characteristics of bad checks include an inappropriate date, written figures that differ from numeric figures on the same check, and smeared ink. Sources of bad checks are varied and include customers who write checks with no funds in their checking account. This may result from customer negligence in personal bookkeeping, and the customer often corrects the problem. Conversely, offenders write bad checks by using stolen checks or by writing checks from a nonexistent account or from one with no funds. Counterfeit checks (e.g., bogus personal checks or bogus payroll checks) are another problem growing worse because of computers, desktop publishing, check-writing software, newer color copier machines, scanners, and laser printers. Government checks frequently are stolen from mailboxes and signatures forged for endorsement.

Various strategies are applied to prevent the problem of bad checks. Retailer policies and procedures include carefully examining checks, not accepting checks over a certain amount, seeking supervisory approval for checks written over a certain amount, prohibiting checks from out of state, and never providing cash for a check. Retail employees should scrutinize customer identification for irregularities. Many employees look at identification cards but do not see irregularities. *Concentration is necessary to match (or not to match) the customer with the identification presented.* Many retailers require two types of identification before a check is accepted. A driver's license, vehicle registration, or credit card is usually acceptable. Many other types of identification (e.g., Social Security cards, birth certificates, and insurance cards) are easier to obtain, forge, and hold for a period without detection. Another approach is an on-line check-clearing service.

A retailer's recovery from a bad check depends on the circumstances. Procedures depend on the state. Usually, a retailer must send the check writer a registered letter requiring payment (if the check writer has a legitimate address). If the letter is not effective, the retailer can sign a warrant against the person who wrote the bad check.

In one jurisdiction, a "bad-check brigade" was formed. A magistrate coordinates the warrants, which are distributed to constables (part-time law enforcers) who are paid for each warrant served. Each week the brigade takes numerous offenders to jail. Retailers should check with public police about local practices. Some jurisdictions require collection through civil procedures. Another strategy, especially for large retailers, is to contract collection work to specialized firms.

If a retailer receives a check returned from a bank stating that there is "no account" or "account closed," then fraud may have been perpetuated. The police should be notified. An altered or forged U.S. government check should be reported to the U.S. Secret Service.

□ □ □ ▬▬▬▬▬▬▬▬▬▬▬▬▬▬▬▬▬▬▬▬

The Counterfeiting of Bar Codes

As technology improves retail operations, it also presents vulnerabilities. The counterfeiting of bar codes is a nuisance to retailers. The fraud involves using a computer to scan bar codes of inexpensive merchandise, printing copies of the bar codes, and placing the counterfeit bar codes onto expensive items. In addition, offenders are assisted by software available on the Internet. In one case, two married couples used counterfeit bar codes to purchase merchandise at Wal-Mart and two other retail chains, and then they returned the items for full value. Their con included entering stores at peak hours when employees were busy. Wal-Mart lost about $1.5 million from the scam. In another case, an offender used counterfeit bar codes to purchase Lego sets for a fraction of the actual value, and then he sold the sets on a Web site for toy collectors (Beaulieu, 2005: 15; Zimmerman, 2006).

▬▬▬▬▬▬▬▬▬▬▬▬▬▬▬▬▬▬▬▬ □ □ □

E-Business

E-business (using Internet-based technologies), phone-order, and mail order are particularly vulnerable to fraud because the customer and the card are not present for the transaction. Offenders obtain card numbers from many sources (e.g., discarded receipts, stealing customer information, and hacking into a business), establish a mail drop, and then place fraudulent orders.

Bednarz (2006) reports that e-business fraud losses for 2006 are predicted at about $3 billion, a 7% increase over 2005. In addition, e-business is predicted to grow by more than 20% from 2005 to 2006. Orders from abroad are riskier than orders from the United States and Canada. Various tools are available to retailers to control fraud. Examples are IP geolocation products that analyze transaction risk based on geographic data, tools that use various metrics (e.g., dollar amounts and frequency) to monitor orders, and lists that show good customers. Other tools are address and card verification services.

In one case, the owner of a computer parts company in New Jersey became concerned when he received a $15,000 order from Bucharest, Romania. The owner tried to contact the credit card authorization company and the bank that works with the processing company to verify the credit cards. However, they were not able to assist, so the owner telephoned the customer and had him fax his Romanian driver's license and other documents to the owner. The owner then shipped the parts via UPS at about the same time the bank became suspicious and called the owner to say that all the cards used in the order were fraudulent. The owner was lucky when the shipment was intercepted in Bucharest.

Other complaints abound of such fraud and the inability of card issuers to assist. E-business owners argue, "there is no financial incentive for the banks and card companies to do anything about the problem because it is the merchant who, in virtually all cases, ultimately bears the cost of fraudulent Internet purchases." Disinterest by law enforcement is another concern because personnel and resources are limited. In another case, an e-business owner in the United States telephoned Canadian police and told them about an individual, living a few miles from the police station, who was attempting to commit credit card fraud against the e-business owner. The police response was that nothing could be done until the e-business owner flew to Canada and posted a $10,000 bond to guarantee a court appearance to testify (Brunker, 2001).

Counterfeiting

Counterfeiting is the unlawful duplication of something valuable to deceive. Counterfeit items can include money, coupons, credit or debit cards, clothes, and jewelry. Here, the emphasis is counterfeit money. The U.S. Secret Service investigates this federal offense.

Persons who recognize that they have counterfeit money will not be reimbursed when they give it to the Secret Service. Because of this potential loss, many people knowingly pass the bogus money to others. The extended chain of custody from the counterfeiter to authorities causes great difficulty during investigations.

Counterfeiting is a growing problem because of the newer color copier machines, scanners, computers, and laser printers that are in widespread use. The best method to reduce this type of loss is through the ability to recognize counterfeit money, and an excellent way to do this is to compare a suspect bill with a genuine bill. The U.S. government has countered counterfeiting through a variety of security features on bills. One should look for the red and blue fibers that are scattered throughout a genuine bill. These fibers are curved, about 1/4 inch long, hair thin, and difficult to produce on bogus bills. Other security features on genuine bills are a security thread embedded in the bill running vertically to the left of the Federal Reserve seal, microprinting on the rim of the portrait, a watermark (hold the bill up to light to see the faint image similar to the portrait), and color-shifting ink (tilt the bill repeatedly to see shifting ink color).

Watch for $1 bills that have counterfeit higher denomination numbers glued over the lower denomination numbers. Also, compare suspect coins with genuine coins.

Another fraud technique that appears to be increasing is the bleaching of a real, lower denomination bill (to wash away the ink), followed by placing the blank bill on a printer to apply a higher denomination bill design. This method of counterfeiting may defeat the use of counterfeit detector pens used by cashiers because the pens react to starch in paper by showing a black mark. However, genuine bills are actually cloth and devoid of starch; the pen will create a golden mark. Again, hold the suspect bill up to light and compare it to a genuine bill.

□ □ □

What do you think is the most serious vulnerability at checkout counters? Support your answer and include countermeasures.

□ □ □

Shoplifting

Shoplifting cost American retailers about $12 billion in 2005, representing about one-third of shrinkage (Hollinger and Langton, 2006: 8). To deal with this serious problem, loss prevention practitioners should have an understanding of the types of shoplifters, motivational factors, shoplifting techniques, and countermeasures.

Types of Shoplifters and Motivational Factors

Amateur shoplifters, also referred to as *snitches,* represents the majority of shoplifters. These persons generally steal on impulse while often possessing the money to pay for the item. Individuals in this category represent numerous demographic variables (e.g., sex, age, social class, ethnicity, and race). The distinguishing difference between the amateur and the professional thief is that the former shoplifts for personal use, whereas the latter shoplifts to sell the goods for a profit.

Generally, *juveniles* take merchandise that they can use, such as clothing and recreational items. Frequently working in groups, their action is often motivated by peer pressure or a search for excitement.

Easy-access shoplifters are neither retail company employees nor customers. Because of their work, these persons have easy access to retail merchandise and are familiar with basic retail operations and loss prevention programs. Delivery personnel, salespeople, repair personnel, and public inspectors make up this category. Even public police and fire personnel have been known to represent this group, especially during emergencies. The motivation is obvious: to get something for nothing. The extent of this problem is difficult to ascertain, but it does contribute to the shoplifting problem.

Fairly easy to detect, *drunk or vagrant shoplifters* usually shoplift liquor, food, and clothing for personal use or shoplift other merchandise to sell for cash. These persons often are under the influence of alcohol and have a previous alcohol-related arrest record.

Addict shoplifters are extremely dangerous because of the illegal drug dependence problem and accompanying desperation. These persons generally peddle stolen loot to a "fence," who pays less than one-third the value of the merchandise. The addicts may also "grab and run."

Professionals or *"boosters"* account for a small percentage of those caught shoplifting. (This low figure could be the result of the professional's skill in avoiding apprehension.) The motive is profit or resale of shoplifted merchandise. Professionals may utilize a *booster box* (a box that looks wrapped and tied, but really contains a secret entrance), hooks inside clothing, or extra long pockets. A criminal record is typical, as are ties to the underworld organization (e.g., fences) that will supply bail money and attorney assistance.

Kleptomania is a rare, persistent, neurotic impulse to steal. Kleptomaniacs usually shoplift without considering the value or personal use of the item, and seemingly want to be caught. This type of shoplifter usually has a criminal record from previous apprehensions and may have been caught several times at the same retail store.

Shoplifting Techniques

The following list presents only a few of the many shoplifting techniques:

1. Shoplifters may work alone or in a group.
2. A person may simply shoplift an item and conceal it in his or her clothing.
3. A person may "palm" a small item and conceal it in a glove.

4. Shoplifters often go into a fitting room with several garments and either conceal an item or wear it and leave the store.

5. An offender may ask to see more items than a clerk can control or send the clerk to the stockroom for other items; while the counter is unattended, items are stolen.

6. A self-service counter can provide an opportunity for a shoplifter to pull out and examine several items while returning only half of them.

7. Merchandise often is taken to a deserted location (e.g., restroom, elevator, stockroom, janitor's supply room, and so on) and then concealed.

8. A shoplifter may simply grab an item and quickly leave the store.

9. A shoplifter may drop an expensive piece of jewelry into a drink or food.

10. Shoplifters arrive at a store early or late to take advantage of any lax situation.

11. Disguised as a priest (or other professional), the shoplifter may have an advantage when stealing.

12. Some bold offenders have been known to impersonate salespeople while shoplifting and even to collect money from customers.

13. Price tags are often switched to allow merchandise to be bought at a lower price; sometimes the desired price will be written on the price tag of a sales item.

14. Shoplifters are aided by large shopping bags, lunch boxes, knitting bags, suitcases, flight bags, camera cases, musical instrument cases, and newspapers.

15. Dummy packages, bags, or boxes ("booster boxes") are used, which appear to be sealed and tied but contain false bottoms and openings to conceal items.

16. Shoplifters may use hollowed-out books.

17. Stolen merchandise is often concealed within legitimate purchases.

18. Expensive items are placed in inexpensive containers.

19. Shoplifters sometimes slide items off counters and into some type of container or clothing.

20. Sometimes shoplifters wear fake bandages or false plastic casts.

21. Professional shoplifters are known to carry store supplies (e.g., bag, box, stapler, or colored tape) to assist in stealing.

22. Baby carriages and wheelchairs have been utilized in various ways to steal.

23. Sometimes items are hidden in a store for subsequent pickup by an accomplice.

24. Various contrived diversions (e.g., appearing to be drunk, dropping and breaking an item, faking a heart attack, fainting, choking, pretending to have an epileptic seizure or labor pains, setting a fire or smoke bomb, breaking a glass, or having someone call in a bomb threat) have been used to give an accomplice a chance to shoplift.

25. Teenagers sometimes converge on a particular retail department, cause a disturbance, and then shoplift.

26. Adult shoplifters have been known to use children to aid them.

27. Sometimes "blind" accomplices with "guide" dogs are used to distract and confuse sales personnel eager to assist the disadvantaged.

28. "Crotchwalking" is a method whereby a woman wearing a dress conceals an item between her legs and then departs.

Prevention and Reduction of Shoplifting through People
People are the first and primary asset for reducing shoplifting opportunities. The proper utilization of people is the test of success or failure in preventing shoplifting. *Good training is essential.*

- *Management:* Management has the responsibility for planning, implementing, and monitoring antishoplifting programs. The quality of leadership and the ability to motivate people are of paramount importance. The loss prevention manager and other retail executives must cooperate when formulating policies and procedures that do not hamper sales.

- *Salespeople:* An antishoplifting program increases a shoplifter's anxiety. One method to accomplish this is to have salespeople approach all customers and say, for instance,

"May I help you?" This approach informs the potential shoplifter that he or she has been noticed by salespeople and possibly by loss prevention personnel. Obviously, the anxiety level will be raised. Sometimes salespeople annoy honest customers by hounding them with persistent offers of assistance. This can hinder sales. A moderate approach is appropriate. For those who have been store detectives, there are few activities as annoying as a salesperson who unknowingly interferes with a potential apprehension of a shoplifter. To avoid this problem, the retailer must formulate and communicate policies and procedures to appropriate employees. One solution may be to have the store detective signal salespeople, for example, by carrying a certain colored bag. The colored bag would signify to salespeople that they should ignore the potential shoplifter.

- *Store detectives or Loss Prevention (LP) professionals: These specialists must have the ability to observe without being observed, remember precisely what happened during an incident, know criminal law and self-defense, effectively interview, testify in court, and recover stolen items.* They perform a variety of duties, such as observing the premises with a CCTV system, helping to reduce shrinkage, and conducting investigations of *suspected* internal theft and shoplifting. When they are on the sales floor and observing a suspect, they should blend in with the shopping crowd and look like shoppers. This can be done by dressing like average shoppers, carrying a package or two and even a bag of popcorn. The antiquated term *floor walkers* should be reserved for historical discussions; this will help to professionalize this important LP position.
- *Uniformed officers:* Only a foolish shoplifter would steal in the presence of an officer who acts as a deterrent. A well-planned antishoplifting program must not lose sight of the systems approach to loss prevention, as described next (Altheide et al., 1978):

The store had four security guards or personnel. These people were also looked upon as "jokes." The security personnel were primarily concerned with catching shoplifting customers. Most of their time was spent behind two-way mirrors with binoculars observing shoppers. Therefore, in reality while the security personnel caught a customer concealing a pair of pants in her purse, an employee was smuggling four pairs of Levi's out the front door. Security was concerned with shoppers on the floor while all employee thefts usually occurred in stockrooms.

- *Fitting-room personnel:* Employees who supervise merchandise passing in and out of fitting rooms play a vital role in reducing the shoplifting problem. Many stores place a limit on the number of items that can be brought into a fitting room.

Training

Employees must realize the economic impact of shoplifting and other crimes. They must understand that, if crime is not prevented, the retail store may go out of business and jobs will be lost. Thus, everyone should play a role in reducing the crime problem. On-line training is cost-effective, and employees at their convenience can study a host of topics (e.g., shoplifting, shrinkage control).

Organized Retail Theft and Countermeasures

Organized retail theft (ORT), also known as organized retail crime, refers to gangs of offenders who victimize retail businesses by stealing and reselling a variety of retail merchandise for illegal profit. Hollinger and Langton (2006: 29), in the NRSS, write that the FBI, working with the National Retail Federation, estimates that retailers lose between $15 billion and $30 billion each year to ORT. They also write that only 37% of retailers responding to their survey are tracking ORT incidents and losses, and only 10% of loss prevention departments have a dedicated task force focused on ORT.

ORT gangs sell stolen merchandise at flea markets and Internet auction sites. They may also work with a network of fences and earn up to 25% of the retail value of the merchandise. The fence sells the items to local residents or back to legitimate retailers. Another type of fence is the *e-fence*, who sells stolen items on-line to a global market. ORT gangs are structured somewhat similar to a terrorist cell, characterized by decentralized operations, and when one cell is apprehended, other cells continue operations. ORT gangs may be involved in funding terrorist groups. To counter ORT, cooperation is essential between retailers and public police, especially since vehicles may be stopped, search warrants executed, and subpoenas obtained for Internet records. Other strategies are retail industry–sponsored educational programs for police; focusing on the fence, besides the shoplifter; utilizing a variety of investigative methods (e.g., informants, undercover operations); forming retailer ORT units; and the use of databases (Talamo, 2007: 23–30).

The **Violence Against Women and Department of Justice Reauthorization Act of 2005** contains many anticrime provisions, including Title XI, Section 1105 that seeks to reduce ORT. It establishes an FBI task force to counter ORT, an ORT database, and training on ORT. The Retail Loss Prevention Intelligence Network (RLPIN), created by the National Retail Federation (NRF), was established in anticipation of the act, and the NRF has worked with the FBI to ensure the RLPIN meets law enforcement and retailer needs. The RLPIN enables the private and public sectors to study crime patterns and take action. By logging on to a secure Web site, users can read about incidents from across the nation and enter data on incidents.

Prevention and Reduction of Shoplifting through Physical Design and Physical Security

Physical design and physical security comprise a second major category of an effective anti-shoplifting program. In reference to physical security, these *systems are only as good as the people operating them*. A retail company can spend millions of dollars on antishoplifting systems; however, money will be wasted if employees are not properly trained and they are not knowledgeable of system capabilities and limitations.

Physical Design

Physical design includes architectural design and store layout (e.g., merchandise displays). Three objectives of physical design are to create an environment that stimulates sales and, for the purposes of this text, to comply with the ADA and to create Crime Prevention Through Environmental Design (CPTED), as covered earlier in the text. The ADA requires the removal of barriers that hinder the disabled. An example of CPTED is increased visibility of customers by retail personnel by designing an employee lounge that is raised above the sales floor and has a large glass window. In addition, POS locations that are raised a few inches increase visibility.

A balance between attractiveness and loss prevention is essential. Counters containing merchandise should be set up to let employees at the POS observe activities down aisles. Adequate lighting is essential. Merchandise or other store features that obstruct the view of employees will aid shoplifters. Eight-foot paneling on display in the middle of a sales floor, for example, would be more appropriate along the store's inner perimeter walls.

Hayes (2006: 46) writes that a retailer can manipulate variables in a store to influence moods and behavior. As examples, he refers to architecture, number of entrances and exits, walkways, flooring, fixture types, aisle width, and employee workstations.

The proper utilization of turnstiles, corrals, and other barriers can limit the circulation of shoplifters and funnel customer traffic to select locations (e.g., toward the POS). Usable exits can be limited and restrooms locked so that customers need to ask for the restroom key.

Other methods to hinder theft include locking display cabinets, displaying only one of a pair, using dummy displays (e.g., empty cosmetic boxes), arranging displays neatly and in a particular pattern to allow for quick recognition of a disruption in their order, having hangers pointing in alternate directions on racks to prevent "grab and run" tactics, and placing small items closer to cash registers.

Electronic Article Surveillance

The electronic article surveillance (EAS) system "watches" merchandise instead of people. Generally, electronic tags are placed on merchandise and removed by a salesperson when appropriate. If a person leaves a designated area with the tagged merchandise, a sensor at an exit activates an alarm.

This device has been on the market since the late 1960s. Because these plastic tags tended to be large (about 3 or 4 inches) and difficult to attach to many goods, they were used on high-priced merchandise such as coats. However, improved technology has permitted manufacturers to develop devices the size of price tags, at a lower cost. The newer device is small, with an adhesive back to allow it to stick to merchandise. Several new types include low-cost disposable labels and higher-cost ($1 to $2) reusable tags.

The *radio frequency* (RF) is the most popular type of EAS system, and it contains a tiny circuit that can be hidden virtually anywhere on a product or in packaging. If the cashier does not remove or deactivate it (which can be done automatically as items are scanned for prices at the POS) and the customer walks between a radio transmitter and a sensor, then the circuit picks up the signal and an alarm is triggered. Its weaknesses are that shoplifters can cover the labels with aluminum foil and that the tags cannot be used on metal objects. At the refund desk, a verifier can be used to check for "live" tags that *may* indicate that an item was not purchased legitimately. A second type, *magnetic*, which is dominant in Europe, employs a metal strip (called an EM strip) that interferes with a magnetic field at an exit. A unique feature of the EM strip is that it can be reactivated, which makes this system especially suitable for libraries. Another type is the *acousto-magnetic system*, which is similar to magnetic tags. These tags are wider and have superior detection in comparison to magnetic tags. Another type of EAS system is *microwave*, which can be costly and is often applied in clothing stores.

Each company contends that its system is best. None is without problems, nor is any foolproof. False alarms or failure of the cashier to deactivate or remove the tag has led to retailers being sued for false arrest. Another problem results from employees who carry an EAS tag on their person and activate the system as a pretext to stop and search suspicious customers. Training and politeness when approaching customers will prevent litigation. Many state that professional shoplifters and the bigger problem of employee theft are not alleviated by EAS. Others view the tags as too expensive to be justified for low-cost merchandise. Many tag only high-shrinkage items.

Research by Read Hayes and Robert Blackwood (Gips, 2007: 26) showed that retail employees routinely ignored EAS alarms; of almost 4,000 alarms studied, employees requested receipts for merchandise in only 18% of cases. Prior to applying EAS, Read and Blackwood recommended strong evidence that a particular item is being shoplifted chainwide and EAS should be made obvious through signs.

Despite the disadvantages of EAS, plus initial costs and maintenance, these systems can be cost effective and are popular. In fact, such systems are used in certain industries to "watch" inventories. Prisoners and patients also are being monitored with such technology.

Innovations have further enhanced EAS technology. Integrated systems use programmable CCTV technology to target an alarm location or "walk a beat." Another type of tag sends out an audible alarm when tampering occurs. **Source tagging** is growing in popularity and involves the manufacturer placing a hidden EAS tag into the product during manufacturing, to be deactivated at the POS. This saves the retailer the labor of tagging and untagging merchandise (Palmer, 2006: 45–50).

Alarms

In addition to EAS, various alarm sensors protect merchandise from theft. *Loop alarms* consist of a cable forming a closed electrical circuit that begins and ends at an alarm device.

This cable usually is attached through merchandise handles and openings. When the electrical circuit is disrupted by someone cutting or breaking it, the alarm sounds. *Cable alarms* also use a cable that runs from the merchandise to an alarm unit. This alarm differs in that a pad attached to the end of the cable is placed on the merchandise. Each item has its own cable pad setup, which is connected to an alarm unit. Cable alarms are useful when merchandise does not have openings or handles. Retailers also use heavy nonalarmed cables that are also woven through expensive items such as leather coats. This cable usually has a locking device. *Wafer alarms* are sensing devices that react to negative pressure. This device, about the size of a large coin, is placed under the protected item; if a thief removes the item, an alarm sounds.

Additional Measures

Numerous security measures are applicable to retail stores to thwart not only shoplifting but also other sources of losses. Figures 17-2 and 17-3 focus on internal space protection and point protection. Chapters 7 and 8 explain a variety of security measures.

CCTV is a popular antishoplifting measure. Comprehensive systems allow personnel to follow suspects through a store. Close communication between the monitoring station and personnel on the sales floor is important to avoid errors in investigations. Modern technology permits CCTV monitoring to take place globally on a variety of devices (e.g., computer or cell phone), as described in Chapter 7.

Two types of *mirrors* used to curb the shoplifting problem are see-through mirrors and wide-angle convex mirrors. These mirrors are relatively inexpensive and provide personnel with advantages that aid in the surveillance of shoplifters. See-through mirrors, also called two-way mirrors, are different from one-way mirrors. A one-way mirror is a regular mirror that reflects light back to the viewer. A see-through mirror enables the observer to see through the mirror; light strikes the surface and travels two ways: back to you as you see yourself and toward the observer on the other side. To detect this type of mirror, use a laser pointer or good flashlight to see the light go through (TwoWayMirrors.net, 2006). Observation booths usually are equipped with see-through mirrors; their location is above the sales floor at various places within a store. Personnel often use binoculars while watching customers (and employees) from these vantage points. A good communication system is necessary to summon aid because, when the observer leaves the booth, the shoplifter's actions are not being watched. If the shoplifter returns the item before being apprehended, the retail store may be faced with a lawsuit. Wide-angle convex mirrors have been placed throughout small and large retail stores to facilitate greater visibility and reduce blind spots around corners. Convex mirrors and regular mirrors can be located along walls, ceilings, at

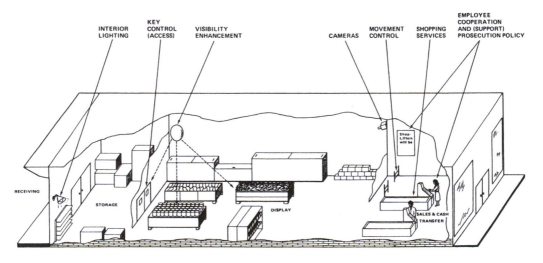

FIGURE 17-2 Internal Space Protection.

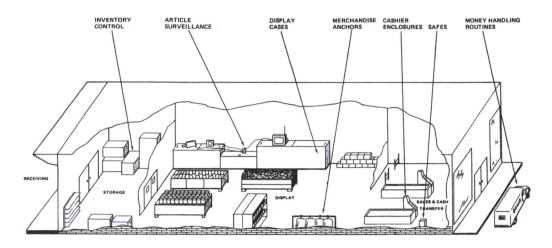

FIGURE 17-3 Point Protection.

support columns, above merchandise displays, and at any point to create greater visibility and thus deter theft.

In one case, a juvenile was shoplifting recorded music items by sliding them into the bottom of a bag that had been stapled closed with a receipt attached. The incident occurred while the store was closing, and more than 20 retail personnel attentively watched the shoplifter in action from the other side of a 7-foot-high partition that had a convex mirror placed above it. The situation was interesting because the music department had been cleared of retail employees, and the juvenile rushed around the department selecting items while nervously watching for people he did not know were watching him via the mirror.

Fake deterrents are debatable loss prevention methods. A dummy camera or a periodic, fake loudspeaker statement (e.g., "dispatch security to main floor") may prevent shoplifting, but the level of effectiveness is difficult to measure. Many stores combine fake and real methods.

Salespersons must carefully control store supplies (e.g., boxes, price tags) to prevent offenders from using the supplies to commit theft.

Confronting the Suspected Shoplifter

Detection and Apprehension

Most suspected shoplifters exhibit the following activities and characteristics before, during, and after a theft: extreme sensitivity to those around them, surveillance of the sales floor, nervousness and anxiety, and walking repeatedly to certain areas. Other characteristics that invite suspicion are a group of juveniles or a person wearing excessive clothing on a warm day.

Two *prerequisites to an apprehension* are *making sure to have seen the suspect conceal the store's merchandise* and *never losing sight of the suspect*. The observer must be positive that he or she saw the item removed from a rack because the customer could have brought the item into the store. If a customer wears a store item out of the store, alters or switches a price tag, store personnel must make sure an eyewitness account is available. Some shoplifters panic on being observed and "ditch" the concealed merchandise or give it to an accomplice. Some people conceal merchandise, return it to the counter unnoticed, and hope to be apprehended in order to sue to collect damages. To help prove intent, store personnel should permit the suspect to pass the last cash register and exit the store. If a register is outside (e.g., at a sidewalk sale), store personnel need to ensure the suspect passes it to strengthen the case.

Juveniles are handled differently than adults. Police and parents usually are called. A loss prevention practitioner should be familiar with local procedures regarding juveniles.

If a retail employee is not certain about a suspect, no apprehension should take place. In this situation, some practitioners recommend the "ghosting technique," which involves an employee carrying a duplicate of the item alleged to have been concealed as he or she walks close to the suspect. No words are spoken, but the message is obvious, if a theft has taken place. This technique has advantages for prevention, but it may permanently frighten customers from the store.

When retail personnel positively witness a shoplifting incident, loss prevention personnel must be notified for apprehension purposes. The detector (e.g., salesperson) should assist as an eyewitness. Additional personnel can stand by in case the subject becomes violent. Only a reasonable degree of force can be used to control the subject. *It is best to avoid a physical confrontation because the subject may be armed and the liability potential is significant. If the suspect flees, personnel should obtain a description and call police.* Immediately on approaching the subject, LP personnel should identify themselves by displaying identification or a badge. Personnel must never threaten the subject. *To reduce the problems associated with error, it is wise not to accuse the subject of stealing; the subject can be asked, "Would you mind answering a few questions about an item?" The next step is to quickly ask the subject to accompany personnel to the loss prevention office.* This perhaps is the most crucial point of the confrontation. At all times, careful observation of the subject is important because the merchandise may be "ditched" or escape may be attempted. If the subject escapes, again, personnel should avoid a physical confrontation and call police.

Detention and Arrest

After entering the LP office, the subject usually is asked to produce some type of identification as well as the concealed merchandise. If the subject does not comply with these requests, the LP officer should call the public police.

After the merchandise is received, a receipt should be requested to reduce the possibility of error. Usually, a shoplifter will state some type of excuse in an attempt to cover up not having a receipt.

Many jurisdictions have adopted the retailer's privilege of detaining shoplifters. *The difference between an arrest and detention is that the former requires the arrester to turn the suspect over to the public police, whereas the latter does not. Conditions for detention involve probable cause (reasonable grounds to justify legal action, such as an eyewitness account) and a reasonable time span, for detention, to accomplish questioning and documentation.* Many shoplifting statutes protect the retailer's right to detain, provided legal action was conducted in a reasonable manner. If an arrest is made, the crime charged by the retailer should be shoplifting (not larceny) to retain the right to detain under the shoplifting statute. Probable cause is a prerequisite for either detention or arrest. The detention of a person can evolve into an arrest. Many attorneys argue that any type of restricted movement placed on the suspect is equal to an arrest. The ultimate decision may rest with a jury in a lawsuit.

LP personnel—or any store personnel—should refrain from touching the subject. If force is used to exercise legal action, it must be reasonable. When a suspect is controlled after a struggle, it would be unreasonable to strike the suspect. Deadly force is restricted to life-threatening situations. *Unreasonable force can lead to prosecution difficulties, as well as criminal and civil action.*

Subsequent to proper detention or arrest, shoplifting statutes generally do not stipulate how merchandise is to be located and recovered from the suspect. Some states permit a search, whereas others forbid it. A shoplifter can be requested to empty his or her pockets and belongings to produce the stolen item(s). Public police should be called for obstinate suspects, and the police should conduct the search.

If the subject complies voluntarily, an arrest has not been made unless specified. The LP officer should ask the offender to sign a civil release form, which is vital before releasing the subject. It provides some protection against civil liability and becomes a record of the incident. The form contains, in addition to basic information (e.g., name, date), a voluntary confession of the store's items stolen, the value, and a statement that retail personnel did not use force or coercion and that the subject's cooperation is voluntary. Although a release may state that the subject agrees not to sue, the retail personnel still can be sued. The release has psychological value in that the subject may believe that a suit is impossible and not seek legal advice, although a claim possibly can be made that the subject signed while under duress. If the subject is obstinate or violent, an arrest is appropriate; handcuffing may be necessary. With this situation, the public police must be summoned; they usually will act in an advisory capacity and transport the prisoner to jail. A decision to call the police and prosecute makes obtaining a signature on the form less important. A criminal conviction perhaps is the best protection against civil liability. If the retailer intends to release the subject without calling public police, then the civil release form is vital for some protection against litigation.

The courts have yet to require private security personnel to state to a suspect the *Miranda* rights (civil liberties) prior to questioning, as public police are required to do. Courts have held that any involuntary confession, gained by public or private police, is inadmissible in court. To strengthen their case, many LP practitioners recite the *Miranda* rights anyway and request that subjects sign a waiver-of-rights form if willing to confess.

If an arrest occurs, the stolen merchandise and the eyewitness to the shoplifting incident (plus a CCTV video recording, if available) will be the primary evidence that will aid in the prosecution. The interviewer must not coerce the subject into a confession by prolonged questioning or tricky tactics. This forceful approach can easily destroy a case.

Throughout the confrontation, at least two retail employees should be present. One employee must be of the same sex as the subject. Problems inevitably develop if an item is forcibly removed from the subject. A video recording can prevent charges related to excessive force, coercion, a bribe, or sexual assault. *Racial profiling* is another potential problem that can result in a lawsuit by a subject who claims that he or she was targeted for surveillance because of racial background. Since recordings of surveillance activities can be taken out of context by a plaintiff's attorney, security personnel should explain to the defense side how surveillance is conducted. Examples include monitoring any customer who continuously looks around to see who is watching or walks into a high-risk area. Also, it may be an employee who is under surveillance rather than the customer (Schmedlen, 2000: 70–73).

Insurance companies write coverage protecting retailers against liability for false arrest, malicious prosecution, willful detention or imprisonment, libel, slander, and defamation of character. These types of insurance are important for retailers. Research by Gabbidon and Patrick (2005: 7) found that in more than two-thirds of shoplifting cases brought to civil court, the plaintiffs were to some extent successful, and almost a third were awarded damages.

Prosecution

The deterrent effect of prosecution is debatable. However, retailers may favor the prosecution of all shoplifters, believing that *shoplifters will avoid a "tough" store that has a reputation for prosecutions.*

Retailers should institute policies that are cost effective. Prevention appears to be less costly than a strict apprehension program.

When a shoplifter is arrested and about to be prosecuted, the witness or LP practitioner probably will be asked to sign a complaint or warrant, the legal document containing the facts making up the essential elements of the crime. The LP practitioner should read the legal documents and safeguard all relevant records and forms. Public police, prosecutors, judges, and juries will be interested in facts. In most cases, the defendant pleads guilty in a lower court, pays a fine, and a trial is avoided. For serious cases, a preliminary hearing may be necessary to give the judge an opportunity to review evidence and to decide on the necessity for a trial. Most defendants waive their rights to a hearing and a trial in exchange for a plea-bargaining opportunity. Some defendants choose to go to trial and retain an attorney. LP personnel facing a criminal trial must have an excellent case; otherwise, an acquittal is likely to lead to a lawsuit.

The testimony of the eyewitness as to the shoplifting incident often is the main evidence in a shoplifting case. CCTV systems provide visual evidence to strengthen cases.

The responsibility for preserving physical evidence for a court appearance is part of the LP practitioner's job. Accurate records are necessary. The evidence should be properly labeled and secured in a box or plastic bag. It should be in a locked location with very limited access to maintain the chain of custody of evidence (see Chapter 10). Two problems exist related to the preservation of physical evidence. First, millions of dollars of confiscated merchandise are not returned to the sales floor at hundreds of retail stores. Court congestion and delays can extend to months and years until the merchandise is out of date. Second, perishable items can deteriorate. A package of eight-month-old chicken breasts would present obvious resale problems when released after it was no longer needed as court evidence.

A solution to these problems involves photographing the stolen and recovered merchandise. Local requirements will vary concerning this procedure. A witness to the photographs can assist in strengthening the case. Color photos that contain a ruler marked with measurements will also aid in the effectiveness of this evidence.

If the prosecution of shoplifters becomes expensive and time consuming, if repeat offenders are not deterred, if the justice system becomes a "revolving door" (i.e., in for prosecution, out to commit another crime), and if cases are not successful, then antishoplifting strategies must be changed.

Civil Recovery

Almost every state has a civil recovery law that holds shoplifters liable for paying damages to businesses. Some states even extend these laws to employee theft. Civil recovery laws vary and may allow retailers, for example, to request three times the actual damages. These civil demand statutes aim to recover attorneys' fees, court costs, and even the cost of security. Essentially, the expense of theft is passed on to thieves.

To recover damages, a retailer sends a shoplifter a demand letter and a copy of the state's civil recovery law. Guidance can be obtained from a state retail association or an attorney. If there is no response, a second letter is sent stating that nonpayment may result in civil court action. With no response after a second letter, a retailer will have to decide whether to pursue the case in small claims court and whether a favorable judgment for damages can be collected.

LP personnel at some businesses may attempt civil recovery while the accused subject is still in custody because the chance for recovery diminishes once the subject leaves the store. The problem with this approach is that the shoplifting case may be based on faulty evidence. In addition, in some states, a guilty verdict may be necessary before civil action is sought. Other states permit simultaneous criminal and civil actions. In addition to the possibility of having a weak case against a suspected shoplifter, civil demand following an apprehension may result in legal action against the retailer for false imprisonment, extortion, and intentional or negligent infliction of emotion distress. The law of the respective state should be carefully studied as a foundation for store policies (Gips, 1997: 10). Research by Hollinger and Langton (2006: 28) shows a trend in less frequent use of civil recovery by retailers. They view this trend as possibly resulting from retailer frustration with the justice system.

Retailers have the option of contracting civil recovery with an outside firm that usually charges 30% of any money collected. Outsourcing saves the retailer the time and expense of operating a civil recovery program.

□ □ □ ▬▬▬▬▬▬▬▬▬▬▬▬▬▬▬▬▬▬▬▬▬▬▬▬▬▬▬

International Perspective: What Deters Shoplifters?
Gill, Bilby, and Turbin (1999: 29–39) interviewed 38 experienced shoplifters in England to assess the effectiveness of antishoplifting strategies. Their research is summarized here:

- *Retail staff:* While 9 out of 38 respondents suggested that retail staff would sometimes deter them, 24 answered "never." They argued that salespeople were too busy or uninterested in shoplifting.
- *Security personnel:* Three-fourths of respondents said that they were able to spot plain-clothed store detectives. Only three claimed to be deterred always. The majority said that they would be deterred if a store detective actively observed them. Respondents claimed that one advantage of being followed by a store detective was that it would help an accomplice.

- *Signs:* Most of the sample claimed that signs stating "shoplifters will be prosecuted" would not deter them, especially because certain retailers do not follow what the sign states.
- *EAS and inktags:* Twenty respondents stated that EAS tags would never deter them, and 14 claimed that they would remove the tags in the store, some with pliers and one with a bottle opener to pop it off. Some respondents avoided EAS tags, which illustrates some deterrent value. Respondents were evenly split on the deterrent effect of inktags. Claims were made that, by putting a condom over it or freezing it before removal, the merchandise would not be ruined. Manufacturers should study shoplifting methods more closely to design systems that are more effective.
- *CCTV:* Thirty-three out of 38 respondents claimed that CCTV would never deter them. Picture quality was perceived to be too poor for prosecution. They claimed that CCTV helped them if they could see where cameras were aimed so they could steal away from the camera's view. Blind spots were also helpful. These research results show the value of dark camera domes so the offender cannot see the camera's direction.

This research demonstrated that offenders make rational choices and that situational crime prevention (i.e., measures that increase risk for the offender) deters crime, but with the respondents in this study who were experienced shoplifters, a minority was deterred. A combination of security methods appears to have more of an impact than any one method. More research is needed to see how security methods impact amateurs.

Research That Examines the Empirical Relationship between LP Strategies and Levels of Shrinkage

Research of 103 retail firms by Langton and Hollinger (2005: 27–44) compared low- and high-shrinkage retailers within the theoretical framework of routine activities theory (see Chapters 3 and 8). Their research found that "in terms of blocking motivated offenders, there do seem to be significant differences between high- and low-shrinkage retailers in the number of pre-employment screening tests used for management and non-management, but not in the number of LP awareness programs implemented." They suggest that it is better to screen offenders out than try to prevent them from stealing once they are hired. Langton and Hollinger also found that background checks and drug tests were used, on average, by more low-shrinkage than high-shrinkage retailers. These researchers noted that they were unable to clearly identify which LP strategies are the most effective solutions to shrinkage, and many LP departments continue to apply the same strategies each year, using a "shot gun" approach, without researching the effectiveness of individual strategies in reducing shrinkage. Langton and Hollinger conclude that the most important difference between low- and high-shrinkage retailers appears to be the employment of capable personnel rather than physical security.

If you were a retailer, what strategies would you implement to prevent and reduce the shoplifting problem?

Robbery and Burglary

Robbery is the taking of something from an individual by force or threat of force. **Burglary** is unlawful entry into a structure to commit a felony or theft.

LP specialists repeatedly call for retailers to prevent burglary by (1) hardening the target, (2) creating a time delay, and (3) reducing the loot. Hardening the target pertains to physical security such as locks and alarm systems. The reasoning behind creation of a time delay is to increase the time necessary to commit the crime and, thereby, frustrate the offender. The offender may abort the offense, or the delay may provide additional time for police apprehension. When the loot is reduced, losses are minimized. Some people may mistakenly favor all three of these measures for *robbery*. In Table 17-1, a robbery/burglary matrix illustrates some problems when all three strategies are incorrectly applied to robbery.

Robbery Countermeasures

According to the Federal Bureau of Investigation (2006), in 2005, there were 417,122 robberies in the United States. Of all violent crime in 2005, robberies had the largest increase at 3.9%, compared with 2004. Although most robberies occur on streets and highways, it is a dangerous and costly crime to retailers. Hollinger and Langton (2006: 30) found in their research of retail firms that on average each robbery resulted in a loss of $8,716.41, with an average of 0.85 robberies per $100 million in total sales.

Employee Socialization of Procedures

- *Opening:* The daily opening of a store is often referred to as the "opening routine." This can be a dangerous time because a "routine" can aid a robber who carefully studies a target. Therefore, a varied opening procedure reduces the chances for robbery. A typical procedure is for one employee to go inside the store while another waits outside; the person returns within 5 minutes and signals that the "coast is clear." If the employee does not signal correctly or fails to appear, the police are called. The signal should be changed periodically to limit routine. Retailers in urban areas frequently open stores in the presence of security people or with a group of three to five employees. Many have permits for handguns.
- *Closing:* Closing procedures should include positioning a trusted store employee either inside or outside the store with a cell phone in hand. Various signaling procedures also are advisable.
- *Cash handling and transportation:* The POS should be located at the front of the store to enhance visibility to those passing by. A self-locking gate or Dutch door prevents access to the register by nonemployees. The cash drawer should require a key or code

Table 17-1 Robbery/Burglary Matrix

	Robbery	Burglary
Harden the target	Yes[a]	Yes
Create time delay	No[b]	Yes
Reduce loot	Yes	Yes

[a] For instance, a retail business hardened for robbery may include an alarm and hidden cameras; however, if the robber becomes trapped because of a metal gate that has blocked the only exit (for example), then violence and a hostage situation may develop.

[b] Once a robbery is in progress, for safety's sake a time delay can be dangerous. The exception would be if there were no threatening situation (unlikely in a robbery); then a time delay might aid in immediate apprehension. Police agencies favor robber–police confrontation outside of the crime scene, away from innocent bystanders.

for access. Reducing the "loot" available will reduce the loss. When cash and other valuables (e.g., checks and credit receipts) accumulate, a pickup system is necessary. Usually, retail managers walk to each cash register for collections while performing associated accountability procedures. Then the money is taken to the store money room. Two retail employees often participate in this operation. After the money is accounted for in the money room, a retail employee (or two) takes the money to a bank, or an armored car pickup takes place. Procedures vary. Employees must know persons handling and transporting cash. If an employee transports money to a bank, use of a moneybag is not advisable. It is better to use an innocuous paper bag. Local police sometimes are available as escorts to banks.

Whatever procedures are employed to protect people and money, there is always the possibility that a present or former employee has provided such information to offenders. Many robberies have a connection to current or former employees. Therefore, *procedures and signals should be changed periodically.*

In the event of robbery, employees should have been trained to act in the following ways:

1. Concentrate on *safety*; do not try to be a hero; accommodate the robber's requests as well as possible.
2. If safety permits, activate alarm and camera; give the robber bait money.
3. Concentrate on details: description of the robber(s); license tag; type of vehicle, if any; and direction of travel.
4. After the robber leaves, telephone the police immediately.

Devices and Services

- *Alarms:* The retail employee activates robbery alarms. A button or foot device signals a silent alarm to authorities. Another type of alarm is activated when money is removed from a money clip within the cash register drawer. The employee must try to prevent the robber from noticing the silent alarm activation by hand or foot movement.
- *CCTV:* A recording of a robbery is helpful in identifying and prosecuting robbers.
- *Safes:* A *drop safe* permits a deposit into the safe without opening it; only management can open the safe. Certain sections of a *time-delay safe* cannot be entered until preset times. *Dual-key locks* on safes require a key from two people, such as a retail employee and an armored car officer. Care must be exercised when designing safe access because a robber may become impatient and resort to violence; warning signs to deter robbers provide some protection.
- *Bait money:* Bait money, also known as *marked money*, has had the banks of issue, denominations, series years, and serial letters and numbers recorded by the retailer. This record should be kept in a safe place. Prosecution of the robber is strengthened if he or she is found with this money. Retail employees should carefully include the bait money with the loot.
- *Security officers:* Armed, rather than unarmed, officers should be used to prevent robbery at high-risk locations. Another method is to hire off-duty police officers.
- *Armored car service:* An armored car service can increase safety for retail employees while providing security for the transportation of money.

□ □ □ ▬▬▬▬▬▬▬▬▬▬▬▬▬▬▬▬▬▬▬▬

Security Manager Looks Bad

A retail executive from headquarters came to a chain store, displayed a company badge on his impressive suit, and systematically collected, with the usual moneybox, more than $2,000 from eight cash registers before leaving the store after the unauthorized collection. The purpose was to test security.

Burglary Countermeasures

According to the Federal Bureau of Investigation (2006), in 2005, there were 2,154,126 burglaries in the United States. It was the only property crime to increase (by 0.5%) in 2005, compared to the previous year. Although most burglaries occurred at residences, the problem is costly to retailers. Hollinger and Langton (2006: 30) found in their research of retail firms that on average each burglary resulted in a loss of $11,363.69, with an average of 1.68 burglaries per $100 million in total sales.

Employee Socialization

Employee socialization can involve the following:

1. Surveying possible burglar entry points
2. Leaving lights on (inside and outside)
3. Overturning cash register money trays on top of opened cash register drawers, at closing
4. Rechecking doors, windows, and alarms at closing
5. Preserving the crime scene to protect any evidence upon discovering a burglary

Physical Security

The burglar's most frequent method of intrusion is by forcing open a door or window. Earlier chapters provide security methods to prevent burglary.

Shopping Mall Strategies

The size of a retail operation has a direct bearing on the extent of its loss prevention program. A small, one-owner retail store obviously will require a different program than a shopping mall. A mall's loss prevention program would include not only countermeasures for crime, fire, accident, and other hazards, but also methods for numerous merchant needs, crowd control, parking lot problems (e.g., traffic, dead batteries, keys locked in autos), and lost people and merchandise. The size and complexity of malls compound loss problems.

A shopping mall's loss prevention program should be centralized and headed by an executive who responds to overall needs. Monthly meetings with merchants will facilitate cooperation and the sharing of problems, ideas, and resources. These meetings can provide an opportunity for a short training program. Special sales and events require further preparation. For malls experiencing many crime incidents, the establishment of a police substation is helpful.

Since the 9/11 attacks, retail shopping malls have been referred to as a "soft target," as have many other locations (e.g., schools, houses of worship). Traditionally, merchant need for easy access by customers limits access controls at malls and retail stores. At this time, malls in the United States will not be protected like airports, unless malls are attacked as they have been in other countries (e.g., Israel). In addition, because of the tight profit margins of retailers, they invest in sales promotion and displays, rather than security. Questions of concern: What are the threats and hazards to U.S. malls today? Is it terrorism? Is it an assailant who enters a mall and shoots people? Is it internal theft and shoplifting? Is it gangs? A risk analysis can help to answer these questions.

Davis et al. (2006) conducted research on the readiness of malls in preventing and responding to terrorist attacks. These researchers view malls as receiving too little attention as "soft targets." They found that malls have not made any significant investment in increased security since the 9/11 attacks. At the same time, they noted that malls have increased antiterrorism training for security personnel, and the majority of mall security directors maintain emergency management plans. The researchers recommended the following: risk assessments and mitigation of risks; emergency planning and partnering with stakeholders (e.g., retailers and first responders); coordination with state homeland security; national guidelines established by DHS; and standardized antiterrorism training courses.

Career: Retail Loss Prevention

The most common perception of the general public regarding the function of retail loss prevention (LP) departments is that they are primarily involved in the recruitment of store detectives or "shoplifter catchers." While it is true that many retailers hire store detectives to prevent and apprehend shoplifters, the responsibilities of LP professionals and the role they play in the overall profitability of the company makes this one of the most critically important functions within retail organizations. Retail companies are plagued by theft and fraud from both internal and external sources. Entry-level retail loss prevention positions generally involve undercover shoplifting apprehensions, LP or safety auditing, and many other such functions and can lead to rapid advancement into more lucrative positions of responsibility. Retail LP positions offer valuable work experience. Part-time work as a store detective is an excellent job while one is in college. Retail LP managers have responsibility for overseeing the store detectives and addressing and resolving internal theft concerns. Depending on the size of the stores and the company, an LP manager may be responsible for the LP functions within a single store or responsible for overseeing LP at a number of locations within a chain.

Entry-level management positions generally require an undergraduate degree from an accredited institution as well as three to five years of experience in retail loss prevention. Salary range is $25,000 to $38,000, depending on many factors.

Mid-level management positions, requiring expertise in multiple security disciplines, require an undergraduate degree in an appropriate discipline, as well as five to eight years of demonstrated success in the field in relevant retail-related LP functions. The Certified Protection Professional (CPP) and Certified Fraud Examiner (CFE) are the preferred designations.

Source: Courtesy of ASIS International. (2005). "Career Opportunities in Security." www.asisonline.org.

The Loss Prevention Foundation launched the Loss Prevention Qualified (LPQ) designation in 2007 for entry-level practitioners and those interested in the profession. The program was designed with input from over thirty retail companies. The on-line coursework focuses on the retail environment, becoming a successful businessperson, and LP basics and tools ("First LP Certification Program Launches June 4th", 2007).

Banks and Financial Businesses

The following information on the banking and financial services sector is from *The National Strategy for the Physical Protection of Critical Infrastructures and Key Assets* (White House, 2003: 63–64). The banking and financial services sector infrastructure consists of a variety of physical structures, such as buildings and financial utilities, as well as human capital. Most of the industry's activities and operations take place in large commercial office buildings. Physical structures to be protected house retail or wholesale banking operations, financial markets, regulatory institutions, and physical repositories for documents and financial assets. Today's financial utilities, such as payment and clearing and settlement systems, are primarily electronic, although some physical transfer of assets does still occur. The financial utilities infrastructure includes such electronic devices as computers, storage devices, and telecommunication networks. In addition to the sector's key physical components, many financial services employees have highly specialized skills and are, therefore, considered essential elements of the industry's critical infrastructure.

The financial industry also depends on continued public confidence and involvement to maintain normal operations. Financial institutions maintain only a small fraction of depositors' assets in cash on hand. If depositors and customers were to seek to withdraw their assets simultaneously, severe liquidity pressures would be placed on the financial system. With this in mind, federal safeguards are in place to prevent liquidity shortfalls. In times of crisis or disaster, maintaining public and global confidence demands that financial institutions, financial markets, and payment systems remain operational or that their operations can be quickly restored. Additionally, in times of stress the Secretary of the Treasury, the Chairman of the Federal Reserve, and the Securities and Exchange Commission proactively address public confidence issues, as was done following the September 11 terrorist attacks. The Department of the Treasury and federal and state regulatory communities have developed emergency communications plans for the banking and finance sector. With regard to retail financial services, physical assets are well distributed geographically throughout the industry. The sector's retail niche is characterized by a high degree of **substitutability**, which means that one type of payment mechanism or asset can be easily replaced with another during a short-term crisis. For example, in retail markets, consumers can make payments through cash, checks, or credit cards. The banking and financial services industry is highly regulated and highly competitive. Industry professionals and government regulators regularly engage in identifying sector vulnerabilities and take appropriate protective measures, including sanctions for institutions that do not consistently meet standards.

Banking and Finance Sector Challenges

Like the other critical sectors, the banking and financial services sector relies on several critical infrastructure industries for continuity of operations, including electric power, transportation, and public safety services. The sector also specifically relies on computer networks and telecommunications systems to assure the availability of its services. The potential for disruption of these systems is an important concern. For example, the equity securities markets remained closed for four business days following September 11, not because any markets or market systems were inoperable, but because the telecommunications lines in lower Manhattan that connect key market participants were heavily damaged and could not be restored immediately. As a mitigation measure, financial institutions have made great strides to build redundancy and backup into their systems and operations.

Overlapping federal intelligence authorities involved in publicizing threat information can cause confusion and duplication of effort for both industry and government. The **U.S. Department of the Treasury**, the lead agency for this sector, organized the Financial and Banking Information Infrastructure Committee (FBIIC) as a standing committee of the President's Critical Infrastructure Protection Board (PCIPB). The FBIIC comprises representatives from 13 federal and state financial regulatory agencies and works to improve the information dissemination and sharing processes.

Banking and Finance Sector Initiatives

The attacks in New York City on September 11 showed that the financial services industry is highly resilient. The strong safeguards and backup systems the industry had in place performed well. Since 1998, the sector has been working with the Department of the Treasury to organize itself to address the risks of the emerging threat environment, particularly cyber intrusions. It was also the first sector to establish an ISAC to share security-related information among members of the industry.

Major institutions in this sector continue to perform ongoing assessments of their security programs. After the September 11 attacks, the industry and its associations initiated lessons-learned reviews to identify corrective actions for the improvement of security and response and recovery programs, as well as to provide a forum for sharing best practices through their trade associations and other interdisciplinary groups.

The Scope of Threats and Legal Responsibilities of the Banking and Finance Sector

The banking and finance sector includes banks, insurance companies, mutual funds, pension funds, and other financial entities. *The National Strategy* cited previously emphasizes the terrorist threat. However, through history, these institutions have faced threats from robbery, burglary, larceny, fraud, and embezzlement. Fraud (e.g., credit and loan) has been especially problematic for this sector, and this crime results in greater losses while being more difficult to detect and solve than other crimes against banks. In addition, money, securities, checks, and other liquid assets make this industry attractive to internal and external culprits. Services that present particular loss problems are automated teller machines (ATMs), after-hours depositories (AHDs), and electronic fund transfer systems (EFTSs). Personnel servicing ATMs and customers have been victimized by armed robbers. AHDs also present a robbery problem, such as when a retailer makes a deposit at the end of the business day. Banks have incurred losses from fraud during the transfer of funds.

Today, the threat environment and the legal responsibilities of this critical infrastructure (CI) sector are immense. The **Bank Protection Act (BPA) of 1968** mandates minimum security measures for protection against robbery, burglary, and larceny, primarily. Besides terrorism and traditional crimes, the challenges include cyber crimes, identity theft, and money laundering. A host of laws and regulations place considerable responsibilities on this sector. The laws include the **Bank Secrecy Act of 1986,** implemented to establish reporting requirements for transactions of money to detect money laundering. The **Anti-Drug Abuse Act of 1988** amended the Bank Secrecy Act and requires banks to report any "suspicious transactions" that may be associated with illegal drug trafficking. The **Antiterrorism and Effective Death Penalty Act of 1996** makes it a criminal offense for persons in the United States, other than those excepted by the government, to engage in financial transactions with countries that condone or encourage terrorism. The **Gramm-Leach-Bliley Act of 1999**, which has broad application, requires safeguards on the privacy and security of customer information. The **USA PATRIOT Act of 2001** contains measures against money laundering and the financing of terrorism. The **Sarbanes-Oxley (SOX) Act of 2002**, which passed in the wake of major corporate scandals, requires public companies to assess internal controls over financial reporting to ensure accuracy.

Regulation H

Regulation H, Code of Federal Regulations, pertains to membership of state banking institutions in the Federal Reserve System. This regulation combines the former BPA and many provisions of the Bank Secrecy Act of 1986 into one document. An increase in crimes against banks and the lack of adequate countermeasures led Congress to enact the BPA, which applied to a variety of financial institutions.

Even though the BPA was designed to counter losses from outsiders, a significant shortcoming of this legislation was that it did not establish standards for internal protection. For example, the **savings and loan (S&L) scandal** of the 1980s and 1990s, where bank executives approved risky loans to friends and relatives (i.e., "the fox was guarding the hen house"), cost U.S. taxpayers billions of dollars (much more than embezzlement and bank robberies combined). Despite these drawbacks, the BPA was the first legislation reinforcing security for a large private commercial enterprise. It is impossible to ascertain the number of crimes that have been prevented because of the BPA.

Security under Regulation H

- Security procedures must be adopted to discourage robberies, burglaries, and larcenies; assist in the identification and prosecution of persons who commit such acts; and maintain records of crimes.
- The institution's board of directors must ensure that a written security program is developed and implemented.

- The board must designate a security officer to administer the security program and receive an annual report from that person.
- Program requirements include opening and closing procedures, warning signals, and safekeeping of currency and other valuables (e.g., vault controls).
- Policies, procedures, and training manuals must be developed, and initial and periodic training must be provided for employees.
- Security devices—alarm systems, tamper-resistant locks, lighting, and safes or vaults—must be selected, tested, operated, and maintained.

A bank security officer's duties may include responsibility for Bank Secrecy Act requirements under Regulation H. This includes ensuring that **suspicious activity reports** (i.e., suspicious financial transactions over a specified amount) are filed with appropriate federal law enforcement agencies and the U.S. Department of the Treasury when violations of federal law are suspected. This includes insider abuse or money laundering.

Money laundering is a huge global problem with a conservative estimate of $600 billion laundered annually. Essentially, it is an attempt to make "dirty" money (i.e., obtained through illegal means, such as the drug trade) appear clean. Offenders often transfer "dirty" money, under disguised ownership, from one bank to another, globally, to increase the difficulty of tracing it (Schroeder, 2001: 1–9; U.S. Drug Enforcement Administration, 2007).

Bank Robbery Countermeasures

A common feature of many financial locations is a warmer, more personal atmosphere gained through the elimination of security barriers. Although this may please customers, robbery—a crime characterized by a threat and the possible use of violence—becomes a serious danger to people. The Federal Bureau of Investigation (2007) reported 6,961 bank robberies in the United States in 2006, with a total loss of $69,776,820.

When a robbery does take place at a bank, the teller is often the only one initially knowledgeable about the crime. The situation of a lone robber passing a holdup note to the teller is typical. In any robbery situation, the danger to life must not be taken lightly. The following suggestions can improve employee reaction:

1. Institute a training program.
2. During a robbery, act cautiously and do not take any chances.
3. Activate an alarm if possible without the robber(s) noticing.
4. Provide the robber with bait money that has the serial numbers recorded. **Tear-gas/dye packs** also are important. These devices look like packs of currency and emit tear-gas and red smoke (which stains clothes and the money) when carried out of a bank. A radio transmitter activates the packet.
5. Study characteristics of the bandit, especially scars, shape of eyes, height, body structure, voice, speech patterns, and other permanent features.
6. Safely note the means of transportation, license number, and vehicle description.
7. Contact public police.

Uniformed officers can offer comfort to customers and act as credible witnesses; however, their use is subject to controversy. They may deter an amateur robber, but not a professional. Tear-gas/dye packs help to apprehend robbers and recover money. However, robbers have threatened violence if they receive one, and detonations have occurred inside banks. Banks are using the **Global Positioning System (GPS)**; a transmitting device is planted in the bait money to track the device via satellite signal, and tracking can be done by police and security through a secure Web site that shows a map on a computer screen. CCTV technology permits remote monitoring, and if a robbery, fraud, or other crime occurs, police (with appropriate equipment) can observe the crime while responding. Security personnel can e-mail a video record to police. Other protection methods include safes and vaults, bullet-resistive bandit barriers, metal detection portals, signage that describes security features, and height markers to help estimate robber height. A mantrap is another option. It consists of double doors capable of trapping a fleeing robber; however, careful planning and construction are essential to promote safety. In addition, the remote teller system can be used whereby business is conducted via CCTV and pneumatic tubes.

Automatic Teller Machines

Robbery and fraud have followed ATM self-service banking. The BPA and the Federal Electronic Funds Transfer Act focus on security of ATMs and fraudulent transactions, rather than the safety of ATM users. Several state and local government bodies have passed ATM safety laws. These bills typically require surveillance cameras, adequate lighting, mirrors and low hedges to enhance visibility, and crime prevention tips to ATM cardholders. Although offenders watch for careless customers who do not protect their identity and PIN numbers, family members or friends commit a considerable amount of ATM fraud.

One low-tech crime victimizing ATMs is theft of the entire machine. A truck and chains or an inexpensive lift truck are used to pull the ATM from its foundation. Countermeasures include placing ATMs at locations busy 24 hours a day and using GPS to deter theft.

Kidnapping and Extortion

The financial executive and his or her family are potential victims of a kidnapper or extortionist. A bank teller is another potential victim. These crimes vary; two scenarios follow. An offender kidnaps a bank employee or family member while he or she is driving the family car or is at home. The kidnapped person is traded for cash. Another approach occurs when an extortionist calls a bank employee at work, claims to be holding a family member, and demands cash for the safe return of the kidnapped victim. The extortionist may even confront the bank employee personally. In these situations, violence is possible, even after cash is delivered.

A precise plan and employee training are essential prior to a confrontation. The following procedures should be observed by the person in contact with the kidnappers:

1. Try to remain calm during the ordeal. Contact public police as soon as possible.
2. If a hostage is involved, ask the caller to allow the hostage to come to the telephone to speak.
3. Repeat demands to the caller to double-check any directions and procedures.
4. Try to arrange for a person-to-person payoff and transfer of the hostage.
5. If prepared, trace the call.
6. After the call, record as much information as possible (e.g., date, time, words spoken, background noises). Management should provide a standard form.
7. If the hostage is brought to the bank or if the offender confronts a bank employee personally, notify other employees with a prearranged signal.
8. Include "bait" money in any payoff.

Embezzlement, On-line Risks, and Fraud

Banks have increased their exposure to crime because they are connected internally through an intranet and externally through on-line banking services. An employee may commit embezzlement by gaining unauthorized access to a bank's accounts payable system and creating fictitious invoices and payments to the employee's post office box. Other internal crimes are to delete all records of a friend's loan, approve fictitious loans, or tap into dormant accounts.

On-line banking risks are varied and include, for example, the hacking of bank Web sites to alter information or to steal customer information. Web spoofing seeks to create a look-alike Web site to trick customers into releasing confidential account information that is exploited or sold by the hacker. Hackers may be less of a threat for banks than vulnerabilities caused by employees—for instance, an employee who leaves the office with a laptop containing customer information and then the laptop disappears (Friedrick, 2006: 19). However, at the same time, financial institutions must balance offering new services to customers with secure on-line systems. A highly publicized bank loss or victimized customer could drive customers away.

Federal regulators are requiring banks to enhance security for on-line banking. Measures emphasize "two-factor authentication" that goes beyond a user name and password. Examples include a customer choosing an image and phrase, or the use of a Universal Serial Bus (USB) token that must be plugged into a computer's USB port to access an on-line account. Another strategy is for banks to install software that monitors each on-line transaction for unusual patterns (Swartz, 2006).

Check swindles, which are a common externally perpetrated fraud, may involve the forgery of stolen checks or the manufacture of fictitious checks. Computer programs permit offenders to create corporate payroll checks that are nearly impossible to distinguish from a genuine one.

Credit card fraud is another problem for banks. Losses can result from a fraudulent application containing a stolen identity, from a stolen card, or from a businessperson who submits fraudulent credit card sales receipts for payment.

Since the 1992 peak of the S&L scandal, the FBI has refocused its resources on other high-priority fraud cases. For example, according to the FBI, mortgage fraud is one of the fastest growing white-collar crimes in the United States. It consists of **fraud for property** and **fraud for profit**. The former involves a single loan whereby the borrower makes misrepresentations, such as higher income and lower debt. The latter involves industry professionals who seek multiple loans with several financial institutions while making gross misrepresentations. In 2005, about 22,000 mortgage fraud suspicious activity reports were filed, and losses were over $1 billion (Federal Bureau of Investigation, 2005).

Because of the growing crimes of identity theft and fraud, banks have been forced to play a greater role in preventing these problems. In reference to *privacy*, the Gramm-Leach-Bliley Act requires financial institutions and insurance companies to disclose to customers the policies on what data they collect, with whom they share it, and how they share it. This is known as the "Privacy Rule," and it limits the disclosure (or selling) of nonpublic personal information to unaffiliated third parties. In reference to *security*, the Gramm-Leach-Bliley Act and the Fair and Accurate Credit Transactions Act of 2003 specify security guidelines for the confidentiality, integrity, and proper disposal of customer information. The guidelines include threat assessments and the implementation of an IT security program.

☐ ☐ ☐ ▬▬▬▬▬▬▬▬▬▬▬▬▬▬▬▬▬▬▬▬▬▬▬▬▬▬▬▬▬

What do you think is the most serious risk facing banks and financial institutions? What are your solutions?

☐ ☐ ☐ ▬▬▬▬▬▬▬▬▬▬▬▬▬▬▬▬▬▬▬▬▬▬▬▬▬▬▬▬▬

Career: Banking and Financial Services Security

Careers in this field include those associated with banking (including retail banking, mortgage, credit/debit cards, Internet banking, commercial and consumer lending), stock brokerages, insurance companies, and other financial institutions. As a key component to the critical infrastructure of every nation, the financial services industry is regulated by various government agencies. Financial institution security directors and managers must deal with a wide variety of concerns including theft, fraud, workplace violence, information security, investigations, executive protection, business continuity, and physical security in order to adequately protect their institution. Security managers must be effective leaders within their organization and able to successfully influence change.

Because of the increasing complexity of the financial services industry, companies continue to seek the best and the brightest from law enforcement agencies, colleges and universities, and from within other private sector companies, both within and outside the financial services sector.

Entry-level management positions in financial services generally require a degree in business, finance, or criminal justice from an accredited institution as well as three to five years experience in either law enforcement or security. The salary range for entry-level positions is $35,000 to $65,000, depending on many factors.

Mid-level management positions, requiring expertise in multiple security disciplines, generally require a bachelor's degree in an appropriate discipline, as well as three to seven years of demonstrated success in the field. Professional certifications such as the Certified Protection Professional (CPP) and Certified Fraud Examiner (CFE) are often desired as an indicator of professionalism and qualification. The salary range for mid-level management positions is $40,000 to $100,000.

Source: Courtesy of ASIS International. (2005). "Career Opportunities in Security." www.asisonline.org.

Educational Institutions

Two major types of educational systems are emphasized here: school districts and higher education campuses. A major difference between school districts and college and university campuses is that, in the former, students normally go home at night and buildings often are empty. On campuses, students often live on the premises in dormitories. Exceptions are community and technical colleges whose students often commute. School districts and campuses both schedule evening and weekend activities such as classes, sports events, and meetings. A major factor for those who plan and implement loss prevention programs for these institutions is that the protection measures must cater to the needs and characteristics of the particular institution (see Figure 17-4).

Threats and Hazards at Educational Institutions

Educational institutions are subject to a host of threats and hazards similar to other segments of society. Examples are crimes of violence, bomb threats, property crimes, cybercrimes, and vandalism. Additional concerns are fire, accident, disaster, terrorism, gangs, suicide, date rape, crowd control for sports and other events, traffic, parking, student activism, and graffiti.

Countermeasures

The following list describes measures for security and safety of school districts and institutions of higher education:

- Establish a security and safety committee and meet at least monthly.
- Ensure that all stakeholders and first responders are involved in security and safety planning and programs.
- Conduct risk analyses.
- Apply CPTED methods.
- Typical security measures are access controls, emergency telephones, intrusion alarms, patrols, lighting, and CCTV.
- Use vandal-resistant construction materials.
- If graffiti is an issue, photograph it before removing it and show the photos to police.
- Carefully consider the use of unarmed students to supplement police and security forces; provide good training.
- Offer counseling services and programs to assist students in crisis.
- Conduct substance abuse education and prevention programs.
- Use an "all-hazards" approach to emergency management (see Chapter 12).

FIGURE 17-4 Protection must cater to the unique needs of institutions. *Courtesy:* Talk-A–Phone.

School Districts

In the 2004–2005 school year, an estimated 54.9 million students were enrolled in prekindergarten through grade 12. Although multiple homicide events at schools have captured headlines in recent years, the chance of suffering a school-associated violent death is very low. Research has shown that students are more likely to be victimized by a violent crime away from school than at school. From July 1, 2004 through June 30, 2005, there were 28 school-associated violent deaths (21 homicides and 7 suicides) of school-age youth (ages 5 to 18) at school in the United States. In 2004, students ages 12 to 18 were victims of about 1.4 million nonfatal crimes at school, including about 863,000 thefts and 583,000 violent crimes (simple assault and serious violent crime)—107,000 of which were serious violent crimes (rape, sexual assault, robbery, and aggravated assault). Violence, theft, drugs, and weapons continue to pose problems in schools (U.S. Department of Justice, Bureau of Justice Statistics, 2006).

In an attempt to reduce school violence, Congress enacted the **Gun-Free Schools Act of 1994,** which requires that each state receiving federal funds under the Elementary and Secondary Education Act must have a state law requiring local educational agencies to expel from school for a period of not less than one year a student who is determined to have brought a weapon to school. Each state's law also must allow the chief administering officer of the local educational agency to modify the expulsion requirement on a case-by-case basis. This law resulted in many schools adopting a **zero-tolerance policy** for weapons being brought to school. In other words, any infraction results in full punishment. This same policy extends to alcohol and drugs. Meadows (2007: 170) writes that the intent of such a policy is both preventive and punitive. He notes the following: "Although zero-tolerance policies have a place in school security, there is the threat of overenforcement, which may undermine school-community relations and label students unfairly."

☐ ☐ ☐ ▬▬▬▬▬▬▬▬▬▬▬▬▬▬▬▬▬▬▬▬▬▬▬▬

Teacher and staff victimization and intimidation in school districts are important topics often not given enough attention.

▬▬▬▬▬▬▬▬▬▬▬▬▬▬▬▬▬▬▬▬▬▬▬▬ ☐ ☐ ☐

A comprehensive school district loss prevention program must involve the community: students, teachers and administrators, parents, public safety agencies, civic groups, and businesses (Decker, 2000: 3). The program can be divided into four components: special programs, personnel, physical security, and emergency management.

Special programs include character education to help students distinguish right from wrong, conflict resolution, diversity, prevention of bullying, anonymous tip lines, and programs that involve parents. Since gangs are a problem in many schools and communities, and they are often linked to violence and drugs, school administrators should be proactive to reduce this problem by, for example, meeting police gang specialists on a regular basis to exchange information and antigang strategies. One popular program is the **Gang Resistance Education and Training (GREAT)** program that provides students with tools to resist the lure and trap of gangs. Modeled after the Drug Abuse Resistance Education (DARE) program, the GREAT program introduces students to conflict resolution skills, cultural sensitivity, and negative aspects of gang life. This program has spread to all 50 states and several other countries (U.S. Department of Justice, Bureau of Justice Assistance, 2007).

All employees at schools should be trained on early warning signs of inappropriate behavior or violence. These signs include feelings of isolation, rejection, and being persecuted, plus behaviors indicating anger or violence, such as threats. Intervention and counseling are vital in response to such signs.

A combined counseling and education approach might reduce student hostility and funnel student time into constructive activities. Traditional suspension from school often sends troublesome students to the streets, where more trouble is likely. On the other hand, if students remain at school in an appropriate program, improved results are probable.

Personnel consist of teachers, teacher aids, administrators, counselors, security officers, and School Resource Officers. SROs are police officers on duty at schools; they provide visibility, create rapport with students, and respond to incidents. Parents and volunteers play an important role in supplementing employees. All those who perform job duties at schools should undergo constant training and clearly understand policies and procedures for day-to-day events, such as student discipline problems and how to care for people during emergencies.

Physical security pertains to a variety of systems and devices that help to protect people and assets. Examples are access control systems, handheld (Figure 17-5) and walk-through metal detectors, and duress alarms. Physical security is a challenge because students must be safe without feeling as if they are in a prison. Depending on the needs of a school district, students can swipe an ID card when they climb onto a bus and when they arrive and leave school; RFID tracks their movements. At the same time, CCTV cameras watch students on buses and on school premises. Visitors can be asked for their driver's license to check against a database of sex offenders, while they wait in a mantrap (Toppo, 2006). *If school security planners argue*

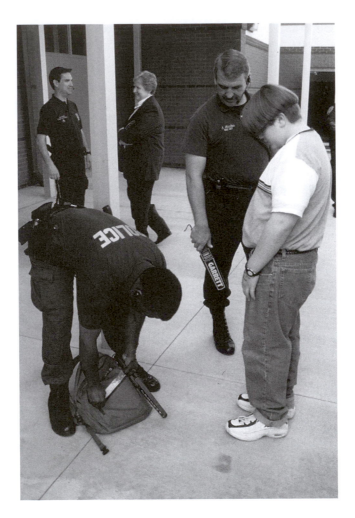

FIGURE 17-5 Police using handheld metal detector at school access point. *Courtesy:* Garrett Metal Detectors.

for more security personnel and hardware to curb school crime, they may be faced with others who see broader solutions to the problem. In addition, whatever strategies are implemented, they should be subject to research and evaluation to produce the best possible solutions and utilization of resources.

Emergency management consists of plans to respond to violence, weapons, hostage situations, bombs/explosions, abused students, aggressive parents who are on the premises, and incidents involving parental rights. Many school districts distribute their crisis plans to public safety agencies that have a ready reference containing maps and building plans, utility shutoffs, staff and parent telephone numbers, a yearbook to identify people, and a set of keys.

☐ ☐ ☐ ▬▬▬▬▬▬▬▬▬▬▬▬▬▬▬▬▬▬▬▬▬▬▬▬▬▬▬

What are the advantages and disadvantages of using unarmed students to supplement police and security forces at high schools?

▬▬▬▬▬▬▬▬▬▬▬▬▬▬▬▬▬▬▬▬▬▬▬▬▬▬▬ ☐ ☐ ☐

Are Educational Institutions "Soft" Targets?

Terrorists search for "soft" targets containing limited security to increase the likelihood of a successful attack. Examples of **"soft" targets** are educational institutions, houses of worship, shopping malls, and theaters. **"Hard" targets** include military bases and fortified government buildings.

Emergency management plans developed by school districts may concentrate on the possibility of a violent and armed person on the premises. However, an "all-hazards" approach to emergency management is best. Schools are subject to a host of threats and hazards as covered in this book, plus others not covered, such as bus accidents, food-borne illnesses, contaminated food recalls, the discharge of toxic substances (e.g., the release of pepper spray in a crowded hall), and the release of an animal in a school.

Emergency management became an important priority at many schools following the 1999 **Columbine High School massacre**. During this incident in Jefferson County, Colorado, two teenage students, armed with a variety of weapons and bombs, killed 12 students and a teacher, wounded 24, and then committed suicide. Prior to the attack, one of the killers showed warning signs of violence through a Web site on America Online, which contained violent threats, information on how to make bombs, and a log of mischief. The massacre fueled debate over gun violence, gun control, and the influence of the media on violence. In addition, the event reinforced attention to warning signs to prevent violence.

Another, more deadly massacre, tied to terrorism, was the **Beslan Elementary School massacre** in 2004. This attack was part of the Chechen war for independence against Russia. Russia has fought an insurgency in the breakaway republic of Chechnya since the 1990s, a time when the former Soviet Union collapsed. The three-day hostage standoff at the elementary school in Beslan, where Chechen rebels rigged bombs around 1,200 hostages, ended in gunfire, explosions, and 338 deaths, mostly children. Each side blamed the other for the battle at the school that caused more controversy over Chechen terrorism and Russian responses.

The carnage began when 32 attackers—armed with AK-47s, a machine gun, grenade launchers, explosives, and two dogs (to protect against chemical attack)—drove to the crowded school and herded children, teachers, and parents into the school gym, which was quickly wired with explosives. Male hostages were forced to build barricades at doors and windows, and when the work was complete, they were executed and their bodies were thrown out of the building. Two female suicide bombers were among the attackers, which illustrated the resolve of the attackers and the possible outcome. The attackers demanded the release of Chechen rebels, the withdrawal of Russian troops from Chechnya, and Chechen independence. The Russian government's options were very limited, and giving in to terrorist demands fuels new hostage events. By the second day, the terrorists continued to refuse water, food, and medicine for the hostages. In their desperation, the hostages began to drink their own urine. On the third day, the terrorists permitted a crew to collect the bodies of 20 male hostages that had been thrown out of the building. At this point, a bomb exploded within the gym, supposedly by accident, a fire began, the roof collapsed, and as hostages escaped, the terrorists shot them. The terrorists were killed, and two that escaped were caught by a mob and lynched. As the disaster unfolded, "finger-pointing" began to explain what went wrong. Explanations were that Special Forces were not ordered to rescue the hostages and assault the building, no one wanted to take responsibility to order the rescue and assault, and armed volunteers interfered with the hostage situation and were not kept back. The disaster shocked the world, and the Russian government promised reform of the police and military (Abdullaev, 2004: 28–35).

Although shootings on U.S. college campuses are rare, on April 16, 2007 the **Virginia Tech massacre** became the worst school mass murder incident in U.S. history when a mentally disturbed student murdered 32 people and then committed suicide. Among the questions that followed the shootings were: Why did it take over two hours to release a notification that a killer was on the loose after two students were found shot earlier in another building? Was the police response quick enough to end the threat of an "active shooter"? These questions are difficult to answer and many factors must be considered. For instance, rushing into a building without a team and a plan is risky. Harwood (2007, 55–65) writes of strategies that require refinement: behavioral threat assessment teams to identify risky students, mass notification systems, and "active shooter" response.

Colleges and Universities

In response to increasing crime on college campuses and the need for more accurate statistics, Congress passed the **Student-Right-to-Know and Campus Security Act of 1990**. This act is also known as the "Clery Act," named after Jeanne Clery, a college student who was raped and murdered in her dorm room. This legislation requires crime awareness and prevention policies at colleges and an annual report of campus crime to the FBI Uniform Crime Reports program, while making these statistics available to students and the general public. Such data, available on the Web, enables comparisons among colleges and universities (Federal Bureau of Investigation, 2006). However, there is conjecture that some schools omit reporting acts of violence to protect recruiting efforts and their reputations (Jaeger, 2001: 6). FBI crime data has been criticized over the years because it represents crimes *reported* to police, and many crimes are never reported or recorded, as shown by victimization studies (Purpura, 1997: 32–36).

In 1992, the **Campus Sexual Assault Victim's Bill of Rights** amended the preceding act, requiring schools to develop policies to deal with sexual assault on campus. This is an important issue, especially in light of Bureau of Justice Statistics research showing 35 incidents of rape per academic year on a campus with 1,000 women (U.S. Department of Justice, Bureau of Justice Statistics, 2000). Further amendments in 1998 added two crimes to reporting—arson and negligent manslaughter—and required schools to report on crime at property owned by a school but not at the main campus. Schools not reporting crime data are subject to a $25,000 fine. In nearly every category of crime, college campuses showed lower incidence of crime than comparable data for the nation as a whole (Office of Postsecondary Education, 2001).

Research by Fisher and Sloan (1993: 67–77) produced guidelines that should be considered when evaluating programs designed to reduce campus crime. Some of their major points follow:

- A comprehensive evaluation requires identifying the individual departments or groups on campus that will be involved and assigning safety and security responsibilities to them.
- A comprehensive approach includes security, faculty members, staff members, students, and public law enforcement personnel.
- Campus administrators should conduct surveys of the campus community to understand the nature and extent of crime and fear, perceptions of the effectiveness of security, and participation in crime prevention programs and whether participants adopted any of the preventive measures. Until evaluations become an integral part of responding to campus crime, administrators will continue to make poor decisions on security strategies.
- Research has confirmed that crime on campuses is influenced by poor lighting, excessive foliage, blocked views, and difficulty of escape by victims. [As we can see, Crime Prevention Through Environmental Design, or CPTED, as discussed earlier in the text, has universal application.]
- Location measures (e.g., proximity to urban areas with high unemployment) are predictors of high campus crime rates.

Numerous campuses have implemented the strategy of many public police agencies, namely, **community policing**. It aims to control crime through a partnership of police and citizens, and it strives to become a dominant philosophy throughout a police department.

Rather than police reacting to the same problem repeatedly, a unique, proactive approach is employed for problem solving.

High priorities for protection on campuses are programs that focus on crime prevention, self-protection, and Neighborhood Watch (so people can look out for one another). Shuttle buses and escorts for students also prevent crime and enhance safety. An essential component of these programs and services is marketing to stimulate interest and participation. This can be accomplished through a brochure, a Web page, and decals with an emergency telephone number that can be placed around campus.

One particular group that has advanced the professionalism of campus safety and security is the International Association of Campus Law Enforcement Administrators (IACLEA). This group began in 1958 with 11 schools, and today it represents 1,000 colleges and universities in 20 countries. The group holds an annual conference; offers training, professional development, and accreditation; and publishes *Campus Law Enforcement Journal*.

In 2004, a National Summit on Campus Public Safety was held in Baltimore, Maryland. It was supported by the U.S. Department of Justice, Office of Community Oriented Policing Services (2005); the IACLEA; the International Association of Chiefs of Police; the U.S. Department of Homeland Security; and the FBI. Some of the main points from this summit are as follows:

- There is a need for a unified approach to campus safety issues; a national agenda on campus public safety to guide government, business, and professional associations; and a national center for campus safety to support information sharing, policy development, model practices, operations, and research.
- National standards, similar to those of the Commission on Accreditation for Law Enforcement Agencies, should be developed for campus police and security operations.
- Since the 9/11 attacks, coordination between senior executives and security/police at colleges and universities remains weak.
- Many campuses house sensitive materials and information and serve as contractors for the Department of Defense, Department of Justice, National Security Agency, other government bodies, and corporations.
- Securing chemical, biological, and radiological materials in an accessible environment, 24 hours a day, 7 days a week, creates security challenges.
- Many campuses have a substantial number of international students who entered the country through student visas. In addition, many U.S. educational institutions maintain campuses overseas.
- Responses to terrorist threats by U.S. educational institutions are varied and fragmented; there is no information exchange or clearinghouse.
- Special events (e.g., sports, graduation, lectures) draw thousands of people to campuses and create vulnerabilities.
- U.S. educational institutions should be more closely linked to local and regional emergency management plans.

□ □ □ ▬▬▬▬▬▬▬▬▬▬▬▬▬▬▬▬▬▬▬▬▬▬▬▬▬

What do you view as the top three strategies to prevent violence at school districts? How would you answer this same question for colleges and universities?

▬▬▬▬▬▬▬▬▬▬▬▬▬▬▬▬▬▬▬▬▬▬▬▬▬ □ □ □

Fire Protection at Educational Institutions

The NFPA 101 Life Safety Code (see Chapter 13) offers guidance to protect educational facilities from fire. Examples of fire hazards endangering life in places of public assembly are (1) overcrowding; (2) blocking, impairing, or locking exits; (3) storing combustibles in dangerous locations; (4) using an open flame without proper precautions; and (5) using combustible decorations. Furthermore, hazards of educational buildings vary with construction characteristics and with the age group of students. Younger students, for example, require protection different from that for older students. The NFPA Life Safety Code specifies that kindergarten and first grade rooms should be on the floor of exit discharge so that stairs do not endanger these students. Because junior and senior high schools contain laboratories, shops, and home economics rooms, these facilities should have fire-resistant construction. School kitchens require similar protection. A fire alarm system is required for all educational buildings. Most schools conduct fire drills for pupils. The Life Safety Code and many good building codes provide numerous standards for increasing fire safety.

For colleges and universities, the Life Safety Code is applied depending on building characteristics and use. If buildings are windowless, the Life Safety Code requirements for special structures are applicable. This includes automatic extinguishing systems, venting systems for smoke, and emergency lighting and power. Because many campus buildings are multistory, specific safeguards are necessary. Fire drills and training are important for residence halls and academic buildings.

☐ ☐ ☐

Career: Educational Institution Security

The primary objective of an educational institution security program is to educate the campus community on the potential for crime both on- and off-campus. The central themes of a campus crime prevention program are awareness, self-protection, and prevention. The level of violence on and around educational institutions has brought about a need for security at public and private educational institutions at both the elementary and secondary school levels. Many educational institutions operate a commissioned police department, which makes police academy training or law enforcement certification a requirement. Interested college students can often enter this field by working for campus security departments on a part-time basis.

Entry-level management positions do not require an academic degree; however, a degree, general security experience, specialty-specific experience, and professional certification are all desired. The salary range is from the low $40,000s to $50,000.

Mid-level management positions also do not require an academic degree; however, a degree, general security experience, specialty-specific experience, and professional certification are all desired.

Source: Courtesy of ASIS International. (2005). "Career Opportunities in Security." www.asisonline.org.

☐ ☐ ☐

Healthcare Institutions

The U.S. Department of Health and Human Services (HHS) is responsible for public health, healthcare, and food (other than meat, poultry, and eggs, which is the responsibility of the U.S. Department of Agriculture). The following information on healthcare challenges and initiatives is from *The National Strategy for the Physical Protection of Critical Infrastructures and Key Assets* (White House, 2003: 41). The public health sector is vast and diverse. It consists of state and local health departments, hospitals, health clinics, mental health facilities, nursing homes, blood-supply facilities, laboratories, mortuaries, and pharmaceutical stockpiles. Hospitals, clinics, and public health systems play a critical role in mitigating and recovering from the effects of natural disasters or deliberate attacks on the homeland (Figure 17-6). Physical damage to these facilities or disruption of their operations could prevent a full, effective response and

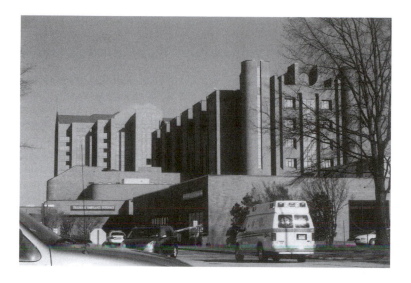

FIGURE 17-6 Healthcare institutions play a critical role in mitigating and recovering from the effects of natural disasters or deliberate attacks on the homeland. Physical damage to these facilities or disruption of their operations could prevent a full, effective response and exacerbate the outcome of an emergency.

exacerbate the outcome of an emergency. Even if a hospital or public health facility were not the direct target of a terrorist strike, it could be significantly impacted by secondary contamination involving chemical, radiological, or biological agents. In addition to established medical networks, the United States depends on several highly specialized laboratory facilities and assets, especially those related to disease control and vaccine development and storage, such as the HHS Centers for Disease Control and Prevention, the National Institutes of Health, and the National Strategic Stockpile.

Public Health Sector Challenges

Public health workers are accustomed to placing themselves in harm's way during an emergency. They may be unlikely, however, to view themselves as potential targets of terrorist acts. Most hospitals and clinics are freely accessible facilities that provide the public with an array of vital services. This free access, however, also makes it difficult to identify potential threats or prevent malicious entry into these facilities. This fact, combined with a lack of means and standards to recognize and detect potentially contaminated individuals, can have an important impact on facility security and emergency operations.

Another significant challenge is the variation in structural and systems design within our hospitals and clinics. On one hand, so-called **immune buildings** have built-in structural design elements that help prevent contamination and the spread of infectious agents to the greatest extent possible. Such features include controlled airflow systems, isolation rooms, and special surfaces that eliminate infectious agents on contact. At the other extreme are buildings with relatively little built-in environmental protection.

Protection of this category of facility presents the greatest challenge. During an epidemic, infectious individuals who continue to operate in the community at large may pose a significant public health risk. The sector needs to develop comprehensive protocols governing the isolation of infectious individuals during a crisis.

Additional public health sector challenges relate to the maintenance, protection, and distribution of stockpiles of critical emergency resources. Currently, other than the National Strategic Stockpile, there are limited resources for rotating and replenishing supplies of critical materials and medicines. Since pharmaceutical companies are taxed on their product inventories, they try to avoid stockpiling finished goods and meet demand through "just-in-time" manufacturing.

The **Emergency Medical Treatment and Active Labor Act** requires hospitals to treat patients requiring emergency care regardless of their insurance status. Disaster situations involving mass casualties tax the resources of critical facilities in terms of labor, medical supplies, and space. As patients are stabilized, it is often necessary to transfer them to other hospitals to free up critical resources for newly arriving casualties. With respect to disaster victims without insurance, however, once treatment is no longer an emergency, hospitals are not bound to treat them. As a result, many second-tier, noncritical hospitals will not or cannot accept uninsured patients, thereby requiring the critical hospital by default to continue nonemergency treatment. Additionally, privacy rules mandated in the Health Insurance Portability and Accountability Act should be reviewed to determine whether they could prevent the sharing of critical data in the event of an epidemic.

Existing security challenges have focused the public health sector on assessing its ability to deliver critical services during a crisis. Many hospitals, however, are faced with operating at limited profit margins and, therefore, have difficulty making appropriate security investments. Finally, specialized medical and pharmaceutical laboratories merit special attention—particularly those handling highly toxic or infectious agents. These facilities are mission-critical with respect to identifying hazardous agents should an attack or outbreak occur. These facilities also enable the containment, neutralization, and disposal of such hazardous materials. Overcoming the protection challenges associated with securing these specialized assets is a top priority.

Public Health Sector Initiatives

Public health HHS protection initiatives are as follows:

- Work with state and local public health officials to identify, appoint, train, and prepare recognized subject matter experts to speak on behalf of the public health sector in times of crisis (e.g., pandemic or bioterrorism).
- Review mission-critical operations, establish protection priorities, and ensure adequate security and redundancy for critical laboratory facilities and services. In partnership with state health departments, HHS and DHS will identify and prioritize national-level critical hospitals and medical centers, as well as their most important component facilities, systems, and services.
- Assist public health sector officials to identify requirements for robust surveillance systems and coordinate links between public health monitoring facilities and healthcare delivery systems.
- Work with state and local health officials to develop isolation and quarantine standards to improve the protection of the unaffected population during a public health crisis. HHS will also work with state and local health officials during consequence management planning to set priorities for the deployment of vaccination and prophylaxis resources in the event of a terrorist incident involving biological or chemical weapons.
- HHS and DHS will work with the healthcare sector to enable the protection of stockpiles of medical supplies and other critical materials, distribution systems, and the critical systems of medical institutions, including basic surveillance capabilities necessary for tracking the spread of diseases and toxic agents. Additionally, HHS will identify providers of critical resources and ensure a ready stockpile of vital medicines for use in an emergency.
- Examine legal and regulatory impediments that could prevent critical health facilities from providing critical services during a crisis. HHS will also explore possible incentives to encourage increased investment in the physical security of facilities in the public health sector.

The Scope of Threats and Legal Responsibilities of Healthcare Institutions

Hospitals, nursing homes, and other healthcare institutions possess specific crime, fire, and safety weaknesses that require countermeasures. Violence is a recurring problem. A large inventory of consumable items is located within healthcare buildings, including food, medical supplies, linens, drugs, and wheelchairs. Thousands of meals and prescriptions are served each day in many of these locations. Assorted crimes are a threat (e.g., assault, theft, kickbacks to purchasers, fraud). Drugs are susceptible not only to internal theft but also to robbery. Expensive medical and office equipment and patient and employee belongings are other tempting targets for offenders. Moreover, the safety of people is a high priority. There is a never-ending flow of employees (doctors, nurses, assorted specialists, nonprofessional support personnel, and volunteers), patients, visitors, salespeople, and repair technicians. A large number of female employees need protection, especially during nighttime shift changes. Patients are particularly vulnerable at all times because of their limited physical capabilities. What makes protection difficult is that these institutions remain open 24 hours a day.

Emergency plans and special equipment are necessary in case of fire, explosion, accident, natural disaster, bomb threat, strike, and other emergencies pertaining to homeland security (explained previously). Flammable medical gases and oxygen support combustion, which necessitates safety precautions. Accumulations of trash as well as safety in the operating rooms are additional considerations.

A host of federal and state laws impacts the healthcare industry. Examples are HIPPA, SOX, and the NLRA (see Chapter 4). The **Health Insurance Portability and Accountability Act of 1996 (HIPAA)** is a law designed to improve healthcare services delivery, lower costs by reducing paper records and claims, enhance electronic transmission of documents, secure medical data and patient information, prevent errors in the healthcare system, and transfer funds more securely.

HIPPA presents a variety of issues for healthcare executives, as explained by Tomes (2005: 75–78). These issues include how to know when security methods are sufficient under the risk analysis and risk management sections of the regulation and how to respond to police demands for patient information that the privacy regulation protects. The regulations require that companies perform a risk analysis to identify risks to the confidentiality, integrity, and availability of the health information they control. Security measures must be documented. They include specific technologies (e.g., encryption) or specific procedures. Guidance is sure to follow from litigation.

HIPPA permits companies to release protected health information to a law enforcement agency under certain specified conditions. For example, a hospital must report certain types of wounds, such as gunshot wounds. Requested information must be disclosed in compliance with a court order, warrant, or judicially or grand-jury-issued subpoena or an administrative subpoena or summons. In addition, information must be disclosed for the purpose of identifying or locating a suspect, fugitive, material witness, or missing person. The HIPPA law preempts federal or state law that is contrary to the statute unless the federal or state law provides more privacy protection. Examples of such laws include statutes covering information on sexually transmitted and communicable diseases, mental health confidentiality, and alcohol and drug abuse confidentiality.

Strategies for Healthcare Institutions

Accountability and Inventory Control

Because much of the inventory in healthcare institutions can be used by employees at home or sold to others, accountability and inventory control can minimize shrinkage. For expensive items (e.g., medical equipment), an asset tracking system (electronic article surveillance) can be useful. Imaginative preventive techniques should also be applied where possible. For example, Russell L. Colling (2001: 459–460), in *Hospital and Healthcare Security*, explains that the loss of hospital scrub suits, which are a popular garment worn by a variety of people, can be reduced by issuing them to individuals, and a soiled suit can be exchanged for a clean one through either an issue window or an automatic uniform dispenser. The dispenser, similar to an ATM, credits a returned suit and issues a clean one; this is another use of an automated access card. Linen and other property permanently imprinted with the name of the institution will also aid shrinkage control efforts. Disposable items (e.g., paper towels) are less expensive but also subject to pilferage. Soiled-linen chutes are convenient hiding places for stolen goods. Offenders often wrap stolen merchandise in dirty linen for later recovery. Daily inspection of soiled linens and trash collection and disposal systems ensures that these theft techniques are impeded.

Auditing

When accounting and other safeguards are checked for deviations, loss prevention programs are strengthened. Are patients being properly billed? How accurate are accounts receivable and accounts payable records? In the food service operation, how careful are the controls over the ordering of foods and food preparation and distribution? The food service area is a prime location for theft. Every loss prevention measure should be audited to make sure it is functioning as designed.

□ □ □ ▬▬▬▬▬▬▬▬▬▬▬▬▬▬▬▬▬▬▬▬▬▬▬▬

Healthcare Fraud

The FBI, along with its federal, state, and local law enforcement partners, the Centers for Medicare and Medicaid Services (CMS), and other public and private sector groups, work together to address fraud and abuse in healthcare. Fraudulent billings to healthcare programs, both public and private, are estimated to be between 3% and 10% of total healthcare expenditures. The problem is expected to rise as people live longer. In 2004, healthcare costs were about $2.1 trillion, which is 15.5% of the Gross Domestic Product. By 2012, CMS estimates total healthcare spending to exceed $3.1 trillion. To combat the fraud, the FBI and the healthcare industry apply data mining techniques to identify patterns of fraud and system weaknesses. An example of one significant case of fraud occurred with Hospital Corporation of America, Inc., the nation's largest for-profit hospital chain. The corporation pleaded guilty to defrauding government healthcare programs. Whistle-blowers had previously accused the corporation of filing false claims for reimbursement from Medicare and Medicaid government health insurance programs, as well as paying kickbacks to doctors for referrals. After a final settlement announced in 2003, the combination of civil fines and criminal penalties resulted in a total of $1.7 billion that the corporation agreed to pay the federal government (Federal Bureau of Investigation, Financial Crimes Section, 2005: C1–C8).

▬▬▬▬▬▬▬▬▬▬▬▬▬▬▬▬▬▬▬▬▬▬▬▬ □ □ □

Applicant Screening

Both professional and nonprofessional staff members cause losses. Equipment and supplies may accompany doctors from a hospital to their private practice. Any other type of employee (and patients and visitors) may steal. An enormous number of items are unguarded at healthcare facilities. Quality applicant screening prevents the hiring of thieves, quacks, and drug and sex offenders.

Access Controls

When entrances to a healthcare facility are limited, unauthorized entry is hindered. Uniformed officers should be stationed at each entrance. Of course, emergency exits are a necessity for safety; but alarms on these doors will deter usage. Identification badges worn by employees assist in recognition by other employees. Outside individuals on the premises (e.g., contractors or technicians) should be issued ID badges.

Koverman (2006: 30–35) writes that access controls in hospitals are especially challenging and require a "tricky balance between appropriate levels of security and appropriate levels of accessibility." The control of visitors must be handled with compassion and empathy. Visitors wanting to see an ill family member are often emotionally upset. Furthermore, the patient's recovery can be aided by visits from loved ones. These factors must be stressed in healthcare training programs. Many locations issue visitor passes to avoid overcrowding in patients' rooms and to inhibit a variety of problems such as the deviant who dresses like a doctor to "examine" female patients.

Patrols, CCTV

Surveillance of interior and exterior areas, with patrols and CCTV, deters crime. Good lighting is an integral aspect of this effort. Large medical centers have a command center for communications and CCTV observation. More intense vigilance usually is needed at night, but assorted crimes are possible at any time. Offenders may break into automobiles in parking lots to obtain valuables. Doctors' automobiles are particularly vulnerable, especially if medical bags are left behind. Aggressive patrolling and surveillance are required during shift changes; women should be escorted to their vehicles to foil attempts at purse snatching, assault, or rape. During slow periods when traffic is limited, uniformed officers should resume patrolling while checking for safety hazards.

Some locations have chosen sports jackets or blazers for loss prevention personnel to create a "nonpolice image." Nevertheless, most facilities seem to favor uniforms to provide a "police image" to reinforce crime deterrence and to signify that the location is protected.

The arming of personnel is controversial. Some medical institutions issue firearms to all officers, whereas other locations issue them only to those assigned to external areas.

Emergency Room

At least one officer must be stationed in the emergency room at all times. Depending on the crime rate, officers may have to be armed; equipped with bullet-resistant vests; and prepared to frisk people, confiscate weapons, and make arrests. Signs prohibiting weapons should be posted as well as notices of metal detectors. Disturbances occur regularly in the emergency room in busy hospitals. Verbal arguments, assaults, and destruction of property may be caused by belligerent patients, visitors who are intoxicated, and rival gangs. Disturbances recurrently are the result of long waiting periods before treatment. Medical personnel can reduce a portion of disturbances if they adequately explain the reasons for delays. Emergency treatment areas should be sealed off if necessary and panic buttons available.

Newborn Nursery

Infant abduction is a particularly disturbing problem for parents, employees, and police. In 1983, the **National Center for Missing and Exploited Children** (NCMEC) created a database on infant abduction that led to the creation of guidelines for hospitals. The NCMEC Web site offers a variety of helpful information for parents, police, and attorneys. Those who abduct infants from hospitals often impersonate medical staff and "case" the nursery prior to the crime. Countermeasures include taking footprints of infants, requiring photo ID cards of all employees and volunteers, restricting visitors, using CCTV, installing an electronic surveillance system that detects infant bracelets, and not releasing birth information. If abduction occurs, hospital staff should immediately notify the police, the FBI, and the NCMEC; conduct a search; check exit points; and begin a thorough investigation. Such "target hardening" at hospitals can displace kidnapping to areas outside the hospital and to the home of the infant. Parents should protect the infant by, for example, not placing pretty bows or a sign outside the home to signify a birth.

□ □ □ ▬▬▬▬▬▬▬▬▬▬▬▬▬▬▬▬▬▬▬▬▬▬▬▬▬▬▬▬▬▬▬▬▬▬▬▬▬

Healthcare Violence and OSHA Guidelines

Certain locations at healthcare facilities have an increased chance of violence. They include emergency rooms, children's hospitals, psychiatric units, and home healthcare. To illustrate, a child in a pediatric unit may require protection following abuse or to prevent kidnapping. If the child's parents are estranged, family strife may spill into the hospital. Protection methods include providing crisis intervention training for healthcare employees, gathering information on the family at the preadmission stage, checking court papers showing parental rights or restraining orders, posting photos of persons to be barred from visiting the child, placing a false name on the nameplate of the patient's room, installing a CCTV camera in the hall near the child's room, and increasing patrols and access controls.

Because of violent crime at healthcare facilities, the federal government and certain states (e.g., California and New Jersey) have developed safety standards to prevent violence in the workplace. On the federal level, the Occupational Safety and Health Administration (1996) published *Guidelines for Preventing Workplace Violence for Health Care and Social Service Workers*. According to OSHA, "All employers have a general duty to provide their employees with a workplace free from recognized hazards likely to cause death or serious physical harm" and "Employers can be cited for violating the General Duty Clause if there is a recognized hazard of workplace violence in their establishments and they do nothing to prevent or abate it." The OSHA guidelines are advisory in nature and focus on management commitment, worksite analysis, hazard prevention and control (e.g., physical security), education and training, recordkeeping, and evaluation.

Pharmacy Protection and Robbery
A small percentage of the population is addicted to drugs and will do anything to obtain them. Colling (2001: 443–450) notes that narcotics addiction among doctors and nurses is a much more serious problem than recognized, and healthcare facilities are a major source of illegal drug traffic involving legal drugs. There have been instances in which medical personnel have withheld drugs from a patient for their own use or sale. One technique is to substitute flour for medication. Hospital administrators are reluctant to report these acts for fear of lawsuits. Another technique is to write a phony prescription or alter an existing one. In one case, a hospital pharmacist diverted thousands of dollars of drugs to his retail drugstore.

The **Controlled Substances Act of 1970**, amended several times, provides the legal foundation for the manufacture, importation, possession, and distribution of certain drugs. The Drug Enforcement Administration (DEA) enforces the act. All states regulate pharmacies.

Pharmacy losses can be prevented through strict accountability and inventory controls. For the protection of the pharmacy, cashiering operations, and the business office, the following measures will deter burglary, robbery, and other crimes: (1) intrusion and holdup alarms integrated with CCTV, (2) bullet-resistant glass, (3) access controls, (4) patrols, and (5) consideration of removing signs identifying the location.

Locker Rooms
Men and women who work in healthcare institutions are accustomed to using separate locker rooms before, during, and after shifts. Locker rooms ordinarily are located in the basement or remote locations. CCTV and patrols can be applied to areas just outside locker rooms. Panic buttons that signal trouble are useful within locker rooms. Loss prevention personnel should conduct occasional locker inspections to deter assorted problems.

Mortuary
The mortuary has been the site of morbid crimes. People, including relatives of the deceased, have stolen jewelry directly from cadavers. Gold dental work has been extracted with a pocket-knife. The rare sexual perversion called necrophilia (i.e., sexual activity with a corpse) is a possibility in the mortuary. In addition, there are cases in which the wrong body was taken away for burial. A complete inventory should be conducted of the personal property of the deceased soon after death. Witnesses and appropriate paperwork should be a part of this procedure.

Patient Property
A recurring puzzle sometimes accompanies patients prior to discharge: jewelry or other personal property is missing. In addition to theft, it is possible that the property is nonexistent,

is at the patient's home, or has been misplaced. A few prevention measures are cost effective. Forms prior to admission can contain a suggestion for the patient to keep valuables at home. The admitting form can contain a statement advising the patient to deposit valuables in a security envelope. These envelopes have the same serial numbers on both the envelope and the receipt. Valuables are inserted and the envelope is sealed in the presence of the patient. The patient and the clerk sign and date both the envelope and the receipt. An adequate safe is needed for these valuables.

Standards and Professionalism

The **Joint Commission on Accreditation of Healthcare Organizations (JCAHO)** is a dominant force in promoting standards in the healthcare field that affect funding from government. JCAHO standard EC 1.4 addresses how hospitals should provide a secure environment for patients, staff, and visitors. Specific written plans for security are required for the "environment of care" (EC) standards. They include maintaining a security management program and addressing security concerns regarding protecting people and assets. Other standards focus on, for example, training and emergency management.

The professionalism of those who protect healthcare institutions is enhanced through the International Association for Healthcare Security and Safety (IAHSS), which was founded in 1968. It is a not-for-profit organization for hospital security and safety administrators. The IAHSS administers the Certified Healthcare Protection Administrator (CHPA) credential and publishes *The Journal of Healthcare Protection Management*. Two important purposes of this group are the development of standards for healthcare security practices and training/certifications. For the various certifications, students study IAHSS manuals and JCAHO security standards.

Fire and Other Disasters

A multitude of fire codes and standards for healthcare institutions emanate from local, state, and federal agencies. The NFPA 101 Life Safety Code refers to a "total concept approach" to the fire problem, consisting of construction, detection/suppression, and staff presence. NFPA 99 Standard for Healthcare Facilities establishes criteria to minimize hazards from fire, explosion, and electricity. Almost all states promote safety through minimum standards and healthcare licensing requirements. The federal government, for example, adopted the Life Safety Code for Medicare and Medicaid regulations in healthcare institutions.

JCAHO has worked closely with the federal government to provide adequate patient care and safety. Legislation has stated that hospitals must meet federal requirements for health and safety if they are accredited by JCAHO. All healthcare locations are subject to OSHA, except those that are federal. At times, overlapping regulations produce confusion between JCAHO and OSHA mandates.

A healthcare facility may require approval for life safety from multiple authorities having jurisdiction (AHJ), meaning the official office enforcing the code. These authorities include the state fire marshal, local building official, fire department, state healthcare licensing agency, JCAHO, U.S. Department of Health and Human Services-Health Care Financing Administration, and the facility's insurance carrier.

Fire protection at healthcare facilities must be a top priority, especially because of immobile patients. The early detection and suppression of fire, plus fire-resistive construction, will play major roles if patients cannot be moved and must be "defended in place." Unique characteristics of these environments must be considered in planning. For example, there is a great deal of disposables, and rubbish must be collected, stored, and eliminated properly; fireproof receptacles are useful. Flammable substances require safe storage, use, and disposal. Operating and delivery rooms are subject to static electricity, which can spark a fire if close to anesthetics. These rooms should be tested for static electricity. A full-time fire marshal, fire engineer, or loss prevention manager should be in charge of fire protection. This individual coordinates training, evacuation plans, drills, equipment evaluation and purchasing, plus other duties; in addition, he or she acts as liaison with local fire agencies.

If a WMD event should occur, healthcare workers would become **first receivers** who treat incoming victims. OSHA information assists hospitals in protecting healthcare workers and creating emergency plans for worst-case scenarios and training. It also offers suggestions for **personal protective equipment (PPE)**. Examples are gloves, mask, and protective eyewear, or a head-to-toes protective suit and respirator. Besides healthcare workers, security officers at hospitals need personal protection and training so they do not become victims themselves. As first receivers treat victims, security officers will likely maintain order and control traffic and access by victims who may be in a state of panic and need to be decontaminated and quarantined. In addition, it is possible that the facility will become overwhelmed, civil disturbance may occur, and the hospital will become a disaster site.

The **Public Health Security and Bioterrorism Preparedness and Response Act of 2002** recognizes emergency room workers as major responders to the problem of terrorism, and it promotes a national curriculum of training to respond to biological agents. It also provides for a real-time surveillance system among emergency rooms, state public health departments, and the **Centers for Disease Control and Prevention (CDC)**—the lead agency, in HHS, if a communicable disease outbreak occurs.

☐ ☐ ☐ ▬▬▬▬▬▬▬▬▬▬▬▬▬▬▬▬▬▬▬▬▬

What do you think is the most serious risk facing healthcare institutions? What are your solutions?

☐ ☐ ☐ ▬▬▬▬▬▬▬▬▬▬▬▬▬▬▬▬▬▬▬▬▬

Career: Healthcare Security

Security in the healthcare industry provides opportunities not only in hospitals, but also in long-term care facilities, clinics, and nursing homes. The healthcare industry is a multifaceted, challenging field, which includes dealing with immobile, unconscious, emotionally disturbed, and distraught patients and their families, and providing security to gift shops, cafeterias, parking lots, pharmacies, and emergency departments. Employee investigation plays a substantial role in asset protection. The work environment is oriented toward patient protection and service, and may include safety and community emergency management. Security opportunities may include being a security supervisor, security director, or public relations person in charge of interacting with the medical community as well as patients.

Entry-level management positions require a bachelor's degree in security or a related field, or equivalent experience. Two years of security supervisory experience are required, and experience in healthcare security or customer service is desired. In addition, training and experience in business management and human resources are desired. Salary range is $30,000 to $50,000.

Mid-level management positions require a bachelor's degree in security or a related field, or equivalent experience. A master's degree is desired. Five years as a senior supervisor or entry-level manager are required, and experience in healthcare security or customer service is desired. In addition, training and experience in business management and human resources are desired. The CHPA and the CPP are preferred designations.

Source: Courtesy of ASIS International. (2005). "Career Opportunities in Security." www.asisonline.org.

☐ ☐ ☐

□ □ □ ▬▬▬▬▬▬▬▬▬▬▬▬▬▬▬▬▬▬▬▬▬

NFPA 730 Guide for Premises Security contains guidelines for retail businesses, educational institutions, healthcare institutions, and other facilities.

□ □ □ ▬▬▬▬▬▬▬▬▬▬▬▬▬▬▬▬▬▬▬▬▬

Search the Web
Here are Web sites relevant to this chapter:

American Bankers Association: www.aba.com
Centers for Disease Control and Prevention: www.cdc.gov
Center for the Prevention of School Violence: www.ncdjjdp.org/cpsv/
International Association of Campus Law Enforcement Administrators: www.iaclea.org/
International Association for Healthcare Security & Safety: www.iahss.org/
Joint Commission on Accreditation of Healthcare Organizations (JCAHO): www.jointcommission.org/
Loss Prevention Research Council: www.lpresearch.org/index.php
National Association of School Resource Officers: www.nasro.org
National Center for Missing and Exploited Children: www.missingkids.com/
National Crime Prevention Council: www.ncpc.org/
National Retail Federation: www.nrf.com
National Shoplifting Prevention Coalition: www.shopliftingprevention.org
School Violence Resource Center: www.svrc.net
The Loss Prevention Foundation: www.losspreventioncertification.com
U.S. Department of Health and Human Services: www.hhs.gov
U.S. Department of Homeland Security: www.dhs.gov
U.S. Secret Service: www.secretservice.gov
University of Florida, National Retail Security Survey: www.crim.ufl.edu/research/srp/NRSS_2001.pdf

▬▬▬▬▬▬▬▬▬▬▬▬▬▬▬▬▬▬▬▬▬ □ □ □

Case Problems

17A. A group of eight merchants who own retail stores at a small shopping center have hired you as a loss prevention consultant. These people are interested in reduced losses and increased profits. Their loss problems are employee theft, losses at the POS, shoplifting, robbery, and burglary. As a loss prevention consultant, what is your plan? Do not forget, you must earn your fee, satisfy the merchants to develop a good reputation, and produce effective loss prevention measures that will reduce losses and increase profits.

17B. As a regional loss prevention manager for a retail chain, you are growing increasingly suspicious of one of the stores in your region. The store manager and employees constantly state that the high shrinkage of 4% at the store is due to shoplifters. The manager argues that very little shrinkage results from damaged merchandise or employee theft. EAS and CCTV systems are functioning at the store, but no security personnel are employed; a variety of nonsecurity employees maintain and operate these systems. What action do you take?

17C. As a bank security director you are faced with the challenge of an upsurge of customer robberies at automated teller machines and after-hours depositories (when retail managers deposit daily sales income). What do you do?

17D. You are a school district security director, and it has been brought to your attention that students in the high school, in certain classes, routinely bring fast food, cell phones, and other electronic devices to their desks and intimidate teachers into permitting these items. The school district superintendent has asked you to work on a solution to this problem. What do you do?

17E. You are a hospital security director, and your new challenge is to prevent the admittance of recidivist patients who fake illness to secure shelter and food. These individuals are often living on the street and use a different identity each time they seek admittance to the emergency room. The problem seems to increase during the cold winter months. What do you do?

17F. Of the four types of entities in this chapter, select two and describe why the ones you chose are unique in terms of loss problems and prevention strategies.

17G. Choose two types of entities from this chapter. For each, establish a priority list of the five most important measures to counter losses. Explain the reasoning behind each ranked list.

17H. Choose two types of entities from this chapter. (1) Refer to additional sources to gather further information, and (2) explain why you would prefer to work in one rather than the other. Maintain a bibliography.

17I. What do you think is the most demanding of the entities discussed in this chapter for a loss prevention manager? Justify your answer.

References

Abdullaev, N. (2004). "Beslan, Russia...Terror! In The Schoolhouse! *Homeland Defense Journal*, 2 (September).

Anderson, T. (2001). "Up and Running." *Security Management*, 45 (January).

Altheide, D., et al. (1978). "The Social Meanings of Employee Theft." *Crime at the Top*. New York: J. B. Lippincott Co.

Beaulieu, E. (2005). "Theft Operation 'Disturbs' Retailers." *Security Director News*, 2 (February).

Bednarz, A. (2006). "Online Merchants Will Lose $3 Billion to Fraud in 2006." *NETWORK WORLD* (November 14). http://www.networkworld.com/news/2006/111406-online-merchants-fraud. html, retrieved February 12, 2007.

Brunker, M. (2001). "Internet Merchants Fight Back." *MSNBC* (May 16). http://www.msnbc. com/news/377221.asp, retrieved May 16, 2001.

Cogswell, P. (2006). "Store-Value Card Fraud: A House of Cards?" *Loss Prevention*, 5 (November-December).

Colling, R. (2001). *Hospital and Healthcare Security*. Boston: Butterworth-Heinemann.

Davis, R. et al. (2006). "An Assessment of the Preparedness of Large Retail Malls to Prevent and Respond to Terrorist Attack." www.asisonline.org/foundation/noframe/mall.pdf, retrieved September 26, 2006.

Decker, S. (2000). "Increasing School Safety through Juvenile Accountability Programs." Washington, D.C.: U.S. Department of Justice.

DiLonardo, R. (2006). "Industry News." *Loss Prevention*, 5 (May-June).

Federal Bureau of Investigation. (2006). *Crime in the United States 2005*. http://www.fbi. gov/ucr/05cius/data/table_01.html, retrieved October 2, 2006.

Federal Bureau of Investigation. (2005). "Financial Institution Fraud and Failure Report." http://www.fbi.gov/publications/financial/2005fif/fif05.htm, retrieved October 4, 2006.

Federal Bureau of Investigation. (2007). "2006 Bank Robbery Statistics Released." http:// seattle.fbi.gov/pressrel/2007/pr010907.htm, retrieved February 24, 2007.

Federal Bureau of Investigation, Financial Crimes Section. (2005). "Financial Crimes Report to the Public." http://www.fbi.gov/publications/financial/fcs_report052005/fcs_ report052005.htm, retrieved March 6, 2007.

"First LP Certification Program Launches June 4th" (2007). *Loss Prevention e-Newsletter*, 3 (May 31). newsletter@losspreventionmagazine.com, retrieved June 1, 2007.

Fisher, B., and Sloan, J. (1993). "University Response to the Campus Security Act of 1990: Evaluating Programs Designed to Reduce Campus Crime." *Journal of Security Administration*, 16.

Friedrick, J. (2006). "Risk of Fraud, Theft Keeps Security Directors at Banks on Their Toes." *Security Director News*, 3 (October).

Gabbidon, S., and Patrick, P. (2005). "Characteristics and Outcomes of Shoplifting Cases in the U.S. Involving Allegations of False Arrest." *Security Journal*, 18.

Gaur, N., and Gilliland, W. (2006). "New Customer Touch Points." *Information Week* (June 1). http://www.informationweek.com/, retrieved February, 13, 2007.

Gill, M., Bilby, C., and Turbin, V. (1999). "Retail Security: Understanding What Deters Shop Thieves." *Journal of Security Administration*, 22.

Gips, M. (2007). "EAS Not a Silver Bullet." *Security Management*, 51 (March).

Gips, M. (1997). "Shoplifter Shakedown?" *Security* (January).

Harwood, M. (2007). "Preventing the Next Campus Shooting." *Security Management*, 51 (August).

Hayes, R. (2006). "Store Design and LP." *Loss Prevention*, 5 (March-April).

Hollinger, R. (2006). "Both Good News and Bad News." *Loss Prevention*, 5 (November-December).

Hollinger, R., and Langton, L. (2006). "2005 National Retail Security Survey, Final Report." www.crim.ufl.edu/research/srp/srp.htm, retrieved February 18, 2007.

Jaeger, S. (2001). "Crime Concerns on Campus." *Security Technology & Design*, 12 (March).

Kelly, M. (2000). "Essentials of Retail Loss Prevention." *Security Technology & Design*, 10 (June).

Koverman, R. (2006). "Assessing and Securing the Hospital Environment." *Security Technology & Design*, 16 (May).

Langton, L., and Hollinger, R. (2005). "Correlates of Crime Losses in the Retail Industry." *Security Journal*, 18.

Levy, M., and Weitz, B. (2001). *Retailing Management*, 4th ed. New York: McGraw-Hill Irwin.

Meadows, R. (2007). *Understanding Violence and Victimization*, 4th ed. Upper Saddle River, NJ: Pearson Prentice Hall.

Occupational Safety and Health Administration. (1996). *Guidelines for Preventing Workplace Violence for Health Care and Social Service Workers*. Washington, D.C.: U.S. Department of Labor.

Office of Postsecondary Education. (2001). "The Incidence of Crime on the Campuses of U.S. Postsecondary Education Institutions." http://www.ed.gov/PressReleases/01–2001/011901m.html, retrieved March 1, 2007.

Palmer, W. (2006). "Considerations for Evaluating EAS Source-Tagging Programs." *Loss Prevention*, 5 (September-October).

Purpura, P. (1997). *Criminal Justice: An Introduction*. Boston: Butterworth-Heinemann.

Purpura, P. (1993). *Retail Security & Shrinkage Protection*. Boston: Butterworth-Heinemann.

Schmedlen, R. (2000). "A Picture of Profiling." *Security Management*, 44 (May).

Schroeder, W. (2001). "Money Laundering." *FBI Law Enforcement Bulletin*, 70 (May).

Swartz, J. (2006). "Banks Pull Out the Big Guns to Guard Online Users." *USA Today* (November 20). http://usatoday, retrieved November 21, 2006.

Talamo, J. (2007). "Organized Retail Crime: Setting the Stage for an ORC Strategy." *Loss Prevention*, 6 (January-February).

Tomes, J. (2005). "Prescription for Data Protection." *Security Management*, 49 (April).

Toppo, G. (2006). "High-Tech School Security Is on the Rise." *USA TODAY* (October 10). http://www.usatoday.com/news/education/2006-10-09-school-security x.htm, retrieved October 10, 2006.

TwoWayMirrors.net. (2006). "Two Way Mirror FAQ." http://www.twowaymirrors.net/mirrorfaq.htm, retrieved March 8, 2006.

U.S. Department of Justice, Bureau of Justice Assistance. (2007). "Gang Resistance Education and Training." http://www.great-online.org/, retrieved February 27, 2007.

U.S. Department of Justice, Bureau of Justice Statistics. (2006). "Indicators of School Crime and Safety: 2006." http://www.ojp.usdoj.gov/bjs/abstract/iscs06.htm, retrieved February 26, 2007.

U.S. Department of Justice, Bureau of Justice Statistics. (2000). "The Sexual Victimization of College Women." http://www.ncjrs.gov/pdffiles1/nij/182369.pdf, retrieved March 3, 2007.

U.S. Department of Justice, Office of Community Oriented Policing Services. (2005). "National Summit on Campus Public Safety." Washington, DC: U.S. Department of Justice.

U.S. Drug Enforcement Administration. (2007). "Money Laundering." http://www.dea.gov/programs/money.htm, retrieved February 24, 2007.

White House. (2003). *The National Strategy for the Physical Protection of Critical Infrastructures and Key Assets* (February). www.whitehouse.gov, retrieved February 23, 2007.

Zimmerman, A. (2006). "As Shoplifters Use High-Tech Scams, Retail Losses Rise." *The Wall Street Journal* (October 25). http://online.wsj.com, retrieved October 30, 2006.

18

Topics of Concern

Objectives

After studying this chapter, the reader will be able to:

1. Discuss the problem of violence in the workplace and what can be done about it.
2. List strategies of personnel protection.
3. Describe the problems and remedies associated with substance abuse in the workplace.
4. List the methods by which an adversary might obtain information assets and list strategies of information security.
5. Explain the array of communications security.
6. Describe Technical Surveillance Countermeasures (TSCM).

KEY TERMS

- workplace violence
- OSHA's general duty clause
- workplace violence prevention program
- conflict resolution and nonviolent response
- personnel protection
- executive protection
- executive protection (or personnel protection) program
- country risk ratings
- creature of habit
- safe room
- substance abuse
- anti-substance abuse program for the workplace
- Anti-Drug Abuse Act of 1988
- specimen validity testing
- trace detection
- alcoholic
- psychological dependence
- addiction
- tolerance
- withdrawal

- information security
- information assets
- espionage
- business espionage
- government espionage
- trade secret
- patent
- trademark
- copyright
- corporate intelligence
- competitive intelligence
- Economic Espionage Act of 1996
- reverse engineering
- "Four Faces of Business Espionage"
- pretext interview
- information security program
- Operations Security (OPSEC)
- communications security
- TEMPEST
- electronic surveillance
- wiretapping
- Technical Surveillance Countermeasures (TSCM)

Workplace Violence

Two important questions on workplace violence are (1) how should it be defined, and (2) how should it be measured? The definition of workplace violence affects not only how it is measured but also its cost. As the definition expanded from "one employee attacks another" to "any violence that occurs on the job" so, too, did the cost.

ASIS International (2005: 8) published the *Workplace Violence Prevention and Response Guideline*. It states: "Any definition of workplace violence must be broad enough to encompass the full range of behaviors that can cause injury, damage property, impede the normal course of work, or make workers, managers, and customers fear for their safety." The *Guideline* defines **workplace violence** as follows: "Workplace violence refers to a broad range of behaviors falling along a spectrum that, due to their nature and/or severity, significantly affect the workplace, generate a concern for personal safety, or result in physical injury or death." At the low end of the spectrum is disruptive and emotionally abusive behavior that creates anxiety and adversely affects the working environment. Next along the spectrum are words or actions that are intimidating, frightening, or threatening and create a concern for personal safety. At the high end of the spectrum is violent behavior.

Kenny (2005a: 45–56) emphasizes that while threats may not result in physical injury, they can leave victims traumatized and fearful. In addition, threats can harm productivity and "serve as the catalyst for progressively more dangerous behaviors." Kenny adds, "Those who ignore, misunderstand or fail to take threats seriously miss an opportunity to identify, diffuse or resolve workplace problems." Research by Kenny (2005b: 55–66) found that women were more likely to be victimized.

The University of Iowa (2001), in a report entitled "Workplace Violence: A Report to the Nation," found that 2 million Americans are victims of workplace violence each year. The report divided workplace violence into four categories: criminal intent (e.g., robbery), customer/client (e.g., health care environment), worker-on-worker, and personal relationship (e.g., domestic violence).

The U.S. Department of Labor (2006) reported 480 homicides in private industry in 2005, with 489 in 2004, and 561 in 2003. In 2005, nearly 5% of the 7.1 million private industry business establishments in the United States had an incident of workplace violence. About a third of these establishments reported that the incident had a negative impact on their workforce. Service providing industries reported much higher percentages of criminal, customer, and domestic violence than goods-producing industries. State government reported higher percentages of all types of workplace violence than did local government or private industry. Thirty-two percent of all state government workplaces reported some form of workplace violence. The higher reported incidence of violence in state and local government workplaces may be attributed to their work environments. These workplaces reported much higher percentages of working directly with the public, having a mobile workplace, working with unstable or violent persons, working in high crime areas, guarding valuable goods or property, and working in community based settings than did private industry.

Workplace violence is costly to businesses. Losses reach into the billions of dollars each year and include medical and psychological care, lost wages, property damage, lost company goodwill, and impact on employee turnover and hiring (Hughes, 2001: 69).

Obviously, incidents of workplace violence (e.g., homicides, assaults, rapes) occurred before increased attention focused on the problem in the early 1990s. What we have witnessed is a change in the way the problem is perceived and counted. This is beneficial for gauging increases and decreases in the problem and as a foundation for planning protection with scarce resources. The United States has been known to maintain good statistics on a number of problems and freely publicize trends. From an international perspective, others may view the United States as the most violent society, when we may simply be the best at gathering data.

□ □ □ ▬▬▬▬▬▬▬▬▬▬▬▬▬▬▬▬▬

Do you think the United States is a violent society, or do we just maintain good data-gathering systems? Explain your viewpoint.

Legal Guidelines

There is no national law addressing violence in the workplace. OSHA has published voluntary guidelines for workers in late-night retail, healthcare, and taxicab businesses, but these guidelines are not legal requirements. Various states have enacted laws to curb violent crime at work, especially for retail establishments and healthcare settings.

ASIS, International (2005: 12) notes: "Under the federal Occupational Safety and Health Act and corresponding state statutes, each employer owes a 'general duty' to protect employees against 'recognized hazards' that are likely to cause serious injury or death. Workplace violence has been identified as one of those hazards, and both federal and state OSHA agencies have issued citations to employers under **OSHA's general duty clause** for failure to protect employees against workplace violence."

Employers not only have a legal responsibility to prevent harm to people on the premises, they must ensure that subjects under investigation are afforded legal rights. Employers who do not take measures to prevent violence in the workplace face exposure to lawsuits. Legal theories at the foundation of such lawsuits include premises liability, negligence, harassment (sexual and other forms), and respondeat superior (see Chapters 4 and 6). Workers' compensation may cover injured employees, but the exposure of employers is much greater.

Contradictions in the law make protection difficult: OSHA requires a safe working environment for employees, but the Americans with Disabilities Act (ADA) can create difficulties for an employer seeking to control an employee with a mental instability. Employees have successfully sued employers for defamation because instability was mentioned. The ADA restricts "profiling" of employees through the observation of traits thought to be potentially violent (Jaeger, 2001: 74).

Protection Methods

What follows is a list of strategies for a **workplace violence prevention program**.

1. Establish a committee to assess risks, plan violence prevention, and to respond to such incidents. Include specialists in security, human resources, psychology, and law.
2. Consider OSHA and ASIS International guidelines to curb workplace violence.
3. Establish policies (Figure 18-1) and procedures and communicate the problems of threats and violence to all employees. Include reporting requirements and procedures.
4. Avoid a strict zero tolerance policy that does not consider mitigating circumstances. Legal problems with zero tolerance may arise with cases involving harassment, labor contracts, disability, and discriminatory practices (Hershkowitz, 2004: 83–88).
5. Although human behavior cannot be accurately predicted, screen employment applicants. The ADA limits certain questions; however, these can be asked: "What was the most stressful situation you faced and how did you deal with it?" "What was the most serious incident you encountered in your work and how did you respond?"
6. Consider substance abuse testing as a strategy to prevent workplace violence. For years, Bureau of Justice Statistics data has shown a relationship between violent crime and substance abuse.
7. A history of threatening or violent behavior can help to predict its reoccurrence. The worker who becomes violent is usually a white male, between 25 and 50 years old, and has a history of interpersonal conflict and pathological blaming. He tends to be a loner and may have a mental health history of paranoia and depression. He also may have a fascination with weapons (Meadows, 2007: 121).
8. Managers and supervisors should be sensitive to disruptions in the workplace, such as terminations. Substance abuse and domestic and financial problems also can affect the workplace; and EAP is especially helpful for such problems.
9. Train managers and supervisors to recognize employees with problems and report them to the human resources department. Include training in **conflict resolution and nonviolent response**. Train in active listening skills, such as repeating to the subject the message he/she is trying to communicate and asking open-ended questions to encourage the subject to talk about his/her problems. Listen and show that you

FIGURE 18-1 Policies are an essential component of a workplace violence prevention program.

are interested in helping to resolve the problem. Do not be pulled into a verbal confrontation; do not argue. Acknowledge and validate the anger by showing empathy, not sympathy. Speak softly and slowly. Ensure that a witness is present. Maintain a safe distance, without being obvious, to provide an extra margin of safety. If a threat is made or if a weapon is shown, call the police. Consistently enforce policies.

10. Remember that outsiders (e.g., visitor, estranged spouse, and robber) may be a source of violence and protection programs must be comprehensive.

11. Ensure that a thorough and impartial investigation is conducted following a reported incident. Follow legal requirements, such as those pertaining to due process, privacy, and labor agreements.

12. If a violent incident occurs, a previously prepared crisis management plan becomes invaluable. Otherwise, a committee should be formed immediately after emergency first responders (i.e., police, EMS) complete their duties on the premises and affected employees and their families are assisted. At one major corporation, management was unprepared when the corporate security manager was shot. A committee was quickly formed to improve security and survey corporate plants. In addition to expenditures for physical security and training, an emphasis was placed on *awareness, access controls,* and *alerts* (Purpura, 1993: 150–157).

□ □ □ ▬▬

"Dozens Sue over Lockheed Shootings"
The following account of workplace violence is from a news article in *The Clarion-Ledger*, Jackson, Mississippi (Hudson, 2004: 1A). Forty-seven employees and relatives of employees filed a federal lawsuit against Lockheed Martin claiming emotional distress following the shooting of 14 people when employees were allegedly forced

back inside the plant for a "live head count." The shooting was the state's deadliest act of workplace violence when plant employee Doug Williams, 48, shot and killed six co-workers and wounded eight others prior to committing suicide. Lockheed Martin allegedly ordered employees to the canteen for a count and that is when employees supposedly walked near victim bodies. The lawsuit also claimed that Lockheed Martin failed to protect employees who complained that Williams threatened to shoot black co-workers, and that the company denied employee requests for security officers prior to the shooting. A Lockheed Martin spokesperson stated: "Lockheed Martin has been cleared of responsibility for this incident by state and federal authorities and is confident that the same conclusion will be reached by the court."

One plaintiff, Henry Odom, a 35-year employee, stated in a court affidavit that he had complained to management about fights and auto thefts at the plant and asked for security officers for the premises. The affidavit stated that Williams shot him in his left arm twice and the second shot also entered his back and punctured a lung. The affidavit noted that the plant now has armed security officers on duty.

The lawsuit claimed that three weeks prior to the shooting, Williams placed a work-issued "bootie" on his head that appeared, according to some, to resemble a Ku Klux Klan hood. Management allegedly confronted him and he supposedly left the plant angry and did not return for about a week. According to the court papers, he was permitted to return to work, but required to attend an ethics course with black co-workers. He allegedly left a meeting and told workers he was angry and going to "take care of this." He allegedly returned to the meeting, fired on some in the room, and then went to the plant floor to shoot others. The lawsuit claimed that Lockheed Martin had sufficient time to stop him and warn employees of the imminent danger he posed.

Workers' Comp Insider (Ryan, 2005) reported that a federal appeals court upheld workers compensation as the exclusive remedy for the nine surviving victims and the families of the six workers who were killed in the Lockheed Martin shooting in Meridien. Ryan noted that this would limit damages to about $150,000. Ryan reported the following: "Exclusive remedy is a strong concept that holds up under repeated legal challenges. Workers comp is no fault by its very nature, a quid pro quo arrangement in which employers agree to provide medical and wage replacement to injured workers, and in turn, this becomes the sole remedy. In all but the most unusual circumstances, employees lose the right to sue their employer for work-related injuries. Sometimes this seems unfair to a worker because benefits are paltry when stacked side by side with enormous awards from civil litigation. But when legal challenges succeed, they weaken the system's underpinnings. Workers comp is essentially a safety net, a system designed to provide the best for the most, not to provide individual redress for every wrong. When litigation is successful at piercing the exclusive remedy shield, it often involves employer misconduct that is highly egregious." ... "Many states require proof of willful intent. It must be demonstrated that the employer had substantial certainty that an injury would occur. In this case, the shooting victims and their surviving families sued the company on the basis of having been deprived of civil rights, alleging that management knew of the threat and '...knew employee Doug Williams' racist views had created a volatile work environment but did too little to defuse the situation.'"

Personnel Protection

At home and abroad, businesses have become the target for kidnappings, extortion, assassinations, bombings, and sabotage. Terrorists use these methods to obtain money for their cause, to alter business or government policies, or to change public opinion. Organized crime groups also are participants in such criminal acts, but in contrast to terrorists, their objective usually is money. It appears that successful criminal techniques employed in one country spread to other countries. This is likely to be one reason why companies are reluctant to release details of an incident or even to acknowledge it. Coca-Cola, Chase Manhattan, B. F. Goodrich, and other companies have been victimized in the past.

Personnel protection is a broad term that focuses on security methods to protect all employees and those linked to them. These links include family; customers, visitors, and contractors; and others depending on the business. **Executive protection** concentrates on security methods to protect key management personnel who are high-value targets because of their position of power and authority and their value to the business. The following paragraphs begin with an emphasis on executive protection methods that are applicable to personnel protection.

Planning

A key beginning for an **executive protection (or personnel protection) program** is to develop a crisis management plan and team. The goals are to reduce vulnerabilities and surprises and develop contingencies. The crisis management plan can consist of threat assessments, countermeasures, policies, procedures, and lines of authority and responsibility in the event of an attack. An interdisciplinary group, if cost effective, can greatly aid the program. The group could consist of top executives, the loss prevention manager, former federal agents, counterterrorism experts, political analysts, insurance specialists, and an attorney–negotiator.

The early stages of the plan, if not the preplanning stages, would be devoted to convincing senior management that executive protection is necessary. This objective can be supported through a quality research report that focuses on risks, seeks to anticipate (not predict) events, and answers the following questions: Which executives are possible targets? Where? When? Which individuals or groups may attack? What are their methods? What are the social and political conditions in the particular country? What role has the specific government played in past incidents? Were the police or military of the foreign country involved in past incidents? Such questions require research and intelligence gathering as well as cooperative ties to government agencies of the United States and other countries. (Sources of assistance are found in the Chapter 10 box, "International Perspective: Overseas Investigations.")

Country risk ratings offered by private firms that conduct research have been used by international corporations for many years. These ratings help businesses gauge risk, decide on travel plans, educate travelers, and for insurers, set premiums. There is inconsistency in how these firms reach their conclusions. Consumers should inquire on the methodology used to prepare these ratings. Firms often acquire information from analysts located globally and from open sources (Elliott, 2006: 36–38).

The U.S. Secret Service completed a study of assassinations of public figures *in the United States* during the second half of the 20th century. The findings showed that threateners do not typically make good on their threats by attacking, and attackers do not usually issue threats to the target before striking. Although threats should not be ignored, this research showed that the most serious threats are unlikely to come from those who communicate threats. So if threats are not a major signal of an attack, what are the indicators? The research found that attackers planned the attack, spoke with others about the attack, followed the target, approached the target in a controlled and secure setting, and attempted repeatedly to contact the target and visit the target's home and a location regularly visited by the target. These latter behaviors signal a probing activity to test protection and attack strategies (Bowron, 2001: 93–97).

Education and Training

Depending on the extent of the executive protection program, many people can be brought into the education and training phase. Executives, their families, and loss prevention personnel (i.e., management, bodyguards, and uniformed officers) are top priorities. However, chauffeurs, servants, gardeners, and office workers also should be knowledgeable about terrorist and other criminal techniques, and countermeasures that include awareness, prevention strategies, personal security, recognizing and reporting suspicious occurrences, the proper response to bomb threats or postal bombs, and skills such as defensive driving.

Most in-house loss prevention personnel are not experts in dealing with executive protection. Therefore, a consultant may have to be recruited.

General Protection Strategies

Gips (2007: 52–60) writes that there are three essential components of executive protection. *Threat assessments* investigate potential harm to a principal and the likelihood of attack. *Advance procedures* focus on visiting the locations where the principal is expected to visit to coordinate comprehensive security. *Operations* involve protecting the principal in the field and this entails countersurveillance (i.e., watching if anyone is observing the principal), assisting the principal with basic tasks to reduce exposure, defense, and rescue.

Principals should maintain a low profile and not broadcast their identity, affiliations, position, address, telephone number, e-mail address, net worth, or any information useful to enemies. Avoidance of publicity about future travel plans or social activities is wise. Those at risk should exercise care when communicating with others on the telephone, via e-mail or postal service, or in restaurants, and should dispose of sensitive information carefully.

Avoidance of Predictable Patterns

The famous Italian politician Aldo Moro, murdered in 1978, is a classic case of a **creature of habit**. Moro was extremely predictable. He would leave his home in the morning to attend mass at a nearby church. Shortly after 9:00 A.M., he was en route to his office. The route was the same each morning, even though plans existed for alternatives. Although five armed men guarded Moro, he met an unfortunate fate. An attack characterized by military precision enabled terrorists to block Moro's vehicle and a following police car. Then, on the narrow street, four gunmen hiding behind a hedge opened fire. Eighty rounds hit the police car. Three police officers, Moro's driver, and a bodyguard were killed. Moro was dragged by his feet from the car. Almost two months later Moro was found dead in a car in Rome.

Recognition of Tricks

A terrorist group or a criminal may attempt to gain entry to an executive's residence or office under the pretext of repairing something or checking a utility meter. Repair people and government employees can be checked, before being admitted, by telephoning the employer. School authorities should be cautioned not to release an executive's child unless they telephone the executive's family to verify the caller.

Hiring bodyguards is a growth industry for the private sector. Bodyguards should be carefully screened and trained. Other employees (e.g., servants or gardeners) surrounding an executive likewise should be screened to hinder employment of those with evil motives.

An executive personnel file should be stored in a secure location at the company's headquarters. If a kidnapping occurs, this data can be valuable to prevent deception by offenders, to aid the investigation, and to resolve the situation. Appropriate for the file are vitae for the executive, family members, and associated employees; full names, past and present addresses and telephone numbers; photographs, fingerprints, voice tapes, and handwriting samples; and copies of passports and other important documents.

Protection at Home

A survey of the executive's home will uncover physical security weaknesses. Deficiencies are corrected through investing in access controls, proper illumination, intrusion alarms, CCTV, protective dogs, and uniformed officers. Burglary-resistant locks, doors, and windows hinder offenders. Consideration should be given to the response time of reinforcements. For a high-risk family, a **safe room** is an asset. This is a fortified room in the house that contains a strong door and other difficult-to-penetrate features. A first-aid kit, rations, and a bathroom are useful amenities. A telephone, two-way radio, and panic button connected to an external monitoring station will assist those seeking help. If weapons are stored in the room, proper training for their use is necessary.

As with security in general, it is best when methods and expenditures for personnel protection remain secret to avoid providing information to an adversary. However, this may not always be possible. The public may have access to protection information. For example, the Associated Press (2006) reported that The Charles Schwab Corporation's proxy filing with the Securities and Exchange Commission revealed that $2.68 million was spent over three years to protect the CEO, Charles R. Schwab, as part of business operations. The news report stated that the firm paid for both a security system at the CEO's residence (based on recommendations of a consultant) and security prior to the installation of the system. The proxy also stated that, in 2005, Schwab earned $4.25 million in salary, bonus, and perquisites.

The following list provides some protection pointers for home and family:

1. Do not put a name on the mailbox or door of the home.
2. Have an unlisted telephone number.
3. Exercise caution when receiving unexpected packages.
4. Do not provide information to strangers.
5. Beware of unknown visitors or individuals loitering outside. Call for assistance.
6. Check windows for possible observation from outside by persons with or without binoculars. Install thick curtains.
7. Make sure windows and doors are secure at all times.
8. Educate children and adults about protection.
9. Instruct children not to let strangers in the home or to supply information to outsiders.
10. When children leave the house, be sure to ascertain where they are going and who will be with them.
11. Keep a record of the names and addresses of children's playmates.
12. Tell children to refuse rides from strangers even if the stranger says that the parents know about the pickup.
13. Provide an escort for children if necessary.
14. Teach children how to seek assistance.

Protection at the Office

As with the residential setting, physical security is important at the executive's office. A survey may reveal that modifications will strengthen executive protection. The following list offers additional ideas:

1. Office windows should be curtained and contain bullet-resistant materials.
2. Equip the desk in the office with a hidden alarm button.
3. Establish policies and procedures for incoming mail and packages.
4. Beware of access by trickery.
5. Monitor access to the office by several controls.
6. Escort visitors.
7. Access during nonworking hours, by cleaning crew or maintenance people, should be monitored by uniformed officers and CCTV.
8. Educate and train employees.

Attacks While Traveling

History has shown that terrorists have a tendency to strike when executives (and politicians) are traveling. Loss prevention practitioners should consider the following countermeasures:

1. Avoid using conspicuous limousines.
2. Maintain regular maintenance for vehicles.
3. Keep the gas tank at least half full at all times.
4. Use an armored vehicle and bullet-resistant clothing and vests.
5. Install an alarm that foils intrusion or tampering.
6. A telephone or two-way radio will facilitate communications, especially in an emergency.

7. A remote-controlled electronic car starter will enable starting the car from a distance. This will help to activate a bomb, if one has been planted, before the driver and the executive come into range.
8. Consider installing a bomb-scan device inside the auto.
9. Headlight delay devices automatically turn headlights off one minute after ignition is stopped.
10. High-intensity lights, mounted on the rear of the vehicle, will inhibit pursuers.
11. GPS can be used to track the executive's vehicle and the executive in case of kidnapping.
12. Protect auto parking areas with physical security.
13. Avoid using assigned parking spaces.
14. Keep doors, gas cap, hood, and trunk locked.
15. Practice vehicle key control.
16. Avoid a personalized license plate or company logo on vehicle.
17. Inspect outside and inside of vehicle before entering.
18. The chauffeur should have a duress signal if needed when picking up an executive.
19. Do not stop for hitchhikers, stranded motorists, accidents, or perhaps "police." It could be a trap. Use a telephone to summon aid, but keep on moving.
20. Screen and train the chauffeur and bodyguards. Include the executive and the family in training.
21. Evasive driver training is vital.
22. Have weapons in auto ready for use.
23. Maintain the secrecy of travel itineraries.
24. Be unpredictable.
25. Know routes thoroughly as well as alternative routes.
26. Use safety belts.
27. If being followed, use the telephone for assistance, continuously sound the horn or alarm, and do not stop.
28. For air travel, use commercial airlines instead of company aircraft. Unless the company institutes numerous security safeguards, the commercial means of air transportation may be safer. Use carry-on luggage to avoid lost luggage or having to wait for workers to locate luggage.
29. Request the second or third floor at a hotel to improve chances of escape in case of fire or other emergency.

Several executive protection strategies are applicable to salespeople, employees attending conferences, and others. A company should take steps to protect all employees to prevent injuries and death. Otherwise, a lawsuit or workers' compensation claim may result. Many risk managers are unaware that their workers' compensation policies do not cover employees in foreign countries (Atkinson, 2001: 19–22).

Avon Products, Inc., provides a superb illustration of an organization seeking to meet the protection needs of its employees. Initiating a global "Women and Security" program, Avon conducted extensive research on vulnerabilities of its female employees as they traveled the globe and faced greater risks than their male coworkers face. The Avon security team found that South Africa, the Philippines, Russia, and Latin America were high-risk areas for women. South Africa, for example, has one of the highest levels of sexual assault in the world. Latin America is noted for abductions at ATMs. The Avon program focused on brochures, self-defense training, and one on-one evaluations. Brochures are country-specific and include tips such as not wearing expensive-looking jewelry because street robbers do not know a genuine from fake and avoiding public restrooms, if possible, because rapists sometimes disguise themselves as females. Employees expressed a need for self-defense training, which was provided. It aims to help women avoid and deter attack. The one-on-one evaluations consist of a security staff member who observes the daily routine of the employee working overseas to offer suggestions for improved protection. The "Women and Security" program has resulted in increased safety, less anxiety, and higher productivity (Shyman, 2000: 58–62).

Kidnap Insurance

As businesses increasingly become globalized, the risk of kidnapping also increases. Corporations obtain kidnap-ransom insurance policies for protection against the huge ransoms that they might be forced to pay in exchange for a kidnapped executive. Each year millions of dollars in premiums are paid to insurance companies for these policies. Of course, the insurance company requires certain protection standards to reduce the premium. Insurance companies are reluctant to admit writing these policies because terrorists may be attracted to the insured company executive. Moreover, these policies often contain a cancellation clause if the insured company discloses the existence of the policy. Insurance should be considered one of the last strategies in a long line of defenses. Insurance acts as the "backup" loss prevention strategy.

According to the Insurance Information Institute (2007), incidents of kidnapping for ransom money are rising. Kidnap and ransom insurance is sold as part of a comprehensive business insurance package, as a stand-alone policy for individuals, and from a few insurers as part of their homeowners insurance policy. Corporate policies generally cover most kidnapping-related expenses including hostage negotiation fees, lost wages, and the ransom amount. Policies for individuals pay for the expenses of dealing with a kidnapping but do not reimburse for ransom payments.

Statistics on global kidnapping are difficult to ascertain, especially since ransom payments are kept confidential and disclosure of a payment can increase the risk of subsequent kidnappings. In addition, many cases are not reported. One insurer's brochure, containing statistics from Control Risks Group, a consulting firm, offers the following: the problem is increasing; more that 14 countries recorded cases of $25 million or more in recent years; and kidnappers usually settle for between 10% and 20% of the demand. The outcomes were listed as follows: 2% escaped; 7% were rescued; 9% resulted in death; 15% were released without payment; and 67% involved payment. Killings usually occur during abduction rather then during negotiation (Petersen International Underwriters, 2003).

□ □ □ ▬▬▬▬▬▬▬▬▬▬▬▬▬▬▬▬▬▬▬▬▬▬▬▬▬

Company Pays Terrorists to "Protect" Workers

In early 2007, Apuzzo (2007) reported that Chiquita Brands International revealed that it had agreed to a $25 million fine after admitting it paid terrorists to protect its workers in a dangerous region of Colombia. The fine was part of a plea-bargaining agreement with the U.S. Department of Justice that investigated the company's payments to right-wing paramilitaries and leftist rebels the U.S. government classifies as terrorist groups. Federal prosecutors said company executives paid about $1.7 million between 1997 and 2004 to the United Self-Defense Forces of Colombia, the National Liberation Army, and the Revolutionary Armed Forces of Colombia. Prosecutors said that Chiquita disguised the payments in company accounting records. Colombia maintains one of the highest kidnapping rates among countries of the world. Companies are known to pay protection money; however, the amount paid is impossible to ascertain. Although companies supposedly have extensive security to protect employees, terrorist groups have fought intensely in Colombia's banana growing region.

□ □ □ ▬▬▬▬▬▬▬▬▬▬▬▬▬▬▬▬▬▬▬▬▬▬▬▬▬

What is your opinion of Chiquita Brands International paying money to terrorists to protect its workers in Colombia?

▬▬▬▬▬▬▬▬▬▬▬▬▬▬▬▬▬▬▬▬▬▬▬▬▬ □ □ □

If Abduction Occurs

After abduction takes place, the value of planning and training becomes increasingly evident. Whoever receives the kidnapper's telephone call should express a willingness to cooperate. The recipient should ask to speak to the victim; this could provide an opportunity to detect a ruse. Asking questions about the hostage (e.g., birth date, mother's maiden name) to either the hostage or the kidnapper improves the chances of discovering a trick. Prearranged codes are effective. The recipient should notify appropriate authorities after the call. If a package or letter is received, the recipient should exercise caution, limit those who touch it, and contact authorities.

People who attempt to handle the kidnapping themselves can intensify the already dangerous situation. Loss prevention personnel and public law enforcement authorities (i.e., the FBI) are skilled in investigation, intelligence gathering, and negotiating. These professionals consider the safety of the hostage first and the capture of the offenders second, although the reverse is frequently true in many foreign countries.

After abduction, the company's policies for action should be instituted. These policies ordinarily answer such questions as who is to be notified, who is to inform the victim's family, what are the criteria for payment of the ransom, who will assemble the cash, and who will deliver it and how. Policies would further specify not disturbing the kidnapping site, whether or not to tap and record future calls, how to ensure absolute secrecy to outsiders, and use of a code word with the kidnappers to impede any person or group who might enter the picture for profit.

The crisis management team should be authorized to coordinate the company's response to the kidnapping. Because a terrorist act can take place at any time, the team members will have to be on call at all times.

Guidelines for the behavior of the hostage are as follows:

1. Do not struggle or become argumentative.
2. Try to remain calm.
3. Occupy your mind with all the incidents taking place.
4. Note direction of travel, length of time, speed, landmarks, noises, and odors.
5. Memorize the characteristics of the abductors (e.g., physical appearance, speech, or names).
6. Leave fingerprints, especially on glass.
7. Remember that an effort is being made to rescue you.
8. Do not escape unless the chances of success are in your favor.

Maximize Technology

Here we cover a sample of technologies that assist in the protection of people (Simovich, 2004: 73–80; Besse and Whitehead, 2000: 66–72). The Web offers input for threat assessments, planning personnel protection, and in helping to convince senior management that protection is necessary. It contains a wealth of government information that is free. Private sources are also available for a fee. Companies that provide information on political violence, terrorism, and so forth, often make the information available through telecommunication devices such as GPS systems and satellite phones; however, some countries prohibit foreigners from entering with such equipment. The Web offers opportunities to check people, businesses, trip routes, and many other subjects of inquiry. The Web also contains information of a negative nature from terrorists, activists, and hate groups. "Sucks.com" sites, such as walmartsucks.com and aolsucks.com, are used to vent at companies. A variety of intelligence can be gathered from such sites. (See Chapter 10 for government and private sector resources and Web sites.)

For advance planning, digital cameras can document travel routes, buildings, airports, etc., and images can be transmitted to headquarters for analysis. Portable, wireless alarm and CCTV systems offer protection for hotel rooms, vehicles, airplanes, and other locations. Pinhole lens cameras, built into almost anything, serve as a witness to an attack and aid in identifying and prosecuting offenders. Thermal imagers, which detect heat rather than light, can be used in total darkness to detect intruders or for search and rescue. Another portable system is the automatic external defibrillator (AED) that delivers electrical shocks to restore normal heart rate for those in cardiac arrest. The GPS system found in vehicles uses a network of satellites that transmit data to ground receivers to navigate and map routes. In addition, it can track the executive's vehicle and monitor speed, direction, and alarms transmitted from the vehicle. Cellular technology can be added to permit audio monitoring and remote start or kill of the engine. Remote systems are vulnerable to hacking, so defenses should include encryption. Although air bags in vehicles offer safety, if protection specialists ram their way out of an attack, or if an attacker backs into the protected vehicle, the activation of an air bag can hinder escape. One option for careful consideration is to disconnect the air bag on the driver's side.

□ □ □ ▬▬▬▬▬▬▬▬▬▬▬▬▬▬▬▬

Who has the advantage when a principal is targeted for attack, the principal and the protection team or the adversary? Explain your answer.

▬▬▬▬▬▬▬▬▬▬▬▬▬▬▬▬ □ □ □

Substance Abuse in the Workplace

Substance abuse refers to human abuse of any substance that can cause harm to oneself, others, and organizations. This problem is pervasive. Millions of people abuse substances. An employee substance abuser can cause harm in several ways. Examples are abusing legal and illegal drugs or other substances (Figure 18-2) and causing production problems or an accident; selling drugs to others in the workplace; and stealing products or information assets to support a drug habit. In addition, drug and alcohol abuse is linked to tardiness, absenteeism, turnover, and violence.

Research has shown that 12% of the workforce reported being heavy drinkers and that 47% of industrial injuries and 40% of deaths in the workplace was linked to alcohol. About 14 million Americans use illegal drugs. As workers, they are 3.6 times more likely to be involved in a workplace accident and five times more likely to file a claim for workers' compensation than nonusers (Elliott and Shelley, 2005). It is estimated that substance abuse by employees costs businesses in the United States more than $250 billion annually in increased medical costs, lost productivity, and workplace accidents (DeCenzo and Robbins, 2005: 94).

No occupation is immune to substance abuse. Those afflicted are from the ranks of blue-collar workers, white-collar workers, supervisors, managers, and professionals.

Countermeasures

Unenlightened managers ordinarily ignore substance abuse in the workplace. As with so many areas of loss prevention, when an unfortunate event occurs (e.g., drug-related crime, production decline, or accident due to substance abuse), these managers panic and react emotionally. Experienced people may be fired unnecessarily, arrests threatened, and litigation becomes a possibility. In contrast, action should begin before the first sign of abuse.

Here is a list of action for an **anti-substance abuse program for the workplace:**

1. Form a committee of specialists to pool ideas and resources.
2. Seek legal assistance from an employment law specialist.

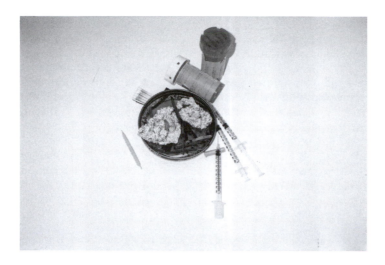

FIGURE 18-2 Abuse of legal and illegal drugs and other substances is a problem in the workplace.

3. Large corporations can afford to hire a substance abuse specialist. Outsourcing is another option. Also, contact the local government-supported alcohol and substance abuse agency.
4. Prepare policies that include input from a variety of employees. Policies should focus on the company's position on abuse of substances, including alcohol; job performance and safety as it relates to substance abuse; drug deterrence such as urinalysis; the consequences of testing positive; the responsibility of employees to seek treatment for abuse problems; available assistance; and the importance of confidentiality.
5. Education and prevention programs can assist employees in understanding substance abuse, policies, and making informed decisions on life choices, health, and happiness. Use signs in the workplace and at entrances, and periodically distribute relevant educational materials.
6. Ensure that supervisors are properly trained to recognize and report substance abuse.
7. Consider an undercover investigation to ascertain drug usage in the workplace.

Employee Assistance Programs (EAPs)

Employee assistance can be traced to the origin of Alcoholics Anonymous (AA), founded in 1935. AA views alcoholism as a disease requiring long-term treatment. Employee assistance programs (EAPs) were first introduced in the 1940s, in U.S. corporations. Thousands of these programs exist today in the public and private sectors, where they incorporate a broad-based approach to such problems as substance abuse, depression, and marital and financial problems. These programs are characterized by voluntary participation by employees, referrals for serious cases, and confidentiality. The goal of EAPs is to help the employee so he or she can be retained, saving hiring and training costs. An organization may establish its own EAP or outsource the program. Initial EAP programs were characterized by "constructive confrontation" (i.e., correct the problem or leave). Today, the philosophy is that a company has no right to interfere in private matters, but it does have a right to impose rules of behavior and performance at work (Elliott and Shelley, 2005; Ivancevich, 2001: 464).

Research is needed on the effectiveness of EAPs, what problems it ameliorates, what problems it shows limited, if any, success, and how it can be enhanced. For instance, research by Elliott and Shelley (2005) found that there were no differences in the accident rates of employees prior to and following EAP interventions.

Legal Guidelines

The federal **Anti-Drug Abuse Act of 1988** is an attempt to create a drug-free workplace. The law requires federal contractors and grantees to prepare and communicate policies banning illegal substances in the workplace and to create drug awareness programs and sanctions or rehabilitation for employees abusing substances. Federal contracts and grants are subject to suspension for noncompliance or excessive workplace drug convictions. Another form of regulation includes industries regulated by the U.S. Department of Transportation, such as airline, motor carrier, and rail, which are required to institute substance abuse programs, including drug testing. Additional mandates that affect substance abuse programs in the workplace include Title VII of the Civil Rights Act of 1964, the Americans with Disabilities Act of 1990, U.S. Department of Defense regulations, state drug testing laws, and state workers' compensation laws (U.S. Drug Enforcement Administration, 2003).

Drug Testing

Risk managers have seen a dramatic decrease in health insurance and workers' compensation claims following drug testing. In addition, insurance companies are encouraging companies to implement drug testing programs to reduce premiums. Furthermore, those companies that do not test become a magnet for those who are abusers (Myshko, 2001: 44–46).

Here is a list of items to assist in planning a drug-testing program (Gips, 2006: 50–58; Smith, 2004):

- Drug testing must be well planned. Questions include the following: What type of test? Who will do the testing? Cost? Who will be tested? What circumstances will necessitate a test? What controls will prevent cheating and ensure accuracy? Do the laboratory and its personnel comply with state or federal licensing and certification requirements? Are all legal issues considered?
- Drug testing focuses on urine, hair, and blood. Of the approximately 55 million drug tests performed in the United States annually, 90% are urine tests. Hair analysis is more expensive. Blood testing is used rarely, such as when an employee is unconscious from an accident and in an emergency room; for a person on dialysis; under a court order; or for a deceased person.
- Following legal research, especially of state law on drug testing and privacy, employers should consider an offer of employment to applicants contingent upon passing a drug test. Include this requirement in employment ads.
- Ensure drug testing is fair and applied equally.
- Randomly drug test, test when an employee shows behavioral or physical indications of substance abuse, and test following an accident.
- Because of an industry of products on the Web to adulterate or substitute for urine specimens, some companies are using multiple drug tests.
- Drug testing of hair is less likely to be tampered with when compared to urinalysis. Hair testing shows evidence of drugs much farther back in time than urinalysis.
- **Specimen validity testing** is gaining momentum from the federal government to ensure specimens are not adulterated or substituted.
- Saliva testing and pupillometry (i.e., measurement of pupils' reaction to light) are in the early stages of development.
- If a company shows that the percentage of drug tests that turn up positive is decreasing, caution is advised because employees may be getting better at subverting drug tests.

Trace detection should be used with caution. It consists of gathering minute particles of drugs in the workplace (e.g., at workstations or rest rooms) by using cloth swabs and then analyzing the swabs with a desktop instrument to detect a variety of drugs. This technique can possibly gauge the types of drugs in the workplace and serve as an aid to drug education and prevention. It presents difficulties if used for investigative and prosecutorial purposes.

□ □ □ ▬▬▬▬▬▬▬▬▬▬▬▬▬▬▬▬▬▬▬▬▬▬▬

What do you think are the most successful countermeasures against substance abuse in society and in the workplace?

▬▬▬▬▬▬▬▬▬▬▬▬▬▬▬▬▬▬▬▬▬▬▬ □ □ □

Alcoholism

An **alcoholic** is defined as someone who cannot function on a daily basis without consuming an alcoholic beverage. *Alcohol is the most abused drug in America.* In the United States, there are about 15 million adults who have alcohol-related problems (Elliott and Shelley, 2005). These figures do not include the millions who are on the fringe of alcoholism. It is often a hidden disease, whereby the alcoholic hides the problem from family, friends, physicians, and himself or herself. Some major indicators are heartburn, nausea, insomnia, tremor, high blood pressure, morning cough, and liver enlargement. The alcoholic often blames factors other than alcohol for these conditions.

Today, many businesses are no longer hiding the problem and rely on an EAP. In addition, Alcoholics Anonymous (AA), an organization for alcoholics and recovered alcoholics, run by people who have had a drinking problem, has had more success than most organizations.

An employee with a drinking problem affecting the workplace is advised of "helping agencies," in addition to internal and external policies and procedures and what is expected of him or her by the employer regarding steps for recovery. Health insurance benefits and company disability income usually are applicable. Unless the employee takes heed in seeking assistance, dismissal may occur because of poor job performance. The threat of job loss jolts many alcoholics into recognizing their serious situation and accepting treatment.

Types of Substances and Abuse

The explanation of four terms can assist the reader in understanding the human impact of various substance abuse categories.

- **Psychological dependence:** Users depend so much on the feeling of well-being from a substance that they feel compelled toward continued use. People can become psychologically dependent on a host of substances. Restlessness and irritability may result from deprivation of the desired substance.
- **Addiction:** Certain substances lead to physiological (or physical) addiction. This happens when the body has become so accustomed to a substance that the drugged state becomes "normal" to the body. Extreme physical discomfort results if the substance is not in the body.
- **Tolerance:** After repeated use of certain drugs, the body becomes so accustomed to the drug that increasing dosages are needed to reach the feeling of well-being afforded by earlier doses.
- **Withdrawal:** A person goes through physical and psychological upset as the body becomes used to the absence of the drug. Addicts ordinarily consume drugs to avoid pain, and possible death, from withdrawal. Symptoms vary from person to person and from substance to substance. An addict's life often revolves around obtaining the substance, by whatever means, to avoid withdrawal.

Five types of substances—narcotics, depressants, stimulants, hallucinogens, and inhalants—are discussed here. According to Gips (2006), marijuana was found most frequently (more than half) in positive drug tests from employees. Cocaine (15%) and amphetamines (11%) followed it. Amphetamines include methamphetamine.

Narcotics

Narcotics include opium, its derivatives, and their synthetic equivalents. Drugs in this category are heroin, morphine, codeine, and methadone, among others. Such drugs are used to relieve pain and induce sleep. The method of consumption is injection, oral, or inhalation. Both psychological and physiological dependence is typical, as well as a tolerance potential.

Depressants

Depressants fall into several categories: barbiturates include phenobarbital and secobarbital (Seconal); tranquilizers include Valium and Librium; nonbarbiturate hypnotics include methaqualone (Quaalude); and miscellaneous depressant drugs include alcohol and chloroform. A depressant affects the central nervous system. Barbiturates ordinarily are prescribed for insomnia, whereas tranquilizers calm anxiety. Other depressants are used prior to surgery. Abuse of these drugs can lead to psychological and physiological dependence. Withdrawal is painful and can be fatal. Depressants have a tolerance potential. These drugs are taken orally or injected. They are obtained by a doctor's prescription or through illegal channels. Symptoms of depressant use are similar to that of alcohol use: drowsiness, slurred speech, disorientation, constricted pupils, irritability, and slow reflexes.

Stimulants

There are several types of stimulants; caffeine, amphetamine, methamphetamine, and cocaine are the most common. These drugs affect the central nervous system and generally cause increased alertness soon after consumption, but restlessness and irritability are characteristic of long-term usage. There is a tolerance potential plus a susceptibility to dependence.

Caffeine is found in coffee, tea, cola drinks, and No-Doz. Increased alertness may be followed by insomnia, gastric irritation, and restlessness.

Amphetamines are widely used stimulants that are swallowed or injected. They are prescribed for narcolepsy (chronic sleepiness). Illegal amphetamines typically originate from legitimate sources. Abuse is characterized by anxiety, talkativeness, irritability, and dilated pupils.

Methamphetamine is chemically related to amphetamine but much more potent, longer lasting, and more harmful to the central nervous system. It can be made in small, illegal laboratories, where its production is dangerous to the people in the labs, neighbors, and the environment. It is referred to by many names, such as "speed," "meth," and "chalk." Methamphetamine hydrochloride, clear chunky crystals resembling ice, which can be inhaled by smoking, is referred to as "ice," "crystal," "glass," and "tina." The intoxicating effects of the drug, whether it is injected or taken in other ways, can alter judgment and inhibition and lead people to engage in unsafe behaviors. Most major metropolitan areas in the United States reported increases in the amounts and purity of methamphetamine smuggled into the United States from Mexico (National Institute on Drug Abuse, 2006).

Legally, cocaine is a narcotic, but physiologically it is a stimulant. It is expensive and the "high" is short-lived. The history of cocaine is interesting. It used to be an ingredient in Coca-Cola. Sigmund Freud experimented with it. The user inhales cocaine into the nose or injects it. Symptoms of abuse are similar to those of amphetamines plus damage to nasal membranes and the potential for hallucinations and hostile behavior.

Crack is a stimulant drug processed from cocaine hydrochloride by using baking soda and water and then heat to remove the hydrochloride. The pebble-sized crystal remaining, called crack, is smoked in a variety of devices. Crack is popular because it is less expensive than cocaine and when smoked it is more rapidly absorbed than snorted cocaine.

Hallucinogens

Hallucinogens can produce a trance, fright, and irrational behavior. Examples are LSD, PCP, mescaline, and psilocybin.

Marijuana is categorized by itself. It is sometimes categorized as a hallucinogen, but its actions are different from that of LSD. Both marijuana and its derivative, hashish, are widely used. Because of widespread cultivation of hemp to produce rope prior to the Civil War, marijuana grows wild in almost every state. Because of so many users today, marijuana use is controversial. Many states have decriminalized (i.e., reduced the penalty for) the offense. The effects of usage depend on the individual and the potency. It may distort perceptions of time and space and reduce concentration, learning, and memory. There is no physiological dependence. Psychological dependence is possible. Research on tolerance is inconclusive. Millions of people smoke marijuana occasionally to feel relaxed and carefree.

LSD was popularized in the 1960s by the youth "counterculture." Use was touted as a consciousness-expanding experience. The effects vary greatly. There is no physiological dependence. Bizarre hallucinations, which can be either beautiful or terrifying, result from usage.

Inhalants

Inhaling volatile chemicals can produce intoxication. This can occur by one's own volition or by accident due to poor ventilation. All employees should understand both causative factors.

Two types of volatile chemicals are volatile solvents and anesthetics. Volatile solvents include a variety of glues or liquid cements, cleaning fluid, paint thinner, and paint remover. Anesthetics are found in medical facilities for surgical purposes. Nitrous oxide (laughing gas) and ether are among the anesthetics.

Those who seek an altered state or "high" gather the substance or gas in a plastic bag and place it over the mouth and nose before breathing. Direct breathing from the container holding the substance is another method. Physiological dependence is nil, but a tolerance and psychological dependence may result. The effects are numerous and varied: intoxication, chemical odor on the person, drowsiness, stupor, and hallucinations.

Information Security

Information security protects an organization's information assets through a broad based, well-planned, and creative program of strategies that consider the widest possible risks from humans, technology, accidents, disasters, or any combination of factors. A balanced information security program avoids overemphasizing perimeter security (Figure 18-3) since the greatest threat is from within. Information security is an extremely challenging undertaking because an organization can expend an enormous amount of resources on the protection of information assets and, as examples, one leak by one employee (e.g., on a telephone, in an e-mail, through another type

FIGURE 18-3 A balanced information security program avoids overemphasizing perimeter security since the greatest threat is from within.

of electronic device, or at a conference) or one intrusion by an outsider (e.g., electronic surveillance or cyber threat), can result in economic loss.

Curtis and McBride (2005: 107–108) write that information security applies numerous strategies to ensure the availability, accuracy, authenticity, and confidentiality of information. Availability ensures that users can access information and not be blocked by, for example, a denial-of-service attack. Accuracy addresses issues of errors (e.g., by an employee) and the integrity of information (e.g., a hacker remotely accesses an IT system to manipulate data). Authenticity means that information and its sender are genuine. Phishing, for instance, can lead to identity theft and loss of sensitive information. Confidentially ensures that only authorized individuals access information.

Information assets contain a combination of economic value, property right, specialized knowledge, and competitive advantage that may be written, verbal, electronic, or in another form. The information often is extremely valuable (e.g., a secret formula) and may represent the lifeblood of an organization. Depending on the source, information assets may be termed "sensitive information" or "proprietary information." ASIS International (2007: 7–8) prepared an *Information Asset Protection Guideline* that offered the following terms and definitions:

> *Proprietary Information: As defined by the Federal Acquisition Regulation (48 CFR 27.402 Policy): A property right or other valid economic interest in data resulting from private investment. Protection of such data from unauthorized use and disclosure is necessary in order to prevent the compromise of such property right or economic interest.*
>
> *Sensitive Information: Information or knowledge that might result in loss of an advantage or level of security if disclosed to others.*

For simplicity, the term "information assets" is emphasized here. Subsequent pages explain corporate intelligence gathering, espionage, and countermeasures. **Espionage** is the act of spying which is a criminal offense. **Business espionage** seeks a competitor's information assets through illegal means. **Government espionage** seeks not only a competitor's information assets, but also military and political secrets. Previous sections of this book elaborate on security, fire protection, and emergency management for assets, besides people. In addition, we must not forget that information pertaining to the privacy of individuals requires protection. This would include credit, medical, educational, and other records protected under various laws as covered earlier.

Common types of information assets that might be sought by a spy are the following: product design, financial reports, engineering data, tax records, secret formulas, marketing strategies, cost reduction methods, research data, client or customer information, trade secrets, human resources records, patent information, computer programs, oil or mineral exploration maps, mergers, and contract information.

A **trade secret**, supposedly known only to certain individuals, is a secret process used to produce a salable product. It may involve a series of steps or special ingredients. A famous trade secret is the formula for Coca-Cola. The holder of a trade secret must take steps to maintain secrecy from competitors. If an employee were to reveal a trade secret to a competitor, the courts could issue an injunction, prohibiting the competitor from using the secret. Money damages might be awarded.

ASIS International (2007: 8) defines trade secret as follows: "All forms and types of financial, business, scientific, technical, economic, or engineering information, including patterns, plans, compilations, program devices, formulas, designs, prototypes, methods, techniques, processed, procedures, programs, or codes, whether tangible or intangible, and whether or how stored, compiled, or memorialized physically, electronically, graphically, photographically, or in writing if (a) the owner thereof has taken reasonable measures to keep such information secret; and (b) the information derives independent economic value, actual or potential, from not being generally known to, and not being readily ascertainable through proper means by, the public."

A **patent** provides protection for an invention or design. If a competitor duplicates the device, patent laws are likely to be violated and litigation would follow. Competitors often engineer around patents.

ASIS International (2007:7) defines patent as follows: "Information that has the government grant of a right, privilege, or authority to exclude others from making, using, marketing, selling, offering for sale, or importing an invention for a specified period (20 years from the date of filing) granted to the inventor if the device or process is novel, useful, and nonobvious."

A **trademark** includes words, symbols, logos, designs, or slogans that identify products or services as coming from a common source. McDonald's golden arches serve as an example.

A **copyright** provides protection for original works in any medium of expression by giving the creator or publisher exclusive rights to the work. This type of protection covers books, magazines, musical scores, movies, art, and computer software programs.

Corporate Intelligence Gathering: Putting It in Perspective

Corporate intelligence involves gathering information about competitors. It ranges from the illegal activity of business espionage to the acceptable, universally applied practice of utilizing salespeople to monitor public business practices of other companies. Corporate intelligence gathering, when done legally, makes good business sense, and this is why companies such as General Electric, Digital Equipment, and Gillette have established formal intelligence programs. Because of unethical and illegal behavior by certain people and firms when gathering intelligence, the whole specialization has earned a bad reputation. However, many avenues for gathering intelligence are legal. Let us first list the reasons for corporate intelligence gathering (Laczniak and Murphy, 1993: 1–4):

- Executives should take advantage of information that is publicly available to fulfill their fiduciary duty to shareholders. Because the Cordis Corporation, a pacemaker manufacturer, for example, was unsure of why its new line did not show improved sales, it asked its salespeople to check the tactics of the competition. The salespeople found that physicians were being offered cars and boats to stay with the competition. When Cordis increased educational support for doctors, added more salespeople, and matched the giveaways, sales increased.
- Competitive intelligence is a basis for strategic planning. One intelligence seminar director found a competitor using a "dirty trick" by enrolling in his course under an assumed name.
- It is necessary, in order to be successful against global competitors. The Japanese have "deployed armies of engineers and marketing specialists" to other countries. Likewise, U.S.-based firms have set up offices abroad to gather information.
- It can be useful for the introduction of a new product. Coors did extensive chemical analysis on Gallo's wine coolers and found that it could not compete on price.

The Society of Competitive Intelligence Professionals (2007) views its vocation as an honorable profession with a code of ethics. The group defines **competitive intelligence** as "the legal and ethical collection and analysis of information regarding the capabilities, vulnerabilities, and intentions of business competitors." Furthermore, the group states

> While some decision makers may attempt to sail blindly through the global marketplace, it is the duty of the trained CI professional to show them alternative courses that will avoid potential dangers, and to take advantage of the tactics and strategies that lead to bottom-line success.
>
> CI is not spying. It is not necessary to use illegal or unethical methods in CI. In fact, doing so is a failure of CI, because almost everything decision makers need to know about the competitive environment can be discovered using legal, ethical means. The information that can't be found with research can be deduced with good analysis, which is just one of the ways CI adds value to an organization.

The following lists provide guidelines for information gathering. Ethical sources include

- Published material and public documents from government
- Purchasing access to business information databases (e.g., LexisNexis; Dun and Bradstreet).

- Disclosures made by competitors
- Market surveys and consultants' reports
- Financial reports and brokers' research reports
- Trade fairs, exhibits, and competitors' brochures
- Analysis of a competitor's products
- Legitimate employment interviews with people who worked for a competitor

A company wishing to detail prohibited activities in its policy should include the following (Horowitz, 2005; Ehrlich, 2002: 11–14):

- Bribery and theft
- Electronic eavesdropping or wiretapping
- Trespassing
- Misrepresenting your identity or that of your company
- Inducing another to violate his duty of confidentiality to his current or former employer
- Accepting trade secret or proprietary information through a confidential relationship which you then violate
- Accepting trade secret or proprietary information from another knowing it was obtained through a violation of law

Economic Espionage Act of 1996

Because intellectual property assets are often more valuable to businesses than tangible assets, Congress passed the **Economic Espionage Act of 1996**. This act makes it a federal crime for any person to convert a trade secret to his or her own benefit or the benefit of others with the intent or knowledge that the conversion will injure the owner of the trade secret. The penalties for any person are up to 10 years of imprisonment and a fine up to $250,000. Corporations can be fined up to $5 million. If a foreign government benefits from such a crime, the penalties are even greater. The act defines *trade secret* broadly as information that the owner has taken "reasonable measures" to keep secret because of the economic value from it. Case law has further defined the act; the greater the protection and value of the information and the fewer people who know about the information, the more likely the courts will recognize its status as a protectable trade secret (Halligan, 2001: 53–58).

The act raises two major concerns for management:

- *Protecting trade secrets:* This would include a comprehensive information security program.
- *Hiring employees from competitors:* Employers may violate the act if they hire employees from other firms who may bring with them trade secrets.

Prevention includes a thorough interview of applicants, ascertaining whether the applicant signed contracts or agreements with others for the protection of sensitive information, and use of a company form that signifies that the new employee understands the act's legal requirements.

The act also links the economic well-being of the nation to national security interests. In addition, it allows the FBI to investigate foreign intelligence services bent on acquiring sensitive information of U.S. companies.

At some point, a company may have to decide whether to report a violation of the act to law enforcement authorities. The disadvantages are lost time and money, unwanted publicity, and the fact that the defendant's attorney may request secrets that could then be revealed in court. Although the act offers some protection for information assets, this protection may depend on how a judge or attorneys in the case interpret the act. Discovery proceedings may result in information loss greater than the original loss. Also, the case may be lost in criminal and civil courts. Therefore, management must carefully weigh decisions on legal action. Another point to consider is that the act requires businesses to protect themselves from losses, which presents liability issues relevant to due diligence (Nolan, 1997: 54–57). *Prevention is seen here, as with many other vulnerabilities, as the key avenue for protection.*

Horowitz (1998: 6) wrote of the confusion and uneasiness for competitive intelligence professionals following the passage of the Economic Espionage Act of 1996. These specialists, and related contract firms and proprietary departments, were unsure of how they should conduct their business of gathering information. Horowitz wrote

> *Herein lies the confusion. While the EEA makes trade secret law a federal criminal matter—this for the first time in U.S. history—the activities it criminalizes were prohibited under state law and/or unacceptable under SCIP's Code of Ethics. In other words, the rules are fundamentally the same, but the consequences of violating them are different. An activity that had always been a violation of state trade secret law can now result in not only state civil liability but federal criminal liability as well.*

Espionage Techniques and the Vulnerabilities of Technology

The techniques used by adversaries to acquire information assets are so varied that defenders must not fall into the trap of emphasizing certain countermeasures while "leaving the back door open." For example, a company may spend hundreds of thousands of dollars defending against electronic surveillance and wiretapping while not realizing that most of the losses of information assets are from a few employees who are really spies for competitors.

Three patterns of illegally acquiring information assets are internal, external, and a conspiracy that combines the two. An *internal attack* can be perpetrated by an employee who sells a secret formula to a competitor, for example. An *external attack* occurs when an outsider gains unauthorized access to the premises and steals product design data. The *combined conspiracy* is seen when an employee "just happens" to leave a secret mailing list on a desk and unlocks a rear door to aid an intruder. Furthermore, information assets are lost through legal means applied by competitors.

Spies use numerous techniques. A spy might assemble trash from a company and an executive's home to "piece together" information. Spies may claim they are a student conducting a survey, as a "pretext" to acquire information. Several spies may each ask certain questions only, and then later, assemble the "big picture." Another method is tricking a key employee into being discovered in a compromising position (e.g., in bed with a prostitute), photographing the incident, and then blackmailing the employee to acquire information. A spy might attempt to gain employment at a target company. Sometimes, proposals for a merger, acquisition, or joint venture are used as a cover to obtain information.

Companies with inadequate information security programs can lose information assets in several easy ways, such as through company speeches, publications, trade meetings, disgruntled employees, consultants, and contractors. Information loss can occur at any location from conversations or phone calls. A spy might frequent a tavern or conference populated by engineers to listen to conversations. Another way in which businesses can lose information assets is when an overly eager salesperson supplies excessive information in an attempt to impress a customer.

Reverse engineering is a legal avenue to obtain a look at a competitor's product. The competitor simply purchases the product and dismantles it to understand the components. Patent applications, which are available to the public, can reveal valuable information. Some companies deliberately patent their failures to lead competitors astray.

Various devices are available to the spy. Wiretapping, electronic listening devices, and pinhole lens cameras are examples. A handheld document scanner, the size of a large pen, can capture numerous pages of text and graphics. A competitor could plant RFID readers to report on the movement of products to collect business data.

In our age of technological marvels, numerous devices we use daily can compromise information security. Ashley (2006: 84–85) describes such vulnerabilities and offers countermeasures. In order to attract customers, communications companies offer a variety of features beyond basic service. For instance, a ringtone is a sound file that is downloaded to a cell phone. If a virus has been loaded into the file, it infects the phone, so use only the ringtones that are with your phone. Bluetooth permits wireless communications over short distances (i.e., 30 feet or less), which facilitates the use of a cordless headset with a cell phone. Victimization may occur if the security feature of Bluetooth is turned off. An offender may be nearby, use a Bluetooth probe, transfer files into the victim's phone, and receive information from the phone. Bluetooth usage with other devices (e.g., laptop or PDA) creates additional vulnerabilities. Cell phones can also be compromised through instant and text messages, so avoid such messages from unknown sources. PDA's are subject to similar attacks.

Piazza (2005: 78–87) further explains the vulnerabilities of Bluetooth technology. This trade name is from a 10th century Danish king. It refers to a short-range wireless radio chip created in the 1990s that is in numerous devices. Bluetooth enables wireless communications in what is called a personal-area network (PAN). Attackers are developing technology that can access PANs from greater distances similar to traditional wireless networks. Several types of attacks can be applied to Bluetooth technology. One type can make an unauthorized connection to a cell phone and copy its contents, including the unique numerical identifier that an offender needs to clone a phone. In one scenario, Piazza describes how a tech-savvy individual was able to access the cell phone of a manager of a chain of coffee shops and retrieved door PIN codes, alarm codes, and safe combinations without the manager's knowledge. Other vulnerabilities include taking control of a victim's cell phone, making calls, sending and reading text messages, and performing other tasks. In another scenario, a tech-savvy individual focused on a group talking at a table in a bar with the cell phone of the victim sitting on the table. A connection was made to the targeted phone, it was signaled to dial the tech-savvy individual's voicemail, and it recorded the conversation without the knowledge of the victims.

Piazza (2007: 48) reports on the threats from USB flash drives. (USB are the initials for Universal Serial Bus, a standard that supports data transfer.) These storage devices can hold an enormous amount of data that can leave the workplace. In addition, if a certain program infects a computer, the program will retrieve data from USB drives or other portable devices connected to the compromised computer. Another program takes the data from the USB drive and sends it out via an e-mail. Flash drives are capable of running software programs and one version allows an employee to circumvent security and visit prohibited Web sites via anonymous proxies.

Miller (2007: 22–30) asks us to think about all the ways we move and store data on mobile devices. She refers to USB ports that support a variety of portable storage devices, such as flash drives, portable hard drives, music and video players, and printers. Miller also refers to data storage on CDs and DVDs and the threat from unprotected WiFi and Bluetooth. WiFi means wireless fidelity. A WiFi enabled device (e.g., laptop, cell phone, or PDA) can access the internet when near an access point called a hotspot. WiFi allows networks to be deployed without cabling; however, WiFi networks can be vulnerable to monitoring and copying data, unless high-quality encryption is employed.

Although an adversary can travel to a targeted company to conduct surveillance, take photographs and video the location, the use of satellite images is increasing. These Internet services are free for basic services. More sophisticated services permit zoom, rotation, and 3D views of facilities and terrain. This vulnerability is challenging to counter. However, consideration should be given to facility design, landscape architecture, and transportation modes that disguise operations.

Mallery (2006: 76) writes of Internet-based methods of removing information assets from organizations. An employee can import their client information into a variety of free e-mail programs. Another Internet-based tool is online data storage that permits users to upload data to a secure site. The data is accessible from anywhere, and when an employee leaves for another employer, or selects to share or sell the data, it is readily available. Countermeasures include a policy, firewall, and periodic checks of Internet activity.

Mallery (2006: 78) also writes of keystroke capturing hardware. This device is installed between a keyboard and a computer; no additional software or power is required for its operation. In addition, keyboards are available that contain an embedded keystroke chip. The potential loss of information assets through this technology is enormous. It is extremely difficult to detect. Although restricted access and CCTV can reduce this threat, installation time is not lengthy and a cleaning crew or service technician can be a risk, as with the installation of other unauthorized devices. At the same time, monitoring software can be installed remotely and discreetly e-mail data to a specified address.

A major point from these descriptions of vulnerabilities is that technology is a "blessing and a burden." Technology makes our lives easier; however, we face a never-ending "cat and mouse" cycle of new technology confronted by offenders seeking to exploit and profit from it as defenses follow.

Furthermore, a good spy does not get caught, and quite often, the victimized firm does not discover that it has been subjected to espionage. If the discovery is made, the company typically keeps it secret to avoid adverse publicity.

The Business Espionage Controls and Countermeasures Association (2007) states

> *The purpose of the association is to research and exchange information about business espionage controls and countermeasures; to establish and encourage a code of ethics within the profession, and to promote our professional image within the business community through a Certified Confidentiality Officer (CCO) program.*
>
> *We identified four primary areas of risk as one of our first BECCA research projects. We called them the "Four Faces of Business Espionage," a term now widely used by controls and countermeasures experts. These risk factors are Pretext Attacks [interviews], Computer Abuse, Technical Surveillance, and Undercover Attacks.*

Pretext interviews are disguised interviews or "surveys" that can take place in a variety of locations (e.g., over the telephone, at trade shows, in chat rooms, in bed). The people gathering information may not know the real reason behind the questions, and the victims may not know the identity of the interviewer. Technical surveillance includes planting a listening device (e.g., a bug).

BECCA stopped charging annual membership dues as of September 11, 2001 as part of their contribution to homeland security. Membership is free to qualified applicants.

Countermeasures

The first step in keeping information assets secure is to identify and classify it according to its value. Top-level executives in a business should perform this subjective job. If a company has a DOD contract, then strict DOD criteria would apply. Each classification has rules for marking, handling, transmitting, storing, and access. The higher the classification the greater are the controls. Table 18-1 shows DOD and corporate classifications, explanations, and illustrations. ASIS International (2007: 37–39) offers the following classification system: unrestricted, internal use, restricted, and highly restricted.

Here is a list of strategies for an **information security program**:

1. *Prevention* is a key strategy to protect information assets, which can be stolen without anything being physically missing, and information assets often are not covered by insurance.
2. Establish formal policies and procedures for such activities as identifying and classifying information assets, handling, use, distribution, release of information on a "need-to-know" basis, storage, and disposal. Other examples are security over passwords and maintaining a "clean desk" policy so important items are not left in the open when they should be in a locked container.

Table 18-1 Classification Systems

	If Unauthorized Disclosure	Illustrations
Government Classification*		
Top Secret	"Exceptionally grave damage" to national security	Vital national defense plans, new weapons, sensitive intelligence operations
Secret	"Serious damage" to national security	Significant military plans or intelligence operations
Confidential	"Identifiable damage" to national security	Strength of forces, munitions performance characteristics
Corporation Classification		
Special Controls	Survival at stake	New process or product; secret formula or recipe
Company Confidential	Serious damage	Process, customer lists; depends on value to business
Private Confidential	Identifiable damage, or could cause problems	Personnel data, price quote

*Classified by the U.S. Department of Defense in National Industrial Security Program Operating Manual, reissued February 28, 2006 (http://www.fas.org/sgp/library/nispom.htm; retrieved July 28, 2007).

3. Provide training and awareness programs for employees on all aspects of information security, including methods used by spies, reporting incidents, investigations, and auditing of the program.

4. Reinforce countermeasures through new employee orientation, the employee handbook, and performance evaluations.

5. Carefully screen employment applicants.

6. Use employee nondisclosure agreements and employee noncompete agreements.

7. Implement physical security and access controls for people and property entering, leaving, and circulating within a facility (Figure 18-4).

8. Secure information assets.

9. Review works written by employees prior to publication and their speeches, ensure protection during trade shows, and control media relations.

10. Control destruction of information assets.

11. Maintain state-of-the-art IT security.

12. Be cautious when logging online in a wireless area. Ensure that your computer is not automatically connected to wireless access points that are unsecured.

13. Mark laptops with company name and telephone number to increase the chances of recovery in case of theft.

14. Protect all forms of electronic communication—e-mail, network, fax, telephone, etc.

15. Establish controls over devices that contain a hard drive (e.g., PDAs, iPods, and MP3 players), electronic storage capacity, or embedded camera. Data are being stored in smaller spaces and so many ordinary items (e.g., pen, knife, watch) can contain a data storage device.

16. Control the variety of office machines (e.g., the combination copy machine, fax, scanner, and printer) that contain hard drives.

17. CDs and DVDs, rather than paper, are increasingly being used to store information. If a duplicator makes a copy of a master CD to its hard drive and then burns multiple copies, the information is available to people who can access the duplicator, unless the data is purged.

FIGURE 18-4 Sen Trac ID uses radio-frequency identification technology to provide hands-free access control and asset management to track people and products within a facility. Courtesy: Sensormatic.

18. Ensure that important data has a backup copy in case data are stolen, a disaster strikes, or a hard drive fails.
19. Use technical surveillance countermeasures (TSCM).
20. Use internal and independent security audits to strengthen protection.

Operations Security

Operations Security (OPSEC) is defined by Isaacs (2004: 104) as follows: "OPSEC is a formal process for looking at the protection of critical information from the viewpoint of an adversary and then denying that adversary the information it needs." It is a government-developed approach to information security that began during the Vietnam War when it was discovered that lives were being lost, not only from espionage, but also from unclassified information that was being analyzed by the enemy. OPSEC is a way of thinking, rather than a series of steps. The components of OPSEC are analyze the threat, identify critical information, examine vulnerabilities, assess risk, and apply countermeasures.

Destruction of Information Assets

Records, documents, computers, hard drives, and other items that contain information assets should not simply be thrown into trash bins or discarded when no longer needed, because spies and other adversaries may retrieve the information. Total destruction affords better information security. Before pollution restrictions against burning, many firms placed unwanted records in incinerators. Today, *strip-cut shredders* (producing long strips of paper 1/4-inch wide) are used by many organizations. However, security is limited. This became painfully evident in 1979, when Iranian militants stormed the U.S. Embassy in Tehran and pieced together top-secret documents that had been shredded by a strip-cut shredder. For increased security, *particle-cut shredders* (smaller pieces of paper) are the alternative (Figure 18-5). *Cross-cut shredders* offer even higher security. The highest level of security is offered by *disintegrators*. These devices produce confetti particles through the action of a rotor and stationary knives. Since the Iranian disaster, the U.S. government requires classified data to be destroyed with either a cross-cut shredder or a disintegrator.

Vendors that sell high-security shredders seek to meet government national security standards. One vendor sells a shredder that delivers a 1 mm × 4 mm particle. An 8 1/2″ × 11″ piece of paper can be reduced to 15,500 particles (Dahle North America, 2007).

FIGURE 18-5 A determined adversary might take the time to put small pieces of paper together for information.

Many companies outsource shredding to service firms that send a mobile shredding truck to the client to shred a variety of items, besides paper. Examples are CDs, DVDs, hard drives, credit cards, and uniforms. Security practitioners should exercise due diligence with shredding service firms and investigate the chain of custody of the shredded product. The National Association of Information Destruction, Inc., promotes professionalism and ethics of its member companies.

Unshredding is a growing specialization. Although unshredding can be done manually, computer technology speeds the process by scanning pieces on both sides and then the computer determines how the strips should be joined. In the Enron accounting case, many documents were fed through a shredder incorrectly, which made the pieces easier to put together. In reference to forensic identification, shredders contain device-specific characteristics that can be used to determine the specific device that shredded an item.

Shredding has increased in popularity because of privacy laws (e.g., FACTA and HIPPA), the problem of identity theft, and the U.S. Supreme Court case, California v. Greenwood, which permits police warrantless search and seizure of garbage left on the street for collection (Wikipedia, 2007).

☐ ☐ ☐ ▬▬▬▬▬▬▬▬▬▬▬▬▬▬▬▬▬▬▬▬▬▬▬▬

Defenders against espionage must not fall into the trap of emphasizing certain countermeasures while "leaving the back door open."

▬▬▬▬▬▬▬▬▬▬▬▬▬▬▬▬▬▬▬▬▬▬▬▬ ☐ ☐ ☐

Communications Security

Communications security involves defenses against interception. The National Security Agency (2000: 10) defines communications security (COMSEC) as follows:

Measures and controls taken to deny unauthorized persons information derived from telecommunications and to ensure the authenticity of such telecommunications. Communications security includes cryptosecurity [i.e., encryption or decryption], transmission security, emission security [i.e., intercept and analysis of emanations from equipment], and physical security of COMSEC material.

In providing a comprehensive approach to protecting information assets, subfields of communications security are listed here (Carroll, 1996: 177–277).

- *Line security* protects communications lines of IT systems, such as a central computer and remote terminals. Line security is effective over lines an organization controls; a wiretap can occur in many locations of a line. Cryptographic security defeats wiretapping.
- *Transmission security* involves communications procedures that afford minimal advantage to an adversary bent on intercepting data communications from IT systems, telephones, radio, and other systems.
- *Emanation security* prevents undesired signal data emanations (e.g., from computer equipment) transmitted without wires (e.g., electromagnetic or acoustic) that could be intercepted by an adversary. **TEMPEST** is the code word used by the National Security Agency for the science of eliminating undesired signal data emanations. "Shielding," discussed soon, is one strategy to reduce data emanations.
- *Technical security*, also called *technical surveillance countermeasures*, provides defenses against the interception of data communications from microphones, transmitters, or wiretaps.

The above methods of attack can be used together, which is one reason why communications security is a highly complex field. What follows here primarily is technical security; however, *we must not lose sight of the importance of a comprehensive approach to protecting information assets.*

Electronic Surveillance and Wiretapping

Electronic surveillance utilizes electronic devices to covertly listen to conversations, whereas **wiretapping** pertains to the interception of telephone communications. The prevalence of these often-illegal activities probably is greater than one would expect. (The legality of such acts is supported by court orders.) Because detection is so difficult, the exact extent of electronic surveillance and wiretapping and what this theft of information costs businesses is impossible to gauge.

Electronic eavesdropping technology is highly developed to the point where countermeasures (debugging) have not kept up with the art of bugging. Consequently, only the most expertly trained and experienced specialist can counter this threat.

Surveillance equipment is easy to obtain. Transmitters are contained in toys and other items found in many homes. Retailers sell FM transmitters or microphones that transmit sound, without wires, to an ordinary FM radio after tuning to the correct frequency. These FM transmitters are advertised to be used by public speakers who favor wireless microphones so they can walk around as they talk without being hindered by wires; the voice is transmitted and then broadcast over large speakers. They are also advertised to listen in on a baby from another room. An electronically inclined person can simply enter a local electronics store or shop on-line and buy all the materials necessary to make a sophisticated bug. Pre-built models are available by mail, or certain retailers will sell them if the buyer signs a statement that they will not be used for audio surveillance.

Miniaturization has greatly aided spying. With the advance of the microchip, transmitters are apt to be so small that these devices can be enmeshed in thick paper, as in a calendar, under a stamp, or within a nail in a wall. Bugs may be planted as a building is under construction, or a person may receive one hidden in a present or other item. Transmitters are capable of being operated by solar power (i.e., daylight) or local radio broadcast.

Bugging techniques are varied. Information from a microphone can be transmitted via a "wire run" or a radio transmitter. Bugs are concealed in a variety of objects or carried on a person. Transmitting devices can be remotely controlled with a radio signal for turning them on and off. This makes detection difficult. A device known as a carrier current transmitter is placed in wall plugs, light switches, or other electrically operated components. It obtains its power from the AC wire to which it is attached. Sound systems with speakers serve as microphones that help spies.

Many spies use multiple systems. Multiple bugs are placed so they will be found, which in many instances satisfies security and management. Other bugs are more cleverly concealed.

Gruber (2006: 280–283) notes that gun microphones are very effective. He writes that they can be aimed at a target from a significant distance and they are used with a headset and amplifier. Gun microphones can be seen at football games. He illustrates the creativity of spies by describing how electrical signals from a microphone can be carried by a clear metallic paint.

Telephones are especially vulnerable. A "tap" occurs when a telephone conversation is intercepted. Telephone lines are available in so many places that taps are difficult to detect. A tap can be direct or wireless. With a direct tap, a pair of wires is spliced to the telephone line and then connected to a recorder. An FM transmitter, similar to a room bug, is employed for a wireless tap. The transmitter is connected to the line and then a receiver and recorder are concealed nearby. Wireless taps (and room bugs) are spotted by using special equipment. Direct taps are difficult to locate. A check of the entire line is necessary.

Because telephone traffic travels over space radio in several modes—for example, cellular, microwave, and satellite—the spy's job is made much easier and safer since no on-premises tap is required. What is required is the proper equipment for each mode. In one case a Mossad agent in Berne, Switzerland, was arrested after he tried to tap the telephone of a Hezbollah target. His technical system was a cellular telephone device that would be activated when the target telephone was put in use. The device would automatically call a second cellular telephone where the target's telephone would be monitored (Business Espionage Controls and Countermeasures Association, 2007).

Another technique transforms the telephone into a listening device whether it is in use or not. Variations of the following technique depend on the technology and design of the telephone. "Hookswitch bypass" short circuits (by changing wires) the telephone hookswitch (the switch that disconnects the microphone in the mouthpiece to the outside when a person hangs up) and transforms the ordinary telephone into a bug. This is easy to detect by hanging up the telephone, placing a radio nearby (for noise), tapping into the telephone line, and listening for the radio.

When guarding against losses of information assets, consideration must be given to a host of methods that may be used by a spy. These include infrared transmitters that use light frequencies below the visible frequency spectrum to transmit information. This can be defeated through physical shielding (e.g., closing the drapes). Another method, a laser listening device, "bounces" laser off a window to receive audio from the room. Inexpensive noise masking systems can defeat this technique (Jones, 2000: 1–17). Kaiser and Stokes (2006: 65) write: "Newer laser microphones are created by feeding two hair-thin strands of fiber-optic cable into the room being monitored. The microphone operates when a laser beam is sent down one of the fibers, where it bumps into a thin aluminum diaphragm and returns on the other fiber with the room conversation." A careful search is required to find this and other devices. Computer, e-mail, facsimile, and other transmissions are also subject to access by spies. A spy may conceal a recorder or pinhole-lens camera on the premises, or wear a camera concealed in a jacket or tie. If drawings or designs are on walls or in sight through windows, a spy, stationed in another skyscraper a few blocks away might use a telescope to obtain secret data, and a lip reader can enhance the information gathering. Or, a window washer might appear at a window for surveillance. Another method is a spy disguised as a janitor to be assigned to the particular site. All of these methods by no means exhaust the skills of spies as covered earlier under "espionage techniques."

Technical Surveillance Countermeasures

ASIS International (2007: 17) states the following:

> **Technical Surveillance Countermeasures (TSCM)** *refers to the use of services, equipment, and techniques designed to locate, identify, and neutralize the effectiveness of technical surveillance activities (electronic eavesdropping, wiretapping, bugging, etc.). Technical surveillance countermeasures should be a part of the overall protection strategy. Individuals within the organization responsible for physical security, facility security, information asset protection, telecommunications, meeting planning and information technology all have a stake in addressing these concerns.*

The physical characteristics of a building have a bearing on opportunities for surveillance. Some of these factors are poor access control designs, inadequate soundproofing, common or shared ducts, and space above false ceilings enabling access. Comprehensive security methods will hinder spies. The in-house security team can begin countermeasures by conducting a physical search for planted devices. If a decision is made to contact a specialist, *only the most expertly trained and experienced consultant should be recruited.*

The Countermeasures Consultant

Organizations often recruit a countermeasures consultant to perform contract work. As a consumer, ask for copies of certificates of TSCM courses completed and a copy of the insurance policy for errors and omissions for TSCM services. What equipment is used? What techniques are employed for the cost? Are sweeps and meticulous physical inspections conducted for the quoted price? Watch for scare tactics. Is the consultant really a vendor trying to sell surveillance detection devices, or a PI claiming to be a TSCM specialist? Will the consultant protect confidentiality? The interviewer should request a review of past reports to clients. Were names deleted to protect confidentiality? These questions help to avoid hiring an unqualified "expert." One practitioner offered clients debugging services and used an expensive piece of equipment to conduct sweeps. After hundreds of sweeps, he decided to have the equipment serviced. A service person discovered that the device was not working properly because it had no battery for one of its components. The surprised "expert" never realized a battery was required.

For a comprehensive countermeasures program, the competent consultant will be interested in sensitive information flow, storage, and retrieval. Extra cost will result from such an analysis, but it is often cost effective.

The employer should use a public telephone off the premises to contact the consultant in order not to alert a spy to impending countermeasures. An alerted spy may remove or turn off a bug or tap and the TSCM may be less effective.

Techniques and Equipment

Detection equipment is expensive and certain equipment is subject to puffing, but useless. A company should purchase its own equipment only if it retains a well-qualified TSCM technician, many sweeps are conducted, and the in-house TSCM program is cost-effective.

Equipment includes the nonlinear junction detector (NLJD), costing about $15,000 and capable of detecting radio transmitters, microphones, infrared and ultrasonic transmitters, recorders, video cameras, cell phones, and other hidden electronic devices, even when they are not working. Gruber (2006: 284–285) offers the following on the NLJD. It transmits a microwave signal through its antenna and an internal receiver listens for a RF response that may mean a device is present. NLJDs are available in various power outputs to the restricted government version. The effectiveness of this equipment is poor in an area containing several electronic devices; in this case, a physical search is best.

The telephone analyzer is another tool designed for testing a variety of single and multi-line telephones, answering machines, fax machines, intercom systems. The spectrum analyzer is another tool. Basically, it is a radio receiver with a visual display to detect airborne radio signals. Other types of specialized equipment are on the market. Buyer beware: the quality and cost of equipment varies widely.

Some security personnel or executives plant a bug for the sole purpose of determining if the equipment of the detection specialist is effective. This "test" can be construed as a criminal offense. An alternative is specially designed test transmitters, commercially available, that has no microphone pickup and therefore can be used without liability. Another technique is to place a tape recorder with a microphone in a drawer.

A tool kit and standard forms are two additional aids for the countermeasures specialist. The tool kit consists of the common tools (e.g., screwdrivers, pliers, electrical tape) used by an electrician. Standard forms facilitate good recordkeeping and serve as a checklist. What was checked? What tests were performed? What were the readings? Where? When? Who performed the tests? Why were the tests conducted? Over a period, records can be used to make comparisons while helping to answer questions.

The following list offers topics of consideration for TSCM (Gruber, 2006: 277–304; Kaiser and Stokes, 2006: 60–68):

- The first step in TSCM is a physical search for devices beginning from outside the building. The physical search, both outside and inside, is very important and time-consuming. On the outside, focus on items such as utilities, wires, ductwork, and openings (e.g., windows). A spy can tap into lines outside the building without needing to ever enter the building. A top executive should establish a cover story to avoid alerting anyone to the TSCM.
- Inside the building, the TSCM technician should check cabling, inside individual office equipment (e.g., telephones, faxes, and computers), and openings. Is there anything in the office equipment that appears odd?
- The technician should be knowledgeable about IT systems, computers, internal network or Local Area Network (LAN), and a connection to the outside or Wide Area Network (WAN). These systems can be bugged or tapped like telephone systems. For example, a LAN analyzer connected to a line can read all e-mail that travels through the line. The technician should have equipment to check what is attached to lines.
- Besides traditional cable, fiber optic cable can also be tapped. A tap on a fiber optic cable can be detected through an Optical Time Domain Reflectometer.
- Since devices may be hidden in walls, the technician can use an ultraviolet light to detect plaster repairs to walls. A NLJD or a portable x-ray machine can be used to detect devices in walls.
- Items in walls that should be checked are power outlets, phone jacks, and network jacks. Tools to check these items and inside walls are a flashlight, dental mirror, and a fiber optic camera.
- Plates at light switches, wall outlets, and HVAC vent covers should all be removed for the search and prior to the sweep.
- If a bug or tap is found, it should be documented and photographed. The device could be booby-trapped. Although police should be contacted for assistance, their response and expertise will vary widely. A difficult question surfaces as to whether the device should remain and fed false information.
- The TSCM technician often finds nothing unusual. Such results afford protection against bugs and taps. However, 100% protection is not possible, because information assets can be lost in so many ways, mostly from humans. Security practitioners should be creative, think like a spy, and not forget about the inexpensive, easy, and obvious methods to steal information assets.

Another strategy to thwart listening devices is "shielding," also called *electronic sound-proofing*. Basically, copper foil or screening and carbon filament are applied throughout a room to prevent acoustical or electromagnetic emanations from leaving. Although this method is very expensive (costing more than $100,000), several organizations employ it to have at least one secure room or to protect information in computers.

Equipment is available on the market that *may* frustrate telephone taps and listening devices. Scramblers, attached to telephones, alter the voice as it travels through the line. However, no device or system is foolproof. Often, simple countermeasures are useful. For instance, an executive can wait until everybody is present for an important meeting, and then relocate it to a previously undisclosed location. Conversants can operate a radio at high volume during sensitive conversations, and exercise caution during telephone and other conversations.

Many businesses and commercial telephony service providers are moving to Voice over Internet Protocol (VoIP) technology because of lower costs and efficiency. Such services may not even make contact with the traditional telephone network. One concern of VoIP technology relates to its inability to provide traditional location identification (i.e., Enhanced 911) for 911 emergency calls made to public safety agencies. Of particular interest for our discussion here is that traditional wiretaps are more difficult to intercept with VoIP infrastructure and end-to-end encryption compounds the challenges for those seeking to wiretap (National Institute of Justice, 2006).

It must be remembered that information assets can be collected in many different ways besides with physical devices. Losses can occur through speeches and publications by employees, in company trash, and by unknowingly hiring a spy. Comprehensive, broad-based information security is necessary.

□ □ □ ▬▬▬▬▬▬▬▬▬▬▬▬▬▬▬▬▬▬

Who do you think has "the edge," those who seek information assets or those who protect it?

□ □ □ ▬▬▬▬▬▬▬▬▬▬▬▬▬▬▬▬▬▬

Search the Web
Here are Web sites relevant to this chapter:

ASIS, International: www.asisonline.org
Business Espionage Controls and Countermeasures Association: www.becca-online.org/
Institute for a Drug-Free Workplace: www.drugfreeworkplace.org/
National Association of Information Destruction, Inc.: www.naidonline.org/
National Clearinghouse for Alcohol and Drug Information: http://ncadi.samhsa.gov/
National Institute for Occupational Safety and Health (NIOSH): www.cdc.gov/niosh/homepage.html
Occupational Safety and Health Administration (OSHA): www.osha.gov
OSHA: www.dol.gov/asp/programs/drugs/workingpartners/dfworkplace/dfwp.asp
Society of Competitive Intelligence Professionals: www.scip.org/
U.S. Department of Labor: www.dol.gov/elaws/drugfree.htm
U.S. Department of State: www.state.gov/travelandbusiness/

▬▬▬▬▬▬▬▬▬▬▬▬▬▬▬▬▬▬ □ □ □

Case Problems

18A. As a security manager, you just received an internal telephone call from a supervisor who complains about a subordinate who became angered by a work assignment and told the supervisor that he knows where he lives and where his kids go to school. What do you do?

18B. You are a security manager at a plant. One day, a former employee shows up at the front gate and demands to see his estranged wife. In addition, he wants to talk with the human resources director about benefits. How do you handle this situation?

18C. John Smith, an employee who has just lost his job because of corporate downsizing, is in the office of the Director of Human Resources holding a pistol in the direction of the Director. As the security manager, you were summoned to the office earlier, not knowing that the pistol had been drawn. You enter the office and you stop upon seeing the pistol. John Smith states: "I've given 10 years of my life to this place." "They had no right doing this to me." "If I can't work, I can't support my family." "It's management's fault and they are going to pay." As the security manager, what do you say and do? (This case problem was prepared with the assistance of Hasselt and Romano, 2004: 12–17).

18D. As the chief security officer for a corporation with plants in the United States and Europe, prepare a list of questions to answer as you plan a personnel protection program.

18E. As a security manager you hear through the grapevine that several employees smoke marijuana during lunch when they go to their vehicles. What do you do?

18F. As the new chief security officer for a corporation, you are reviewing the methods of information collection of the in-house competitive intelligence unit. The list includes using the Internet, public documents, public documents from government, private investigators, subscriptions to news services, purchasing securities to receive annual financial reports of competitors, collecting garbage from competitors, attending seminars and speeches of competitors, and purchasing competitor products for study. Do any of these methods necessitate closer attention? Explain and justify your answer.

18G. As the security director for a corporation engaged in research, you see the need for an information security consultant to improve protection. What criteria would you list to select such a specialist? What questions would you ask applicants during the selection process?

18H. Of the major topics in this chapter, which one would you select as a specialization and career? Why? How would you develop such a specialization and career?

References

ASIS International. (2007). *Information Asset Protection Draft Guideline*. www.asisonline. org, retrieved February 9, 2007.

ASIS International. (2005). *Workplace Violence Prevention and Response Guideline*. www. asisonline.org, retrieved March 8, 2007.

Apuzzo, M. (2007). "Chiquita to Pay $25M in Terror Case." Associated Press (March 14). http://biz.yahoo.com/ap/070314/terrorism_bananas.html?.v=5, retrieved March 16, 2007.

Ashley, S. (2006). "Cell Phone Vulnerabilities." *Law Officer Magazine*, 2 (July).

Associated Press. (2006). "Schwab: $2M for CEO Security." *Security Director News*, 3 (May).

Atkinson, W. (2001). "Safe Travel." *Risk & Insurance*, 12 (April 1).

Besse, W., and Whitehead, C. (2000). "New Tools of an Old Trade." *Security Management*, 44 (June).

Bowron, E. (2001). "All the World's a Staging Ground." *Security Management*, 45 (April).

Business Espionage Controls and Countermeasures Association. (2007). "About BECCA." http://www.becca-online.org/, retrieved March 18, 2007.

Business Espionage Controls and Countermeasures Association. (2001). "News of Hostile Activity" http://www.espionbusiness.com, retrieved June 6, 2001.

Carroll, J. (1996). *Computer Security*, 3rd ed. Boston: Butterworth-Heinemann.

Curtis, G., and McBride, R. (2005). *Proactive Security Administration*. Upper Saddle River, NJ: Pearson Prentice Hall.

Dahle North America. (2007). http://www.dahle.com/high_security.htm, retrieved March 19, 2007.

DeCenzo, D., and Robbins, S. (2005). *Fundamentals of Human Resource Management*, 8th ed. Hoboken, NJ: John Wiley & Sons Pub.

Ehrlich, C. (2002). "Liar, Liar: The Legal Perils of Misrepresentation." *Competitive Intelligence Magazine*, 5 (March-April).

Elliott, R. (2006). "What's Behind Country Risk Ratings?" *Security Management*, 50 (August).

Elliott, K., and Shelley, K. (2005). "Impact of employee assistance programs on substance abusers and workplace safety." *Journal of Employment Counseling*, 42 (September).

Gips, M. (2006). "High on the Job." *Security Management*, 50 (February).

Gips, M. (2007). "My Short Life as an EP Specialist." *Security Management*, 51 (March).

Gruber, R. (2006). *Physical and Technical Security: An Introduction*. Clifton Park, NY: Thomson Delmar Learning.

Halligan, R. (2001). "Do Your Secrets Pass the Test?" *Security Management*, 45 (March).

Hasselt, V., and Romano, S. (2004). "Role-Playing: A Vital Tool in Crisis Negotiation Skills Training." *FBI Law Enforcement Bulletin*, 73 (February).

Hershkowitz, R. (2004). "Zero Tolerance Equals Trouble." *Security Management*, 48 (October).

Horowitz, R. (2005). "A Comment on Drafting Corporate Competitive Intelligence Policies." http://www.rhesq.com/CI/Comment%20on%20CI%20Policies.html, retrieved March 18, 2007.

Horowitz, R. (1998). "The Economic Espionage Act: The Rules Have Not Changed." *Competitive Intelligence Review*, 9. http://www.scip.org/pdf/9(3)horowitz.pdf, retrieved March 22, 2007.

Hudson, J. (2004). "Dozens Sue over Lockheed Shootings." *The Clarion-Ledger* (July 3).

Hughes, S. (2001). "Violence in the Workplace: Identifying Costs and Preventive Solutions." *Security Journal*, 14.

Insurance Information Institute. (2007). "What does kidnap and ransom insurance cover?" http://www.iii.org/individuals/business/optional/kidnapandransom/, retrieved March 11, 2007.

Isaacs, R. (2004). "How Not to Tell all." *Security Management*, 48 (May).

Ivancevich, J. (2001). *Human Resource Management*, 8th ed. Boston: McGraw-Hill Irwin.

Jaeger, S. (2001). "The Age of Rage." *Security Industry & Design*, 11 (February).

Jones, T. (2000). *Surveillance Countermeasures in the Business World*. Cookeville, TN: Research Electronics International.

Kaiser, M., and Stokes, R. (2006). "Who's Listening?" *Security Management*, 50 (February).

Kenny, J. (2005a). "Threats in the Workplace: The Thunder before the Storm?" *Security Journal*, 18 (3).

Kenny, J. (2005b). "Workplace Violence and the Hidden Land Mines: A Comparison of Gender Victimization." *Security Journal*, 18 (1).

Laczniak, G., and Murphy, P. (1993). "The Ethics of Corporate Spying." *Ethics Journal* (Fall).

Mallery, J. (2006). "The Hidden Data Thieves." *Security Technology & Design*, 16 (March).

Meadows, R. (2007). *Understanding Violence and Victimization*, 4th ed. Upper Saddle River, NJ: Pearson Prentice Hall.

Miller, S. (2007). "Gone in a Flash." *Information Security*, 10 (March).

Myshko, D. (2001). "Just Say Yes to Drug Testing." *Risk and Insurance*, 12 (April 16).

National Institute of Justice (2006). "Telephony Implications of Voice over Internet Protocol." www.ncjrs.gov/pdffiles1/nij/212976.pdf, retrieved June 18, 2007.

National Institute on Drug Abuse. (2006). "NIDA InfoFacts: Methamphetamine." http://www.nida.nih.gov/Infofacts/methamphetamine.html, retrieved March 9, 2007.

National Security Agency. (2000). "National Information Systems Security (INFOSEC) Glossary." (UNCLASSIFIED). http://security.isu.edu/pdf/4009.pdf, retrieved March 22, 2007.

Nolan, J. (1997). "Economic Espionage, Proprietary Information Protection: Difficult Times Ahead." *Security Technology and Design* (January-February).

Petersen International Underwriters. (2003). "A Kidnap and Ransom Insurance Plan" (Brochure). http://www.eglobalhealth.com/files/Epic.pdf, retrieved March 12, 2007.

Piazza, P. (2005). "From Bluetooth to RedFang." *Security Management*, 49 (March).

Piazza, P. (2007). "The ABCs of USB." *Security Management*, 51 (January).

Purpura, P. (1993). "When the Security Manager Gets Shot: A Corporate Response." *Security Journal* (July).

Ryan, L. (2005). "Exclusive remedy upheld in Lockheed Martin shooting case." *Workers' Comp Insider* (July 21). http://www.workerscompinsider.com/archives/2005_07.html, retrieved March 10, 2007.

Shyman, R. (2000). "Women at Work." *Security Management*, 44 (February).

Simovich, C. (2004). "To Serve and Protect." *Security Management*, 48 (October).

Smith, S. (2004). "What every employer should know about drug testing in the workplace." *Occupational Hazards*, 66 (August).

Society of Competitive Intelligence Professionals. (2007). "About SCIP." http://www.scip.org/2_overview.php, retrieved March 18, 2007.

U.S. Department of Labor. (2006). "Injuries, Illnesses, and Fatalities." http://www.bls.gov/iif/home.htm, retrieved March 8, 2007.

U.S. Drug Enforcement Administration. (2003). "Guidelines for a Drug-Free Workforce." http://www.usdoj.gov/dea/demand/dfmanual/09df.htm, retrieved March 14, 2007.

University of Iowa. (2001). "Workplace Violence: A Report to the Nation." http://www.public-health.uiowa.edu/IPRC/NATION.PDF, retrieved March 8, 2007.

Wikipedia. (2007). "Paper Shredder." http://en.wikipedia.org/wiki/Paper_shredder, retrieved March 19, 2007.

19

□□□
□□□
□□□

Your Future in Security and Loss Prevention

Objectives

After studying this chapter, the reader will be able to:

1. Discuss security and loss prevention in the future.
2. List at least 10 trends affecting security and loss prevention.
3. Discuss security and loss prevention education, research, and training.
4. Explain how to seek employment opportunities in the security and loss prevention profession.

KEY TERMS

- smart security
- automatic factory
- cycle of protection
- criminal entrepreneurs
- multinational and multicultural workforce
- United States Commission on National Security/21st Century
- five wars of globalization
- market forces
- decentralized networks
- clinical experience model
- evidence-based model
- DHS Centers of Excellence
- programmed, self-paced instruction
- distance learning online

Security and Loss Prevention in the Future

Seeking to accurately predict the future is difficult and risky. However, a professional will consider many variables when making educated guesses to anticipate future events. What follows here are possibilities for the future to which the reader can apply critical thinking skills.

Periodically, we hear older, experienced folks speak about how much simpler life was years ago. However, this view is subject to debate because technology, for example, has made life and work easier in many ways. At the same time, security and loss prevention practitioners face numerous problems in their work today, brought about by numerous factors. These factors include the needs of businesses as they seek to survive and return a profit, globalization, an array of threats and hazards, limited security budgets, and government laws and regulations. Our world is likely to continue to be increasingly complicated, and as difficult as it may be at times, problems should be perceived as challenges that have solutions and/or present opportunities.

As we know, technology has enhanced security in many ways. We have "smart cards" and "smart cameras," and we will see many more systems and devices that contain **"smart security,"** which means that never-ending enhanced technology will be built into systems and devices. We will see increasingly "smart"—fences, contraband detection systems, WMD sensors, robot guards, and cybersecurity. Artificial intelligence will continue to surpass human capabilities. For instance, rather than security officers watching numerous CCTV monitors and becoming fatigued, the artificial intelligence that we have today will continue to help them to spot events deserving attention and response. Facial recognition systems will improve and eventually be capable of identifying offenders wherever they may be while they are moving.

Future integrated security systems will perform an array of loss prevention activities beyond what is accomplished today. For example, if an intruder enters a building, not only will a system pinpoint the entry location, via a series of sensors, and activate CCTV, but also simultaneously, it will dispatch a robot to apprehend the intruder and positively identify the intruder and his or her background.

Access control systems will no longer use cards. An individual will stand in front of sophisticated sensors, and positive identification will be made by the analysis of a number of biometric characteristics: bone structure, teeth, and body odor, to name a few. It would be especially difficult for an offender to duplicate several of these characteristics. The same sensors could be placed at many locations to monitor personnel, such as parking lots, building entrances, elevators, high-security locations, copying machines, lunchrooms, and restrooms. Obviously, with such a system, it would be possible to know exactly where all employees are at every minute of every workday. If a fire developed or a crime occurred, the recorded location of everyone would aid loss prevention personnel. However, will employees welcome IT records revealing how many times and for how long they visit the restroom or other locations? Suppose a system had the capability to record every conversation, every day, within a building. This could give management the opportunity to "weed out" employees who are counterproductive to organizational goals. In addition, because this system would be capable of "recognizing" any conversations pertaining to losses, the loss prevention department could review these conversations and investigate vulnerabilities. With these possibilities in mind, one realizes the blessing and burden of technology. Are such intense measures worth sacrificing privacy? Certainly not. *Countermeasures must strike a balance between preventing losses and protecting privacy. In the future, as today, the courts will be watching and ruling as technological innovations and loss prevention strategies are applied.*

As we progress in the era of the **automatic factory** (AF), loss prevention methods will change to meet the new technology. The AF operates machines that transform raw materials into finished products with limited human input. Robots with self-contained computers are an essential part of the AF. Activities such as material handling, assembly, inspection, and quality control are automated. Human input comes from a computer control center. Widespread use of "just-in-time production" also contributes to manufacturing's need for fewer workers. Production is based on the needs of retailers, which avoids costly inventory holding and producing items that do not sell well (U.S. Department of Labor, 2000: 31).

The future use of robots is promising. They operate 24 hours a day without a coffee break or vacation. A salary and fringe benefits such as hospitalization and pensions are unnecessary for robots. Also, robots are immune to heat, cold, noise, radiation, and other hazards.

Imagine loss prevention for a plant operated by only three managers and six technicians. If internal pilfering occurred, the number of suspects would be narrowed to nine, excluding robots. Parking lots, frequently a source of crime and requiring traffic control, would be smaller. Fires and accidents, which are often caused by human error, would be reduced.

□ □ □ ▬▬▬▬▬▬▬▬▬▬▬▬▬▬▬▬▬▬▬▬▬▬▬▬▬▬▬▬▬▬▬▬▬▬▬▬▬▬▬

Can you describe an example of a clash between technology and civil liberties? What were the issues and solutions?

▬▬▬▬▬▬▬▬▬▬▬▬▬▬▬▬▬▬▬▬▬▬▬▬▬▬▬▬▬▬▬▬▬▬▬▬▬ □ □ □

Trends Affecting Security and Loss Prevention

To begin with, the primary drivers of security and loss prevention practitioners, programs, and services are the needs and objectives of organizations and the changes within our society and world. Protection at a hotel will differ from protection at a nuclear power plant. The loss prevention needs of a retail chain in the United States will differ from the loss prevention needs of a multinational corporation with business interests in the Middle East. Although the protection needs of organizations differ, there are trends that affect all security and loss prevention programs.

The 21st century will continue to see no shortage of threats and hazards facing businesses and institutions. The list that follows presents trends and challenges that impact protection programs and the types of specialists required for security and loss prevention and, thus, employment opportunities:

- The challenges of crimes, fires, accidents, and disasters will remain but increase in complexity.
- Terrorism will become increasingly sinister and surprising because of the proliferation of WMD, mass casualties, severe economic harm, and its successes.
- Security and loss prevention metrics (see Chapter 2) will grow in importance to measure and enhance the success of protection programs. Campbell (2007: 60) writes: "Metrics are a tool used to facilitate influence, to demonstrate, argue, support, and convince."
- We often hear about security and loss prevention departments "doing more with less." Budget cuts are a fact of life requiring prioritization and creativity. The challenges can be enormous. However, "doing more with less" has its limitations, and a variety of outcomes is possible. Examples are victimization of people, financial losses, and ethical and legal issues.
- Risk analysis will become more challenging. Improved research methodologies for risk analyses must be sought for better decisions.
- Research shows that security managers are gaining new duties including risk management, safety, background investigations, and travel security. They are also harnessing their computers for broader applications such as incident tracking, sharing information internally via an intranet, and conducting training ("Security's Burden Increases," 2001: 18).
- Many security departments are facing either placement under another department (e.g., facilities management), outsourcing, or even elimination.
- The market for security services and systems will continue to grow globally (see Chapter 2). Although many businesses and institutions will maintain proprietary security departments, we will see an increase in the outsourcing of partial and entire security departments. Service firms will continue to provide security officers, investigations, integrated systems, and cybersecurity, among other services.
- Numerous specializations will grow in importance. Examples are risk management, business continuity planning, emergency management, life safety, fire protection, homeland security, protection of critical infrastructures and key assets, border security, cybersecurity, fraud prevention and investigation, workplace violence prevention, personnel protection, and information security.
- The **cycle of protection** will remain: as new technology is developed, offenders will exploit it, and security specialists and offenders will remain in constant competition—one group striving to protect, the other striving to circumvent defenses. Both sides will win "battles," but neither will win the "war."
- Cybercrime will increase. The number of cybercrime cases reported to police will also increase and require additional resources and training for police, prosecutors, and judges. "The largest computer crime problem affecting local law enforcement representing the largest number of victims and the largest monetary loss will be Internet fraud, including fraud via identity theft." Virtual crimes will require new criminal and civil laws and new methodologies for prevention and investigation. Organized crime and terrorist groups will increasingly become involved in cybercrime (Taylor et al., 2006: 354–383).

- Public police, especially on the local level, will continue to lag behind the technical expertise of cybercriminals. Consequently, the private sector will continue to fill the void.
- Information security will increase in intensity. Taylor et al., (2006: 374) write: "The character of espionage will continue to broaden into the arenas of information warfare, economic espionage, and theft of intellectual property."
- As we become a cashless society, offenders will be ready to gain illegally from system weaknesses.
- E-business will increase along with protection needs.
- Senior management in criminal organizations is becoming increasingly well educated and trained. Criminals increasingly will have college degrees and experience in IT, engineering, money management, investments, accounting, and law. In addition, offenders will use just about all the technology available to government and businesses.
- **Criminal entrepreneurs,** who seek illicit profits from a wide variety of enterprises and launder the proceeds, are becoming increasingly knowledgeable of the operations of financial institutions and related vulnerabilities. They will continue to infiltrate and manipulate financial institutions for their own purposes (e.g., money laundering), as this target becomes a top priority. Financial security professionals will continue to be challenged not only by external offenders but by internal ones as well.
- Counterfeiting will continue to be a huge business for organized criminals, especially in designer clothes, software, entertainment items, vehicle parts, and medical supplies. Counterfeiters have production facilities and distribution networks ready for new product lines.
- Twenty-first century crime groups increasingly will own shares of multinational corporations and be involved in management decisions. This will create new challenges for security professionals.
- Satellites increasingly will assist security through instantaneous communications throughout the world. People and assets will be more easily tracked. Such technology will assist in the investigations of kidnappings and hijackings.
- Corporate and institutional changes have had an impact on employee morale. The objectives of generating profit and improving quality while downsizing, and other workplace issues, have taken a toll on loyalty among workers. Loyalty has been an asset to protection programs. Its deterrent value today must be questioned and studied. New innovative strategies are required.
- Women, the elderly, and the disadvantaged will make up a greater portion of the workforce. Such groups present new challenges for security. Women and the elderly require protection not only in the workplace, but also at home and while traveling. Cases of domestic violence, sexual harassment, and stalking are likely to occupy more of the security professional's time. Women and the elderly will be involved in more workplace crime. If increasing numbers of disadvantaged workers are employed, they may bring with them problems of gangs and illegal drugs ("Here Comes the 21st Century: What Does It Hold for Security?" 1997: 4–7).
- More research is needed on issues of minority group members and women in security positions. The majority of women in one study of women security managers felt they experienced relatively high levels of sex discrimination, sexual harassment, and on-the-job stress; they also felt they were not paid the same as men for the same work. Despite these issues in this male-dominated vocation, the study showed three-fourths of the women surveyed were satisfied with their careers ("Survey Studies Women in Security," 1996: 87–88).
- Security must adapt to a **multinational and multicultural workforce.** As the workforce changes, security professionals must be aware of diversity and use it to the advantage of the business. Good communication can improve security and business, and even help develop new markets.
- Global markets require security to be aware of each culture and related risks.

- Twenty-first century police will spend most of their resources and time curbing violent crimes, while their efforts against property crimes will take a lower priority. Consequently, the private sector will fill the void.
- More and more citizens and business people are realizing that the police have limited ability and resources to curb crime. Police are primarily "reactive"; that is, they respond to calls for service and investigate. They often are under great pressure to solve serious cases. Because of limited resources, police are not able to be more "proactive." Again, the private sector will fill the void.
- A panel of law enforcement specialists predicted that, in 2035, private security agencies will perform more than 50% of all law enforcement responsibilities (Tafoya, 1991: 4).
- Ritter (2006: 8) writes: "There's no question that terrorism, the growth of multicultural populations, massive migration, upheavals in age-composition demographics, technological developments, and globalization over the next three or more decades will affect the world's criminal justice systems."
- First responders (i.e., police, firefighters, and EMS) will continue to have limited resources. Businesses and institutions must prepare for emergencies.
- As the world's population increases, competition for natural resources (e.g., oil, drinking water) will intensify.
- Three key factors to assist protection professionals today and in the future are a broad-based education (e.g., business, security, IT), the skill to show that protection strategies have a return on investment, and the flexibility to deal with rapid change.
- Trends affecting the security and loss prevention profession point to employment opportunities in many organizations (both proprietary and contract), government agencies, and in many specialized areas.

The **United States Commission on National Security/21st Century** (1999: 1–8), commonly known as the Hart-Rudman Task Force on Homeland Security, produced a series of reports. Phase 1 focused on trends in the future, as outlined in the following list. Phase 2 explained an American strategy based on U.S. interests and objectives. Phase 3 recommended comprehensive institutional and procedural changes throughout the executive and legislative branches in order to meet the challenges of 2025.

1. Institutions designed for another age may not be appropriate for the future.
2. Authoritarian regimes will increasingly collapse as they try to insulate their populations from free-flowing information and new economic opportunities.
3. An economically strong United States is likely to remain a primary political, military, and cultural force in the world through 2025.
4. Weapons of mass destruction and weapons of mass disruption (e.g., information warfare) will continue to proliferate.
5. Adversaries will resort to forms and levels of violence shocking to our sensibilities. Americans will likely die on American soil, possibly in large numbers.
6. Emerging technologies, such as advances in biotechnology, will create new moral, cultural, and economic divisions and an antitechnology backlash.
7. Energy, especially fossil fuel, will continue to have major strategic significance.
8. Minorities will be less likely to tolerate prejudicial government. Consequently, new states, international protectorates, and zones of autonomy will be born in violence.
9. Space will become a competitive military environment.
10. U.S. intelligence will face more challenging adversaries, and even excellent intelligence will not prevent all surprises.

The National Intelligence Council, which reports to the Director of National Intelligence and serves in a strategic thinking role, reports from its "2020 Project" that the magnitude and speed of change from globalization will be a defining feature of the world to 2020. Other trends noted by this group are: new global players of increasing influence will be China and

India; political Islam will have an increasingly significant impact; there will be a sense of insecurity, including terrorism; and the U.S. will retain enormous advantages that no other state will match, however, more countries will be in a position to make the U.S. pay a heavy price for military action. Furthermore, more firms will become global; the world economy is likely to continue to grow; large pockets of poverty will persist globally; and governments will struggle to keep up with change (Flynn, 2007).

☐ ☐ ☐ ▬▬▬▬▬▬▬▬▬▬▬▬▬▬▬▬▬▬▬▬▬▬▬▬

What trends do you anticipate in the security and loss prevention profession?

☐ ☐ ☐ ▬▬▬▬▬▬▬▬▬▬▬▬▬▬▬▬▬▬▬▬▬▬▬▬

Five Wars of Globalization
As in the past, the private sector, as well as the public sector, will continue in the future to contend with what Naim (2003) calls the "**five wars of globalization.**" These are the illegal trade in drugs, arms, intellectual property, people, and money. He emphasizes that religious zeal or political goals drive terrorists, whereas profit drives the other wars, and all of the wars result in murder, mayhem, and global insecurity. According to Naim, governments have been fighting the five wars for centuries and losing them. He does not include terrorism in this statement. Naim explains why governments cannot win the five wars of globalization:

- Criminal cartels can manipulate weak governments by corrupting politicians and police.
- International law, including embargoes, sanctions, and conventions, offer criminals opportunities to profit from illegal goods.
- Al-Qaida members are stateless and so are criminal networks involved in the five wars. Whereas terrorists and other criminals can seek refuge in and take advantage of porous borders, traditional notions of sovereignty frustrate governments.
- These wars pit governments against **market forces**. Thousands of independent, stateless organizations are motivated by large profits gained by exploiting international price differentials, unsatisfied demand, or the cost advantages resulting from theft (i.e., no cost to produce the product).
- These wars pit bureaucracies against networks. The same network that smuggles illegal drugs may be involved in counterfeit watches that are sold on the streets of Manhattan by illegal immigrants. Highly **decentralized networks** can act swiftly and flexibly, while often lacking a headquarters and central leadership to be targeted. Governments often meet the challenge by forming task forces or creating new bureaucracies.

Naim claims that governments may never be able to eliminate the international trade from the five wars, but they can and should do better. He offers four areas capable of producing ideas to meet the challenges from these wars:

- Negotiate more flexible notions of sovereignty. Since stateless networks regularly violate laws and cross borders to trade illegally, nations should develop agreements to "manage" sovereignty to combat criminal networks.
- Naim calls for stronger multilateral institutions (e.g., multinational police efforts such as Interpol). However, nations do not trust each other, some assume that criminals have infiltrated the police agencies of other countries, and today's allies may become tomorrow's enemies.

- The five wars render obsolete many institutions, legal frameworks, military doctrines, weapons systems, and law enforcement techniques that have been applied for numerous years. Rethinking and adaptation are needed to develop, for instance, new concepts of war "fronts" defined by geography and new functions for intelligence agents, soldiers, and enforcement officers.
- In all five wars, government agencies battle networks motivated by profits created by other government agencies that create an imbalance between demand and supply that makes prices rise and profits skyrocket. Since beating market forces is next to impossible, reality may force governments, in certain illegal markets, to change from repressing the markets to regulating them. In addition, creating market incentives may be better than creating bureaucracies to curb the excesses of markets. In certain instances, technology can possibly be used to replace government policies (e.g., encryption to protect software on CDs).

☐ ☐ ☐ ▬▬▬▬▬▬▬▬▬▬▬▬▬▬▬▬▬▬▬

What can businesses and protection programs do to prevent and reduce losses from the "wars of globalization"?

▬▬▬▬▬▬▬▬▬▬▬▬▬▬▬▬▬▬▬ ☐ ☐ ☐

Education

How relevant is a college education to the loss prevention careerist? A college degree will not guarantee a job or advancement opportunities. However, with a college degree, a person has improved chances of obtaining a favored position. If two, equally experienced people are vying for the same professional loss prevention position and person A has a college degree while person B does not, person A probably will get the job. Of course, other characteristics within a person's background will improve job opportunities. Education and experience are top considerations. Training also is important. Two other characteristics are personality and common sense. As used here, *personality* pertains to one's ability to get along with others. Many consider this factor to be one-half of a person's job. *Common sense* is a subjective term that is used widely. It refers to an analysis of a situation that produces the "best" solution that most people would favor.

Loss Prevention Education: Today and Tomorrow

Although business degree programs are an excellent location for security and loss prevention courses, the criminal justice (CRJ) degree programs at hundreds of campuses in the United States today are the greatest driving force behind security and loss prevention academic programs. Many institutions offer criminal justice degrees with an emphasis in security and loss prevention. In addition, several institutions maintain distinct departments focusing on security and loss prevention degree and certificate programs.

During the late 1960s, many police science degree programs advanced to law enforcement and then to CRJ degree programs. As CRJ programs developed, so did the spectrum of course offerings: from primarily narrow police science courses, CRJ programs began offering courses relating to the entire justice system (i.e., police, courts, corrections). CRJ programs became multidisciplinary because the answers to complex problems are more forthcoming from a broader spectrum of study. Likewise, security and loss prevention academic programs will evolve into broader-based, multidisciplinary programs and include the study of business, risk management, cybersecurity, terrorism, and homeland security.

Since the 9/11 attacks, hundreds of new academic and training programs have been implemented. Universities, four-year colleges, and two-year colleges have increased their offerings of degree programs, certificates, and courses in homeland security (HS), emergency management (EM), and related disciplines. Other sources of education and training include proprietary schools, corporations, government agencies, unions, and associations. Despite an increase in education and training programs relevant to HS, there is no consensus of what constitutes a common body of knowledge to establish HS as an academic discipline. Furthermore, course content in this field of study varies among institutions and training programs. HS in higher education is being developed in a wide variety of academic disciplines and focusing on various audiences and needs. Part of the problem is that the DHS is continuously developing its mission under changing circumstances and events. In addition, the public and private sectors are trying to determine what knowledge and skills are required for HS. Also, perspectives on HS differ among specialists.

In reference to academic programs in EM, these programs have a longer history than academic programs in HS. Both are evolving at an erratic pace with no uniformity, while being influenced by catastrophic events followed by government action.

The many issues of HS were discussed and debated at the 2005 ASIS Academic-Practitioner Symposium, whose attendees work to enhance education and research in the discipline of security. David Gilmore, a security practitioner and educator who chairs the annual event, expressed the sentiment of most participants that the concept of HS is not clearly defined and its meaning varies (Davidson, 2005: 74). Dr. Wayne Blanchard, who hopes to make EM a legitimate academic discipline, spoke at the symposium. He noted that most EM academic programs are oriented toward the public sector, but the private sector is larger, and perhaps academia should offer more programs on preventing and responding to emergencies in the private sector. He was asked how HS differs from EM. "Dr. Blanchard observed that since EM covers all hazards, all actors, and all phases, a program dealing only with terrorist threats would not be considered an EM program. However, such distinctions and definitions change over time. The work done by FEMA used to be called civil defense, then emergency management, and perhaps one day might be called homeland security" (ASIS International, 2005: 23).

Over several years, an HS body of knowledge and standardization of curricula will evolve to strengthen HS as an academic discipline. At the same time, diverse academic departments will continue to clash as decisions are made as to which department will house HS. EM has been going through such an evolutionary process for a longer period, and it will continue. Although a major source of direction for HS education and training is the National Strategy for Homeland Security, future events, challenges, legislation, and government policy will shape curriculum design (Purpura, 2007: 452–454).

Research

The criminal justice profession is one source for research direction for the security and loss prevention profession. The following perspectives on criminal justice research are verbatim from the *National Institute of Justice Journal* (Ritter, 2006: 8–11).

David Weisburd [University of Maryland] believes that the nature of criminal justice in 2040 will depend in large part on the primary research methodology. Is the criminal justice community better served by relying on the experiences and opinions of practitioners (the **clinical experience model**) or by research that tests programs and measures outcomes (the **evidence-based model**)?

Currently, the clinical experience model is the research path most frequently followed. Policies and technologies are based primarily on reports from practitioners about what they have found to work or not work. Sharing approaches and programs that seemed to work in one community with another community allows for quick application of successful ideas. The downside of this model is that a program may be widely adopted before scientific research demonstrates its efficacy in more than one place or application. For example, in one youth program aimed at reducing delinquency, counselors and parents believed that the treatments were effective, based on initial measures of success. However, subsequent evaluation revealed that participation in the program actually increased the risk of delinquency.

In the evidence-based model, a new program undergoes systematic research and evaluation before it is widely adopted. Now dominant in medicine—and becoming more popular in other areas such as education—the evidence-based model has been used successfully in criminal justice. For example, hot-spot policing (a policy adopted in the early 1990s that focuses police resources in high-crime areas) was preceded by studies that demonstrated its effectiveness.

But the evidence-based model also has shortcomings. Research requires a large investment of time and money, and many practitioners understandably would rather spend resources implementing an innovation than wait for confirming research. Time—always a precious commodity for policymakers and practitioners—can be a particularly frustrating component of the evidence-based model. Credible research requires time to adequately test an approach, often in more than one jurisdiction, before communities can adopt it on a large scale.

"Policymakers want to improve things while they have the power," Weisburd says. "They are under pressure to make an impact—so there is tension between the slowness of the evidence-based process and the pressure to move quickly."

Weisburd proposes making the evidence-based model "more realistic." He believes this can be done by

- Streamlining the process of developing evidence and conducting evaluations.
- Building an infrastructure to ensure that studies do not reinvent the wheel.
- Devising methods for getting studies off the ground faster, such as encouraging funders to help in the development of high-quality randomized experimental studies.
- Reinforcing a culture that emphasizes the exploration of which programs and practices do and do not work.

Weisburd also argues that federal investment in the scientific evaluation of new practices and programs must be increased. Researchers and practitioners must insist that "if you want us to make intelligent policy and not waste money by prematurely innovating in hundreds of departments, you must give us more money."

In what ways can the perspectives of Weisburd be applied to research in the security and loss prevention profession?

The most practical question for loss prevention researchers to address is as follows: What strategies are best to prevent and reduce losses from crimes, fires, accidents, and other threats and vulnerabilities? Ongoing evaluative research is instrumental in strengthening successful strategies while eliminating those that are less useful.

Additional directions for research include protection against terrorism, WMD, protection of critical infrastructures, key assets and "soft targets," IT security, security metrics, model training programs, determination of the most appropriate courses for relevant degree programs, effective job applicant screening, model statutes for licensing and regulation of the security industry, model for regulatory bodies, criteria for the selection of security services and systems, evaluation of services and systems, legal issues and liabilities, strategies to improve public–private sector cooperation, privatization, private justice system, centralized data bank for compiling loss statistics, the feasibility of tax deductions for implementing loss prevention strategies by a variety of entities and residential settings, and the use and effect of robots and other technological innovations.

As well as college and university criminal justice and loss prevention programs sharing these research questions, other curricula are capable of providing valuable input. They include business, risk management, insurance, emergency management, safety, fire protection, public health and medicine, architecture, landscape architecture, and engineering degree programs. A multidisciplinary research effort is most beneficial. Without adequate research, loss prevention practitioners will be hindered in their decision-making roles.

Universities have been actively fulfilling the research needs of homeland security and defense. Funding for university research for homeland security and defense is provided by federal departments (e.g., DHS, DOD) and agencies (e.g., CIA, EPA) and the private sector and state governments.

The DHS is involved in numerous research initiatives through its Office of Science and Technology. The DHS partners with other government agencies, universities, and industry to find and develop innovative ideas. A major area of focus is protection against catastrophic terrorism that could result in large-scale loss of life and major economic harm.

Homeland Security Presidential Directive-7 (HSPD-7) calls for a national critical infrastructure protection research and development (R&D) plan. *The National Plan for Research and Development in Support of Critical Infrastructure Protection* (The Executive Office of the President, Office of Science and Technology Policy and The Department of Homeland Security Science and Technology Directorate, 2004) is essentially a roadmap for investment and protection that integrates cyber, physical, and human elements. This R&D plan was developed in coordination with the *National Infrastructure Protection Plan*.

Through the Homeland Security Act of 2002, Congress mandated the DHS to enhance U.S. leadership in science and technology aimed at homeland security issues. This goal is supported through DHS funding of undergraduate and graduate fellowships and scholarships, and establishing **DHS Centers of Excellence** (HS-Centers). HS-Centers (i.e., universities) are overseen by the Office of University Programs within the Science & Technology directorate and are designed to create learning and research environments that bring together experts who focus on numerous topics including WMD, risk analysis related to the economic consequences of terrorism, infrastructure protection, biological threats and diseases, agro-security, and the behavioral aspects of terrorism and its consequences.

Larger sources of research on homeland security issues are the over 700 federally funded research and development laboratories and centers throughout the United States. These sites include federal labs, college and university labs, and private industry labs. Each year billions of dollars support homeland security R&D.

☐ ☐ ☐ ▬▬▬▬▬▬▬▬▬▬▬▬▬▬▬▬▬▬▬▬▬▬▬▬▬▬▬▬▬▬

What directions for research can you suggest for the security and loss prevention profession?

▬▬▬▬▬▬▬▬▬▬▬▬▬▬▬▬▬▬▬▬▬▬▬▬▬▬▬▬▬▬ ☐ ☐ ☐

Training

The future direction of training largely depends on organizational needs and objectives, threats and vulnerabilities, technological innovations, and loss prevention strategies. Practitioners will need to know how to operate in an environment of new countermeasures and complex systems. But even though loss prevention will change, many key topics taught in the training programs of today also will be taught tomorrow. Strategies against crimes, fires, accidents, and disasters will still be at the heart of training programs.

State involvement in training proprietary and contract service practitioners probably will increase for greater public safety. Uniformity in training will ensure that practitioners receive adequate information on basic topics such as laws of arrest, search and seizure, use of force, weapons, fire protection, safety, and emergency response. An interdisciplinary group would be the best choice to provide input for state-mandated training programs.

The training curriculum of tomorrow will continue to cater to the ever-increasing goal of professionalizing loss prevention personnel. The end product will be a thoroughly knowledgeable and skilled practitioner, able to provide a useful service to the community. Greater mutual respect will follow as public police and private-sector personnel share similar characteristics in education, training, salary, and professionalism.

Improved training helps to prevent costly liability suits; for example, from excessive force used by a uniformed officer. The quality of training, in terms of duration, intensity, and topics covered, is a prime consideration in such liability cases.

Programmed, self-paced instruction with the aid of computers will increase. This type of instruction is cost-effective, especially when an organization is faced with the challenge of turnover. Furthermore, new employees who learn quickly can move through the instructional program without having to wait for slower students. A varied training program may include not only programmed, self-paced instruction, but also lectures, audiovisual productions, role-playing, and demonstrations. **Distance learning online** will increase in popularity as students learn from remote locations.

The Concept of the Security Institute

Every state should maintain a security institute, preferably at a college or university. Three goals of a security institute are as follows:

1. Develop and conduct college and continuing education courses based on the needs of customers.
2. Work with the state government agency that regulates the private security industry to develop training programs, conduct research, and professionalize the field.
3. Offer the institute's service area crime prevention initiatives involving security and criminal justice college students who are an unrealized and underutilized national resource to control crime.

Employment

Many employment opportunities can be found in the security and loss prevention profession. Chapter 2 provides information on this industry and career specializations. The related profession of criminal justice, which includes police, courts, corrections, probation, and parole, plus the growth of privatization, provides opportunities and specialization for employment applicants.

Entry-level security officer positions vary widely in pay, benefits, and training. Generally, these positions do not pay as well as public police. However, there are many opportunities for employment and advancement and many part-time positions; the hours offer some flexibility; and the duties are less risky than public policing. Supervisors in security have mastered the tasks of security officers, possess broader skills, and have good human relations qualities. Managers generally have more education, training, experience, and responsibilities than supervisors do. They are involved in planning, budgeting, organizing, marketing, recruiting, directing, and controlling. Other careers in this profession include sales, self-employment (e.g., private investigations, consulting), and government security. The career boxes in previous chapters, courtesy of ASIS International, offer salary ranges for various positions.

Sources of Employment Information

- *Online services:* The Internet is a major source of employment information. There are several advantages: offerings are broad, time is saved by reviewing opportunities open worldwide, it is more up-to-date than most publications, and you can respond electronically. Be aware that confidentiality is limited. Look for services that are free.
- *Periodicals:* Within these sources, trends in employment and employment opportunities are common topics.
- *Professional associations:* Professional organizations serve members through educational programs, publications, and a variety of strategies aimed at increasing professionalism.
- *Trade conferences:* People with a common interest attend trade conferences, which are advertised in trade publications. By attending these conferences, a loss prevention

practitioner or student can learn about a variety of topics. The latest technology and professional seminars are typical features. Trade conferences provide an opportunity to meet practitioners who may be knowledgeable about employment opportunities or are actively seeking qualified people.

- *Educational institutions:* Security and loss prevention and criminal justice degree programs are another source of employment information. Usually, these programs have bulletin boards, near faculty offices, that contain career opportunities. College or university placement services or faculty members are other valuable sources.
- *Libraries:* A wealth of information for a career search is available at libraries. Examples include periodicals, newspapers, telephone books, directories, books on career strategies, and online services.
- *Government buildings:* Public buildings often contain bulletin boards that specify employment news, especially near personnel offices. Government agencies frequently search for practitioners to maintain security and safety at government buildings and installations.
- *Newspapers:* By looking under "security" in classified sections, one can find listings for entry-level positions. In large urban newspapers, more specialized positions are listed.
- *Public employment agencies:* These agency offices operate in conjunction with the U.S. Employment Service of the Department of Labor. Personnel will provide employment information without cost and actually contact recruiters or employers.
- *Networking:* An informal network consists of people the applicant knows from past educational or employment experiences. It is a good idea for any professional to maintain contact, however slight, with peers. When employment-related challenges develop and solutions are difficult to obtain, networking may be an avenue for answers. Likewise, this mutual assistance is applicable to employment searches.
- *Telephone books:* The addresses and telephone numbers of both private and public entities are abundant in telephone books. By looking up "security," "guards," "investigators," and "government offices," one can develop a list of locations for possible employment opportunities.
- *Private employment agencies:* Almost all urban areas have private employment agencies that charge a fee. This source probably will be a last resort, and one should carefully study financial stipulations. At times, these agencies have fee-paid jobs, which mean that the employer pays the fee.

Career Advice

1. Read at least two current books on searching for employment and careers; both the novice and the experienced person will learn or be reminded of many excellent tips that will "polish" the career search and instill confidence.
2. Begin your search by first focusing on yourself—your abilities and background, your likes and dislikes, and your personality and people skills.
3. If you are new to the security and loss prevention profession, aim to "get your foot in the door." As a college student, look for an intern position, work part-time, or do volunteer work. *Aim to graduate with experience.* As a retired government employee, or if you are beginning a new career in security, market and transfer your accumulated skills and experience to this profession.
4. Most people will enter new careers several times in their lives.
5. Searching for a career opportunity requires planning, patience, and perseverance. Rejections are a typical part of every search. A positive attitude will make or break your career.
6. When planning elective courses in college or when training opportunities arise, consider that employers want people with skills (e.g., writing, speaking, interviewing, information technology).
7. Many students do not realize that a college education and some training programs teach the student *how to learn.* Although many bits of information studied and reproduced

on examinations are forgotten months after being tested, the skills of how to study information, how to read a textbook or article, how to critically think and question, how to do research and solve problems, and how to prepare and present a report are skills for life that are repeated over and over in one's professional career. In our quickly changing information age, these skills are invaluable.

8. If you are fortunate enough to have a choice among positions, do not let salary be the only factor in your decision. Think about career potential and advancement, content of the work, free training, benefits, travel, and equipment.
9. Exercise due diligence on potential employers. For example, speak to present employees and check the organization's financial health.
10. Five key factors influencing an individual's chances for promotion are education, training, professional development and certification, experience, and personality.
11. Avoid quitting a job before you find another. Cultivate references, even in jobs you dislike; such jobs are a learning experience (Purpura, 1997: 366–384).

☐ ☐ ☐ ▬▬▬▬▬▬▬▬▬▬▬▬▬▬▬▬▬▬▬▬

The employment situation in the security and loss prevention profession reflects a bright future. Good luck with your career!

☐ ☐ ☐ ▬▬▬▬▬▬▬▬▬▬▬▬▬▬▬▬▬▬▬▬

Search the Web
Here are Web sites relevant to this chapter:

Academy of Security Educators and Trainers: www.asetcse.org/index.htm
ASIS International: www.asisonline.org
Central Intelligence Agency: www.cia.gov
Department of Homeland Security, Research & Technology: www.dhs.gov
FEMA Emergency Management Institute: http://www.training.fema.gov/emiweb/edu/
LawEnforcementJobs.com: www.lawenforcementjobs.com/content.cfm?ESID
    =find&ACTION=&SearchBy=location&SearchWhereClause=AND+S.
    StateID=42#joblist
National Academic Consortium for Homeland Security: http://homelandsecurity.osu.
    edu/NACHS/index.html
Nation Job Network: www.nationjob.com/security/
The Homeland Security/Defense Education Consortium: www.hsdec.org
U.S. Department of Labor, Occupational Outlook Handbook: www.bls.gov/oco
U.S. Office of Personnel Management: www.usajobs.gov/homeland.asp
World Future Society: www.wfs.org
Yahoo! Hot Jobs: http://hotjobs.yahoo.com/jobs-Law_Enforcement_Security-all

▬▬▬▬▬▬▬▬▬▬▬▬▬▬▬▬▬▬▬▬ ☐ ☐ ☐

Case Problems

19A. As a contract security supervisor with a major security service firm, you are faced with a major career decision. You have a bachelor's degree and have been with your present employer for a total of 7 years: 2 years part-time while in college, and 5 years full-time since graduating. These years have been spent at a hospital where you would like to advance to site security manager, but you face competition from one other supervisor, who also has a bachelor's degree, the same certifications and training that you possess, and about the same years of experience. The present contract site security manager is a former detective who wants to retire within the next year or two. You have repeatedly asked managers from the security service firm (i.e., your employer) about advancement opportunities, but nothing is available. Recently, you were offered the position of in-house security and safety training officer with a nearby, urban school district. The pay is $800 less annually than what you are earning now. However, you would receive additional insurance and retirement benefits and work only day shifts, Monday through Friday. You would be the only college-educated officer on the school district security force, which is primarily composed of contract officers. The director of security is the only other in-house security officer, a retired police officer with no college degree. What career choice do you make?

19B. As a regional loss prevention manager with a major retailer, you have 12 years of retail loss prevention experience. You earned bachelor's and master's degrees and a CPP. The territory you work covers nearly 100 stores in six southeastern states. You are on the road each day responding to challenges and wish you could spend more time with your spouse and two children. After 8 years with the same company, and no chance for advancement, you decide to consider an offer as loss prevention director with a major retailer in the New York City area. The pay is $8,000 more than what you are earning now, with similar benefits. You would have additional responsibilities, but you would travel much less. Your spouse and children do not want to move because of family and friends. What career choice do you make?

References

ASIS International. (2005). "Proceedings of the 2005 Academic/Practitioner Symposium." Alexandria, VA: ASIS International.

Campbell, G. (2007). "Security Metrics in Context." *Security Technology & Design*, 17 (March).

Davidson, M. (2005). "A Matter of Degrees." *Security Management*, 49 (December).

Flynn, D. (2007). "Mapping the Global Future: Report of the National Intelligence Council's 2020 Project." *Strategic Insights*, VI (June).

"Here Comes the 21st Century: What Does It Hold for Security?" (1997). *Security Management Bulletin* (March 25).

Naim, M. (2003). "The Five Wars of Globalization." *Foreign Policy* (January/February).

Purpura, P. (1997). *Criminal Justice: An Introduction*. Boston: Butterworth-Heinemann.

Purpura, P. (2007). *Terrorism and Homeland Security: An Introduction with Applications*. Burlington, MA: Elsevier Butterworth-Heinemann.

Ritter, N. (2006). "Preparing for the Future: Criminal Justice in 2040." *NIJ Journal* (November).

"Security's Burden Increases." (2001). *Security Management*, 45 (May).

"Survey Studies Women in Security." (1996). *Security Management* (February).

Tafoya, W. (1991). "The Future of Law Enforcement? A Chronology of Events." *C J International*, 7 (May–June).

Taylor, R., et al. (2006). *Digital Crime and Digital Terrorism*. Upper Saddle River, NJ: Pearson Prentice Hall.

The Executive Office of the President, Office of Science and Technology Policy and The Department of Homeland Security Science and Technology Directorate. (2004). *The National Plan for Research and Development in Support of Critical Infrastructure Protection*. http://www.dhs.gov/xlibrary/assets/ST_2004_NCIP_RD_PlanFINALApr05.pdf, retrieved April 1, 2007.

United States Commission on National Security/21st Century. (1999). *New World Coming: American Security in the 21st Century* (September 15). http://www.fas.org/man/docs/nwc/nwc.htm, retrieved March 31, 2007.

U.S. Department of Labor. (2000). "Futurework: Trends and Challenges for Work in the 21st Century." *Occupational Outlook Quarterly* (Summer). http://www.bls.gov/opub/ooq/2000/Summer/art04.pdf, retrieved March 29, 2007.

Index